'Inles  ̄ ̄ ̄

**JOSEPH A. SCHUMPETER**

LAUREL AHLSTRÖM

# JOSEPH A. SCHUMPETER

## THE ECONOMICS AND SOCIOLOGY OF CAPITALISM

*Edited by Richard Swedberg*

PRINCETON UNIVERSITY PRESS    PRINCETON, NEW JERSEY

**Copyright © 1991 by Princeton University Press**
Published by Princeton University Press, 41 William Street,
Princeton, New Jersey 08540
In the United Kingdom: Princeton University Press, Oxford
All Rights Reserved

*Library of Congress Cataloging-in-Publication Data*
Schumpeter, Joseph Alois, 1883–1950.
The economics and sociology of capitalism / Joseph A. Schumpeter ;
edited by Richard Swedberg.
p.   cm.
Includes bibliographical references.
ISBN 0-691-04253-5 (alk. paper) — ISBN 0-691-00383-1 (pbk. : alk. paper)
1. Schumpeter, Joseph Alois, 1883–1950. 2. Capitalism.
I. Swedberg, Richard. II. Title.
HB119.S35S36   1991
330.12'2—dc20   90-35148   CIP

This book has been composed in Linotron Baskerville

Princeton University Press books are printed
on acid-free paper and meet the guidelines
for permanence and durability of the Committee
on Production Guidelines for Book Longevity
of the Council on Library Resources

*Frontispiece*: Drawing based on a cartoon that appeared in the
Austrian press in 1919, when Joseph Schumpeter was finance
minister. (Drawing by Laurel Ahlström.)

Printed in the United States of America by
Princeton University Press, Princeton, New Jersey

10  9  8  7  6  5  4  3  2  1

# Contents

# Preface _____

ALTHOUGH Joseph Schumpeter commands a renowned reputation as an economist, one sometimes gets the impression that in reality his works are not very much read and that little is known about his life. This anthology has been compiled in the hope that Schumpeter will receive more notice: He is a rich thinker, and many aspects of his work have yet to be explored. His life is also fascinating: Schumpeter was born in the last days of the Austro-Hungarian Empire; he became finance minister in the new Austria just after World War I; he then served as head of a small Viennese banking house, which collapsed; and after some years at the University of Bonn, he emigrated to the United States, where he became a professor of economics at Harvard University. As is explained in the Introduction, his life had its tragic side as well.

The emphasis in this anthology is mainly on Schumpeter's work in economics in a broad sense, and some of his most important contributions to sociology and history have therefore been included. Schumpeter felt that these two neighboring social sciences were both integral parts of economics. Indeed, Schumpeter tried throughout his life to find a way to connect "theoretical economics," "economic sociology," "history," and "statistics" to each other in one broad concept of economics that he called "social economics" or *Sozialökonomik*. This effort, which is also connected to the work of Max Weber, has been forgotten—but perhaps needs to be resurrected since mainstream economics has tended to isolate itself from the other social sciences during the twentieth century.

_____

In assembling this anthology, I have had the support and help of many people whom I would like to thank. During the year 1987–1988 I had the pleasure of being at Harvard University, and I am especially grateful for financial support during this year from The American Council of Learned Societies. I spent much of this time in the Harvard University Archives, going through the Schumpeter Collection. The staff in Pusey Library, as well as Clark A. Elliott, its associate curator, were extremely helpful and are hereby warmly thanked. I soon came to know many of the other researchers in the

Archives, such as Bill Buxton, Howard Brick, and Larry Nichols—all of whom generously shared their knowledge of archival work. Other libraries that have provided assistance while working on this anthology include the Schlesinger Library at Radcliffe College, Baker Library at the Harvard Graduate School of Business Administration, the Royal Library in Stockholm, and the Frescati Library in Stockholm. I am also grateful to Dr. Paul Schmidt of the Archive of the University of Bonn, Dr. Dieter Krüger of the Bundesarchiv/Militärarchiv in Freiburg, Dr. Kurt Mühlberger of the Archive of the University of Vienna, and Hofrat Dr. Berthold Waldstein-Wartenberg of the Allgemeines Verwaltungsarchiv in Vienna. As part of my work, I also interviewed many people who had been Schumpeter's colleagues or students. They were all very forthcoming, and I would especially like to thank Hugh G. J. Aitken, Abram Bergson, Thomas C. Cochran, James Duesenberry, John Kenneth Galbraith, Gottfried Haberler, David Landes, Richard Musgrave, Carl Kaysen, Edward Mason, Paul Samuelson, Robert Solow, and James Tobin. Many other people who are interested in Schumpeter helped me as well, including Massimo Augello, Daniel Bell, Lewis Coser, Erik Dahmén, Lutz Köllner, Dirk Käsler, Wolfgang Mommsen, Yuichi Shionoya and George Homans. (Massimo Augello, who compiled the bibliography of Schumpeter's work at the end of this volume, would like to express his thanks to Springer-Verlag for permission to reprint this section from his book, *Joseph A. Schumpeter: A Reference Guide* [Berlin, 1990]. He extends particular thanks to Dr. W. A. Müller, economics executive editor at Springer-Verlag, who supplied him with unpublished correspondence held in the Springer archives between Schumpeter and Ferdinand Springer concerning the publication of a textbook in economics.)

A special thanks should be given to Wolfgang Stolper and Robert Loring Allen, both of whom have given of their wide knowledge about Schumpeter's work and life, and to Guy Oakes, who very skillfully translated Schumpeter's essay on Max Weber. Without the enthusiasm and energy of Jack Repcheck of Princeton University Press, this volume would not exist. My English owes much to the skillful editing of Karen M. Verde. For financial support I am also grateful to the Jan Wallander Foundation for Social Science Research in Stockholm. Finally, I would like to thank my parents, Hans and Dagmar Swedberg, and my wife, Marta Cecilia Gil-Swedberg, for their patience, ideas, and love.

# JOSEPH A. SCHUMPETER

# Introduction ——————————————————

## The Man and His Work

### JOSEPH A. SCHUMPETER: A BIOGRAPHICAL PROFILE

The first thing you notice when you enter the conference room of the economics department at Harvard are the rows of photographs of previous members of the department. Your eyes wander from one stern-looking gentleman to the next, recognizing a few and trying to determine the identity of the others. You suddenly realize that one photograph is in some way different from the others—that of Schumpeter. After looking at it for a while, you figure out the reason: While all the other photographs are in black and white, that of Schumpeter is in color.

It is clear that Schumpeter's personality as well as his work are considerably more colorful than those of most economists. Joseph Alois Schumpeter was born on February 8, 1883, in Triesch (Třešť) in the Austro-Hungarian Empire, which is in present-day Czechoslovakia.[1] His mother, Johanna Schumpeter (born Grüner), was the daughter of a physician. His father, Joseph Schumpeter, Sr., was a cloth manufacturer who also owned a factory in Triesch. The paternal grandfather, Alois Schumpeter, had founded the factory, and his son expanded and mechanized it, replacing horse power with mechanical power. By the time Joseph was born in the early 1880s, the Schumpeters were a well-established and respected family in the small town of Triesch.

The Schumpeter family was Catholic and belonged to the German minority in a town of about five thousand people, the majority of whom were Czech. It seems that the family came to the region after the Reformation. There has been speculation that "Schumpeter" is a German version of the Italian "Giampietro," and that the origin of the family is Italian. There exists no proof for this—or for the colorful legend which circulated in the Schumpeter family, that an early member of the family was a robber knight who was beheaded and demoted from the nobility at Nuremburg in the 1200s. According to the same legend, the Schumpeters thereafter made their living as glassblowers and weavers. The family then became prosperous; individual members were several times offered positions within the nobility by the Austrian emperor, but never accepted.[2]

Schumpeter—affectionately called "Jozsi" (pronounced "Yoshi") by family members and friends—was the only child of Joseph, Sr. and Johanna. On January 14, 1887, when Schumpeter was four years old, his father died of unknown causes. The widow and her little boy continued to live in Triesch, but then moved to Graz. They probably moved so that Johanna could be near the person who was to become her second husband, the recently retired field marshal–lieutenant Sigismund von Kéler. Joseph, Jr. therefore entered primary school (*Volksschule*) in Graz, in 1888. In 1893, when he had completed the first stage of his education, his mother and von Kéler, who was thirty-three years older than she, were married and the whole family moved to Vienna. Schumpeter's stepfather had earlier been stationed in Vienna where, by virtue of his position and family name, he had good contacts. Von Kéler used these to get the young boy into the famous school Theresianum, where the aristocracy of the Austro-Hungarian Empire traditionally sent their children. The education Schumpeter attained here was roughly the equivalent of American high school and two years of college.[3]

Little is known about Schumpeter's stay in Theresianum, which began in 1893. However, there exists a photo of him from 1898 (which incidentally is the earliest photo of him), and it depicts a shy and unsure boy.[4] In all other photos of Schumpeter, he virtually *radiates* self-confidence and determination, so one might assume that he felt somewhat out of place in this prep school for the aristocracy. He was also a day student, which put him in a special category. One of the goals of Theresianum was to teach the students to look at the world from different perspectives and not to adhere to any one view; this was intended to be good training for the day when the students would be taking over the administration of the Empire with all its nationalities and ethnic groups. According to Schumpeter's lifelong friend, Felix Somary, this attitude at Theresianum was to have a profound impact on Schumpeter's character:

> Schumpeter . . . never seemed to take anything in life seriously. He had been educated in Theresianum, where the pupils were taught to stick to the issue and not let personal feelings interfere. One should know the rules of all parties and ideologies, but not belong to any party or believe in any one opinion. And Schumpeter knew how to play all political games superbly, from the extreme left to the extreme right.[5]

According to the pupils, the unofficial motto of Theresianum was, "To be a bit stupid means that you come from a good family" (*A bisserl blöd is vornehm*). On this account too, Schumpeter must pretty quickly have shown that he came from the wrong circles in society. He excelled in Greek and Latin as well as in French, English, and Italian. He was also very interested in sociology and philosophy.[6] And his grades were excellent when he graduated from Theresianum in 1901.

Later in 1901, Schumpeter enrolled at the University of Vienna and began to study economics. He first focused on social history and the history of law, but this was soon followed by "a sharp turn" toward economic theory.[7] In 1906 he received his Ph.D., and at this point he was pretty well set on his course in life: He wanted to be an economist.

But before we say anything more about Schumpeter's career as an economist, we need to pause for a moment. A person's character is to a large extent shaped by what happens in childhood; and since Schumpeter was a very complex person, it is necessary to look more carefully at his first years. When we do this, however, we are struck by how little knowledge there is. All that is known covers little more than a page, and most of it has been presented here. What is especially lacking is some insight into Schumpeter's character. How did he react to the death of his father? What was his relationship to his mother? And what did he think of his stepfather?

Insofar as Schumpeter's relationship to his father is concerned, there exists no information whatsoever. We know a little bit more about what he thought of his stepfather. According to a friend, Schumpeter did not look upon von Kéler as a father, but he did regard him with a certain admiration.[8] Later in life he would hint that von Kéler was the supreme commander of all troops in Vienna—rather than just a retired officer with a generous pension. Our knowledge of Schumpeter's mother—and this is probably the greatest lacunae of them all—is also very sketchy. Schumpeter supposedly idolized his mother, and he described her as "handsome, talented, and ambitious for her son."[9] Schumpeter, we are told by the same source, was extremely attached to his mother: "His devotion to her continued without diminution or disillusion not only to the end of her life but to the end of his." After having left Austria in 1925, Schumpeter returned only once in his life to his native country, and that was for his mother's funeral.

Given what we know about Schumpeter being admitted to Theresianum through von Kéler's connections, the description of Schumpeter's mother as ambitious for her son makes sense. There also exist many stories which confirm that Schumpeter desperately wanted to be successful; unfortunately, it appears that his hopes were consistently dashed. He never could live up to his mother's expectations.

Still, we need to know much more about Schumpeter as a child and as a youngster to understand his personality when he was ready to enter adulthood as a student in Vienna. There exists no autobiographical fragment on this point; Schumpeter did not like to write about his past, nor did he preserve material about himself.[10] There are not even any anecdotes about his early life; the anecdotes that Schumpeter liked to tell about himself are all about his life as an adult. There is, however, one document, which, in the eyes of one of Schumpeter's closest friends, gives some clues to his psychology. It is the outline to a novel entitled *Ships in the Fog*. Schumpeter probably wrote the outline in the early 1930s, and it was found among his papers after his death. The novel itself was never written.[11]

It is often the case that people who write fiction for the first time produce thinly veiled autobiographical stories. This seems to have been true of Schumpeter and his projected novel. The hero in *Ships in the Fog*—Henry—is an only child. When he is four years old, his father has an accident and is killed. The widowed mother does not have much money, but she does her best to see to it that her son gets a good start in life: "She had connections which she resolutely exploited for her darling." And how did Henry see his mother? According to the outline, she was "an excellent woman, strong and kind." After the death of her husband, she became "the one great human factor in Henry's life." Her ancestry was British and was rather plain compared to that of Henry's father, "which racially was a mixture defying analysis." The father's family came from "Trieste" in the Austro-Hungarian Empire and had "Greek, German, Serb, and Italian elements."

And how was Henry himself—the central figure—portrayed by Schumpeter? First of all, Henry had a pervasive feeling of homelessness. Even though he loved his mother, he could not really identify with her, and he did not feel English at all: "Where was he at home? Not really in England! Often he had thought so but ancestral past had asserted itself each time." But neither did he feel at home in his father's home country: "Certainly not . . . in what had been the Austro-Hungarian Empire." Henry was also confused about which social group to identify with: "More important than country means class—but he did not with subconscious allegiance belong either to society or the business class or the professions or the trade union world, all of which provided such comfortable homes for everyone he knew." The only stable point in Henry's life was work. He had "no family," "no real friends," and "no woman." Work was "all that is left."

There are indeed several sides to Schumpeter's personality that cannot be found in his portrait of Henry. Schumpeter, for example, was a bit of a snob and a showman—not to mention that he also was a brilliant scientist. Still, there are striking parallels between the character Henry and Schumpeter. Both were fatherless early in life and had strong mothers; and both often felt lost and unhappy.

———————

In 1901, the eighteen-year-old Schumpeter registered as a student at the Faculty of Law at the University of Vienna. While there, he specialized in the study of economics. He had several famous teachers, in particular Eugen von Böhm-Bawerk and Friedrich von Wieser. After six years of studies, Schumpeter received his doctorate of law (*Doctor utriusque juris*; literally, "doctor of each of the two laws—Roman law and canon law"). When his university education was completed, Schumpeter applied for his *Habilitation* or permission to lecture in three areas: economics, statistics, and sociology.[12] This was granted on suggestion by the two referees, Böhm-Bawerk and von Wieser. Schumpeter also could have taught law and political science. In addition, he had acquired some knowledge of mathematics, even if he never was to become particularly skillful in this area. Mathematics, incidentally, was frowned upon by the Austrian economists—especially by von Wieser—and Schumpeter had to attend lectures in mathematics on his own. While he was a student in Vienna, he became exposed to Marxist ideas, but little is known about Schumpeter's early reaction to Marxism. We do know that in 1905–1906, Schumpeter participated in a very lively seminar together with the two famous Marxists Otto Bauer and Rudolf Hilferding. Böhm-Bawerk had published a harsh critique of Marxism a few years earlier, which had created quite a stir in Marxist circles. "In the heated debates between Böhm-Bawerk and the Marxists," according to one of the participants in the seminar, "Schumpeter attracted general attention through his cool, scientific detachment. The seemingly playful manner in which he took part in the discussion ... was evidently mistaken by many for a lack of seriousness or an artificial mannerism."[13]

The University of Vienna was an extremely interesting place to be at the turn of the century for someone like Schumpeter. Carl Menger had just stopped teaching when Schumpeter arrived in 1901, but his spirit was very much alive in the teachings of his two foremost disciples, Eugen von Böhm-Bawerk and Friedrich von Wieser. Schumpeter took courses from both, as well as from Eugen von Philippovich

and Karl Theodor von Inama-Sternegg. The latter was a famous statistician and economic historian, for whom Schumpeter wrote a series
of brilliant statistical papers. It is generally considered that it was von
Wieser and Böhm-Bawerk who had the greatest influence on Schumpeter in Vienna. In his first book, *Das Wesen und der Hauptinhalt der
theoretischen Nationalökonomie* (*The Nature and Essence of Theoretical Economics*, 1908), Schumpeter says that von Wieser and Walras are the
two economists to whom he owes the most.[14] And in his next work,
*Theorie der wirtschaftlichen Entwicklung* (*The Theory of Economic Development*, 1911), it is Böhm-Bawerk whom Schumpeter explicitly mentions.[15] However, there seems to have been a third professor in Vienna to whom Schumpeter also felt indebted. When Schumpeter
applied for his *Habilitation* in 1909, he did not single out von Wieser
or Böhm-Bawerk. Instead he wrote: "My studies have . . . first of all
been influenced by the Counciller von Philippovich."[16]

After he received his doctorate in law on February 16, 1906,
Schumpeter seems to have been unsure about what to do next. Since
he had no private fortune, he needed a profession. There were a few
alternatives open to him. First, he could become an academic and
teach. To do this, however, he first needed his *Habilitation* (that is, a
second doctorate to qualify for academic teaching posts), and that
would take several years of further study. In addition, Schumpeter
had already developed a taste for the good life and no doubt had
dreams of a lifestyle better than that of a professor. His second alternative was to become a lawyer. This was certainly more lucrative than
being a professor, but he would first have to work for years as a law
clerk and then pass a bar examination. Schumpeter was very young
when he got his doctorate—he was only twenty-three years old—and
after a summer term at the University of Berlin (where he studied
economics), he decided to go abroad. In an autobiographical letter,
written many years later, Schumpeter says that after having taken his
degree in Vienna and "following up on an impulse which early asserted itself, I then travelled about for a few years studying economics from various standpoints."[17]

Schumpeter first visited England. He stayed there for about a year,
and according to a friend, it was the happiest year of his life.[18]
Schumpeter liked England immensely, especially its aristocratic side.
The British political system—"tory democracy"—was from this point
on his political ideal. The young Schumpeter seems to have enjoyed
English social life as well: He attended balls, he socialized in the best
circles, and he practiced his favorite sport, riding. In a passage which
breathes joyous recollection, Schumpeter was many years later to
write that "I . . . lived in England as a young man and a great snob."[19]

But his stay was not only hedonistic; Schumpeter also worked hard. He spent long days in the British Museum, where he added to his already profound knowledge of economic literature. For a while he was affiliated with the London School of Economics as a "research student." And he made a tour of Oxford and Cambridge, visiting Edgeworth and Marshall. It is clear that Schumpeter was very eager to visit the great minds in economics, whose works he had studied. Sometimes, however, these meetings did not turn out as he had expected. He was, for example, advised by Marshall to give up the hope of ever becoming a good economic theorist!

Schumpeter started to dabble in the study of British common law while in England. But this led nowhere because, to cite Schumpeter himself, "he couldn't stand eating the requisite meals in the Temple."[20] It is likely that what sparked Schumpeter's interest in law at this point was that he had fallen in love. The target of his affections was Gladys Ricarde Seaver, the daughter of a high dignitary of the Church of England. The two were married in 1907. Very little is known about Schumpeter's first wife except that she was "stunning."[21] "In the few references I remember Schumpeter making to this marriage," a friend has recalled, "he said that whatever good manners he had, he owed to his first wife."

It is in any case clear that once Schumpeter was married, he needed a well-paying job. He eventually found one as a lawyer in Egypt, where no previous experience was needed to practice law at the so-called International Mixed Court. It seems that Schumpeter became associated with an Italian law firm in Cairo as the junior partner. Various colorful anecdotes exist from these years about how Schumpeter administered the fortune of an Egyptian princess; how an Arab sheik threatened to whip him for making a Moslem accept interest; and the like. In any case, Schumpeter seems to have done very well financially as a lawyer, and he lived in high style, with a race horse to his name. His work was also progressing well, and it was in Cairo that he signed the preface to his first great book, *The Nature and Essence of Theoretical Economics* (1908). This work was the result of many years of study and hard work in his spare time as a lawyer. The book was dedicated to Schumpeter's mother and not to his wife. Exactly what his relationship to his wife was like and how long they actually lived together is unclear. Schumpeter hinted to one of his friends that the relationship only lasted "a few months."[22] According to other sources, however, the two lived together from the marriage in 1907 until at least 1914, when Gladys used the outbreak of World War I as an excuse not to return to Austria from England. In any case, it is generally agreed that it was an ill-conceived marriage. The divorce could not be finalized until 1920, probably for formal reasons.

After two years in Cairo, Schumpeter contracted Malta fever, a painful infectious disease, and decided to return to Vienna. He applied for the right to lecture in economics and related topics and was granted his *Habilitation* at the University of Vienna on January 25, 1909. He delivered his *Habilitation* lecture, "The Verification of Abstract Theorems by Statistics," on February 15, and he became *Privatdozent* with effect of March 16. The reason Schumpeter decided to leave his career as a lawyer is not known—probably he had wanted to be an economist since his days as a student, and the positive reception of his 1908 book no doubt was encouraging. Schumpeter's first academic appointment was as associate professor (*ausserordentlicher Professor*) at the University of Czernowitz. In those days Czernowitz was situated in the easternmost part of the Austro-Hungarian Empire (today, it is called Chervotsy and is part of the Ukrainian Soviet Socialist Republic). It seems that Schumpeter liked the city of Czernowitz, and later in the United States he would entertain his colleagues with stories from these days "that might well have come out of the Arabian Nights."[23] One of these anecdotes was about how Schumpeter challenged the local librarian to a duel over the right of his students to use the books more freely. Schumpeter won, after having scratched his opponent. Schumpeter apparently also clashed with his university colleagues, whom he found dull and provincial. Their small-town manners annoyed Schumpeter: "He liked to shock them by appearing at faculty meetings in riding boots and aroused unfavorable comment by dressing for dinner when he and his wife were dining alone."[24]

Schumpeter taught courses in economics and general social science at the University of Czernowitz. His scientific creativity flourished, and it was in Czernowitz that Schumpeter completed what was to be his most famous work in economics: *The Theory of Economic Development*. The book was finished and published in 1911 (not in 1912, as it says on the cover).[25] At the time Schumpeter was only twenty-eight years old, and the publication of this book no doubt confirmed his theory that the third decade in a scientist's life is a "decade of sacred fertility."[26]

Schumpeter's own creativity, however, continued unabated even after his thirtieth birthday. This is clear from his publication record at the University of Graz, where he moved as full professor (*ordentlicher Professor*) in 1911. The Graz faculty was dominated by historical economics, and Schumpeter's type of theoretical economics was not appreciated. When Schumpeter applied for the position, he was initially placed well below several other candidates. His book from 1908 on economic theory was criticized for being filled with "empty generalizations," "trivialities," and so on.[27] The decision by the Graz faculty to appoint someone other than Schumpeter was, however, overruled by an imperial decision—possibly because of the intervention of Böhm-Bawerk.[28] Hence, Schumpeter became the youngest full professor at the University of Graz.

He was also the only professor of economics in Graz, and as such he had a heavy teaching load. He had to lecture on all aspects of economics as well as in social science. This must have been very tiring, especially since he also chose to be a lecturer at the Graz University of Technology, but it does not seem to have slowed Schumpeter down. His third major work in economics was published during this period, *Epochen der Dogmen- und Methodengeschichte* (*Economic Doctrine and Method*, 1914).[29] He also wrote a small book on the history of the social sciences as well as a number of important articles. According to a letter to a publisher from these years, Schumpeter was also working on several other projects, including a book on public finance, one regarding political sociology, and one on feminism.[30]

According to what Schumpeter later told his friends, he was not very happy in Graz. The town apparently lacked the redeeming features of Czernowitz, and during most of his stay in Graz, he was alone. The local faculty also seems to have been uncommonly dull. In 1913, however, he found a way to escape: He became a visiting professor at Columbia University. His year in the United States was very successful and he left Columbia with an honorary degree (Litt.D., 1914). It appears that Schumpeter enjoyed himself thoroughly during his stay in the United States, and in a farewell letter to an American colleague, written on the day of his departure for Europe, he wrote:

> I have seen, and given addresses at, seventeen American universities and am taking with me the pleasantest impressions of men and institutions. Truly this is a great country and I am awfully sorry to have to leave it. I always felt that in the inspiring company of American colleagues I could turn out much better things than I shall be able to over there. [31]

Once back in the unstimulating environment of Graz, Schumpeter tried to escape as often as possible. Vienna was just a three-hour train ride away, and he preferred to be there. From 1918 onward he was offered—and accepted—various full-time commissions, mainly of a political nature, which took him away from Graz. In 1920 he returned and taught for a while. In 1921, however, he handed in his resignation. A life different from that of the scholar was tempting him.

———————

Schumpeter used to entertain his American students with the following anecdote. "As a young man," Schumpeter said, "I had three ambitions in life: to become the world's greatest economist, the world's greatest lover, and the world's greatest horseman." Silence. "I never became the world's greatest horseman." But this popular anecdote fails to tell the whole story of the young Schumpeter and his ambitions. Schumpeter admitted as much at a lunch, held in his honor at the University of Wisconsin in 1943. On this occasion he was asked point blank if the famous story about his three ambitions was true. Well, Schumpeter said, he had actually had two more ambitions as a young man: He had also wanted to become a successful politician and an accomplished connoisseur of art.[32]

Schumpeter's interest in art persisted throughout his life and seems to have given him much pleasure. He was especially interested in cathedrals and often took the opportunity, while touring the Mediterranean countries for vacation or business, to study the local churches. His diaries are filled with postcards of favorite Gothic cathedrals and drawings he liked to make of particular details. Schumpeter was also fond of the classics, and read them in their original form. After his death in 1950, Homer's *Odysseus*—in Greek—was found on his desk, with favorite passages underlined.

Schumpeter's interest in art, however, does not qualify as a burning ambition; and it never interfered very much with the rest of his life. His interest in politics, on the other hand, did exactly that. Indeed, it not only interfered with his life, it also created havoc in it. As a result, Schumpeter was always reluctant to discuss the various political episodes of his life, and it is only during the last few years—more precisely since the mid-1970s—that we have come to know more about Schumpeter's political activities.[33]

Schumpeter's first involvement with politics probably occurred during World War I. Schumpeter viewed the war as a "bloody madness" which was "devastating Europe." His attitude has been described as pro-Western—especially pro-British—anti-German, and pacifist.[34] What seems to have galvanized Schumpeter into action, however, was his Austrian patriotism and the rumor during the war that secret negotiations had been initiated between Austria and Germany about a customs union. The general context was the following. During the war the notion of a German-led "Middle Europe" had become popular in Germany. By uniting all German-speaking parts of Europe, it was hoped that Germany would finally have the strength to stand up to both the West and the East. When Schumpeter heard the rumor of an impending customs union between Austria and Germany, he became very worried and contacted one of his former professors at the University of Vienna, Heinrich Lammach. Schumpeter had studied law and foreign policy under Lammach, who was a well-known political figure in Vienna with strong ties to the emperor. Lammach encouraged Schumpeter to put down his ideas in a memorandum, which he promised to try to show to the emperor, Franz Joseph I. Whether the emperor actually read Schumpeter's memorandum is not clear. But we do know that in 1916–1917, Schumpeter wrote several political memoranda, which were circulated in great secrecy in the highest Catholic, conservative circles in Vienna. Schumpeter would later hint at meetings he had had with the emperor during the war, yet little is known about the actual impact of Schumpeter's writings.

The memoranda and the correspondence with Lammach give us a picture of Schumpeter's political ideas when he was in his early thirties. Two beliefs stand out most vividly. The first is Schumpeter's strong concern for Austria's independence and his suspicion of German foreign policy vis-à-vis Austria. He did not want Austria to be "chained to Prussia" in a customs union; Austria's industry and financial system were so underdeveloped that the Austro-Hungarian Empire would soon be dominated by Germany. A German *Mitteleuropa* would be a disaster: "Then the Austria we know and love would not exist any longer."[35]

The second element that stands out in Schumpeter's political writings from these years is his political recipe for how the Austro-Hungarian Empire should be ruled. What Schumpeter essentially wanted was a form of tory democracy or a mixture of aristocratic elitism and bourgeois democracy. The monarchy should remain and a government be formed of the "historical families" of the Empire, that is, of members from the highest aristocratic circles. The parliament should be loyal to the monarch, and the liberty of the press minimal. Schumpeter rounded off his vision of a conservative democracy with a few welfare measures, such as compensation to victims of the war, and the like.

World War I spelled the end of a world—the world that Schumpeter had both grown up in and in which he felt most at home. A new Europe and a new Austria now emerged, where different men with different ideas held power. As a sign that the world had indeed changed, Schumpeter received an offer in late 1918 to enter the po-

litical world—not from Heinrich Lammach and the aristocratic circles
he had been courting during the war, but from two of his Marxist
fellow students at the University of Vienna, Rudolf Hilferding and
Emil Lederer. They wanted to know if he would be interested in serving on the Socialization Commission which had just been formed in
Germany. Schumpeter, who believed in the sanctity of private property and that socialization basically was theft, accepted the offer.
Later he was to quip that the reason he had been asked was that "if
somebody wants to commit suicide, it is a good thing if a doctor is
present."[36]

As part of the German Socialization Commission, Schumpeter
spent a couple of months in Berlin in late 1918 and early 1919.[37] The
commission consisted of a mixture of Marxists and liberals. About
half of the members were economists and the other half trade union-
ists; Karl Kautsky was the chairman and Eduard Heimann the secretary. Formally, the commission was connected to the German government, but it soon demanded—and was granted—status as an
independent research group. The main question that the commission discussed was socialization. What type of socialization was
needed? What role should the state play in socialized enterprises?
And how could one get former leaders of private enterprises to work
in socialized enterprises?

The answer to these and similar questions can be found in the various reports that were issued by the commission. Schumpeter signed
the general report, like all the other members. He also signed the
majority report together with the Marxists, in which it was argued
that socialization was necessary to increase the efficiency of the economy. By "socialization," it should be noted, the committee neither
meant that the state should be running the economy nor that the
workers should. What was needed was some kind of intermediary socialist agency. A former member, himself a liberal and signer of the
minority report, has this to say about Schumpeter's role in the commission:

> Certainly Schumpeter's presence added much brilliance and interest to our
> internal discussions and our very informal conversations outside the Com-
> mittee Room. In fact Schumpeter sided mostly with the more extreme
> propagators of immediate and integral socialization, i.e., more with Led-
> erer who, at that time, was rather radical and doctrinaire in his intention
> to bring forth "Socialism in our time," as against Hilferding who—as always
> in practical matters—was more compromising and willing to yield to the
> arguments of his opponents. In a private conversation with Schumpeter
> and some other members, after the official close of a session, I expressed a

certain surprise about his position, whereupon he answered, "I don't know whether or not Socialism is a practical possibility, but I am convinced that it is impossible if not applied integrally. At any rate, it will be an interesting experiment to try it out."[38]

In the early spring of 1919, Schumpeter was asked to become finance minister in the new Austrian government. He immediately accepted, and thus begins one of the most spectacular chapters in Schumpeter's life. On March 15, 1919, he moved into his new office in one of Vienna's most magnificent baroque palaces. But this would end in a nightmare for Schumpeter, and after a few months he was forced to resign. Popular rage at the impossible financial situation in the country was turned against Schumpeter personally, and he became overnight "one of the more disliked persons in the new Austria."[39]

The government that Schumpeter entered in the spring of 1919 was a coalition government made up of the Social Democrats and members of the Christian Social Party, a Catholic conservative party. The head of the government was Karl Renner, a Marxist of the reformist type. Schumpeter did not formally belong to any party and was therefore brought in as a "technical" minister. It has been suggested that Schumpeter was asked to become finance minister because neither party wanted to assume responsibility for the financial situation in Austria. Whether this is true is unclear. It was in any case on the suggestion of the Marxists—more precisely Rudolf Hilferding and Otto Bauer—that Schumpeter was brought into the government. They knew him fairly well from the days at the University of Vienna and in the Socialization Commission in Berlin. In addition, Schumpeter had publicly advocated a financial policy during the last years of the war that was broadly similar to that of the Social Democrats. But he was not a socialist; beginning in his youth, Schumpeter was a confirmed conservative.

Austria's finances were in terrible shape in 1919. The income of the state, which mainly came from taxation, was simply not enough to cover the expenses. Money had to be found for the war debt, for the unemployed, for food subsidies, and for the enormous bureaucracy that the small republic had inherited from the Austro-Hungarian Empire. There was very little food in the country and many people lived at a starvation level, especially in the capital. One study has determined that the calorie intake of individuals in Vienna averaged 1,270 in 1919, as opposed to the recommended 2,300. Unemployment was skyrocketing and more than trebled during December 1918–May 1919. In brief, the economic situation was close to hopeless.[40]

When he entered the government, Schumpeter had very clear ideas about how to attack Austria's financial problems. There were three major points on his program: to impose a capital levy; to stabilize the currency; and to import capital from abroad. The Social Democrats were also advocating a capital levy, and this may be one reason why Schumpeter was offered the position as finance minister in the first place. Schumpeter, however, wanted the capital levy primarily for purposes of currency reform, while Otto Bauer and the Marxists saw it more as a tool for the socialization of the economy. In terms of stabilizing the currency, Schumpeter first of all wanted to acknowledge the existing devaluation of the Austrian crown. And to get the economy going, Schumpeter felt that capital should be imported from abroad.

It is generally agreed that Schumpeter was a failure as a finance minister. Some argue that *no one* could have succeeded—that Schumpeter's financial plan was brilliant, but that the situation was just hopeless.[41] Whether the situation was indeed hopeless is hard to judge. But it is clear that Schumpeter was not a skillful politician and that his personality was not an asset for a public figure. The Austrian press from 1919 contains many sarcastic comments about Schumpeter's chameleonic personality. Just a few days after he took office, he was greeted by a satiric verse in *Der Morgen* to the effect that he was a person with "three souls"—one conservative, one liberal, and one left wing.[42] And a few days before he was dismissed in October 1919, the *Arbeiter-Zeitung* said that he "always adjusted his speeches according to whom he spoke"; when he spoke to the workers, he sounded like a Social Democrat, and so on. To Karl Kraus, the great Austrian satirist, Schumpeter had "more different views than were necessary for his advancement."[43]

What especially turned Schumpeter's Marxist colleagues in the government against him was his opposition to their plan for Austria's *Anschluss* to Germany. The plan for a German *Mitteleuropa*, which Schumpeter had already fought against during World War I, was adopted after the war by some of the Austro-Marxists. What they had in mind was not so much a strong German state as a Social Democratic Middle Europe, which could hold its own against the capitalist West as well as the Soviet Union. Schumpeter, however, would have none of this and began to criticize the government's policy, both publicly—in speeches and interviews—and in private, at the British and French missions in Vienna. This infuriated Renner and Bauer, and Schumpeter was several times severely rebuked. On October 17, 1919, he was fired.

Schumpeter also angered his Marxist colleagues in the government by his attitude toward their socialization program. In Berlin, Schumpeter had signed the majority report and many people had the impression that he was a proponent of radical socialization. And during the first few months as finance minister, Schumpeter indeed seemed to advocate socialization. On March 20, 1919, for example, he said in a public speech that "We shall have to intervene on a massive scale in the private economy. Socialization is the decisive issue of our time."[44] A few weeks later, however, Schumpeter was talking about "limited socialization measures." Schumpeter also infuriated his Marxist colleagues by letting foreign interests buy up Austria's largest steel and iron producer, the famous Alpine Montan Corporation. That the owner was a foreigner made it impossible for the government to nationalize the corporation. Schumpeter was accused of having done nothing to stop the transaction in order to undercut the government's socialist plans. Schumpeter himself, however, saw the whole affair in a different light. As far as he was concerned, there was no reason for him to stop the affair with the Alpine Montan Corporation; he saw no reason to do so and, even if he had wanted to do it, he said that he had no legal right to do so.[45]

By mid-October 1919, the Social Democrats had had enough of Schumpeter's intrigues. And Schumpeter had no support from any other group to fall back on. The government members from the Christian Social Party did not defend him since he was too closely identified with the Marxists. He was also known as a "Jewfriend."[46] And the officials at the Treasury had from the beginning distrusted the brilliant young finance minister. The propertied classes, finally, were angered by Schumpeter's "socialist" policies, such as his advocacy of a capital levy and socialization. Schumpeter also offended many people simply by his flashy lifestyle and snobbish mannerisms. A respected newspaper editor, Gustav Stolper, later wrote that Schumpeter's lifestyle was regarded as totally "un-Austrian." Stolper was convinced that the elegant Schumpeter with his "silk shirts, silk handkerchiefs, and . . . race horse" made many people worried. Where did he get all the money for this?[47] When Schumpeter was forced to resign on October 17, quite a few people apparently drew a sigh of relief.

Why did Schumpeter fail as a finance minister? As already mentioned, there are those who feel that Schumpeter had no talents for politics, and others who claim that the situation was hopeless. My own feeling is that Schumpeter gave many people—including his Marxist colleagues in the government—the impression that he was considerably less conservative than he actually was. And this easily led to situations where Schumpeter's actions surprised and dismayed those around him: They felt he was unreliable and dishonest.

In any event, after his dismissal from the government Schumpeter returned briefly to the University of Graz. However, teaching at a minor university was not what he wanted at this stage of his life. In 1921 he became president of a small and highly respected Viennese banking house, the Biedermann Bank. Schumpeter was not involved in the daily affairs of the bank; being the president was apparently more of a ceremonial task.[48] In any case, Schumpeter's venture into banking ended badly. In 1924 the bank became insolvent, due to a combination of bad times and dishonest dealings of some of Schumpeter's associates. Schumpeter had to resign, and the bank was liquidated in 1926. In retrospect, it is clear that Schumpeter had gone into banking at exactly the wrong moment; the Biedermann Bank was just the first in a long series of banks in Austria and Germany that collapsed in the 1920s and 1930s. In the end, Schumpeter had to assume responsibility for 120,000 Austrian schillings (roughly the equivalent of $250,000 today), and this meant that he had to borrow a considerable amount of money. After his debacle as a banker, Schumpeter's popularity in his country reached a new low. "In the Austria of 1925," a contemporary observer notes, "Schumpeter was a 'nonentity.' "[49]

In 1924, Schumpeter was forty-one years old, and he must have been very disappointed. He had left academia and entered politics and business, only to fail miserably. He had also accumulated a mountain of debts—for unpaid taxes, for living expenses in Vienna, and for the trouble at the Biedermann Bank. The great hopes that his mother had had for him were crushed by these events. She was still a very important factor in his life, especially after the failure of his first marriage. Schumpeter later wrote, "Disappointment was in store for her. Disappointment all the more bitter because realization was so near; all the more bitter, in a sense, because precisely in every other respect he gave her satisfaction and always not only felt but also manifested in every word and act his unconditioned attachment to her. . . ."[50]

Schumpeter's precarious situation in the early 1920s made him reevaluate his plans for the future. It seems that he finally decided to leave politics and business permanently and continue his pursuit of academia. His students from the late 1920s remember him often discussing the pros and cons of life as a businessman and a politician, on the one hand, and life as an academic, on the other. But it was not without a struggle that Schumpeter came to his decision to become an academic again. He later wrote to a friend, who had just received a university appointment, "I welcome you back to academic activities which as in the fifth century in Rome are perhaps the least distasteful ones to indulge in, in the world as it is."[51] For the rest of his life Schumpeter would always feel drawn to the world of politics. His American students remember that he would often begin his digressions on politics with the words, "If I were among the living, I should [do this and that]...."[52] Schumpeter was undoubtedly a political animal at heart. But he never gave in to his impulse to reenter politics; he had made his decision to stay out of politics and he stuck to it.[53]

The first offer that Schumpeter received to return to academia came from Japan, where he was invited as a guest professor. Schumpeter accepted this offer, but a short time later, in 1925, he was offered a chair in public finance at the University of Bonn, and he decided to take this offer instead. The person who had pushed for his appointment—against a certain resistance in Berlin—was Arthur Spiethoff, a fellow economist and friend of Schumpeter's. Schumpeter's social and financial situation quickly improved, even though he had to work painfully hard for many years to pay off his debts. Schumpeter seems to have enjoyed teaching at Bonn, which was clearly a better university than Graz and Czernowitz. His lectures were truly innovative, as Schumpeter introduced his students to a host of new economic theories which the historically minded economists had succeeded in keeping out of the German universities. According to Schumpeter's students, his lectures were always very well delivered. Schumpeter spoke freely, and he used only a few small notes on which a couple of lines had been jotted down.[54] Schumpeter lavished attention on his students, and he was very much liked in return. He would give an inordinate amount of time to every student who wanted his help. When the student was also the son of a good friend, he would of course get special treatment, as the following charming account by Wolfgang Stolper makes clear:

I had the good fortune of being probably Schumpeter's only tutee [in Bonn]. This procedure too, he deliberately introduced from England. Every Monday evening I appeared to read and discuss a paper he had assigned to me the week before. But that was really only a small part of my education. Every Monday noon I had to appear to order dinner and select a wine, for this too was part of the education of a gentleman. In the evening Schumpeter would approve my choice (since his wine cellar was excellent that was not really too difficult) and we would discuss anything that came to his mind: Goethe's poems or his letters to Frau von Stein, Gothic cathedrals about which he knew an enormous amount, Picasso and Braque. I do not remember ever discussing music, however, which was my special love. At about ten o'clock we would retire to the glassed-in veranda with a magnificent view of the Rhine and the Seven Mountains (Schumpeter had rented the house used by the emperor as a student) and until one in the morning we would discuss economics. . . .[55]

Soon after his appointment at the University of Bonn, Schumpeter remarried. His new bride, Annie Reisinger, was about twenty years younger than Schumpeter, and very little is known about her except that she was uncommonly graceful and beautiful. Annie was the daughter of the caretaker in the apartment house in Vienna where Schumpeter's mother (by now divorced from von Kéler) was living. Apparently Schumpeter had taken a strong liking to Annie when she was very young—twelve years in one account, a few years older in another—and decided to marry her when she came of age.[56] Together with his mother, Schumpeter decided on a suitable education for Annie in Paris and Switzerland, for which he also paid. Exactly how old Annie was when she and Schumpeter married is not clear. A good guess is that she was twenty-two years old and that the marriage took place in 1925. One thing, however, is beyond doubt: Schumpeter was extremely happy with Annie. She was his great love in life—"the great wonder of my life" ("das grosse Wunder meines Lebens"), as he would later describe her in a letter.[57] The newly married couple had a very active social life. "Years later," we are told, "stories continued to circulate in Bonn of the gay and lavish parties the Schumpeters gave, how they were the most desirable couple on any hostess's list."[58]

Schumpeter's happiness with Annie was to be very brief. On August 3, 1926, she died in childbirth. The child, a little boy, also died. According to the death certificate, "Joseph Schumpeter" only became "three and three-quarters hours" old.[59] Adding to Schumpeter's sorrow was his mother's sudden death a little more than a month before, on June 22. It is clear that this was a turning point for Schumpeter. One of his closest friends says that "after that time a streak of resignation and pessimism was unmistakable in his character."[60] Other friends noticed the change as well; and from then on it seems that Schumpeter was basically a very unhappy person.

This unhappiness was expressed in many ways. Schumpeter became very restless and eagerly seized every opportunity to leave Bonn. During the academic year of 1927–1928 he was at Harvard. A large part of 1930 was spent in the United States as well, teaching at Harvard again. On the way back from the United States, Schumpe-

ter spent some time in Japan, where he gave a number of greatly appreciated lectures.

In Germany, Schumpeter also traveled and gave lectures. Unlike his trips abroad, however, these were motivated largely by his desperate efforts to pay off his debts. His private correspondence from these years contains many despairing comments about the "prostitution" he had to endure. He more or less lectured for anyone who offered a good honorarium, and he wrote a huge number of articles in various economic magazines. This wore him down and it also made him depressed. "This slave chain has no end," he wrote to a friend in 1928, "this forced labor can last for twenty years."[61]

The period in Bonn (1925–1932) is usually considered very productive in terms of scholarship for Schumpeter. And it is true that he buried himself in work after Annie's death. During the years spent in Bonn, he published a long stream of articles as well as a second and thoroughly revised edition of *The Theory of Economic Development* (1926). In 1930 Schumpeter also helped to found the Econometric Society in the United States. But despite these accomplishments, all was not well with the intellectual Schumpeter. He had difficulty concentrating, and he was unable to produce a major work in economics, as he had in previous decades. In a letter to a friend, written while in Singapore in 1931, Schumpeter wrote that "the sense of decay, physical and mental . . . always accompanies me."[62] We know that Schumpeter's main intellectual project during the years in Bonn was a treatise on money. He had very high hopes for this work, entitled *Geld und Währung* (*Money and Currency*). During 1930 in particular, he worked furiously to finish the manuscript, but failed. That same year Keynes also published his *Treatise on Money*, and when Schumpeter read it, he found to his dismay that most of what he had written Keynes had already anticipated. According to one account, Schumpeter tore up his manuscript and started a new one. According to another version, Schumpeter began to rewrite his manuscript. Ultimately, however, Schumpeter worked on his treatise on money until his death. He sometimes announced its impending publication, but he could never bring himself to finish the manuscript.[63] In brief, things were not coming as easily to Schumpeter as when he was a young man.

In the 1930s, however, Schumpeter's academic star was still shining brightly, and he received several job offers—including one from Japan and another from Harvard. Apparently he was not particularly interested in either. What he really wanted was the chair in economic theory at the University of Berlin, and when this position became available, Schumpeter immediately made it known that he was inter-

ested. But he did not get it. Instead it went to Emil Lederer, a German economist and one-time collaborator with Schumpeter in the
German Socialization Commission. Exactly why Schumpeter did not
get the chair in Berlin is not clear. It is rumored that he had enemies
at the Prussian Ministry of Education, who had already tried to block
his appointment at the University of Bonn. There was also "resistance" at the University of Berlin itself, where it was feared that
Schumpeter's debts would interfere with his scientific activities.[64] In
any case, Schumpeter was bitterly disappointed when he did not get
the chair in Berlin in 1931. In addition to this setback, he was faced
with several other irritations in his life as well: His new relationship
with Mia Stöckel, his secretary, was not going anywhere, and he was
disgusted with the political situation in the Weimar Republic, especially with the role of labor.[65] Disappointed and without much enthusiasm, Schumpeter decided to accept the offer from Harvard in 1932.

On June 20, 1932, Schumpeter gave a farewell speech to his students in Bonn. The theme he had chosen was "Where is economics
going?" and Schumpeter particularly emphasized that economics was
an objective science, where each new piece of knowledge has to prove
its true value:

> Unlike in business and politics, what matters in science is not momentary
> success. All we can say is that if in science something wins through, it will
> have proved its right to exist; and if the thing is not worth anything, it will
> surely wither. For my part, I am willing to accept the judgment of future
> generations.[66]

Schumpeter also said that if the National Socialists came to power,
young economists should take the chance to influence them: "What
giant subjective possibilities this constitutes for a young man!"[67]

––––––––––

Schumpeter was to live in the United States from 1932 until his death
in 1950. He would never visit his native Austria again, and the last
time he saw Europe was in 1935. In February 1933 he had already
written to the U.S. immigration authorities and announced his intention to become a citizen. When he left Germany in 1932 he left behind a sizable number of books, letters, and manuscripts, which he
never sent for. Schumpeter seemed to prefer leaving his old life behind completely.

Schumpeter arrived in the United States on September 25, 1932,
and proceeded immediately to Cambridge. For the next few years he
would stay with F. W. Taussig, who lived in a pleasant house at 2

Scott Street near the Harvard campus. Taussig took a fatherly interest in Schumpeter, who responded by trying to behave like a good
son. The first letters that Schumpeter wrote from his new country
breathed optimism and contentment. "I feel quite happy at Harvard
which in fact is an old love of mine," he wrote to Adolph Löwe a few
weeks after his arrival.[68] And at Christmas 1932 he summed up his
first impressions to another friend with the following words: "Academic life goes its pleasant course as usual at Harvard. I like the place
immensely."[69]

Schumpeter must have received a warm welcome from his new colleagues in the economics department when he arrived at Harvard. In
1927 the department had decided that they needed an "outstanding
man," and that Schumpeter was it. A vote had been taken, which
Schumpeter easily won (followed by Gustav Cassel and Edwin Can-
nan). The choice of Schumpeter was articulated to the dean by Allyn
Young in the following words:

> Schumpeter, beyond doubt, is the most distinguished of the younger gen-
> eration of economists on the continent of Europe. . . . He is, I imagine,
> about forty-five years old. His English is good, and his special interests are
> such that he could handle precisely the graduate courses which I have been
> giving. He is well known in America, and his coming to this country would
> create a great deal of interest among American economists, and would be
> very distinctly a feather in our cap.[70]

When Schumpeter arrived at Harvard, the economics department
was in a period of transition. Historical economics had traditionally
dominated the department. Interestingly, Harvard's economics department also taught the sociology courses, since there was no separate sociology department. But this was increasingly considered outmoded, and historical economics as well as sociology were in the
process of being phased out. The department was looking for something more in tune with the times. Schumpeter, who all his life had
been a fervent advocate of the introduction of mathematics into economics, fit perfectly into the new type of department that was now
taking shape. He quickly succeeded in assembling a Committee on
Instruction in Mathematical Economics, and in the fall of 1933 he
taught the first course in mathematical economics at Harvard.

The department was also going through a generational change in
the early 1930s. Taussig was getting old, and it was Schumpeter who
first took over his famous graduate course in economic theory, Ec-11.
The Harvard department attracted several other excellent economists in addition to Schumpeter in the 1930s, such as Wassily Leontief, Gottfried Haberler, and Alvin Hansen. The result was an intel-

lectually stimulating and exciting milieu for Schumpeter. In the 1930s, Harvard's economics department became one of the best in the United States. The two theories that were to attract the most attention there were Chamberlin's theory of monopolistic competition and Leontief's input-output analysis. Still, to quote a standard article on the history of the Harvard department, "Joseph Alois Schumpeter . . . was, without doubt, the outstanding member of the department in the 1930s and 1940s."[71]

The economics students at Harvard were also particularly brilliant during these years. They included Paul Samuelson, Richard Goodwin, James Tobin, Abram Bergson, Wolfgang Stolper, and many more. The junior faculty included such people as Paul Sweezy—a particular favorite of Schumpeter—and John Kenneth Galbraith. Schumpeter got along very well with the students and, as always, he gave generously of his time. In addition to office hours, every week he circulated a sheet among his graduate students, urging them to sign up for a half hour of discussion. Schumpeter used to amuse his students with a string of anecdotes from old-time Europe, and he consistently gave them inflated grades.[72] With his various European mannerisms, Schumpeter must have been as exotic to his American students as a cowboy would have been to the students in Heidelberg. Paul Samuelson has given the following picture of his teacher in 1935 in the famous Ec-11:

> After, and not before, the students had assembled for the class hour, in would walk Schumpeter, remove hat, gloves, and topcoat with sweeping gestures, and begin the day's business. Clothes were important to him: he wore a variety of well-tailored tweeds with carefully matched shirt, tie, hose, and handkerchief. My wife used to keep track in that period of the cyclic reappearance of the seemingly infinite number of combinations in his wardrobe: the cycle was not simple and it was far from random.[73]

Another picture of Schumpeter from these early days at Harvard, which also hints at the pleasure Schumpeter seems to have taken in his role as a Harvard professor, can be found in John Kenneth Galbraith's memoirs. Galbraith describes his older colleague in the following manner:

> Schumpeter was a slightly swarthy man of solid frame and a little less than average height. He had an amused and expressive face and an unremitting love for company and conversation. That Cambridge lacked the style of Franz Josef's Vienna he never doubted, but he was determined to compensate as best he could. He held court each afternoon in a small coffee shop across Massachusetts Avenue from Widener Library. . . .[74]

Schumpeter also appeared to have been satisfied with the way his work was going during these first years in the United States. This was clearly very important to him since work had become his main existential reason for living after Annie's death. "My work is my only interest in life," he wrote in a letter to Irving Fisher in the mid-1930s.[75] Schumpeter produced a steady stream of articles at Harvard, all in brilliant English prose, which earned him many admirers. An English translation of *The Theory of Economic Development* appeared in 1934 and got excellent reviews in the mainstream economic journals. Schumpeter was also very active in the 1930s in the Econometric Society. But most important, Schumpeter had high hopes for his two major intellectual projects during these years: a massive work on business cycles, and a more tentative, theoretical work entitled *The Theoretical Apparatus of Economics*.

Adding to Schumpeter's well-being during these first years at Harvard was the fact that by 1935 he had paid off all his debts. Schumpeter also remarried in 1937, and so left Taussig's house and moved into a home of his own, first at 15 Ash Street and then from June 1938 on at 7 Acacia Street in Cambridge. Schumpeter's new wife also had a beautiful, large house in Connecticut—"Windy Hill" in Taconic—to which Schumpeter was immediately attracted.

Schumpeter's third wife was Elizabeth Boody, and she came from a well-to-do New England family. She had been married before—to a book dealer named Maurice Firuski—but was divorced since 1933. As a student Elizabeth attended Radcliffe and earned a Ph.D. in 1934 in economics with economic history as her specialty. Thereafter she supported herself as a researcher at Harvard and Radcliffe, specializing in the economy of Japan, in which she succeeded in publishing several scholarly articles, especially about the economy of Japan. Elizabeth Boody Schumpeter was clearly the most accomplished of Schumpeter's wives and she no doubt deserves more scholarly attention than she has received until now.[76] Many friends felt that Schumpeter appealed primarily to Elizabeth's protective instincts, and that she wanted to take care of him and shelter him from the world. The house on Acacia Street, for example, had been chosen because it was situated on a calm side street, so Schumpeter would not be disturbed by the noise from passing cars. There was only one telephone in the house, which had been placed in the kitchen to prevent Schumpeter from hearing it ring. Elizabeth explained these arrangements in the following way in a letter from 1939:

He [Schumpeter] has had many heavy responsibilities and many difficult situations to face in the past. As a consequence his nervous system has become more or less disorganized. He is able to carry on his work at Harvard only if he has fairly long periods of complete quiet and rest. He is, of course, being subjected to careful medical treatment.[77]

Just as earlier in his life, the picture of Schumpeter as a private person differs radically from the image he projected in public. We can get a glimpse of what Schumpeter did *not* want his students and colleagues to find out through some dramatic letters that Elizabeth wrote to him during the summer of 1937, just before they were married. Elizabeth clearly felt that Schumpeter was a sick man and in need of immediate care. More precisely, he was periodically given to severe depressions, which he did nothing about. In Elizabeth's words:

> You mellow in my society and then you go away and think dark thoughts. I have been willing to try to draw you back again and again because I love you and because it seemed to me that almost any life would be preferable to the one you are leading with its concomitant state of mind. It is, of course, your mind much more than your body which makes you feel ill and weak.[78]

What Elizabeth in another letter called Schumpeter's "pendulum-like movements" refers both to swings in his mood and in his attitude to Elizabeth herself. It is clear that Schumpeter felt ambivalent about marrying Elizabeth, and she reacted to this ambivalence with sadness and anger. In response to Schumpeter's refusal to come and visit her in Taconic about a month before their marriage, she lashed out: "You really will have a breakdown if you go on leading the ridiculous existence you lead at present."[79] It was clear that to Elizabeth, Schumpeter's choice was between, on the one hand, herself and some peace of mind and, on the other, breakdown and despair. Perhaps Schumpeter also came to see it that way. In any case, on August 16, 1937, they were married in Community Church in New York.

There were negative aspects to Schumpeter's new life in the United States as well, and as time went on, they became more pronounced. For example, he could never reconcile himself to the heavy teaching load at Harvard. It wore him down and added to his depressions. "The teaching load is terrible and enough to kill a bull," he wrote to a friend.[80] As the years went by, Schumpeter also felt increasingly snubbed by the administration at Harvard. By 1940 he was so fed up that he seriously contemplated accepting an offer from Yale. He declined only after long deliberations and after the faculty and the students had made it unambiguously clear that they really wanted him to stay.

Schumpeter's work did not go very well in the late 1930s either.

In 1936 Keynes published his *General Theory* and thereby upstaged Schumpeter for the second time. Keynes had written exactly the kind of work that Schumpeter himself would have liked to produce: a brilliant work which immediately was recognized as a classic. When Schumpeter's *Business Cycles* appeared in 1939, it went almost unnoticed; in any case, it was not very much appreciated. The Harvard students, who under Alvin Hansen's influence had become fervent Keynesians, also began to desert Schumpeter. This hurt him, since he had grown accustomed to a fan club of admiring students.[81] When *Business Cycles* appeared, a seminar was held at which the graduate students made clear what they thought of Schumpeter's book. Schumpeter, who rarely could be coaxed into discussing his own theories, nearly lost his temper and said that they should at least have made an attempt to understand what he was trying to say. The whole thing was a "disgrace," Lloyd Metzler later said.[82]

The political developments during the 1930s also upset Schumpeter. He was disgusted by the strong anti-Franco sentiments in the United States—even among people who, in his opinion, should have known better. "Many good conservatives," he wrote in dismay to an acquaintance, "take sides with the anarchist and communist rabble." How they could do this was a mystery to him: "The government headed by Franco . . . is really the most national and democratic imaginable."[83] Schumpeter also detested Roosevelt with a passion. Time and again he lambasted "the political doctor" and the "violent cures" the president was prescribing for "the economic patient."[84] In Schumpeter's opinion, the Depression could not be alleviated by interventions of the state. The business cycle should not be disrupted; it had to work itself out, through the downs as well as the ups. Schumpeter was also afraid that Roosevelt would get the United States involved in World War II. He felt that this would only strengthen the anti-capitalist forces in the United States and drive the country a step further in the direction of socialism. "I cannot help feeling this will be the end of the American way of life," he wrote to a friend of similar mind. He added gloomily that Roosevelt's politics also meant that "the likes of us will disappear."[85]

A few months after these words were written, the Japanese attack on Pearl Harbor brought the United States into the war. The years 1942 to 1945, all of Schumpeter's friends agree, were to be particularly hard and unhappy for him. He was increasingly isolated because of his controversial political opinions, and he responded by withdrawing more or less completely into his work. He was often depressed and only Elizabeth fully supported him. According to Galbraith, "he secluded himself over in the library at the Business School, reading and working away . . . and feeling that the Europe he knew and loved was tearing itself to pieces."[86] He wrote in his private diary in January 1942: "This is no longer my world. I am a stranger to the mortals and their doings. . . ."[87]

What most people in Schumpeter's milieu reacted against during these years were Schumpeter's violent attacks on the president and his ambivalent statements about the enemy regimes. Gottfried Haberler tells the following story, which gives an indication of what was going on:

> Schumpeter was extremely critical of Roosevelt and his New Deal. In 1944, when Roosevelt was running for his fourth term as president, a lady who was unaware of Schumpeter's intense aversion asked him at a cocktail party whether he would vote for Roosevelt. He answered: "My dear lady, if Hitler runs for President and Stalin for Vice President, I shall be happy to vote for that ticket against Roosevelt."[88]

Several of Schumpeter's friends in Cambridge, including Haberler and Galbraith, felt that Schumpeter was definitely *not* pro-Nazi, and they urged him to restrain himself since he was giving people the impression that he supported the German regime. They were not too successful in this, judging from the comments of another close friend of Schumpeter. According to Richard Goodwin, it was perfectly clear that Schumpeter was "pro-Hitler, saying, to anyone who cared to listen, that Roosevelt and Churchill had destroyed more than Jenghis Kan."[89] What Schumpeter really felt about Nazism is difficult to establish, even now. On the one hand, it is clear that his own political ideal was always much closer to British conservatism than to German fascism. On the other hand, however, it is just as clear that in the choice between fascism and communism, he would choose the former any day. It is in this sense that statements like "Germany and Japan" being "our two natural bulwarks" should be understood.[90]

Schumpeter's only wholehearted supporter during these years was his wife, and the two grew closer together. Elizabeth was actually in a similar situation to Schumpeter since she had apparently been blacklisted by the administration in Washington for her pro-Japanese statements. The FBI also kept an eye on her during the war. Going through the records more than thirty years later, one gets a feeling that her reputation as a rabid right-winger and a potentially disloyal citizen was unfair. It is also clear that her academic career was damaged by these rumors, and that the whole misunderstanding would torment her until her death.[91] In any case, her situation probably made her sympathize even more with Schumpeter's semi-ostracized status. Both of them also deeply admired Japan and were upset by the anti-Japanese sentiments that swept the country.

In 1942 Schumpeter published *Capitalism, Socialism and Democracy*, which soon became a huge success. But this did not give Schumpeter much pleasure, and he seems to have regarded the book more as a diversion than as a serious scientific effort. Galbraith says that Schumpeter "once told me that among his books this one inspired his special loathing. It lacked, he said, scientific depth and precision."[92] Galbraith ascribes Schumpeter's disparaging remarks to his elitism: Schumpeter did not want to write for the common reader but only for the elected. This might be true, but Schumpeter was also going through a serious personal crisis during the war years, which made it hard for him to enjoy anything completely.

It seems that Schumpeter during these years was becoming more and more preoccupied with the thought of his own death. He wanted to sum up his life, to see where he had gone wrong and find out why he always felt so miserable. One entry in his private diary from 1942 is particularly revealing in this regard. Schumpeter here writes:

> Funny when I survey my life and my present situation I see that I was favored in many respects, and I also see a mosaic of many successes. Yet as a whole and in a worldly sense, and quite apart (tho' perhaps not so "apart" after all) from the fact that subjectively I was unhappy most of the time, it was a failure. And the reason is quite clear—even in my scientific activity and in spite of an "oeuvre" a fraction of what would have been enough for "fame," I do not carry weight: for I am typically "unleaderly"—in fact I am a man without an aura (and without antennae). . . .[93]

In 1945 Schumpeter ends a similar retrospective entry in his diary with the words, "Ease me gently to my grave."[94]

---

Schumpeter was to live only a couple of years after World War II. According to a friend, he withdrew even further into himself during this time. There were several reasons for this. For one thing, the war had destroyed much of the world he held dear, and it had released political forces in many countries that he heartily disliked. Some of the family and friends he had left in Europe had also fared badly. Gradually he learned of their fates. For instance, in 1947 he received a letter explaining how his old companion, Mia Stöckel, had been killed together with her husband during the war. In January 1942 the Nazis had moved into the small Serbian town of Neusatz, where she and her husband lived, and started executing everyone thought to be potentially disloyal—including, like Mia, all the members of the local English Club.[95]

During the years after the war, Schumpeter was also increasingly alienated from his colleagues and students. To these people Schumpeter seemed a leftover from another age—he was "just a showman" and "someone who could say 'marginal utility' in seventeen languages," to quote some of the uncharitable comments of his colleagues and students from these years.[96] Schumpeter wrote to a friend in 1949 that "[I] cannot say that I experience much stimulus from my surroundings. Scientifically, Leontief is the only man who is really alive and he is now so much buried in administrative work, running the big research organization which he has built up, that not so very much remains of him either."[97]

But even if Schumpeter's colleagues and students at Harvard were not very interested in his work, Schumpeter's standing with the economics profession was still excellent. In 1948 he was elected president of the American Economic Association and only his death prevented him from becoming the first president of the International Economic Association. During his last years Schumpeter also began to redirect his work away from economic theory, which he felt was becoming sterile, to economic history. For example, he supported Arthur Cole, who was head of the Research Center in Entrepreneurial History at Harvard (1948–1958). He also wrote more on economic history and distanced himself from the nonhistorical and over-mathematized type of economics that was now becoming popular. Schumpeter still spoke of having several books to write—one on conservatism, one on sociology, one on money, and so on. But all of them had to wait until he had finished his main task: the giant *History of Economic Analysis*, on which he was feverishly working.

Schumpeter died in his sleep during the night of January 7–8, 1950, in his own bed in the house in Taconic, Connecticut. The medical reason was cerebral hemorrhage, even if some suspected that the real reason was overwork in combination with a lack of will to live. Elizabeth arranged for a funeral with Episcopalian services at St. John's Church in Salisbury, Connecticut. She then spent the next few years trying to honor his memory in various ways. Money was collected for a Schumpeter Prize Fund and his private papers were put together and given to Harvard. Elizabeth sold the house on Acacia Street and used half of the money to put *History of Economic Analysis* into order. Elizabeth herself was to live another couple of years in the house in Taconic. Then she too passed on.

## SCHUMPETER'S WORK: ITS UNITY AND CONTEXT

There exists a distinct unity to Schumpeter's work that is essential to keep in mind if one wants to understand his individual writings and appreciate his greatness as an economist. This anthology is dedicated to this unity. Its subtitle—"The Economics and Sociology of Capitalism"—is actually a quote from *Business Cycles*, and it also recurs many times in Schumpeter's other writings. To some extent one is no doubt justified in equating this unity in Schumpeter's work with what he himself called his "vision." All economists, as Schumpeter says in *History of Economic Analysis*, are driven by a "preanalytic" view of things; and all great works in economics draw as much on this vision as on the analytical skills of the author.[98] And it is true that Schumpeter's vision was uncommonly broad: It included not only economics but also sociology, history, and (more peripherally) political science. It is no doubt this broad vision of Schumpeter that some of his Harvard colleagues had in mind when they put together a collection of essays in his memory and called it *Schumpeter, Social Scientist*.[99]

Today, when mainstream economics has essentially cut off its links to the other social sciences, it is important to recall that economics is a member of the family of the social sciences and that it has much in common with history, sociology, and political science. One of the purposes of this anthology is to remind us of this fact. It contains the majority of Schumpeter's writings in sociology and a few others with direct relevance to history and political science.

It would, however, not be correct to leave the reader with the vague impression that Schumpeter just had an "interdisciplinary" approach to economics; and that he, for this reason, could have a salutary influence on contemporary economics. This is much too simple, and Schumpeter's own position was much more complex. As we shall see, Schumpeter spent considerable time analyzing the relationship between economics and the other social sciences, and he was constantly trying to work out different ways of integrating them in his concrete analyses. It is also very important to note that he did this within a very specific economic discourse, which has largely been forgotten today. To reestablish the proper intellectual context of Schumpeter's work represents a crucial task when one is trying to come to terms with his writings half a century later. As we shall see, Schumpeter struggled to express his "vision" within a distinct body of German-Austrian economics which was called *Sozialökonomik* and which had emerged around the turn of the century as a direct reaction to the *Methodenstreit*. At various times, Schumpeter suggested different solutions to the problem of how to put economics back together again and thereby overcome the artificial separation into "abstract economics" and "historical economics" which had developed as a result of the battle of the methods.[100]

Before taking a closer look at Schumpeter's work, a few words about *Sozialökonomik* are in order. The person who gave the name to this effort to reintegrate economics around the turn of the century in Germany was Max Weber. He, in turn, had picked up the term from Heinrich Dietzel, an economist at the University of Bonn.[101] Weber basically tried to have *Sozialökonomik* (translated by Schumpeter into English sometimes as "social economics" and sometimes just as "economics" and "scientific economics") accepted as a replacement for "political economy," which was on its way out of economic discourse in Germany as in other countries around the turn of the century. According to Schumpeter, Weber launched a real campaign to popularize the new term.[102] For example, when he became editor for *Archiv für Sozialwissenschaft und Sozialpolitik* in the early 1900s, he tried to turn it into a platform for *Sozialökonomik*. It was actually in connection with this that Weber sketched the intellectual program for this new type of economics. What Weber had in mind with *Sozialökonomik* was first of all a broad kind of economic analysis, which would encompass not only economic theory but also historical economics. It is clear that Weber was very disturbed by the *Methodenstreit*, which in his formulation had split economics into "*two* sciences"—Menger's new type of economic theory and Schmoller's historical economics.[103] Weber wanted to bring these two back together into a single, much richer concept of "economics."

But Weber's vision of economics was even broader than that. He also wanted *Sozialökonomik* to include something he called "economic sociology" (*Wirtschaftssoziologie*). Exactly how the various bits were to fit together caused Weber considerable headache; and he tried different solutions in his writings, just as Schumpeter would later do. Since he first and foremost was a sociologist, it is natural that Weber was personally most interested in "economic sociology." But even if his own inclinations went in this direction (as well as in that of economic history), it is obvious that Weber's basic stance was that economics as a science should be broad enough to encompass all three of them: *economic theory, economic history,* and *economic sociology*. According to Weber, the point was not so much to synthesize and coordinate their methods and results—this was unrealistic and could even be unsuitable. The point was rather to reintroduce into German academics a new and richer concept of economics, which would thrive on a dialogue between these three different viewpoints. Economic theory—

especially in its novel, Austrian form—was certainly necessary, but so were economic history and economic sociology.

But the advancement of these theories did not go as Weber had hoped. The term *Sozialökonomik*, as Schumpeter would write in retrospect, "never caught on."[104] And instead of overcoming the artificial separation between theoretical economics and historical economics, which characterized the situation around the turn of the century in Germany, the former won a devastating victory over historical economics. As the twentieth century advanced, history was increasingly forced out of economics and transferred to a new group of academics, the economic historians. Economic theory was systematically dehistorized and desociologized; and practically all the links between economics and the other social sciences were severed. The project of a broad-based *Sozialökonomik* vanished in this process to the point where it is not even mentioned in today's histories of economic thought. There therefore exist two good reasons today to draw attention to the vision of "social economics." First, the contemporary concept of "economics" has shrunk to what was known as "theoretical economics" around the turn of the century; and some would argue that this has led to an intellectual impoverishment of economics as a science. And second, the notion of *Sozialökonomik* gives us a vantage point from which to understand the greatness of Schumpeter's work.


### The European Period

Schumpeter's work can conveniently be divided into two periods, his European period and his American period. The former starts in the early 1900s—more precisely in 1906, when he published his first major article in economics—and it ends in 1932, when Schumpeter left Germany and the University of Bonn for the United States. The American period begins with Schumpeter's arrival at Harvard and it ends in 1950 with his death. This division places roughly twenty years of scholarship into each period. Schumpeter's first three major works belong to his early period: *The Nature and Essence of Theoretical Economics* (1908), *The Theory of Economic Development* (1911), and *Economic Doctrine and Method* (1914). His last three major works belong to his American period: *Business Cycles* (1939), *Capitalism, Socialism and Democracy* (1942), and *History of Economic Analysis* (posthumously published in 1954). During his early period, Schumpeter was the *enfant terrible* of European economics; and during his late period he was a mature and respected economist in the United States. During his time in Europe, Schumpeter outlined his famous theory of the entre-

preneur; in the United States he focused mainly on the development
of capitalism.

The division of Schumpeter's work into a European part and an
American part is convenient for a variety of reasons, and it is this
distinction that will be used here. Schumpeter's writings in this volume have been arranged chronologically, and the items from before
1932 will be presented in conjunction with Schumpeter's early works;
while those produced after this date will be discussed with his later
works. A few qualifying remarks regarding the basis for this group-
ing of his works into a European and an American period are, however, in order. First, it is clear that Schumpeter had a burst of creativity during a rather brief period of his youth. It was roughly during
the years 1905–1914 that Schumpeter's first three major works were
written—during a time span, in other words, that was considerably
shorter than his "European period." After that, more than twenty
years pass until a new major work appears: *Business Cycles* (1939). It
is also evident that Schumpeter's writings from his American period
were strongly prefigured by those of his youth. *Business Cycles* (1939)
is in many ways a follow-up to *The Theory of Economic Development*
(1911); and *History of Economic Analysis* (1954) is an elaboration upon
themes in his history of economic thought from 1914. There is, in
brief, no sharp conceptual break between his European period and
his American period.

It is clear that Schumpeter's major achievement during his early
period was *The Theory of Economic Development* (1911) in which he presented his famous theory of the entrepreneur. There is, however,
more to Schumpeter's work during these early years than his theory
of economic change. For example, he also wrote a small book on the
history of social science; he made a vigorous plea for "theoretical economics" in another book-length study; and he wrote the history of
*Sozialökonomik* in yet another volume. Before returning to Schumpeter's ideas in *The Theory of Economic Development*, we shall take a look
at some of these lesser known works in order to get a better picture
of how Schumpeter viewed *Sozialökonomik*.

Schumpeter's broad interests in the social sciences and in the way
these are related to each other was one of the factors that made him
sympathetic to Weber's idea of a *Sozialökonomik*. That Schumpeter
himself had a thorough knowledge of several different social sciences
is clear from his studies of the tax state and imperialism as well as
from his general writings on social science. Two of these more general writings deserve special attention, namely a pamphlet called *Wie
studiert man Sozialwissenschaft?* (*How to Study Social Science*, 1910), and
a small book, entitled *Vergangenheit und Zukunft der Sozialwissenschaften*

(*The History and Future of the Social Sciences*, 1915).[105] Both of these were published by the Academic Social Science Association in Czernowitz, in which Schumpeter was a very active member while he taught at the local university.

From these two writings it is possible to get a picture of how Schumpeter looked at the division of labor between the social sciences—a theme of great importance to *Sozialökonomik*. According to Schumpeter, the social sciences do not constitute an organic unity, where each social science has its own, determined place. The situation is rather one of chaos, and the different social sciences have often developed by historical accident. Sometimes the development of a social science has been determined by its method and sometimes by its object. The result is that the same problem is often analyzed by several different social sciences. As Schumpeter put it: "There basically does not exist one social science—only different social sciences, whose circles often intersect."[106]

The picture of the history of the social sciences that Schumpeter draws in these early works illustrates well his thesis that the social sciences have not developed according to some architectural blueprint, but rather as the result of historical fiat. In Schumpeter's opinion, social science was basically born during the Renaissance and the Reformation, when traditional society experienced very rapid and dramatic changes. It was during this period that the first attempts were made to free human thought from the yoke of religion. According to Schumpeter, social science emerged primarily out of the natural law tradition. The eighteenth century was the golden century in social science; it was then that natural law began to give birth to the individual social sciences. "What the Nile was to Egypt, natural law was to social science thinking in the eighteenth century."[107] Economics, according to Schumpeter, was one of the sciences born out of the natural law tradition, and so was sociology.

During the nineteenth century social science made few advances. The critical spirit of the eighteenth century was now replaced by an emphasis on historical individuality, romanticism, and hostility to rationalism. All of this prevented the social sciences from flowering. But Schumpeter was not pessimistic about the future of the social sciences. Something of a revival in social science was already taking place, Schumpeter said; and this revival was inspired by the insight that all the major areas of human activity—art, politics, economics, and so on—could be analyzed in terms of social action. We are now living in a time when "the sociological way of thinking" ("*Soziologisieren*") is becoming increasingly important, and when much energy is directed toward the creation of "a cultural theory." Our time, Schumpeter concludes, will "have its run"—but only provided we remember that the division of labor is necessary in social science, and that personal and political values must always be kept out of the analysis.[108]

The most precise picture of how Schumpeter saw *Sozialökonomik* during his early European period can be found in *Economic Doctrine and Method* (1914). This work had been commissioned by Max Weber for *Grundriss der Sozialökonomik*, the giant handbook in economics that Weber had started to edit around the turn of the century. Schumpeter's book, in other words, was not intended as a conventional history of economics but rather as a history of *Sozialökonomik*. It therefore deals not only with economics in a more narrow sense ("economic theory"), but also with "economic sociology" and with "history." In the course of going through the development of economics, Schumpeter carefully outlines what in his mind are the proper tasks for "economic theory," "economic sociology," and "history." He stresses that one must not fuse these three perspectives into a single type of economic analysis; that would just be harmful. Each of them has its own distinct role to play within the broad framework of *Sozialökonomik*.

In his history of economic thought Schumpeter traces the origin of *Sozialökonomik* to Aristotle. After Aristotle, little progress was made until the Renaissance, which gave birth to the natural law perspective. A new scientific spirit was born that was rationalistic and anti-metaphysical in nature. Modern scientific economics has its roots in this natural law tradition, more precisely in the works of the physiocrats. To Schumpeter the first major accomplishment in economics was the discovery by Quesnay of "the circular flow." Adam Smith had in Schumpeter's mind synthesized the ideas of many other economists, but was not a particularly original thinker of his own.

In general, Schumpeter had a positive opinion of the classical economists. He felt that they were basically inspired by the natural law tradition and that they had made several significant contributions to economic theory. There were, however, also some serious limitations to their works. For one thing, their "economic sociology" was very poor, when it was not nonexistent. By this term (*ökonomische Soziologie* in German) Schumpeter essentially meant an analysis of economics as a social phenomenon as opposed to an exclusively economic phenomenon. The classical economists had made several assumptions about socio-economic reality, which they then mistakenly treated as if they were true pictures of reality. They thought, for example, that individuals maximize; that there is perfect competition; and so on. To Schumpeter, this was clearly wrong. One could indeed make assumptions about reality; that was the proper way to proceed in economic theory. But it was naive to believe that an assumption is the same as reality. In Schumpeter's mind, this proved that you did not understand the central epistemological distinction between "objects of knowledge" ("*Erkenntnisobjekt*") and "real objects" ("*Realobjekt*").

During much of the nineteenth century there was a strong reaction to the rationalist spirit of the eighteenth century. According to Schumpeter, romanticism was destructive to the advancement of economic theory. It was on the other hand congenial to the development of "economic sociology." The nineteenth century also saw the birth of the work of Karl Marx, to which Schumpeter devotes an enormous footnote in his history of economic thought.[109] According to Schumpeter, it was clear that Marx had a "scientific talent of the highest calibre." One, however, has to make a distinction between Marx's "sociology" and his "economic theory"; and it is obvious that Schumpeter preferred Marx the Sociologist to Marx the Economist. Marx's foremost achievement as a sociologist, Schumpeter says, was clearly his "economic interpretation of history." Marx's basic intuition—that the economic reality of society influences its social structure—was extremely valuable, even if it could easily be misused.

Schumpeter's attitude to the role that "history" should play in *Sozialökonomik* comes out with great clarity in the section of his book that is devoted to the *Methodenstreit*. According to Schumpeter, it was self-evident that historical research was part of economics. "If we counted all 'empiricists' as members of the Historical School of Economics, it would include absolutely all economists."[110] Some people, no doubt, preferred historical studies to theoretical studies and vice versa. But to elevate this personal preference to a principled contradiction between "theory" and "history" was a grave mistake. "Economic science," Schumpeter says, "has in all periods and in all countries contained historical and theoretical elements . . . without this in itself constituting a contradiction in principle."[111] It was simple—for some kinds of work you basically need a historical approach, and for others, a theoretical approach.

If there was no principled opposition between theory and history, why did the *Methodenstreit* take place? There were several reasons for this in Schumpeter's opinion, including the fact that Schmoller and his followers had tried to take over economics in Germany and constitute themselves as a school—a tabu to someone like Schumpeter, who believed that no schools should exist in economics.[112] It was also true that economic theory had never succeeded in getting a real foothold in German economics; it was a "foreign flower," which had never been properly transplanted. History, on the other hand, had always had an extremely privileged position in German academics, and this had helped to legitimize the Historical School of Economics.

The *Methodenstreit*, as Schumpeter saw it, had gone through three fairly distinct stages. During the first stage the debate was really not about methodology but rather about the political ideology of the classical economists—whether their advocacy of free competition and their hostility to state intervention in the economy was justified or not. During the second stage of the battle of the methods, the key issue shifted to the opposition between "induction" and "deduction"; should one use one or the other? To Schumpeter this opposition was nonsensical; any serious analysis in economics had to include inductive as well as deductive elements. Only during the third stage of the *Methodenstreit* was something productive accomplished. During this stage, Schumpeter said, it was realized that Menger and Schmoller were both advocating a *mixture* of "theory" and "history." Another important development was that someone like Weber now introduced new epistemological theories into the debate, which helped the participants to realize that the contradiction between "theory" and "history" was superficial. The point was brought home, Schumpeter says, that assumptions that had to be made for theoretical purposes should not be regarded as statements about reality. In the days of classical economics, Schumpeter concludes, economics was the only sophisticated social science around, and it was natural to extend its way of thinking to other topics. Today, however, the situation is different; and when economists need to analyze social reality, they should make use of the neighboring social sciences, like history and sociology.

It is obvious that Schumpeter himself—in contrast, for example, to Weber—was more interested in economic theory than in any other part of *Sozialökonomik*. This is evident from his first two books, *The Nature and Essence of Theoretical Economics* (1908) and *The Theory of Economic Development* (1911), which were both studies in economic theory. It is also clear that Schumpeter in principle drew sharp lines between "economic theory," "economic sociology," and "history." These were all sciences with different tasks and methods, and they should not be confused with one another. What is not so clear to contemporary researchers, however, is that what Schumpeter called "economic theory" is *not* the same as conventional economic theory, neither in Schumpeter's day nor today. The "economic theory" that Schumpeter advocated as part of *Sozialökonomik* has a structure different from conventional economic theory, and it also has much stronger links to "economic sociology" and "history."

To elaborate, let us look at Schumpeter's critique of conventional economic theory, which in his opinion only dealt with the "circular flow," and at his attempt to partially replace conventional economic theory with a theory of economic development. Schumpeter's appreciation of conventional economic theory is often exaggerated, something which comes from the fact that his first major work was written as a high-spirited defense of Walras's type of economics. This defense, however, had more to do with Schumpeter's opinion that "theoretical economics" had been neglected in Germany than with a belief that Walras's type of analysis represented the future in economics. Schumpeter was definitely appreciative of Walras's equilibrium theorem, which he always regarded as a magnificent scientific achievement. But he was also deeply critical of Walras's failure to deal with changes in the economy. Schumpeter's critique is expressed in a particularly poignant manner in a preface that he wrote in the 1930s for the Japanese edition of *The Theory of Economic Development*. Schumpeter here says that he soon came to realize that Walras's type of economics is only applicable to a "stationary" economic process, that is, to a process which does not change on its own accord. To Walras, Schumpeter wrote, "economic life is essentially passive," and whatever changes it goes through are exclusively a result of the impact of various *external* forces, such as wars and natural catastrophies. Schumpeter then continues:

> I felt very strongly that this was wrong, and that there was a source of energy within the economic system which would of itself disrupt any equilibrium that might be attained. If this is so, then there must be a purely economic theory of economic change which does not merely rely on external forces propelling the economic system from one equilibrium to another. It is such a theory I have tried to build [in *The Theory of Economic Development*] and I believe now, as I believed then, that it contributes something to the understanding of the struggles and vicissitudes of the capitalist world and explains a number of phenomena, in particular the business cycle, more satisfactorily than it is possible to explain them by means of either the Walrasian or the Marshallian apparatus.[113]

Schumpeter's notion of "the circular flow" constitutes the first step in his effort to recast economic theory in a more dynamic direction. The circular flow essentially depicts an isolated community, where the economic life remains the same year after year. The demand always finds its supply, and the various bits of the economic process fit together perfectly. The enterprises are run by managers, who obey the demand of the market in a mechanical fashion. The money in the system is sufficient, so no new money has to be infused. Everything, in brief, runs in the same channels year in and year out.

Schumpeter then asks whether one can improve conventional economic theory by using "history" and "economic sociology" rather than "theoretical economics." He firmly rejects both of these options; changes in the economy should not be explained either through "historical evolutionary forces" or through "economic sociology" with its emphasis on "the social framework of the economic course of events."[114] To Schumpeter this would be the same as giving up on economic theory and handing over its main task to social sciences, which were never intended to deal with "economic mechanisms." A new approach was needed, namely a purely economic theory which could account for changes through an analysis of developments *internal* to the economic system, as opposed to changes in its social and political environment. What was needed was a way to analyze a *dynamic* economy, as opposed to a static one.

The last stage in Schumpeter's argument was to construct such a theory with the help of his ideas about the entrepreneur. Certain aspects of Schumpeter's attempt to create a dynamic version of "theoretical economics" are particularly relevant from the viewpoint of *Sozialökonomik*. For one thing, Schumpeter's theory might originally have been intended as a *complement* to Walras and the idea of the circular flow. But as the analysis progresses in *The Theory of Economic Development*, it is clear that it increasingly came to *replace* it. The following phenomena could in Schumpeter's opinion only be explained through a theory of economic development: profits, interest, capital, savings, the money market, enterpreneurship, and business cycles. This amounts to a huge part of economic theory; and it is probably correct to say that it was the theory of the circular flow that ended up as a complement to Schumpeter's theory of economic development rather than the other way around.

Another fact that should be noted is that Schumpeter's dynamic theory broke with several of the key assumptions of conventional economic theory, which were particularly hard to square with a social perspective on economics. Schumpeter states, for example, that the entrepreneur is no "homo economicus." The entrepreneur is not driven by a desire for hedonistic enjoyment but by a different set of motives, such as "the joy of creating," "the will to conquer," and "the dream . . . to found a private kingdom."[115] It is also clear that in Schumpeter's theory of economic development the consumers and their tastes play a different role than in conventional economic theory. To Schumpeter, it is "the producer who as a rule initiates economic change, and consumers are educated by him if necessary; they are, as it were, taught to want new things, or things which differ in some respect or other from those which they have been in the habit of using." Schumpeter then concludes: "Therefore, while it is permissible and even necessary to consider consumers' wants as an independent and indeed the fundamental force in a theory of the circular flow, we must take a different attitude as soon as we analyze change."[116]

What also makes Schumpeter's new version of "theoretical economics" so different from conventional economic theory is that on several points it is very close to a sociological and a historical analysis of economics. Schumpeter, as we know, was in principle against confounding "economic theory" with "economic sociology" and "history." In practice, however, he often let his economic theory slip into historical and sociological ways of reasoning. There are many examples of this in Schumpeter's early work. The two most obvious ones in *The Theory of Economic Development* pertain to the spread of innovations and Schumpeter's idea that the actions of entrepreneurs structurally affect the system of stratification in capitalist society. Once an innovation has been made, Schumpeter says, a swarm of entrepreneurs emerge and eventually a whole business cycle is set in motion. This process, which is clearly sociological in nature, constitutes what Schumpeter terms "the second act of the drama" of economic change. To break through the initial resistance to change—the first act in the drama, so to speak—a heroic act is needed, and also here a sociological process is involved: "Any deviating conduct by a member of a social group," Schumpeter writes, "is condemned, though in greatly varying degrees according as the social group is used to such conduct or not. Even a deviation from social custom in such things as dress or manner arouses opposition, and of course all the more so in the graver cases."[117]

How closely Schumpeter ties stratification—another sociological topic par excellence—to economic development becomes clear in the part of *The Theory of Economic Development* where Schumpeter discusses the struggle between old and new firms. After having stressed that "new combinations" are often introduced by people other than those who are in charge of already established firms, Schumpeter moves from economics into sociology: "Especially in a competitive economy, in which new combinations mean the competitive elimination of the old, [this] explains on the one hand the process by which individuals and families rise and fall economically and socially and which is peculiar to this form of organisation, as well as a whole series of other phenomena of the business cycle, of the mechanism of the formation of private fortunes, and so on."[118]

In brief, economic theory in Schumpeter's version is not the same as conventional economic theory. Schumpeter's version of "theoretical economics" is much more dynamic and social in nature, and it also has far more direct links to the social and historical type of analysis. To have formulated this novel and more social type of "theoretical economics" represents one of Schumpeter's most important contributions to *Sozialökonomik*.

It should also be noted in this context that it is Schumpeter's "theoretical economics" that in most economists' minds constitutes his major contribution to mainstream economics. It is sometimes argued that Schumpeter was the first to raise the whole issue of economic change in modern economics. More often, however, Schumpeter's fame among mainstream economists rests on his attempt to introduce *technical change* into marginal utility analysis. It is generally agreed that neoclassical economics cannot deal effectively with technical change, and that technical change is central to modern economies. Schumpeter's *Theory of Economic Development* (as well as his later ideas about the positive role of monopoly in furthering technical innovations) is praised for its bold attempt to solve this problem—even if it is often added that Schumpeter's theory ultimately fails to provide what is needed the most, namely a formal theory of technical change.[119]

### The European Period: Schumpeter's Works in This Volume

Some of the writings in this anthology belong to Schumpeter's early period. These include a speech that Schumpeter gave in Japan in 1931 (Chapter 5); Schumpeter's necrology over Max Weber from 1920 (Chapter 3); and the three famous studies: "The Crisis of the Tax State" (1918), "The Sociology of Imperialisms" (1918–1919), and "Social Classes in an Ethnically Homogeneous Environment" (1927) (Chapters 1, 2, and 4). Since the last three writings are all studies in sociology, this provides an opportunity to take a closer look at how Schumpeter viewed sociology and its role in *Sozialökonomik*. First, however, a few words should be said about the Japanese lecture and the necrology of Weber, since these two writings are important for our understanding of *Sozialökonomik*.

Schumpeter probably gave the speech, on which "Recent Developments of Political Economy" is based, in Osaka-Kobe on February 9, 1931 (Chapter 5 in this volume).[120] Schumpeter had stopped in Japan on his way back from the United States to give a number of lectures. A few days after his departure, Schumpeter wrote to a friend that "the time in Japan was one continuous rush of addresses and excursions of all sorts" and that he had "enjoyed it greatly."[121] His original plan, according to the same letter, was "to work out half a dozen addresses [given in Japan] for publication." In the end little came of this plan; and only one of Schumpeter's speeches was actually published. Most of the notes he had made for his talks in Japan were left in Germany when he moved to the United States in 1932. Schumpeter, however, did bring with him the manuscript to two of the lectures he gave in Japan as well as a few notes. After his death these were discovered in a closet in Schumpeter's house in Cambridge and then donated to Harvard by his wife. One of them was published in *The Journal of Economic Literature* in 1982 as "The 'Crisis' in Economics— Fifty Years Ago"; and the second is being made available in this volume. Both of these essays—to cite a note attached to the original manuscripts (and probably written by Paul Sweezy)—are "splendid elaborations of J.A.S.'s central theme that economics is a science and that, being a science, there is essentially no room for disagreement."

Beyond this common theme, however, the two essays differ considerably. "Recent Developments of Political Economy," for example, contains a very thorough and illuminating discussion of the different principles according to which schools of thought are formed in economics—and also why all of them are invalid in Schumpeter's opinion. For instance, it is unacceptable to organize a school in economic theory according to one's political or philosophical convictions. What economists think in these matters has absolutely nothing to do with science. It is also wrong to talk of different national schools; there is no specifically "French," "English," or "German" school in economics—that is nonsense. Schumpeter concludes that schools are "evil things," and he hopes that "they will fall away from us as science progresses."

The Japanese lecture also contains some parts which help to clarify how Schumpeter saw *Sozialökonomik*. There is first of all his argument that no single method should have a monopoly on how to analyze economic phenomena. The tendency to elevate one method into a universal method, equally valid for all problems, is dangerous and had in his opinion helped to foster the *Methodenstreit* (which he described as "one of the greatest misfortunes" in economics). It was important to realize that while one had to start the analysis in "theoretical economics" with the individual, this was *not* suitable in other types of analyses. For some sociological problems, "methodological individualism" (which incidentally was a term that Schumpeter had coined in his 1908 book) cannot be used.[122] "Economic institutions," such as "private property" and "inheritance," Schumpeter says in his Japanese lecture, have for example to be approached in a different way from the topics that belong to economic theory.

In this same lecture, Schumpeter also has some comments on "the fourth field" of *Sozialökonomik*—that is, "statistics" (the other three being "theory," "economic history," and "economic sociology").[123] Schumpeter explains that it is extremely important to have a close collaboration between "theorists" and "statisticians," since this makes economics more precise and scientific. The American economists in particular, he says, had recently been trying to introduce quantitative data into their theories. In doing this, they were in Schumpeter's mind helping to inaugurate "a new epoch in economic science."

Schumpeter's Japanese lecture also contains some interesting remarks about sociology, and it is in this sense similar to the essays on imperialism, social classes, and the tax state. Schumpeter, as we know, had been interested in sociology since his days in Theresianum, but he was never formally trained in this field. One reason for this was simply that sociology did not exist as a separate topic at the University of Vienna when Schumpeter was a student. It seems that the only lectures in sociology that he ever attended were those of Edward Westermarck at the London School of Economics.[124] Still, Schumpeter appears to have read quite a bit on his own and when he got his *Habilitation* in 1909, he declared that aside from being qualified to give courses in "economics" and "statistics," he was also ready to give a course in "sociology" on "The Foundations of Sociology and Its Present State."[125]

Schumpeter's interest in sociology was probably also influenced by the positive attitude to this topic among some of his professors at the University of Vienna. It can be said that it was *through economics* that Schumpeter came to know and appreciate economic sociology. All his teachers in economics agreed that economics was a very broad topic, and that it should include not only economic theory but also historical and social approaches. This had been Carl Menger's opinion as well as that of his two foremost disciples, von Wieser and Böhm-Bawerk. Von Wieser was especially interested in sociological aspects of the economy, and when he produced a major treatise in economics in the early 1910s, he called it *Theorie der gesellschaftlichen Wirtschaft*. This work had been commissioned by Weber for *Grundriss der Sozialökonomik* (it actually appeared in the same volume as Schumpeter's history of economic theory) and was eventually translated into English as *Social Economics* (1927).[126]

Contact with other economists also caused him to become interested in sociology. For example, he was influenced by Marxist economists. It is true that not one of Schumpeter's professors in Vienna was a Marxist, but Marxism was an integral part of intellectual life in turn-of-the-century Vienna and young intellectuals were supposed to be well versed in it. Also, the historical economists looked at reality in a sociological-historical manner. That someone like Schumpeter, who had a lively interest in history, would study their works very carefully is rather obvious—and also clear from his history of economics from 1914.

The group of economists with which Schumpeter most closely identified when it came to sociology, however, was the so-called Youngest Historical School. Its key members were Max Weber, Werner Sombart, and Arthur Spiethoff. Schumpeter was to be a lifelong friend of Spiethoff, and he worked for several years together with Sombart and Weber as editor (1916–1933) for the famous social science magazine *Archiv für Sozialwissenschaft und Sozialpolitik*. Schumpeter could not stand Sombart but was on friendly terms with Weber.[127] Weber and Schumpeter collaborated on the *Grundriss der Sozialökonomik* and as fellow editors of *Archiv für Sozialwissenschaft und Sozialpolitik*, which Weber tried to steer in the direction of *Sozialökonomik*. Both were members of the German Sociological Association as well as the *Verein für Sozialpolitik*; and they fought on the same side in the famous "battle of the values" ("*Werturteilstreit*"). The issue in this dispute was whether social science should be a policy science or objective and value-free; Schumpeter, like Weber, argued forcefully for the latter option.[128] When Weber died in 1920, Schumpeter wrote a moving necrology in which he praised Weber's moral stature and acknowledged his outstanding achievements in sociology.[129]

From this necrology—which is reprinted in this volume as Chapter 3 in a fine translation by Guy Oakes—it is clear that Schumpeter deeply admired Weber. He saw Weber as a true leader, in scientific as well as in political matters. Schumpeter especially admired how Weber had solved the *Methodenstreit*—a task for which not only a tremendous methodological knowledge was needed, in Schumpeter's opinion, but also true leadership and strength of character. As to Weber's scientific accomplishments, Schumpeter stressed that Weber was first and foremost a sociologist and only secondly an economist. Still, he was a sociologist who was primarily interested in economic matters, and his work contains a wealth of insights for the broadly minded economist. *Grundriss der Sozialökonomik*, Schumpeter says, was originally intended to be a real encyclopaedia in economics, but this was stopped by the outbreak of World War I.

There is no doubt that Weber and Schumpeter influenced each other. Weber's annotated copy of *The Theory of Economic Development* can still be inspected at the Max-Weber-Arbeitsstelle in Munich, and several people have pointed to the similarities that exist between the charismatic leader in Weber's work and the entrepreneur in Schumpeter's work.[130] It is also clear that Weber came to influence Schumpeter on the issue of *Sozialökonomik* and "economic sociology." This having been said, however, it should also be noted that the emphasis in Schumpeter's work differed considerably from that in Weber's work. While Weber increasingly came to see himself as a sociologist, Schumpeter decided early on that he wanted to be an economic theorist. In a private letter he says that "dropping early sociological and historical interests, I became an economic theorist."[131] In brief, while Weber and Schumpeter agreed that economics should be a broad science, which drew on economics as well as on sociology and history, they each chose to concentrate on different aspects of it in their own works.

It appears that during his early period Schumpeter was more interested in producing concrete studies in sociology than in theorizing about sociology. Yet it is still possible to piece together a picture of how he viewed sociology during these years.[132] Sociology is essentially defined as the science about interactions between individuals in a group. As opposed to history and ethnology, sociology is an *analytical* science. This roughly means that one does not start the analysis by collecting facts, as in history and ethnology, but rather by some conceptual and theoretical work. In this sense sociology is similar to economics. But this is also where the similarity to economics ends; sociology and economics basically study different things and in different ways.

But this does not mean that economists and sociologists should not cooperate. In his 1908 book Schumpeter stresses that "sociology can accomplish much that we [economists] cannot do, but which is of interest to us."[133] According to Schumpeter, this is especially true for "economic sociology" or "*Wirtschaftssoziologie*." What Schumpeter meant by this term, which he probably had picked up from Weber, is not totally clear. Schumpeter is most explicit about "economic sociology" in a famous article from the mid-1920s on Schmoller. In "Gustav v. Schmoller und die Probleme von heute" (1926), Schumpeter points out that economic theory usually contains statements about "social institutions," such as "property," "inheritance," and "the family," and that these institutions are "partly economic" and "partly noneconomic" in nature.[134] Social institutions therefore cannot be analyzed with conventional economic theory; pure economic theory is only applicable to topics such as value, price, and money. Something else is needed—a "theory of economic institutions, basically within economic theory." And this something else is "economic sociology."

Schumpeter's attempt to outline the task of "economic sociology" in the essay on Schmoller may seem of little importance. But this is not necessarily the case. In several European countries, a vigorous debate had begun about "economic sociology" after the destructive *Methodenstreit*, and Schumpeter's essay was part of this. One person who, for example, picked up on Schumpeter's comment about economic sociology was Adolph Löwe in his book *Economics and Sociology: A Plea for Co-operation in the Social Sciences* (1935). Löwe himself, however, wanted a much more organic mixture of economics and sociology than Schumpeter. Schumpeter's "economic sociology," Löwe said, was basically "a kind of borderline science," where "only the outworks of the two sciences [economics and sociology] are in contact with each other." He summarized his critique of Schumpeter's type of economic sociology in this way:

> It renders the theoretical propositions of economics more concrete and appropriate to individual cases. But these generalizations themselves, the fundament of economic analysis, appear as an entirely independent body of knowledge, not requiring sociological research though certainly concerned with a particular section of society.[135]

Löwe's critique is justified up to a point, at least insofar as Schumpeter's theoretical statements about economic sociology and economic theory are concerned. In his concrete analyses, however, we already know that Schumpeter did not always stick to his principles but often followed his scientific instincts. This is also true for his famous analyses of the tax state, imperialism, and social classes. In theory, these were all studies in "sociology" and not in "economic theory" or "history." But, as we soon shall see, this distinction is hard to maintain once one takes a closer look at them. These essays are of obvious interest to the sociologist, but they are also excellent historical studies and helpful to the economic theorist.

This is especially true for "The Crisis of the Tax State" (Chapter 1 in this volume). This essay is based on a speech that Schumpeter gave in 1918 to the Viennese Sociological Society, and it was published in a sociological magazine later that year. In 1954 an English translation by Wolfgang Stolper and Richard Musgrave—both students of Schumpeter—appeared in *International Economic Papers*. The main question that Schumpeter addresses in this essay is whether the capitalist state ("the tax state" in his terminology) will be able to withstand the financial pressures after World War I, or whether it will break down. Schumpeter's answer is basically that it will be able to handle the financial difficulties, but that capitalism is still doomed to be replaced by socialism. "*That* too is certain," as the essay ends.

Within this general framework Schumpeter also addresses the following three topics: how to study the state; how the tax state has emerged historically; and how the Austrian state should handle the economic difficulties, once World War I is over. Schumpeter argues that the state is best studied within the new field of "fiscal sociology." *Finanzsoziologie* had been introduced by the Austrian sociologist and political activist Rudolf Goldscheid in his book *Staatssozialismus und Staatskapitalismus* (1917). Goldscheid here says that in order to understand the state, one must study its finances. As he put it in a famous phrase, which Schumpeter liked to cite: "The budget is the skeleton of the state stripped of all misleading ideologies."[136] Schumpeter fully agreed with Goldscheid that an analysis of the budget and the tax system offered an excellent vantage point for analyzing the state. The state apparatus is actually so much formed by its financial tasks that Schumpeter called it "the tax state" or "the tax-collecting state" ("*Steuerstaat*"). Taxation has also influenced "the spirit of a people, its cultural level, its social structure."[137] Schumpeter concludes that "fiscal sociology" is an important new field in sociology, of which much is to be expected. On this last point, incidentally, Schumpeter was wrong in his prognosis: with a few exceptions, sociologists have ignored this field.[138]

Why Schumpeter chose to call the state "the tax state" becomes even more clear in the historical section of the essay. This part describes how the state in Austria and Germany was born toward the end of the Middle Ages out of the financial needs of the princes.[139] They had mismanaged their finances for a long time; they had maintained too costly courts in order to pacify rival aristocrats; and they needed endless sums of money for the war against the Turks. At one stage during the fourteenth and fifteenth centuries, however, the princes succeeded in persuading the estates that wars were not just the personal responsibility of the prince but rather a "common exigency." It was at this point, Schumpeter says, that the modern state was born. The state soon transformed the old, communal economy into a private and a public sector in its search for new subjects to tax. The state machinery also became an important source of power, which led to bitter fights between the prince and the estates over who should control it. The prince won this battle in most countries. In the modern democracies, however, the prince has had to relinquish his power over the state to the general public.

The modern state, as Schumpeter explains it in his essay, is dependent on the existence of a healthy private economy; if no income is produced, there is nothing to tax. The state should therefore not interfere with the economy, and Schumpeter outlines in detail which kinds of taxes are proper for different kinds of income. Taxation of entrepreneurial profit should, for example, be lenient, while the profit of cartels can be taxed much more harshly. It is also important to realize, Schumpeter says, that if people demand more and more public services, the state will eventually collapse. Too high taxes will kill the desire to work; and in a capitalist economy people will only work as long as it pays for them to do so. If taxation is held within reasonable limits, however, there is no reason why the tax state should not survive.

The last question that Schumpeter addresses in "The Crisis of the Tax State" pertains to the future of the tax state in Austria. Will it have to be replaced by a new kind of state—a socialist state perhaps which will administer the economy rather than tax it—or will the Austrian state be able to handle the tremendous financial problems that it will have to confront, once World War I is over? Schumpeter's answer is that the state in Austria will *not* collapse, if the appropriate financial measures are taken; and in the last section of his essay he outlines what these measures are. According to one commentator, Schumpeter probably owes some of his appointment as a finance minister in 1919 to the measures he suggested in this article.[140] This may or may not be true, but it is true that some of Schumpeter's policy measures, such as the idea of a capital levy, were seriously debated by the Austrian politicians once the war was over.

During the war, Schumpeter was not only preoccupied with the situation in Austria but also with the problem of imperialism. The result was the essay called "The Sociology of Imperialisms," which appeared in 1918–1919 in *Archiv für Socialwissenschaft und Sozialpolitik* (Chapter 2 in this volume). In 1951, one year after Schumpeter's death, it appeared in an excellent English translation by Heinz Norden. Schumpeter's essay has been called "a minor classic" by Karl Deutsch, and Schumpeter also seems to have been quite satisfied with it. From his private correspondence it is clear that he regarded the essay on imperialism and the one on social classes as his two most important sociological works.[141] Both of them were also reproduced in the volume of Schumpeter's sociological writings, which was published in Germany in 1953 as *Aufsätze zur Soziologie*.[142]

Schumpeter's essay on imperialism is frequently cited in scholarly literature, but it is clear that what he tried to say is frequently misunderstood. This occurs so often, in fact, that one is justified in arguing that a new reading of "The Sociology of Imperialisms" is necessary today. Such a new interpretation should first of all try to do more justice to what Schumpeter actually says. It is especially important to avoid the two most common errors in interpreting Schumpeter's theory of imperialism, namely that it is purely psychological in nature or, alternatively, purely economic.[143] According to the first of these interpretations, Schumpeter mainly saw imperialism as the result of "psychological attitudes," "the dark powers of the subconscious," and the like. This, however, is a misreading of Schumpeter's essay; Schumpeter makes quite clear that the psychological element in imperialism cannot operate on its own but always needs the support of a social structure. According to the second erroneous interpretation, Schumpeter's theory can be reduced to the thesis that "capitalism is by nature anti-imperialist." In reality, however, Schumpeter's argument is much more complicated than that; and he of course acknowledges a historical link between early modern capitalism and imperialism. Schumpeter's theory of imperialism, in brief, is neither psychological nor economic in nature; it is predominantly *sociological* and to some extent it also draws on economic theory.

Schumpeter's essay on imperialism falls into two clearly defined parts. In the first he defines imperialism and he also discusses a series of historical examples. The main point here is to reject the Marxist theory of imperialism (which Schumpeter knew mainly through the works by Rudolf Hilferding and Otto Bauer—not Lenin) and to present an alternative theory which is more flexible and sociological in nature. Early in the essay we also find Schumpeter's famous definition of imperialism: "Imperialism is the objectless disposition on the part of the state to unlimited forcible expansion."[144] Schumpeter then proceeds to analyze a series of historical examples of imperialism, from Antiquity to the absolute monarchies in the seventeenth and eighteenth centuries. What all of these historical examples have in common, Schumpeter says, is that they show that imperialism is the result of a certain social structure. This social structure is characterized primarily by the central position it assigns to warriors or warlike groups—groups that must all expand in order to avoid extinction.

The second part of the essay focuses on the relationship between imperialism and capitalism. Schumpeter first points out that insofar as there is "a purely capitalist world," there will be no impulses toward imperialism. It is precisely at this point that the influence of economic theory on Schumpeter's reasoning is the most obvious. He argues that if there are free trade and competitive markets everywhere, there will be peace. It does not matter in this situation what nationality the buyers and the sellers are; the market alone will decide who gets what at a fair price. All energy in this type of free trade-capitalist society goes into industry, just as it goes into war in the feudal type of society. Schumpeter, however, also acknowledges that we do *not* live in "a purely capitalist world" where there is no imperialism. There exists indeed something he terms "modern imperialism." The reason for this is the following. Nations defend their markets through various protective measures; this protectionism breeds monopolies; and monopolies breed nationalistic rivalries. Protectionism, Schumpeter says, is an example of political interference in the market, and it is fundamentally to be characterized as a survival from the era of the absolutist monarchy. Today's imperialism, in brief, is an inheritance from bygone days. The essay closes with the sentence, "The dead always rule the living."

It should be clear from this brief account that Schumpeter's theory of imperialism is neither psychological nor economic in nature. The psychological element is dependent on the social structure and the purely economic element plays a minor role. It is also clear that Schumpeter's attempt to introduce elements of economic theory into his theory of imperialism is not very successful. The transition from the economic argument about free trade to the thesis that capitalism is by nature peaceful is not convincing. The reason for this, as for example Otto Hintze has made clear, is essentially that capitalism has been shaped just as much by political as by economic forces.[145] There exists, in brief, a historical link between "economics" and "politics" and therefore also between capitalism and war. What shall one do in this situation—reject Schumpeter's theory as wrong and forget his essay? That would be unwise; Schumpeter's one-hundred-page essay is filled with numerous interesting insights which would then be lost. Instead of rejecting Schumpeter's main theory, it would perhaps be better to eliminate the part on the inherently peaceful nature of capitalism. The result would then be a purely sociological theory of imperialism. Karl Deutsch, who advocates proceeding in exactly this manner with Schumpeter's theory, presents a revised Schumpeterian theory of imperialism in these words:

> Schumpeter's theory has a second and more dynamic implication. Whenever new social changes create a set of military habits, politically influential groups or classes, and important social institutions, all dependent for their continued functioning on sustained politics of warfare or at least war preparations, there the pattern of seemingly irrational imperialistic behavior— in the crude Assyrian or the more polished Roman manner—may come to be acted out all over again. Where such warlike habits and institutions have once again been developed, rational discussion of aims of foreign policy might once again be beside the point. Only domestic changes in the distribution of economic and political influence and in popular habits of political behavior might then be able to deflect or reverse the drift to unending armed conflicts.[146]

It is true that Schumpeter's theory becomes less provocative when the link to the theory of the inherent peacefulness of capitalism is cut off, in the manner that Deutsch suggests. But it is also evident that Schumpeter's theory of imperialism becomes considerably more flexible and realistic in Deutsch's "middle-range" interpretation.

Schumpeter's essay on social classes—Chapter 4 in this anthology—was originally published in 1927 in *Archiv für Sozialwissenschaft und Sozialpolitik*. However, it was already conceived during the 1910s, just as were the studies on the tax state and imperialism. Schumpeter says in the preface that he got "the basic idea" for the essay on classes in 1910 and that he worked on it until 1916. During these years he gave courses on social classes at the University of Czernowitz ("State and Society," in 1910–1911) and at Columbia University ("The Theory of Social Classes," in 1913–1914). In November 1926 he gave a lecture entitled "Leadership and Class Formation" at the University of Heidelberg, and this finally provided him with an opportunity to write down his ideas. The essay on social classes appeared the next year in German but not until 1951 in English translation. U.S. sociologists therefore did not come to know Schumpeter's ideas on this topic until much later. Still, they immediately recognized the essay as an important contribution to social stratification.[147] When, for example, Reinhard Bendix and Seymour Martin Lipset a few years later put together their famous reader in stratification, *Class, Status, and Power* (1953), they included an excerpt from Schumpeter's essay.

In his essay on classes Schumpeter links up "theoretical economics" and "sociology" in a much more successful way than in his study of imperialism. He makes clear that the concept of class can be understood in two very different ways, which must not be confused. On the one hand, "class" can be used in economic theory as a classificatory concept. One is, for example, perfectly justified in economic theory to place a manager and a worker in the working class, since both receive a salary. In sociology, however, this is not acceptable. Here "class" denotes something else, namely a specific, collective reality; and from this perspective, a worker and a manager have little in common. Drawing primarily on Durkheim, Schmoller, and Spann for his concept of class, Schumpeter says that "every social class is a special social organism, living, acting, and suffering as such and in need of being understood as such."[148] People who belong to a certain class interact much more with one another than with people from other classes; and one especially does not marry someone from another class. The "true unit" in social classes, Schumpeter says, is the family and not the individual.

After having outlined these general principles for how to look at social class, Schumpeter proceeds to analyze three specific problems: social mobility within classes; social mobility between classes; and the rise and fall of whole classes. Individuals may come and go, Schumpeter says, but social classes remain: "Each class resembles a hotel, . . . always full, but always of different people."[149] What propels a family upward within the same class or across class lines into a different class is usually some novel, extraordinary action. This is especially true for industrial society, Schumpeter says, where a bourgeois family of good standing will decline unless entrepreneurial profit is continuously added to its bank account. The link between Schumpeter's "sociology" and his "theoretical economics" is obvious on this point; and Schumpeter also explicitly refers the reader to a chapter in *The Theory of Economic Development*. Finally, the essay on social classes contains some interesting comments on the entrepreneur, which complement the portrait in his famous book from 1911.[150]

Mere entrepreneurial aptitude, however, does not account for all social mobility. There also has to be some insight into the specific problems that a family faces in its environments. A family, in other words, has to know how to adapt itself to society. The theme of adaptation becomes even more central in another section of the essay where Schumpeter discusses the rise and fall of whole classes. The fate of a class, he says, always depends on how well it can fulfill its "function" in society and how highly this "function" is evaluated by others. If a ruling class, for example, starts to evade its basic function, it will eventually lose its social power. An example of this is the feudal class. The primary function of this class was to fight: "In case of need the lord would mount his horse and defend himself, sword in hand, against dangers from above or below."[151] Gradually, however, feudal society was transformed into capitalist society; and there was less and less place for the warrior-aristocrat. The warlord himself also contributed to this development by becoming increasingly reluctant to fight himself and by rather hiring mercenaries to do the fighting for him. "In the end he [that is, the warlord] was likely to don armor only when his portrait was to be painted."[152]

It is evident that today's experts in stratification have surpassed Schumpeter in many ways. Still, Schumpeter's essay on social classes has much to teach when it comes to providing a broad, historical perspective on class society. Schumpeter's picture of the decline of feudal society is particularly successful; and it belongs to the tradition of Max Weber, Otto Hintze, and Norbert Elias with its " 'interpretive' history of class structure," as Schumpeter puts it.[153] It should also be noted that Schumpeter is much more successful in this essay than in the one on imperialism when it comes to linking up his "sociology" with "economic theory." In the essay on imperialism, economic theory is suddenly and rather unconvincingly brought into the analysis

in the form of the argument that there can be no imperialism in a
purely capitalist society with free trade. In the essay on social classes,
the transition from economic theory to sociology is more organic.
Schumpeter here ties the role of the entrepreneur, as outlined in *The
Theory of Economic Development*, directly to the rise and fall of classes.
With his notion that classes always have to fulfill certain "functions"
in society, Schumpeter also succeeds in introducing a sense of historical evolution into the analysis. The result is a fine mixture of "sociology," "economic theory," and "history" in accordance with the basic
principles of *Sozialökonomik*.

## The American Period

Schumpeter's American period began in 1932, when he arrived in
the United States for good; and it ended some eighteen years later
with his death in 1950. During these years Schumpeter produced a
stream of articles—all in impeccable, elegant prose. Many of these are
still worth reading, and the interested reader is referred to *Essays*
(1951) and *Ten Great Economists* (1951). However, Schumpeter's major
effort during this period was dedicated, as it had been in Europe, to
his books. And just as Schumpeter had produced three important
books as a young scholar, he now produced three more: *Business Cycles* (1939), *Capitalism, Socialism and Democracy* (1942), and *History of
Economic Analysis* (posthumously published in 1954). Of these three
books, two are more than a thousand pages long. The short one—
*Capitalism, Socialism and Democracy*—was written because Schumpeter
"sought relaxation";[154] and it ended up being only four hundred
pages!
   The herculean effort that went into these books gives a hint of the
seriousness with which Schumpeter regarded his scientific work. It
seems that he was first and foremost interested in finishing the work
he had begun in his youth. *Business Cycles* is thus a continuation of
*The Theory of Economic Development* (1911), and *History of Economic
Analysis* is an enormously enlarged version of *Economic Doctrine and
Method* (1914). In an elegant metaphor from *Business Cycles* Schumpeter says that he had provided "the analytical scaffolding" in his earlier work and that he now wanted to build "the house."
   The effort to finish his work and carry through his ideas to their
logical conclusion pushed Schumpeter during these years to go beyond "theoretical economics" and explore the economic phenomenon in its totality, in accordance with the notion of *Sozialökonomik*.
*Business Cycles*, for example, represents an attempt to tie together

"theory," "history," and "statistics"; "economic theory" was now to get its "statistical and historical complement," as Schumpeter put it.[155] "Sociology" was consciously left out of *Business Cycles* since Schumpeter felt it would be too cumbersome to handle the whole economic phenomenon all at once. In *Capitalism, Socialism and Democracy*, however, Schumpeter set out to analyze all that he had deliberately omitted from *Business Cycles*, namely those phenomena that threatened to undermine the whole economic system. The main focus in this latter work is therefore on "the sociology of capitalism" or on those forces that affect the economy without being part of the economic phenomenon in a more restricted sense. That Schumpeter, during his years in the United States, was interested in exploring the economic phenomenon in a wide sense is also clear from *History of Economic Analysis*, with its detailed account of the four fields of *Sozialökonomik*. What Schumpeter wanted to capture in this work is also something that is much broader than "economic theory," namely the full scientific attempt throughout the ages to understand economic phenomena.

There was finally a tendency in Schumpeter's later works to emphasize the importance of "history" in economic analysis. During his years in the United States, Schumpeter often criticized those who argued that "economic theory" is sufficient to fully explain economic phenomena. Sometimes Schumpeter even said that, if anything, "history" is *more* important than "economic theory"; the main point, however, was usually that both of them (as well as "statistics" and "sociology") are needed for a full analysis. It was also during these years that Schumpeter made his often-quoted remark that "I wish to state right now that if, starting my work in economics afresh, I were told that I could study only one [field in economics] but could have my choice, it would be economic history that I should choose."[156]

The picture of Schumpeter's later works given here differs from the popular interpretation of Schumpeter, according to which he always set "economic theory" first, but started to criticize it during his last year of life. In one of the articles in *Schumpeter, Social Scientist* (1951) it is, for example, argued that "only in the last year of his life" did Schumpeter express the opinion that history was more important than economic theory.[157] The author then asks what could possibly lie behind this "uncharacteristic performance"; and he rejects "old age" as a possible explanation. Instead he settles for Schumpeter's tendency to always embrace unpopular causes ("he loved to oppose the popular side"). This line of argument, however, has to be rejected because it is wrong and trivializes an important theme in Schumpeter's writings, beginning in his youth. Even in his first works Schumpeter expressed a lively interest in a broad concept of economics and in the relationship between "economic theory" and "history" and "sociology."[158] Later, in the introduction to *Business Cycles*, we read an eloquent passage that captures Schumpeter's stance:

> It is always of the utmost importance for us to be thoroughly masters of the economic history of the time, the country or the industry, sometimes even of the individual firm in question, before we draw any inference at all from the behavior of time series. We cannot stress this point sufficiently. General history (social, political, and cultural), economic history, and particularly industrial history are not only indispensible but really the most important contributors to the understanding of our problem. *All other materials and methods, statistical and theoretical, are only subservient to them and worse than useless without them.*[159]

Schumpeter's main goal in *Business Cycles*, he says, is indicated by its subtitle: "A Theoretical, Historical, and Statistical Analysis of the Capitalist Process." He found it perfectly normal to simultaneously draw on these three fields of *Sozialökonomik* for his analysis, and he explicitly denied that "there is anything novel in my combination of historical, statistical, and theoretical analysis—as far as that goes I have merely moved with the general tendency toward their mutual peaceful penetration."[160] Schumpeter, as was earlier mentioned, consistently excluded the fourth field of *Sozialökonomik*—"sociology"—from his analysis. He does not explicitly say why he did this, but it is obvious from the text that he felt it was challenging enough to simultaneously try to handle "theory," "history," and "statistics."

The chapters in *Business Cycles* fall very naturally into the three fields of "economic theory" (Chapters 2–4), "history" (Chapters 6–7, 14–15), and "statistics" (Chapters 5, 8–13). Schumpeter begins his analysis by outlining a theoretical model, which in principle is self-contained and ahistorical. This model is very similar to the one that he had presented nearly thirty years earlier in *The Theory of Economic Development*. Again we meet the entrepreneur, who upsets the equilibrium in the economic system by an innovation. A series of other economic changes is then ignited by the original innovation, and a wave-like movement is set off through the economy. The economic system eventually reaches a new equilibrium, and the whole process starts over again. Wave after wave is produced in this fashion by entrepreneurial innovations. In Schumpeter's "first approximation" he works with a model of a wave or a cycle which has only two phases, "prosperity" and "recession." In his "second approximation" two further phases are added, "depression" and "recovery." According to the third and last approximation, there are three cycles which simultaneously roll on: long waves of about fifty years in duration (Kondratieffs), intermediate waves of about nine to ten years (Juglars), and short waves of about forty months (Kitchins). Schumpeter emphasizes that the idea of there being three cycles is not to be regarded as a hypothesis; it is merely a convenient way of describing the economic process in capitalist society.

Schumpeter makes clear in *Business Cycles* that he does not equate "economic theory" with explanatory hypotheses. Theory proper belongs to a deeper level of scientific work, which essentially pertains to conceptual clarification and innovation. Theory makes us see what we would otherwise not see. Once new concepts have been constructed, they are to be worked into models, and these models provide "the analytical scaffolding" for the concrete analysis. Schumpeter emphasizes that theory is not sufficient by itself; it must always be complemented with historical and statistical material. By itself theory is just a "skeleton of economic life"—"bloodless" and in need of "live fact."[161]

"History"—the second field in *Sozialökonomik*—plays a key role in *Business Cycles*. At one point Schumpeter actually presents the whole purpose of his work in terms of history:

> Since what we are trying to understand is economic change in historic time, there is little exaggeration in saying that the ultimate goal is simply a reasoned (conceptually clarified) history, not of crises only, nor of cycles or waves, but of the economic process in all its aspects and bearings to which theory merely supplies some tools and schemata, and statistics merely part of the material. It is obvious that only detailed historic knowledge can definitely answer most of the questions of individual causation and mechanism and that without it the study of time series must remain inconclusive, and theoretical analysis empty.[162]

The kind of historical material that Schumpeter finds particularly useful is, on the one hand, general economic histories and, on the other, monographs on individual industries. The former describe the economic process, Schumpeter says, while the latter often contain interesting information on the rise and fall of individual industries.

Despite these positive statements by Schumpeter on the role of history in economic analysis, it is clear that he kept seeing himself primarily as an "economic theorist" also during his last years. At one point in *Business Cycles*, Schumpeter explains that "he is no more of a historian than he is a mathematician" (and it is well known that Schumpeter did not consider himself much of a mathematician). He says that he did have some training in history as a young man, and that he even did some archival work at one point. He, however, stresses that "he has never acquired, still less kept up, that wide knowledge of historical fact that would really be necessary to substantiate some of the views submitted [in *Business Cycles*]."[163]

The third area of *Sozialökonomik*, which Schumpeter draws on for *Business Cycles*, is "statistics." The book contains a theoretical chapter on this topic as well as some chapters in which the analysis is centered around statistical material. It is apparent from these sections that Schumpeter considered it essential for an economist to be well versed in statistics. But he was also fairly skeptical of the tendency of many economists to rely exclusively on aggregate data, such as total output, total income, and total profits. These measures, in Schumpeter's opinion, tend to keep the analysis on the surface of things and prevent it from penetrating to the individual industrial processes: "It invites a mechanistic and formalistic treatment of a few isolated contour lines and attributes to aggregates a life of their own and a causal significance that they do not possess."[164]

Despite these reservations from Schumpeter's side, he stressed that there are many instances when statistics must be used. In *Business Cycles* he also makes an argument for using a special statistical method for time-series analysis, which calls for the establishment of certain inflection points and which had just been invented by Ragnar Frisch. The argument is rather technical but basically boils down to the fact that in Schumpeter's mind this method made it easier to establish the terminal dates of business cycles. Schumpeter has been much criticized for using Frisch's method, especially by Simon Kuznets in a famous review of *Business Cycles* in *The American Economic Review*.[165] According to Kuznets, Schumpeter fails to show that Frisch's method is at all useful in this context. In addition, Kuznets attacks Schumpeter's use of statistics in *Business Cycles* very severely, and argues that Schumpeter is unable to connect his theoretical model to concrete data. Though Kuznets does not say so explicitly, the reader is left with the impression that he considered Schumpeter to be fairly incompetent as a statistician.

Kuznets's review also contains a sharp attack on Schumpeter's theory of innovations and on the use of Kondratieff waves in *Business Cycles*. Kuznets could not understand why innovations necessarily had to come in "swarms," as Schumpeter said. Why couldn't they equally well come in a continuous stream? Kuznets also found Schumpeter's empirical proof for Kondratieff waves unconvincing; other people, he said, had failed to prove their existence, and Schumpeter did not add anything new to the debate. Reviewing the whole issue of whether Schumpeter was right or wrong in *Business Cycles*, W. W. Rostow recently came to the conclusion that Kuznets's critique is still valid. Whoever wants to rehabilitate Schumpeter's theory of business cycles will therefore first have to confront Kuznets's arguments in his 1940 article.[166]

This having been said, it should also be pointed out that Kuznets's critique does not invalidate the analysis in *Business Cycles*. One of its strengths, as we have tried to show, resides in the attempt to tie together several different fields of study within the general framework of a *Sozialökonomik*. Three of these have already been discussed— "theory," "history," and "statistics"—and we shall now proceed to the fourth, "sociology." To review, Schumpeter wanted in principle to keep "sociology" out of the analysis in *Business Cycles*. This primarily meant that an assumption was made that the "institutional framework" did not change for the period under study. But just as in his earlier economic-theoretical works, there are several points at which Schumpeter's analysis leads into sociology in a very natural way; and these are of special interest for a discussion of Schumpeter and *Sozialökonomik*.

One of these points relates to the issue of class; and at one place in *Business Cycles* Schumpeter explicitly refers to his 1927 analysis of social classes. In a discussion of how entrepreneurship is related to social class, Schumpeter says that this is not the place to discuss this issue in detail, but that in principle "economic theory and sociology should combine to account for [the] institutional patterns [of social classes]."[167] At another point Schumpeter refers to his essay on imperialism and raises some questions about its validity. He says that "the deepest question of the economic sociology of our epoch" is whether imperialist tendencies grow out of the internal logic of capitalism or whether they rather are distortions of it, due to extracapitalist influences. Schumpeter also says in *Business Cycles* that he does not accept his own "atavism theory" of imperialism any longer.[168] Precisely what Schumpeter meant by this is somewhat unclear, especially which alternative theory he now preferred.[169] For our purposes, however, it is enough to point out that Schumpeter did not see the transition from conventional economic theory to sociology in the same unproblematical way as before.

It was noted earlier that Schumpeter's theory of innovation leads in a natural way into a sociological analysis. This is, for example, true for the description in *The Theory of Economic Development* of how innovations are diffused and how they encounter resistance once they appear. In *Business Cycles* Schumpeter emphasizes another side of the innovation process, which is sociological in nature as well, namely the struggle between new firms and old firms. Schumpeter says that his innovation theory "stresses that kind of economic change that is particularly likely to break up existing patterns and to create new ones, thereby breaking up old and creating new positions of power and civilizations, valuations, beliefs, and policies which from this standpoint are, therefore, no longer 'external.' "[170] In *Business Cycles* Schumpeter also makes a statement to the effect that his theory of innovation is in his mind applicable not only to changes within the economy, but also to changes within other areas of society: "The writer believes, although he cannot stay to show, that the theory here expounded is but a special case, adapted to the economic sphere, of a much larger theory which applies to change in all spheres of social life, science and art included."[171]

Finally, a close reading of *Business Cycles* along the lines of *Sozialökonomik* also gives us a clue to how Schumpeter came to write a "sociological" work like *Capitalism, Socialism and Democracy* immediately after his study of business cycles. At one point in *Business Cycles* Schumpeter argues that it is quite natural, when analyzing the two first Kondratieff waves (1787–1842, 1843–1897), to make the assumption that there is, on the one hand, an economic system and, on the other, an institutional setting. When one comes to the "Neo-Mercantilist Kondratieff," which begins in the 1890s, however, this way of reasoning becomes more problematical. The reason for this is that the social-institutional setting during this period directly interferes with the workings of the economy by producing discontented intellectuals, an atmosphere that is hostile to capitalism, and so on. Or, to phrase it differently, in order to understand the contemporary economy one must also pay attention to what happens in the social structure.

*Capitalism, Socialism and Democracy* (1942) is an exceptionally rich work. The main theme is whether capitalism can survive (Schumpeter said "no") and whether socialism is a viable alternative ("yes"). But the book contains much more than this. It starts, for example, with a long and brilliant dissection of Marx's thought; it includes a history of socialist parties; and it also contains an extraordinary section on the theory of democracy. The part on democracy is really the only example we have of a study in political theory by Schumpeter, and it deserves to be highlighted for this if for no other reason. As it turns out, it is also a superb piece of political theorizing which raises serious questions about the classical doctrine of democracy. Schumpeter basically criticizes earlier theoreticians for seeing democracy mainly as *a value in itself*. In its stead he suggests the following approach, which emphasizes democracy as *a method*: "The democratic method is that institutional arrangement for arriving at political decisions in which individuals acquire the power to decide by means of a competitive struggle for the people's vote."[172] This emphasis on the democratic

THE MAN AND HIS WORK

method in Schumpeter's theory of democracy has not earned him many friends among reformists, but it represents an important step forward in terms of realism. Throughout his discussion of democracy Schumpeter also draws parallels between the entrepreneur and the political leader. In *An Economic Theory of Democracy* Anthony Downs refers explicitly to *Capitalism, Socialism and Democracy* and states that "Schumpeter's profound analysis of democracy forms the inspiration and foundation for our whole thesis, and our debt and gratitude to him are great indeed."[173] Schumpeter, in other words, helped to inspire the public choice approach.

Despite its brilliance, *Capitalism, Socialism and Democracy* is not the kind of work that hangs together in a very organic way. Its five different parts do not fit particularly well together, and there is really no single scientific argument that runs through the whole book. Instead there is a little for everyone, including the general public. Insofar as *Sozialökonomik* is concerned, Schumpeter's discussions of the decline of capitalism and of Marxism are of particular interest. In the section entitled "The Marxian Doctrine," Schumpeter argues vigorously against the kind of synthesis that one can find in Marx's work and which to Schumpeter's mind was both wrong and premature. Marx's work only becomes useful, Schumpeter says, if one divides it up into different parts, such as "economic theory," "sociology," and "prophecy." Schumpeter then proceeds to analyze each of these parts. For example, he finds most of Marx's economic theory to be of little or no interest. The labor theory of value is invalid, and the main part of what is known as "Marxian economics" has no value whatsoever for a professional economist. There is, however, one great quality to Marx's work, and that is his idea that the economy is constantly transforming itself and generating new changes. On this point Marx was indeed working on "the economic theory of the future."

To Schumpeter, Marx's contribution to "sociology" was much more valuable than his contribution to "economic theory." Schumpeter considered Marx's "economic interpretation of history" to be one of the great intellectual accomplishments of all time, and he also praised Marx for his astute analysis of class. Schumpeter, however, was at the same time critical of Marxist sociology, both in its original version and in its later incarnations. *Capitalism, Socialism and Democracy* contains, for example, a sharp attack on the Neo-Marxist theory of imperialism (as well as a further attempt by Schumpeter himself to develop his own ideas on this topic).[174] Schumpeter also warns against the dogmatic side of Marx and points out that most of his sociology has to be toned down in order to be useful. In particular, he criticizes Marx's way of mixing "economic theory" and "sociology." What often starts out as "sociology" in Marx suddenly becomes "economic theory," and vice versa. This way economic theory may appear less abstract and sociology more analytical, but "a valuable economic theorem may by its sociological metamorphosis pick up error instead of richer meaning and vice versa."[175] In brief, "synthesis in general and synthesis on Marxian lines in particular might easily issue in both worse economics and worse sociology."[176]

In Schumpeter's view, Marx was much more successful in uniting "economic theory" with "economic history" than with "sociology." Economists, he says, have often tried to combine "economic theory" and "economic history," but usually they have failed. "The facts of economic history were assigned to a separate compartment. They entered theory, if at all, merely in the role of illustrations, or possibly of verifications of result."[177] With Marx, however, it was different; and the mixture was truly profound: "He was the first economist of top rank to see and to teach systematically how economic theory may be turned into historical analysis and how the historical narrative may be turned into *histoire raisonnée*."[178] Schumpeter sums up his analysis by saying that Marx failed to draw "economic theory" and "sociology" properly together; that he was much more successful with "economic theory" and "economic history"; and that he never tried his hand at "economic theory" and "statistics."

From the viewpoint of *Sozialökonomik*, *Capitalism, Socialism and Democracy* is mainly of interest for two reasons. First, it contains an interesting critique of conventional economic theory. And second, its main focus is on the institutional setting of capitalism or on its "sociology." According to a succinct statement in *Capitalism, Socialism and Democracy*, "economics is . . . an observational and interpretative science."[179] Schumpeter is also very critical of the various fictions which are used in conventional economic theory, such as the idea of perfect competition. *Capitalism, Socialism and Democracy* contains a vigorous attack on this idea as well as a defense of monopoly. As Schumpeter saw it, the process of "creative destruction" made monopolies feel the threat of competition and also forced them to act accordingly. Monopolies were consequently not the enemies of progress; on the contrary, they helped progress along in ways that were impossible for small firms.

Schumpeter's main argument in *Capitalism, Socialism and Democracy* has to do with the future of capitalism. In his article from 1918 on the tax state, Schumpeter had already said that capitalism could probably not survive very much longer, and similar statements can also be found in several other of his writings, especially "The Instability of Capitalism" (1928). But it is first in *Capitalism, Socialism and Democracy*

that Schumpeter explores this theme in any real detail. His argument
on this point essentially falls into two parts. The first is a narrow economic argument; and here the main point is that capitalism is indeed
still a viable force. Schumpeter then presents a broader and more
"sociological" argument, from which he concludes that capitalism will
soon break down and be replaced by socialism.

From a purely economic viewpoint, Schumpeter says, it is clear that
capitalism is doing fine and that it can probably even double the standard of living during the next couple of decades. But this is on the
assumption that the economic institutions on which it rests remain
the same—and this assumption simply does not hold for contemporary capitalism. In chapter after chapter Schumpeter enumerates the
reasons for the coming downfall of capitalism. The intellectuals are
allowed to attack capitalism without penalty; the institutions of property and contract are being hollowed out; and the protective strata
from feudal society are slowly disappearing. There are other reasons
as well. The modern corporations are more congenial to managers
than to creative entrepreneurs. Society as a whole is becoming more
rationalized. And last but not least, the bourgeois have lost all confidence in themselves. Capitalism will die from internal wounds,
Schumpeter says, and not from attacks from the outside.

When Schumpeter had finished *Capitalism, Socialism and Democracy*
in the early 1940s, he immediately set out to work on what was to
become *History of Economic Analysis*. His wife tells us that he had originally intended only to translate and revise his history of economic
theory from 1914. But he must have changed his mind quickly, for
he worked on the new version all through the 1940s until his death
in 1950. At that time the manuscript was about five times as long as
the 1914 book, although the structure was basically the same. According to Schumpeter's wife, who edited the whole unwieldy manuscript
after his death, the book was essentially finished by this time.

The main bulk of *History of Economic Analysis* is devoted to a detailed account of the development of economics from the Greeks to
around World War I. Most commentators point out that *History of
Economic Analysis* is a proof of Schumpeter's truly encyclopaedic
knowledge of economics, but that the author's idiosyncracies sometimes steer him wrong or at least in peculiar directions. Schumpeter
says, for example, that there is really not one new idea in *The Wealth
of Nations* and that Ricardo's work can best be characterized as a "detour." Many other similar examples can be cited.

According to Schumpeter, his work was intended as a history of
"economic analysis" and not of "economic thought." By "economic
analysis" he basically means concepts or "tools" of economic theory,

as opposed to just any thoughts and ideas about economic topics ("economic thought"). It is "analytical work," Schumpeter says in his book, that is "the hero throughout our play."[180] Schumpeter presents the way these "tools" have emerged throughout the centuries and, in doing so, he pays much attention to the social conditions of the time or to "the sociology of economics," as he calls it. Schumpeter also says that great economists always start with a "vision," which they then try to hammer into "economic tools." Being preanalytic by definition, these visions also contain ideological elements. Indeed, Schumpeter warns repeatedly in his book that "ideology" represents a major danger to economics. That Schumpeter attached great importance to this topic is also clear from the fact that he chose "Science and Ideology" as the theme for his presidential address to the the American Economic Association in 1948.

*History of Economic Analysis* is an extremely rich work with erudite accounts of a multitude of economists and plentiful excursions into the sociology of science. The book also contains a detailed account of how Schumpeter viewed economics in general. One gets the impression that Schumpeter, after a lifetime of experience as an economist, wanted to set the record straight. The result, as we shall see, is the most complete account of *Sozialökonomik* which can be found in Schumpeter's work.

The focus in *History of Economic Analysis*, Schumpeter says, is on "(scientific) economics" or, to use the German term, *Sozialökonomik*.[181] Given the rather haphazard division of labor in the social sciences, we are told, it is no surprise that a topic like economics is "an agglomeration of ill-coordinated and overlapping fields of research."[182] This means that there do not exist sharp and clear boundaries between the various social sciences; economics rather has a series of zones in common with some of its scientific neighbors. Economics, Schumpeter says, basically consists of four "fundamental fields": "economic history," "statistics," "theory," and "economic sociology." Three of these fields—all but "theory"—can also be conceptualized as zones in common with the other social sciences.

The first of these four fundamental fields is economic history, and it is also "by far the most important."[183] Schumpeter gives three main reasons why economists should always take economic history into account. First, economics is about processes in historical time. Second, history helps us in a very natural way to understand how the economic and noneconomic parts of a phenomenon are related. And third, most of the errors that are committed in economics are caused by a lack of knowledge of economic history. Economic history,

Schumpeter sums up, is "part of economics," and a competent economist should also be able to do historical research.

The second fundamental field of *Sozialökonomik* is statistics, and at various points in his book Schumpeter traces the history of this field from the sixteenth century to the present. He points out that economic theory and statistics have been "almost completely divorced" until our own day, and that this has had a negative impact on the development of economics. A competent economist, Schumpeter emphasizes, should be familiar with the techniques of "statistical economics." To be ignorant about the way statistics are put together represents a real danger to the economist.

The third field of economic analysis is theory. Schumpeter notes that economic theorems fall into two broad categories; they can either be "economic theorems that are logical" or "economic theorems that are directly based on observations."[184] In both cases, economic theory is quite different from the mere formulation of hypotheses. Theorizing is about something else, namely the formulation of fundamental economic concepts, such as "marginal utility," "accelerator," and so on.

The picture that Schumpeter draws of economic theory in *History of Economic Analysis* is reminiscent of the one that can be found in *Business Cycles*. As opposed to the latter work, however, Schumpeter says in the former that *Sozialökonomik* also has a "fourth fundamental field"—*"economic sociology."*[185] Economic theory, he explains, always takes place within an institutional framework; this is something that economic history teaches us. When we look at certain parts of this institutional framework, however, we realize that they do not really consist of unique facts of the type that history studies. To describe them we therefore need "a sort of generalized or typified or stylized economic history"—in short, we need "economic sociology."[186]

At a few points in *History of Economic Analysis* Schumpeter attempts to define "economic sociology." This field of *Sozialökonomik*, he says, deals mainly with the way people have come to behave the way they do in economic matters; while economic theory deals with the way people do behave and what economic consequences this has. There is, in other words, a historical dimension to economic sociology. But its main focus is on economic institutions, such as inheritance, private property, and contract.[187] Schumpeter clearly wants more interaction between economists and sociologists, and he bemoans the fact that "ever since the eighteenth century both groups have grown steadily apart until by now the modal economist and the modal sociologist know little and care less about what the other does, each preferring to use, respectively, a primitive sociology and a primitive economics of his own to accepting one another's professional results—a state of things that was and is not improved by mutual vituperation."[188] Schumpeter, however, does not want economic theory and sociology to be pushed too closely together; as he views it: "Cross-fertilization might easily result in cross-sterilization."[189]

It is sometimes said that Schumpeter does not really accomplish what he sets out to do in the introduction to *History of Economic Analysis*. In one sense this is true; what Schumpeter proposed to do was so radically new that it is uncertain whether anyone could have done it successfully. Still, Schumpeter made a real effort to follow the development of his four "fields" through the centuries and map out what the interaction had been between economic theory, on the one hand, and economic sociology, statistics, and economic history, on the other. In various ingenious ways Schumpeter also tried to theorize about the way these four fields should be connected to each other. The intellectual effort that it must have taken Schumpeter to write the history of *Sozialökonomik* in such detail was probably enormous. But like so many of the economists whose work he discusses in *History of Economic Analysis*, Schumpeter was himself driven by a powerful vision that he wanted to express.

### The American Period: Works in This Volume

The writings from Schumpeter's years in the United States which have been included in this volume are primarily of interest for a fuller understanding of Schumpeter's views of the role of history and sociology in *Sozialökonomik* and for his thoughts about the decline of capitalism. One of Schumpeter's most brilliant writings on economic history and sociology—"Comments on a Plan for the Study of Entrepreneurship" (more commonly known as "The Creative Response in Economic History")—is here presented for the first time in a complete version (Chapter 10). That Schumpeter, however, was not ready to reject economic theory is clear from his 1940 paper on "The Meaning of Rationality in the Social Sciences," which also is presented here for the first time in its entirety (Chapter 7). Schumpeter's speech from 1945 on "The Future of Private Enterprise in the Face of Modern Socialistic Tendencies" (Chapter 9) is primarily known for its political content. But it is also of methodological interest, mainly for the questions it raises about Schumpeter's attempt to keep "value judgments" out of his writings.

As to the second theme in the writings from this period—the decline of capitalism—a special mention should be made of the Lowell

Lectures, "An Economic Interpretation of Our Time," which are here published for the first time (Chapter 8). Additional information on how Schumpeter viewed capitalism during the last period of his life can be found in "Wage and Tax Policy in Transitional States of Society" (Chapter 11) and in "American Institutions and Economic Progress" (Chapter 12). Like the Lowell Lectures, these two writings are also of interest for their sociological content. Finally, to give the reader a sense of what it must have been like to listen to Schumpeter in person, a transcript of one of his speeches—"Can Capitalism Survive?" from 1936 (Chapter 6)—has been included.

"Comments on a Plan for the Study of Entrepreneurship" (Chapter 10) is one of the essays that most clearly testifies to Schumpeter's renewed interest in history during his years in the United States. It was in all likelihood written in 1946 on the suggestion of Arthur H. Cole and circulated privately among interested scholars. In 1947 Schumpeter presented his "Comments" at the meeting of the Economic History Association, and the article was later published in a shorter version as "The Creative Response in Economic History" in *The Journal of Economic History*.[190] Arthur H. Cole, who was a business historian as well as a librarian at Baker Library, had since the early 1940s tried to breathe new life into economic history by advocating research on entrepreneurship. By the mid-1940s he was ready to start an interdisciplinary center at Harvard but needed support and resources from the faculty members. One of the people he turned to was Schumpeter, who helped Cole considerably in founding the Research Center in Entrepreneurial History at Harvard (1948–1958). Schumpeter lobbied for funds; he lent his name to the whole effort by becoming one of the Center's four "senior members"; and he also gave the first public speech at the Center. "Without his zeal and support," Cole wrote after Schumpeter's death, "the Center might readily have 'died aborning.'"[191]

The "plan for the study of entrepreneurship" that Schumpeter refers to in the title to his essay had been authored by Cole and presented in 1946 as Cole's presidential address to the Economic History Association. Schumpeter applauded Cole's suggestion that more research should be devoted to economic change and the entrepreneur. Many of the ideas on the entrepreneur that Schumpeter presents in his "Comments" to Cole's speech can already be found in his earlier writings, beginning with the 1911 book. What is definitely novel in Schumpeter's essay, however, is its strong emphasis on the need for empirical verification. Throughout his article, Schumpeter enumerates various areas which would be suitable subjects for historical research; and he repeatedly says that we just do not know what to expect in terms of empirical results. Referring, for example, to his own theory that the entrepreneurial function is declining in modern society, he says: "But this is at present only an impression. It is for the historian to establish or refute it."[192]

Even though it might be correct to say that Schumpeter in the 1940s was feeling a certain conflict between economic theory and economic history or empirical research, it is also obvious that Schumpeter was not at all interested in reducing economic theory to economic history.[193] This comes out very clearly in "Comments." Schumpeter stresses, for example, that the role of history is different in different parts of economic science: "The relation between historical and theoretical work varies widely from one type of field of economic inquiry to another. In our case [that is, in the case of economic change], the theory itself is historical in nature."[194] But even if the theory of economic change might be more open to empirical-historical research than, say, the theory of money, Schumpeter always insisted that the kind of economic history he had in mind was analytical in nature. The main emphasis of his argument in "Comments" was really that the economic theorist could be of assistance to the historian by indicating which parts of economic reality needed to be studied in more detail. The result of the study of economic change should ideally be *"an analytic history of enterprise"*—not just ordinary economic history. It was also of primary importance that the researcher be openminded; economic history and economic theory needed to be complemented by a "sociology of enterprise."

That Schumpeter did not want economic history to replace economic theory is equally clear from his paper on rationality in this volume (Chapter 7). The following is the background to the article. In the fall of 1939 Schumpeter formed a small faculty seminar at Harvard on "rationality in the social sciences."[195] Schumpeter seems to have enjoyed arranging this type of seminar, and the one on rationality was by no means the only one he was involved with. The first meeting probably took place in late October 1939 and the whole seminar ended in May 1940; altogether there were around a dozen meetings. Apart from Schumpeter, the two key people were Talcott Parsons and D. V. McGranahan. Other more or less permanent members included Abram Bergson, John Dunlop, Wassily Leontief, Wilbert E. Moore, and Paul Sweezy. Schumpeter opened the seminar series with a talk on "rationality in economics." He made his presentation in two parts, on October 27 and on November 13, 1939, and he later circulated a typed version of the speech and the comments made during the discussion.[196] In May 1940 Schumpeter met with Parsons and McGranahan, and it was decided that they should try to put together a book based on the seminars. A number of seminar members were contacted, but only a few actually handed in their papers, and the book was never published.[197]

Schumpeter was one of the persons who handed in his paper to Parsons. He noted on the manuscript, which he finished on June 12, that it was "still only a sketch." The very same day he also wrote to Parsons that "though I have rewritten and amplified (also modified), I am not yet pleased with the thing."[198] Schumpeter added that since the paper was going to be a chapter in a book, he would hopefully get another opportunity to work through it. This, however, was not to be; and the version published in this volume is the one Schumpeter completed on June 12.

Rationality was a topic that had interested Schumpeter for many years, and he often touches on it in his various writings. Yet he does not seem to have been very satisfied with his ideas. A couple of months before the Harvard seminar he wrote to Chester Barnard that "as a theorist I am naturally very interested in this problem [of rationality] which I have never been able to handle to my satisfaction."[199] In his 1940 paper Schumpeter mainly tried to tackle the problem of rationality by introducing two novel distinctions: one between what he called "rationality of the observer" and "rationality of the object," and another between "subjective rationality" and "objective rationality." By "rationality of the observer" Schumpeter just meant that in any science, be it a natural science or a social science, the intellectual procedure has to be rational. It has to be rational regardless of what is being studied, which can be irrational phenomena just as well as rational phenomena ("rationality of the object"). In the latter case, a further distinction is useful: The rationality can be "objective" or "subjective." If it is "subjective," the actor is conscious of acting in a rational manner. But if it is objective, he or she is not. "Objective rationality" is mainly used in model building, Schumpeter says, such as in economics.

In his article on rationality Schumpeter also criticizes economists for having blurred the line between "objective rationality" and "subjective rationality." They have "almost invariably," he says, exaggerated the element of conscious rationality and thereby become easy targets for criticism. This, however, does not mean that models of the type that economists use are without value; on the contrary, they are extremely helpful. It must also be realized that "objective rationality" is much more common than we think. "The reason for this," to cite the early version of Schumpeter's paper, "is of course that experience is handed to us not by the rational procedures of the classroom but in the form of rules of thumb which we never bother to analyze but which may be perfectly rational all the same." Schumpeter concludes: "This is why we cannot as a rule hope to arrive at the meaning of anyone's behaviour and of the *Sinnzusammenhang* involved, by the naive method of interviewing people."[200] In brief, rational models are needed in social science research.

Another article in this volume, which is of interest for an understanding of Schumpeter's methodology, is "The Future of Private Enterprise in the Face of Modern Socialistic Tendencies" (Chapter 9). This article is primarily known in the Schumpeterian literature for its frank political message—Schumpeter here advocates a reconstruction of society along corporatist lines. But besides the light that this article sheds on Schumpeter's political views, it also raises another important question: How successful was Schumpeter in actually eliminating value judgments from his own scientific writings? Judging from this essay, he was not very successful: The transition from statements of "facts" to "value judgments" is unmistakable. Our intention in saying this, however, is not to intimate that Schumpeter in his own works often failed to draw the sharp line between "facts" and "values" that he always advocated for others. That would be an unfair charge. Still, the fact remains that many of Schumpeter's writings are strongly colored by an essentially conservative vision; and that this is something one should be aware of when his scientific works are analyzed.

The invitation to give the talk on "The Future of Private Enterprise" came from one of Schumpeter's students at Harvard, Emile Bouvier, who was a Jesuit priest.[201] After having finished his studies in Cambridge, Bouvier returned to Canada, where he became the director for the Section on Industrial Relations at the University of Montreal. He was also heavily involved with a Catholic organization for employers, called l'Association Professionelle des Industriels. This organization—which organized the meeting at which Schumpeter gave his speech—advocated a reorganization of society along Catholic lines, as suggested by Leo XIII in *Rerum Novarum* (1891) and by Pius XI in *Quadragesimo Anno* (1931). The general goal was to introduce Christian principles into industrial life and to bring about a harmonious cooperation between employers and employees with the help of professional organizations, organized along corporatist lines.

Schumpeter gave his speech to the Association on November 19, 1945, at a hotel in Montreal. According to one reporter, the audience—which mostly consisted of Canadian businessmen—was "a bit surprised" when they heard the famous economist from Harvard argue that the only effective remedy to the problems of our time was to organize society along the lines of *Quadragesimo Anno* by Pius XI.[202] This was all the more astonishing, the reporter said, since Schumpeter was not even Catholic. Anyone familiar with Schumpeter's writings would have been equally surprised, since they do not contain any references whatsoever to Catholic-corporatist ideas of this type. Still, Schumpeter's vision was essentially conservative; and ideas that advocate a harmonious cooperation between employers and employees are part of this tradition. Schumpeter himself had also been a personal advisor in 1919 to Ignaz Seipel, who was to become one of the leading advocates of Austro-corporatism.[203] It can finally be noted that on a few other occasions in the 1940s Schumpeter would return to his ideas on *Quadragesimo Anno*. He did this, for example, in his famous 1949 speech to the American Economic Association on "The March into Socialism."[204] On some level, in short, the corporatist vision answered to something deep within Schumpeter.

Since it has been said that Schumpeter's speech in Montreal contains "an outright appeal for a fascist order, based on Catholic principles," it is important to establish what Schumpeter did say and what he did not say in his speech—at least insofar as it is possible to do this on the basis of the printed version of his speech.[205] Schumpeter argues in his article that any society or social group contains elements of conflict as well as elements of cooperation. Conflict is as necessary as cooperation in keeping the group together. But usually, a group is also held together by a "common culture" or "faith." In modern society, however, this is not the case; the governing class is incapable of exerting true "leadership," and there is "social decomposition" and "disintegration" as a result. Socialism represents one way out of this dilemma, but Schumpeter rejects it on the ground that socialism is just a form of "authoritarian statism." Corporatism offers a superior alternative in this situation, especially in its Catholic version: "It will be necessary to turn to corporate organization in the sense advocated by *Quadragesimo Anno*."[206] One essential difference between socialism and corporatism, Schumpeter says, is that "the corporate principle organizes but it does not regiment."

Is the plan for the reorganization of society that Schumpeter here proposes "fascist"? Definitely not; it is rather a form of social program, which is reminiscent of Durkheim's proposal for how to deal with "anomie" in *Division of Labor in Society* (1902). Whether Schumpeter's proposal for the reorganization of society is "solidarism" with elitist overtones or just an anti-bureaucratic form of corporatism is not easy to decide. But it is not fascism, either in its German or Italian version.

Several of Schumpeter's later writings, which can be found in this volume, have as their major theme the decline of capitalism. They are also all in the form of lectures, which were never published during Schumpeter's lifetime. Perhaps this is a sign that even though Schumpeter was increasingly feeling the need to analyze noneconomic factors and institutions during these years, he was still somewhat reluctant to publish them and step forward as a sociologist. Schumpeter, to recall, always saw himself as a professional economist— never as a historian or a sociologist.[207]

The renewed interest for social institutions and sociology that one can find in Schumpeter's writings in the 1940s also went against the mainstream, insofar as the economic profession was concerned. Just as economics had become independent of history in the United States, it had also cut off its links to sociology. At Harvard this separation between economics and sociology took considerably more time than in most other places. Indeed, sociology had been taught in the economics department since the early 1890s, and it was not until 1931—one year before Schumpeter arrived in Cambridge to stay— that Harvard established its own sociology department.[208] In the 1930s it is evident that Schumpeter was mainly concerned with mathematizing economics, and he seems to have had little time for anything else. He did, however, keep in contact with Parsons—he was actually one of the original reviewers of the famous *Structure of Social Action*[209]—and Parsons, as we know, also played a key role in the seminar on rationality in 1939–1940. In the 1940s Schumpeter appears to have become more interested in sociology again. When he was president of the American Economics Association in 1948, he tried to get economists and sociologists together in a special session at the annual meeting. According to Schumpeter, the American Economics Association and the American Sociological Association used to have sessions in common—e.g., in 1913—and it was now time to revive this tradition. For a variety of practical reasons, this attempt did not work out as well as Schumpeter had hoped. One session with economists and sociologists was, however, held at the 1948 meeting in Cleveland. The topic was "The Sociology and Economics of Class Conflict," and Parsons participated with a paper.

The first item on the theme of the decline of capitalism—"Can Capitalism Survive?" (Chapter 6)—has primarily been included because it is the only known transcript of a lecture by Schumpeter. By reading through the lecture and the exchange with the audience afterward, one gets a vivid picture of what it must have been like to listen to Schumpeter in person. The jokes, the playful formulations, the bold perspectives—everything is there but Schumpeter's thick Viennese accent and his vivid gestures. The exact date on which Schumpeter gave this particular speech is not known. Most likely it was on January 18, 1936, in Washington, D.C., at the United States

Department of Agriculture Graduate School.[210] The person who had arranged the speech was probably Mordecai Ezekiel, who worked at the Bureau of Agricultural Economics at the Department of Agriculture in Washington, D.C.

The central ideas in "Can Capitalism Survive?" are also found in *Capitalism, Socialism and Democracy* (1942). The speech therefore shows that by the mid-1930s Schumpeter already had some of the main arguments for *Capitalism, Socialism and Democracy* in mind. Schumpeter's audience in 1936 was told that capitalism, from a purely economic viewpoint, has a great future; but that capitalism will probably decline anyway and that socialism was on the horizon. The theme of the speech, from a methodological viewpoint, is that when something like capitalism is analyzed, the whole "social system" must be included in the analysis. To Schumpeter, "no social system is ever going to survive when allowed to work out according to its own logic."[211]

The most important of Schumpeter's unpublished writings on the decline of capitalism is unquestionably "An Economic Interpretation of Our Time" or the Lowell Lectures (Chapter 8). In the spring of 1941 Schumpeter delivered eight public lectures in Boston as part of the Lowell Institute's program for the general public. The lectures were given on Tuesdays and Fridays, beginning on March 4 and ending on March 28, in the Lecture Hall of the Boston Public Library on Boylston Street near Copley Square. Admission was free, but tickets had to be ordered in advance. Schumpeter had started to prepare for the lectures by the fall of 1940, and Elizabeth was of great assistance to him. In December 1940 she wrote to a friend, "I am helping him [that is, Schumpeter] work up the material and we plan eventually to do a book together on the material of the Lowell lectures."[212] The book never materialized, but Schumpeter did a substantial amount of work on it. What is presented here is in all likelihood a first version, and Schumpeter seems to have had a considerably longer end product in mind.[213] In October 1941—roughly half a year after the lectures were given—Schumpeter wrote to a friend that he hoped to have the book ready "within the next few months."[214] In the meantime, however, Schumpeter got increasingly involved with his *History of Economic Analysis*. The last time that the book is referred to is in 1943, when Schumpeter says that he still hopes to get the time to do the book "some day."[215]

The Lowell Lectures are in many ways reminiscent of *Capitalism, Socialism and Democracy*: both have the decline of capitalism as their main theme, and their focus is much more on social institutions than on economic mechanisms. But there also exist some important differ-

ences; and it should be remembered that the Lectures were intended
to be a separate book. While *Capitalism, Socialism and Democracy* pulls
in many directions with its theory of democracy, its analysis of Marx,
and its history of socialist parties, "An Economic Interpretation of
Our Time" is exclusively devoted to one topic—the development of
capitalism between 1871 and 1940 in the United States and some European countries. In the first lecture Schumpeter discusses the period
before World War I ("intact capitalism"), and in the following lectures
he traces how capitalist society is slowly being undermined by its own
internal dynamic, a process that had been accelerated first by World
War I, then by the Depression, and now probably also by World War
II. The lectures end with some speculations, from the vantage point
of 1941, of what World War II will mean for the United States.
Schumpeter fears that the war will spell the end of the American way
of life. A possible geo-political scenario is that the world will split into
four blocks: a European block, an Anglo-American block, a Russian
block, and a Japanese block. The United States will do well, Schumpeter notes, even if Hitler wins.

The Lowell Lectures are mainly sociological in nature; and the title—"An Economic Interpretation of Our Time"—is an allusion to
what Schumpeter always saw as Marx's greatest sociological accomplishment, "the economic interpretation of history." Schumpeter
makes clear, however, that one has to go beyond Marx. His own analysis, as Schumpeter puts it, starts with Marx but does not end with
Marx. It is evident, for example, that the bourgeoisie dominated the
capitalist period, as Marx says. But Marx drew the wrong conclusion
from this, namely that economic interests always determine the social
structure and the values of society. In reality, however, the social
structure often affects the economy, and this means that a certain
measure of interaction between social and economic factors has to be
allowed for in the analysis. The "economic interpretation of history,"
in brief, needs to be adjusted and made into a more flexible tool of
analysis.

In presenting his "sociological diagnosis" of capitalist society in the
Lowell Lectures, Schumpeter also makes some important remarks
about the limits of determinism in a socio-historical type of analysis.
Even though society is fundamentally "historically and economically
conditioned," he says, there is "much room for personal or groupwise
failure or success."[216] There is "ineluctable necessity" as well as
"chance events." In the long run it is, for example, clear that the social structure of "intact capitalism" had to fall. But what happened in
the short run was a different story. Russia did not have to attack Serbia at the opening of World War I; and the Russian Revolution was

by no means a necessity. And "the long run consists of a succession of short runs. . . ."[217]

"Wage and Tax Policy in Transitional States of Society" (Chapter 11) is the outline to a lecture series that Schumpeter gave in January 1948 at the National University of Mexico in Mexico City. During the first half of his lecture tour Schumpeter gave a course on recent economic theory. The outline to these lectures was published by Elizabeth Boody Schumpeter as part of *History of Economic Analysis* under their original title, "The Progress of Theoretical Economics during the Last Twenty-Five Years."[218] The outline to the lectures on wage and tax policy, on the other hand, has not been published before, and it essentially testifies to Schumpeter's increasing interest in sociological and institutional matters during his last years. Wages and taxes can be analyzed from a purely economic perspective, but Schumpeter here chose to emphasize the ambivalent role that they have come to play in twentieth-century capitalist society. Private ownership is still the rule, but the motive for the businessman to work hard is, for example, undermined by huge taxes. It can also be noted that the Mexican lectures continue a line of thought that had already begun with the discussion of "fiscal sociology" in "The Crisis of the Tax State" (1918), and that they contain a very fine account of what Schumpeter saw as the contradictory character of the capitalist society of his days. Capitalist society was essentially in a "transitional state"—its "civilization" no longer matched its "class structure"—and different parts of its "civilization" were at war with each other.

The last item in this volume is "American Institutions and Economic Progress" (Chapter 12). This text is essentially an outline for a series of lectures that Schumpeter was scheduled to give in January 1950 at the Charles R. Walgreen Foundation in Chicago. He had been invited to give the lectures in the spring of 1949, and by the late fall most of the arrangements were ready. It was agreed that Schumpeter should give six lectures during the period January 9–January 20 and that the theme should be "American Institutions and Economic Progress." On December 22, Schumpeter sent an outline for his lectures to the secretary of the Foundation. By early January 1950, Schumpeter was all set to go, and a ticket for the night train to Chicago had been ordered for January 8. It was during the night before he was scheduled to leave that Schumpeter died.

According to one of his colleagues, Schumpeter had actually been working on the Walgreen Lectures during the night of his death.[219] Regardless of whether "American Institutions and Economic Progress" is the last article that Schumpeter worked on or not, it is in many ways a remarkable text. Schumpeter, for example, addresses several basic sociological problems. He discusses what he considers to be the real agents in the social process ("groups and classes"), and he defines what he means by an institution ("all the patterns of behavior into which individuals must fit under penalty of encountering organized resistance . . . and the agencies for their production or enforcement"). The Walgreen Lectures also contain some interesting statements in political sociology. Politicians "struggle for their positions by competing for the popular vote," and bureaucrats "struggle for their positions by competing for 'appointment.' "[220] One can usually assume, Schumpeter adds, that the interests of politicians and bureaucrats are "entirely different" from those of the people they represent.

In the Walgreen Lectures, Schumpeter also brings up a topic of great interest from the viewpoint of *Sozialökonomik*; namely, how is one to connect sociological and economic analyses to each other? When you make a purely economic analysis, Schumpeter says, you basically "freeze" the social institutions: You make the assumption that the institutions do not change, and you then go on with the analysis itself. Maybe one could also do this process "in reverse," Schumpeter suggests. You would then "freeze" the economic factors, so that only the social institutions can change. It would then be possible to distinguish between three different types of social changes. First, there are the changes that come about because people just attend to their business as usual. Then there are the changes that are caused by purely external factors, say an earthquake. And finally, there are the changes that come about through the internal dynamic of the social institutions themselves. Schumpeter says apropos this last type of change that "an interesting analogy with the economic concept of profit will be noticed [here]"; and it is clear that the three types of social change are closely patterned on Schumpeter's theory of economic change.[221]

Another problem in this context, Schumpeter continues, is that the interaction between "economic factors" and "social institutions" must be taken into account. Marx is wrong in assuming that it is always the economy that changes the social institutions; it is just as much the other way around. The analysis is also complicated by the fact that factors other than economic and social factors have to be taken into account in order to explain processes of change. There are, for example, pure "chance events." The inflow of precious metals into sixteenth-century Europe from the New World is an example of this. There is also the question of human nature and biology. Biological factors influence, for example, the capacity of a people as soldiers and warriors. Schumpeter notes that questions of this type are not popular and adds that a still more unpopular topic is the influence that "exceptional individuals" exert.

The Walgreen Lectures do not solve the problems that are inherent in bringing together economics and sociology; they are far too schematic for that. But they do show that until the end of his life Schumpeter kept thinking about various ways in which a purely economic analysis can be enriched through the neighboring social sciences. This problematique, it should be stressed, is just as much with us today as it was in the 1940s. Indeed, the isolation of "economic theory" from the other social sciences has grown considerably since Schumpeter's death in 1950. This is in many ways a negative and anomalous development, which must be overcome if economics and nearby types of analyses—such as economic history and economic sociology—are to really flourish again. In the end, this is one reason why Schumpeter's ideas on *Sozialökonomik* are still of great interest to us today.

## Notes

1. The information here and in the following biographical sections comes— unless otherwise indicated—from the following standard sources on Schumpeter's life: Gottfried Haberler, "Joseph Alois Schumpeter, 1883–1950," *Quarterly Journal of Economics* 64 (1950): 333–72; Erich Schneider, *Joseph A. Schumpeter* (Lincoln: BBR Monograph Nr. 1, University of Nebraska–Lincoln, 1975); Christian Seidl, *Joseph Alois Schumpeter in Graz* (Graz: Research Memorandum Nr. 8201, Department of Economics, University of Graz, 1982) and "Joseph Alois Schumpeter: Character, Life and Particulars of His Graz Period," in Christian Seidl, ed., *Lectures on Schumpeterian Economics*, 187–205 (Berlin: Springer-Verlag, 1984); Arthur Smithies, "Memorial: Joseph Alois Schumpeter," in S. E. Harris, ed., *Schumpeter, Social Scientist*, 11–23 (Cambridge: Harvard University Press, 1951); and Wolfgang Stolper, "Joseph Alois Schumpeter—A Personal Memoir," *Challenge* (January–February 1979): 64–69. Some information on the history of the Schumpeter family has also been taken from Frank Meissner, "The Schumpeters and Industrialization of Třešť," *Zeitschrift für die gesamte Staatswissenschaft* 135 (1979): 256–62. The author's attention was drawn too late to Yuichi Shionoya's "The Schumpeter Family in Trest," *Hitotsubashi Journal of Economics* 30 (1989): 151–71. It can be noted that no major biography has been published about Schumpeter. One, however, exists in manuscript form: Robert Loring Allen, "The Life and Work of Joseph Schumpeter." Here, as elsewhere in this introduction, the Schumpeter material from the Harvard Archives is quoted by permission of the Harvard University Archives, and the material from the Schlesinger Library by permission of Radcliffe College.

2. Edda Gigers (born Schumpeter), March 6, 1951, to Elizabeth Boody Schumpeter. The letter is today part of the Schumpeter collection at the Harvard University Archives. The key section, charmingly written by a non-native English speaker, is the following:

> About the origin of our family there is an old legend, which as far as I know could not be verified: The family is said to descend from barons of the Roman Empire of German Nation; one of them was decapitated at Nüremberg as [a] robber knight under the Emperor Rudolph (1273–1291). The whole posterity were sentenced to lose the nobility and "banished for ever from the country." At Nüremberg, so is told, it is a little church in which there is a sepulcre of a "Reichsfreiherr" of Schumpeter. Nobody of our family, nor weselves, were interested in those things and so we can't say if there is somewhat true in this legend.
>
> Then the Schumpeters appear in the Böhmerwald as glassblowers and later in the Sudetengebirge as clothweavers. Then they settled at Triesch about 200 years ago and acquired a big fortune, houses, factories, fields and forests. I am born there and I remember clearly the house, the garden, the horses and the old servants. It is certain that the Schumpeters were an old patrician family with high freemanspirit and democratic feelings, and they refused several times titles of nobility, offered them by the Austrian Emperor.

According to a "persistent" rumor about Schumpeter, which circulated in the United States, Schumpeter was "the illegitimate son of a very highly placed Austrian noble" (Richard Goodwin, "Schumpeter: The Man I Knew," *Ricerche economiche* 4 [1983]: 610). There does not seem to be any basis for this rumor.

3. The Austro-Hungarian Empire was, according to one author, "the most rigidly aristocratic society of all the nations of Old Europe" (Erich Streissler, "Schumpeter's Vienna and the Role of Credit in Innovation," in Helmut Frisch, ed., *Schumpeterian Economics*, 60 [New York: Praeger, 1982]). The two highest circles in the Empire were known as the "first society" and the "second society." To the former—the upper upper class—belonged all those who were entitled to be addressed as "Excellency." By virtue of being a fieldmarshal-lieutenant (*Feldmarschalleutnant*), Schumpeter's stepfather belonged in this category. The "second society"—the lower upper class—consisted of upper civil service men, high officers, and rich financiers. Entrepreneurs like Schumpeter's father and grandfather were not part of either the first or the second society.

4. The photo can be found in Smithies, "Memorial," 22.

5. Felix Somary, *Erinnerungen aus meinem Leben* (Zürich: Manesse Verlag, 1959), 170–71.

6. See Schumpeter's contribution to *Stammbuch (II) der Philosophischen Fakultät der Universität Bonn* at the archives of the University of Bonn.

7. This "sharp turn" was first toward Menger's type of economics and then toward mathematical economics—Schumpeter's contribution to *Stammbuch (II)*.

8. Smithies, "Memorial," 11.

9. Schneider, *Joseph A. Schumpeter*, 27, and Smithies, "Memorial," 11.

10. See, for example, Schumpeter's letter to Lewis H. Haney, April 22, 1949, Harvard University Archives, in which he discusses some objections to autobiographies by scientists.

11. The outline is reprinted in Smithies, "Memorial," 16–17. On October 19, 1936, Schumpeter wrote in his private diary, "A few plays and novels bubble in my brain—well, I suppose I better do my work" (Harvard University Archives).

12. This is based on the material Schumpeter handed in when he applied for his *Habilitation* in 1909. See Akt Nr. 9501, 8 März 1909 des K. K. Ministerium für Kultus und Unterricht, Dep. Nr. VII, Allgemeines Verwaltungsarchiv, Vienna.

13. Haberler, "Joseph Alois Schumpeter," 338.

14. Joseph A. Schumpeter, *Das Wesen und der Hauptinhalt der theoretischen Nationalökonomie* (Leipzig: Duncker & Humblot, 1908), ix. This work was Schumpeter's *Habilitationsschrift*. Note that it was not necessary to write a doctoral dissertation to earn the degree *doctor utriusque juris*.

15. Joseph A. Schumpeter, *Theorie der wirtschaftlichen Entwicklung* (Leipzig: Duncker & Humblot, 1912), 324.

16. See the act on Schumpeter at the Verwaltungsarchiv in Vienna, as mentioned in note 12. Schumpeter also explicitly mentioned four non-Viennese professors, all of whom Schumpeter was probably in contact with in England, namely Karl Pearson ("modern statistics"), Francis Edgeworth ("modern statistics"), Alfred Cort Haddon ("ethnology"), and Edward Westermarck ("sociology").

17. Schumpeter to Stewart S. Morgan, May 18, 1934, Harvard University Archives.

18. Smithies, "Memorial," 11.

19. Schumpeter to George W. Stocking, September 19, 1949, Harvard University Archives.

20. Stolper, "Joseph Alois Schumpeter," 65.

21. Ibid., 66.

22. Wolfgang Stolper, "Schumpeter, Joseph A.," in *International Encyclopaedia of the Social Sciences*, vol. 14, 67 (London: Macmillan, 1968).

23. Haberler, "Joseph Alois Schumpeter," 338.

24. Smithies, "Memorial," 12.

25. See for example Schumpeter to David T. Pottinger, June 4, 1934, Harvard University Archives. Schumpeter writes in this letter, "When this book appeared in 1911 . . . it met almost universal hostility." *Theorie* was translated into English in 1934 as *The Theory of Economic Development* and published by Harvard University Press.

26. That there also could be certain problems in being so young and brilliant as Schumpeter comes out very clearly in the following anecdote, as told by William Jaffé. Some time before 1910 Schumpeter visited the aging Léon Walras to pay his respects. Walras greeted Schumpeter by asking him to thank his father for sending *The Nature and Essence of Theoretical Economics*.

Jaffé writes, "In vain Schumpeter tried to correct the misunderstanding. As Schumpeter took his leave, L. W. again complimented Schumpeter's father on the excellent book" (William Jaffé, ed., *Correspondence of Léon Walras and Related Papers* [Amsterdam: North-Holland Publishing Company, 1965], vol. 3, 385). In this context it can also be mentioned that a few letters between Walras and Schumpeter have been preserved. In one of these, dated October 9, 1908, Schumpeter writes that his 1908 book (which he sent to Walras) is "a book by a disciple" and that "I will always try to follow in your footsteps and to continue your work" ("Moi, je m'efforcerai toujours de travailler sur les bases indiqués par vous, de continuer votre oeuvre"). In a letter to Georges Renard, dated December 24, 1908, Walras characterizes Schumpeter's 1908 book as "a very handsome and important work" (Ibid., 378, 384).

27. Seidl, *Joseph Alois Schumpeter in Graz*, 6–12, for Schumpeter's appointment at the University of Graz.

28. The role that Böhm-Bawerk played in this appointment is disputed. See for example Smithies, "Memorial," 12; Schneider, *Joseph A. Schumpeter*, 4; and Seidl, "Joseph Alois Schumpeter: Character," 195.

29. Translated into English as *Economic Doctrine and Method: An Historical Sketch* (New York: Oxford University Press, 1954). Schumpeter was examined for possible military service in December 1914 and found fit. However, since he was the only professor in economics in Graz, he was exempted from military service at the request of the dean. See Seidl, "Joseph Alois Schumpeter: Character," 191.

30. See Schumpeter to Paul Siebeck, June 16, 1916, Graz, Harvard University Archives. This is incidentally one of the few letters from his European time that Schumpeter brought with him to the United States. Most of his own correspondence from these years seems to have been left behind (probably in Jülich). Schumpeter's book on feminism is referred to in the letter to Siebeck in the following way: "a book on themes surrounding the woman question." Wolfgang Stolper also tells the following story, which may be of interest in this context:

> While still in high school, Schumpeter . . . wrote a petition to the Ministry of Education protesting the denial of rights to women students. Squirting soda water, he physically defended the right of women to attend particular lectures against a hostile professor and his hostile students (Stolper, "Joseph Alois Schumpeter," 66).

31. Schumpeter to Fetter, March 21, 1914, as cited in Frank Whitson Fetter, "An Early Memoir of Joseph Schumpeter," *History of Political Economy* 6 (1974): 94.

32. Theodore Morgan, Letter to the Editor, *The Economist*, December 24, 1983, 4. In an interview from 1944 Schumpeter also said, "Early in life I formed an idea of a rich and full life to include economics, politics, science, art, and love." See "Professor Schumpeter, Austrian Minister, Now Teaching Economic Theory Here," *The Crimson* (Harvard University), April 11, 1944.

33. Especially important in this process was the publication in 1976 of Ste-

phan Verosta, "Joseph Schumpeter gegen das Zollbündnis der Donaumon-
archie mit Deutschland und gegen die Anschlusspolitik Otto Bauers (1916–
1919)," in *Festschrift für Christian Boda*, 373–404 (Vienna: Europaverlag,
1976). The standard work is otherwise a collection of Schumpeter's political
writings, edited by Wolfgang Stolper and Christian Seidl as Joseph A.
Schumpeter, *Aufsätze zur Wirtschaftspolitik* (Tübingen: J.C.B. Mohr, 1985).

34. See Haberler, "Joseph Alois Schumpeter," 344–45. The quotation is
from "The Crisis of the Tax State" (1918).

35. Schumpeter to Heinrich Lammach, February 21, 1916, as cited in Verosta, "Joseph Schumpeter," 384–85.

36. Haberler, "Joseph Schumpeter," 345. Haberler was told this anecdote
by Albert Hahn, according to a letter from Haberler to Theodor W. Vogelstein, December 20, 1950, Harvard University Archives.

37. The following account of Schumpeter and the Socialization Commission mainly draws on Wolfgang Stolper, "Schumpeter and the German and
Austrian Socialization Attempts of 1918–1919," *Research in the History of Economic Thought and Methodology* 3 (1985): 161–85; and Theodor W. Vogelstein,
"Joseph A. Schumpeter and the Sozialisierungskommission," Harvard University Archives. See also *Bericht der Sozialisierungskommission über die Frage der
Sozialisierung des Kohlenbergbaues vom 31. Juli 1920* (Berlin: Verlag Hans Robert Engelmann, 1920); and *Verhandlungen der Sozialisierungskommission über
den Kohlenbergbau im Winter 1918/1919* (Berlin: Verlag Hans Robert Engelmann, 1921). It should finally be pointed out that Schumpeter himself
touches on this issue in some of his works. See especially Schumpeter, *Capitalism, Socialism and Democracy* (New York: Harper & Brothers, 1942), 300.

38. Vogelstein, "Joseph A. Schumpeter," 4–5.

39. Stolper, "Joseph Alois Schumpeter," 67.

40. Eduard März, "Joseph A. Schumpeter as Minister of Finance of the
First Republic of Austria, March 1919–October 1919," in H. Frisch, *Schumpeterian Economics*, 162–63.

41. Stolper, "Schumpeter and the German and Austrian Sozialization Attempts," 180.

42. The verse, reproduced in Stolper and Seidl, 5 in Schumpeter, *Aufsätze*,
begins like this:

**Schumpeter**
Von Max und Moritz
Wie lieblich ist's, drei Seelen zu vereinen!
Die eine zieht nach rechts, ist streng feudal,
Inmitten steht die zweite liberal,
Die linke scheint die and'ren zu verneinen

43. Jürgen Osterhammel, "Varieties of Social Economics: Joseph A.
Schumpeter and Max Weber," in W. J. Mommsen and J. Osterhammel, eds.,
*Max Weber and His Contemporaries*, 109 (London: Allen & Unwin, 1987). The
quote by Kraus originally comes from *Die Fackel*.

44. März, "Joseph A. Schumpeter," 167–68.

45. This whole affair is discussed in Stolper, "Schumpeter and the German and Austrian Sozialization Attempts," and in Charles A. Gulick, *Austria: From Habsburg to Hitler* (Berkeley: University of California Press, 1948), vol. 1, 134–43. Gulick consulted Schumpeter for his book, and Schumpeter answered him in a letter dated August 7, 1944, in which he stated: ". . . the fact is that I had neither a motive nor the power to initiate or to prevent any buying campaign [of shares in the Alpine Montan Corporation] on the stock exchange" (140). Stolper's article is a defense of Schumpeter's actions, basically arguing that Schumpeter had said yes to a certain type of socialization in Berlin and that he only changed his mind when Otto Bauer wanted to use socialization for socialist purposes. In Stolper's version, in other words, it is Bauer and not Schumpeter who changes his mind.

46. Stolper and Seidl, 7 in Schumpeter, *Aufsätze*. According to many accounts, Schumpeter was antisemitic (see for example Samuelson, in Leonard Silk, *The Economists*, 13–14 (New York: Avon Books, 1976), and in a personal communication to the author on January 11, 1988; Goodwin, "Schumpeter: The Man," 610–11; Karl-Heinz Paqué, "Einige Bemerkungen zur Persönlichkeit Joseph A. Schumpeter" (Kiel: Institut für Weltwirtschaft, Arbeitspapier Nr. 193, 1983, 6–7). Schumpeter himself denied that he was antisemitic and is supported on this account by Wolfgang Stolper in a personal communication to the author on June 21, 1988. In a letter to Ragnar Frisch, dated December 3, 1932, Schumpeter wrote, "Nor am I or have I ever been an anti-Semite" (Harvard University Archives). Finally, according to Galbraith, Schumpeter was *not* antisemitic—but he would often enough make antisemitic sounding statements to shock his surroundings; personal communication to the author on January 8, 1988.

47. Gustav Stolper to Arthur Spiethoff, August 22, 1925, as cited in Stolper and Seidl, 33–34 in Schumpeter, *Aufsätze*.

48. What Schumpeter actually did during his years as president of the Biedermann Bank is somewhat of a mystery if his function was only ceremonial (as is stated in a personal communication to the author from Wolfgang Stolper, June 21, 1988). It is also not known what Schumpeter did in between his resignation as finance minister in October 1919 and his entrance into banking "about two years after he left the government," to cite Haberler; see Haberler, "Joseph Alois Schumpeter," 353.

49. Schneider, *Joseph A. Schumpeter*, 26.

50. "He" refers to Henry, and the excerpt comes from Schumpeter's autobiographical novel, *Ships in the Fog*, as cited in Smithies, "Memorial," 17.

51. Schumpeter to Shigito Tsuru, August 10, 1949, Harvard University Archives.

52. März, "Joseph A. Schumpeter," 21.

53. "I have made it a rule for myself not to take part in any public action that is not directly related to the professional duties and competence of an economist." Schumpeter to Carl Landuaer, December 21, 1940, Harvard University Archives.

54. For a portrait, filled with vivid details, of how Schumpeter appeared

to his students in 1929, see M. Ernst Kamp and Friedrich H. Stamm, "Joseph Alois Schumpeter 1883–1950," in *Bonner Gelehrte: Beiträge zur Geschichte der Wissenschaften in Bonn*, 63–64 (Bonn: Ludwig Röhrscheid Verlag, 1969).

55. Stolper, "Joseph Alois Schumpeter," 68.

56. According to one source, Schumpeter had known Annie for at least five years when they got married; see Smithies, "Memorial," 13. According to another source, however, Annie was only twelve years old when they met: "He [that is, Schumpeter] once told me an awe-inspiring, specific number for the women he had known sexually. But he was no simple sexist. When in Bonn he fell in love with a porter's daughter, who was only twelve or so years of age, he asked that he be allowed to arrange for her education and to marry her when she came of age" (Goodwin, "Schumpeter: The Man," 611). It can also be mentioned that the earliest letter that exists from Annie to Schumpeter is dated 1920—that is five years before they were married. Annie here says that she must refuse to meet with Schumpeter since he is still married; since he lives with another woman; and since he has a bad reputation. See Annie Reisinger to Schumpeter, September 30, 1920, Harvard University Archives.

57. Schumpeter to "G," August 22, 1926, as quoted in Eduard März, *Joseph Alois Schumpeter: Forscher, Lehrer und Politiker* (Munich: R. Oldenbourg, 1983), 171. *Emphasis added.*

58. Stolper, "Joseph Alois Schumpeter," 67.

59. According to the death certificate of Schumpeter's wife, which can be found at the Harvard University Archives, "Anna Reisinger" was "twenty-four years old." Schumpeter, however, refers to her as "twenty-three years old" on the very day of her death; see Schumpeter to "G," August 3, 1926, as cited in März, *Joseph Alois Schumpeter*, 170.

60. Haberler, "Joseph Alois Schumpeter," 354. One of the most curious items in the Schumpeter collection at the Harvard University Archives is a box with ten book-size diaries labeled "Mostly extraxts from Annie's Diary." These were written during 1933–1949 and contain mostly a mixture of what appears to be Schumpeter's own memories of his life with Annie, plus extracts from Annie's diaries, as copied by Schumpeter.

61. Schumpeter to "G," September 21, 1928, as cited in März, *Joseph Alois Schumpeter*, 179. Throughout the 1920s Schumpeter also promised different publishers that he would finish a textbook in economic theory. (I am grateful on this point to Massimo Augello for having made the correspondence between Schumpeter and Julius Springer available to me.)

62. Schumpeter to "G," March 13, 1931, as cited in März, *Joseph Alois Schumpeter*, 183. *Emphasis added.*

63. The details surrounding Schumpeter's book on money are unclear. See for example Joseph A. Schumpeter, *Das Wesen des Geldes* (Göttingen: Vandenhoeck & Ruprecht, 1970); Erich Schneider, "Review of Schumpeter, *Das Wesen des Geldes*," *German Economic Review* 8 (1970): 348–52; and Bernd Kulla, "Spiethoff, Schumpeter und *Das Wesen des Geldes*," *Kyklos* 42 (1989): 431–34.

64. März, *Joseph Alois Schumpeter*, 12.

65. In a letter to Waldemar Gurian, dated February 5, 1943, Schumpeter wrote: "I will confess to you in confidence that among the personal motives which I had for leaving Germany and accepting Harvard's invitation (it is not much to my credit as a political analyst that I had no idea whatsoever of Hitler's impending rise to power) was that I did not wish to live under a laborite regime of that kind if I could possibly help it. Motives of scientific work were more important but that motive also played a role" (Harvard University Archives).

66. Schumpeter, "Das Woher und Wohin unserer Wissenschaft," in *Aufsätze zur ökonomischen Theorie*, 603 (Tübingen: J.C.B. Mohr, 1952).

67. Ibid., 606. It should be pointed out that the speech cited here only exists in a shorthand version, which Schumpeter himself never corrected. The shorthand version was printed with the approval (and slight changes) of Elizabeth Boody Schumpeter and Gottfried Haberler for a volume of Schumpeter's essays. In a note appended to the printed version, the editors— Erich Schneider and Arthur Spiethoff—say that the spirit of the text is unmistakably Schumpeter's. Since the passage about National Socialism on page 606 is of interest for an understanding of Schumpeter's political attitude at the time, the full text is given here:

> A young man, who understands to supply himself with tools of knowledge that others do not have, is necessarily superior to these others all his life; and this means something even in our bureaucratized world. Just think about the situation our fatherland is in today! We are witnessing a giant movement which is unique in history. No organization has ever succeeded in prevailing upon the established parties. This giant power apparatus can be compared to a colossus of infinite impulses; and it can—dependent on how it is used—mean catastrophe or glory to the German people. But how important it is that this colossus gets the right kind of economic advice; and that there are people in it which have national-socialistic feelings—and despite this do not despise economic technique. What giant subjective possibilities this constitutes for a young man! One only has an impact, where nothing has been thought through yet. That one must turn to parties with nonrational programs is something all important politicians know.

It should finally be mentioned that when Arthur Spiethoff, who was one of the editors of the book in which the speech was reprinted, wanted to eliminate this passage from the public version, Elizabeth Boody Schumpeter and Gottfried Haberler refused to do so; see the correspondence from May 1952 between Elizabeth Boody Schumpeter and Spiethoff at the Schlesinger Library at Radcliffe College. Erich Schneider, the other editor, would later refer to the version he had himself published in 1952 as "inaccurate" (Schneider, *Joseph A. Schumpeter*, 59).

68. Schumpeter to Adolph Löwe, November 19, 1932, Harvard University Archives.

69. Schumpeter to Dennis H. Robertson, December 24, 1932, Harvard University Archives.

70. Allyn Young to Clifford H. Moore, March 23, 1927, Harvard University Archives. I thank Larry Nichols for having drawn my attention to this letter.

71. Edward S. Mason, "The Harvard Department of Economics from the Beginning to World War II," *Quarterly Journal of Economics* 47 (1982): 420.

72. Schumpeter, for example, used to tell his students that it was not until he came to the United States that he learned what a "mailbox" is; in Europe you just leave the mail on the silver tray in the hall and then it is gone by the morning. It was also said that Schumpeter only gave A's to three categories of students. There were first the Jesuits, who all got A's. Then there were the women, and they got all A's too. And finally there were all the others—who also all got A's. I am grateful to Carl Kaysen for telling me these anecdotes, which he picked up as a student at Harvard in the 1940s.

73. Paul A. Samuelson, "Schumpeter as a Teacher and Economic Theorist," in S. E. Harris, *Schumpeter*, 50.

74. John Kenneth Galbraith, *A Life in Our Times: Memoirs* (Boston: Houghton Mifflin Company, 1981), 49.

75. Schumpeter to Irving Fisher, March 19, 1936, Harvard University Archives.

76. The author has used two sources on Elizabeth Boody Schumpeter: Elizabeth Waterman Gilboy's memoir "Elizabeth Boody Schumpeter, 1898–1953," in Elizabeth Boody Schumpeter, *English Overseas Trade Statistics, 1697–1808*, 5–7 (Oxford: Clarendon Press, 1960); and the collection of Elizabeth Boody Schumpeter's papers at the Schlesinger Library, Radcliffe College.

77. Elizabeth Schumpeter to J. C. Roraback, June 2, 1939, Schlesinger Library at Radcliffe College.

78. Elizabeth Boody to Joseph Schumpeter in a folder with the title "Letters from EBF—Summer 1937," Harvard University Archives.

79. Elizabeth Boody to Joseph Schumpeter, July 8, 1937, Harvard University Archives.

80. Schumpeter to Kenneth Boulding, March 15, 1939, Harvard University Archives.

81. From interview with James Duesenberry, Cambridge, March 10, 1988.

82. Stolper, "Joseph Alois Schumpeter," 69.

83. Schumpeter to Albert Pratt, May 12, 1937, Harvard University Archives.

84. See for example Schumpeter to Tryggve J. B. Hoff, May 19, 1933, Harvard University Archives.

85. Schumpeter to Charles C. Burlingham, May 21, 1941, Harvard University Archives.

86. Interview with John Kenneth Galbraith, Cambridge, January 8, 1988.

87. Schumpeter in his private diary on January 5, 1942, Harvard University Archives.

88. Haberler, "Schumpeter's *Capitalism, Socialism and Democracy* after Forty Years," in A. Heertje, ed., *Schumpeter's Vision*, 74 (New York: Praeger, 1981).

89. Goodwin, "Schumpeter: The Man," 610.

90. Schumpeter in his private diary on May 14, 1944, Harvard University Archives. To this statement should perhaps be added that Schumpeter always felt that Hitler's access to power in 1933 was justified by the excesses of the preceding government. There are several letters to this effect from the spring of 1933, including one to Edmund E. Day, dated May 2, 1933, Harvard University Archives, in which Schumpeter says that "I know something of the government which preceded Hitler's and I can only say that I am quite prepared to forgive him much by virtue of comparison." In general it has to be emphasized that a full study of Schumpeter's attitude toward German fascism must not neglect the material in Schumpeter's private diary, which is mainly written in an old-fashioned, Austrian form of shorthand. To give a flavor of the material in this diary, we may cite an entry from 1939 where Schumpeter argues that the Western powers have driven Hitler into the arms of Stalin; and that if Hitler wins, there will be "a much more stable state of things—the structure of Europe better balanced and strains removed and more hope for peace for a long time past." Schumpeter then asks, "And what about Hitlerism?" His answer is:

> Well history should have taught us that it is no good fighting a religion, that's why nobody would think about fighting bolshevism: If it is to stay it will stay. But even so it is not unlikely that it will settle down—possibly after success—whereas I don't see what is to be done if Germany is *beaten*.

91. This statement is based on the material on Elizabeth Boody Schumpeter at the Schlesinger Library at Radcliffe College. This material, it should be stressed, represents a selection of what Elizabeth herself wanted to keep and what her friend Lucy Talcott (who seems to have put together the papers for the Schlesinger Library) wanted posterity to know. Elizabeth would after the war try to find out who had spread the rumors about her in Washington. She would also try—unsuccessfully—to be hired by the CIA.

92. John Kenneth Galbraith, "Review of *Capitalism, Socialism and Democracy*," *New Society*, April 14, 1977, 74.

93. Schumpeter in his diary on November 23, 1942, Harvard University Archives.

94. Smithies, "Memorial," 23. The full entry reads:

> Looking back on these months and on the weeks that are still left, and looking back on my life in the process, three things stand out:
>
> 1. Always the same mistakes committed and the same type of strength and weakness displayed.
>
> 2. The story might be written in terms of lost opportunities (though of course that stands out in retrospect); there were those that were seized and used promptly enough.
>
> 3. Yet there is no regret—if I had used every one of those opportunities I should not have done a better job of it all—perhaps even contrary, for

success up to the hilt with any one of them would have stuck me in the particular line and not only narrowed me but landed me in uncomfortable situations.

95. Otto Stöckel to Schumpeter, May 1, 1947, Harvard University Archives.

96. Both statements come from interviews that were made by the author with a series of Schumpeter's colleagues and students in 1987–1988.

97. Schumpeter to Shigito Tsuru, August 10, 1949, Harvard University Archives.

98. Schumpeter, *History of Economic Analysis*, 41–42, 561–62. See also Schumpeter, "Science and Ideology," in *Essays*, 267–81 (Reading, Mass.: Addison-Wesley, 1951).

99. S. E. Harris, ed., *Schumpeter*.

100. In the 1944 *Crimson* interview, which was referred to in note 32, Schumpeter said that his research program had "varied but always stayed on the same plane—that of evolving a comprehensive sociology with a single aim." For some information on Schumpeter and *Sozialökonomik*, see the two excellent essays by Jürgen Osterhammel, "Joseph A. Schumpeter und das Nicht-Ökonomische in der Ökonomie," *Kölner Zeitschrift für Soziologie und Sozialpsychologie* 39 (1987): 40–58; and "Spielarten der Sozialökonomik: Joseph A. Schumpeter und Max Weber," in W. J. Mommsen and W. Schwentker, eds., *Max Weber und seine Zeitgenossen*, 147–95 (Göttingen: Vandenhoeck & Ruprecht, 1988). In this context, see also Erich Schneider's already cited book (whose original title is *Joseph A. Schumpeter: Leben und Werk eines grossen Sozialökonomen*).

101. Dietzel—who was actually Schumpeter's predecessor at the University of Bonn—introduced the term *Sozialökonomik* first through an article in 1883 and then in *Theoretische Sozialökonomik* (1895), which was published as a volume in Wagner's handbook of political economy; see Johannes Winkelmann, *Max Webers hinterlassenes Hauptwerk: Die Wirtschaft und die gesellschaftlichen Ordnungen und Mächte* (Tübingen: J.C.B. Mohr, 1986), 11–12. Dietzel himself traces the term *Sozialökonomik* to some early Italian economists and especially to Jean-Baptiste Say, who uses it in the introduction to *Cours complet d'économie politique* (1828–29). Also, John Stuart Mill, who was the first to use the term in its English version ("social economy"), traces its ancestry to Say— see John Stuart Mill, "On the Definition of Political Economy" (1838), in *Essays on Some Unsettled Questions*, 136–37 (London: John W. Parker, 1844). In Mill's opinion, Say equates "social economy" with "every part of man's nature, insofar as influencing the conduct or constitution of man in society." Dietzel himself, however, defined *Sozialökonomik* somewhat differently. He was first of all interested in finding a substitute for the terms *Nationalökonomik* and *politsche Ökonomik*, which he felt misrepresented economics by connecting it to "the nation" and "politics." Dietzel himself defined *Sozialökonomik* in an organic and holistic manner.

102. See Schumpeter, *History of Economic Analysis*, 21, 535.

103. Max Weber, *The Methodology of the Social Sciences* (New York: The Free

88 INTRODUCTION

Press, 1949), 63. Weber's most important essay on *Sozialökonomik* is " 'Objectivity' in Social Science and Social Policy" (1904), where Weber tried to lay out the new editorial policy for *Archiv für Sozialwissenschaft und Sozialpolitik*. This essay, which is reprinted in the Free Press edition on methodology, can be said to contain Weber's program of socio-economics. Another important source in this context is of course *Economy and Society*, which was part of *Grundriss der Sozialökonomik*. A definition of *Sozialökonomik* can, for example, be found here: "Sociological economics [*Sozialökonomie*] . . . considers actual human activities as they are conditioned by the necessity to take into account the facts of economic life" (Max Weber, *Economy and Society* [Berkeley: University of California Press, 1978], 311–12).

104. Schumpeter, *History of Economic Analysis*, 535. The meaning that Weber tried to impose on the term was also soon forgotten. This development was no doubt speeded up by the alternative definitions of *Sozialökonomik* that were suggested in such works as Adolph Wagner's *Theoretische Sozialökonomik oder Allgemeine und theoretische Volkswirtschaftslehre* (1907), and Gustav Cassel's *Theoretische Sozialökonomie* (1918).

105. The publication date of the former work is given as 1910 by the National Union Catalogue and other sources, but as 1915 in the note accompanying the reprint in Schumpeter, *Aufsätze zur ökonomischen Theorie* (Tübingen: J.C.B. Mohr, 1952). The author has been unable to inspect the original edition.

106. Schumpeter, *Vergangenheit und Zukunft der Sozialwissenschaften* (Munich: Duncker & Humblot, 1915), 4.

107. Ibid., 38.

108. Ibid., 136.

109. Schumpeter, *Epochen der Dogmen- und Methodengeschichte* (Tübingen: J.C.B. Mohr, 1914), 81–83.

110. Ibid., 101.

111. Ibid.

112. Schumpeter would later correct this rather negative picture of Schmoller. See Schumpeter, "Gustav v. Schmoller und die Probleme von heute," *Schmollers Jahrbuch* 50 (1926): 19, note 1.

113. Schumpeter, "Preface to Japanese edition of *Theorie der wirtschaftlichen Entwicklung*," 160 in *Essays*.

114. Schumpeter, *The Theory of Economic Development* (Cambridge: Harvard University Press, 1934), 60.

115. Ibid., 93.

116. Ibid., 65.

117. Ibid., 86–87.

118. Ibid., 67.

119. For an emphasis on Schumpeter as having introduced economic change into economics, see for example Erik Dahmén, "Schumpeterian Dynamics: Some Methodological Notes," *Journal of Economic Behavior and Organization* 5 (1984): 25–34. For the view that Schumpeter tried to fill the gap of technical change in marginal utility analysis, see for example Mark Blaug,

*Economic Theory in Retrospect* (Cambridge: Cambridge University Press, 1983), 462–63. It can finally be noted that research on the entrepreneur—a figure that Schumpeter helped to introduce into economics—is today much more popular in business schools than among mainstream economists.

120. That Schumpeter probably gave his speech on February 9, 1931 is confirmed by Robert Loring Allen in his introduction to this article, as published (in a slightly different form from here) in *Kobe University Economic Review* 28 (1982): 1–15. The original title of the lecture was "The Present State of Economics on Systems, Schools and Methods." For some other material on Schumpeter's Japanese lectures, see the folder marked "Cambridge Closet— Japan—(nature of economics)" at the Harvard University Archives.

121. Schumpeter to Justin H. Moore, February 13, 1931, Harvard University Archives.

122. In *The Nature and Essence of Theoretical Economics*, Schumpeter devotes chapter 6 in Part I to "Der methodologische Individualismus." Even if it is clear that Schumpeter was the first to use the term "methodological individualism" (mainly in order to distinguish it from "political individualism"), it is generally considered that it was Carl Menger who "invented" it. See on this point, for example, Lars Udéhn, *Methodological Individualism—A Critical Appraisal*, unpublished Ph.D. thesis, Department of Sociology at Uppsala University, 1987, 6–48. It can finally be noted that in his later writings Schumpeter was to add a third type of individualism to his terminology: "sociological individualism." By this term he essentially means an outmoded attempt to explain sociological phenomena through the actions of the individual as opposed to that of the group. See Schumpeter, *History of Economic Analysis*, 888–89.

123. Schumpeter discusses the four fields of *Sozialökonomik* in *History of Economic Analysis*, 12–21. (See also the section titled "The American Period" in this introduction.)

124. This was probably in 1906 and/or 1907. In addition, most of Schumpeter's own notes on sociology from the pre-1932 period have been lost. As previously mentioned, when Schumpeter emigrated to the United States in 1932 he left behind several trunks of books, notes, manuscripts, and the like in Jülich. According to a list of their contents, which Schumpeter compiled, one of these trunks—which was destroyed by the bombings during World War II—contained "Sociology; in case of death to be destroyed. Also a thick envelope in regards to *Capital*." See Harvard University Archives.

125. Schumpeter outlined the content of this course in the following way: "(1) How sociology emerged and why it is necessary. (2) What belongs to the field of sociology. (3) Its problems. (4) Its methods and present results. (5) Main currents of sociology. (6) The sociology of everyday life; the sociological insights of artists." (For the exact reference, see note 12.)

126. For an introduction to von Wieser as a sociologist, see Hermann Strasser, "Macht und Klassenbildung bei Friedrich von Wieser: Zur Erinnerungen an einen soziologischen Wegbereiter," *Kölner Zeitschrift für Soziologie und Sozialpsychologie* 33 (1981): 576–89. According to Carl Menger, "econom-

ics" consisted not only of "economic theory" but also of "the practical economic sciences"; see Carl Menger, *Untersuchungen über die Methode der Sozialwissenschaften und die Politischen Ökonomie* (Leipzig: Duncker & Humblot,
1883), 8–9. In Böhm-Bawerk's opinion, the historical method constituted "a
wide and important province in economic theory; see Eugen von Böhm-
Bawerk, "The Historical vs. the Deductive Method in Political Economy," *Annals of the American Academy of Political and Social Science* 1 (1891): 248.

127. For a discussion of Schumpeter's personal difficulties with Sombart,
see his letter to Paul Siebeck, June 16, 1916, Harvard University Archives.
Karl Jaspers tells the following anecdote about a meeting between Schumpeter and Weber, which took place just after World War I:

> Both had met in a Vienna coffeehouse, in the presence of Ludo Moritz
> Hartmann and Somary. Schumpeter remarked how pleased he was with
> the Russian Revolution. Socialism was no longer a discussion on paper, but
> had to prove its viability. Max Weber responded in great agitation: Com-
> munism, at this stage in Russian development, was virtually a crime, the
> road would lead over unparalleled human misery and end in a terrible
> catastrophe. "Quite likely," Schumpeter answered, "but what a fine labo-
> ratory." "A laboratory filled with mounds of corpses," Weber answered
> heatedly. "The same can be said of every dissecting room," Schumpeter
> replied. Every attempt to divert them failed. Weber became increasingly
> violent and loud, Schumpeter increasingly sarcastic and muted. The other
> guests listened with curiosity, until Weber jumped up, shouting "I can't
> stand any more of this," and rushed out, followed by Hartmann, who
> brought him his hat. Schumpeter, left behind, said with a smile: "How can
> a man shout like that in a coffeehouse?"

This quotation comes from Karl Jaspers, *Three Essays: Leonardo, Descartes, Max
Weber* (New York: Harcourt, Brace & World, 1964), 222. Jaspers, in his turn,
had found the anecdote in Felix Somary, *Erinnerungen*, 171–72. There exists
one more account of a meeting between Schumpeter and Weber: Walter
Tritsch, "A Conversation between Joseph Schumpeter and Max Weber," *History of Sociology* 6 (1985): 167–72. It is clear from this article that Weber and
Schumpeter were usually on more friendly terms than the Somary-Jaspers
anecdote would indicate.

128. See especially Schumpeter's contribution to *Äusserungen zur Wertur-
teilsdiskussion im Ausschuss des Vereins für Sozialpolitik*, 49–50, privately printed
in 1913. For the general context of the debate see Franz Boese, *Geschichte des
Vereins für Sozialpolitik 1872–1932* (Berlin: Duncker & Humblot, 1939); and
Dieter Lindenlaub, *Richtungskämpfe im Verein für Sozialpolitik* (Wiesbaden:
Franz Steiner Verlag, 1967).

129. For information about Weber and Schumpeter, see for example Jürgen Osterhammel, "Spielarten der Sozialökonomik"; Ronan Macdonald,
"Schumpeter and Max Weber—Central Visions and Social Theories," *Quarterly Journal of Economics* 79 (1965): 373–96; and N. M. Hansen, "Schumpeter
and Max Weber: Comment," *Quarterly Journal of Economics* 80 (1966): 488–

91. According to a personal communication from Wolfgang Mommsen on June 1, 1989, there only exists a small number of letters between Weber and Schumpeter, none of which is particularly illuminating.

130. See for example Edward A. Carlin, "Schumpeter's Constructed Type: The Entrepreneur," *Kyklos* 9 (1956): 27–43.

131. Schumpeter to Lloyd S. Huntsman, May 26, 1941, Harvard University Archives.

132. The following is primarily based on Schumpeter, *Wie studiert man Sozialwissenschaft?*, in *Aufsätze zur ökonomischen Theorie*, 555–65.

133. Schumpeter, *Das Wesen*, 539.

134. See especially Schumpeter, "Gustav v. Schmoller," 33–35.

135. Adolph Löwe, *Economics and Sociology: A Plea for Co-operation in the Social Sciences* (London: George Allen & Unwin, 1935), 31–32.

136. Schumpeter, "The Crisis of the Tax State," 6. For an introduction in English to Goldscheid's thought, see Rudolf Goldscheid, "A Sociological Approach to Problems of Public Finance," in R. A. Musgrave and A. T. Peacock, eds., *Classics in the Theory of Public Finance*, 202–13 (London: Macmillan & Co, 1958). An accessible source in German is Rudolf Hickel, ed., *Die Finanzkrise des Steuerstaats* (Frankfurt am Main: Suhrkamp Verlag, 1976), which contains the key texts of Goldscheid as well as of Schumpeter.

137. Ibid., 7.

138. That sociologists have ignored "fiscal sociology" is clear, for example, from Daniel Bell's comments in Chapter 6 ("The Public Household: On 'Fiscal Sociology' and the Liberal Society") in *The Cultural Contradictions of Capitalism* (New York: Basic Books, 1976). Since the 1970s, however, there has been a certain revival of interest, much due to James O'Conner's book *The Fiscal Crisis of the State* (1973). See in this context Fred Block, "The Fiscal Crisis of the Capitalist State," *Annual Review of Sociology* 7 (1981): 1–27. In the United States, as in Europe, economists have been more interested in fiscal sociology than sociologists. See for example Fritz Karl Mann, "The Sociology of Taxation," *The Review of Politics* 5 (1943): 225–35; and "The Fiscal Component of Revolution: An Essay in Fiscal Sociology," *The Review of Politics* 9 (1947): 331–49; Herbert Sultan, "Finanzwissenschaft und Soziologie" in *Handbuch der Finanzwissenschaft* (Tübingen: J.C.B. Mohr, 1952), 66–98; Rolf Richard Grauhan and Rudolf Hickel, eds., *Krise des Steuerstaats?* (Opladen: Westdeutscher Verlag, 1978); Richard Musgrave, "Theories of Fiscal Crises: An Essay in Fiscal Sociology," in H. J. Aaron and M. J. Boskin, eds., *The Economics of Taxation*, 361–90 (Washington, D.C.: The Brookings Institution, 1980); and Lutz Köllner, "Bemerkungen zur Finanzsoziologie heute," *Jahrbuch für Nationalökonomie und Statistik* 203 (1987): 26–42.

139. Schumpeter has been challenged on this point with the argument that the state arose as much out of political needs as out of financial needs. See for example Rudolf Braun, "Taxation, Sociopolitical Structure, and State-Building: Great Britain and Brandenburg-Prussia," in C. Tilly, ed., *The Formation of National States in Western Europe*, 245–46 (Princeton: Princeton University Press, 1975).

140. Eduard März, "Joseph A. Schumpeter," 162.

141. In a letter to Stewart S. Morgan from May 18, 1934, Schumpeter refers to the essays on imperialism and social classes as "[my] two sociological pieces of work"; and in a letter to Lewis H. Haney, dated April 22, 1949, as "my excursions into sociology" (both letters can be found in the Harvard University Archives). From the 1949 letter it is clear that he felt that *Capitalism, Socialism and Democracy* belonged to a special category and that it "contains some purely economic chapters." After Schumpeter's death a note was found, according to which it was clear that Schumpeter regarded "his most important works" to be *The Nature and Essence of Theoretical Economics* (1908); *The Theory of Economic Development* (1911); *Business Cycles* (1939); *Capitalism, Socialism and Democracy* (1942); and the two essays on imperialism and social classes (Paul Sweezy, "Schumpeter on 'Imperialism and Social Classes'," in S. E. Harris, ed., *Schumpeter*, 119).

142. Aside from the essays on the tax state, imperialism, and social classes, this volume also contains "Das sociale Anlitz des Deutschen Reiches" from 1929 ("The Social Structure of Germany"). *Aufsätze zur Soziologie* was put together by two economists, Erich Schneider and Arthur Spiethoff, and their statement that it contains all of Schumpeter's sociological works in German is somewhat exaggerated. Schumpeter wrote several small sociological articles and book reviews during his European period, which have not been included in *Aufsätze*. See for example "Die 'positive' Methode in der Nationalökonomie" (1914) and "Ökonomie und Soziologie der Einkommensteuer" (1929).

143. For some examples, see Horace B. Davis, "Schumpeter as Sociologist," *Science and Society* 24 (1960): 13–35; and Keith Griffin and John Gurley, "Radical Analyses of Imperialism, the Third World, and the Transition to Socialism: A Survey Article," *Journal of Economic Literature* 23 (1985): 1098. A critical essay that can be recommended is: Murray Greene, "Schumpeter's Imperialism—A Critical Note," *Social Research* 19 (1952): 453–63.

144. Schumpeter, *Imperialism and Social Classes* (New York: Meridian Books, 1971), 6.

145. The reference to Schumpeter can be found in Otto Hintze's important essay on Sombart, "Economics and Politics in the Age of Capitalism," in *The Historical Essays of Otto Hintze*, 426 (New York: Oxford University Press, 1975).

146. Karl W. Deutsch, "Joseph Schumpeter as an Analyst of Sociology and Economic History," *Journal of Economic History* 16 (1956): 50.

147. Otis Dudley Duncan found Schumpeter's essay "refreshing" with its "broad approach to social change." Reinhard Bendix said that "current studies of stratification . . . will profit from Schumpeter's sociological writings." And according to Robert Merton, "These essays [that is, "The Sociology of Imperialisms" and "Social Classes"] build a bridge carrying two-way intellectual traffic between economics and sociology." "It will be of immense benefit to American social scientists," Merton added, "to have these works available." See Otis Dudley Duncan, "Review of J. A. Schumpeter, *Imperialism and Social Classes*," *Rural Sociology* 16 (1951): 412; Reinhard Bendix, "Review of J. A.

Schumpeter, *Imperialism and Social Classes*," *American Journal of Sociology* 57 (1951): 198–200; and Robert K. Merton as cited on the back of J. A. Schumpeter, *Imperialism and Social Classes* (New York: Meridian Books, 1971).

148. Schumpeter, *Imperialism and Social Classes*, 105.

149. Ibid., 126.

150. The reader is referred to the section in the essay on social classes, where Schumpeter talks about "that extraordinary physical and nervous energy" of the entrepreneur which makes him realize new possibilities also late at night "when few men manage to preserve their full force and originality" (ibid., 122–23).

151. Ibid., 146.

152. Ibid., 150.

153. Ibid., 163.

154. Schumpeter, *History*, v.

155. Schumpeter, *Business Cycles*, v, 111.

156. Schumpeter, *History*, 12. In a first draft of Chapter 1 in *History*, Schumpeter formulated his ideas slightly differently: "Moreover, I wish to testify to my belief that if for the training of an economist I had to choose one of the three fundamental fields [of economic analysis] to the exclusion of the other two, my choice would not be theory but economic history" (Schumpeter, "Some Questions of Principle," *Research in the History of Economic Thought and Methodology* 5 [1987]: 115).

157. Paul Samuelson, "Schumpeter as a Teacher and Economic Theorist," 48–53 in S. E. Harris, *Schumpeter*. It should be stressed that Samuelson's essay contains a superb picture of Schumpeter which in artistry is comparable to the best in the genre—Keynes's portraits of economists in *Essays in Biography*.

158. See for example Schneider on this point: "What mattered to him [that is, Schumpeter] was to make quite distinct the limitations of theoretical analysis and to stress that *theory is a necessary, but not sufficient, instrument for the comprehension of economic reality*. This noncontroversial view pervades his entire life-work—from his first book, *Essence and Principal Contents*, to the *History of Economic Analysis*" (Schneider, *Joseph A. Schumpeter* 44; *emphasis in text*).

159. Schumpeter, *Business Cycles*, 13. *Emphasis added*.

160. Ibid., v.

161. Ibid., 31, 137–38, 222.

162. Ibid., 220.

163. Ibid., 223. In "Comments on a Plan for the Study of Entrepreneurship," Schumpeter says that "In my youth, I did, for instance, under a man who was considered an authority, some work in the history of strategy and tactics."

164. Ibid., 43–44.

165. Simon Kuznets, "Schumpeter's Business Cycles," *American Economic Review* 30 (1940): 257–71.

166. W. W. Rostow, "Review of Alfred Kleinknecht, *Innovation Patterns in Crisis and Prosperity*," *Journal of Economic Literature* 26 (March 1988): 111–13.

167. Schumpeter, *Business Cycles*, 104.

168. Ibid., 696.
169. See for example Sweezy, "Schumpeter on 'Imperialism and Social Classes,' " 122.
170. Schumpeter, *Business Cycles*, 696.
171. Ibid., 97, n. 2.
172. Schumpeter, *Capitalism, Socialism and Democracy*, 269.
173. Anthony Downs, *An Economic Theory of Democracy* (New York: Harper & Row, 1957), 29. Gary Becker, who worked on an economic theory of democracy during the 1950s (but published little), also acknowledges his debt to Schumpeter. See Gary Becker, "Competition and Democracy," *Journal of Law and Economics* 1 (1958): 106, and "Pressure Groups and Political Behavior," 120 in R. D. Coe and C. K. Wilber, eds., *Capitalism and Democracy: Schumpeter Revisited* (Notre Dame: University of Notre Dame, 1985). See in this context also William C. Mitchell, "Schumpeter and Public Choice, I-II," *Public Choice* 42 (1984): 73–88, 161–74. It should finally be added that Weberian scholars claim that Schumpeter's theory of the politician as an entrepreneur owes much to Weber. (See for example Wolfgang J. Mommsen, *Max Weber and German Politics, 1890–1920* [Chicago: University of Chicago Press, 1984], 406–7 and David Beetham, *Max Weber and the Theory of Modern Politics* [Cambridge: Polity Press, 1985], 111.) The great success of Schumpeter's new theory of democracy is according to two authors ascribed to the fact that Weber's ideas were not yet known in the United States. They also note that Schumpeter "minimized" the extent to which his ideas on this score actually had their origin in Weber's work (see Stephen P. Turner and Regis Factor, *Max Weber and the Dispute over Reason and Value* [London: Routledge and Kegan Paul, 1984], 2–3).
174. Schumpeter, *Capitalism*, 49–55. On page 404, Schumpeter refers to his 1918–1919 article on imperialism and suggests a new definition of imperialism: "Imperialism is a policy that aims at extending a government's control over groups other than co-national ones against their will." It can be mentioned that Schumpeter was planning to write an article on imperialism for *Foreign Affairs* at the time of his death.
175. Ibid., 46.
176. Ibid.
177. Ibid., 44.
178. Ibid.
179. Ibid., 107.
180. Schumpeter, *History of Economic Analysis*, 39.
181. Schumpeter naturally uses the English term throughout his work. For explicit references to *Sozialökonomik*, see especially pp. 21 and 535 (and also pp. 10, 817, and 819) in *History of Economic Analysis*.
182. Ibid., 10.
183. Ibid., 13.
184. Ibid., 17.
185. According to Elizabeth Boody Schumpeter, who edited Schumpeter's work from a bewildering number of finished and half-finished manuscripts,

THE MAN AND HIS WORK

economic sociology is just a *"possible* fourth field." But given the fact that
Schumpeter wrote the key section on "economic sociology" as late as 1949
and that the work contains several sections on "economic sociology" (which
are organically worked into the main argument of the history of economic
analysis), it seems clear that Schumpeter indeed saw economic sociology as a
fourth field. See Schumpeter, *History of Economic Analysis*, 20–21, 544–48,
886–88, 1190.

186. Ibid., 20.

187. Ibid., 21, 544. Another good definition of economic sociology from
this period can be found in "The Communist Manifesto in Sociology and
Economics" (1949): "By 'economic sociology' (the German *Wirtschaftssoziologie*) we denote the description and interpretation—or 'interpretative description'—of economically relevant institutions, including habits and all forms of
behavior in general, such as government, property, private enterprise, customary or 'rational' behavior" (Schumpeter, *Essays*, 286–87).

188. Schumpeter, *History of Economic Analysis*, 26–27.

189. Ibid., 27.

190. This information on "Comments" is based on letters to the author
from Hugh G. J. Aitken, April 1988, and from Thomas C. Cochran, May 5,
1988. Cochran writes: "As co-editor of *The Journal of Economic History*, I reti-
tled one of his [that is, Schumpeter's] articles 'The Creative Response,' and S.
accepted this."

191. Arthur H. Cole, "Joseph A. Schumpeter and the Research Center in
Entrepreneurial History," *Explorations in Entrepreneurial History* 2, 2 (1950):
56. For the history of the Center, see especially Adrien Taymans, "Le 'Research Center' in Entrepreneurial History," *Economie Appliquée* 3 (1950): 615–
35; Hugh G. J. Aitken, "Entrepreneurial Research: The History of an Intellectual Innovation," in H.G.J. Aitken, ed., *Explorations in Enterprise*, 3–19
(Cambridge: Harvard University Press, 1965); and Ruth Crandall, *The Research Center in Entrepreneurial History at Harvard University, 1948–1958*, unpublished manuscript, 1960.

192. Schumpeter, "Comments on a Plan for the Study of Entrepreneurship," 13.

193. In a letter to the author from May 5, 1988, Thomas C. Cochran
writes, "The Research Center in Entrepreneurial History was certainly more
sociological in its views and interests than neo-classical economic. The real
split was our emphasis on tentative empirically based hypotheses as against
deductive theory, and there is perhaps no reconciliation of this difference. I
believe that Schumpeter was up against this dilemma in his later thinking,
and was moving toward empiricism." For some additional comments along
these lines, see also Richard Swedberg, "Introduction," xxii–xxvii in Schumpeter, *Essays* (New Jersey: Transaction Press, 1989).

194. Schumpeter, "Comments," 3.

195. The following is primarily based on information about the Seminar
on Rationality in the Social Sciences at the Harvard University Archives. I am
also grateful to Wassily Leontief for additional information.

196. Schumpeter, "Discussions on the Meaning of Rationality in Action" (9 pages).

197. Parsons was in charge of putting together the book. In a letter to Wilbert E. Moore at the Harvard University Archives, Parsons wrote on March 2, 1941, that he had just run into Schumpeter in the Harvard Yard and that Schumpeter had asked him what was happening with the book. Parsons answered that several of the people who were supposed to write papers had not done so. This is the last time any reference is made to the book. Parsons described the rationality seminar in the following manner in an autobiographical essay from 1970 (Talcott Parsons, "On Building Social Systems Theory: A Personal History," *Daedalus* 99 [1970]: 834):

> After my formal transfer to sociology, Schumpeter organized a small discussion group with younger people, mostly graduate students, on problems of the nature of rationality. After a few meetings he proposed to me that the group should aim at producing a volume, of which he and I should be at least coeditors, if not coauthors. Though not specifically rejecting the proposal, at least immediately, I remember having reacted rather coolly, and in fact I let it die. I am not wholly clear about my motives, but I think they had to do with the feeling that I needed a relatively complete formal break with economics.

198. Schumpeter to Talcott Parsons, June 12, 1940, Harvard University Archives. I am grateful to William Buxton for having drawn my attention to this letter.

199. Schumpeter to Chester I. Barnard, January 6, 1939, Harvard University Archives. See also Schumpeter's letter to Barnard from January 30, 1939.

200. Schumpeter, "Discussions," 7.

201. The following information comes from Elizabeth Schumpeter's file at the Schlesinger Library and from Dale L. Cramer and Charles G. Leathers, "Schumpeter's Corporatist Views: Links among His Social Theory, *Quadragesimo Anno*, and Moral Reform," *History of Political Economy* 13 (1981): 745–71.

202. Anonymous, "Un economiste préconise le corporatisme," *Ecole Sociale Populaire*, novembre 1945, as cited in Association professionelle des industriels, *Premier congrès patronal: Comment sauvegarder l'entreprise privée* (Montreal: L'Association, 1946), 140–41.

203. See Cramer and Leathers, "Schumpeter's Corporatist Views," 766–67.

204. In "The March into Socialism," Schumpeter stresses that the ideas in *Quadragesimo Anno* constitute a good alternative to socialism but is perhaps only practicable in Catholic countries. See Schumpeter, *Capitalism, Socialism, and Democracy* (New York: Harper & Row, 1975), 416. In *History of Economic Analysis*, Schumpeter notes that *Quadragesimo Anno* outlines the notion of a corporatist state. He then adds, "Since it [that is, the encyclical of Pius XI] is a normative program and not a piece of analysis, no more will be said about it in this book" (Schumpeter, *History*, 765).

205. The rumor about Schumpeter's speech being fascist was told to the author by Paul Samuelson in an interview on January 11, 1988. According to the two translators of the Montreal speech, the written version of the speech is "substantially expanded" in relation to the actual speech delivered; see Michael G. Prime and David R. Henderson, "Schumpeter on Preserving Private Enterprise," *History of Political Economy* 7 (1975): 293.

206. Schumpeter, "The Future of Private Enterprise in the Face of Modern Socialistic Tendencies," *History of Political Economy* 7 (1975): 297.

207. Schumpeter sometimes mocked sociology and said that it was a suitable pastime for old economists, well past their prime. One example is the following entry on Pareto in Schumpeter's private diary from March 19, 1942: "Say what you will and respect as much as you like the many good things in the Trattato di Sociologia Generale—it *is* a work of bourgeois rancune! and, more than that, it *is* senile and displays sociology's senile quality. Yes, sociology is the economist's second childhood." From an interview with Paul Samuelson on January 11, 1988; Schumpeter's diary from 1942, Harvard University Archives.

208. See especially Robert L. Church, "The Economists Study Society: Sociology at Harvard 1891–1902," 18–90 in R. L. Church, et al., eds., *Social Sciences at Harvard 1860–1920* (Cambridge: Harvard University Press, 1965); Edward Mason, "The Harvard Department of Economics," 398–403; and Lawrence T. Nichols, "The Establishment of Sociology at Harvard: A Case of Organizational Ambivalence and Scientific Vulnerability," unpublished manuscript. I am especially grateful to Larry Nichols for having explained the emergence of Harvard sociology to me.

209. In his report on *The Structure of Social Action* to the Committee on Research in the Social Sciences (which had financed Parsons's research), Schumpeter mockingly wrote: "The author has in fact so deeply penetrated into the German thicket as to lose in some place the faculty of writing clearly in English about it, and some turns of phrase become fully understandable only if translated into German." See the papers of the Committee on Research in the Social Sciences, Harvard University Archives.

210. This is based on information in a folder called "Can Capitalism Survive? Reprint and Notes" in the Harvard University Archives and in the preface to the 1942 edition of *Capitalism, Socialism and Democracy*. Schumpeter, it can be added, lectured on the theme "Can Capitalism Survive?" at several other times, including twice in 1940. There also exists a ten-page mimeographed version with the same title, which was published in November 1936 by the United States Department of Agriculture Graduate School. It is possible that Schumpeter, when reading through the transcript to his January speech, decided, as was his habit, that he better rewrite the whole speech for publication.

211. Schumpeter, "Can Capitalism Survive?," 6.

212. Elizabeth Boody Schumpeter to Vera Dean, December 12, 1940, Schlesinger Library at Radcliffe College. In another letter Joseph Schumpeter says that the book will be just as much Elizabeth's as his own. See Schum-

peter to Hugh J. Kelly of McGraw-Hill, February 21, 1941, Harvard University Archives.

213. Chapters 1 and 2 exist in substantially longer, handwritten versions at the Harvard University Archives. Given their length, one would guess that the final version would have been two to three times as long as the version printed here.

214. Schumpeter to Leslie Hastings, February 21, 1941, Harvard University Archives.

215. Schumpeter to Thurlow Field Collier, May 21, 1943, Harvard University Archives.

216. Schumpeter, "An Economic Interpretation of Our Time," lecture 8, 14.

217. Ibid., 15.

218. Schumpeter, *History*, 1140–45. Elizabeth Boody Schumpeter included the lectures because Schumpeter never finished the part of *History of Economic Analysis* that was to deal with contemporary economic theory.

219. Schneider, *Joseph A. Schumpeter*, 49.

220. Schumpeter, "American Institutions and Economic Progress," 2.

221. Ibid.

# *One*

## The Crisis of the Tax State

### I. Issues

Many people assert, and indeed in some circles it has become axiomatic, that the fiscal problems left in the wake of the war cannot be solved within the framework of our prewar economic order.[1] This order was a mixture of highly contradictory elements. Only by heroic abstraction could it be called an economy of free competition; yet whatever drive and success it had were due to such elements of free competition as remained in spite of everything—in spite even of those attempts at state tutelage which, though reinforced by the war, were by no means created by it. Will this economic order collapse under the weight of the war burden or, indeed, must it collapse? Or will the state have to alter it so much as to make it something entirely new? The answer tends not to rest on dispassionate analysis. As usual, everyone endeavors to proclaim the fulfillment of his own wishes to be a necessary consequence of the war. Some foresee that "high capitalism," having culminated in the war, must now collapse; others look forward to more perfect economic freedom than before, while yet others expect an "administered economy" fashioned by our "intellectuals." This is bound to happen because the state—so says the bourgeois smugly—or because the free economy—so says the intellectual enthusiastically—have failed. Neither of them, though possibly the socialist a little more than the other, attempts to justify his judgment in a manner which bears even a faint resemblance to scientific habits of thought. This discussion, unpleasant like almost every expression of today's culture or lack thereof, goes to prove that there remains free competition at least in slogans: the cheapest wins. In no other field of knowledge would such a performance be possible. Only in economic matters does everyone consider himself called upon to speak as an expert; every Tom, Dick, and Harry feels entitled ingenuously to recite age-old fallacies and naively to declare his own most subjective economic or ideological interest to be the last word of wisdom. In these pages, however, we shall only touch upon this question. Whoever expects an exhaustive discussion of it should lay down this pamphlet. For our main concern is with other matters.

If the initial assertion is true then we face a crisis of much greater scope than is indicated by the catchword which has provided us with our title. If the tax state were to fail and another form of providing for the wants of the community ensued, this would, on the one hand, mean much more than that a new fiscal system replaces the prewar one. Rather, what we call the modern state would itself change its nature; the economy would have to be driven by new motors along new paths; the social structure could not remain what it is; the approach to life and its cultural contents, the spiritual outlook of individuals—everything would have to change. On the other hand, it should be pretty clear that a continuous failure of the tax state could never be the fortuitous result of any disturbance, however big—as if, for example, an otherwise perfectly healthy tax state had suddenly become impossible owing to the world war and its aftermath. Even the simplest considerations show that, at most, the war could have brought to light a much more basic inadequacy of the particular society whose fiscal expression the tax state is; that, at most, it could have been the occasion which laid bare the structural weaknesses of our society and thus precipitated a collapse which was inevitable for deeper reasons. Here we come to the sociologically important vista which the fiscal position opens before us and which is our main concern. What does "failure of the tax state" mean? What is the nature of the tax state? How did it come about? Must it now disappear and why? What are the social processes which are behind the superficial facts of the budget figures?

## II. Fiscal Sociology

It is Goldscheid's enduring merit[2] to have been the first to have laid proper stress on this way of looking at fiscal history: to have broadcast the truth that "the budget is the skeleton of the state stripped of all misleading ideologies"—a collection of hard, naked facts which yet remain to be drawn into the realm of sociology. The fiscal history of a people is above all an essential part of its general history. An enormous influence on the fate of nations emanates from the economic bleeding which the needs of the state necessitates, and from the use to which its results are put. In some historical periods the immediate formative influence of the fiscal needs and policy of the state on the development of the economy and with it on all forms of life and all aspects of culture explains practically all the major features of events; in most periods it explains a great deal and there are but a few periods when it explains nothing. Our industrial organism cannot be understood the way it actually is if this is overlooked. And our people have become what they are under the fiscal pressure of the state. It is not merely that economic policy has, up to the turn of the century, been motivated primarily by fiscal considerations: exclusively fiscal motives determined, for example, the economic policy of Charles V; led in England up to the sixteenth century to the domination by foreign merchants under the protection of the state; led in Colbert's France to the attempt at subjecting the whole country to the guild order; and led in the Great Elector's Prussia to the settlement of French artisans. All of this created economic forms, human types, and industrial situations which would not have grown in this manner without it. All of this, too, continues to have an effect to this day. More than that, fiscal measures have created and destroyed industries, industrial forms, and industrial regions even where this was not their intent, and have in this manner contributed directly to the construction (and distortion) of the edifice of the modern economy and through it of the modern spirit.[3] But even greater than the *causal* is the *symptomatic* significance of fiscal history. The spirit of a people, its cultural level, its social structure, the deeds its policy may prepare[4]— all this and more is written in its fiscal history, stripped of all phrases. He who knows how to listen to its message here discerns the thunder of world history more clearly than anywhere else.

Most important of all is the insight which the events of fiscal history provide into the laws of social being and becoming and into the driving forces of the fate of nations, as well as into the manner in which *concrete* conditions, and in particular organizational forms, grow and pass away. The public finances are one of the best starting points for an investigation of society, especially though not exclusively of its political life. The full fruitfulness of this approach is seen particularly at those turning points, or better epochs, during which existing forms begin to die off and to change into something new, and which always involve a crisis of the old fiscal methods. This is true both of the causal importance of fiscal policy (insofar as fiscal events are an important element in the causation of all change) and of the symptomatic significance (insofar as everything that happens has its fiscal reflection). Notwithstanding all the qualifications which always have to be made in such a case, we may surely speak of a special set of facts, a special set of problems, and of a special approach—in short, of a special field: fiscal sociology, of which much may be expected.

Of these approaches, the development of which lies as yet in the lap of the gods, there is one which is of particular interest to us: the view of the state, of its nature, its forms, its fate, as seen from the fiscal side. The word "tax state" is a child of this view, and the following investigations are concerned with the implications quite clearly contained in this term.

## III. The Crisis of the Desmesne Economy at the Close of the Middle Ages

The modern tax state whose "crisis" is debated today has, in its turn, grown out of the crisis of its predecessor, the feudal relationship. At least so far as Germany and Austria are concerned (and our material will in substance be limited to these two countries) it is well known that the modern tax state is not rooted in the tax state of antiquity,[5] either in the sense of continuity or in the sense of resuscitation or "migration of culture." It is rooted instead in the highly autochthonous circumstances of the territories of the *Reich* and the princes of the fourteenth to the sixteenth centuries. Its genesis can be told in a few words.[6] The pressure of the times created it. The fourteenth- and fifteenth-century prince was not the absolute ruler of his country that he became after the Thirty Years' War. He was confronted by the solid position of the estates, that is primarily the nobility of various degrees, to a lesser extent the clergy, still less the burghers of the towns, and finally and least important, the remains of free peasantry, particularly in the Tyrol and in Eastern Frisia. The estates held their position vis-à-vis the prince by their own power and in their own right, and it was a position essentially similar to that of the prince, resting on essentially the same sanctions and consisting of essentially the same elements. The position of the prince, too, consisted merely of a sum of the rights of dukes, counts, various feudal officials, landowners, etc., as did the rights of all other land- and relatively independent allodial lords. The difference between the overlord and the others was at first only one of degree; he was *primus inter pares*. Only gradually was this overshadowed by the fact that his dependence on the Emperor and the *Reich* through vassalage and otherwise evaporated more and more while the subordination of the great lords of the territories, which rested on the particular titles, not only remained intact but grew and finally merged into the whole of sovereign rights—into a special "sovereignty." This sovereignty was one of the germs of state power,[7] as was the position of the nonsovereign feudal lords, though to a lesser extent and partly in other spheres. Even then the prince, supported by the logic of the facts and aided by Roman patterns of thought, assumed the bearing and the phraseology of state power. There did remain in this sovereignty something of the organic position of earlier days, something of the deposable dignitary of the Carolingian and Ottonian *Reich*.[8] But it was not yet state power, for it did not rest on any general sovereignty, the representative and personification of which the prince might have felt himself to be and from the sanction of which the rights of the remaining powers which confronted the prince within the territory might have derived. The prince owned his sum of rights and positions of power for his own benefit, so that his phrases of public welfare then and much later had no other meaning than, for example, similar expressions uttered by a factory owner of today. The natural law distinction between the *persona publica* and the *persona privata* of the prince did, therefore, not simply remain unrecognized at the time because of deficient legal or sociological analysis,[9] but it had no factual basis and would have been meaningless. The prince did not look upon his territory then as a modern estate owner looks upon his cattle. All this came later. But he did look upon the sum of his rights precisely like this—as a *patrimonium* of which he could dispose in a manner which was nobody else's business.

Nor was the prince the only one who considered his prerogatives in this way. Everyone else did too, in particular the other "lords" of the country whose opinion alone counted. Certainly, they took a stand as to the manner in which the prince used his rights. But they did so in no sense other than that in which interested persons of every industry or every region today take a stand vis-à-vis the possibly vexatious or anti-social behavior of a landlord or factory owner. We think this strange, but unjustly so. For it was impossible then to speak of any point of view of common welfare, which is what we miss. Nobody represented such a point of view and it was not founded on any social power.

Of course, many of these princely rights did, at the time, serve the needs of the community, especially the right of jurisdiction. But this does not make them anything "public" or "governmental." The community needs shoes, too, but this does not by any means make shoe manufacturing a public affair, though it could be one. Altogether, there is nothing which *could* not be a "general" or "public" affair, once the state exists; and nothing which *must* fall within the "public" or "state" sphere in the sense that we could not otherwise speak of a state.[10] As long as the state does not exist as a separate and real power, the distinction of public and private law has simply no meaning. The statement that during the middle ages public law was shot through with aspects of private law or that there existed only private law is as illegitimate a projection of *our* modes of thought into the past as is the opposite assertion.[11] The concept of the state is inapplicable to the circumstances then existing, but not in the sense that what we see today within the sphere of the state was absent and that only the private sphere remained; instead, the organizational forms of that time combined both what we nowadays call the public and the private sphere in one essentially different unity.

So far as the economy of the prince was concerned, it followed that he had to meet all the expenses of any policy which was his private affair and was not the policy of the state. For instance, he himself had to meet the cost of a war against "his" enemies, at least unless he had a right to the necessary contributions by virtue of particular titles, such as the vassals's obligation to render military service. Neither the means at the prince's disposal for this purpose nor his sovereignty derived from any centralized state power. The one was the sum of revenues of the most diverse kind, the other a sum of diverse rights. Most important were the revenues from his own lands, that is, the dues of his subjects, the peasant-serfs, whose landlord he was. Since the thirteenth century these dues were paid mostly in money. Until the sixteenth and seventeenth centuries these revenues were considered the foundation of the princely economy as well as the core of the fiscal problem connected with the domains' administrative reform which took place everywhere between the thirteenth and the sixteenth centuries. In addition there were diverse feudal rights, such as the mint, market, customs, mining, or protection-of-jewry regalia and all the rest of them, and finally the revenues from those powers which he had as a dispenser of justice or as lord over towns and bailiwicks. Apart from that there were traditional gifts of vassals, the highly controversial contributions of the church, but no general right to "taxes."[12] At most the towns were an exception. Though they did not as yet know the idea of a state, they did have the "idea of the town" and in this as in other matters they anticipated developments which in the country did not come about until much later. Aside from this neither the freeman nor even the dependent nobleman paid taxes as a rule.

During the fourteenth and fifteenth centuries the princes got into more and more difficult financial straits which contrasted oddly with their rise in every other respect—both in relation to the *Reich* and to the other powers of the territory—and which frequently led to tragicomical situations. At the turn of the fifteenth and sixteenth centuries, and in individual cases as early as in the fourteenth century, the situation became untenable: a crisis of the fiscal economy was at hand. Let us look more closely at the situation of Austria, or the "five Lower-Austrian *Länder*," to use the traditional terminology. The immediate reason why the prince got into debt to such an extent that he finally could not carry on was that he mismanaged his affairs, that he administered his domain inefficiently. If that had been all we could speak of a crisis of the economy of individual princes, but not of a crisis of the whole fiscal system. Every fiscal system can occasionally break down. But this by no means signifies the collapse of its *principle*. So long as the cause is accidental, i.e., so long as it does not follow from the inner logic of the system and so long as remedies can be found within the system (in this case more efficient management), so long the collapse may be of interest perhaps to the historian, but not to the sociologist. In such a case we cannot conclude that there is an underlying social process of change. The broken-down economy is somehow liquidated and thereafter things proceed as before.[13] This is important for a precise definition of what we mean by "crisis"—also when applied to the tax state.

Another cause for the difficulties of the princes is much more interesting: this is what historians refer to as courtly waste. It was the maintenance of all the nobles in the service of the lord which made the court so expensive. But this particular expense was neither accidental nor avoidable. Profitable service at the court transformed a recalcitrant country nobility into a pliable court-, official-, and military nobility, and if the prince wanted to gain ground vis-à-vis the estates he had to offer such court service when the ties of the vassal relationship began to loosen. But the prince's means had not been intended for such expenses and proved insufficient to meet them. Here we have both a *factor* and a *symptom* of a process of social change as well as a cause of the failure of the fiscal economy of the prince. It is a cause which does have an interest from the point of view of "principle."

The most important cause of the financial difficulties, however, consisted in the growing expenses of warfare. The emergence of mercenary armies (which confronted the prince with a situation similar to that which a modern aristocratic household had to face when it had to pay each servant the wage determined by the industrial labor market) was, of course, not the consequence of the invention of gunpowder, as the high school textbook puts it with involuntary humor. The feudal army could have learned the use of firearms quite as well. And the hired soldier for a long time rode his steed into the enemy much as the nobleman would have done. However, the feudal ban, first of all, was simply not numerically sufficient, particularly not against the Turkish armies. Moreover, the nobility increasingly resisted the fulfillment of its obligations and more and more failed the enemy. The prince finally realized that it became useless and in the sixteenth century used his right to call up the feudal ban only to wear down recalcitrant estates. How did this come about? It was simply due to the fact that life was breaking through the feudal organization, that after the fiefs had *de facto* become hereditary a long time ago the vassals began to feel as independent lords of their soil and began to detach themselves in spirit from the vassalage, the essence of which was continuous fighting, continuous conquest, and knightly life in the sense of the early middle ages.[14] This is one of the forms of the process which I usually refer to in my private use as "Patrimonialization of the Personality." The mercenary army was also an expression of this process, and so were the fiscal needs thereby created. These in turn became the driving forces for further development. Around A.D. 1500 the normal income of the electorate of Cologne was, for example, 110,000 Rhenish guilders, that of Mayence 80,000, that of Treves 60,000, and that of Brandenburg 40,000. The house of Hapsburg towered over them all with 300,000 guilders received from its hereditary Austrian territories alone. But even this sum would have paid for only 6,000 foot soldiers or 2,500 "armored horses" during a year. And with these 6,000 foot soldiers or 2,500 knights the prince would have been free to oppose the 250,000 Turks whom the Sublime Porte could have sent into the field at any time. Here we have with the clarity of a textbook example what we mean by the crisis of a fiscal *system*: obvious, ineluctable, continuous failure due to unalterable social change.

The prince did what he could: he got into debt. When he could borrow no more, he turned begging to the estates. He acknowledged that he had no right to demand, declared that accession to his plea was not to prejudice the rights of the estates, promised never again to beg—this is the content of those *Schadlosbriefe* (letters of indemnity) which, had this development continued without a break, might have come to take the place that in England is taken by the Magna Charta. The prince pointed to his insolvency and suggested that matters such as the Turkish wars were not merely his personal affair but a "common exigency." The estates admitted this. The moment they did so a state of affairs was acknowledged which was bound to wipe out all paper guarantees against tax demands. This state of affairs meant that the old forms were dead which had encompassed the whole personality in a super-personal system of aims; that the individual economy of each family had become the center of its existence; and that thereby a private sphere was created which was now to be confronted by the public sphere as a distinguishable element. Out of the "common exigency" the state was born.

At first the concession of taxes by no means implied a general tax duty. The previously sketched view of the nature of the medieval political community is confirmed by the observed facts, which are fully concordant with that nature and are reoriented only step by step in the direction which corresponds to the modern idea of the state. Not only was the concession of taxes valid only for the estates which granted it and perhaps for their own vassals—from whom they could in Austria, with the consent of the prince, in any case recoup part of their taxes since 1518—rather than for the whole country as such; but at first only those who had themselves voted for the tax concession were committed, while he who had mounted his horse before the concession and had ridden off did not have to pay.[15] This speaks a clear language. Tax liability on the basis of a majority decision, even more so general tax liability and a legally controlled distribution of the tax burden among lords and vassals—all this came about but very slowly. In this process it is of interest to us, though we cannot go into details, that this development kept pace with the emergence of the state along all other lines and that the fiscal element was frequently the driving element[16] and in all cases the faithful image of the development of social affairs.

The estates did not trust their prince. Frequently the funds that had been raised were channeled to their intended purpose through the estates' own agents, and always, except in disagreeable cases of difficult collection, the estates opposed the intervention of the prince as to the way in which the voted sums were to be raised. This led to the growth of an estate tax system, administered by a bureaucracy of the estates, which reached its peak during the second half of the sixteenth century and became the basis of estate autonomy also in other matters. The newly born state acquired a solid framework, created its own organs, became a separate power. Taxes were no longer raised merely for the purposes for which the prince had asked them but also for others. The estates of Styria and Carinthia, for instance, did much for public schools and in general a free, attractive, autonomous cultural life developed. True, all this served the freedom, the culture, and the policy of a class. The peasant was suppressed with an iron fist. Yet it was the freedom, culture, and policy appropriate to the spirit of the age. It takes all the narrowness of the liberalizing type of historian biased in favor of the princely bureaucracy to take the side of the prince in this fight between prince and estates and to stylize him as the father of his country, solicitous of its welfare, and fighting for the suppressed against the brutal class of lords. However this may be: the tax state had arrived—its idea and its machinery.

Everywhere in Europe the princes took up the fight for the conquest of this state. In England the fight ended on the scaffold of Charles I. Everywhere else it ended with the victory of the prince because he and his soldiery were the only unbroken powers on the soil devastated by the religious wars. Now the prince tore the sharp weapon, "the state," out of the hands of the estates which had begun to forge it. And then in turn the modern democracies of the continent wring the state from the hands of the prince, but it is now a state formed by his interests and his tendencies which will continue to have an effect for a long time to come. Everywhere on the continent *his* bureaucracy became the state bureaucracy, his power the state power. All the prince's former rights and positions went over into state power, except for a residue which could not be assimilated and which later became the private law sphere of the prince. But the first thing that happened was that the "patrimonial" concept of the rights of the prince was transferred to the power of the state which he had conquered: *now* he really stood in his country like a landowner on his property, now *he* was the state—the real power in the public sphere.[17]


## IV. The Nature and the Limits of the Tax State

We have seen that without financial need the immediate cause for the creation of the modern state would have been absent. In its turn, the appearance of this need and its satisfaction precisely by the method of tax demands is explained by the process of disintegration of medieval forms of life. This process itself may very well be traced through all intermediate causes to changes in the very foundations of the economy; it ends up in the free economy of the individual family. This is the reason why this manner of looking at the facts opens a path to the furthest depths of social development. The tax is not merely a surface phenomenon, it is an expression of this development which it summarizes in a particular direction.

Taxes not only helped to create the state. They helped to form it. The tax system was the organ the development of which entailed the other organs. Tax bill in hand, the state penetrated the private economies and won increasing dominion over them. The tax brings money and calculating spirit into corners in which they do not dwell as yet, and thus becomes a formative factor in the very organism which has developed it. The kind and level of taxes are determined by the social structure, but once taxes exist they become a handle, as it were, which social powers can grip in order to change this structure. However, the whole fruitfulness of this approach can here only be hinted at.

Since "state" and "tax" have so much to do with each other it is natural to try to penetrate the nature of the state from this point of view.[18] Insofar as the word "state" signifies the factor of social life which we see at work around us rather then simply a synonym for "community" or "social organization," there is, in the first place, no room for the special phenomenon of the "state" where *all* areas of social life are "socialized" and where all the activities of the individual merge in the social whole. This is why a primitive horde has no state. Its social organization is an entity which *also* fulfills those functions that later fall to the state, but from which no separate state has as yet developed. If we wanted to find a state here we would have to identify it with social order as such.

For the same reason a socialistically organized people would have no state. Of course, such a socialist community, too, would be a subject of international law and in this sense a state in the meaning of international law. However, in its internal organization there would be no state power distinguishable from other social powers. If socialism became a reality through the conquest of the economy by the power of the state, the state would annul itself by its very expansion.

This would also be true of a lord-and-vassal community in its pure and complete form. No doubt this never existed, just as the free economy does not occur in its pure form; but we nevertheless must imagine it for theoretical purposes if we are to approach a particular historical situation with clear concepts. The very ideal of life in such a lord-vassal community would be fulfilled in the community. The community would be the origin of the guiding principles of individual life finding its own meaning in what is one of the closest approximations to the super-personal and absolute known to social reality. True, some parts of the people would remain outside this circle. But they too belong to this world—as its working animals. Without the dues of the peasant-serfs the castle of the Holy Grail was impossible. Only, they had as little part in it as the slaves of antiquity had in the spirit of Athens. There was God and the lord and the knight—the expression of the form of life of the age—but no state except in the sense in which we might speak of a state of the bees. When the stream of productive revolutions sweeps away this world, when the knight forgets the Holy Grail and bethinks himself of his property, then this order breaks up like a corpse swollen with putrefying gases—and it breaks up into individuals and families with a thousand conflicting interests.

Only where individual life carries its own center of gravity within itself, where its meaning lies in the individual and his personal sphere, where the fulfillment of the personality is its own end, only there can the state exist as a real phenomenon. Only there does the state become necessary, and there it arises, either by a "common need" finding its spokesman in the future master of the state, or because the all-embracing community which breaks up retains certain functions—whatever they may be—which the newly created individual autonomies are unwilling or unable to take over. For this reason the state can never be its own end but only a machine for those common purposes. It is part of its nature that it opposes individual egotism as a representative of the common purpose. Only then is it a separate, distinguishable social entity.

The economy, of course, is of the essence. So long as the economy is the concern of the whole group or at least is subject to a super-individual system—a consciously regulated system and not merely, as is true of any economy, a system of automatic interactions of individual or family egotisms—so long does the economy carry with it that essential unity of all cultural life[19] which simply leaves no room for the state. The individual economy disrupts this unity. How the individual economy has grown from these forms can be understood in essentially economic terms, even if only through numberless intermediate links and ideological fire magics, just as can the opposite process if it should ever occur in the future. The individual economy makes the individual—or the family—dependent upon himself and forces him, as the apple in paradise, to open his eyes to the economic realities of the world and to read his purpose out of his interest. His horizon narrows, his life settles down in his own spiritual house, and he looks at the world only through his window—and not very far at that, for soon his view is obstructed by the walls of other such houses. The individual now runs his economy for himself, and anything that is not in some individual's interest as a rule remains, both in principle and in fact, denuded of all economic means—unless, as is the case of the church, it can place itself on a separate economic basis. This is why fiscal demands are the first sign of life of the modern state. This is why "tax" has so much to do with "state" that the expression "tax state" might almost be considered a pleonasm. And this is why fiscal sociology is so fruitful for the theory of the state.

It goes without saying that there is more to the state than the collection of taxes necessitated by the common need that was their origin. Once the state exists as reality and as a social institution, once it has become the center of the persons who man the governmental machine and whose interests are focused upon it, finally, once the state is recognized as suitable for many things even by those individuals whom it confronts—once all this has happened, the state develops further and soon turns into something the nature of which can no longer be understood merely from the fiscal standpoint, and for which the finances become a serving tool. If the finances have created and partly formed the modern state, so now the state on its part forms them and enlarges them—deep into the flesh of the private economy.

Apart from the character of the state as a machine for certain fairly narrowly circumscribed ends (which machine is *confronted* by the whole of the nation's cultural life with its essential driving forces) it is, however, decisive for a realistic understanding of the phenomenon of the state to recognize the importance of that group of persons in whom it assumes social form, and of those factors which gain domination over it.[20] This explains the state's real power and the way in which it is used and developed. At first, the actual master of the state was usually the prince from whose hands the modern democracy of the Continent received the state or is about to receive it. Later, one could say more frequently of the bureaucracy that it was the state. And finally the state could penetrate so deeply into the consciousness of the people—and the fist of the prince has contributed to this—that it was really able to become something impersonal, a machine manner only by serving, not by dominating spirits. This kind of state may perhaps continue to exist as a mere habit of thought of its citizens. Perhaps it has already come to this in some countries.

In any case, the state has its definite limits. These are, of course, not conceptually definable limits of its field of social action, but limits to its fiscal potential. These vary considerably in each specific case according to the wealth or poverty of the country, to the concrete details of its national and social structure, and to the nature of its wealth. There is a great difference between new, active, and growing wealth and old wealth, between entrepreneurial and rentier states. The limits of their fiscal potential may also differ according to the extent of military expenses or the debt service, to the power and morality of its bureaucracy, and to the intensity of the "state-consciousness" of its people. But they are always there and they may be theoretically determined in general terms from the nature of the state.

The bourgeois tax state of the present time does not exist anywhere as a pure type. Everywhere it is shot through with elements of the past, everywhere the shadows of future developments can more or less clearly be seen to fall upon it. Yet everywhere this tax state is today still the expression of the most creative forces. Everywhere it leads a separate existence not only vis-à-vis the individuals and families whose private lives are for them their center and purpose but also vis-à-vis the totality of these individuals. Everywhere it confronts the private economies with relatively few means—private economies whose meaning and drive are service for the private sphere and which produce only for the latter—while the state is dependent on what it can wring from them. Though the state may be felt everywhere, and notwithstanding the phraseologies hammered into the citizens by its organs from their childhood, it remains something peripheral, something alien to the proper purpose of the private economy, even something hostile, in any case something derived.

Here we have arrived at the fact which can become the leading principle for the theoretical understanding of the economic capacity of the tax state. In the bourgeois society everyone works and saves for himself and his family, and perhaps for some ends he has chosen himself. What is produced is produced for the purposes of the private economic subjects. The driving force is individual interest—understood in a very wide sense and by no means synonymous with hedonistic individual egotism. In this world the state lives as an economic parasite. It can withdraw from the private economy only as much as is consistent with the continued existence of this individual interest in every particular socio-psychological situation. In other words, the tax state must not demand from the people so much that they lose financial interest in production or at any rate cease to use their best energies for it. This is a different amount depending on the manner in which particular people view a particular state in a particular historical situation which necessitates the tax. In times of patriotic fervor, tax payments are consistent with extreme productive adaptation of strength which *normally* would make production cease altogether. However, though the limits are nearer or farther away in different situations, they are nevertheless in every case recognizable on the basis of our principle.

Let us consider first how much indirect taxes can contribute. The effects which emanate from them through the process of shifting and of curtailment of consumption cannot be described briefly in their enormous complexity. However, we are not interested in the manner in which, retarding and destroying, they affect first the economy, then the way of life, and thus finally the cultural level. Nor are we interested in investigating the extent to which the low intellectual and moral level of the majority of the population in most countries today can in the final analysis be traced back to these effects. All we are concerned with is that indirect taxes are for the time being an indispensable and certainly the most important element of the mechanism of the tax state, and the fact that for the tax load on each article and thus for the receipts from indirect taxes as a whole there exists a level beyond which further tax increases mean not an increase but a decrease of yield. The determination of that level which yields the maximum revenue meets with two great practical difficulties. There is first the fact that every significant indirect tax enforces technical and commercial changes in the productive apparatus, the consequences of which are most difficult to follow. Second, there is the difficulty that the situation in which the tax was imposed does not remain unchanged in other respects; there are practically always other "disturbances" which may weaken the effect of a tax on the consumer (such as an accidental expansion of production of the article in question abroad) or which accentuate the effect of the tax on the consumer and dampen it for the producer (such as a simultaneous increase in population). Leaving aside fiscal ineptness which is largely responsible, these difficulties explain in part why to our days almost all countries have shot way beyond the mark in this or that case of indirect taxation and have burdened some articles to such an extent that the fiscal interest of the state itself has been hurt and a tax reduction would lead to an increase in revenues. The most brilliant examples of such a policy of raising revenue by diminishing taxes have been furnished by the younger Pitt and by Gladstone. But there always is a point of maximum yield of any indirect tax beyond which returns fall and, given sufficient knowledge of the facts, it should always be possible to determine it. No fiscal system can extract more from indirect taxes than this maximum amount which is thus a datum independent of the will of the state. Once this limit has been reached we have also reached the limit of the effectiveness of this method of taxation. No need for more funds can push it further out.

With direct taxes things are, in practice, less clear but only apparently different. Let us investigate only the taxes of individual types of income: entrepreneurial profit, monopoly profit, profit, interest, rent, and wages. We can limit ourselves in this way because a reasoning very similar to that we have indicated for indirect taxes is also applicable to the special taxes upon individual forms of those income categories, such as taxes on buildings, dividends, etc. In any case, income tax is for everyone simply a tax on the returns which make up his income. There is only one tax which is in a category by itself, and that is a property tax which is not, as is the case with the Prussian one, to be paid out of income and therefore simply a special kind of income tax, but which is meant to be a real cession of property. But it is only a rare expedient and we shall overlook it here. We shall return to it in the next section.

Entrepreneurial profit proper—as distinct from interest with which it used to be combined, from the risk premium which obviously is no net income, and from the wages of the entrepreneur which is a special case of wages—arises in the capitalist economy wherever a new method of production, a new commercial combination, or a new form or organization is successfully introduced. It is the premium which capitalism attaches to innovation. As it arises continuously so it disappears continuously through the effect of competition which, baited by the profit, follows up immediately on the innovator. If this profit were taxed away, that element of the economic process would be lacking which at present is by far the most important individual motive for work toward industrial progress. Even if taxation merely reduced this profit substantially, industrial development would progress considerably more slowly, as the fate of Austria plainly shows. We are not here concerned with the obvious consequences for the economy and thus in the last analysis also for the finances of the state. Only one thing is important for us: that there is a limit to the taxation of entrepreneurial profit beyond which tax pressure cannot go without first damaging and then destroying the tax object. An ideally perfect tax practice, which would give individual treatment to each individual case of entrepreneurial profit as it arises, could collect much higher sums than the actual practice which in spite of relatively small success nevertheless brutally destroys many possibilities for economic development. Yet even the most ideal tax technique would reach a limit and would reach it fairly soon.

This is not true for monopoly profit and ground rent. The monopoly profit of a cartel, for instance, that is the difference between the net return and the sum which is necessary to pay for the means of production employed (including interest) may be almost completely taxed away without any unfavorable repercussions. So can pure ground rent, i.e., that element of the net return of a rural or urban piece of land which remains after deduction of interest on the capital invested (which already includes the wage sums spent on installation of fixed capital and operation)—but not, of course, after deduction of interest on the purchase price! Since this pure ground rent is merely the payment of the productive accomplishments of nature which would remain even if the owner received no return, and since the motive for the utilization of a piece of land lies in the return to labor and capital which it can yield and which remains even when the ground rent is taxed away, such a tax never reflects back on the productive process. The same is true of all windfall profits which are not the result of special economic activities. Inheritances hardly ever fall into this category, but the various forms of "unearned increments of value" frequently do, though most of the time it is very difficult to single out among the mass of phenomena which the layman calls an unearned increase in value, those cases to which the epithet really applies, in particular those in which the increase in value does not fulfill the function of a risk premium or of an interest element. In all these cases we have ideal tax objects, provided one can always recognize them beyond doubt, separate them from others which look similar but are very different, and provided that a correct tax technique for their treatment can be devised. This has never been done successfully so far. In practice we mostly find something like an attempt to load a sack of flour on the shadow of an ass. Even here there exists a limit. But it is determined only by the existence and magnitude of such taxable objects.

In the case of interest and wages the tax cannot penetrate too deeply into the tax object. Since we are here considering the taxation of *all* forms of capital yield and wages, we need not worry about a shift of capital and labor into alternative uses. And since we are here dealing with a problem common to *all* tax states, with a problem of the system and not of a particular state, we shall disregard also the tendency of capital and labor to migrate to countries of lower taxation, however important this is precisely for Austria. But even so there are still two reactions which occur both with capital and with labor. Insofar as they result in higher interest or wages which entrepreneurs have to pay, taxes counteract the expansion of production which would have occurred without them. Insofar, however, as these taxes are a charge on the income of the capitalists or the workers, they may even sometimes result in more saving and more work than without them. But such cases are rare exceptions for capital and are significant for labor only if the working day was relatively short prior to the imposition of the tax. In all other cases capital formation is paralyzed and may even turn into capital consumption through lack of amortization and repairs. And additional taxation of higher labor incomes, which are the only ones which matter in practice, discourages all above-average effort wherever the effort is not its own end. Again, the economic effects of these taxes do not interest us here. What matters to us is that the possible tax yield is limited not only by the size of the taxable object less the subsistence minimum of the taxable subject, but also by the nature of the driving forces of the free economy. The layman, of course, thinks of the big incomes as almost inexhaustible sources of taxes. And our intellectual whose whole outlook is basically petit-bourgeois is inclined to set the limit which demarcates the big incomes just above the salary rank or other income which he hopes to attain himself. However, neither the numbers nor the size nor the capacity to bear taxes[21] of the big incomes is all that large, and hardly anywhere smaller than with us (in Austria). The case of the childless millionaire living off his inherited rents, whose income is given once and for all and can therefore be taxed without fear of diminution, this case is rare, though the time may come when the whole bourgeoisie will be nothing but a childless rentier-millionaire.

The tax state is not altogether limited to derived revenues. It has not only the mostly small inheritance of its predecessor, but it can also create its own economic sphere within the world of capitalism and can become an entrepreneur itself. I do not mean here the "profit sharing" with private industries, for this is but another word for a tax. I mean enterprises which the state itself runs. In so doing it does, indeed, transgress its own limits. However, as long as the state has not swallowed all or most of the economy it remains essentially what it was. The decisive criterion is whether, apart from any monopoly position which it might secure for itself, the state does or does not continue to work within the framework of a free economy whose data and methods it has to accept in its own enterprises. If it does and thus works in a capitalistic spirit toward as high a money profit as possible, then its possible profits are limited by the economic laws of capitalist production. And these limits are narrower than the layman believes. Since the state must work with money capital just as any other entrepreneur, and since it can raise this money only through loans, it is unlikely that the remaining profit will be much larger than what could have been extracted from the same industry by direct and indirect taxes including taxes on the income of this industry. This is likely to be true even with extreme fiscal exploitation of a possible monopoly position and even if we disregard the small entrepreneurial ability which the state in fact has.

It can now be seen how untenable is the phrase that with the public economy and contrary to the private economy, income depends on outgoings. The fiscal capacity of the state has its limits[22] not only in the sense in which this is self-evident and which would be valid also for a socialist community, but in a much narrower and, for the tax state, more painful sense. If the will of the people demands higher and higher public expenditures, if more and more means are used for purposes for which private individuals have not produced them, if more and more power stands behind this will, and if finally all parts of the people are gripped by entirely new ideas about private property and the forms of life—then the tax state will have run its course and society will have to depend on other motive forces for its economy than self-interest. This limit, and with it the crisis which the tax state could not survive, can certainly be reached. Without doubt, the tax state *can* collapse.

## V. Must the Tax State Collapse?

Tax states have collapsed innumerable times. Even more frequently has their collapse been expected, even in England which has the longest unbroken tradition of fiscal solvency. However, these breakdowns were always considered as particular accidents or crimes; never has one despaired of the system. And correctly so. However much mismanagement there was and however big the mistakes in particular cases, the system has successfully survived the Turkish wars, the world wars against the Spanish threat, the Thirty Years' War, the world wars against *ancien régime* France, and the world war against Napoleon. And if the expenditures were smaller than they are nowadays, so were the means to at least the same degree.

One might almost forget the above-described limits of the tax state as one views its huge expansion through the centuries. What a path from the three-and-a-half million pounds of government revenues of the Restoration (1680) to the 188.8 million of the British fiscal year 1912–13 to the gigantic figures of the last war budget! Austria has during the years of the dual monarchy gone from 281.24 million guilders in 1868 to 514.5 million guilders in 1888, and from there to about 3 billion crowns in the last year of peace. But the figures themselves do not matter. The point is that the system of the tax state has so far met all challenges, and whenever it has failed to do so in particular causes, special causes can be found which are not inherent in its nature. Its best period on the continent was the turn of the century, and in England the Gladstone era. At that time it had everywhere risen above all tribulations, above its previous disgrace. At that time it wallowed in surpluses. This was brought to an end quantitatively not so much by the rising social expenditures as by the financial shadow of the approaching world war. Yet the former were much more ominous for the tax state than the latter, for it is from that side that it may be conquered. In any case, our great problems, financial as well as other, all have their roots in prewar circumstances. The war has not created any new problems, it has only accentuated an existing situation. It is a superficial view to link to the war the question of life and death of the tax state or, for that matter, of any social institution. However, at this stage we too want to do just that.

Nowhere is this question so obvious as in Austria. Indeed, if there were to be a collapse of the tax state, it would have to be a local Austrian affair (not even an Austro-Hungarian affair). The collapse of Russia is a very special case which does not belong here. What collapsed in Russia was that peculiar tyranny which had been grafted onto a peasant democracy. This tyranny had been only just strong enough to prevent the formation of an upper class capable of political action, so that, parenthetically, the Russian revolution as such is in a very untypical special position. The fiscal collapse in Russia, too, was only a consequence of the anti-capitalistic *will*. Given even the most unfavorable judgment of the development of Russia's finances since 1890, the colossus which has such unlimited possibilities need not have broken down. Incidentally, the return to the tax state is certain particularly in the Russian case, so that it is as impossible to speak of the defeat of its principle as of its hopeless failure. None of the other warring nations, however, will be forced to abandon the tax state.[23] Great Britain indeed has from the very beginning covered a substantial part of her war needs by taxes. The question whether Great Britain will be able to bear her war burden within the framework of a free economy must be answered with a clear-cut Yes. No reasonable doubt can be entertained as to Germany's ability to carry on with the means of the tax state. Even in Italy things are not desperate. And France? *If* she collapsed, this would be due solely to the devastation of her northern parts. Against *this* no community has any ready means. However, France will not collapse. Indeed all this will be overcome not only with the means of the tax state but essentially with its *old* means. The fiscal policy of our days has no new ideas nor altogether much talent.

Thus we shall limit ourselves to Austria. If *her* tax state can stand the test, the others can do so *a fortiori*. Let us specify the question: if it is said that the tax state will fail in the face of the problems which the war will leave behind, one or both of two things are meant. One is the problem of the war burden, of covering the cost of the war; the other is the reconstruction of the dislocated economy. It is implied that the tax state cannot bear the financial burden of the war with its own means, and that it cannot carry through the tasks of reconstruction. The two problems are not of the same kind. Rather, they lie in two different spheres which have to be kept strictly separate in a discussion of economic matters and the confusion of which is a typical lay error.

The first problem is fiscal. It is, in concrete terms, a matter of *money*: money which the state needs to fulfill its obligations and to get rid of its deficit. It is not a matter of goods, such as war materials, food and clothing for the army, etc. To be sure, the true costs of the war lie in the goods sphere: the used-up goods, the devastation of parts of the country, the loss of manpower, these are the real "cost" of war to the economies. It was the procurement of the mass of goods needed for the conduct of the war that was the great problem within which the raising of the necessary sums of money was a relatively subordinate problem of fiscal technique. However, this problem is already solved. What the armies and the peoples needed for warfare in the way of goods, we have raised already by hook or by crook and we shall continue to raise it during the war. The problem which *then* remains is merely a "question of money." We shall be in the position of a businessman whose factory has burned down and who now faces the task of expressing this loss in his books. Like a huge conflagration the war has devoured a large part of our national wealth, the economy has become poorer. This has already happened, nothing can change it, and whatever goods were necessary for the purposes of war will have been supplied by the end of the war. However, in money terms the economy has not become poorer. How is this possible? Simply so that claims on the state and money tokens have taken the place of stocks of goods in the private economies. The state cannot replace the goods it has taken out of the private economies—it could after all only take them from the economy itself. What is needed is simply an adjustment of money values which would return them to harmony with the world of goods, that is to say, a large-scale writing-down of book values. And this can be done only by the state covering its monetary obligations out of the money claims and money stocks of the economy. Therein lies the meaning of the problem of the covering of the war cost, which is a specific problem of the tax state since only the form of the tax state and of the free economy of private property explains the way in which the war is financed and with it the origin of the problem. The war was financed as an enterprise through the purchase of goods and credit operations, the only exception being military service which is a great payment in kind. Therein lies also the guarantee that the problem is soluble.

The problem of reconstruction is a different matter. This is not, or at least not in the last resort, a question of raising *money* but a question of securing *goods*. The peace economy has yet to accomplish after the conclusion of peace what the war economy is already accomplishing during the war. This problem is not specifically one of the tax state. Every form of organization would encounter it. Money to cover the cost of the war is needed only by the tax state because only it is forced to enter into obligations toward individuals in order to carry on the war. The goods for reconstruction are needed in any case, in whatever form of organization we may live.

Now consider the first problem: the absolute level of the financial war burden is irrelevant for our discussion since with it comes increased inflation and hence the monetary expressions of yields, incomes, and property. For this reason we need not concern ourselves either with the question of when the murderous insanity which devastates Europe will end. Merely in order to make our presentation more precise let us assume that peace will be concluded in the autumn of this year. Even then our data cannot be very precise, for it cannot be foreseen what will be needed for disablement payments, demobilization cost, reconstruction of devastated areas, and war damage compensation proper. These items are to be counted as part of the cost of warfare, not of reconstruction. Just how much will be needed for them in any case depends largely on political intrigues and much less on objective considerations. Furthermore, the real cost of war, even counted only in money, cannot be known until later. However, if these items are added and the permanent burdens capitalized, the sum of 100 billion (crowns) is probably too low rather than too high. This sum will consist of war bonds, bank debts, and bank advances, or will soon be converted into one or the other of these forms. Of this amount, large parts are available to the state at purely nominal rates of interest, so that, notwithstanding the inevitable increase in the rate of interest after the war, we remain amply within likely limits if we assume an average interest of 5 percent, that is an increase in the annual debt service of 5 billion (crowns). Since we believe we can include *all* war expenditures in the wildest sense within those 100 billion, there remain the figures of the last peacetime budget. Some of these have not been increased at all by inflation, notably the debt service. Others have increased tenfold. A good many, particularly civil service pay, have not so far risen appropriately, but will inevitably soar if circumstances remain as they are. And these circumstances will by their nature continue as long as the present use of the printing press and will probably deteriorate even further. It is impossible to foretell the outcome. It is a conservative estimate if we suppose that the Minister of Finance who next New Year's Day—i.e., on our assumptions a few weeks after the conclusion of peace though this is rather improbable considering the difficulties of peace negotiations—surveys his budget, will have to reckon at least that the 3 billion of the last peacetime budget will have risen to 10 billion. On our assumption, therefore, the peace budget would amount to 15 billion, compared with 23 billion of the last war budget. We assume that it will be covered to the extent of 5 billion out of taxes as was the case with the last war budget. This means a deficit of 10 billion compared with the last wartime deficit of 18 billion. To be sure, the deficit of the first peace year will be larger, but anything additional belongs properly in the 100 billion war cost. We repeat: the figures are merely for example's sake; they are as little a prophecy as is the assumption that the war will end in the autumn.

What can the tax state do in such a situation? Three things immediately come to mind. First, the fact that it got into such a situation in the first place is not the fault of the *system* of the tax state so that even if it failed this would not prove anything against its principle. The enormity of the burden was in the first place a consequence of such limitless waste as no system could bear. Without such waste, the situation would still be serious, but much less so than it is now. Second, the weight of the burden was the consequence of the equally uninhibited paper money economy. The example of Great Britain alone shows that this is not by any means a necessary consequence of the system of the tax state. It is clear, furthermore, that strictly speaking we could have squeezed the necessary money out of the private economy just as the goods were squeezed out of it. This could have been done by taxes which would have looked stifling but which would in fact have been no more oppressive than the devaluation of money which was their alternative. The individual economies would then have had fewer monetary units but they would have paid lower prices in exactly the same proportion and the sacrifices would have been distributed more evenly and rationally. Things would have been better and not worse than with the chosen method. Now it so happens that it is everywhere impossible completely to cover the cost of war by taxation, from the point of view both of politics and fiscal technique. Nowhere is this more true than in Austria. Nevertheless much more could have been achieved than was achieved in fact. Second, we shall refuse even to discuss the possibility of raising those annual 10 billion through further note issue, because of the social and economic consequences. Even apart from everything else, this would become an endless spiral since with the price level, public expenditures too would rise to heights which would make the present prices and budget figures look puny. Third, we equally refuse to consider the methods of 1811 and 1816. We do so with all the greater decisiveness as the voices which demand them are never completely silent. Already then these methods were more than ignominious, they were nonsensical. Now they would be incomparably more so.

There remain two ways. The first begins with the recognition, which at any rate is a reason for solace for us in Austria, albeit a melancholy one, that the figures of our budgets are not quite as oppressive as they would be if money still had its prewar value. The amount of goods which 15 billion signify is not what it would have been four years ago. And what matters is precisely the amount of goods and means for the satisfaction of wants a money payment of 15 billion would withdraw from the economy. If the stock of money is not reduced then, as peace comes, only the other cause of high prices can disappear, namely the scarcity of goods due to interrupted production and imports. Prices would in this case have to remain well above peacetime levels. On the average, incomes will adapt themselves to these prices, and the 15 billion will not be five times as much as the peacetime burden, perhaps not even twice as much. Now it is of course impossible to increase every state revenue fivefold, if only to make allowance for those incomes which have not risen or have not risen correspondingly. But this is just the reason why some other incomes have risen more than proportionately—and by no means only the incomes of the "rich."[24] On the *average* such an increase in the revenues of the state certainly lies within the realm of possibilities, whatever the technical difficulties that may arise in detail. It may be argued that there is not sufficient moral energy in Austria for such an effort. If so, this is Austria's affair and not the fault of the tax state. It is particularly important that such a tax burden would not by any means be crushing, would not mean want and poverty, neither so far as direct nor as indirect taxes are concerned: whoever can pay five times as high a price for his consumers' goods—and to the extent to which this is not yet the case it is bound to happen since the artificial maximum prices are in the long run untenable if inflation continues—can also pay five times as high a consumption tax.[25] Inflation will make sure that he can do it; if this appears harsh it is only because we still think in terms of the old purchasing power of the crown. But it is a defect of this way out that it presupposes continuance of the inflation and abandonment of order in our monetary system.

The other way out leads not only to fiscal but at the same time to monetary order. It has the further advantage that it counteracts at least in part the emergence of a class of war bond rentiers. I mean a once-and-for-all capital levy high enough to enable the state not only to repay its bank loans and advances but also to redeem a significant part of the war bond issue. The latter is necessary because repayment of the bank debt means an end to the flood of bank notes and therefore a sharp decline in the price level, or, what comes to the same thing, an increase in the purchasing power of money. Thereby the real value of the public debt in the form of war bonds is raised as regards both principal and interest and the economic burden the state has to bear increases. In another respect the increase in the value of money due to this method would work in favor of the state. It need then not raise the salaries of its civil servants and would have to pay less for the goods it requires, such as buildings or locomotives. In such an event the expenditures of the peacetime budget need not be assumed to be much higher. Revenues of 6 or 7 billion crowns might do, including the debt service for the remaining war bonds.

I confess that I was once quite taken with this mode of saving the situation, and that I still consider it correct in principle. If I have learned in the meantime to doubt its success, this is due to considerations which have nothing to do with the economics of the matter. Only a strong government on the broadest political base, impressing the public with real power and leadership, could dare to attempt the task of overcoming all resistance, in particular of preventing the levy from hitting only a small fraction of the private economy—too small for success—yet hitting that fraction with destructive force. The man who is to solve this task needs real political and fiscal ability—and he needs that brilliance of willpower and word which nations trust. In addition, the treatment of the problems of our fiscal policy to date has almost prejudged an expert solution. But this is irrelevant here. What matters is neither political feasibility nor the technique of execution, but the proof that the thing can be done in principle. If we can prove this, no practical failure, if it occurred, will invalidate the proof,[26] even if it should turn out that really unsurmountable difficulties of the Austrian situation are responsible and not other reasons. Once more, *Austria* would have failed, and not the tax state.

It may sound strange to expect from an economy impoverished by the war a capital levy which is not to eradicate the financial evils but to reduce them to manageable proportions. Is the diminished wealth to be diminished further, is even what remains to be wrested from the citizen? Is this not to advocate a course amounting to a confession of the failure of the tax state and the substitution of moral for fiscal bankruptcy—or, to quote the popular phrase, the substitution of the "people's bankruptcy" for that of the state? No, the capital levy does not demand further surrender of *goods* from the economy. This sacrifice has been made already. The tax object is not that which has declined during the war, namely *real* national wealth, but only that which has risen during the war and the rise of which is completely irrelevant, namely the *money value* of national wealth. Only the money value is reduced by that method, not the real wealth of the economy. This is particularly true of Austria; it is even more true of Russia, but much less so everywhere else. For this reason the problem of a capital levy in Austria is something special which makes the measure much more harmless here than elsewhere. In other countries a capital levy would have to be defended, if at all, with considerably more reservations and in any case with quite different reasons. *The levy is not to hand over any goods to the state but only money and claims.*[27] And it is to do so only in order that this money and these claims may be destroyed, not in order to finance expenditures. If this were not so I would not only admit that that would be no salvation but a partial defeat of the tax state, nor would I assert that it would not be destructive of wealth. It is important to emphasize this in order to distinguish our position clearly from those voices which advocate the transfer to the state for permanent operation precisely of real sources of income, such as land, factories, etc. In the form in which the capital levy is

proposed here it is, however, not only compatible with a free economy, it is the very method which is appropriate to the principle of
economic freedom and which preserves it intact, exactly opposite to
the method which considers a capital levy a suitable measure for nationalization.

The possibility of repaying even the whole war debt of the state
through a capital levy is proven by the mere consideration that this
debt is for the overwhelming part owned by our own citizens;[28] it is
conceivable, though of course not practicable, to impose upon them
a tax to the full extent of their claim on the state. Let us imagine the
whole process in the manner of an old thought experiment of Soet-
beer: if all the liabilities of the state, including bank debts and bank
and departmental advances, were converted into war bonds which
would then amount to 100 billion (crowns), and if all citizens had invested the same percentage of their wealth in these war bonds, a capital levy of that same percentage would obviously finish the whole
affair and would equally obviously not kill anybody. The practical difficulties are simply the result of the facts that not all private fortunes
contain the same percentage of war bonds and that not all the liabilities of the state consist of or can be converted into war bonds. However, these difficulties prevent only a complete, not an adequate success.

We could certainly speak of adequate success if the result
amounted to about 40 billion, on our assumptions. The other 60 billion would remain outstanding in war bonds or would be converted
into war bonds. After such energetic ordering of the budget they
could certainly be converted into 5 percent issues. A yield of 40 billion would, at an assumed tax rate of 20 percent, presuppose taxable
wealth in the amount of 200 billion. *Unless the formation of such wealth
is artificially prevented* it will amply exist. It is surely a very moderate
assumption that, after the conclusion of peace and prior to a reduction in the circulating quantity of money, prices on the average will
be five times their prewar level. According to Fellner's certainly not
excessive estimate our national wealth amounted to about 80 billion
before the war. Fivefold prices mean fivefold returns and fivefold returns mean fivefold capitalized values, that is 400 billion.[29] Now, it is
of course true that there will be a number of exceptions: the devastated parts of the country must be excluded, postwar production will
at first fall short of war production in quantitative terms, many returns, such as controlled rents, and therefore their capitalized values
cannot for particular reasons rise appropriately, and small properties, say up to 20,000 crowns, are difficult to assess. However, we need
only half the 400 billion. If we do not get them, it will be our own

fault, in particular the fault of the senseless hostility to capital which drives capital to Hungary, prevents a corresponding rise of stocks and shares and thereby destroys or diminishes important taxable objects, thus achieving exactly the opposite of the desired end as is always the case with irrational hostility to capital. Even more radical measures could be considered. A solution which leaves an inheritance of 60 billion in government bonds is not ideal and would hardly make a complete return to prewar prices seem desirable from the standpoint of public finances. But it is a way out and this is enough for us.

Whatever will actually happen, the proposal need not fail because of technical difficulties. It must be realized that what is at issue is the salvation of the state from shame and evil rather than popular slogans, or in particular popular petty persecution of unpopular circles. The levy could be a fairly simple matter if for the sake of the purpose progression were foregone and with it the only reason for inquisition. Instead, the levy should be made a charge on the taxable object and its owner be left to deduct the appropriate amount of the tax from his creditors' claims. The problem involved would be that of estimating the market values. With joint stock companies other techniques could be used. The state would of course be among the debtors entitled to exemption. The enormous liquidity of the economy facilitates such a payment. War bonds would, of course, have to be accepted in payment. Only in a minority of cases would there be any economic justification for postponement of the payment of the tax or for its distribution over a number of years—whatever may be *politically* feasible.

This very liquidity helps to overcome whatever economic hesitations one may have. Anyone who has cash or war bonds, or bank deposits with which to buy war bonds, is in no danger even if he pays the levy out of his working capital. Though he will have fewer monetary units, their purchasing power will be the same and in certain circumstances even bigger than that of the greater amount had been before. Anyone who has neither cash, nor war bonds, nor bank deposits, has to borrow one of them and then to pay them back gradually. This is *always* possible since war bonds, cash, and deposits are in ample supply and there *must* be people who have more of them than the amount of the levy they have to pay. It follows that the levy cannot involve either a freezing of means needed by firms and households or further inflation through additional credit creation, provided the levy is carried through in a businesslike manner, decisively, and with a reassuring impartiality rather than with the bearing of a burglar.

The operation ends in the furnace in which all cash and titles which fall into the hands of the state must be burned. In the case of stock certificates the state would, of course, not burn them but exchange them against cash or war bonds. The meaning of the operation lies in the restoration of the parallelism between the worlds of goods and paper values which was disturbed by excess consumption and the paper mess of the war. There can be no question of any unbearable burden, of impoverishment, of anything whatsoever which might make us curse the tax state and prefer every alternative. Of course, more would remain to be done. New taxes, tax increases, even government monopolies would still become necessary. But the bulk of the work can be done by the capital levy. It can clear the way along which the tax state can go forward into a better future without breakdown and without becoming a torture chamber—although an unskillfully executed capital levy creates the most beautiful opportunities for just that. Failure would simply be due to lack of moral strength and technical competence. The capital levy is a possible course. This was all we wished to demonstrate.

Yet the tax state could still founder on the rock of reconstruction. This implies in this connection that the "free economy," the competitive economy of entrepreneurs and capitalists could fail. For the free economy is the complement of the tax state which by its very nature must leave reconstruction to the market no less than normal economic activity. We have proved nothing with the above argument if failure were to be expected in this field. It would be useless if the tax state could save itself but if the economy were to perish in the process or be condemned to misery. It is not our concern here to investigate whether the free economy is the "absolutely best" method of solving the tasks of reconstruction. This is always a question of imponderable prejudices and of partisanship based on nonscientific reasons; nor would it be possible in the present context to consider all aspects in detail. In any case, the answer is irrelevant for our purposes. We do not care about what usually underlies this kind of discussion, namely a hidden accusation against the competitive economy or an apotheosis of its excellence. We merely want to assess what may be expected from the competitive economy at present, in our concrete historical situation, in order to see whether this economy is capable of bringing about economic reconstruction without delay—as compared to the only practicable alternative: a far-reaching administrative economy of the state.

In such a general form the question of the sufficiency of the free economy would, of course, have to be answered in the negative. In a situation where everything is disturbed and much is destroyed, where work toward reconstruction is the paramount task of the whole society, the machine of the tax state must, of course, contribute what it can. The liquidation of abnormal war developments, in particular of the human agglomerations of the armies; emergency situations beyond the capacity of the private economy; the restitution of the nervous system of the economy through the administrative machinery—in all these and other matters the mediating and facilitating action of the state will be needed and in some cases will become permanent, the classic example being the labor exchanges. This is, however, self-evident. The decisive question is whether the motive force can remain that of the free economy or whether the state has to take its place; and whether the *essential* task can be solved only by state intervention. This essential task is "recapitalization," to use Goldscheid's expression. Here we have to deal with two matters, both of which are problems of securing goods and not of raising money.

First, "war economy" essentially means "switching" the economy from production for the needs of a peaceful life to production for the needs of warfare. This means in the first place that the available means of production are used in some part to produce different final goods, chiefly of course war materials, and in the most part to produce the same products as before but for other customers than in peacetime. This means, furthermore, that the available means of production are mainly used to produce as many goods for immediate consumption as possible to the detriment of the production of means of production—particularly machinery and industrial plant—so that that part of production which in peacetime takes up so much room, namely the production for the maintenance and expansion of the productive apparatus, decreases more and more. The possibility to do just this, that is to use for the production of immediate consumption goods, labor, and capital which previously had made producer's goods and thus only indirectly contributed to the production of consumer's goods (i.e., which made "future" rather than "present" goods to use the technical terminology), this possibility was our great reserve which has saved us so far and which has prevented the stream of consumer's goods from drying up completely. This possibility explains the capability of the modern productive apparatus. But it explains also why the latter may exhaust itself rather quickly, as Lederer has pointed out. Our poverty will be brought home to us to its full extent only after the war. Only then will the worn-out machines, the run-down buildings, the neglected land, the decimated livestock, the devastated forests, bear witness to the full depth of the effects of the war. The reconstruction of this apparatus and its return to the production for peacetime uses, this is the first task of recapitalization. It will at first make the shortage of consumer's goods even more acute.

Now it is obvious that the enormous industrial achievement of switching the economy over to the exigencies of war was due at least 90 percent to the automatism of the free economy and to the play of self-interest. We owe to it not merely the equipment and supply of the army and most of what remained for the home front; we owe it also, and to a much greater degree than the public will generally admit, a distribution of the product which does at least keep the mass of the population alive. The worker does not owe his livelihood to any government measures but to the daily wage of 40 or 50 crowns which the automatism of the competitive economy sends his way in favorable cases. The contribution of the state exists beyond doubt only in those cases where the analogy with a beleaguered fortress is proper, a simile by which our intellectuals live and which the public therefore sees as through a magnifying glass. In every other case we have to judge the successes achieved not only by their immediate results but by their effects on supply, if the judgment is to be more than a partisan phrase or the expression of some personal interest. The reconversion to a peace economy differs in one essential respect from the conversion to a war economy which the market has successfully accomplished, though in a manner the comparative merits and shortcomings of which one will never be able to judge impartially and which will probably forever remain the victim of insidious phrases. While the transition to a war economy demanded the use of productive resources for the supply of present instead of future goods, reconversion requires the opposite process. The former is an act of economic waste, an action under the stimulus of immediate necessity; the latter is an act of saving, the counteracting of the very stimulus to waste. The former would in the last resort have come easily to the initiative of the collective economy; however, it would have proved itself as regards the enormous entrepreneurial achievements necessary even there. The latter demands, beside entrepreneurial activity, something which can do without private motives as little today as it could in the youth of capitalism and which is achieved with particular promptness if the motivation of the private economy is given a completely free rein. If the free economy succeeded in converting to war, it will, *a fortiori*, also succeed in the reconversion to peace. We shall not raise here the old question whether state direction of the economy can bring about that commitment of the whole personality, "that desperate energy" which alone can lead to success in the foreseeable future and which is precisely that which characterizes the achievements of the entrepreneur. Indeed, there has been no difference of opinion on this point among economists of all schools since the middle of the eighteenth century, the socialists not excluded. Nor shall we point out that nine-tenths of all industrial experience and all industrial talent are at the disposal of private industry and not of the governmental bureaucracy. Nor shall we show that the hardships involved in the method of a free economy are essential motors of success, that these hardships mean benefits for the future and for the coming generations. It suffices to insist that the organizational form of the competitive economy can reconstruct the economy after the war exactly as it has created the modern economy in its essence and that therefore its public counterpart, the tax state, has an effective method of reconstruction and will not come to grief on *this* task. It is indeed a highlight of the Communist Manifesto to have demonstrated the effectiveness of this method with such classical precision. The tax state can further the reconstruction most effectively if in its tax policy it makes allowances for this necessity to save and generally refrains from disturbance, but particularly if it knows how to raise that enormous treasure of energy which in Austria is wasted in the fight against the chains into which irrational legislation, administration, and politics have thrown the personality, which take the entrepreneur away from his organizational, technical, and commercial tasks and which leave him merely the backstairs of politics and administration as the only path to success.

The second task of recapitalization consists of arranging for the supply of those goods, particularly raw materials, which have to come from abroad. It is frequently said that the private economies will be unable to procure the necessary supplies and that for this reason we have to go beyond the essential nature of the tax state. Anyone who has the slightest idea about these things knows that any good bank has better access to foreign credits and will be accommodated much more readily abroad than the state. In the difficult postwar situation with its struggle for raw materials, it is clearly just that business ingenuity which in our as yet "capitalistically diseased" world is set in motion by the prospect of large private gain, that will be able to find ways and means here and there to wrest one or the other shipload out of the hands of stronger purchasing power and make it available to Austria. Those firms which belong to the combinations financed by the big banks may rest assured on this point. And so may many others. It is, of course, certain that in the process we will not get the distribution of raw materials which anyone considers ideal and that many entrepreneurs may need government subsidies; but it is equally certain that this is of no importance at a time in which the real question is to get anything at all of those goods that we need most. The wage level and the amount of liquid working capital will ensure that these essential imports will be the most profitable ones from the standpoint of the private economy. Let them insist that an ideally functioning state could perform better. This it is idle to discuss. It is certain that a private economy can *also* do it, and do it quickly and promptly if the bureaucracy does not get in its way and piles up a mountain of paper between us and the necessary raw materials. It is also a form of state aid not to penalize the importer who brings us what we need and to pursue a policy which will enable foreign countries to accommodate us; in fact this may be the kind of aid which gets us furthest at this moment. And if to this we add the tax and monetary policy which we have sketched earlier one can import as much as one wants and can get it without having to fear for the exchange rate.

The validity of our argument has two limitations. First, our argument concerns only the question whether the tax state and the organizational form of a free economy *can* cope with the postwar situation without breakdown and without oppressive hardships. This question can only be answered by an unequivocal Yes. It is not our concern here whether there may not be other reasons which might induce nations to abandon this organizational form voluntarily. But they are not forced to abandon it by any failure of the tax state; nor is the war and its heritage a sufficient reason. *In this, the only essential meaning, there is no "crisis of the tax state."*

Our argument applies, secondly, only to the particular historical moment in which we live. It is not intended as an apotheosis of the free economy as the last word of wisdom. I am not in the habit of crowning our bourgeoisie with laurel wreaths. However, it can do *exactly* what is needed now. No recognition of its narrowness and cultural poverty detracts from this fact. Marx himself, if he lived today, could not be of a different opinion. And he would laugh grimly at those of his disciples who welcome the present administrative economy as the dawn of socialism—that administrative economy which is the most undemocratic thing there is, that step back to what preceded the competitive economy which alone can create the preconditions for true socialism and finally evolve socialism itself. The social form of the society of the future cannot grow out of an impoverished economy thrown backward in its development, nor out of instincts run wild. It has been the tragedy of all attempts to realize the new social order, most recently of the Russian one, that people could be won over only when whipped up by dire need and when a situation existed in which true success could not be hoped for—a situation which precisely the bourgeois businessman with precisely his mentality and precisely his experiences and methods could meet successfully.

And yet it is the first precondition for the socialized community

that capitalism has done its work and an economy exists which is sa-
tiated with capital and thoroughly rationalized by entrepreneurial
brains. Only then is it possible to look forward calmly to that inevitable slowing down of merely economic development which is the con-
comitant of socialism, for socialism means liberation of life from the
economy and alienation from the economy. This hour has not yet
struck. The war has postponed it. The hour that is belongs to private
enterprise, to economic effort to the very limit of its strength. And
with private enterprise the hour also belongs to the tax state. Only at
the price of heavy sacrifices for all, including the interests of the
workers, may the hour be torn from these hands. That much is certain.

Nevertheless the hour will come. By and by private enterprise will
lose its social meaning through the development of the economy and
the consequent expansion of the sphere of social sympathy. The signs
of this are already with us and it was inherent in the tendencies of
the second half of the nineteenth century, whose perhaps final aberration was all that which culminated in the world war. Society is growing beyond private enterprise and tax state, not because but in spite
of the war. *That* too is certain.

## Notes

1. This essay represents an enlarged version of a lecture Schumpeter gave
before the Wiener Soziologische Gesellschaft. It was originally published in
1918 under the title "Die Krise der Steuerstaates" as issue number 4 of *Zeitfragen aus dem Gebiet der Soziologie*. An English translation, prepared by Wolfgang F. Stolper and Richard A. Musgrave, appeared in 1954 as number 4 of
*International Economic Papers*. For more information on this essay, see the section titled "The European Period: Schumpeter's Works in This Volume" in
the Introduction.

2. R. Goldscheid, *Staatssozialismus oder Staatskapitalismus*, 1917. The scientific significance of this highly intelligent book lies in the fundamental idea
of a fiscal sociology; the reason for its success lies in the practical proposals
for the solution of the fiscal problem. Here we are not concerned with these
practical proposals even though some parts of the last section of the present
sketch are an implied criticism of them; at the same time we both agree regarding a once-and-for-all capital levy, notwithstanding the fact that G. and
I judge its significance in an entirely different manner.

3. This has frequently been insufficiently appreciated. However, the historian is often inclined to overestimate the influence of the state on the formation of the economy. At no time have economy and budget formed a really uniform "state economy," never has the state been able to create

something lasting which the free economy would not have created, though perhaps to a larger or smaller extent. Old market privileges, for example, explain to this day the location of some industries. But such cases are on the whole mere aberrations from the economically determined locations.

4. Anyone who knows how to read in budgets and who carefully followed events in the international money markets could see the world war coming for at least ten years.

5. To be sure, Brentano has asserted (e.g., *Schmoller's Jahrbuch*, Vol. 41) that modern life has, through the mediation of Byzantium, been in continuous connection with antiquity and that it can only thus be understood; and even that the teutonic manorial system could only be explained in terms of the example of the Roman latifundia. This undoubtedly places vastly exaggerated importance on the phraseologies which were indeed frequently taken over—and we can say this without rejecting Brentano's idea entirely. This is particularly true of tax history. The analogies are, of course, clear enough but they prove only that the same causes have the same effects. See also A. Rambaud, *L'Empire Grec au Dixième Siècle*, 1870; F. Chalandon, *Essai sur le Règne d'Alexis Iᵉʳ*, 1900; Bussell, *The Roman Empire*, 1910.

6. Every one of these words is debatable. It is the merit of Sander's book *Feudalstaat und bürgerliche Verfassung*, 1906, to have shown that the clouds of ambiguity which hover over German constitutional history have their origin only partly in the matter itself, i.e., in the marked poverty of some of the material and the frequently blurred outline of events, and that they arise in part from the lack of an adequate conceptual apparatus. As Sander has also seen, this latter defect is in turn due not only to the historians' (even legal historians') frequently careless use of juridical concepts; but rather to the fact that they use juridical concepts at all to the exclusion of others and that they use any concepts they need in a juridical meaning. Juridical concepts as such are not suitable for the interpretation of historical series, especially not for the comparative characterization of types of conditions which are historically given, or better, which have to be *abstracted* from history. It is just this comparison that is at issue here. For these types are children of particular legal systems, therefore also of particular social situations and of the jurisprudence attaching thereto. Outside their proper setting these types lose their true meaning, though this is obscured by the fact that later epochs cling to the name.

The concepts of sociology are not conditioned by legal systems, nor are they juridical, but rather theoretical. It is, therefore, not to jurisprudence but to sociology that the historian, and the constitutional historian too, must turn when concerned with the interpretation and the conceptual formation of social (including constitutional) conditions, rather than with specifically legal questions. When it comes to legal concepts, the historian is perfectly right with his almost stereotyped warning that an intellectual approach born out of one era must not be projected into another, and that in particular modern concepts must not be "projected" back into the middle ages. To this extent there is some truth in Jellinek's assertion (*Allgemeine Staatslehre*, p. 446) that the phenomena of widely separated epochs can yield no common constitutional concepts. However, this must not be taken to mean, as undoubtedly it frequently is, that there can be no concepts at all—e.g., economic or sociological ones—which could exist in all or in many different historical climates. If this were correct, there could not only be no comparison, but no scientific observation whatsoever in the field of human action and suffering.

Nevertheless, what little we want to say could be considered pretty much *communis opinio* even of the history of law, especially if the use of the concept of the state is left aside. In support of the *facts* on which we base ourselves we could quote in our favor a long string of authorities of different complexion from Hegel to Gierke, not excluding Brunner and, among historical sociologists, Schmoller; and an almost equally long list could be quoted in support of our *interpretation* of the facts in most points. For this very reason we must at once mention also the most important authority who, falling back in part on previously accepted scientific views, takes the opposite standpoint with particular energy: G. v. Below. His book *Der Deutsche Staat des Mittelalters*, Vol. I, 1914, is dedicated primarily to the proof of the thesis intimated in all the well-known works of this author that the medieval state was a state in the modern sense, that its law was "public" law, and that the idea of the public-law vassal relationship was never entirely dead. Insofar as this means that a "private law" interpretation of medieval constitutional conditions is impracticable and in particular that a satisfactory derivation of state sovereignty from land ownership is impossible there can, of course, be no objection from the standpoint taken in the text. I should like to stress this. Insofar, however, as v. Below wants to prove the opposite, he appears to come to grief because he neglects the point of view which Sander was the first to stress. He begins (p. 107) with the recognition, most gratifying in a historian, that conceptual clarity is essential in these problems. However, he seems to know of none but juridical concepts to apply to his data and this contrasts strangely with his good intentions (p. 109) "to take all the formative elements of our century into account." Similarly, the historical anti-theoretical rigorism to which v. Below has frequently confessed can hardly be reconciled with his tendency, which is *really* inconsistent with such rigorism, to save the honor of the middle ages, let alone with his criticism of Emperor Otto I which smacks of modern newspaper politics. For that matter, the *facts* which he presents can hardly have been unknown to anyone, and their *interpretation* is a sociological problem toward the solution of which he contributes little of value, certainly much less than Sander whom he condemns so harshly.

7. Social conditions always contain remnants of the past and seeds of the future; and it is these seeds that are especially noticeable to the researcher looking back through the spectacles of a later time. *Natura non facit saltum*, and it is only by way of abstraction that one can speak of any condition in the sense of a definitely defined type. But such abstractions are simply necessary as an economy of thinking. Furthermore, each actual situation in its totality (*not* as an abstraction) gives birth to the succeeding situation in its totality. However, a type arrived at through abstraction need not create a succeeding

type of the same logical character since the elements of the actual historical object which are taken into the abstraction are at best only part of the effective real causes. This is one of the difficulties of every "theory of development." It is correct, as v. Below stresses, that the social powers of the middle ages cannot be reduced to "private" relations and that the "common purpose" has never been entirely absent. To be sure, there is an exaggeration in the pointedness and generality of Gierke's contention that the "banalities" of the peasant and the territorial powers of the king both fall under the one concept of territorial property law. On the other hand, neither the "irreducibility" nor the "common purpose" are sufficient to justify the use of the term "state," if this term is to have anything in common with what we mean by it. Nor does this recognition exempt us from the task of specifying in their purest form those features of a social condition which seem to us essential for the purposes of scientific research.

A social condition may furthermore combine several types which are inconsistent in their "inner logic" and which have to be worked out separately. To this extent v. Below's distinction between *Lehensstaat* and *Feudalstaat* makes just as good sense as, for example, does Rotteck's distinction between *Lehenswesen* and *Allodialwesen*. However, the latter distinction means the opposite of two principles while the former uses *Feudalstaat* as the broader concept which includes within it the special *Lehensstaat*. All such attempts lie in the direction of a conceptual classification of historical matter which alone can be the way to clarity. It is true that the *Lehenswesen* has never completely penetrated the social body. Yet from the ninth to the thirteenth centuries it was nevertheless the characteristic form of social organization alongside of which another form of feudal state gradually developed, which in turn was to dominate the succeeding centuries.

8. The Margrave of the Ostmark, for example, was until the tenth century a removable official. Even so, it would still be a question of interpretation whether his position was more similar to that of a modern governor or to that of a private employee administering an estate independently—or to that of a tenant. Of course, none of these modern categories fit.

9. v. Below (*Der Deutsche Staat*) gives examples intended to prove the opposite. However, the distinction between *Reich* property and royal property which can be found, the possibility of conflicts between "emperor" and "*Reich*" which is admitted, etc., are surely to be understood otherwise than in the sense of the recognition of a "public" besides a "private" sphere. Clearly, things were in part different in the *Reich* from those in the territories. Here we are speaking only of the latter.

10. Of course, *we* are used to look at particular social functions as specifically within the sphere of the state and others as specifically "private." However, no borders exist between the two unless one is content to say that "public" is whatever is considered "public" at a particular time. But this presupposes the existence of a state. For this reason it is hopeless to try and define the state by means of certain necessarily public functions. Just as hopeless is the opposite attempt to derive the "limits of its effectiveness" from the

"essence " of the state. Such attempts were made a hundred years ago and are still being made now and then. In particular, the "common purpose" is not the same as the "purpose of the state."

For our purposes it will be convenient to treat the attributes "state" and "public law" as coinciding because only the emergence of the state gives full meaning to the distinction between private and public law. We thereby use a terminology which is contradictory to that used by Sander without, however, wishing to deny the "justification" of that terminology. We would not, incidentally, do this in a more detailed discussion.

11. See note 6. Besides Gierke cf. also v. Schulte, *Lebenserinnerungen*, Vol. III, Essays: "Feudalstaat und Moderner Staat." In this essay v. Schulte denies the existence of a *Reich* army and of *Reich* revenues since the Hohenstaufen era. No general vassal relationship then existed, so he asserts, but only a league of princes, lords, cities. Similar conditions are said to have obtained in the territories. This description does not do justice to all details. Yet the general impression it creates is not for this reason wrong. The "tax" of that era he describes as an impost which is a charge on the soil and connected with predial bondage.

12. Occasionally we find something which could be compared to modern taxes, for example, when King Henry I had to raise the tribute promised to the Magyars. This was a payment for *Reich* purposes, but it was restricted to Saxony. Notwithstanding certain attempts, e.g., by Henry IV, Henry V, and Otto IV, the *Reich* did not develop taxes until the time of the "Kammerzieler," the "gemeine Pfennige," the "Römermonate," i.e., until the end of the fifteenth century. By that time similar developments had already begun in the territories. There indirect taxation grew out of the regalia which in the times of the Stauffer fell to the territorial powers. The Austrian duke, for example, received the fiscal rights of the crown in the twelfth century; this strengthened his position considerably and, the privilege of 1156 having also loosened the vassal dependence, he called himself *dominus terrae* after 1192. It is a debatable question what was the character of the impost which is found, as far as I know, in all German territories during the twelfth and thirteenth centuries under the name of *Bede* (*Schoss, petitio, tallia*). In his publications (particularly "Die direkten Staatssteuren in Jülich und Berg," *Zeitschrift des Berg. Gesch. Ber.* 26, 28, 29) v. Below has always emphasized the "public law" character of these taxes and has finally treated them entirely like a modern land and real estate (in his article "Bede," *Handwörterbuch der Staatswissenschaften*). Partly under his influence the monographs on this special problem accepted this almost without exception, while some writers, and Gierke particularly sharply, denied that there was any generic difference between ground rents and this land tax. There is no reason to attach any more weight to the fact that on the one hand the *Bede* did later frequently merge into the ground rent, than to the fact that on the other hand the literature at the time of the commutation of dues overwhelmingly took the position that the *Bede* was a "public" impost which was to be abolished without compensation. However, the numerous exceptions from the "tax liability" delimit a circle of taxable

persons which corresponds roughly to the realm of jurisdictional power. Indeed, Zeumer (*Deutsche Städtesteuern*) derived the *Bede* from the jurisdictional power. In that case what is true of jurisdictional power would also be valid for the *Bede*. The right or the power of the juridical lord to levy dues would then depend on a "particular relation" to those under his jurisdiction, just as his and the other nobles' right to other payments. There is no need to go as far as G. L. v. Maurer or Lamprecht or v. Inama-Sternegg, who construct all medieval powers on the basis of feudal land ownership. However, from the rejection of this view to the notion that penal judicature and "tax rights" have derived from state power is a long road quite insufficiently marked by documents. For literature, see the article by v. Below. Since the *Bede* is seen in its purest form where the peasantry predominates, the most interesting situation so far as Austria is concerned is that in the Tyrol, about which we have the publications of F. Kogler, and secondly the situation in Silesia about which Knies and Rachfahl may be consulted. For the older view on these matters, see K. H. Lang, *Historische Entwicklung der Teutschen Steuerverfassung*, 1793. About the Bohemian Berna, cf. Lippert, *Sozialgeschichte Böhmens in vorhussitischer Zeit*, 1896. Mone (in *Zeitschrift für die Geschichte des Oberrheins*, Vol. VI) considers the *Bede* to be a remainder of Roman times. Gliemann ("Einführung der Akzise in Preussen," *Tübinger Zeitschrift*, 29) believes that the *Bede* was originally paid also by the nobility and that the fifteenth- and sixteenth-century territorial tax which should be mentioned developed out of it. Hoffmann ("Geschichte der direkten Steuern in Bayern," *Schmollers Forsch.*, 1883) puts it that way that *Bede* and tax during the thirteenth century "frequently had private law character" but nevertheless contained seeds of a public institution. Schönberg (*Finanzverhältnisse der Stadt Basel*, 1879) believes that taxes in our sense developed first in the cities. It should be stressed that Zeumer (*Deutsche Stadtsteuern*) expresses himself quite vaguely and that, while considering "taxes" (which he takes to be of the same nature as the *Bede* while others contrast these two expressions) to be a right relating to the office of a feudal official (*Vogt*), he leaves open in many cases the possibility of a feudal origin. Schmoller (in *Schmollers Jahrbuch*, Vol. I) declares the *Bede* of the Mark Brandenburg of the thirteenth century (it was commuted in 1280) simply to be a "general property tax." Dopsch ("Beiträge zur Geschichte der Finanzverwaltung Österreichs im 13. Jahrhundert," *Mitteilungen des Instituts für österreichische Geschichtsforschung*, Vol. 18) sees the *Marchfutter*, the *Landpfennige*, the *Burgwerk*, as payments of a public law nature and accepts the opinion (which used to be current and is still maintained by Brunner) that it was a payment made by that part of the population which was not bound to serve in war. Cf. also Schalk ("Österreichs Finanzverwaltung unter Berthold von Mangen," *Blätter des Vereins für Landeskunde von Niederösterreich*, 1881). Bruder declares expressly that "taxes proper" existed in Austria only from the vassals of the prince and from the subvassals of the feudal lords over whom the duke had a right to jurisdiction—although there were occasional attempts, for example in 1235 and 1336, to go beyond them. We cannot here enter into this problem further. However, what we have quoted may be sufficient to justify the account given in the text. As a matter of fact what we have said would not be changed in its essence (though of course in individual points) if we had to speak of a "public" character of the *Bede* as, following v. Below, is done for example by Brennecke and Hübner. Incidentally, Hübner in his *Grundzüge des Deutschen Privatrechts* (1908) nevertheless rejects the distinction between private and public law for that period.

13. Analogy: If nowadays any enterprise collapses this is of no particular interest. If however the capitalist enterprise necessarily had to collapse for internal reasons, then we would be faced with what the socialist theory of the collapse of capitalism means, namely a passing of the enterprise form of production.

14. In this manner a new form of organization took the place of the decaying vassal relationship. First the vassal relationship had disintegrated the Carolingian Reich, which, if it really was as it seems to look on paper (cf. v. Dungern, *Staat und Volk durch die Jahrhunderte*, 1911; for facts particularly: Dopsch, *Karolingerzeit*) indeed came so close to the form of a state that much is to be said for Sohm's view according to which the Franconian *Reich* was a state and only later lost this character. In just the same way the vassal relationship now came to be disintegrated through a process of patrimonialization or allodification of the fiefs, and there arose a new egocentric mode of living in which a separate state is a social necessity. The old *civitas*, the association of the tribal kingdom, the Franconian *Reich*, the vassal relationship, the seignioralty: all these are different medieval types which follow each other historically but not by immanent development.

15. Lords whose castles were far distant, as for instance in the Tyrol the counts of Arco and Lodron, exploited their favorable situation to the full. (Cf. v. Sartori-Montecroce, *Das landständische Steuerwesen Tirols*.) Here too the literature is plentiful. Concerning the situation in Bohemia, which differed in some respects, cf. Gindely, *Geschichte der böhmischen Finanzen*, 1526–1618, Akad. Vol. 18.

16. The finances were the driving element particularly in the domestic policy of the princes, whose tendencies—for example their friendliness toward the peasants and generally their assumption of the role of representatives of the interest of the "country as a whole"—are explicable chiefly in terms of their fiscal interest and of the position into which the class attitude of the estates forced them. It was chiefly fiscal necessities which drove the princes forward and forced the estates to beat a retreat.

17. This is the moment in the life of nations when the theory of Haller, the German Burke, fits best. However, it is not this which is his merit, but rather that he was one of the first to try to take a realistic sociological view of the phenomena of the state and to help this point of view to its rightful place against juridical schemata. His attempt which, to be sure, is not entirely successful has to be considered as a "Natural History of the State" in the sense of C. Frantz, and though his text sometimes gives a somewhat primitive impression, it contains much sound sense.

18. In judging such attempts three things have to be kept in mind: *First,*

there is the infinite variety of points of view from which the nature of the state is of interest. But something different matters to each of these points of view. Depending on the point of view, the nature of the state itself differs and different things are true of it; this is difficult for us to recognize and it is this which, if misunderstood, gives rise to so many useless controversies and "pseudo problems." The plane and horizon of those who wish to explore the metaphysical meaning of the state do not touch ours. Those who define the state for juridical purposes have nothing in common with our aims. What matters to us is simply to understand a historically given, precisely character- ized factor of social life. *Second*, we must recognize that the mere under- standing of the genesis of a social phenomenon by itself does not reveal the latter's "essence," its "meaning," its "cultural significance," its "inner logic." If the point of view of fiscal sociology permitted us no more than to understand the emergence of the state, we might still be in the situation of the man who tries to "explain" the impression of a landscape by studying its geology. Ob- serve that we do not fall into the error of looking for the essence of a phe- nomenon in the driving forces of its genesis and that we do not obliterate the peculiar character of a type once created by dissecting it retrospectively into its furthest origins. *Third*, any realistic analysis of the state finds, as it were, an already spoiled ground. The tendency of the modern state worshipper to see in the state in as many respects as possible a superlative, something "high- est," "all-embracing," has expanded the state for the modern consciousness far beyond its true dimensions—much as the façade technique did to many Renaissance churches. Just as, by hardly credible aberration, all culture is subordinated to the objectives of the state, so the scope of the state becomes an enormous abstraction which devours the whole of social life, all its insti- tutions and other essential features. He who speaks of the state wherever there is any social organization at all will, of course, find the state every- where—but he also loses everything which is characteristic of the state. The same naturally also holds true for the conception of the state as the very essence of norm, as order itself.

19. This serves to explain what is termed "objectivity" of culture, a view of cultural phenomena as norms with super-individual sanctions as contrasted with the subjective atomization of the culture of the free economy.

20. One should really never say "the state does this or that." It is always important to recognize who or whose interest it is that sets the machine of the state in motion and speaks through it. Such a view must be repulsive to anyone for whom the state is the highest good of the people, the acme of its achievement, the sum of its ideals and forces. However, only this view is re- alistic. It also contains that which is correct in the otherwise wrong theory that the state is nothing but the ruling classes' means of exploitation. Neither the aspect of a class state nor the idea of the state as something above all parties and classes which is simply the organized "totality" is adequate to the nature of the state. Yet neither of the two is taken out of thin air. The state does always reflect the social power relations even though it is not merely their reflection. The state does necessitate the emergence of an idea of the

state to which the peoples give more or less content depending on circumstances, even if it is not the offspring of an abstract idea of the state embracing the social whole.

21. Incidentally, it is only from the standpoint of modern ideals of equity that the capacity to bear taxes of large incomes is greater than that of the same amount distributed over small incomes, except where the latter approach the subsistence minimum. In general there is no essential difference of the *economic* capacity, i.e., those reactions to taxation which are discussed in the text occur in general with large as well as with small incomes.

22. The closer the tax state approaches these limits the greater is the resistance and the loss of energy with which it works. A bigger and bigger army of bureaucrats is needed to enforce the tax laws, tax inquisition becomes more and more intrusive, tax chicanery more and more unbearable. The picture of absurd waste of energy shows that the meaning of the organization of the tax state lies in the autonomy of the private economy and of private life and that this meaning is lost when the state can no longer respect this autonomy.

23. It is no accident that the voices which speak of the insufficiency of the tax state come almost all from Austria, and particularly that R. Goldscheid is an Austrian. And if in Austria one frequently meets with the phrase that Austria's desperate situation should not be taken too tragically since "all the others are just as badly off," then this is simply not true.

24. This is one of the points which in public life are always treated in a misleading phraseology, something which fiscal problems in particular cannot stand. Except for a relatively narrow circle of large businessmen, the real war profiteers—to tell the unpopular truth—i.e., the people whose incomes have risen by more than corresponds to the fall in the value of money, are by no means to be found primarily among the upper strata of capitalist society. The capitalists—both shareholders and owners of fixed-interest bearing securities—mostly belong to the "war losers," for only in a few cases have their dividends risen correspondingly and their interest payments in the narrow sense never at all. Compared with them the workers are in a much more favorable position. This is quite natural since their incomes have risen not only according to the fall in the value of money, but also under the influence of the diminution in the supply of labor due to military service. In agricultural circles—and no one familiar with the situation can deny this—the peasants are the true war profiteers, while the large land owners were for a number of reasons prevented from using their opportunity to the full. The answer to these points is usually an outburst of furious howls. But this is hardly suited to further recognition of the facts.

25. Consumption taxes would under present circumstances not fall entirely on the consumer; hence the political resistance against such taxes.

26. I insist on this point in view of the probable course of events. The worst one can do is to approach such a task with inadequate political means and with patent uncertainty.

27. In this point the proposed measure differs from the capital levy ad-

vocated by R. Goldscheid. However, let it be stressed that I am not here discussing the problem of the latter nor arguing against it, but that I merely wish to show for a narrowly circumscribed purpose the feasibility of the tax solution.

28. Foreign holdings probably have to be estimated at approximately 15 billion crowns, but this is not a percentage which would shift the center of gravity of the problem.

29. I am well aware that the figures given in the text are open to a flood of objections if it is not borne in mind in what sense they are meant. In particular it must not be forgotten that the monetary value of wealth which we are discussing is not that of reality but that which would result from an appropriate fiscal policy and that my purpose is merely to give the reader a very rough outline of the matter. It would therefore be completely inadmissible to quote in rebuttal Vogel's results published in *Österreichischer Volkswirt*, December 22, 1917, and January 5, 1918, even if they were wholly beyond question from his own standpoint. Fellner's estimate, by the way, which was our starting point, was, as Vogel emphasizes, much too low even for peacetime quite apart from the fact that after 1911, the last year for which Fellner has given estimates, national wealth must have increased further up to the war and that for purposes of a capital levy the state's liabilities toward its own citizens have to be added to the national wealth though, of course, the amount of state property as well as of the property of other juridical subjects to be exempted from the tax have to be subtracted. Vogel has treated the capital gains during the war quite inadequately and in a manner which is methodologically not correct. It goes without saying that a comparison with Prussian figures, for example, would also be quite inadmissible since inflation has progressed much less there. In case there are still some doubts left: Alone the taxation of the claims of individuals on the state would raise 20 billion on our assumptions. Should it really be impossible to raise an equal amount from other property at a time when one *Joch* (a little less than one-and-a-half acres) of the best land costs up to 10,000 crowns and when the sales value (which alone is relevant) of agricultural properties without buildings or other improvements is estimated much too low at 100 billion? Vogel's pessimistic result is explained by the particular methods of tax technique which he seems to have in mind. I cannot go into this here in spite of the reproach which was made against me that I did not exhaust this question as well in a fifty-minute lecture which was devoted to a sociological topic and which covered quite a large amount of ground, from the nature of a medieval community to our own fiscal situation. To be sure: inquisition, the raised fist of criminal prosecution of tax offenses, achieves only a *sauve qui peut* which necessarily prevents success no matter how vexatious the procedure.

# Two

## The Sociology of Imperialisms

### I. The Problem

Our problem arises from the fact that aggressive attitudes on the part of states—or of such earlier organizational structures as history may record—can be explained, directly and unequivocally, only in part by the real and concrete interests of the people.[1] Examples will best illustrate what we mean. When two tribes come into conflict over essential salt deposits or hunting grounds; or when a state, hemmed in on all sides by customs and communication barriers, resorts to aggression in order to gain access to the sea, we have a case in which aggression is explained by interests. It is true that there are many methodological difficulties in speaking of the interests of a people as such. Here, however, reference to "concrete" interests explains everything that would seem to stand in need of explanation. A concrete interest need not be economic in character. When a state resorts to aggression in order to unite its citizens politically, as was the case with Piedmont in 1848 and 1859, this likewise betokens a real, concrete interest, explaining its conduct. The interest, moreover, need not necessarily extend to the *entire* population of the state. When a planter aristocracy prevails upon its government to seize some foreign base of operations for the slave trade, this too is explained by a real, concrete interest. The interest that actually explains a warlike act need not, finally, be openly admitted—or of the kind that *can* be openly admitted; it need not, to use our own term, be an *avowed* interest. Such cases nevertheless come under the present heading if the concrete interests of a sufficiently powerful class are accessible to scientific consideration. There are, on the other hand, certain cases that do *not* belong here, such as that of a group of people who contrive to have a declaration of war issued because they gain financially from the waging of war, or because they need a war as a diversion from domestic political difficulties. Here there is no concrete interest, in the sense that applies to the aforementioned cases. True, there must be *some* concrete interest. There must be a reason for the declaration of war. But that *reason* is not the *cause*. The true cause, of course, must also lie in an interest. But that interest is not in the concrete war aims. It is not a question of the advantages offered by the attainment of those aims, but of an interest in the waging of war as such. The questions that then arise are how the people came to acquire such a generally belligerent disposition and why they happened to choose this particular occasion for war. Thus, mere reference to a concrete interest is satisfactory under only three conditions: In the first place, such a concrete interest *must be present*, in the sense that has now been made clear—an interest which the observer can grasp as such, of course taking into account the social structure, mentality, and situation of the people in question. In the second place, the conduct of the state which is under study must be calculated to *promote* this interest, with the sum total of predictable sacrifices and risks in some proportion to the anticipated gains. In the third place, it must be possible to *prove* that this interest, whether avowed or not, is actually the *political driving force* behind the action.

In the individual case it may often become difficult to establish whether these conditions obtain. The fabric of social interests is so closely woven that scarcely ever can there be any action on the part of a state that is not in keeping with the concrete interest of someone, an interest to which that action can be reduced without manifest absurdity. To this must be added the belief, inculcated into the people, especially in the present age, that concrete interests of the people dictate the behavior of the state and that concrete advantages for all classes are to be expected. Government policies are always officially justified in this way, and often, without the slightest doubt, in perfect good faith. Finally, current fallacies, especially of an economic character, may serve to create the semblance of an adequate, concrete interest in the mind of the people—and occasionally even in the mind of the scientific observer, especially the historian. In such cases the true background is laid bare only by an inquiry into the manner in which the people came to their belief. But the individual case does not concern us. We are concerned only with the fact, which is beyond doubt, that the three above-mentioned conditions are frequently not fulfilled. Whenever such is the case, a problem arises. And among the problems of this nature is the problem of imperialism.

No one calls it imperialism when a state, no matter how brutally and vigorously, pursues concrete interests of its own; and when it can be expected to abandon its aggressive attitude as soon as it has attained what it was after. The word "imperialism" has been abused as a slogan to the point where it threatens to lose all meaning, but up to this point our definition is quite in keeping with common usage, even in the press. For whenever the word "imperialism" is used, there is always the implication—whether sincere or not—of an aggressiveness,

the true reasons for which do not lie in the aims which are temporarily being pursued; of an aggressiveness that is only kindled anew
by each success; of an aggressiveness for its own sake, as reflected in
such terms as "hegemony," "world dominion," and so forth. And history, in truth, shows us nations and classes—most nations furnish an
example at some time or other—that seek expansion for the sake of
expanding, war for the sake of fighting, victory for the sake of winning, dominion for the sake of ruling. This determination cannot be
explained by any of the pretexts that bring it into action, by any of
the aims for which it seems to be struggling at the time. It confronts
us, independent of all concrete purpose or occasion, as an enduring
disposition, seizing upon one opportunity as eagerly as the next. It
shines through all the arguments put forward on behalf of present
aims. It values conquest not so much on account of the immediate
advantages—advantages that more often than not are more than dubious, or that are heedlessly cast away with the same frequency—as
because it *is* conquest, success, action. Here the theory of concrete
interest in our sense fails. What needs to be explained is how the will
to victory itself came into being.

Expansion for its own sake always requires, among other things,
concrete objects if it is to reach the action stage and maintain itself,
but this does not constitute its meaning. Such expansion is in a sense
its own "object," and the truth is that it has no adequate object beyond
itself. Let us therefore, in the absence of a better term, call it "objectless." It follows for that very reason that, just as such expansion cannot be explained by concrete interest, so too it is never satisfied by the
fulfillment of a concrete interest, as would be the case if fulfillment
were the motive, and the struggle for it merely a necessary evil—a
counterargument, in fact. Hence the tendency of such expansion to
transcend all bounds and tangible limits, to the point of utter exhaustion. This, then, is our definition: imperialism is the objectless disposition on the part of a state to unlimited forcible expansion.

Now it may be possible, in the final analysis, to give an "economic
explanation" for this phenomenon, to end up with economic factors.
Two different points present themselves in this connection: First, an
attempt can be made, following the basic idea of the economic interpretation of history, to derive imperialist tendencies from the eco-
nomic-structural influences that shape life in general and from the
relations of production. I should like to emphasize that I do not
doubt in the least that this powerful instrument of analysis will stand
up here in the same sense that it has with other, similar phenomena—
if only it is kept in mind that customary modes of political thought
and feeling in a given age can never be mere "reflexes" of, or coun-

terparts to, the production situation of that age. Because of the persistence of such habits, they will always, to a considerable degree, be dominated by the production context of past ages. Again, the attempt may be made to reduce imperialist phenomena to economic class *interests* of the age in question. This is precisely what neo-Marxist theory does. Briefly, it views imperialism simply as the reflex of the interests of the capitalist upper stratum, at a given stage of capitalist development. Beyond doubt this is by far the most serious contribution toward a solution of our problem. Certainly there is much truth in it. We shall deal with this theory later. But let us emphasize even here that it does not, of logical necessity, follow from the economic interpretation of history. It may be discarded without coming into conflict with that interpretation; indeed, without even departing from its premises. It is the treatment of this factor that constitutes the contribution of the present inquiry into the sociology of the *Zeitgeist*.[2]

Our method of investigation is simple: we propose to analyze the birth and life of imperialism by means of historical examples which I regard as typical. A common basic trait emerges in every case, making a single sociological problem of imperialism in all ages, though there are substantial differences among the individual cases. Hence the plural, "imperialisms," in the title.

## II. Imperialism as a Catch Phrase

An example will suffice. After the split over the question of repealing the Corn Laws in the year 1846, the Conservative Party in England, reconstituted around Stanley, Bentinck, and Disraeli, was in an extremely difficult situation. During long years of unbroken dominance, ever since the Napoleonic wars, it had at bottom lacked even a single positive plank in its platform. Its entire program may be summarized in the word "No!"[3] Its best heads soon recognized that they could get away with such a policy in wartime, but not under normal circumstances. Canning was the first to grasp this truth, and it was he who created that highest type of Conservative policy which consists in refusing to shrink from the great necessities of the day, and instead seizes upon them realistically and constructs Conservative successes on what would otherwise have become Conservative defeats. One of his two great accomplishments was his struggle for national freedom throughout the world—a struggle that created a background of international goodwill that was to mean so much in the future; the Catholic emancipation was the other. When Peel moved up to leadership, he could not follow the same policy, for his followers would have rebelled. He chose to fight against electoral reform, which played into the hands of the Whigs under Lord Grey and helped them to their long rule. Yet at the height of his power (1842–1846) Peel did conduct himself in the spirit of Canning. He made the cause of free trade his own. The great undertaking succeeded—an accomplishment I have always regarded as the greatest of its kind in the history of domestic politics. Its fruits were a sharp rise in prosperity, sustained social peace, sound foreign relations. But the Conservative Party was wrecked in the process. Those who remained loyal to Peel—the Peelites—first formed a special group, only to be absorbed by the legions of Liberalism later on. Those who seceded formed the new Conservative Party, for the time being essentially agrarian in character. But they lacked a platform that would have attracted a majority, a banner to be flung to the breezes of popular favor, a leader whom they trusted. That was shown after the death of Lord George Bentinck, who at least had been a convinced partisan of the Corn Laws; and it was shown especially in 1852 when the chances of the parliamentary game put Stanley (by then Lord Derby) and Disraeli in the saddle. To strengthen their minority—they could not hope for a majority—they dissolved Parliament. But in the ensuing election campaign they were so unsure of their cause that their opponents were able to claim with some justification that Derby candidates were protectionist in rural districts and free trade in urban ones. It could scarcely have been otherwise, for it was not hard to see that a return to the Corn Laws was out of the question, while the Conservative Party had nothing else to offer to the hard core of its followers. Failure was inevitable under such circumstances, nor was it long delayed. Thus when Disraeli picked up the reins a second time, once again with a minority (1858–1859), he ventured along a different course. He usurped the battle cry of electoral reform. This was a plausible policy from the Conservative point of view. An extension of the franchise was bound to give a voice to population segments that, for the time being at least, were more susceptible to Conservative arguments than the bourgeoisie which did not begin to swing over to the Conservative side until the seventies. At first Disraeli failed, but in 1866–1867 he succeeded all the better. Again in the minority, facing the latent hostility of his own people, reviled as no English statesman had been since Bute and North, beset with problems on every side, he yet revolutionized the electoral law—an unparalleled triumph of political genius. Disraeli fell, but in the midst of disaster the essence of victory was his. True, it was Gladstone's hour. All the forces and voices of victory fought for him. But as early as 1873 it was plain that the meteoric career of his first cabinet—or his second, if he be counted the actual head of Russell's cabinet—was drawing to a close. Reform legislation always brings in its wake a renascence of conservative sentiment. The Conservative election success of 1874 was more and more clearly foreshadowed. And what program did Disraeli, the Conservative leader, have to offer? The people did not ask for much in a positive way. They wanted a breathing space. Criticism of Gladstone's acts was highly rewarding under the circumstances. Yet some positive policy had to be offered. What would it be?

The Conservative leader spoke of social reform. Actually he was only reverting to Conservative traditions (Ashley) which he himself had helped to shape in earlier years. Besides, such a policy might split off a few radicals from Gladstone's camp. A certain kinship between the Conservatives and the radicals was of long standing—did not, in fact, cease, until the radicals had got the better of the Whigs within the Liberal Party. But the situation was unfavorable for "Tory democracy." For the moment, Gladstone had done more than enough in this field. The slogans were shopworn. There was prosperity. The working people turned every official trip of Gladstone's into a triumphal procession. No, there was little capital to be made on that score. It was no better with the Irish question—the cause of the Ulstermen and the High Church. In this predicament Disraeli struck a new note. The election campaign of 1874—or, to fix the date exactly, Disraeli's speech in the Crystal Palace in 1872—marked the birth of imperialism as the catch phrase of domestic policy.

It was put in the form of "Imperial Federation." The colonies—of which Disraeli in 1852 had written: "These wretched colonies . . . are a millstone round our necks" (Malmesbury, *Memoirs of an Ex-Minister*, p. 343)—these same colonies were to become autonomous members in a unified empire. This empire was to form a customs union. The free soil of the colonies was to remain reserved for Englishmen. A uniform defense system was to be created. The whole structure was to be crowned by a central representative organ in London, creating a closer, living connection between the imperial government and the colonies. The appeal to national sentiment, the battle cry against "Liberal" cosmopolitanism, already emerged sharply, just as they did later on in the agitation sponsored by Chamberlain, on whom fell Disraeli's mantle. Of itself the plan showed no inherent tendency to reach out beyond the "Empire," and "the Preservation of the Empire" was and is a good description of it. If we nevertheless include the "Imperial Federation" plan under the heading of imperialism, this is because its protective tariff, its militarist sentiments, its ideology of a unified "Greater Britain" all foreshadowed vague aggressive trends that would have emerged soon enough if the plan had ever passed from the sphere of the slogan into the realm of actual policy.

That it was not without value as a slogan is shown by the very fact that a man of Chamberlain's political instinct took it up—characteristically enough in another period, when effective Conservative rallying cries were at a premium. Indeed, it never vanished again, becoming a stock weapon in the political arsenal of English Conservatism, usurped even by many Liberals. As early as the nineties it meant a great deal to the youth of Oxford and Cambridge. It played a leading part in the Conservative press and at Conservative rallies. Commercial advertising grew very fond of employing its emblems—which explains why it was so conspicuous to foreign (and usually superficial) observers, and why there was so much discussion in the foreign press about "British Imperialism," a topic, moreover, that was most welcome to many political parties on the Continent. This success is readily explained. In the first place, the plan had much to offer to a whole series of special interests—primarily a protective tariff and the prospect of lucrative opportunities for exploration, inaccessible to industry under a system of free trade. Here was the opportunity to smother consumer resistance in a flood of patriotic enthusiasm. Later on, this advantage weighed all the more heavily in the balance, for certain English industries were beginning to grow quite sensitive to the dumping tactics employed by German and American exporters. Equally important was the fact that such a plan was calculated to divert the attention of the people from social problems at home. But the main thing, before which all arguments stemming from calculating self-interest must recede into the background, was the unfailing power of the appeal to national sentiment. No other appeal is as effective, except at a time when the people happen to be caught in the midst of flaming social struggle. All other appeals are rooted in interests that must be grasped by reason. This one alone arouses the dark powers of the subconscious, calls into play instincts that carry over from the life habits of the dim past. Driven out everywhere else, the irrational seeks refuge in nationalism—the irrational which consists of belligerence, the need to hate, a goodly quota of inchoate idealism, the most naive (and hence also the most unrestrained) egotism. This is precisely what constitutes the impact of nationalism. It satisfies the need for surrender to a concrete and familiar super-personal cause, the need for self-glorification and violent self-assertion. Whenever a vacuum arises in the mind of a people—as happens especially after exhausting social agitation, or after a war—the nationalist element comes to the fore. The idea of "Imperial Federation" gave form and direction to these trends in England. It was, in truth, a fascinating vision which was unfolded before the provincial mind. An additional factor was a vague faith in the advantages of colonial possessions, preferably to be exploited to the exclusion of all foreigners. Here we see ancient notions still at work. Once upon a time it had been feasible to treat colonies in the way that highwaymen treat their victims, and the possession of colonies unquestionably brought advantages. Trade had been possible only under immediate military protection and there could be no question that military bases were necessary.[4] It is because of the survival of such arguments that colonialism is not yet dead, even in England today, though only in exceptional circumstances do colonies under free trade become objects of exploitation in a sense different from that in which independent countries can be exploited. And finally, there is the instinctive urge to domination. Objectively, the man in the street derives little enough satisfaction even from modern English colonial policy, but he does take pleasure in the idea, much as a card player vicariously satisfies his primitive aggressive instincts. At the time of the Boer War there was not a beggar in London who did not speak of "our" rebellious subjects. These circumstances, in all their melancholy irony, are serious factors in politics. They eliminate many courses of action that alone seem reasonable to the leaders. Here is an example: In 1815 the Ionian Islands became an English protectorate, not to be surrendered until 1863. Long before then, however, one foreign secretary after another had realized that this possession was meaningless and untenable—not in the absolute sense, but simply because no reasonable person in England would have approved of the smallest sacrifice on its behalf. Nevertheless, none dared surrender it, for it was clear that this would have appeared as a loss and a defeat, chalked up against the cabinet in question. The only thing to do was to insist that Corfu was a military base of the highest importance which must be retained. Now, during his first term as head of the government, Gladstone had frequently made concessions—to Russia, to America, to others. At bottom everyone was glad that he had made them. Yet an uncomfortable feeling persisted, together with the occasion for much speech-making about national power and glory. The political genius who headed the opposition party saw all this—and *spoke* accordingly.

That this imperialism is no more than a phrase is seen from the fact that Disraeli *spoke*, but did not *act*. But this alone is not convincing. After all, he might have lacked the opportunity to act. The crucial factor is that he *did* have the opportunity. He had a majority. He was master of his people as only an English prime minister can be. The time was auspicious. The people had lost patience with Gladstone's peace-loving nature. Disraeli owed his success in part to the slogan we have been discussing. Yet he did not even try to follow through. He took not a single step in that direction. He scarcely even mentioned it in his speeches, once it had served his purpose. His foreign policy moved wholly within the framework of Conservative tradition. For this reason it was pro-Austrian and pro-Turkish. The notion that the integrity of Turkey was in the English interest was still alive, not yet overthrown by the power of Gladstone's Midlothian speeches which were to change public opinion on this point and later, under Salisbury, invade even the Conservative credo. Hence the new Earl of Beaconsfield supported Turkey, hence he tore up the Treaty of San Stefano. Yet even this, and the capture of Cyprus, were of no avail. A tide of public indignation toppled his rule soon afterward.[5]

We can see that Beaconsfield was quite right in not taking a single step in the direction of practical imperialism and that his policy was based on good sense. The masses of the British electorate would never have sanctioned an imperialist policy, would never have made sacrifices for it. As a toy, as a political arabesque, they accepted imperialism, just so long as no one tried it in earnest. This is seen conclusively when the fate of Chamberlain's agitation is traced. Chamberlain was unquestionably serious. A man of great talent, he rallied every ounce of personal and political power, marshaled tremendous resources, organized all the interests that stood to gain, employed a consummate propaganda technique—all this to the limits of the possible. Yet England rejected him, turning over the reins to the opposition by an overwhelming majority. It condemned the Boer War, did everything in its power to "undo" it, proving that it was merely a chance aberration from the general trend.[6] So complete was the defeat of imperialism that the Conservatives under Bonar Law, in order to achieve some degree of political rehabilitation, had to strike from their program the tariffs on food imports, necessarily the basis for any policy of colonial preference.

The rejection of imperialism meant the rejection of all the interests and arguments on which the movement was based. The elements that were decisive for the formation of political willpower—above all the radicals and gradually the labor representatives as well—showed little enthusiasm for the ideology of world empire. They were much more inclined to give credence to the Disraeli of 1852, who had compared colonies to millstones, than to the Disraeli of 1874, to the Chamberlain of the eighties rather than the Chamberlain of 1903. They showed not the least desire to make presents to agriculture, whether from national or other pretexts, at the expense of the general welfare. They were far too well versed in the free-trade argument—and this applies to the very lowest layers of the English electorate—to believe the gloomy prophecies of the "yellow press," which insisted that free trade was sacrificing to current consumer interests employment opportunities and the very roots of material welfare. After all, the rise of British export trade after 1900 belied this argument as plainly as could be. Nor had they any sympathy for military splendor and adventures in foreign policy. The whole struggle served only to demonstrate the utter importance of jingoism. The question of "objective interest"—that is, whether and to what extent there is an economic interest in a policy of imperialism—remains to be discussed.[7] Here we are concerned only with those political notions that have proved effective—whether they were false or true.

What effect the present war will have in this respect remains to be seen. For our purposes what has still to be shown is how this anti-imperialist sentiment—and especially anti-imperialism in practice—developed in England. In the distant past England did have imperialist tendencies, just as most other nations did. The process that concerns us now begins with the moment when the struggle between the people and the crown ended differently in England from the way it did on the Continent—namely, with the victory of the people. Under the Tudors and Stuarts the absolute monarchy developed in England much as it did at the same time on the Continent. Specifically, the British Crown also succeeded in winning over part of the nobility, the "cavaliers," who subsequently sided with it against the "roundheads" and who, but for the outcome of the battles of Naseby and Marston Moor, would surely have become a military palace guard.[8] Presumably England, too, would then have seen the rise of an arbitrary military absolutism, and the same tendencies which we shall discover elsewhere would have led to continual wars of aggression there too. That is why the defeat of the king and his party represent so decisive a juncture for our subject, a break in continuity. For by way of Charles I's scaffold, of Cromwell, of the Restoration, and of the events of 1688, the way led to freedom—at first, it is true, to the freedom of only one class, even to the dominance of a privileged class. But this was a class that could maintain its position only because—and so long as—it assumed leadership of those segments of the population which counted in politics—the urban population (even those without the franchise had ways of making themselves felt), yeomen, farmers, clerics, and "intellectuals." It was a class, in other words, that very soon had to learn how to behave like a candidate for public office. It might on occasion depart from such an attitude, but each time it paid dearly. The crown might seek to intervene, but each time such an effort ended in a more or less humiliating setback. The electorate may have been very narrowly circumscribed, but the ruling class depended on it—and even more on public opinion—much as on the Continent it was dependent on the monarch. And that made a great difference. In particular, it turned foreign policy into something altogether different from what it was on the Continent. The entire motivation of continental monarchial policy gave way to something different. This does not mean that a policy made by the monarch and his courtiers was impossible—it merely became one of many factors. It had to curry favor, was strictly controlled, and, if it transcended the formulated will of a party that commanded a sufficiently powerful segment of the public, always succumbed in the end to a storm which no minister's nerves could stand up to.[9] From that time on, secret diplomacy in England survived only in the literal sense—in the sense that a circle of professionals rallied around the man responsible for foreign policy, a circle that was susceptible to irresponsible influences of various kinds and often, in ways that were obscure to the public, acted in a manner that would never have been approved, had the true facts of the matter become known. But there was no secret diplomacy in the deeper sense, no circle that was able, in secret, to determine the whole course of foreign policy, as the councilors of a continental sovereign could. As soon as the results of their actions came to light, British statesmen were subject to the verdict of Parliament and of public opinion, which were able to mete out punishment where they did not approve. This made foreign policy part and parcel of partisan politics, the concern of the people who mattered in a political sense.

It is important to grasp the full implications of these facts. The parties succeeded each other in power, and each one had different aims and policies. One might declare war and wage it victoriously, only to be brought down by the other, which might at once conclude peace and surrender some of the gains which had been won. One might enter into alliances which the other would dissolve. One might bask in national glory, while the other would calculate the costs to the people. In this way England, since 1688, has lacked an unbroken, planned political line. If there was the appearance of such a thing, it was only the consequence of the fact that certain iron necessities prevailed in the face of all deliberate efforts to escape them; in part, also, the consequence of biased interpretation. True, even the policies of continental states were not necessarily governed by strict logic. But in the case of the advisers of such sovereigns the driving forces, interests, traditions, and motivations behind policies were firmly fixed. They brought a certain consistency to the whole picture, while in England it was precisely the driving forces and interests that so frequently alternated. There was only one point on which the parties

were always in agreement. This was to prevent the rise of a professional army; and when that rise had become unavoidable, to keep the
army as small as possible and prevent it from growing into a separate
occupational estate with independent power and distinct interests.
This element always worked in the same direction: it served to eliminate any factor that might have continually pressed for aggression.

We see this even at the outset of the new era. A peace party as such
arose at once, and has persisted ever since, to act as a brake on any
policy of aggression. At first it consisted of the Tories, the clerical
party, the small landowners, the yeomen, the farmers. All of them
wanted to go riding and hunting, or till the soil, in peace. They
looked on all war as sheer Whig deviltry. European policies and overseas struggles were matters of supreme indifference to them, which
was not at all true of the tax burden which at that time fell primarily
on them.

The Whigs, for their part, were all the more belligerent. They were
the party of the great lords on the one hand, and the City on the
other. For, in the first place, colonial possessions at that time really
meant more than they do today. War was then still something it has
no longer been since about the time of the French Revolution—good
business. Again—and this is something that is overlooked unbeliev-
ably often—it behooved the Whigs to defend the newly won freedom—and with it their own position—against unquestionable aggressive intentions on the part of France. Finally, it was up to them to
hold those national positions throughout the world that had been
captured by their individual co-nationals rather than by the state as
such.

These last two factors make it appear doubtful whether it is proper
to speak of eighteenth-century English imperialism in our sense. At
the very least, it would be a very special imperialism, quite different
from the continental brand. As in the case of Spain, England at first
merely *defended* itself against France. True, the defense was so successful that it passed over into conquest. And it is also true that appetite appeared in the eating. The first of our three factors certainly
supported any and every predisposition toward war. The wars of that
period were commercial wars, *among other things*, but to describe them
*only* as commercial wars is simply historically untrue—for the French
as well as the English side of the question. It is noteworthy, furthermore, that it was not the English *state* that conquered the colonial
empire. Usually the state intervened in a protective capacity—generally with extreme reluctance and under duress—only when a colony
was already in existence. More than that, it cannot even be said that
it was "the people" who conquered the whole empire, that the leading

men embarked on conquest to the plaudits of the public. The conquerors were of an altogether different stripe—adventurers who were unable to find a solid footing at home, or men driven into exile. In the latter case there was the simple necessity for finding a new home. In the former it was a question of elements who, on the Continent, would have joined the armies of the sovereigns and vented their belligerent instincts on their own people or on some other European state. Since England had no sovereign who could have hired or paid them, they ventured out into the world and waged war on their own—"private imperialists," as it were. But the people refused to go along. No one was more unpopular than the slave trader, or the "nabob" who returned with his pockets full of plundered gold. Only with great effort could such a man secure social position. The public attitude toward him was similar to the reaction toward "war profiteers" nowadays. As often as not, he was hauled into court. But of course it is true that every war creates groups interested in that war. Armaments always create a predisposition toward war. And every war is father to another war.

England's attitude toward revolutionary France, like that of the continental states, was doubtless in part determined by lust for booty. But that attitude is seen in its true light only when it is compared with the character of the rule of the younger Pitt before the French Revolution. That character was most clearly expressed in the French Treaty of 1786. Pitt was a typical minister of peace. It was to peace, free trade, and the dissolution of mercantilism that England aspired under his leadership. Thus, the English attitude toward the France of the Revolution and of Napoleon must be understood as a departure from the prior trend rather than as a step along that line of evolution.[10] The period that followed showed that the Napoleonic wars were but an interlude. At first, England followed in the wake of the Holy Alliance,[11] which was anything but imperialist. And the earliest stirrings of an independent policy—in Huskisson's campaign for free trade—were linked to Pitt's prerevolutionary principles. As for Canning, his Greek policy struck a new note which, as we can see today, was intimately linked with free-trade trends and which may be summarized in the single word: *anti-imperialism*.

The two great parties, Tories and Whigs, maintained the foreign policy positions that have been indicated about as long as they did their names, to about 1840. Even the last typical Whig foreign ministers (and prime ministers), Palmerston and Russell, were "activist" in character. Yet all that was really left to them was the old bias, for the actual direction of their "activism" was forced on them by changed circumstances. They intervened everywhere in the world, generally in a challenging tone, ready to throw out military threats. They defended even unimportant interests with aggressive vigor— the classic expression of this aspect of their policy is Lord Palmerston's *Civis Romanus* speech of 1850. Toward the colonies, they stressed the claim of the central power to submission. But the people compelled them, first, to give a wide berth to what is called "economic imperialism"—a matter we have yet to discuss. Both were or became free traders. Both fought against the slave labor. And the people compelled them, second, to act on behalf of national liberation and against oppression, misgovernment, and imperialism, whenever they transcended England's immediate sphere of interests. This they did, and thus these men, whose political genealogy certainly had its roots elsewhere, became advocates of national, political, and religious self-determination throughout the world.[12] It has become the custom to describe this as "hypocrisy." But we are not at all concerned with the individual motives of these two statesmen. Suppose they were hypocrites, in the subjective sense—though it is far from easy for anyone to pretend a whole life long. Suppose this policy was mainly determined by the realization that it would open up to England inexhaustible resources of power and sympathy—which was what actually happened. The point that concerns us is that their policy was the only one that was tenable in England, in the parliamentary sense, that it was a means for winning political victories at home. It follows that it must have been in accord with the true intentions of the "important people" and, beyond them, of the masses. And the masses are never hypocritical.

It is not difficult to find an explanation. Moral progress is here directly linked with the "conditions of production." The sociological meaning of the process lies in the relationship between this policy and contemporary free-trade trends. The interests of trade and everyday life in England had turned pacifist, and the process of social restratification that marked the Industrial Revolution brought these interests to the fore. It was a process that only now bore all of its political fruits, and the interests it carried to the top were those of industry, in contradistinction to those of the trade monopolists of the seventeenth and eighteenth centuries. The principles of free trade were now carried to victory by Sir Robert Peel's Conservatives and later accepted even by Disraeli's new party. This was the original occasion for that "regrouping" of forces behind the political parties that ultimately led the industrial-capitalist class (including the banking fraternity) and almost the entire high aristocracy into the Conservative camp, while Liberalism became more and more the party of the Nonconformists and intellectuals—except for most clerics and lawyers—and, for a time, of working-class interests as well. And it was the great ministry of Sir Robert Peel that inaugurated, with complete logic, the policy that, despite many relapses into former habits, has become more and more the policy of England; a policy adopted by the Liberal Party through the instrumentality of Gladstone and under the influence of the rising power of the radicals, while the opposing trends gathered under the Conservative banner; a policy that for the first time seriously applied the full consequences of free trade,[13] emancipating itself from the old notions of the tasks of diplomacy; a policy that may be summarized under the following principles: never to intervene, unless vital interests are gravely and immediately threatened; never to be concerned about the "balance of power" on the Continent; not to arm for war; to reduce, by means of understandings, those areas of friction with other spheres of interest that were particularly extensive because of the lack of planning in the global structure of empire; to relieve tension and conflict by appropriate yielding, to the point where the remaining British sphere would be at least halfway tenable. That policy encountered immense difficulties in the acquired habits of political thought and emotional reaction, in concrete situations taken over from earlier times, in individual interests, and above all in the fact that championing it in Parliament in each case was generally a thankless task, offering ready-made points of attack to the opposition. Nevertheless, in spite of all aberrations, it prevailed time and again, because it was in accord with the objective interests of the politically important segments of the population, including, after the eighties, above all the industrial workers. From Peel to Lansdowne and Grey, it continually reasserted itself, like the level of a storm-tossed ocean.

We see therefore that the imperialist wave that in recent decades has been beating against the mainland of social evolution in England did not rise from the true depths of that evolution but was rather a temporary reaction of political sentiment and of threatened individual interests. Aggressive nationalism (to which we shall revert), the instincts of dominance and war derived from the distant past and alive down to the present—such things do not die overnight. From time to time they seek to come into their own, all the more vigorously when they find only dwindling gratifications within the social community. But where, as in England, there is a lack of sufficiently powerful interests with which those trends might ally themselves, an absence of warlike structural elements in the social organization, there they are condemned to political impotence. War may call them back to life, even lead to a more closely knit organization of the country, one that appears more aggressive toward the outside. But it cannot alter the basis of social and political structure. Even in England imperialism will remain a plaything of politics for a long time to come. But in terms of *practical* politics, there is no room left for it there—except possibly as a means for defense—nor any support among the real powers behind the policies of the day.[14]

## III. Imperialism in Practice

What imperialism looks like when it is not mere words, and what problems it offers, can best be illustrated by examples from antiquity. We shall select the Egyptian, Assyrian, and Persian empires and later add certain examples from a more recent period of history. We shall find characteristic differences among them, as well as one basic trait common to all, even the most modern brand of imperialism—a trait which for that reason alone cannot very well be the product of modern economic evolution.

The case of Egypt, down to the Persian occupation, is particularly instructive, because here we see the imperialist trend toward expansion actually in the making. The Egyptians of the "Old" and "Middle" empires—down to the Hyksos invasion—were a nation of peasants. The soil was the property of a hereditary, latifundian nobility which let it out to the peasants and which ruled in the political sense as well. This fundamental fact found organizational expression in a "regional" feudalism, an institution that was for the most part hereditary, rooted in real property, and, especially during the Middle Empire, quite independent of the crown. This social structure bore all the outward marks of force, yet it lacked any inherent tendency toward violent and unlimited expansion. The external situation ruled out such a trend; for the country, while easy to defend, was quite unsuitable as a base for a policy of conquest in the grand manner. Nor was it demanded by economic requirements—and indeed, no trace of such a policy is apparent. Throughout the period of the "Old" Empire of Memphis we learn of but one warlike undertaking (except for unimportant fighting on the Sinai peninsula). This was the campaigns in southern Syria under the Sixth Dynasty. In the "Middle" Empire of Thebes things were not quite so peaceful; still, fighting revolved essentially only about the defense of the frontiers. The single conquest was Nubia (under Amenemhat I and Usertesen III).

Things changed only after the expulsion of the Hyksos (whom Manetho counts as the Fifteenth and Sixteenth Dynasties), in the "New" Empire. The immediate successors of the liberator, Aahmes I, already conquered upper Cush to the third cataract and then reached farther into Asia. They grew more and more aggressive, and campaign followed campaign, without the slightest concrete cause. Dhutmes III and Amenhotep III were conquerors, pure and simple. In the end Egyptian rule reached to the Amanes and beyond the Euphrates. Following a reversal under the Nineteenth and Twentieth Dynasties, this policy was resumed, and after the Assyrian invasion (662) and the liberation by Psamtik I, Egypt, reunited under Necho II, again passed over to the attack, until the Battle of Karkamish (604) put an end to its Asiatic undertakings. Why did all this happen?

The facts enable us to diagnose the case. The war of liberation from the Hyksos, lasting a century and a half, had "militarized" Egypt. A class of professional soldiers had come into being, replacing the old peasant militia and technically far superior to it, owing to the employment of battle chariots, introduced, like the horse, by the Bedouin Hyksos. The support of that class enabled the victorious kings, as early as Aahmes I, to reorganize the empire centrally and to suppress the regional feudal lords and the large, aristocratic landowners—or at least to reduce their importance. We hear little about them in the "New" Empire. The crown thus carried out a social revolution; it became the ruling power, together with the new military and hierarchical aristocracy and, to an increasing degree, foreign mercenaries as well. This new social and political organization was essentially a war machine. It was motivated by warlike instincts and interests. Only in war could it find an outlet and maintain its domestic position. Without continual passages at arms it would necessarily have collapsed. Its external orientation was war, and war alone. Thus, war became the normal condition, alone conducive to the well-being of the organs of the body social that now existed. To take the field was a matter of course, the reasons for doing so were of subordinate importance. *Created by wars that required it, the machine now created the wars it required.* A will for broad conquest without tangible limits, for the capture of positions that were manifestly untenable—this was typical imperialism.

The case of the Persians is distinct from that of the Egyptians in that the former appear as a "warrior nation" from the very outset. What does that term mean? Manifestly, a nation whose social structure is oriented toward the military function, that does not need to be readjusted to that function by the power of the crown and a new warrior class, added at some time to the previously existing classes; a nation where the politically important classes—but not necessarily *all* the classes—view warfare as their main profession, are professional soldiers, do not need to be specially trained as such. The crucial point is *not* the mere capacity or inclination to resort to arms when the need arises. The landlords and even the peasants of Egypt were originally no strangers to the profession of arms. But it was *not* their profession as such. They took up arms much as the modern "civilian" joins the army—when they had to. Their lives were centered in the private rather than the military sphere. War was a nuisance—an abnormal emergency. What *is* the crucial point is that in a warrior nation war is never regarded as an emergency interfering with private life; but, on the contrary, that life and vocation are fully realized *only* in war. In a warrior nation the social community is a war community. Individuals are never absorbed into the private sphere. There is always an excess of energy, finding its natural complement in war. The will to war and violent expansion rises directly from the people —though this term is here not necessarily used in the democratic sense, as we shall see later. Hence the term "people's imperialism," which today is unquestionably nonsense, is in good standing when applied to a warrior nation.

The Persians offer a good example of such a warrior nation. True, even *their* organization did not emerge full-fledged until the conquest of Elam (second half of the sixth century). True, even with *them* the crown grew powerful only in the ensuing period of triumphs. And, despite continued adherence to universal, compulsory military service, they saw the rise of a more narrowly circumscribed standing army of personal followers that was to become the ruling class within the world empire. But despotism was a consequence of conquest, rather than the basis for the inauguration of a policy of conquest, the source of imperialist tendencies. Limitations on the royal power survived for a long time, as did the autonomy of the aristocracy, especially the ruling houses of the seven original tribes. This fact is readily understandable because the imperialist policy of the crown, instead of being at odds with the aristocracy, *rested on* it, merely formulated its policy. And the Persian people continued to occupy a position of preference within the empire. The king treated them with extreme care, offering them bounties and freedom from tribute. They constituted themselves the master class, though with a great measure of moderation. It was unnecessary to subject them to a special new system of military rule.

But the mere statement that we are here dealing with a "warrior nation" does not, of course, say everything. Indeed, this very character of the Persians as a warrior nation requires explanation. That explanation does not lie far afield. True, we do not know a great deal about the Persians before they entered into the limelight of history, but we do know enough about the prehistory of all Iranian Aryans to be able to reconstruct the prehistory of the Persians as well. It was geographic factors that made warriors of the Iranian Aryans. For them, war was the only method for keeping alive, the only possible form of life in a given environment. Warriors by environment, the Persians very probably reached the regions where history first finds them with sword in hand. And the psychological dispositions and organizational forms gained from such a mode of life persisted, continuing in an "objectless" manner. This is in accord with psychological developments that can be verified everywhere. The miser originally saves for good reasons, but beyond a certain point his hoarding ceases to be rational. The modern businessman acquires work habits because of the need for making a living, but labors far beyond the limits where acquisition still has rational meaning in the hedonist sense. Such phenomena have familiar parallels in the evolutionary facts of physical organisms and further parallels in the evolutionary facts of social phenomena, such as law, custom, and so on. Imperialism is such a phenomenon. The imperialism of a warrior nation, a people's imperialism, appears in history when a people has acquired a warlike disposition and a corresponding social organization *before* it has had an opportunity to be absorbed in the peaceful exploitation of its definitive area of settlement. Peoples who were so absorbed, such as the ancient Egyptians, the Chinese, or the Slavs, never of themselves develop imperialist tendencies, though they may be induced to do so by mercenary and generally alien armies. Peoples who were not preoccupied in this fashion—who were formed into a warlike pattern by their environment before they settled permanently, while they were still in a primitive stage of tribal or even clan organization—remain natural-born imperialists until centuries of peaceful work wear down that warlike disposition and undermine the corresponding social organization.

In the case of the Persians, we can thus understand what would otherwise remain incomprehensible—why the brief struggle for liberation from the Medes under Kurush II automatically turned into a war for the subjection of these former overlords and why this war reached out farther and farther. The Bactrians and Armenians were subjected. Babylon and Sardis were conquered. In the end Persian rule reached to the coast of Asia Minor, to the Caucasus and the Indus. A characteristic case was the conquest of Egypt by Cambyses. The invasion was made as a matter of course. One side prepared for it, the other side anticipated it, just as though any other course were out of the question. And, as history testifies, the Hellenic world was utterly baffled as to the reasons for the campaign. Just as happens today, public opinion looked primarily to personal motives on the part of the ruling men—a line of inquiry that turns history into a form of gossip richly embroidered with romance. As for Cambyses, he was a warrior and the overlord of a mighty power. He needed deeds, for himself and for it. Egypt was not a particularly suitable object of aggression—but there it was, and so it was attacked. The truth of this interpretation is proved by the fact that the Persians never dreamed of stopping in Egypt but were intent on pushing on, to Siwah and Carthage on the one hand, and to the south on the other—even though there were no princesses to offer convenient pretexts for war. These further advances largely miscarried, and the difficulties in the way of further penetration proved to be insurmountable. But we have here a failure of military power rather than of the will to conquest. This was also true of the conquests of Darius I, who developed the despotic police state without bringing about a change in policy.

True, pretexts for war were always found. There is no situation in which such pretexts are altogether lacking. What matters here is that the pretexts are quite unsuitable to form links in the chain of explanation of historic events—unless history is to be resolved into an account of the whims of great lords. This, after all, is precisely the point at issue—why to some peoples any pretext was good enough for war, why to them war was the *prima* rather than the *ultima ratio*, the most natural activity in the world. This is the question of the nature of the imperialist mentality and constitutes our problem.

Even less satisfactory than the explanation by flimsy pretexts is the theory that points to the interest in booty and tribute, or in commercial advantages. Of course such elements are never lacking. Yet the Persians, of all conquerors, were remarkably mild toward the peoples they subjugated. They never even remotely exploited them to the extent that would have been possible. Naturally they did seek some return from their conquests, once they had been made. The Persian king would become king of the country in question—as in the case of Egypt—or impose tribute or military levies on it. Yet there were never any cessions of privately owned land to Persians. The social organization of the conquered country usually remained intact. Religion, language, economic life suffered no harm. The leading men were often elevated to the imperial Persian aristocracy. Any concrete advantages were more in the nature of tokens of victory, esteemed as such, than of goals sought and exploited for their own sake.[15] Specifically nationalist trends are nowhere in evidence. The Persians did not "Persianize." In their proclamations, the kings often used several different languages. Unquestionably we have here a case of "pure" imperialism, unmixed with any element of nationalism. Any explanation derived from the cultural consequences which wars of conquest (at that time at least) could bring would be altogether inadmissible. Even today such cultural consequences are never consciously sought, in the sense that they could provide a decisive motive. Usually no one can foresee them clearly. There is no social force behind them. Moreover, they would be too much in the nature of "long-term promissory notes." In any event, they are beyond the mental horizon of the protagonists.

The religious element is conspicuously absent, with the Persians as with the Egyptians, a fact that is particularly noteworthy in the latter case. Both were tolerant to the point of indifference, especially the Persians, who actually fostered foreign cults. Outwardly this distinguishes their imperialism from that of the Assyrians. The Assyrians were Semites who migrated to Mesopotamia. They stuck to the upper reaches of the Tigris, where history finds them and whence they spread out, relatively undiluted by heterogeneous ethnic elements. Even Mesopotamia was not all—or nearly all—theirs until after the ninth century. Like the Persians, they were from the outset a "warrior nation," in the sense that has been defined; but, in contrast to the Persians, their organization, while aristocratic from earliest times, was along strictly despotic lines. The king himself was not divine, as in Egypt; he was merely the mandatory of the gods; yet despotism among the Assyrians was much more sharply marked than in Egypt, where it was regulated by a law higher than that of the king. Yet there is no evidence that a policy of imperialism was foisted on the Assyrian people by despotism. There was no special class of mercenaries, foreign or domestic. Down to the fall of Nineveh (606), massed native foot soldiers played an important role in the army. Battle chariots and cavalry were the weapons of the nobles, but they did not fight separately. War was the natural vocation of king and people. Culture, customs, script, religion, technology all came from Babylonia. The sovereigns who reigned in ancient Assur around 2000 called themselves Patisi, priest-kings. Not until about 1500, under Assur-bel-nishê-shu, did the royal title appear. This sacred character persisted in the Assyrian kingdom and in Assyrian policy. Assyrian wars were always, among other things, wars of religion, a fact that may be linked to their unmerciful cruelty. The enemy was always an "enemy of Assur."

At first Assyria expanded to the east and north, mostly at the expense of Babylonia. Once the borders of oldest Assyria, in the narrowest sense, had been crossed (under Assuruballit about 1400), there ensued a bloody struggle for command over the surrounding peoples and against Babylonia, a struggle that led to one success after another and, after a temporary setback in the thirteenth century, to

a pinnacle under Tuklâtî-pal-ísharra I (1115–1100). Then came a
time of quiescence for the peoples round about, but under Rammân-
nirâri II (911–890) and especially Assurnasirpal (884–860) the policy
of conquest that created the Assyrian world empire was inaugurated.
Although interrupted by domestic strife and brief periods of exhaustion, it endured until the Scythian assault weakened it to such an extent that it succumbed quite suddenly to the Median-Babylonian coalition. Year after year king and people took the field to conquer, lay
waste, pillage, and murder, with pretext or without. The vanquished
were crucified, impaled, flayed, immured alive by the thousands, or
had their eyes put out or limbs struck off. Conquered cities were usually destroyed, the inhabitants often burned with them. Expressions
like "grind into the dust" or "tinge the mountains with the blood of
the foe" recur time and again in the annals of the kings. A relief
sculpture from Khorsabad shows the king himself putting out the
eyes of prisoners with a lance, holding the victim's head firm by
means of a line fastened to a ring in his lower lip—an arrangement
indicating that this was a routine procedure. It was not that the kings
proceeded in this fashion only occasionally—say, in times of particular agitation. They all did it, without a single exception. The reason
was, in part, that these wars were often intended as wars of annihilation. The enemy population was often resettled in the interior of the
conquered country and replaced by Assyrians, and the survivors were
subjected to a pitiless regime of exploitation. There was an effort at
colonization and nationalization in order to weld into a single unit at
least the regions that lay closest to old Assyria.

The first attacks were aimed at Babylonia—which defended itself
longest—and at Armenia and Kurdistan. Then Syria and all the
countries to the Phoenician shores of the Mediterranean were conquered, and finally portions of Asia Minor and even Egypt. Any hesitation to undertake a campaign seems to have been regarded as an
extraordinary event. It *was*, in fact, exceptional, and when it occurred
repeatedly, as under Assur-nirâri (755–746), it weakened the position
of the crown. Yet not many complete successes were won. Babylonia
was vanquished only at a late date (709 and 689), and then only temporarily. Other peoples were never subdued. Despite all the furious
energy, the policy of violence failed time and again. Despite all the
measures of annihilation, territory that had already been conquered
had always to be conquered anew. The mistreated peoples defended
themselves with savage desperation. Uprisings in the end passed over
into wars of annihilation against the conqueror, and in 606 came the
dramatic end.

What answer would we get if we were to ask an Assyrian king:

"Why do you conquer without end? Why do you destroy one people after another, one city after another? Why do you put out the eyes of the vanquished? Why do you burn their habitations?" We would be told the official—perhaps even the conscious—motive. Tuklâtî-pal-ísharra I, for example, replied: "The God Assur, my Lord, commanded me to march. . . . I covered the lands of Saranit and Ammanit with ruins. . . . I chastized them, pursued their warriors like wild beasts, conquered their cities, took their gods with me. I made prisoners, seized their property, abandoned their cities to fire, laid them waste, destroyed them, made ruins and rubble of them, imposed on them the harshest yoke of my reign; and in their presence I made thank offerings to God Assur, my Lord." Characteristically, this account reads much like Assurnasirpal's report of a hunt: "The gods Nindar and Nirgal, who cherish my priestly office, gave the beasts of the desert into my hands. Thirty mighty elephants I killed, 257 huge wild bulls I brought down with arrows from my open chariot, in the irresistible power of my glory."

Such an answer from the king does not help us much. It is scarcely permissible to assume that he was lying or pretending—nor would that matter, one way or the other. But we can scarcely be disputed when we insist that the God Assur commanded and his prophet—in this case the king himself—proclaimed merely what was in keeping with the acquired habits of thought and emotional response of the people, their "spirit," formed by their environment in the dim past. It is also plain that conscious motives—no matter whether, in the concrete case, they were always religious in character—are seldom *true* motives in the sense of being free of deceptive ideologies; and that they are never the *sole* motives. Human motivation is always infinitely complex, and we are never aware of all its elements. The Assyrian policy of conquest, like any similar policy, must have had many auxiliary motives. Lust for blood and booty, avarice and the craving for power, sexual impulses, commercial interests (more prominent with the Assyrians than the Persians)—all these, blended to varying degrees, may have played their part in motivating individuals and groups; also operative was the unrestrained will to gratify instincts—precisely those instincts to which a warlike past had given predominance in the mentality. Such real motives are powerful allies of official motives (whether religious or otherwise), increase their striking power, or usurp their guise. This aspect of imperialism emerges more sharply in the Assyrian case than in any other. But it is never altogether absent, not even today.

Here too, however, the actual foundation of the religious motive—and here is the crucial formulation—is the urge to action. The direction of this urge, determined by the nation's development, is, as it were, codified in religion. It is this, too, that makes the God Assur a war god and as such insatiable. For the fact of definite religious precepts can never be accepted as ultimate. It must always be explained. In the case of the Assyrians this is not at all difficult. That is why I placed the hunting account beside the war report. It is evident that the king and his associates regarded war and the chase from the same aspect of *sport*—if that expression is permissible. In their lives, war occupied the same role as sports and games do in present-day life. It served to gratify activity urges springing from capacities and inclinations that had once been crucial to survival, though they had now outlived their usefulness. Foreign peoples were the favorite game and toward them the hunter's zeal assumed the forms of bitter national hatred and religious fanaticism. War and conquest were not means but ends. They were brutal, stark naked imperialism, inscribing its character in the annals of history with the same fervor that made the Assyrians exaggerate the size of the muscles in their statuary.

Naturally, imperialism of this kind is worlds removed from the imperialism of later ages. Yet in its innermost nature the imperialism of Louis XIV, for example, ranks beside that of the Assyrians. True, it is more difficult to analyze. The "instinctual" element of bloody primitivism recedes, is softened and overgrown by the efforts of both actors and spectators to make these tendencies comprehensible to themselves and others, to found them on reason, to direct them toward reasonable aims—just as the popular mind seeks to rationalize ancient customs, legal forms, and dogmas, the living meaning of which has been lost. In an objective sense the results of such efforts are nearly always fallacious, but that does not mean that they lack all significance. They indicate functional changes in social habits, legal forms, and so on. They show how these modes of thought and behavior can either be adapted to a new social environment and made useful or be weakened by rationalist criticism. That is why the newer imperialisms no longer look like the Assyrian brand, and that is why they are more easily misunderstood. Only a more searching comparison will put them in their proper light. But we shall now add to the examples already cited—which were to introduce us to the nature and the problem of imperialism—certain others that will enable us to discuss individual points of interest and that will serve as a bridge to modern times.

In order to illuminate especially the character of the religious brand of imperialism, let us briefly discuss the case of the Arabs. The relevant facts are simple and uncontroverted. The Arabs were mounted nomads, a persistent warrior type, like the nomadic Mongol

horsemen. At heart they have remained just that, despite all modifications of culture and organization. Only at a late date and incompletely did portions of the Arab people relinquish the equestrian profession—no one readjusts so slowly and with such difficulty as the
mounted nomad. Such people are never able to support themselves
alone, and in Arabia they constituted a master class that systematically
exploited for its own purposes, sometimes by means of outright robbery, the (likewise Semitic) population that had settled here and there
and was engaged in agriculture and trade. Internally the Arabs were
organized along thoroughly democratic lines, again like all mounted
nomads. It was a gentile and patriarchal type of democracy, in keeping with the "relations of production" that prevailed among a nation
of herdsmen and horsemen, and quite different from agrarian and
urban democracy—but democracy all the same in the sense that all
members of the nation carried political weight and that all political
expression grew from the people as a whole. The Arabs were divided
into loosely knit tribes, headed by a freely elected sheik or emir who
was dependent, in all affairs of importance, on the assent of the clan
chiefs. The stock from which the tribes developed constituted the primary community, the fundamental social bond.

There were three elements that brought this Arab world to the
stage of ferment. First of all, there was the alien rule of the Byzan-
tines and Persians, of which, by the end of the sixth century, only
Hejaz, Nejd, and Yemen had rid themselves. Second, in the realm of
ideas, there was the religious bond that existed between the tribes.
This was objectified in the ancient sanctuary of the Kaba at Mecca,
where all the tribes met and were exposed to religious currents of
every description, especially from the Semitic world, and where they
created a cultural as well as a religious center. The center itself, the
breeding place of new trends, was in the possession of a single tribe,
the Koreishites, who thereby assumed a privileged position, often at
odds with other interests. Even with the Koreish tribe the holy place
was in charge of a special clique, as always happens in such cases. In
the third place, an urban commercial culture, reaching out to draw
in certain individuals, clans, and tribes, developed in the centers of
communication, especially Mecca. This was bound to wear down
many corners of the old order and way of life and thinking, at the
same time opening a gulf between the elements so affected and the
simple, old-style Bedouins, to whom these things appeared alien and
dissonant. There appeared, at first purely by way of reaction, a movement of social reform or revolution, beginning in the early seventh
century. Pristine simplicity, a softening of the contrasts between poor
and rich, a voluntary relinquishment of the pursuit of profit—these

were Mohammed's first thoughts. He threw down the gage of battle to established interest and "acquired right," and his first practical demand was for a purge of the stain of money-grubbing by means of alms-giving.

Whatever his adherents may have thought, the interests that were threatened recognized the situation with the clarity peculiar to them and acted promptly. But their measures failed to destroy Mohammed, merely driving him out, and only a year after the Hegira he was able to make himself master of Medina. Thus, all they succeeded in doing was to force him, first, onto the defensive and, then, the offensive, with a corresponding shift in his viewpoint. The reformer of the sacred tribe became the aggressive fighter against the "infidels." Inner communion gave way to the call for war on behalf of the faith—the jihad—as the most important practical demand, the normal outward attitude of the faithful. Partly as a cause of this ideological orientation, partly as its consequence, there came into being a practical fighting organization, which reduced the element of inner communion to the role of a means for self-discipline on the part of the warrior, and to which the Bedouins took like ducks to water. Both ideology and organization proved their vitality and grew with the task for which they had been created—the struggle for Mecca and the unifying conversion of the Arab tribes. And when, suddenly, they had arrived, become firm, grown into a power, they followed the impulse they had received. Mohammed himself attempted to reach beyond Arabia (the campaign of Said), though without success. Abu Bekr, having developed the new politico-military organization and secured it against uprisings, invaded Syria without difficulty. Yet the new clerical warrior state remained democratic, despite the Caliph's wealth of temporal and clerical power. It could do so, because it had grown straight from the people. Loot was community property, to be distributed according to military rank. Not until Othman was the acquisition of land in the conquered countries permitted. The original idea had been that the Arabs would remain a master class, merely establishing garrisons. Under Omar, Persia was invaded—without any good reason, but with brilliant success. Byzantine Syria suffered the same fate at almost the same time. Then came Palestine, Phoenicia, Egypt. Christians and Jews were expelled from Arabia, forbidden to use Arab script and language. After a period of confusion came the culmination, under the Omayyads (661–750), when the center of empire shifted to Damascus. Ideology and organization began to lose their original impact. There was increasing differentiation and division of labor. The Arabs began to fuse with the conquered countries, and developing despotism did its work. Rigid centralism succumbed and the Occidental Caliphate separated from the Oriental. The Arab wave spent itself against Byzantium. But the basic outlines remained. North Africa and Spain were conquered. Frankish might rather than any lack of Arab will put an end to further penetration. In Asia it was the same story. Many armed actions still succeeded. A halt was called only when it was impossible to push on. And whenever a halt was called, internal difficulties erupted, destroying the empire in the end.

The diagnosis is simple. We are here face to face with a "warrior nation" and must explain from its circumstances how it came to be one. We see how internal struggles gave rise to a unified war organization behind which rallied all the popular forces—including those in the ideological sphere—a war machine that, once in motion, continued so long as there was steam behind it and it did not run up against a stone wall.[16] War was the normal function of this military theocracy. The leaders might discuss methods, but the basic issue was never in question. This point emerges with particular clarity, since the Arabs, for the most part, never troubled to look for even flimsy pretexts for war, nor did they even declare war. Their social organization needed war; without successful wars it would have collapsed. War, moreover, was the normal occupation of the members of the society. When there was no war, they would rebel or fall upon each other over theological controversies. The older social doctrine, especially the tendency to guard against merging with the conquered land and to keep the people fixed in the profession of arms, served the needs of this situation. Whenever that failed, whenever a new environment beckoned in another country with a richer background, whenever the Arabs settled down there, especially when they acquired land—then the impetus of war was spent and there developed such cultural centers as Cordoba, Cairo, and Bagdad. The energies of the best elements were diverted to other goals. We have, then, a typical case of "objectless," violent expansion, born of past necessities of life, grown to the proportions of a powerful drive by virtue of long habit, persisting to the point of exhaustion—a case of imperialism which we are able to view historically, precisely, and completely from its very origins to its death in the functional transformation of its energy.

What was the role played by the religious element, the commandments of Allah, the doctrine of the Prophet? These pervaded and dominated Arab life with an intensity that has few parallels in history. They determined daily conduct, shaped the whole world outlook. They permeated the mentality of the believer, made him someone who was characteristically different from all other men, opened up an unbridgeable gulf between him and the infidel, turning the latter into the arch enemy with whom there could be no true peace. These influences can be traced into every last detail of Arab policy. And most conspicuous of all in the whole structure of precepts is the call to holy war that opens wide the gates of paradise.

Yet if one sought to conclude that the religious element played a causative role in the Arab policy of conquest, that imperialism rooted in religion must therefore be a special phenomenon, one would come up against three facts. In the first place, it is possible to comprehend Arab policy quite apart from the religious element. It rises from factors that would have been present even without Allah's commandments and presumably would have taken effect even without them— as we saw in the example of the Persians. Some aspects of Arab imperialism may make sense only in the light of the Word of the Prophet, but its basic force we must clearly place elsewhere. In the second place, it was by no means true that religion was an independent factor that merely happened to be tending in the same direction as the imperialist drive for conquest. The interrelation between the Word of the Prophet and the data of the social environment (that by themselves already explain that drive) is too obvious to be overlooked. It was the Prophet of the mounted nomads who proclaimed war everlasting—not just *any* prophet. We simply cannot ignore the fact that such preachments came naturally to the Prophet and his followers. We cannot dispose of the question by positing a theoretical dominance and creative social force somehow peculiar to the religious element—as though some mysterious and unfathomable vision, remote from environmental pressures, had given rise to the Word of the Prophet in a vacuum, as it were, and as though that Word alone had driven the people forward *in agmen, in pulverem, in clamorem*. It is pointless to insist that the Word of the Prophet is an ultimate fact beyond which social science analysis cannot go, any more than it can transcend the data of physical nature—when that fact becomes easily understandable from the very social, psychic, and physical background that is itself quite adequate to explain fully what the Word of the Prophet is otherwise left to explain alone. Quite apart from trying to explain the unknown through the still less known, we would be resorting to a crutch that is quite unnecessary. But suppose we do accept the theory that the Prophet's doctrine existed *in vacuo*. In trying to understand its success, we would—to mention the third point— inevitably come up against the same situation that confronted us when we sought to grasp its basic spirit. It is only necessary to visualize what might have happened if the jihad had been preached to the unmilitary "fishermen" of Galilee, the "little people" in Palestine. Is it really farfetched to assume that they would not have followed the call, that they *could* not have followed it, that, had they tried any such thing, they would have failed wretchedly and destroyed their own community? And if, conversely, Mohammed had preached humility and submission to his Bedouin horsemen, would they not have turned their backs on him? And if they *had* followed him, would not *their* community have perished? A prophet does more than merely formulate a message acceptable to his early adherents; he is successful and comprehensible only when he also formulates a policy that is *valid* at the moment. This is precisely what distinguishes the successful—the "true"—prophet from his unsuccessful fellow—the "false" prophet. The "true" prophet recognizes the necessities of the existing situation—a situation that exists quite independently of him—and when these necessities subsequently change, he manages to adopt a new policy without letting the faithful feel that this transition is treachery.

I do not think this view can be disputed. What it means is that even in this highly charismatic case no causative role can be ascribed to the Word of the Prophet and that Arab imperialism must not be looked on as something unrelated to other imperialisms. What is true of Arab imperialism is true of any imperialism bearing a religious "coloration"—as we may now put it. This applies to states and peoples, but not, of course, to the expansive drives of religious communities as such—that of the Catholic Church in the Middle Ages, for example. It too did not shrink from brute force and resort to religious warfare. Too often it exploited the instinct for conquest—which played an important part in the Crusades, for example—and often served the instinct for power as well—as in the case of many a Pope. Whenever it was dominated by a state, as happened at times, for example under the Roman emperors and later under Charlemagne and Henry III, the expansive drive of the faith at once showed signs of merging into the expansive trend of the state in question; and if this did not happen on a more intensive scale, it was only because the relationship between the universal state and the Church never endured for very long. Such incidents, however, remained accessory aberrations; for, by and large and to an ever increasing degree, the Church maintained itself as a specifically clerical, super-governmental, and supernational power, not merely ideologically but also practically, in accordance with the power resources and organizational methods at its disposal. Hence its will to conquest remained a mere will to convert. In the course of this mission of conversion and in the political interests of the Church, the military subjugation of one country by another might on occasion be desirable, but it was never an end in itself. Conversion without such conquest would have been—and usually was—sufficient in such cases. The ideologically appropriate method—and the customary one—was the sermon. What needed to be spread was the rule of dogma and the corresponding organization of religious, not political, life. In this process natural instincts of pugnacity could be vented only incidentally and rarely. This is clearly seen from the characteristic fact that the devoutly Catholic Spaniards never dreamed of giving a religious motivation to their overseas conquests, though these conquests did indeed serve the interests of the Church.[17] Here, then, there is an essentially different element that would stamp such a religious imperialism as something distinct, something with outright religious causation—if, that is, we can really speak of imperialism in this case. We do not propose to do so and are holding this phenomenon up to view only to the extent that it interacts with the imperialisms of nations and states.

The Arabs, for their part, did not proselytize. When the inhabitants of conquered countries adopted Mohammedanism *en masse*, this was not the result of a deliberate plan by the conquerors, though it was an entirely plausible process of adaptation. Nor did the Arabs annihilate the infidels. On the contrary, they were treated with remarkable mildness. Neither conversion nor annihilation would have accorded with the Arab brand of war on behalf of the faith. From the viewpoint of their interests, neither course would have paid, for they were dependent on the labor and tribute of subjugated peoples for their livelihood, for their chance to remain a parasitical warrior and master nation. Once the infidel was converted or killed, an object of exploitation was lost, an element that was necessary to Arab life and social organization was sacrificed. Thus, the Arabs were quite content to leave the infidels their faith, their lives, and their property. Let them remain infidels. What mattered was that they must serve the faithful. There was never any objection that such a policy might be wrong since it perpetuated the existence of infidels—an argument that should carry much weight with religious sentiment and that was, indeed, always decisive in the case of Christian sentiment as embodied in the Catholic Church. However this policy may fit into the inner logic of the Mohammedan religion,[18] it *was* Arab practice. And this is precisely what characterizes the position of the religious element in this case. The meaning of the struggle was not the spreading of the faith but the spreading of Arab rule—in other words, war and conquest for their own sake.

This does not, of course, mean that we deny the significance of religious commandments in the consciousness of the people. Had an Arab been asked why he fought, he might, as a born warrior, on proper reflection have countered with the question as to why one lived. That is how self-evident, how far above all rational thought, war and the urge for expansion were to him. But he would not have given such a reply. He would have said: "I fight because Allah and his Prophet will it." And this reply gave him an emotional prop in his struggle, provided him with a mode of conduct that preserved his character as a warrior. Religion was more than a mere reflex, certainly within the body social. It is not my intention to pursue this approach to the extreme, particularly since we here touch on problems that reach far too deeply to be disposed of within the framework of our topic. It was for that reason that I emphasized just now the possibility of the religious idea's taking on a social life of its own, in the example of Christianity. But the imperialism of a people or a state can never be explained in this fashion.

Arab imperialism was, among other things, a form of popular imperialism. In examining this type at greater length, let us select the example of the ancient Germans. We know far too little of their prehistory to be able to assert that they were a warrior nation in our sense during that period. It is probable that they were not—this is indicated by the high stage of development that agriculture had attained among them—which does not rule out that certain tribes, at an early date, acquired warlike habits by piracy, enslavement, and so on. True, the picture of them drawn by Tacitus does not accord with the assumption that the Germans were an agricultural people, with an aristocracy that was neither large nor exalted. Other reports likewise fail to support such a view, which, nevertheless, prevailed rather uniformly among historians down to the year 1896. Wittich, Knapp, and Hildebrand then raised their voices in opposition, though it does not seem that their views will prevail. In any event, the Great Migrations made warrior nations of the Germanic tribes (similar circumstances had had this result even earlier in the case of the Cimbrians and Teutons)—especially those tribes that had to traverse great distances. Even these, however, usually lacked the imperialist *élan*. They were looking for new areas of settlement, nothing more. When they found such areas, they were content. They did not reach farther and farther—they were too weak for that. It is true that the East and West Goths, the Vandals, and the Lombards did constitute themselves as military master peoples, but that was a necessity from the point of view of self-preservation. We find only one indubitable case of imperialism—that of the Salian Franks. Since the third century, alliances had welded together their various tribes and in the fourth and fifth centuries they spread westward across the Rhine, following the retreating Roman legions. All the while they clung to their tribal territory, but on the other hand they displaced or destroyed the Roman-Celtic population, actually and continually expanding their national domain. This paved the way for the far-reaching policies of Clovis I, who first began vigorous attacks on the Roman power (Battle of Soissons, 486) and shifted the center of his empire to Paris, then exterminated his Frankish co-princes, thereby uniting all Franks, and finally subjugated even Germanic tribes (first the Alemanni, then the Burgundians, and at last the West Goths in Aquitania). Despite the division of the empire, Clovis's successors continued his policies, at first with some success (subjugation of Thuringia, completion of the conquest of Burgundy, adherence of Bavaria). This policy of conquest was typical imperialism. Without any regard for "interests" or "pretexts"—though the latter, of course, were always at hand—indeed, sometimes without the slightest pretext at all, Clovis and his immediate successors simply reached out as far as their power permitted—into limitless space, as it were. There was not even a major organizational principle, as is shown by the division of the empire. The Franks were simply driven forward by instincts of war and power. The report by Gregory of Tours reads like a report about the Assyrian kings. The religious element played precisely the same role. Gregory has his hero say, before the attack on Aquitania: "I am furious that these Arians rule any part of Gaul. With God's help we shall take the field and subject the land to our will." The account of the murders of the other Frankish princes closes with these words: "Thus, day after day, God felled the enemies of Clovis the Christian under His fist, for Clovis walked in the path of righteousness and his deeds were pleasing in the eyes of the Lord."

This was a popular imperialism. True, the royal power grew with its successes, with the direct acquisition of vast areas of land—quite apart from the controversial question of its "sovereignty" over all land—with control over the Church, and, finally with the allegiance of an ever-growing number of warriors and other beneficiaries of war who were directly dependent on the crown. Yet the whole people still participated—insofar as they carried political weight. This meant not merely the uppermost stratum—although even then the organization of society was rather aristocratic in character—nor did it mean a special warrior class. The kings still depended on the approval of broad groups much more than on the "powerful." Their own power was neither so unlimited nor so firm that they could afford to pursue unpopular policies. There may be much room for controversy about the social structure of the Merovingian period, but the conclusion is inescapable that the imperialist will to battle and conquest was the people's will, and that the king could have been no more than the leader and spokesman of this widespread disposition.

This is entirely plausible. Struggles for the maintenance and extension of their area of settlement had temporarily made a warrior nation of the Franks. In this fashion alone can an entire people become oriented toward imperialism, and that is what happened to the Franks. Our example enables us to observe not only the origin but also the gradual disappearance of imperialist tendencies. In the case of the Franks, the "habit of conquest" did not go back far enough to become enduringly fixed, as in the case of the Arabs. Even while they were engaged in conquest, the Franks remained predominantly tillers of the soil. Unlike the Arabs, they did not constitute themselves an armed camp in enemy territory. Thus, the popular will to conquest as such soon vanished, once large numbers of Franks had ensconced themselves comfortably in new areas of settlement—the upper strata, in part, also among alien populations of the empire. Once again they were swallowed up by the private sphere of agriculture, hunting, local guerrilla warfare—the life of village, estate, and province. The people very soon lost all interest in imperial politics, all contact with the central power. They insisted vigorously on protecting themselves against excessive central authority at home and adventure abroad. This explains why the empire was always on the verge of flying apart, why the temporal and clerical powers so readily obtained the "Magna Carta" of 614, why after the middle of the seventh century local authorities arose everywhere. Despite the prospect of booty and the opportunities which war then opened up to individuals, the masses began to resent universal military service, the nobles their feudal service. True, the Franks did remain a belligerent people. They eagerly resorted to arms. But they could no longer be enlisted on behalf of plans of unlimited conquest, for a policy that would remove them from their homes and interests too often for long periods of time. We see that not every warlike nation tends toward imperialism. There must be other circumstances, especially forms of social organization. Above all, in order to exhibit a continual trend toward imperialism, a people must not live on—or at least not be absorbed by— its own labor. When that happens, the instincts of conquest are completely submerged in the economic concerns of the day. In such a case even the nobles—unless a special military class arises—cannot evade the economic pressure, even though they themselves may remain parasitical in economic sense. They become content with the peaceful administration of their estates and offices, with hunting and local skirmishing.

In this connection it is interesting to compare the second, Carolingian wave of Frankish imperialism with the Merovingian wave that preceded it. If Merovingian imperialism was definitely "popular" in character, Carolingian just as certainly was not. Even the older Car-

olingians, who reunited the empire before Charlemagne, had to resort to special measures to muster an army against the Arabs. They
were compelled to organize a special warrior class with an economic
base of its own, professional knights, subsisting on Church lands. The
people failed to support the crown, except in the case of an undertaking in the immediate vicinity of their homes, and the crown thus
had to create a special group of vassals. These had to be enabled to
live without working, if they were to be readily available—in other
words, they needed benefices. Thus the feudal system arose, the technical innovation of the mounted army being far more a consequence
than a cause of this social development. True, Charlemagne still resorted to the general levy, but in the face of rising resistance, as seen
from the importance popularly attributed to draft indemnities. The
people fled from the imperialism of the crown into protective dependence on local authority. And it was the vassals who were the main
support of Charlemagne's imperialist policies, even in a political
sense. This emerged quite characteristically early in his reign, in his
differences with Carloman. It was precisely imperialism that was at
stake in this controversy. Carloman sought peace with the Lombards,
and he was supported by the people who "counted." Charlemagne
wanted war with them, as a first step along his path of a universal
imperialism embroidered with Roman and religious elements. Charlemagne and his policies prevailed. But his successors failed because
their peoples, though aristocratically organized, were basically anti-
imperialist.

   Let us add that these observations also apply to the imperialism,
centering in Italy, of the German kings of the Middle Ages. Historians are fond of speculating what may have persuaded Otto I to undertake his Italian campaign, for they rightly find his motives obscure. Such inquiry into personal motivation is futile and irrelevant.
All the German kings who pursued such a policy faced the same situation. Their power rested primarily on the political and economic
position of their dynasties, which was independent of the royal title.
As the chiefs of their tribes they had estates, vassals, legitimate usufructs within their territory, and the opportunity to exploit their people even beyond legal limits. Acquisition of the crown gained them
imperial estates and usufructs, sovereignty over the independent cities, and intimate contact with high ecclesiastics and imperial vassals.
Actually, however, their fellow dukes and princes could be counted
among these royal vassals to only a limited degree. Instead, they felt
themselves to be relatively independent powers in their own right.
Each king had to win their allegiance anew, sometimes actually to
subdue them. They were unwilling either to let the king interfere in

the internal affairs of their territories, or to give unconditional support to any foreign policy. These territories, after all, were not mere
administrative districts, but living political entities with interests of
their own. For every one of the Ottonians, Salians, and Hohenstaufens, the conquest of power within the empire was the primary task.
When that had been solved to some degree, each of them had a fighting organization of his own, a feudal army enlisted under his banner
which needed work and subsistence. At the same time each of them
knew how narrow was the foundation on which he stood, how quickly
success, once gained, might be frittered away. Above all, in order to
rule Germany they needed money, for the amount of land that could
be handed out was limited and, besides, every enfeoffment soon
alienated the liegeman from the crown. Germany was unable to offer
such funds to the crown, not because of poverty, but because of its
form of organization. The kings therefore needed a territory where
they might rule absolutely, not merely as feudal overlords. Italy was
such a territory. Its conquest would preoccupy the feudal army—satisfy it, tie it firmly to the king, weld it into a professional army. Had
it really been possible to conquer Italy, all the German elements that
were avid for war and booty would have rallied to the royal colors.
The king would have been able to pay them and perhaps to conquer
the entire Mediterranean basin. This would have automatically made
him master of Germany as well, for the local centers of authority
would have lost their warriors to him—would have become deflated,
as it were. Whatever may have been in the mind of Otto I, this was
the situation and this was the meaning of the Italian policy. We see it
most clearly in Frederick II, who quite probably pursued it in full
awareness of the goal of ruling Italy by the power of German knighthood, and ruling Germany by the power of Italian money, making
both countries his base for a far-reaching policy of conquest. Thus,
a policy otherwise suggesting an almost incredible lack of political sa-
gacity becomes entirely comprehensible. It was quite safe to dole out
the remaining imperial and dynastic lands in Germany, to surrender
one royal prerogative after another to the princes, to sacrifice even
the cities responsible directly to the crown—in other words, to deprive the royal power in Germany of its basis—for the sake of a temporary respite. All this was quite safe—*if* there was the hope of creating in Italy, far more effectively than by guerrilla warfare with the
German princes, a mighty bastion of power that would serve to re-
gain the relinquished positions in Germany. Frederick II came close
to attaining his goal. He created the state of Naples for himself and
was able to function as its despot. Had he met with success against the
Pope and the Lombards, he would have become master of the situa-

tion even in Germany; and undoubtedly enterprises in the nature of crusades—such as Frederick II actually inaugurated—would have followed, as would have, perhaps, attacks on France and Spain. But full success was wanting, and the whole policy ended in disaster for the imperial power. The essential meaning of the policy had been to strengthen the royal power even in Germany, but when only its negative rather than its positive fruits were realized, it appeared as a policy of surrender to regional authority, the pointless pursuit of a phantom. In essence the policy was imperialist. But it was the imperialism of a ruler rather than of a people. That is precisely why it failed, for the people and the nobles would have none of it. And because it failed, the royal power bled to death. Here we have an interesting example of an anti-imperialist warrior aristocracy.

Within the framework of the present study, we can be concerned only with examining our problem with the help of certain typical examples; yet we shall briefly glance at two further instances where the diagnosis is subject to certain doubts. The first case is the imperialism of Alexander the Great. The essential feature is that here, instead of the founding of a new world empire by piling conquest on conquest—which takes much time, a sharply focused will on the part of the ruling classes of a people, or a long succession of despots—instead of this, the central power of an already existing empire was overturned by a swift blow, only to be picked up by the victor. It would not have been very much different if some Persian satrap had led a successful rebellion and lifted himself into the saddle. That this was so is clearly seen from the fact that Alexander, once he had reached his goal, at once established himself as a Persian king. While he was intent on rewarding his Macedonians and preserving their military power, he could not even dream of making them a ruling people. True, he penetrated beyond the frontiers of the Persian empire, but this was nothing but an essentially individual adventure. He availed himself of the Macedonian military machine, which had grown to maturity, first in the struggle for the coast of Macedonia itself, and then in a miniature imperialism against the Scythians and Greeks, and which was on the verge of attacking Persia even without him; yet he transformed the situation into a policy that was anything but Macedonian imperialism. Nor was there anything that one might be tempted to call Greek cultural imperialism. Obviously the domain of Greek culture expanded by virtue of Alexander's conquests, but not substantially more than it would have done in the course of times even without him. What was aggressive in this situation was neither Greek culture, nor Greek commercial interest, but a warrior who saw the tempting bait of a great empire before him. This was neither the imperialism of a state, nor that of a people, but rather a kind of individual imperialism that is of no further interest to us, akin but not identical to the imperialism of the Caesars, that is to say, of politicians whose stature rises with their military missions, who need ever new military successes to maintain their position—men like Julius Caesar himself and Napoleon I, for example.

The second case on which we shall touch is the imperialism of Rome. We must bear in mind above all in this connection that the policy of the empire was directed only toward its preservation and therefore was not imperialist within our definition. True, there was almost continuous warfare, because the existing situation could be maintained only by military means. Individual emperors (Germanicus, for example) might wage war for its own sake, in keeping with our definition, but neither the Senate nor the emperors were generally inclined toward new conquests. Even Augustus did no more than secure the frontiers. After Germanicus had been recalled, Tiberius tried to put into effect a policy of peace toward the Germans. And even Trajan's conquests can be explained from a desire to render the empire more tenable. Most of the emperors tried to solve the problem by concessions and appeasement. But from the Punic Wars to Augustus there was undoubtedly an imperialist period, a time of unbounded will to conquest.

The policies of this epoch are not as naively manifest as those in the other cases discussed so far. Here is the classic example of that kind of insincerity in both foreign and domestic affairs which permeates not only avowed motives but also probably the conscious motives of the actors themselves—of that policy which pretends to aspire to peace but unerringly generates war, the policy of continual preparation for war, the policy of meddlesome interventionism. There was no corner of the known world where some interest was not alleged to be in danger or under actual attack. If the interests were not Roman, they were those of Rome's allies; and if Rome had no allies, then allies would be invented. When it was utterly impossible to contrive such an interest—why, then it was the national honor that had been insulted. The fight was always invested with an aura of legality. Rome was always being attacked by evil-minded neighbors, always fighting for a breathing space. The whole world was pervaded by a host of enemies, and it was manifestly Rome's duty to guard against their indubitably aggressive designs. They were enemies who only waited to fall on the Roman people. Even less than in the cases that have already been discussed, can an attempt be made here to comprehend these wars of conquest from the point of view of concrete objectives. Here there was neither a warrior nation in our sense, nor, in the beginning, a military despotism or an aristocracy of specifically military orientation. Thus, there is but one way to an understanding: scrutiny of domestic class interests, the question of who stood to gain.

It was certainly not the Italian peasant. The conquests gained him nothing—on the contrary, they made possible competition on the part of the foreign grain, one of the causes for his disappearance. He may not have been able to foresee that eventuality in the republican period, but he did feel all the more keenly the burden of military service that was always interfering with his concerns, often destroying his livelihood. True, it was this class that gave rise to the caste of professional soldiers who remained in the military service beyond the minimum term of enlistment. But in the first place, the rise of that estate was only a consequence of the policy of war, and, in the second place, even these people had no real interest in war. They were not impelled by savage pugnacity, but by hope for a secure old age, preferably the allotment of a small farm. And the veteran would much rather have such a farm at home than somewhere in Syria or Britain. As for war booty, the emperor used it to pay his debts or to stage circuses at Rome. The soldiers never saw much of it. The situation of the Roman proletariat was different. Owing to its peculiar position as the democratic puppet of ambitious politicians and as the mouthpiece of a popular will inspired by the rulers, it did indeed get the benefit of much of the booty. So long as there was good reason to maintain the fiction that the population of Rome constituted the Roman people and could decide the destinies of the empire, much did depend on its good temper, and mass corruption was the stock-in-trade of every political career. But again, the very existence, in such large numbers, of this proletariat, as well as its political importance, was the consequence of a social process that also explains the policy of conquest. For this was the causal connection: The occupation of public land and the robbery of peasant land formed the basis of a system of large estates, operating extensively and with slave labor. At the same time the displaced peasants streamed into the city and the soldiers remained landless—hence the war policy.

The latifundian landowners were, of course, deeply interested in waging war. Quite apart from the fact that they needed slaves, whom war provided in the cheapest way, their social and economic position—that of the Senatorial aristocracy—would have become untenable the moment the Roman citizen thought he was menaced by an enemy and might have to fight for the interest or the honor of the country. The alternative to war was agrarian reform. The landed aristocracy could counter the perpetual threat of revolution only with the glory of victorious leadership. Had it remained an aristocracy of large yeomen or become one of landed nobles—as was the aristocracy of the German Middle Ages and of the later empire—its position would not have been so dangerous. But it was an aristocracy of land-lords, large-scale agricultural entrepreneurs, born of struggle against their own people. It rested solely on control of the state machine. Its only safeguard lay in national glory. Its only possible course was pre-occupation with the foreign-policy contingencies of the state, which were in any case a mystery to the citizens.

This does not mean that the individual senator, when he pleaded for another war, was always mindful of these circumstances. Such things never rise into full consciousness. An unstable social structure of this kind merely creates a general disposition to watch for pretexts for war—often held to be adequate with entire good faith—and to turn to questions of foreign policy whenever the discussion of social problems grew too troublesome for comfort. The ruling class was al-ways inclined to declare that the country was in danger, when it was really only class interests that were threatened. Added to this, of course, were groups of every description who were interested in war, beginning with the political type we have called the Caesar—a type that often went farther than the Senate liked, creating situations where it sometimes became necessary to apply the brakes—and reaching down to army suppliers and those leeches in the conquered provinces, the procurators who represented the conquering military leaders. But here too we deal with consequences rather than causes. And another consequence that always emerges in imperialism was the phenomenon that the policy of conquest inevitably led to situations that compelled further conquests. Once this road was entered upon, it was difficult to call a halt, and finally the results far transcended what anyone had originally desired or aspired to. Indeed, such a pol-icy almost automatically turned against the very aims for the sake of which it had been designed. The empire became ungovernable, even by an aristocracy as highly gifted in a political sense as was the Ro-man. It evaded the rule of that aristocracy, and in the end military despotism went over the heads of the aristocrats and passed on to the order of the day. History offers no better example of imperialism rooted in the domestic political situation and derived from class struc-ture.

## IV. Imperialism in the Modern Absolute Monarchy

At the threshold of modern Europe there stands a form of imperial-ism that is of special interest to us. It is rooted in the nature of the absolutist state of the seventeenth and eighteenth centuries which was, everywhere on the Continent, the result of the victory of the monarchy over the estates and classes. Everywhere on the Continent, in the sixteenth and seventeenth centuries, these struggles broke the political back of the people, leaving only the prince and his soldiers and officials on the devastated soil of earlier political factions. Of the whole family of constitutions in western and central Europe, only the English constitution maintained itself. Whenever there was enough power and activity in the autocratic state, imperialist tendencies began to stir, notably in Spain, France, and the larger territories of Germany. Let us take France as an example.

Of the eight virtually independent principalities that threatened to divide the West Frankish empire among themselves on the decline of the Carolingians, the duchy of France, through the rise of the Capets, came to be the foundation not only of the royal title but also of a royal policy that, despite certain relapses, continued steadfastly. Even Abbé Suger, under Louis VI and Louis VII, had already formulated the principles that were ultimately to lead that policy to victory. The obvious aims were to fight against the other seven principalities and against the rural nobility, which in France, too, enjoyed virtual independence and lived only for its private feuds and its own undertakings abroad. The obvious tactics were the representation of the interests of the Church, the cities, and the peasantry, with the help of a small standing army (*maison du roi*, originally formed from a few hundred poor noblemen). The Hundred Years' War with England served to develop national sentiment and to bring the kingship to the fore. It had the effect of rallying the immense war potential of the aristocracy to the crown and of gradually disciplining the aristocracy as well. Crusades and other foreign operations were contributory factors. As early as St. Louis, the kingship rested on a broad political foundation which was quite equal to the revolts of the nobles that kept breaking out all the time, and also to the power of the Popes. As early as the last Capet an orderly tax administration had developed. The house of Valois continued the policy—more accurately, the policy continued under that dynasty, for nothing is further from our mind than to seek to explain a historical process simply by the actions of individuals. Charles V temporarily subdued the nobility and mastered the cities for good, subjecting them to a policy of mercantilism. Under Charles VII the army was reorganized along modern lines (1439) and a larger standing army was established. Louis XI completed the construction of the unified national state, and under him the provincial estates lost much of their importance. The internecine warfare among the nobles during the religious wars of the sixteenth century

did the rest, and from there the road led, by way of Sully and Riche-
lieu, to the culmination of this development in Louis XIV. Let us examine his situation.

He was master of the machinery of state. His ancestors had gradually created this position by military force; or rather, in a military
sense, it had been created in the course of the development of the
national state, for that course manifested itself in military struggle,
and the centralized state could arise only when one of the military
powers originally present triumphed over the others, absorbing what
was left of them in the way of military strength and initiative. In
France, as elsewhere, the absolutist national state meant the military
organization of the martial elements of the nation, in effect a war
machine. True, this was not its entire meaning and cultural significance. Now that national unity was achieved, now that, since the victory over Spain, no external enemy offered a serious threat any
longer, there might have been disarmament—the military element
might have been permitted to recede. The state would not have
ceased to exist or failed to fulfill its function on that account. But the
foundations of royal power rested on this military character of the
state and on the social factors and psychological tendencies it expressed. Hence it *was* maintained, even though the causes that had
brought it to the fore had disappeared. Hence the war machine continued to impress its mark on the state. Hence the king felt himself
to be primarily a warlord, adorned himself preeminently with military emblems. Hence his chief concern was to maintain a large, well-
equipped army, one that remained active and was directly tied to his
person. All other functions he might delegate to his subordinates.
But this one—supreme command of the army and with it the direction of foreign affairs—he claimed as his own prerogative. When he
was unable to exercise it, he at least made a pretense of personal military efficiency. Any other inadequacy he and the dominant groups
might have pardoned. Military shortcomings, however, were dangerous, and when they were present—which doubtless was the case with
Louis XIV—they had to be carefully concealed. The king might not
actually be a hero in the battle, but he had to have the reputation of
being one.

The necessity for this attitude flows from the social structure of the
period. In a political sense neither the peasantry nor the working
masses carried weight—and this was true in the social sense as well.
In its fight against the nobility, the crown had occasionally champi-
oned both, but essentially they were and remained helots, to be disposed of at will—not only economically exploited but even, against
their will, trained to be blindly obeying soldiers. The urban middle

class was also virtually beholden to the crown, though not quite so unconditionally. Once a valuable ally in the struggle against the nobility, it had become a mere servant. It had to obey, was molded by the crown along the lines of greatest financial return. The Church likewise paid for its national opposition to Rome with strict submission to the royal power. To this extent the king was actually, not merely legally, the master. It was of little concern to him—within eventually quite wide limits—what all these people who were forced to submit to him thought. But that was not true of the aristocracy. It too had had to submit to the crown, surrendering its independence and political rights—or at least the opportunity to exercise them. The stiff-necked rural nobility that once had both feet firmly planted in the soil amid its people had turned into a court aristocracy of extreme outward servility. Yet its social position remained intact. It still had its estates, and its members had retained their prestige in their own immediate neighborhoods. The peasants were more or less at its mercy. Each of the great houses still had its dependent circle among the lower nobility. Thus, the aristocracy as a whole was still a power factor that had to be taken into account. Its submission to the crown was more in the nature of a settlement than a surrender. It resembled an election—a compulsory one, to be sure—of the king as the leader and executive organ of the nobility. Politically the nobility ruled far more completely *through* the king than it once did while it challenged his power. At that time, after all, the still independent cities did form a modest counterpoise to the nobility. Had the king, for example, conceived the notion of translating into action his pose as the protector of the lowest population strata, the nobility would have been able to squelch any such attempt by mere passive resistance—as happened in Austria in the case of Joseph II. The nobles would have merely had to retire to their chateaus in order to bring into play, even outwardly, the actual foundations of their power, in order to become again a reasonably independent rural nobility which would have been capable of putting up a good fight.

The reason they did no such thing was, in essence, because the king did what they wanted and placed the domestic resources of the state at their disposal. But the king was aware of the danger. He was carefully intent on remaining the leader of the aristocracy. Hence he drew its members to his court, rewarded those that came, sought to injure and discredit those that did not. He endeavored successfully to have only those play a part who had entered into relations with him and to foster the view, within the aristocracy, that only the *gens de la cour*—court society—could be considered to have full and authoritative standing. Viewed in this light, those aspects that historians customarily dispose of as court extravagance and arbitrary and avoidable mismanagement take on an altogether different meaning. It was a class rather than an individual that was actually master of the state. That class needed a brilliant center, and the court had to be such a center—otherwise it might all too readily have become a parliament. But whoever remained away from his estates for long periods of time was likely to suffer economic loss. The court had to indemnify him if it wished to hold him—with missions, commands, offices, pensions— all of which had to be lucrative and entail no work. The aristocracy remained loyal only because the king did precisely this. The large surplus beyond the requirements of debt service and administration which had existed at the outset of the era of Louis XIV, together with all the borrowings the crown was able to contrive—all this fell only nominally to the crown. Actually it had to be shared with the nobility which, in this fashion, received a pension from the pockets of the taxpayers.

A system of this kind was essentially untenable. It placed shackles of gold on real ability that sought outlet in action, bought up every natural opportunity for such talent to apply itself. There they were at Versailles, all these aristocrats—socially interned, consigned to amuse themselves under the monarch's gracious smile. There was absolutely nothing to do but to engage in flirtation, sports, and court festivities. These are fine pastimes, but they are life-filling only for relatively rare connoisseurs. Unless the nobles were to be allowed to revolt, they had to be kept busy. Now all the noble families whose members were amusing themselves at Versailles could look back on a warlike past, martial ideas and phrases, bellicose instincts. To ninety-nine out of a hundred of them, "action" meant military action. If civil war was to be avoided, then external wars were required. Foreign campaigns preoccupied and satisfied the nobility. From the viewpoint of the crown they were harmless and even advantageous. As it was, the crown was in control of the military machine, which must not be allowed to rust or languish. Tradition—as always surviving its usefulness—favored war as the natural pursuit of kings. And finally, the monarchy needed outward successes to maintain its position at home—how much it needed them was later shown when the pendulum swung to the other extreme, under Louis XV and Louis XVI. Small wonder that France took the field on every possible occasion, with an excess of enthusiasm that becomes wholly understandable from its position[19] and that left it quite indifferent to the actual nature of the occasion. Any war would do. If only there was war, the details of foreign policy were gladly left to the king.

Thus, the belligerence and war policy of the autocratic state are explained from the necessities of its social structure, from the inherited dispositions of its ruling class, rather than from the immediate advantages to be derived by conquest. In calculating these advantages it is necessary to realize that possible gains to the bourgeoisie were not necessarily valid motives. For the king was in control of foreign policy, and bourgeois interests, on the whole rather impotent, weighed in the balance only when the king stood to gain by them. Certainly he stood to gain tax revenue when he promoted trade and commerce. But even then wars had already grown so costly that they might be doubtful risks to the king even though they offered indubitable advantages to business. Moreover, from the contemporary economic perspective—which is the one that must be adopted—by no means all the undertakings of Louis XIV were calculated to promote commercial interests. On the contrary, he showed little discrimination, eagerly seizing both on plans asserted, sometimes falsely, to be commercially advantageous (such as the subjugation of the Netherlands), and on those for which no one put forward any such claim (such as the plan of the "reunions"). Indeed, the king actually showed a certain indifference toward commercial and colonial undertakings,[20] seeming to prefer small and fruitless undertakings in nearby Europe that appeared easy and promised success. The one man, incidentally, who, if anyone, should have been the driving power behind economically motivated wars, Colbert, was an avowed opponent of the war policy. It is time for the estimate of the share that mercantilism had in international military involvements at that time to be reduced to its proper dimensions. The theory that the wars of the late seventeenth and the eighteenth centuries were commercial wars does represent an advance over the superficial judgment of political history expressed in the phrase "cabinet wars"—which does not mean that that phrase lacks all significance—but the commercial theory involves considerable exaggeration. Industrial life was then only in its infancy. It was only just beginning to discard craft forms. Capital exports—which is the thing that would really be relevant in this connection—were quite out of the question, and even production was quantitatively so small that exports could not possibly occupy a central position in the policies of the state. Nor did they, in fact, occupy such a position. The monarchs may have been avaricious, but they were far too remote from commercial considerations to be governed by them. Even colonial questions impinged only slightly on the European policies of the great powers. Settlers and adventurers were often allowed to fight out such problems on the spot, and little attention was paid to them. That the basic theory of mercantilism was quite adequate to justify violent measures against foreign powers, and that in every war economic interests, as conceived by mercantilism, were safeguarded whenever possible—these facts tend to exaggerate the mercantilist element. Certainly it made a contribution. But industry was the servant of state policy to a greater degree than state policy served industry.

We do not seek to underestimate the immediate advantages, at the time, of an expansion of the national domain. This is an element that then had a significance much greater than it has today. At a time when communications were uncertain, making military protection of commerce necessary, every nation undoubtedly had an interest in national bases overseas as well as in Europe, and in colonies too, though not so much in the conquest of other European countries. Finally, for the absolute monarch conquest meant an increment in power, soldiers, and income. And had all the plans of Louis XIV succeeded, he would undoubtedly have "made a go of it." The inner necessity to engage in a policy of conquest was not distasteful to him. Yet that this element could play a part is explained only from the traditional habit of war and from the fact that the war machine stood ready at hand. Otherwise these instincts would have been inhibited, just as are predatory instincts in private life. Murder with intent to rob cannot be explained by the mere desire for the victim's money, any more than analogous suggestions explain the expansion policy of the absolutist state.

At the same time, it remains a peculiarity of this type of imperialism that the monarch's personal motives and interests are far more important to an understanding of its individual aspects than is true in the case of other types. The prince-become-state made foreign policy his own personal business and saw to it that it was the concern of no one else. His personal interests became the interests of the state. Hereditary claims, personal rancor and idiosyncrasy, family politics, individual generosity and avarice, and similar traits cannot be denied a role as real factors shaping the surface situation. These things may have been no more than individual manifestations of a social situation, social data processed through an individual temperament; but superficially, at least, they did make history to the extent that they, in turn, had consequences that became elements of the social situation. It was this period that gave rise to the notion, so deeply rooted in the popular mind down to recent times, that foreign policy can be explained by the whims of sovereigns and their relations to one another. It gave rise to the whole approach that judges events from the viewpoint of monarchial interest, honor, and morality—an approach stemming directly from the social views of the time (as seen, for example, in the letters of Mme. de Sevigné) and one that adapts itself only slowly to changing times.

Invaluable evidence in this respect is furnished by the memoirs of Frederick the Great, mainly because his keen mind analyzed itself with far less prejudice than our Assyrian king ever did. In all cases of this kind the psychological aspects were surely determined by the desire to shine, to play an important role, to become the cynosure of discussion, to exploit existing power resources—all the while pursuing one's own advantage. Tradition and the availability of appropriate means are entirely sufficient to explain why these motives tended toward war. Domestic contingencies were subordinate, for in Germany, at least, the sovereign had triumphed over the nobility to such an extent that little political effort was required in that direction. The farther east we go, the more completely we see the sovereign able to regard state and people as his private property—with the noteworthy exception of Hungary, which can be compared only with England. The absolute monarch who can do as he pleases, who wages war in the same way as he rides to hounds—to satisfy his need for action— such is the face of absolutist imperialism.

The character of such absolutism is nowhere plainer than in Russia, notably the Russia of Catherine II. The case is particularly interesting because the Slavic masses never have shown and do not now show the slightest trace of militancy or aggressiveness. This has been true ever since the distant past, the time of settlement in the swamplands of the Pripet. It is true that the Slavs soon mingled with Germanic and Mongol elements and that their empire soon embraced a number of warlike peoples. But there never was any question of imperialist trends on the part of the Russian peasant or worker. Czarism triumphant rested on those Germanic and Mongol elements, elaborated its empire, created its army, without essentially impinging on the sphere of the peasant except to levy taxes and recruits for the army. In the time of feudalism as well as later, after the liberation of the peasants, we have the singular picture of a peasant democracy— one that was at times sorely oppressed by the nobility, but on which a bureaucratic and military despotism was superimposed in only superficial fashion. Once this despotism was securely established—and this occurred definitively under Peter the Great—it immediately exhibited that trend toward limitless expansion which our theory readily explains from the objectless "momentum of the machine in motion," the urge to action of a ruling class disposed to war, the concern of the crown to maintain its prestige—but which becomes quite incomprehensible to any rational approach from existing interests. Such interests—that is, those springing from vital needs—ceased to exist in the case of Russia from the moment that access to the Baltic and the Black Seas was won. This is so obvious that the argument of vital interest has not even been put forward. Instead, *ex post* explanations have been concocted, both inside Russia and out, which have gained considerable credence and are held to be verified by the otherwise unexplained tendencies to expansion—an example of reasoning in a circle, by no means uncommon in the social sciences. Among the motives thus postulated are the urge for Pan-Slav unification, the desire to liberate the Christian world from the Mohammedan yoke— even a mystical yearning for Constantinople on the part of the Russian people! And as often happens when such analysis encounters difficulties, refuge is sought in the allegedly bottomless depths of the "national soul." Actually, the continued momentum of acquired forms of life and organization, fostered by domestic interests, is entirely adequate to explain the policies of, say, Catherine II. True, from the subjective viewpoint a war policy undoubtedly recommended itself to her as the natural outcome of tradition, and, in addition, presumably as an interesting toy. Moreover, there was the example of the great lords whom she was copying. War was part of their settled order of life, so to speak—an element of sovereign splendor, almost a fashion. Hence they waged war whenever the occasion was offered, not so much from considerations of advantage as from personal whim. To look for deep-laid plans, broad perspectives, consistent trends is to miss the whole point.

## V. Imperialism and Capitalism

Our analysis of the historical evidence has shown, first, the unquestionable fact that "objectless" tendencies toward forcible expansion, without definite, utilitarian limits—that is, nonrational and irrational, purely instinctual inclinations toward war and conquest—play a very large role in the history of mankind. It may sound paradoxical, but numberless wars—perhaps the majority of all wars—have been waged without adequate "reason"—not so much from the moral viewpoint as from that of reasoned and reasonable interest. The most herculean efforts of the nations, in other words, have faded into the empty air.[21] Our analysis, in the second place, provides an explanation for this drive to action, this will to war—a theory by no means exhausted by mere references to an "urge" or an "instinct." The explanation lies, instead, in the vital needs of situations that molded peoples and classes into warriors—if they wanted to avoid extinction—and in the fact that psychological dispositions and social struc-

ture acquired in the dim past in such situations, once firmly established, tend to maintain themselves and to continue in effect long
after they have lost their meaning and their life-preserving function.
Our analysis, in the third place, has shown the existence of subsidiary
factors that facilitate the survival of such dispositions and structures—factors that may be divided into two groups. The orientation
toward war is mainly fostered by the domestic interests of ruling
classes, but also by the influence of all those who stand to gain individually from a war policy, whether economically or socially. Both
groups of factors are generally overgrown by elements of an altogether different character, not only in terms of political phraseology,
but also of psychological motivation. Imperialisms differ greatly in
detail, but they all have at least these traits in common, turning them
into a single phenomenon in the field of sociology, as we noted in the
introduction.

Imperialism thus is atavistic in character. It falls into that large
group of surviving features from earlier ages that play such an important part in every concrete social situation. In other words, it is an
element that stems from the living conditions, not of the present, but
of the past—or, put in terms of the economic interpretation of history, from past rather than present relations of production.[22] It is an
atavism in the social structure, in individual, psychological habits of
emotional reaction. Since the vital needs that created it have passed
away for good, it too must gradually disappear, even though every
warlike involvement, no matter how nonimperialist in character,
tends to revive it. It tends to disappear as a structural element because the structure that brought it to the fore goes into a decline,
giving way, in the course of social development, to other structures
that have no room for it and eliminate the power factors that supported it. It tends to disappear as an element of habitual emotional
reaction, because of the progressive rationalization of life and mind,
a process in which old functional needs are absorbed by new tasks, in
which heretofore military energies are functionally modified. If our
theory is correct, cases of imperialism should decline in intensity the
later they occur in the history of a people and of a culture. Our most
recent examples of unmistakable, clear-cut imperialism are the absolute monarchies of the eighteenth century. They are unmistakably
"more civilized" than their predecessors.

It is from absolute autocracy that the present age has taken over
what imperialist tendencies it displays. And the imperialism of absolute autocracy flourished before the Industrial Revolution that created the modern world, or rather, before the consequences of that
revolution began to be felt in all their aspects. These two statements

are primarily meant in a historical sense, and as such they are no more than self-evident. We shall nevertheless try, within the framework of our theory, to define the significance of capitalism for our phenomenon and to examine the relationship between present-day imperialist tendencies and the autocratic imperialism of the eighteenth century.

The floodtide that burst the dams in the Industrial Revolution had its sources, of course, back in the Middle Ages. But capitalism began to shape society and impress its stamp on every page of social history only with the second half of the eighteenth century. Before that time there had been only islands of capitalist economy imbedded in an ocean of village and urban economy. True, certain political influences emanated from these islands, but they were able to assert themselves only indirectly. Not until the process we term the Industrial Revolution did the working masses, led by the entrepreneur, overcome the bonds of older life-forms—the environment of peasantry, guild, and aristocracy. The causal connection was this: A transformation in the basic economic factors (which need not detain us here) created the objective opportunity for the production of commodities, for large-scale industry, working for a market of customers whose individual identities were unknown, operating solely with a view to maximum financial profit. It was this opportunity that created an economically oriented leadership—personalities whose field of achievement was the organization of such commodity production in the form of capitalist enterprise. Successful enterprises in large numbers represented something new in the economic and social sense. They fought for and won freedom of action. They compelled state policy to adapt itself to their needs. More and more they attracted the most vigorous leaders from other spheres, as well as the manpower of those spheres, causing them and the social strata they represented to languish. Capitalist entrepreneurs fought the former ruling circles for a share in state control, for leadership in the state. The very fact of their success, their position, their resources, their power, raised them in the political and social scale. Their mode of life, their cast of mind became increasingly important elements on the social scene. Their actions, desires, needs, and beliefs emerged more and more sharply within the total picture of the social community. In a historical sense, this applied primarily to the industrial and financial leaders of the movement—the bourgeoisie. But soon it applied also to the working masses which this movement created and placed in an altogether new class situation. This situation was governed by new forms of the working day, of family life, of interests—and these, in turn, corresponded to new orientations toward the social structures as a whole. More and more, in the course of the nineteenth century, the typical modern worker came to determine the overall aspect of society; for competitive capitalism, by its inherent logic, kept on raising the demand for labor and thus the economic level and social power of the workers,[23] until this class too was able to assert itself in a political sense. The working class and its mode of life provided the type from which the intellectual developed. Capitalism did not create the intellectuals—the "new middle class." But in earlier times only the legal scholar, the cleric, and the physician had formed a special intellectual class, and even they had enjoyed but little scope for playing an independent role. Such opportunities were provided only by capitalist society, which created the industrial and financial bureaucrat, the journalist, and so on, and which opened up new vistas to the jurist and physician. The "professional" of capitalist society arose as a class type. Finally, as a class type, the rentier, the beneficiary of industrial loan capital, is also a creature of capitalism. All these types are shaped by the capitalist mode of production, and they tend for this reason to bring other types—even the peasant—into conformity with themselves.

These new types were now cast adrift from the fixed order of earlier times, from the environment that had shackled and protected people for centuries, from the old associations of village, manor house, clan fellowship, often even from families in the broader sense. They were severed from the things that had been constant year after year, from cradle to grave—tools, homes, the countryside, especially the soil. They were on their own, enmeshed in the pitiless logic of gainful employment, mere drops in the vast ocean of industrial life, exposed to the inexorable pressures of competition. They were freed from the control of ancient patterns of thought, of the grip of institutions and organs that taught and represented these outlooks in village, manor, and guild. They were removed from the old world, engaged in building a new one for themselves—a specialized, mechanized world. Thus, they were all inevitably democratized, individualized, and rationalized.[24] They were democratized, because the picture of time-honored power and privilege gave way to one of continual change, set in motion by industrial life. They were individualized, because subjective opportunities to shape their lives took the place of immutable objective factors. They were rationalized, because the instability of economic position made their survival hinge on continual, deliberately rationalistic decisions—a dependence that emerged with great sharpness. Trained to economic rationalism, these people left no sphere of life unrationalized, questioning everything about themselves, the social structure, the state, the ruling class.

The marks of this process are engraved on every aspect of modern culture. It is this process that explains the basic features of that culture.

These are things that are well known today, recognized in their full significance—indeed, often exaggerated. Their application to our subject is plain. Everything that is purely instinctual, everything insofar as it is purely instinctual, is driven into the background by this development. It creates a social and psychological atmosphere in keeping with modern economic forms, where traditional habits, merely because they were traditional, could no more survive than obsolete economic forms. Just as the latter can survive only if they are continually "adapted," so instinctual tendencies can survive only when the conditions that gave rise to them continue to apply, or when the "instinct" in question derives a new purpose from new conditions. The "instinct" that is *only* "instinct," that has lost its purpose, languishes relatively quickly in the capitalist world, just as does an inefficient economic practice. We see this process of rationalization at work even in the case of the strongest impulses. We observe it, for example, in the facts of procreation. We must therefore anticipate finding it in the case of the imperialist impulse as well; we must expect to see this impulse, which rests on the primitive contingencies of physical combat, gradually disappear, washed away by new exigencies of daily life. There is another factor too. The competitive system absorbs the full energies of most of the people at all economic levels. Constant application, attention, and concentration of energy are the conditions of survival within it, primarily in the specifically economic professions, but also in other activities organized on their model. There is much less excess energy to be vented in war and conquest than in any precapitalist society. What excess energy there is flows largely into industry itself, accounts for its shining figures—the type of the captain of industry—and for the rest is applied to art, science, and the social struggle. In a purely capitalist world, what was once energy for war becomes simply energy for labor of every kind. Wars of conquest and adventurism in foreign policy in general are bound to be regarded as troublesome distractions, destructive of life's meaning, a diversion from the accustomed and therefore "true" task.

A purely capitalist world therefore can offer no fertile soil to imperialist impulses. That does not mean that it cannot still maintain an interest in imperialist expansion. We shall discuss this immediately. The point is that its people are likely to be essentially of an unwarlike disposition. Hence we must expect that anti-imperialist tendencies will show themselves wherever capitalism penetrates the economy and, through the economy, the mind of modern nations—most strongly, of course, where capitalism itself is strongest, where it has advanced furthest, encountered the least resistance, and preeminently where its types and hence democracy—in the "bourgeois" sense—come closest to political dominion. We must further expect that the types formed by capitalism will actually be the carriers of these tendencies. Is such the case? The facts that follow are cited to show that this expectation, which flows from our theory, is in fact justified.

1. Throughout the world of capitalism, and specifically among the elements formed by capitalism in modern social life, there has arisen a fundamental opposition to war, expansion, cabinet diplomacy, armaments, and socially entrenched professional armies. This opposition had its origin in the country that first turned capitalist—England—and arose coincidentally with that country's capitalist development. "Philosophical radicalism" was the first politically influential intellectual movement to represent this trend successfully, linking it up, as was to be expected, with economic freedom in general and free trade in particular. Molesworth became a cabinet member, even though he had publicly declared—on the occasion of the Canadian revolution—that he prayed for the defeat of his country's arms. In step with the advance of capitalism,[25] the movement also gained adherents elsewhere—though at first only adherents without influence. It found support in Paris—indeed, in a circle oriented toward capitalist enterprise (for example, Frédéric Passy). True, pacifism as a matter of principle had existed before, though only among a few small religious sects. But modern pacifism, in its political foundations if not its derivation, is unquestionably a phenomenon of the capitalist world.

2. Wherever capitalism penetrated, peace parties of such strength arose that virtually every war meant a political struggle on the domestic scene. The exceptions are rare—Germany in the Franco-Prussian war of 1870–1871, both belligerents in the Russo-Turkish war of 1877–1878. That is why every war is carefully justified as a defensive war by the governments involved, and by all the political parties, in their official utterances—indicating a realization that a war of a different nature would scarcely be tenable in a political sense. (Here too the Russo-Turkish war is an exception, but a significant one.) In former times this would not have been necessary. Reference to an interest or pretense at moral justification was customary as early as the eighteenth century, but only in the nineteenth century did the assertion of attack, or the threat of attack, become the only avowed occasion for war. In the distant past, imperialism had needed no disguise whatever, and in the absolute autocracies only a very transparent

one; but today imperialism is carefully hidden from public view—even though there may still be an unofficial appeal to warlike instincts. No people and no ruling class today can openly afford to regard war as a normal state of affairs or a normal element in the life of nations. No one doubts that today it must be characterized as an abnormality and a disaster. True, war is still glorified. But glorification in the style of King Tuklâtî-pal-ísharra is rare and unleashes such a storm of indignation that every practical politician carefully dissociates himself from such things. Everywhere there is official acknowledgment that peace is an end in itself—though not necessarily an end overshadowing all purposes that can be realized by means of war. Every expansionist urge must be carefully related to a concrete goal. All this is primarily a matter of political phraseology, to be sure. But the necessity for this phraseology is a symptom of the popular attitude. And that attitude makes a policy of imperialism more and more difficult—indeed, the very word "imperialism" is applied only to the enemy, in a reproachful sense, being carefully avoided with reference to the speaker's own policies.

3. The type of industrial worker created by capitalism is always vigorously anti-imperialist. In the individual case, skillful agitation may persuade the working masses to approve or remain neutral—a concrete goal or interest in self-defense always playing the main part—but no initiative for a forcible policy of expansion ever emanates from this quarter. On this point official socialism unquestionably formulates not merely the interests but also the conscious will of the workers. Even less than peasant imperialism is there any such thing as socialist or other working-class imperialism.

4. Despite manifest resistance on the part of powerful elements, the capitalist age has seen the development of methods for preventing war, for the peaceful settlement of disputes among states. The very fact of resistance means that the trend can be explained only from the mentality of capitalism as a mode of life. It definitely limits the opportunities imperialism needs if it is to be a powerful force. True, the methods in question often fail, but even more often they are successful. I am thinking not merely of the Hague Court of Arbitration but of the practice of submitting controversial issues to conferences of the major powers or at least those powers directly concerned—a course of action that has become less and less avoidable. True, here too the individual case may become a farce. But the serious setbacks of today must not blind us to the real importance or sociological significance of these things.

5. Among all capitalist economies, that of the United States is least burdened with precapitalist elements, survivals, reminiscences, and

power factors. Certainly we cannot expect to find imperialist tendencies altogether lacking even in the United States, for the immigrants
came from Europe with their convictions fully formed, and the environment certainly favored the revival of instincts of pugnacity. But we
can conjecture that among all countries the United States is likely to
exhibit the weakest imperialist trend. This turns out to be the truth.
The case is particularly instructive, because the United States has
seen a particularly strong emergence of capitalist interests in an imperialist direction—those very interests to which the phenomenon of
imperialism has so often been reduced, a subject we shall yet touch
on. Nevertheless the United States was the first advocate of disarmament and arbitration. It was the first to conclude treaties concerning
arms limitations (1817) and arbitral courts (first attempt in 1797)—
doing so most zealously, by the way, when economic interest in expansion was at its greatest. Since 1908 such treaties have been concluded with twenty-two states. In the course of the nineteenth century, the United States had numerous occasions for war, including
instances that were well calculated to test its patience. It made almost
no use of such occasions. Leading industrial and financial circles in
the United States had and still have an evident interest in incorporat-
ing Mexico into the Union. There was more than enough opportunity for such annexation—but Mexico remained unconquered. Racial
catch phrases and working-class interests pointed to Japan as a possible danger. Hence possession of the Philippines was not a matter of
indifference—yet surrender of this possession is being discussed.
Canada was an almost defenseless prize—but Canada remained independent. Even in the United States, of course, politicians need slogans—especially slogans calculated to divert attention from domestic
issues. Theodore Roosevelt and certain magnates of the press actually
resorted to imperialism—and the result, in that world of high capitalism, was utter defeat, a defeat that would have been even more
abject, if other slogans, notably those appealing to anti-trust sentiment, had not met with better success.[26]

These facts are scarcely in dispute.[27] And since they fit into the
picture of the mode of life which we have recognized to be the
necessary product of capitalism, since we can grasp them adequately
from the necessities of that mode of life and industry, it follows that
capitalism is by nature anti-imperialist. Hence we cannot readily derive from it such imperialist tendencies as actually exist, but must evidently see them only as alien elements, carried into the world of capitalism from the outside, supported by noncapitalist factors in
modern life. The survival of interest in a policy of forcible expansion
does not, by itself, alter these facts—not even, it must be steadily emphasized, from the viewpoint of the economic interpretation of his-

tory. For objective interests become effective—and, what is important, become powerful political factors—only when they correspond to attitudes of the people or of sufficiently powerful strata. Otherwise they remain without effect, are not even conceived of as interests. The economic interest in the forcible conquest of India had to await free-booter personalities, in order to be followed up. In ancient Rome the domestic class interest in an expansive policy had to be seized upon by a vigorous, idle aristocracy, otherwise it would have been ruled out on internal political grounds. Even the purely commercial imperialism of Venice—assuming that we can speak of such a thing, and not merely of a policy of securing trade routes in a military sense, which was then necessary—even such a policy needed to have examples of a policy of conquest at hand on every side, needed mercenary groups and bellicose adventurers among the *nobili* in order to become true imperialism. The capitalist world, however, suppresses rather than creates such attitudes. Certainly, all expansive interests within it are likely to ally themselves with imperialist tendencies flowing from noncapitalist sources, to use them, to make them serve as pretexts, to rationalize them, to point the way toward action on account of them. And from this union the picture of modern imperialism is put together; but for that very reason it is not a matter of capitalist factors alone. Before we go into this at length, we must understand the nature and strength of the economic stake which capitalist society has in a policy of imperialism—especially the question of whether this interest is or is not inherent in the nature of capitalism—either capitalism generally, or a special phase of capitalism.

It is in the nature of a capitalist economy—and of an exchange economy generally—that many people stand to gain economically in any war. Here the situation is fundamentally much as it is with the familiar subject of luxury. War means increased demand at panic prices, hence high profits and also high wages in many parts of the national economy. This is primarily a matter of money incomes, but as a rule (though to a lesser extent) real incomes are also affected. There are, for example, the special war interests, such as the arms industry. If the war lasts long enough, the circle of money profiteers naturally expands more and more—quite apart from a possible paper-money economy. It may extend to every economic field, but just as naturally the commodity content of money profits drops more and more, indeed, quite rapidly, to the point where actual losses are incurred. The national economy as a whole, of course, is impoverished by the tremendous excess in consumption brought on by war. It is, to be sure, conceivable that either the capitalists or the workers might make certain gains as a class, namely, if the volume either of capital or of labor should decline in such a way that the remainder receives a greater share in the social product and that, even from the absolute viewpoint, the total sum of interest or wages becomes greater than it was before. But these advantages cannot be considerable. They are probably, for the most part, more than outweighed by the burdens imposed by war and by losses sustained abroad. Thus, the gain of the capitalists as a class cannot be a motive for war—and it is this gain that counts, for any advantage to the working class would be contingent on a large number of workers falling in action or otherwise perishing. There remain the entrepreneurs in the war industries, in the broader sense, possibly also the large landowner—a small but powerful minority. Their war profits are always sure to be an important supporting element. But few will go so far as to assert that this element alone is sufficient to orient the people of the capitalist world along imperialist lines. At most, an interest in expansion may make the capitalists allies of those who stand for imperialist trends.

It may be stated as being beyond controversy that where free trade prevails *no* class has an interest in forcible expansion as such. For in such a case the citizens and goods of every nation can move in foreign countries as freely as though those countries were politically their own—free trade implying far more than mere freedom from tariffs. In a genuine state of free trade, foreign raw materials and foodstuffs are as accessible to each nation as though they were within its own territory.[28] Where the cultural backwardness of a region makes normal economic intercourse dependent on colonization, it does not matter, assuming free trade, which of the "civilized" nations undertakes the task of colonization. Dominion of the seas, in such a case, means little more than a maritime traffic police. Similarly, it is a matter of indifference to a nation whether a railway concession in a foreign country is acquired by one of its own citizens or not—just so long as the railway *is* built and put into efficient operation. For citizens of any country may use the railway, just like the fellow countrymen of its builder—while in the event of war it will serve whoever controls it in the military sense, regardless of who built it. It is true, of course, that profits and wages flowing from its construction and operation will accrue, for the greater part, to the nation that built it. But capital and labor that go into the railway have to be taken from somewhere, and normally the other nations fill the gap. It is a fact that in a regime of free trade the essential advantages of international intercourse are clearly evident. The gain lies in the enlargement of the commodity supply by means of the division of labor among nations, rather than in the profits and wages of the export industry and the carrying trade. For these profits and wages would be reaped even if there were no export, in which case import, the necessary complement, would also vanish. Not even monopoly interests—if they existed—would be disposed toward imperialism in such a case. For under free trade only *international* cartels would be possible. Under a system of free trade there would be conflicts in economic interests neither among different nations nor among the corresponding classes of different nations.[29] And since protectionism is not an essential characteristic of the capitalist economy—otherwise the English national economy would scarcely be capitalist—it is apparent that any economic interest in forcible expansion on the part of a people or a class is not necessarily a product of capitalism.

Protective tariffs alone—and harassment of the alien and of foreign commodities—do not basically change this situation as it affects interests. True, such barriers move the nations economically farther apart, making it easier for imperialist tendencies to win the upper hand; they line up the entrepreneurs of the different countries in battle formation against one another, impeding the rise of peaceful interests; they also hinder the flow of raw materials and foodstuffs and thus the export of manufacturers, or conversely, the import of manufacturers and the export of raw materials and foodstuffs, possibly creating an interest in—sometimes forcible—expansion of the customs area; they place entrepreneurs in a position of dependence on regulations of governments that may be serving imperialist interests, giving these governments occasion to pervert economic relations for purposes of sharpening economic conflicts, for adulterating the competitive struggle with diplomatic methods outside the field of economics, and, finally, for imposing on peoples the heavy sacrifices exacted by a policy of autarchy, thus accustoming them to the thought of war by constant preparation for war. Nevertheless, in this case the basic alignment of interests remains essentially what it was under free trade. We might reiterate our example of railway construction, though in the case of mining concessions, for example, the situation is somewhat different. Colonial possessions acquire more meaning in this case, but the exclusion from the colonies of aliens and foreign capital is not altogether good business since it slows down the development of the colonies. The same is true of the struggle for third markets. When, for example, France obtains more favorable tariff treatment from the Chinese government than England enjoys, this will avail only those French exporters who are in a position to export the same goods as their English confrères; the others are only harmed. It is true, of course, that protectionism adds another form of international capital movement to the kind that prevails under free trade—or rather, a modification of it—namely, the movement of cap-

ital for the founding of enterprises inside the tariff wall, in order to
save customs duties. But this capital movement too has no aggressive
element; on the contrary, it tends toward the creation of peaceful
interests. Thus, an aggressive economic policy on the part of a country with a unified tariff—with preparedness for war always in the
background—serves the economy only seemingly rather than really.
Actually, one might assert that the economy becomes a weapon in the
political struggle, a means for unifying the nation, for severing it
from the fabric of international interests, for placing it at the disposal
of the state power.

This becomes especially clear when we consider which strata of the
capitalist world are actually economically benefited by protective tariffs. They do harm to both workers and capitalists—in contrast to entrepreneurs—not only in their role as consumers, but also as producers. The damage to consumers is universal, that to producers almost
so. As for entrepreneurs, they are benefited only by the tariff that
happens to be levied on their own product. But this advantage is substantially reduced by the countermeasures adopted by other countries—universally, except in the case of England—and by the effect
of the tariff on the prices of other articles, especially those which they
require for their own productive process. Why, then, are entrepreneurs so strongly in favor of protective tariffs? The answer is simple.
Each industry hopes to score *special* gains in the struggle of political
intrigue, thus enabling it to realize a net gain. Moreover, every decline in freight rates, every advance in production abroad, is likely to
affect the economic balance, making it necessary for domestic enterprises to adapt themselves, indeed often to turn to other lines of endeavor. This is a difficult task to which not everyone is equal. Within
the industrial organism of every nation there survive antiquated
methods of doing business that would cause enterprises to succumb
to foreign competition—because of poor management rather than
lack of capital, for before 1914 the banks were almost forcing capital
on the entrepreneurs.[30] If, still, in most countries virtually *all* entrepreneurs are protectionists, this is owing to a reason which we shall
presently discuss. Without that reason, their attitude would be different. The fact that all industries today demand tariff protection must
not blind us to the fact that even the entrepreneur interest is not unequivocally protectionist. For this demand is only the consequence of
a protectionism already in existence, of a protectionist spirit springing from the economic interests of relatively small entrepreneur
groups and from noncapitalist elements—a spirit that ultimately carried along all groups, occasionally even the representatives of working-class interests. Today the protective tariff confers its full and im-

mediate benefits—or comes close to conferring them—only on the large landowners.

A protectionist policy, however, does facilitate the formation of cartels and trusts. And it is true that this circumstance thoroughly alters the alignment of interests. It was neo-Marxist doctrine that first tellingly described this causal connection (Bauer) and fully recognized the significance of the "functional change in protectionism" (Hilferding). Union in a cartel or trust confers various benefits on the entrepreneur—a saving in costs, a stronger position as against the workers—but none of these compares with this one advantage: a monopolistic price policy, possible to any considerable degree *only* behind an adequate protective tariff. Now the price that brings the maximum monopoly profit is generally far above the price that would be fixed by fluctuating competitive costs, and the volume that can be marketed at that maximum price is generally far below the output that would be technically and economically feasible. Under free competition that output *would* be produced and offered, but a trust cannot offer it, for it could be sold only at a competitive price. Yet the trust *must* produce it—or approximately as much—otherwise the advantages of large-scale enterprise remain unexploited and unit costs are likely to be uneconomically high. The trust thus faces a dilemma. Either it renounces the monopolistic policies that motivated its founding; or it fails to exploit and expand its plant, with resultant high costs. It extricates itself from this dilemma by producing the full output that is economically feasible, thus securing low costs, and offering in the protected domestic market only the quantity corresponding to the monopoly price—insofar as the tariff permits; while the rest is sold, or "dumped," abroad at a lower price, sometimes (but not necessarily) *below* cost.

What happens when the entrepreneurs successfully pursue such a policy is something that did not occur in the cases discussed so far— a conflict of interests between nations that becomes so sharp that it cannot be overcome by the existing basic community of interests. Each of the two groups of entrepreneurs and each of the two states seeks to do something that is rendered illusory by a similar policy on the part of the other. In the case of protective tariffs *without* monopoly formation, an understanding is sometimes possible, for only a few would be destroyed, while many would stand to gain; but when monopoly rules it is very difficult to reach an agreement for it would require self-negation on the part of the new rulers. All that is left to do is to pursue the course once taken, to beat down the foreign industry wherever possible, forcing it to conclude a favorable "peace." This requires sacrifices. The excess product is dumped on the world market at steadily lower prices. Counterattacks that grow more and more desperate must be repulsed on the domestic scene. The atmosphere grows more and more heated. Workers and consumers grow more and more troublesome. Where this situation prevails, capital export, like commodity export, becomes aggressive, belying its ordinary character. A mass of capitalists competing with one another has no means of counteracting the decline in the interest rate. Of course they always seek out the places where the interest rate is highest, and in this quest they are quite willing to export their capital. But they were unable to adopt a policy of forced capital exports; and where there is freedom of capital movement they also lack the motive. For any gaps which might be opened up at home would be filled by foreign capital flowing in from abroad, thus preventing a rise of the domestic interest rate. But *organized* capital may very well make the discovery that the interest rate can be maintained above the level of free competition, if the resulting surplus can be sent abroad and if any foreign capital that flows in can be intercepted and—whether in the form of loans or in the form of machinery and the like—can likewise be channeled into foreign investment outlets. Now it is true that capital is nowhere cartelized. But it is everywhere subject to the guidance of the big banks which, even without a capital cartel, have attained a position similar to that of the cartel magnates in industry, and which are in a position to put into effect similar policies. It is necessary to keep two factors in mind. In the first place, everywhere except, significantly, in England, there has come into being a close alliance between high finance and the cartel magnates, often going as far as personal identity. Although the relation between capitalists and entrepreneurs is one of the typical and fundamental *conflicts* of the capitalist economy, monopoly capitalism has virtually fused the big banks and cartels into one. Leading bankers are often leaders of the national economy. Here capitalism has found a central organ that supplants its automatism by conscious decisions. In the second place, the interests of the big banks coincide with those of their depositors even less than do the interests of cartel leaders with those of the firms belonging to the cartel. The policies of high finance are based on control of a *large* proportion of the national capital, but they are in the actual interest of only a *small* proportion and, indeed, with respect to the alliance with big business, sometimes not even in the interest of capital as such at all. The ordinary "small" capitalist foots the bills for a policy of forced exports, rather than enjoying its profits. He is a tool; his interests do not really matter. This possibility of laying all the sacrifices connected with a monopoly policy on one part of capital, while removing them from another, makes capital exports far more lucrative for the favored part than they would otherwise be. Even capital that is independent of the banks is thus often forced abroad—forced into the role of a shock troop for the real leaders, because cartels successfully impede the founding of new enterprises. Thus, the customs area of a trustified country generally pours a huge wave of capital into new countries. There it meets other, similar waves of capital, and a bitter, costly struggle begins but never ends.

In such a struggle among "dumped" products and capitals, it is no longer a matter of indifference who builds a given railroad, who owns a mine or a colony. Now that the law of costs is no longer operative, it becomes necessary to fight over such properties with desperate effort and with every available means, including those that are not economic in character, such as diplomacy. The concrete objects in question often become entirely subsidiary considerations; the anticipated profit may be trifling, because of the competitive struggle— a struggle that has very little to do with normal competition. What matters is to gain a foothold of some kind and then to exploit this foothold as a base for the conquest of new markets. This costs all the participants dear—often more than can be reasonably recovered, immediately or in the future. Fury lays hold of everyone concerned— and everyone sees to it that his fellow countrymen share his wrath. Each is constrained to resort to methods that he would regard as evidence of unprecedented moral depravity in the other.

It is not true that the capitalist system as such must collapse from immanent necessity, that it necessarily makes its continued existence impossible by its own growth and development. Marx's line of reasoning on this point shows serious defects, and when these are corrected the proof vanishes. It is to the great credit of Hilferding that he abandoned this thesis of Marxist theory.[31] Nevertheless, the situation that has just been described is really untenable both politically and economically. Economically, it amounts to a *reductio ad absurdum*. Politically, it unleashes storms of indignation among the exploited consumers at home and the threatened producers abroad. Thus, the idea of military force readily suggests itself. Force may serve to break down foreign customs barriers and thus afford relief from the vicious circle of economic aggression. If that is not feasible, military conquest may at least secure control over markets in which heretofore one had to compete with the enemy. In this context, the conquest of colonies takes on an altogether different significance. Nonmonopolist countries, especially those adhering to free trade, reap little profit from such a policy. But it is a different matter with countries that function in a monopolist role *vis-à-vis* their colonies. There being no competition, they can use cheap native labor without its ceasing to be cheap;

they can market their products, even in the colonies, at monopoly prices; they can, finally, invest capital that would only depress the profit rate at home and that could be placed in other civilized countries only at very low interest rates. And they can do all these things even though the consequence may be much slower colonial development. It would seem as though there could be no such interest in expansion at the expense of other advanced capitalist countries—in Europe, for example—because their industry would merely offer competition to the domestic cartels. But it is sufficient for the industry of the conquering state to be superior to that of the one to be subjugated—superior in capital power, organization, intelligence, and self-assertion—to make it possible to treat the subjugated state, perhaps not quite, but very much like a colony, even though it may become necessary to make a deal with individual groups of interests that are particularly powerful. A much more important fact is that the conqueror can face the subjugated nation with the bearing of the victor. He has countless means at his disposal for expropriating raw material resources and the like and placing them in the service of his cartels. He can seize them outright, nationalize them, impose a forced sale, or draft the proprietors into industrial groups of the victor nation under conditions that ensure control by the domestic captains of industry. He can exploit them by a system of quotas or allotments. He can administer the conquered means of communication in the interests of his own cartels. Under the pretext of military and political security, he can deprive the foreign workers of the right to organize, thus not only making cheap labor in the annexed territory available to his cartels, but also holding a threat over the head of domestic labor.

Thus we have here, within a social group that carries great political weight, a strong, undeniable, economic interest in such things as protective tariffs, cartels, monopoly prices, forced exports (dumping), an aggressive economic policy, an aggressive foreign policy generally, and war, including wars of expansion with a typically imperialist character. Once this alignment of interests exists, an even stronger interest in a somewhat differently motivated expansion must be added, namely, an interest in the conquest of lands producing raw materials and foodstuffs, with a view to facilitating self-sufficient warfare. Still another interest is that in rising wartime consumption. A mass of unorganized capitalists competing with one another may at best reap a trifling profit from such an eventuality, but organized capital is sure to profit hugely. Finally there is the political interest in war and international hatred which flows from the insecure position of the leading circles. They are small in numbers and highly unpopular. The essential nature of their policy is quite generally known, and most of the people find it unnatural and contemptible. An attack on all forms of property has revolutionary implications, but an attack on the privileged position of the cartel magnates may be politically rewarding, implying comparatively little risk and no threat to the existing order. Under certain circumstances it may serve to unite all the political parties. The existence of such a danger calls for diversionary tactics.

Yet the final word in any presentation of this aspect of modern economic life must be one of warning against overestimating it. The conflicts that have been described, born of an export-dependent monopoly capitalism, may serve to submerge the real community of interests among nations; the monopolist press may drive it underground; but underneath the surface it never completely disappears. Deep down, the normal sense of business and trade usually prevails. Even cartels cannot do without the custom of their foreign economic kin. Even national economies characterized by export monopoly are dependent on one another in many respects. And their interests do not always conflict in the matter of producing for third markets. Even when the conflicting interests are emphasized, parallel interests are not altogether lacking. Furthermore, if a policy of export monopolism is to be driven to the extremes of forcible expansion, it is necessary to win over all segments of the population—at least to the point where they are halfway prepared to support the war; but the real interest in export monopolism as such is limited to the entrepreneurs and their ally, high finance. Even the most skillful agitation cannot prevent the independent traders, the small producers who are not covered by cartels, the "mere" capitalists, and the workers from occasionally realizing that they are the victims of such a policy. In the case of the traders and small producers this is quite clear. It is not so clear in the case of the capitalists, because of the possibility of "dumping" capital in order to raise the domestic interest rate. Against this, however, stands the high cost of such a policy and the curtailment of the competition of entrepreneurs for domestic capital. It is of the greatest importance, finally, to understand that export monopolism injures the workers far more unequivocally than the capitalists. There can be no dumping of labor power, and employment abroad or in the colonies is not even a quantitative substitute. Curiously enough, this injury to the working class is a matter of controversy. Even neo-Marxist doctrine—and not merely those writers properly characterized as "vulgar Marxists," who in every respect resemble their ilk of other persuasions—is inclined to admit that the workers derive temporary benefits from export monopolism,[32] limiting the polemic against it to proof that the ultimate effects—economic and especially political—are doubtful, and that even the temporary benefits are purchased by an injury to foreign workers which conflicts with the spirit of socialism. There is an error here. Apparently it is assumed that production for export—and, to the extent that it fosters such production, monopoly capitalist expansion as well—increases the demand for labor and thus raises wages. Suppose we accept as correct the premises implied in this argument, that the increase in demand will outweigh any decrease flowing from monopolistic labor saving production methods, and also that it will outweigh the disadvantage flowing from the fact that the workers are now confronted, rather than by many entrepreneurs in a single industry, by a single party of the second part who, on the local labor market at least, can engage in monopolistic policies with respect to them, both as workers and as consumers. Even if we accept these premises—which seem doubtful to me—the balance is not even temporarily in favor of the workers. We have already pointed out that the interest of workers in export, even when free trade prevails, is essentially a consumer interest; that is, it is based on the fact that exports make imports possible. But as a producer the worker will usually fare no worse without exports, since the lack of exports must also eliminate imports. The workers, moreover, have no interest whatever in exports that may result from a policy of export monopolism—in other words, that would not otherwise be exported at all. For if it were impossible to dump these quantities they would by no means remain unproduced. On the contrary, most, if not all, would be offered at home, in general affording the same employment opportunities to the workers and in addition cheapening consumption. If that is not possible—that is to say, if the profit from the increased supply at home, together with the profit from the reduced supply abroad, fails to cover total costs including interest—then the industry in question is expanded beyond economically justifiable limits, and it is in the interest of all the productive factors concerned, excepting only the cartel magnates, for capital and labor to move into other industries, something that is necessary and always possible. This constellation of interests is not altered by the circumstance that export monopolism is often able and willing to do things for its workers in the social welfare sphere, thus allowing them to share in its profits.[33] For what makes this possible is, after all, nothing but exploitation of the consumer. If we may speak of the impoverishment of the workers anywhere within the world of capitalism, then a tendency to such impoverishment is apparent here, at least in a relative sense—though actually that tendency has slowed up since the turn of the century. If it is ever true that there is not a trace of parallelism of economic interests between entrepreneurs and workers, but instead only a sharp economic conflict—and usually there is much exaggeration in such statements—then this is true here. Chamberlain had every reason to appeal to national sentiment, to mock the petty calculation of immediate advantage, and to call out to the workers: "Learn to think imperially!" For the English worker knew what he was about, despite the banner headlines on the front pages of the yellow press: "Tariff Reform Means Work For All," and so on.

The fact that the balance sheet of export monopolism is anything but a brilliant success, even for the entrepreneurs, has been glossed over only by an upswing that stemmed from sources other than export monopolism itself. The hope of a future of dominion, to follow the struggles of the present, is but poor solace for the losses in that struggle. Should such a policy become general, the losses—admitted or not—of each individual nation would be even greater, the winnings even smaller. And if the export monopolists have not done too well, the nonmonopolist industries of England have hardly suffered from the dumping policies followed by other nations. The British steel industry may have suffered (though it was by no means in serious danger), but in return all the other English industries actually enjoyed, at the expense of the foreign dumpers, a production premium in the form of abnormally low prices for iron and ferrous products. The sugar industry may have been unable to maintain itself in England, but in return sugar-using industries developed in England as they did nowhere else. To those entrepreneurs, moreover, who never succeeded in gaining leading positions in the cartels, the enjoyment of an assured return is often but a poor substitute for lost opportunities for growth. Thus, we can understand the fact that even in entrepreneurial circles dissatisfaction with such a policy arose, and while one group entertained the thought of forcible expansion as a last resort, another was led into an attitude of opposition. In all the protectionist countries, therefore, we have had, for the past twenty years, anti-dumping legislation, primarily as an instrument of tariff policy. This legislation, it is true, is directed primarily against foreign dumping rather than against dumping by domestic enterprise, and hence it becomes a new weapon in the hands of the monopoly interests. But it is also true that its political basis lies partly in circles and attitudes opposed on principle to export aggression and for this reason anxious to make such a policy impossible for domestic enterprise. It must be admitted that such opposition often suffers from inappropriate techniques and from the influence of lay catchwords. But given peaceful development, it may be assumed that the opposition would gradually turn directly against dumping by domestic cartels.

This countermovement against export monopolism, within capitalism rather than opposed to it, would mean little if it were merely the political death struggle of a moribund economic order which is giving way to a new phase of development. If the cartel with its policy of export aggression stood face to face with noncartelized factory industry, as that industry once faced handicraft industry, then even the most vigorous opposition could scarcely change the ultimate outcome or the fundamental significance of the process. But it cannot be emphasized sharply enough that such is not the case. Export monopolism does *not* grow from the inherent laws of capitalist development. The character of capitalism leads to large-scale production, but with few exceptions large-scale production does *not* lead to the kind of unlimited concentration that would leave but one or only a few firms in each industry. On the contrary, any plant runs up against limits to its growth in a given location; and the growth of combinations which would make sense under a system of free trade encounters limits of organizational efficiency. Beyond these limits there is no tendency toward combination inherent in the competitive system. In particular, the rise of trusts and cartels—a phenomenon quite different from the trend to large-scale production with which it is often confused—can never be explained by the automatism of the competitive system. This follows from the very fact that trusts and cartels can attain their primary purpose—to pursue a monopoly policy—only behind protective tariffs, without which they would lose their essential significance. But protective tariffs do not automatically grow from the competitive system. They are the fruit of political action—*a type of action that by no means reflects the objective interests of all those concerned* but that, on the contrary, becomes impossible as soon as the majority of those whose consent is necessary realize their true interests. To some extent it is obvious, and for the rest it will be presently shown, that the interests of the minority, quite appropriately expressed in support of a protective tariff, do not stem from capitalism as such. It follows that *it is a basic fallacy to describe imperialism as a necessary phase of capitalism, or even to speak of the development of capitalism into imperialism.* We have seen before that the mode of life of the capitalist world does not favor imperialist attitudes. We now see that the alignment of interests in a capitalist economy—even the interests of its upper strata—by no means points unequivocally in the direction of imperialism. We now come to the final step in our line of reasoning.

Since we cannot derive even export monopolism from any tendencies of the competitive system toward big enterprise, we must find some other explanation. A glance at the original purpose of tariffs provides what we need. Tariffs sprang from the financial interests of the monarchy. They were a method of exploiting the trader which differed from the method of the robber baron in the same way that the royal chase differed from the method of the poacher. They were in line with the royal prerogatives of safe conduct, of protection for the Jews, of the granting of market rights, and so forth. From the thirteenth century onward this method was progressively refined in the autocratic state, less and less emphasis being placed on the direct monetary yield of customs revenues, and more and more on their indirect effect in creating productive taxable objects. In other words, while the protective value of a tariff counted, it counted only from the viewpoint of the ultimate monetary advantage of the sovereign. It does not matter, for our purposes, that occasionally this policy, under the influence of lay notions of economics, blundered badly in the choice of its methods. (From the viewpoint of autocratic interest, incidentally, such measures were not nearly so self-defeating as they were from the viewpoint of the national economy.) Every customs house, every privilege conferring the right to produce, market, or store, thus created a new economic situation which deflected trade and industry into "unnatural" channels. All tariffs, rights, and the like became the seed bed for economic growth that could have neither sprung up nor maintained itself without them. Further, all such economic institutions dictated by autocratic interest were surrounded by manifold interests of people who were dependent on them and now began to demand their continuance—a wholly paradoxical though at the same time quite understandable situation. The trading and manufacturing bourgeoisie was all the more aware of its dependence on the sovereign, since it needed his protection against the remaining feudal powers; and the uncertainties of the times, together with the lack of great consuming centers, impeded the rise of free economic competition. Insofar as commerce and manufacturing came into being at all, therefore, they arose under the sign of monopolistic interest. Thus, the bourgeoisie willingly allowed itself to be molded into one of the power instruments of the monarchy, both in a territorial and in a national sense. It is even true that the bourgeoisie, because of the character of its interests and the kind of economic outlook that corresponded to those interests, made an essential contribution to the emergence of modern nationalism. Another factor that worked in the same direction was the financial relation between the great merchant houses and the sovereign. This theory of the nature of the relationship between the autocratic state and the bourgeoisie is not refuted by pointing out that it was precisely the mercantile republics of the Middle Ages and the early modern period that initially pursued a policy of mercantilism. They were no more than enclaves in a world pervaded by the struggle among feudal powers. The Hanseatic League and Venice, for example, could maintain themselves only as military powers, could pursue their business only by means of fortified bases, warehousing privileges, protective treaties. This forced the people to stand shoulder to shoulder, made the exploitation of political gains more important than domestic competition, infused them with a corporate and monopolistic spirit. Wherever autocratic power vanished at an early date—as in the Netherlands and later in England—and the protective interest receded into the background, they swiftly discovered that trade must be free— "free to the nethermost recesses of hell."

Trade and industry of the early capitalist period thus remained strongly pervaded with precapitalist methods, bore the stamp of autocracy, and served its interests, either willingly or by force. With its traditional habits of feeling, thinking, and acting molded along such lines, the bourgeoisie entered the Industrial Revolution. It was shaped, in other words, by the needs and interests of an environment that was essentially noncapitalist, or at least precapitalist—needs stemming not from the nature of the capitalist economy as such but from the fact of the coexistence of early capitalism with another and at first overwhelmingly powerful mode of life and business. Established habits of thought and action tend to persist, and hence the spirit of guild and monopoly at first maintained itself, and was only slowly undermined, even where capitalism was in sole possession of the field. Actually capitalism did not fully prevail *anywhere* on the Continent. Existing economic interests, "artificially" shaped by the autocratic state, remained dependent on the "protection" of the state. The industrial organism, such as it was, would not have been able to withstand free competition. Even where the old barriers crumbled in the autocratic state, the people did not all at once flock to the clear track. They were creatures of mercantilism and even earlier periods, and many of them huddled together and protested against the affront of being forced to depend on their own ability. They cried for paternalism, for protection, for forcible restraint of strangers, and above all for tariffs. They met with partial success, particularly because capitalism failed to take radical action in the agrarian field. Capitalism did bring about many changes on the land, springing in part from its automatic mechanisms, in part from the political trends it engendered—abolition of serfdom, freeing the soil from feudal entanglements, and so on—but initially it did not alter the basic outlines of the social structure of the countryside. Even less did it affect the spirit of the people, and least of all their political goals. This explains why the features and trends of autocracy—including imperialism—proved so resistant, why they exerted such a powerful influence on capitalist development, why the old export monopolism could live on and merge into the new.

These are facts of fundamental significance to an understanding of the soul of modern Europe. Had the ruling class of the Middle Ages—the war-oriented nobility—changed its profession and function and become the ruling class of the capitalist world; or had developing capitalism swept it away, put it out of business, instead of merely clashing head-on with it in the agrarian sphere—then much would have been different in the life of modern peoples. But as things actually were, neither eventuality occurred; or, more correctly, both are taking place, only at a very slow pace. The two groups of landowners remain social classes clearly distinguishable from the groupings of the capitalist world. The social pyramid of the present age has been formed, not by the substance and laws of capitalism alone, but by two different social substances, and by the laws of two different epochs. Whoever seeks to understand Europe must not forget this and concentrate all attention on the indubitably basic truth that one of these substances tends to be absorbed by the other and thus the sharpest of all class conflicts tends to be eliminated. Whoever seeks to understand Europe must not overlook that even today its life, its ideology, its politics are greatly under the influence of the feudal "substance," that while the bourgeoisie can assert its interests everywhere, it "rules" only in exceptional circumstances, and then only briefly. The bourgeois outside his office and the professional man of capitalism outside his profession cut a very sorry figure. Their spiritual leader is the rootless "intellectual," a slender reed open to every impulse and a prey to unrestrained emotionalism. The "feudal" elements, on the other hand, have both feet on the ground, even psychologically speaking. Their ideology is as stable as their mode of life. They believe certain things to be really true, others to be really false. This quality of possessing a definite character and cast of mind as a class, this simplicity and solidity of social and spiritual position, extends their power far beyond their actual bases, gives them the ability to assimilate new elements, to make others serve their purposes—in a word, gives them *prestige*, something to which the bourgeois, as is well known, always looks up, something with which he tends to ally himself, despite all actual conflicts.

The nobility entered the modern world in the form into which it had been shaped by the autocratic state—the same state that had also molded the bourgeoisie. It was the sovereign who disciplined the nobility, instilled loyalty into it, "statized" it, and, as we have shown, imperialized it. He turned its nationalist sentiments—as in the case of the bourgeoisie—into an aggressive nationalism, and then made it a pillar of his organization, particularly his war machine. It had not been that in the immediately preceding period. Rising absolutism had at first availed itself of much more dependent organs. For that very reason, in his position as leader of the feudal powers and as warlord, the sovereign survived the onset of the Industrial Revolution, and as a rule—except in France—won victory over political revolution. The bourgeoisie did not simply supplant the sovereign, nor did it make him its leader, as did the nobility. It merely wrested a portion of his power from him and for the rest submitted to him. It did not take over from the sovereign the state as an abstract form of organization. The state remained a special social power, confronting the bourgeoisie. In some countries it has continued to play that role to the present day. It is in the *state* that the bourgeoisie with its interests seeks refuge, protection against external and even domestic enemies. The bourgeoisie seeks to win over the state for itself, and in return serves the state and state interests that are different from its own. Imbued with the spirit of the old autocracy, trained by it, the bourgeoisie often takes over its ideology, even where, as in France, the sovereign is eliminated and the official power of the nobility has been broken. Because the sovereign needed soldiers, the modern bourgeois—at least in his slogans—is an even more vehement advocate of an increasing population. Because the sovereign was in a position to exploit conquests, needed them to be a victorious warlord, the bourgeoisie thirsts for national glory—even in France, worshipping a headless body, as it were. Because the sovereign found a large gold hoard useful, the bourgeoisie even today cannot be swerved from its bullionist prejudices. Because the autocratic state paid attention to the trader and manufacturer chiefly as the most important sources of taxes and credits, today even the intellectual who has not a shred of property looks on international commerce, not from the viewpoint of the consumer, but from that of the trader and exporter. Because pugnacious sovereigns stood in constant fear of attack by their equally pugnacious neighbors, the modern bourgeois attributes aggressive designs to neighboring peoples. All such modes of thought are essentially noncapitalist. Indeed, they vanish most quickly wherever capitalism fully prevails. They are survivals of the autocratic alignment of interests, and they endure wherever the autocratic state endures on the old basis and with the old orientation, even though more and more democratized and otherwise transformed. They bear witness to the extent to which essentially imperialist absolutism has patterned not only the economy of the bourgeoisie but also its mind—in the interests of autocracy and against those of the bourgeoisie itself.

This significant dichotomy in the bourgeois mind—which in part explains its wretched weakness in politics, culture, and life generally; earns it the understandable contempt of the Left and the Right; and proves the accuracy of our diagnosis—is best exemplified by two phenomena that are very close to our subject: present-day nationalism and militarism. Nationalism is affirmative awareness of national character, together with an aggressive sense of superiority. It arose from the autocratic state. In conservatives, nationalism in general is understandable as an inherited orientation, as a mutation of the battle instincts of the medieval knights, and finally as a political stalking horse on the domestic scene; and conservatives are fond of reproaching the bourgeois with a lack of nationalism, which, from their point of view, is evaluated in a positive sense. Socialists, on the other hand, equally understandably exclude nationalism from their general ideology, because of the essential interests of the proletariat, and by virtue of their domestic opposition to the conservative stalking horse; they, in turn, not only reproach the bourgeoisie with an excess of nationalism (which they, of course, evaluate in a negative sense) but actually identify nationalism and even the very idea of the nation with bourgeois ideology. The curious thing is that both of these groups are right in their criticism of the bourgeoisie. For, as we have seen, the mode of life that flows logically from the nature of capitalism necessarily implies an anti-nationalist orientation in politics and culture. This orientation actually prevails. We find a great many anti-nationalist members of the middle class, and even more who merely parrot the catchwords of nationalism. In the capitalist world it is actually not big business and industry at all that are the carriers of nationalist trends, but the intellectual, and the content of *his* ideology is explained not so much from definite class interests as from chance emotion and individual interest. But the submission of the bourgeoisie to the powers of autocracy, its alliance with them, its economic and psychological patterning by them—all these tend to push the bourgeois in a nationalist direction; and this too we find prevalent, especially among the chief exponents of export monopolism. The relationship between the bourgeoisie and militarism is quite similar. Militarism is not necessarily a foregone conclusion when a nation maintains a large army, but only when high military circles become a political power. The criterion is whether leading generals as such wield political influence and whether the responsible statesmen can act only with their consent. That is possible only when the officer corps is linked to a definite social class, as in Japan, and can assimilate to its position individuals who do not belong to it by birth. Militarism too is rooted in the autocratic state. And again the same reproaches are made against the bourgeois from both sides—quite properly too. According to the "pure" capitalist mode of life, the bourgeois is unwarlike. The alignment of capitalist interests should make him utterly reject military methods, put him in opposition to the professional soldier. Significantly, we see this in the example of England where, first, the struggle against a standing army generally and, next, opposition to its elaboration, furnished bourgeois politicians with their most popular slogan: "retrenchment." Even naval appropriations have encountered resistance. We find similar trends in other countries, though they are less strongly developed. The continental bourgeois, however, was used to the sight of troops. He regarded an army almost as a necessary component of the social order, ever since it had been his terrible taskmaster in the Thirty Years' War. He had no power at all to abolish the army. He might have done so if he had had the power; but not having it, he considered the fact that the army might be useful to him. In his "artificial" economic situation and because of his submission to the sovereign, he thus grew disposed toward militarism, especially where export monopolism flourished. The intellectuals, many of whom still maintained special relationships with feudal elements, were so disposed to an even greater degree.[34]

Just as we once found a dichotomy in the social pyramid, so now we find everywhere, in every aspect of the bourgeois portion of the modern world, a dichotomy of attitudes and interests. Our examples also show in what way the two components work together. Nationalism and militarism, while not creatures of capitalism, become "capitalized" and in the end draw their best energies from capitalism. Capitalism involves them in its workings and thereby keeps them alive, politically as well as economically. And they, in turn, affect capitalism, cause it to deviate from the course it might have followed alone, support many of its interests.

Here we find that we have penetrated to the historical as well as the sociological sources of modern imperialism. It does not *coincide* with nationalism and militarism, though it *fuses* with them by supporting them as it is supported by them. It too is—not only historically, but also sociologically—a heritage of the autocratic state, of its structural elements, organizational forms, interest alignments, and human attitudes, the outcome of precapitalist forces which the autocratic state has reorganized, in part by the methods of early capitalism. It would never have been evolved by the "inner logic" of capitalism itself. This is true even of mere export monopolism. It too has its sources in absolutist policy and the action habits of an essentially precapitalist environment. That it was able to develop to its present dimensions is owing to the momentum of a situation once created, which continued to engender ever new "artificial" economic structures, that is, those which maintain themselves by political power alone. In most of the countries addicted to export monopolism it is also owing to the fact that the old autocratic state and the old attitude of the bourgeoisie toward it were so vigorously maintained. But export monopolism, to go a step further, is not yet imperialism. And even if it had been able to arise without protective tariffs, it would never have developed into imperialism in the hands of an unwarlike bourgeoisie. If this did happen, it was only because the heritage included the war machine, together with its socio-psychological aura and aggressive bent, and because a class oriented toward war maintained itself in a ruling position. This class clung to its domestic interest in war, and the pro-military interests among the bourgeoisie were able to ally themselves with it. This alliance kept alive war instincts and ideas of overlord-ship, male supremacy, and triumphant glory—ideas that would have otherwise long since died. It led to social conditions that, while they ultimately stem from the conditions of production, cannot be explained from capitalist production methods alone. And it often impresses its mark on present-day politics, threatening Europe with the constant danger of war.

This diagnosis also bears the prognosis of imperialism. The pre-capitalist elements in our social life may still have great vitality; special circumstances in national life may revive them from time to time; but in the end the climate of the modern world must destroy them. This is all the more certain since their props in the modern capitalist world are not of the most durable material. Whatever opinion is held concerning the vitality of capitalism itself, whatever the life span predicted for it, it is bound to withstand the onslaughts of its enemies and its own irrationality much longer than essentially untenable export monopolism—untenable even from the capitalist point of view. Export monopolism may perish in revolution, or it may be peacefully relinquished; this may happen soon, or it may take some time and require desperate struggle; but one thing is certain—it *will* happen. This will immediately dispose of neither warlike instincts nor structural elements and organizational forms oriented toward war—and it is to their dispositions and domestic interests that, in my opinion, much more weight must be given in every concrete case of imperialism than to export monopolist interests, which furnish the financial "outpost skirmishes"—a most appropriate term—in many wars. But such factors will be politically overcome in time, no matter what they do to maintain among the people a sense of constant danger of war, with the war machine forever primed for action. And with them, imperialisms will wither and die.

It is not within the scope of this study to offer an ethical, aesthetic, cultural, or political evaluation of this process. Whether it heals sores or extinguishes suns is a matter of utter indifference from the viewpoint of this study. It is not the concern of science to judge that. The only point at issue here was to demonstrate, by means of an important example, the ancient truth that the dead always rule the living.

## Notes

1. This essay was originally published under the title "Zur Soziologie der Imperialismen" in 1918–1919 in *Archiv für Sozialwissenschaft und Sozialpolitik*. It appeared in an English translation in 1951 as one of the two essays in Joseph Schumpeter, *Imperialism and Social Classes* (New York: A. M. Kelley; Oxford: Blackwell, 1951). For more information on this essay, see the section titled "The European Period: Schumpeter's Works in This Volume" in the Introduction. The translation into English has been made by Heinz Norden.

2. The author proposes to devote another study to the latter topic. Still another study by the author, *Die Krise des Steuerstaats* (Graz, 1918) [reproduced in English as Chapter 1 in this volume], seeks to approach the problem of the *Zeitgeist* from another angle. The discussion of economic problems in the present study is necessarily held to relatively brief length and is to be supplemented by a study of neo-mercantilism, yet to be published. Another study, *Die Ideenseele des Sozialismus*, likewise as yet unpublished, is to deal with a related complex of ideas.

3. To be sure, there were accomplishments in various fields. Above all, the currency was restored. It is also true that coming events were casting their shadows before them—in Huskisson's tariff policy. But overall orientation with respect to the great questions of the day was purely negative.

4. We shall revert to this point repeatedly in the following.

5. It is true that certain other acts of Disraeli's could be adduced. But the Zulu War was really the act of the local commander, Sir Bartle Frere, who earned a reprimand from the cabinet. The annexation of the Transvaal (1877), revoked only by the Treaty of London (1884) under Gladstone, was the result of a very difficult situation vis-à-vis the natives. The Afghanistan adventure, likewise reversed by Gladstone, was a countermove to a Russian advance. And the title of "Empress of India" was a gesture that serves to demonstrate to the hilt the verbal character of this imperialism.

6. Egypt was Gladstone's conquest, but a conquest against his will. From the very outset it was intended to leave Egypt to Turkey, and negotiations on this point reached a stage where it was solely Turkey's fault that this intention was not realized. Even so, there was no annexation, though such action would

have been diplomatically quite feasible and would even have met the approval of Germany. Later on the situation changed, first because of the gathering agitation among the Mohammedan population and later because of the general worsening of world conditions.

7. It scarcely seems worthwhile still to discuss the stock phrase about "commercial jealousy," which has now been pretty generally abandoned. It has been shown rather conclusively, first, that there were no grounds for such sentiments, and second, that they played a part—and a relatively unsuccessful one at that—only in one segment of the press. This is shown by the very fact that the free-trade policy continued. We shall, however, come upon this question in another context.

8. Of course this is not meant to imply that political developments on the domestic scene in any country are somehow dependent on the "fortunes of war." The result of these battles was a natural reflection of social circumstances, especially of the relative security from external enemies which placed the crown at a disadvantage in developing its instruments of power. The sentences that follow must likewise be read with this in mind.

9. Was, then, the policy of Lord North in accordance with public opinion? No, but he took a beating too. Even in this instance, by the way, the crown had to have a majority in Parliament behind its policies. It obtained this majority by means of corruption. In the end even this method failed whenever crown policy departed too far from the will of the masses. Even the great aristocratic coteries could not in the long run survive without popular favor. As early as the middle of the eighteenth century, that favor was powerful enough to prevail over the crown and the aristocracy, as the career of the elder Pitt shows. It was also powerful enough to make the position of a minister untenable, even though he was the king's favorite, as is shown by Bute's misfortunes.

10. A policy that would have been in accord with the past as well as the future was represented by Fox, whose position was weak in Parliament, but relatively strong outside. The mere fact that such an opposition policy could exist supports the argument of the text.

11. The Holy Alliance resembled a cartel. It was, to be sure, a cartel of imperialist interests, but by nature it was directed toward conservation rather than aggression.

12. The outstanding monument of this policy is Russell's note of October 27, 1860, in which he backed Piedmont against Naples and the Pope, in a tone that was then quite unusual in diplomacy. From the "objective" point of view, the Crimean War was a betrayal of this policy, but "subjectively" it appears in the light of a defensive war against imperialism.

13. Characteristically, it was Cobden, the leader in the struggle for free trade, who first successfully represented this policy in public. In his treatise on Russia (1840) he opposed the literary exponent of interventionism at the time, David Urquhart (founder of the magazine *Portfolio* in 1835 and author of, among other works, *Turkey and Its Resources; England, France, Russia, and Turkey*; and *Sultan Mahmud and Mehemet Ali*). What happened paralleled the

fate of every point argued by utilitarianism and the Manchester school. Both trends were so unpopular in England, accorded so little with popular inclination, that every politician who desired to get ahead and play a role of importance, carefully eschewed them. Yet in different verbal guise one of their points after another was usurped and realized. The most conspicuous milestone in this process was Gladstone's speech in the *Don Pacifico* debate of 1850.

14. On the pacifist character of English foreign policy in the time prior to the first world war, see Reventlow, *Deutschlands auswärtige Politik*, 1st ed., *passim*.

15. The psychological aspect here resembles the case of the modern captain of industry, whose actions likewise cannot be viewed as a balancing of hedonist purpose against effort which is experienced as disagreeable. See my *Theory of Economic Development*.

16. This is no mere analogy of the kind rightly held in contempt. We are dealing with the fact that every purposive organization by its mere existence adapts its members to its purpose.

17. This applies to the Turkish wars, waged mainly by Catholic nations. These wars were not crusades and though the religious element often emerges in them, it never appears as the motivation.

18. In later times Mohammedanism also knew expansion by means of conversion, notably in India and among the Mongols. But this does not change our diagnosis of Arab imperialism.

19. To the need for action there was added the fighting instinct. Royal policy gave direction to both. A mass of subsidiary motives were also present, among which lust for booty, murder, and destruction was by no means absent.

20. Thus, he never carried further Leibniz's plan for the conquest of Egypt. Conquests in the western part of the North African coast would have been even more plausible, but were never considered. Warfare in the colonies was conducted with considerable lassitude and financed only meagerly.

21. This is not meant to prejudice the question of whether such efforts, in the final reckoning, achieved objective cultural gains or not, a subject falling outside our present province. Personally, I take a predominantly negative view of their significance. But my arguments along these lines are again beyond the present study.

22. Imperialism is one of many examples of the important fact, already alluded to in the beginning, that the application of the economic interpretation of history holds out no hope of reducing the cultural data of a given period to the relations of production of that same period. This always serves to support objections to the basic economic approach, particularly since one of the consequences of the cited fact is that relations of production in a given period may often be reduced to existing economic sentiments that are independent of those relations. For example, the constitutional and political order of the Normans in southern Italy cannot be explained by the relations of production prevailing in that country. The very economy of the Normans in

southern Italy becomes comprehensible only by reference to their capacity and wishes. But this does not actually refute the economic interpretation, for the mentality of the Normans was not something that existed outside the economic sphere. Its sources are found in the economic background from which the Normans came to southern Italy.

23. There is here a conflict (not elaborated in the present study) with Marxism, primarily with the theories of increasing misery and the reserve army, but indirectly also with the basic conception of the whole process of capitalist production and accumulation.

24. See in this connection especially Lederer, "Zum sozialpsychischen Habitus der Gegenwart," *Archiv für Sozialwissenschaft und Sozialpolitik*, vol. 44.

25. This parallelism, of course, cannot be traced in every individual case. Countries and ideas differ far too greatly for that. Kant, for example, certainly did not have a pronounced capitalist background, though English influences did play an important part with him. His case, by the way, offers the occasion to point out that we mean our assertions to apply to *all* types formed by capitalism, not merely, or primarily, to capitalistic classes in the sense of *propertied* classes—in other words *the* capitalist class. A misunderstanding in this respect would be regrettable. It should be further emphasized that utilitarianism was not a philosophy of capitalists, either by origin or social tendency, although it was a *capitalistic* philosophy in the sense that it was possible only in a world of capitalism. Indeed, the "capitalist class" in England preponderantly and sharply rejected utilitarianism, from its early beginnings to its culmination in the younger Mill, and so did the big landowners. This fact is commonly ignored, because utilitarianism fits in so well with bourgeois practice. It does so, however, only so long as its distorted journalistic projection is confounded with its true character, only when it is taken at face value. Actually it shows an unmistakable kinship to socialism, in its philosophic approach, its social orientation, and many of its practical demands. It is the product of capitalist development, but by no means of capitalist *interests*. Pacifism, for example, can be shown to flow from it—though not from it alone. Present-day pacifist tendencies have their roots largely elsewhere, notably in Christian thought, which, of course, preceded the capitalist era, though it could become effective in this direction only in the capitalist world. Unfortunately it is not possible here to set forth these things at length and thus to guard our views against the danger of being misunderstood.

26. It is an interesting fact, by the way, that while the peace policy is certainly not rooted in the capitalist upper class, some of the most eminent exponents of the political interests of the trusts are among the most zealous promoters of the peace movement.

27. Rather, imperialist and nationalist literature is always complaining vociferously about the debility, the undignified will to peace, the petty commercial spirit, and so on, of the capitalist world. This in itself means very little, but it is worth mentioning as confirming a state of affairs that can be established from other indications.

28. The stubborn power of old prejudices is shown by the fact that even

today the demand for the acquisition of colonies is justified by the argument that they are necessary to supply the demand for food and raw materials and to absorb the energies of a vigorous, rising nation, seeking world outlets. Since the flow of food and raw materials from abroad is only impeded by tariffs at home, the justification has no rhyme or reason even in our world of high protective tariffs, especially since in the event of war traffic with colonies is subject to the same perils as traffic with independent countries. For the rest, the element of war danger circumscribes what has been said in the text to the extent that it creates an interest in the control of such food and raw material producing countries as are situated so as to offer secure access even in wartime. *In the case of universal free trade, however, the danger of war would be substantially less.* It is in this sense that the sentence about dominion of the seas, which follows in the text, must be understood.

29. Even with free trade there would be capital exports to the countries offering the highest interest rate at any given time. But that flow would be lacking in any aggressive character, just as would be true of export of commodities, which would be regulated by the law of costs, or, if capital and labor were but incompletely mobile, by the law of comparative costs. Any forcing of exports, whether of commodities or of capital, would be senseless.

30. Workers too may be temporarily placed in dire straits by a shift to other industries or methods that becomes necessary in such a case. For some individuals a shift to occupations for which they are not qualified may be altogether impossible. As a class, however, and in the long run, workers only gain through such a process—unless the industries forced out of business by competition employ relatively more workers than those which proceed to occupy the places made vacant. For in general, under free trade, production opportunities are better exploited, greater quantities are produced, and, all other things being equal, more workers are employed too. To be sure, these "other things" are by no means always equal, but that does not change the core of the argument. The fear that domestic industry will be undersold by the foreign products of cheaper labor and that wages will be consequently depressed stems from popular superstition. Actually such a danger exists to but a trifling degree. But we cannot deal with all of these questions here.

31. Capitalism is its own undoing but in a sense different from that implied by Marx. Society is bound to grow beyond capitalism, but this will be because the achievements of capitalism are likely to make it superfluous, not because its internal contradictions are likely to make its continuance impossible. This is not properly part of our subject. I do wish, however, to preclude any interpretation that I regard capitalism as the *final* phase of social evolution, as something that exists of natural necessity, that cannot be adequately explained. Still less do I regard it as an ideal in any sense. I do not go along with Hilferding, incidentally, in anticipating that trustification will bring about a stabilization of capitalism.

32. The reasons may, in part, lie in the fact that orthodox socialism has always been inclined to regard the question of protective tariff vs. free trade as something of essential concern only to the bourgeoisie, something almost

unworthy of socialist attention, to be left to literary polemicists who are in the habit of compromising with the existing order. Tactically this attitude can scarcely be maintained any longer today, nor *is* it maintained with respect to export monopolism. Yet it was tactically comprehensible in Marx's own time, for any other stand would have compelled him to admit a community of interests between the proletariat and the contemporary bourgeoisie—in England an interest in free trade, in Germany an interest in an "educational tariff," which he and Engels acknowledged. The stand, however, did impair theoretical understanding. It was one of the elements in the incorrect total evaluation of the effects of the system of free competition: especially of what Marx called the "anarchy of production," but also of the suicidal stimulus of profit, and finally, of the movement toward concentration. What was indirectly at stake was the entire concept underlying the theory of underconsumption, impoverishment, and collapse. Adherence to these views, regarded as essential to "scientific socialism," has led to far too favorable an evaluation of export monopolism, which is supposed to have brought "order" into "anarchy." See Lederer's excellent study: "Von der Wissenschaft zur Utopie," *Archiv für die Geschichte des Sozialismus und der Arbeiterbewegung*, vol. VII.

33. An imperialism in which the entrepreneurs and other elements woo the workers by means of social welfare concessions which appear to depend on the success of export monopolism may be called "social imperialism," a term appropriate to the factual situation, but certainly not implying imperialism on the part of the working class. Social imperialism in the sense of an imperialism rooted in the working class does not exist, though agitation may, of course, succeed in kindling such a mood locally and temporarily in the working class. Social imperialism in the sense of imperialist interests on the part of the workers, interests to which an imperialist attitude ought to correspond, if the workers only understood it correctly—such an imperialist policy oriented toward working-class interests is nonsensical. *A people's imperialism is today an impossibility.*

34. Methodologically, it is interesting to note here that, though nationalism and militarism are not "reflexes" of the capitalist alignment of interests, neither did they emerge as what they are today during the periods in which they had their roots. Yet they do not necessarily escape the focus of the economic interpretation of history. They are the forms assumed in the environment of the modern world by habits of emotions and action that originally arose under primitive conditions.

# *Three*

## Max Weber's Work

HE WAS life among the shadows. No one—least of all the German economist himself—denies that for some time, German science has generally produced neither achievements nor personalities of the first class in economics and the social sciences in general; and with regard to personalities, it has produced neither first-class scholars nor teachers.[1] It is not difficult to indicate some of the causes of this fact. Most important are the circumstances of political life in Germany. Because there was no more or less satisfactory form that a political career in Germany could take, some who otherwise would have gone into politics became professors of economics in Germany. This led to a preponderance of political factors in the theory and research of an academic, professorial science, with the result that the considered and thorough excavation into the depths of a problem detached from mundane considerations—the only sort of work that leads to more significant results—became more infrequent. Political circumstances were also influential in another respect. Consider a people for whom not even the greatest shock could awaken as much as a desire for what passes for freedom elsewhere. On the contrary, as we see, these shocks led only to the result that the lifeless body of the state, which lay with a crushing weight on every area of German life, became even more burdensome and oppressive. Among such a people, it was inevitable that the professor, whose main purpose was and is to train officials of every sort, was judged on the basis of convictions that were predominantly political. Although this does not explain everything, it explains a great deal. It explains not only weak achievements and personalities, but also that atmosphere of infirmity in which everything among these people—both in and outside science—becomes conventional, an atmosphere in which we can invariably predict what a man will say before we read a page or listen to a speech. We have to be familiar with this background in order to experience the brilliance that surrounds the figure of Max Weber.

He was not conventional. He had never been broken in. He was his own man. But that is not all. These qualities would be compatible with a career of isolated and ineffectual self-absorption. However, he led. He was able to steer against the current. He was strong enough to transcend this atmosphere and carry with him the best of his time and his circle. He was an imposing figure. You submitted to him, whether or not you wanted to. Energy resounded from his every word, flowed—we might say—from every pore of his being. Energy in all the varieties that can be distinguished, especially energy united in an extremely unusual combination: intellectual and at the same time moral. Together with his unbound intellectual and moral courage, he also had all the qualities associated with courage, above all candor in friendship and enmity, tempered with generosity and a sense of duty. There was nothing in this sense of duty that was at all servile. It was rooted solely in the pleasures of work, on the one hand, and in a self-conscious pride, on the other.

This is not a complete portrait of the man, nor is it intended to be. Since my personal acquaintance with him was much too limited, I would be quite incompetent to offer such a sketch. Here I want only to convey to the reader the impression that this total image stood over and above each of his individual characteristics. You could love it or hate it, but you could never ignore it. Above all, he was loved: by his students and followers with an intensity for which I know no other example in our time; and by a larger circle with a feeling of awe that often bordered on helplessness. He had triumphed among specialists in his science. You accepted this triumph and swallowed what was perhaps not altogether to your liking. I can offer no judgment on the position he took in political matters, although I have often considered the faces that would be made by the banal political figures of today if this Lohengrin with his silver moral armor suddenly appeared among them.

There is no doubt that we have lost an intellectual leader. Not a leader in the sense in which the word is debased, like the "Sir" in the address of a modern letter. Nor in the sense in which every member of the liberal professions thinks that he is a leader. But rather a leader in the full sociological meaning of the word: someone who forms and dominates intellectual trends, a man whose influence, both as a symptom as well as a cause, belongs to the history of Germany today, not merely to the history of its specialized science.

At this point it is my task to describe, as well as I can, the roots of his significance. One caveat should be entered at the outset. This significance does not lie in the economic policies he may have generated or recommended for his people. The significance of a scholar can never lie in this arena. Among the things that Max Weber himself forced on a recalcitrant community of scientific specialists is a conviction that most of its members now share: It cannot be the business of science to tell us what should be the case or what should happen.

Moreover, in this area he had nothing to say that would add to the existing intellectual inventory of economic policy. It is true that he was an energetic participant in politics, or at least in controversy concerning political ideas, with all the courage, common sense, and vigor that were his characteristics—and in the final years of his life, this engagement became a matter of passionate interest. Naturally we must take note of the position he took from the beginning of his career as an advocate of social welfare policy, and also the position he took at the end of his career as a defender of private initiative and an opponent of an administratively controlled economy. Nevertheless, there is no economic policy that can be linked with his name in the way that we associate free trade with the name of Adam Smith, the educational tariff with the name of Friedrich List, or social welfare policy with the names of the older academic socialists.

And yet one aspect of his achievement lies outside the sphere of purely scientific research and theory. He labored mightily at the political education of his people, above all the young people in the universities. He taught hundreds how to see political and cultural matters and how to think about them. He assailed with a fury the mentality of the rootless, jargon-fed intellectuals of our time, the mentality of the "literati," as he called them, and on this subject the truths that he declared were innumerable. Only a few of his original publications are devoted to this purpose, for example his book *Parliament and Government in a Reconstructed Germany*.[2] He was ruthless, but without being embittered in the attempt to clear away the rubbish of worthless phraseology that prevents the "educated classes" of today from seeing the realities of politics—with his word or his pen, in conversations and newspaper articles, and in addresses, two brilliant examples of which have just been published: "Politics as a Vocation" and "Science as a Vocation."[3] Those who were influenced by him achieved from that time on a clearer and more sound position.

This aspect of his life's work sets him apart from the community of scientific specialists. However, the essential significance of his work naturally lies within this community. In the first place, he did something here that is intimately related to the extra-scientific achievement just mentioned. He encountered a state of methodological confusion in German science, that strife among methodological factions characteristic of our science, which was so detrimental to the progress of positive work and led to stereotypical formulas and phrases on every page. The problem posed by this situation demanded not only prodigious methodological knowledge and a real insight into the inner workings of science. Since group interests were also implicated in these methodological controversies, it also required the same forceful leadership and firmness of character needed in a political struggle. That is why he was the man for the job. Before Weber, there were countless occasions on which the distinction between knowledge and the aims of economic policy were both recognized and demanded as a necessity. However, this distinction is a matter not just of knowledge, but also of self-discipline. It requires resignation, resignation of the cherished desire of the economist: to regard himself, wherever possible, as the practical leader of his people and to invest his partisan views with the authority of science.

In addition to the struggle for the distinction between science and politics, there was also the struggle for the distinction between science and philosophy. Naturally, the process of the disengagement of the social sciences, first from the major premises of theology, then from those of philosophy, is as old as the problematics of the social sciences. In the natural sciences, this disengagement proceeded automatically and essentially painlessly. In the sphere of the difficult issues of human behavior, matters were different, and until quite recently metaphysical influences inhibited the development of social science. More than virtually anyone else, Max Weber was the man to attack these issues. Because he was not a scholar who confined himself to his study, he could demonstrate by his own example that one can participate in politics with the most profound passion and still expel it from science; and because he was also a man of the most profound metaphysical understanding and philosophical aptitude, he was especially qualified for the task of showing how one could still pursue a metaphysically neutral positive science.

This brings us to his original individual contributions to the methodology of the social sciences. They were not speculative, they were focused on concrete problems, and they are inextricably connected with his great sociological works. They were primarily concerned with conquering the stronghold of epistemological difficulties, the scientific treatment of history. The major questions of principle concerning historical causation, historical necessity, and historical development; the relation between social conditions and the sociopsychological "superstructure"; the relations between concrete social processes and general nomological knowledge have never been handled with so much positive substantive knowledge and, at the same time, such logical rigor. In no other author do we find a comparable fusion of methodological theory and productive research. Each of his special studies mirrors the totality of his reflections on questions of principle. Every account of his reflections on questions of principle pulsates with the life of his individual investigations. In every line of both we find his entire personality.

Thus, his epistemological works became an arsenal not only of sociological methodology, but also of sociological theory. The following
works are primarily relevant here: "Roscher and Knies: The Logical
Problems of Historical Economics," a series of articles published in
*Schmollers Jahrbuch*,[4] in which Weber unsparingly revealed the entire
wretched state of conceptual chaos in the so-called older historical
school of economics and made the first attempt to bring the discussion to the surface out of this world of slogans and shibboleths and
launch defensible conceptions. When he became a member of the editorial board of the *Archiv für Sozialwissenschaft*, he inaugurated his
activity, to which the *Archiv* owes so much, with his treatise " 'Objectivity' in Social Science and Social Policy."[5] This was followed by his
"Critical Studies in the Logic of the Cultural Sciences,"[6] and finally by
" 'Energetische' Kulturtheorien."[7] The point of departure for these
studies was always critique. A critique replete with honesty and seriousness, and occasionally of such fervor that it threw out the baby
with the bath water in the attempt to strike down every source of
unclarity as such, without asking whether a fuzzy expression or an
erroneous phrase might not also conceal a grain of truth. Weber was
absolutely tireless in passing judgment on the epistemological dilet-
tantism of historians and sociologists. However, he did not rest content with mere criticism. An increasingly wide circle of students was
able to gain positive enlightenment and to learn, among other things,
modesty from these powerful discussions.

The substantive complement to these accomplishments are his
works "The Protestant Ethic and the Spirit of Capitalism"[8] and "The
Economic Ethics of the World Religions."[9] Both were published in the
*Archiv für Sozialwissenschaft*, and both produced a powerful effect.
They are not only the best sociological achievements of German science. They are also the center of a German school of sociologists, and
they have been infinitely productive. One may accept or reject the
basic conception of the social phenomenon that they propound.
However, they certainly represent the greatest endeavors in the area
of the scientific analysis of world-historical events thus far produced.
It lies in the nature of the subject matter that the results of such investigations, which are based on the principle of the theoretical mastery of an immense body of material, cannot be set out in a few sentences. The goal to which the entire effort of the author is directed is
to give the reader a total impression of the nature of the relations
between sociopsychological processes and economic states. Consider
the type of view of history for which Marx's economic conception of
history provides the great landmark. Here for the first time it is sub-

stantially advanced from the level of an impression and a mere demand to the level of fulfillment.

Both publications are only two pillars, perceptible to a more extensive readership, of an immense edifice. This edifice, whose broad halls open up a prospect onto an unlimited horizon, was Weber's great scientific achievement.

Thus, Weber was a sociologist above all. Even though he was a sociologist with a penchant for things that are primarily concerned with economics, he was an economist only indirectly and secondarily. His interest in economics does not focus on the mechanism of economic life as described by economic theory, nor on the real historical phenomenon for its own sake, but rather on the sequence of historical types and their sociopsychological profusion. Partisanship in favor of any school or party-line was quite foreign to his way of thinking. In the sphere of science, he is a good example of the truth, also valid for the arts, that only second-class minds can accept the sort of "party-line" that is characteristic of a school. Every work of the highest quality combines elements of all possible schools of the present, the past, and the future.

From time to time—and this brought him the leading role in scientific life that corresponded to the magnitude of his personality—he took a lively interest in specifically economic research that explored one new path or another. His memorandum—printed as a manuscript by the *Verein für Sozialpolitik*—on surveys dealing with adaptation and selection, the occupational choice, and the occupational fate of workers in large-scale industrial enterprises belongs under this heading.[10] It opened up a comprehensive field of fruitful empirical research. However, Weber himself did no further work in this area. If, in spite of this consideration, this initiative and a number of similar projects should be included in the total picture of his life's work, there are numerous surveys and speeches concerning problems in political economy that are related only tenuously to this picture. Even his great, purely scientific works in economics—such as his studies on the stock exchange[11] and his Roman agrarian history[12] or his very first work on medieval trading companies[13]—were treated by Weber as mere opportunities for learning, enlarging his general conceptual system, and confirming his immense body of knowledge. For us and our successors, they are examples of his mode of work. In many respects they are models. However, his reputation has only a little to gain from the individual achievements they represent and only a little to lose from the individual errors they commit. In the last years of his life, he assumed more and more responsibilities of this sort, which may conveniently be described as the governmental affairs of a scientific prince. Thus, he devoted much effort to the German Sociological Society and to the publication of the *Grundriss der Sozialökonomik*,[14] the programmatic expansion of which into an encyclopedia of economic theory was prevented by the war.

His passionate appetite for knowledge led him to consume, without ever flagging, an unbelievable mass of facts. Factual knowledge by itself does not signify scientific greatness. However, the mastery of a vast multitude of concrete facts was an essential presupposition of Weber's special mode of thought and work. He began with studies in law and history. As the years passed, he expanded his historical knowledge in an astonishing fashion to include the totality of all extra-European material accessible to us. He never observed the boundaries that social scientists generally draw in these matters. Whenever boundaries were at stake, his zeal surmounted all obstacles. For example, he learned Hebrew expressly for these purposes; not with the intention of undertaking specific pieces of work for their own sake, but only to gain a better insight and to make his own judgments.

It virtually goes without saying that German economists can be expected to have philosophical interests. In most cases, however, these interests are not profound. This did not hold true for Weber. He struggled with all the questions of philosophy and psychology, and he did his own research and spoke on these questions. Although he never claimed the authority of an expert, he did lay claim to the authority of a man who knows the ground on which he stands. His multitudes and mountains of facts nourished an endlessly animated world of ideas. He was not one of those minds in which the coals put out the fire. What we all admired so much about this knowledge was its immediacy and the unparalleled ease with which he could juxtapose masses of facts of the most diverse origin imaginable and then theoretically fuse them, often outraging the guilds of historians or ethnologists.

From a purely scientific standpoint, this was probably also the greatest experience of his audience. I never heard him speak myself. Without being a good speaker in the usual sense, he is said to have cast a distinctive spell over his listeners. He was an effective, productive, and thoroughly conscientious teacher. Following the unconventionally framed studies of his university years, he began teaching quite early, first in Berlin, then in Freiburg, and finally in Heidelberg, where, since 1897, he created around himself that atmosphere of all kinds of intellectual work and intellectual interests that will remain an unforgettable experience for all the many who were touched by it.

The above judgments are not altered by the fact that in 1903 he resigned his teaching position. In view of his mode of work, in the long run its burdens must have become unbearable. The ordeal of stress to which he subjected himself, constantly struggling in an intellectual world of such dimensions, was too much for his nerves. The last few years, in which he resumed teaching in Vienna and then in Munich, finally proved to be too much. What everyone who loved and admired him had welcomed with so much satisfaction—the resumption of his immediate influence from the lecture platform—may have cost him his life. Faced with the choice between slackening and collapse, a man of his nature could choose only the latter. In undiminished brilliance and up to the final moment a vital force in German intellectual life, he suddenly departed. Weber was one of those men of whom it cannot be asked whether they can be replaced, one of the fortunate who gave the world the feeling that it has received only a small part of what they could offer.

## Notes

1. This article was originally published as "Max Webers Werk" in *Der österreichische Volkswirt* 12 (1920): 831–34. It was translated for this anthology by Guy Oakes, who is also responsible for the footnotes. For more information on this essay, see the section titled "The European Period: Schumpeter's Works in This Volume" in the Introduction.

2. *Parlament und Regierung im neugeordneten Deutschland*, Munich and Leipzig: Duncker & Humblot, 1918. English translation of the first five of the six sections of this essay: "Parliament and Government in a Reconstructed Germany," translated by Guenther Roth, 1381–1469 in Max Weber *Economy and Society*, edited by Guenther Roth and Claus Wittich (Berkeley: University of California Press, 1978).

3. *Politik als Beruf*, Munich and Leipzig: Duncker & Humblot, 1919. English translation: "Politics as a Vocation," 77–128 in *From Max Weber: Essays in Sociology*, translated, edited, and with an introduction by H. H. Gerth and C. Wright Mills (New York: Oxford University Press, 1958). *Wissenschaft als Beruf* (Munich and Leipzig: Duncker & Humblot, 1919). English translation: "Science as a Vocation," 129–56 in *From Max Weber*.

4. "Roscher und Knies und die logischen Probleme der historischen Nationalökonomie," *Jahrbuch für Gesetzgebung, Verwaltung und Volkswirtschaft im Deutschen Reich* 25 (1903): 1181–1221; 29 (1905): 1323–84; and 30 (1906): 81–120. Reprinted in Max Weber, *Gesammelte Aufsätze zur Wissenschaftslehre*, 3rd edition, revised and enlarged, edited by Johannes Winckelmann, Tübingen: J.C.B. Mohr, 1968, 1–145. English translation: *Roscher and Knies: The Logical Problems of Historical Economics*, translated and edited, with an introduction by Guy Oakes (New York: The Free Press, 1975). For many years, the *Jahrbuch für Gesetzgebung, Verwaltung und Volkswirtschaft* was edited by Gus-

tav Schmoller, the Berlin economist and historian, doyen of the German historical school of economics, chairman of the executive committee of the *Verein für Sozialpolitik* since its foundation, and perhaps the most influential of the *Kathedersozialisten*—that fragmented collection of social scientists who became known, somewhat contemptuously, as "academic socialists" or "socialists of the lectern." Thus, the *Jahrbuch* was more conventionally known as *Schmollers Jahrbuch*.

5. "Die 'Objektivität' sozialwissenschaftlicher und sozialpolitischer Erkenntnis," *Archiv für Sozialwissenschaft und Sozialpolitik* 19 (1904): 22–87. Reprinted in *Wissenschaftslehre*, 146–214. English translation: " 'Objectivity' in Social Science and Social Policy," 49–112 in Max Weber, *The Methodology of the Social Sciences*, translated and edited by Edward A. Shils and Henry A. Finch (New York: The Free Press, 1949). In 1903, Weber, Edgar Jaffe, and Werner Sombart assumed joint editorship of the *Archiv*, now regarded as one of the most distinguished scholarly journals in the history of the social sciences. During their joint editorship, work of extraordinarily high quality appeared in the *Archiv*, including essays by Robert Michels, Gustav Radbruch, Georg Simmel, Ottmar Spann, Ferdinand Toennies, and many contributions by Weber himself. Much of the work for which Weber is remembered—including *The Protestant Ethic and the Spirit of Capitalism* and the entire series of studies on the economic ethics of the world religions—originally appeared as monographs in the *Archiv*.

6. "Kritische Studien auf dem Gebiet der kulturwissenschaftlichen Logik," *Archiv für Sozialwissenschaft und Sozialpolitik* 22 (1906): 143–207. Reprinted in *Wissenschaftslehre*, 215–90. English translation: "Critical Studies in the Logic of the Cultural Sciences," 113–88 in *Methodology of the Social Sciences*.

7. " 'Energetische' Kulturtheorien," *Archiv für Sozialwissenschaft und Sozialpolitik* 29 (1909): 575–98. Reprinted in *Wissenschaftslehre*, 400–26.

8. "Die protestantische Ethik und der 'Geist' des Kapitalismus," *Archiv für Sozialwissenschaft und Sozialpolitik* 20 (1904): 1–54; 21 (1905): 1–110. Weber's revised version, expanded by the addition of new notes, is published in his *Gesammelte Aufsätze zur Religionssoziologie*, I, Tübingen: J.C.B. Mohr, 1920. The English translation—*The Protestant Ethic and the Spirit of Capitalism*, translated by Talcott Parsons (New York: Scribner's, 1958)—employs the 1920 version.

9. "The Economic Ethics of the World Religions" is constituted by a core of three monographs: the first on Confucianism, the second on Hinduism and Buddhism, and the third on ancient Judaism. These monographs are prefaced by a lengthy theoretical introduction and a *Zwischenbetrachtung* or digression, inserted between the first and second studies. The circumstances of publication are as follows. "Die Wirtschaftsethik der Weltreligionen. Religionssoziologische Skizzen. Einleitung. Der Konfuzianismus, I & II," *Archiv für Sozialwissenschaft und Sozialpolitik* 41 (1915): 1–87; "Die Wirtschaftsethik der Weltreligionen. Der Kunfuzianismus, III & IV. Zwischenbetrachtung: Stufen und Richtungen der religiösen Weltablehnung," *Archiv für Sozialwissenschaft und Sozialpolitik* 41 (1915): 335–421; "Die Wirtschaftsethik der Welt-

religionen. Hinduismus und Buddismus," *Archiv für Sozialwissenschaft und Sozialpolitik* 41 (1916): 613–744; 42 (1917): 687–814; "Die Wirtschaftsethik der Weltreligionen. Das antike Judentum," *Archiv für Sozialwissenschaft und Sozialpolitik* 44 (1917): 52–138; 44 (1918): 349–443, 601–26; 46 (1918): 40–113; 46 (1919): 311–66, 541–604. The entire series was revised by Weber shortly before his death and published under the title "Die Wirtschaftsethik der Weltreligionen. Vergleichende religionssoziologische Versuche" in his *Gesammelte Aufsätze zur Religionssoziologie*, I–III (Tübingen: J.C.B. Mohr, 1920–1921). The "Einleitung" is translated as "The Social Psychology of the World Religions," 267–301 in *From Max Weber*. "Der Konfuzianismus" is translated as *The Religion of China*, translated and edited by H. H. Gerth (Glencoe, IL: The Free Press, 1951). The "Zwischenbetrachtung" is translated as "Religious Rejections of the World and Their Directions," 323–59 in *From Max Weber*. "Hinduismus und Buddismus" is translated as *The Religion of India*, translated and edited by H. H. Gerth and Don Martindale (Glencoe, IL: The Free Press, 1958). And "Das antike Judentum" is translated as *Ancient Judaism*, translated and edited by H. H. Gerth and Don Martindale (Glencoe, IL: The Free Press, 1952).

10. *Erhebung über Auslese und Anpassung (Berufswahl und Berufsschicksal) der Arbeiterschaft der geschlossenen Grossindustrie* (Altenburg: Stephan Geibel & Co., 1908).

11. In the mid-1890s, Weber published a series of analyses of German stock exchanges. See "Die Börse," *Göttinger Arbeiterbibliothek* 1 (1894): 17–48; 2 (1896): 49–80; "Die Ergebnisse der deutschen Börsenenquete," *Zeitschrift für das Gesammte Handelsrecht* 43 (1895): 83–219, 457–514; 44 (1896): 29–74; 45 (1896): 69–156.

12. *Die römische Agrargeschichte in ihrer Bedeutung für das Staats- und Privatrecht* (Stuttgart: Enke, 1891).

13. *Zur Geschichte der Handelsgesellschaften im Mittelalter. Nach südeuropäischen Quellen* (Stuttgart: Enke, 1889).

14. On Weber's editorial leadership of the project for a multi-volume series on the "Fundamental Elements of Socio-Economics," see Wolfgang Schluchter, "Wirtschaft und Gesellschaft: Das Ende eines Mythos," 597–634 in his *Religion und Lebensführung*, vol. 2 (Frankfurt: Suhrkamp, 1988).

# Four

## Social Classes in an Ethnically Homogeneous Environment

### Prefatory Note

The basic idea here briefly set forth dates back to the year 1910 and was first presented in a lecture course for laymen on the subject of "State and Society" which I delivered at the University of Czernowitz (Cernauti) in the winter of 1910–1911.[1] Subsequently, at Columbia University in the winter of 1913–1914, I presented it at length in a course entitled "The Theory of Social Classes." Since that time I have never altogether stopped developing my thoughts and analyzing the material on the subject, but after 1916 the topic took second place to other interests. Hence I am glad to seize upon the occasion of a lecture, delivered on November 19, 1926, at the University of Heidelberg, under the title "Leadership and Class Formation," to formulate once again and to publish for the first time a line of reasoning which, according to my present plan of work, I shall be able to work out fully only years from now, if at all. I offer this by way of explanation, though not of excuse, for the gaps and unevennesses in the following presentation, which stand in regrettable contrast to the length of time during which the thoughts matured and the amount of effort that went into them.

The qualifying phrase, "in an ethnically homogeneous environment," is not meant to deny the significance of racial differences in explaining concrete class formations. On the contrary, my early thinking on the subject followed the paths of the racial theory of classes, as it is found in the works of Gumplowicz, upon which I came while I was still at school. One of the strongest impressions of my apprenticeship came from Haddon, the ethnologist, who, in a course given at the London School of Economics late in 1906, demonstrated to us the differing racial types of various classes of Asiatic peoples, with the aid of countless photographs. Nevertheless, this is not the heart of the matter, not the reason why there are social classes. True, even the cursory outline, imperfect in every respect, which I present in the following, must at one point take account of this factor—since no explicit presentation would be possible otherwise. But in order not to complicate the basic features of the picture, I thought it best to exclude the racial factor in what I have to say. When it comes to investigating the "essential nature" of a social phenomenon, it is often proper and necessary to ignore certain external factors that may be quite characteristic or at least common. They may be "essential" in many respects, but not for the purposes in hand.

The theory of social classes has not attracted an amount of study truly commensurate with its fundamental importance. Marx, for example, who recognized its importance and even exaggerated it in one direction, offered a theory of the evolution of classes, but not really a theory of classes themselves. Even so, it is scarcely fair for Sombart to say (*Sozialismus und Soziale Bewegung*, p. 2) that in the works of Guizot, Mignet, and Louis Blanc we "can read everything that can be stated to this day about the nature and growth of social classes." Sombart's own definition (*loc. cit.*, p. 1) offers more than that and deserves to be recognized here as a contribution to the subject. And the widely known theories of the past fifty years do more than merely echo the thoughts of the aforementioned authors (and of Ferguson as well), nor are they made of thin air. Our own views rest, in more or less important points, on the work of Schmoller, which includes much more than merely the element of the division of labor; and on Durkheim and Spann (note the latter's reduction of "class" to "estate," in the *Handwörterbuch der Staatswissenschaften* article, "Klasse und Stand"). In many respects, furthermore, we hark back to Simmel, A. Bauer (*Les Classes sociales*, 1902), and Overberg ("La Classe sociale," *Extrait des Annales de la Société belge de Sociologie*, 1905); as well as to the theory of Bücher, so wittily expressed in the well-known simile about the *mariage de convenance* between occupation and property— though it is a theory that never goes much beneath the surface or past the foreground. The book by P. E. Fahlbeck, excellent in many individual sections, seems to us to be merely skirting the problem, which rears its head often enough. As for the book by Niceforo, it represents no more than a first step along a promising avenue of approach and hence, understandably, succeeds only in part. We are compelled to forego debating the views of all these authors, to whom we should have to add the majority of sociologists and "historians of society" (such as Riehl and Rossbach), though such a method of presentation might best serve to set forth our own concepts in detail and to buttress them against objections.

Our subject owes much more to legal and social history; to ethnology (where, unfortunately, the wrong questions are often asked and there is lack of a real grasp of the problem); to the study of the family; and to eugenics—for those, that is, who know how to recognize the relevance of what these disciplines have to offer. Beyond all this, the subject—and this is what constitutes its fascination—poses a wealth of new questions, offers outlooks on untilled fields, foreshadows sciences of the future. Roaming it, one often has a strange feeling, as though the social sciences of today, almost on purpose, were dealing with relative side issues; as though some day—and perhaps soon—the things we now believe will be discounted. But this is not an aspect that I wish to bring to the fore. Quite the contrary. My purpose is to present, not only as briefly but as soberly as possible, a sharply delimited series of problems, together with their corresponding solutions. The wider vistas must open up to the reader spontaneously or not at all.

## I. The Problem of Classes

1. We here mean by classes those social phenomena with which we are all familiar—social entities which we observe but which are not of our making. In this sense every social class is a special social organism, living, acting, and suffering as such and in need of being understood as such.[2] Yet the concept of class occurs in the social sciences in still another meaning—a meaning shared with many other sciences. In this sense it still corresponds to a set of facts, but not to any specific phenomenon of reality. Here it becomes a matter of classifying different things according to certain chosen characteristics. Viewed in this sense, class is a creation of the researcher, owes its existence to his organizing touch. Those two meanings are often annoyingly mixed up in our social-science thinking, and we therefore emphasize what should be self-evident, namely, that there is not the slightest connection between them as a matter of necessity. Whenever there is any actual coincidence of their contents, this is either a matter of chance, or—if it is really more than that—must be demonstrated, generally or specifically, by means of pertinent rules of evidence. It can never be assumed as a matter of course. This word of caution applies especially to the field in which theoretical economics operates. In theoretical economics, a landlord—the very term implies the confusion we oppose—is anyone who is in possession of the services of land. But not only do such people not form a social class. They are divided by one of the most conspicuous class cleavages of all. And the working class, in the sense of economic theory, includes the prosperous lawyer as well as the ditch digger. These classes are classes only in the sense that they result from the scholar's classification of economic subjects. Yet they are often thought and spoken of as though

they *were* classes in the sense of the social phenomenon we here seek to investigate. The two reasons that explain this situation actually make it more troublesome than it would otherwise be. There is, first, the fact that the characteristic by which the economist classifies does have some connection with the real phenomenon. Then there is the fact that the economic theorist finds it exceedingly difficult to confine himself strictly to his problems, to resist the temptation to enliven his presentation with something that fascinates most of his readers—in other words, to stoke his sputtering engine with the potent fuel of the class struggle. Hence the amusing circumstance that some people view any distinction between economic theory and the facts of social class as evidence of the most abysmal failure to grasp the point at issue; while others see any fusion of the two as the most abysmal analytical blundering. Hence, too, the fact that the very term "class struggle," let alone the idea behind it, has fallen into discredit among the best minds in science and politics alike—in much the same way that the overpowering impression of the Palazzo Strozzi loses so much by its inescapable juxtaposition with the frightful pseudo-architecture of modern apartment houses.

2. Of the many sociological problems which beset the field of class theory—the scientific rather than the philosophical theory, the sociological rather than the immediately economic—four emerge distinctly. First, there is the problem of the *nature* of class (which is perhaps, and even probably, different for each individual scientific discipline, and for each purpose pursued within such a discipline)—and, as part of this problem, the function of class in the vital processes of the social whole. Fundamentally different, at least theoretically, is the problem of class *cohesion*—the factors that make of every social class, as we put it, a special living social organism, that prevent the group from scattering like a heap of billiard balls. Again fundamentally distinct is the problem of class *formation*—the question of why the social whole, as far as our eye can reach, has never been homogeneous, always revealing this particular, obviously organic stratification. Finally, we must realize—and we shall presently revert to this point—that this problem is again wholly different from the series of problems that are concerned with the *concrete causes and conditions* of an individually determined, historically given class structure—a distinction that is analogous to that between the problem of the theory of prices in general and problems such as the explanation of the level of milk prices in the year 1919.

We are not, at this point, seeking a definition that would anticipate the solution of our problem. What we need, rather, is a characteristic that will enable us, in each case, to recognize a social class and to dis-

tinguish it from other social classes—a characteristic that will show on
the surface and, if possible, on the surface alone; that will be as clear
or as fuzzy as the situation itself is at first glance. Class is something
more than an aggregation of class members. It is something else, and
this something cannot be recognized in the behavior of the individual
class member. A class is aware of its identity as a whole, sublimates
itself as such, has its own peculiar life and characteristic "spirit." Yet
one essential peculiarity—possibly a consequence, possibly an intermediate cause—of the class phenomenon lies in the fact that class
members behave toward one another in a fashion characteristically
different from their conduct toward members of other classes. They
are in closer association with one another; they understand one another better; they work more readily in concert; they close ranks and
erect barriers against the outside; they look out into the same segment of the world, with the same eyes, from the same viewpoint, in
the same direction. These are familiar observations, and among explanations which are traditionally adduced are the similarity of the
class situation and the basic class type.

To this extent the behavior of people toward one another is a very
dependable and useful *symptom* of the presence or absence of class
cohesion among them—although it does not, of course, go very
deeply, let alone constitute a cause. Even more on the surface—a
symptom of a symptom, so to speak, though it hints at a far-reaching
basic orientation—is the specific way in which people engage in social
intercourse. These ways are decisively influenced by the degree of
"shared social *a priori*," as we might say with Simmel. Social intercourse within class barriers is promoted by the similarity of manners
and habits of life, of things that are evaluated in a positive or negative
sense, that arouse interest. In intercourse across class borders, differences on all these points repel and inhibit sympathy. There are always a number of delicate matters that must be avoided, things that
seem strange and even absurd to the other class. The participants in
social intercourse between different classes are always on their best
behavior, so to speak, making their conduct forced and unnatural.
The difference between intercourse within the class and outside the
class is the same as the difference between swimming with and
against the tide. The most important symptom of this situation is the
ease or difficulty with which members of different classes contract
legally and socially recognized marriages. Hence we find a suitable
definition of the class—one that makes it outwardly recognizable and
involves no class theory—in the fact that intermarriage prevails
among its members, socially rather than legally.[3] This criterion is especially useful for our purposes, because we limit our study to the

class phenomenon in a racially homogeneous environment, thus eliminating the most important additional impediment to intermarriage.[4]

3. Our study applies to the third of the four questions we have distinguished—to the others only to the extent that it is unavoidable. Let us begin by briefly discussing three difficulties in our way—a consideration of each of them already constituting an objective step toward our goal.

First: We seek to interpret the class phenomenon in the same sense in which we understand social phenomena generally, that is, as *adaptations* to existing needs, grasped by the observer—ourselves—as such. We shall pass over the logical difficulties inherent in even this simple statement, such as whether it is admissible to apply our own conceptual modes to cultures remote from us. There is also the question of the extent to which the condition of culturally primitive peoples in our own time may be taken as a clue to the past state of modern civilized peoples, and the even more important question of the extent to which historical data are at all valid for theoretical purposes. One difficulty, however, we must face. Unless specifically proven, it is an erroneous assumption that social phenomena to which the same name has been applied over thousands of years are always the same things, merely in different form. This is best seen in the history of social institutions. Anyone will realize that common ownership of land in the ancient Germanic village community—supposing, for the moment, that its existence had been proven—is something altogether different from common land ownership in present-day Germany. Yet the term "ownership" is used as though it always implied the same basic concept. Obviously this can be true only in a very special sense, to be carefully delimited in each case. When taken for granted, it becomes a source of one-sided and invalid constructions. The fact that there may occur in the language of law and life of a given period expressions that we regard as equivalent to our chosen concept, proves nothing, even when those expressions were actually used in an equivalent sense. Similarly, the actuality of the institution we call marriage has changed so greatly in the course of time that it is quite inadmissible to regard that institution always as the same phenomenon, from a general sociological viewpoint and without reference to a specific research purpose. This does not mean that we renounce the habit, indispensable in analysis, of seeking, wherever possible, the same essential character in the most diverse forms. But the existence of that character must be a fact, its establishment the result of study, not a mere postulate. This applies to our problem as well. When we speak of "the" class phenomenon and take it to mean that group differences in social values, found everywhere, though under varying conditions, are everywhere explained by the same theory, that is not even a working hypothesis, but merely a method of presentation in which the result is anticipated—a result that has meaning only from the viewpoint of the particular theory in question. "Master classes," for example, do not exist everywhere—if, indeed, the concept of "master" has a precise content at all.

Second: The class membership of an individual is a primary fact, originally quite independent of his will. But he does not always confirm that allegiance by his conduct. As is well known, it is common for nonmembers of a class to work with and on behalf of that class, especially in a political sense, while members of a class may actually work against it. Such cases are familiar from everyday life—they are called fellow travelers, renegades, and the like. This phenomenon must be distinguished, on the one hand, from a situation in which an entire class, or at least its leadership, behaves differently from what might be expected from its class orientation; and, on the other hand, from a situation in which the individual, by virtue of his own functional position, comes into conflict with his class. There is room for differences of opinion on these points. For example, one may see in them aberrations from the normal pattern that hold no particular interest, that have no special significance to an understanding of society, that are often exceptions to the rule more apparent than real. Those who view the class struggle as the core of all historical explanation will generally incline to such opinions and seek to explain away conflicting evidence. From another viewpoint, however, these phenomena become the key to an understanding of political history—one without which its actual course and in particular its class evolution become altogether incomprehensible. To whatever class theory one may adhere, there is always the necessity of choosing between these viewpoints. The phenomena alluded to, of course, complicate not only the realities of social life but also its intellectual perception. We think that our line of reasoning will fully answer this question, and we shall not revert to it.

Third: Every social situation is the heritage of preceding situations and takes over from them not only their cultures, their dispositions, and their "spirit," but also elements of their social structure and concentrations of power. This fact is of itself interesting. The social pyramid is never made of a single substance, is never seamless. There is no single *Zeitgeist*, except in the sense of a construct. This means that in explaining any historical course or situation, account must be taken of the fact that much in it can be explained only by the survival of elements that are actually alien to its own trends. This is, of course, self-evident, but it does become a source of practical difficulties and diagnostic problems. Another implication is that the coexistence of essentially different mentalities and objective sets of facts must form part of any general theory. Thus, the economic interpretation of history, for example, would at once become untenable and unrealistic— indeed, some easily demolished objections to it are explained from this fact—if its formulation failed to consider that the manner in which production methods shape social life is essentially influenced by the fact that the human protagonists have always been shaped by past situations. When applied to our problem, this means, first, that any theory of class structure, in dealing with a given historical period, must include prior class structures among its data; and then, that any general theory of classes and class formation must explain the fact that classes coexisting at any given time bear the marks of different centuries on their brow, so to speak—that they stem from varying conditions. This is in the essential nature of the matter, an aspect of the nature of the class phenomenon. Classes, once they have come into being, harden in their mold and perpetuate themselves, even when the social conditions that created them have disappeared.

In this connection it becomes apparent that in the field of our own problem this difficulty bears an aspect lacking in many other problems. When one seeks to render modern banking comprehensible, for example, one can trace its historical origins, since doubtless there were economic situations in which there was no banking, and others in which the beginnings of banking can be observed. But this is impossible in the case of class, for there are no amorphous societies in this sense—societies, that is, in which the absence of our phenomenon can be demonstrated beyond doubt. Its presence may be more or less strongly marked, a distinction of great importance for our solution of the class problem. But neither historically nor ethnologically has its utter absence been demonstrated in even a single case, although there has been no dearth either of attempts in that direction (in eighteenth-century theories of culture) or of an inclination to assume the existence of classless situations.[5] We must therefore forego any aid from this side, whatever it may be worth,[6] though the ethnological material nevertheless retains fundamental significance for us. If we wanted to start from a classless society, the only cases we could draw upon would be those in which societies are formed accidentally, in which whatever class orientations the participants may have either count for nothing or lack the time to assert themselves—cases, in other words, like that of a ship in danger, a burning theater, and so on. We do not completely discount the value of such cases, but quite apparently we cannot do very much with them. Any study of classes and class situations therefore leads, in unending regression, to other classes and class situations, just as any explanation of the circular flow of the economic process always leads back, without any logical stopping point, to the preceding circular flow that furnishes the data for the one to follow. Similarly—though less closely so—analysis of the economic value of goods always leads back from a use value to a cost value and back again to a use value, so that it seems to turn in a circle. Yet this very analogy points to the logical way out. The general and mutual interdependence of values and prices in an economic situation does not prevent us from finding an all-encompassing explanatory principle; and the fact of regression in our own case does not mean the nonexistence of a principle that will explain the formation, nature, and basic laws of classes—though this fact naturally does not necessarily furnish us with such a principle. If we cannot derive the sought-for principle from the genesis of classes in a classless state, it may yet emerge from a study of how classes function and what happens to them, especially from actual observation of the changes in the relationship of existing classes to one another and of individuals within the class structure—*provided* it can be shown that the elements explaining such changes also include the reason why classes exist at all.

## II. The Rise and Fall of Families within a Class

4. We have said that allegiance to a certain class is a foreordained fact for the individual—that he is *born* into a given class situation. This is an objective situation, quite independent of what the individual does or wants to do, indeed limiting the scope of his behavior to a characteristic pattern. The individual belongs to a given class neither by choice, nor by any other action, nor by innate qualities—in sum, his class membership is not individual at all. It stems from his membership in a given clan or lineage. The family, not the physical person, is the true unit of class and class theory.[7]

We shall for the moment postulate given class situations, as though every social class that ever existed were made up simply of a certain number of family units, which, for some reason or other, had chanced into their class and had persisted in it, forbidding other people access to it—in other words, as though class barriers were insurmountable. Now it is beyond dispute that within a class the relative position of families is forever shifting, that some families rise within their class, while others fall. And we are interested in the reasons *why* this happens. This can best be studied in individual historical situations. The scope of our own study imposes certain limitations on us, and we therefore choose but two examples that demonstrate the points in question—the German aristocracy of the Hohenstaufen period, and the industrial bourgeoisie of capitalism at its prime. It will be seen at once that the arguments to be enumerated apply beyond the cases under consideration.

One reason for the rise or fall of a family manifestly applies so generally that it can be discussed without reference to a specific example. This is chance. We take this to mean the occurrence of favorable or unfavorable events that are independent of the behavior of the family in question, or of its position.[8] Only in rare instances is an event of this nature significant enough to exert a critical and enduring effect on the fate of a family, in a way that might not have happened otherwise. Even rarer are those cases in which not only the occurrence but also the effect of the event on the family's position is independent of its behavior—for even where chance operates, its effects are usually exploited or overcome. An example might be the gain in wealth and position accruing to the few aristocratic families who happened to own the land on which present-day London is built. The position of the Grosvenors (Westminster), for example, rests wholly on this chance, while that of the Russells (Bedford) and Howards (Norfolk) was greatly enhanced thereby. The significance of such accidents in the total picture of family history is too slight to figure as more than an aberration, important only to an understanding of individual cases or groups of cases. We can also assess as quite insignificant the number of cases in which a series of unrelated chances, each one alone unimportant, but the sum total carrying great weight, lifts up a family or depresses it. For, by the law of probability, such events are bound to cancel each other out. Of course, this does not necessarily happen in the individual case. But no valid theory to account for the constant shifting of family positions can be built on such a foundation.

5. The German nobility of the Hohenstaufen period formed not one class, but two: first, the princes (small in number after the Hohenstaufen reforms) and princely lieges [*Fürstengenossen*] (who numbered in the hundreds, though most families of that position in the thirteenth century were extinct by the fifteenth); and second, the mere knights [*ritterliche Burgherren*]. There were differences between these two classes, not only in rank but also in law, mode of life, and power; nor did they intermarry. It was in the upper of the two that the restratification took place which found expression in the so-called constitutional reform of the Hohenstaufen period; but in both classes certain families, in terms of wealth and prestige, rose high above the

level at which we find them at the outset of the period; while others sank down, languished, and grew impoverished. Why?

In the first place, there is an automatic increment to a position once elevated. To the family that looms above its fellows accrue new vassals, tenants, and properties, which slip from the grasp of families in decline. The rising family has better chances and is able to exploit them more effectively than the family on the downgrade. Rising power always invests in new power. But the explanatory value of this factor is greatly limited by the fact that it already presupposes an elevated or rising position. Of itself it would evidently account for only a modest increment, beyond which further gains would be dependent on new successes—as demonstrated by the rapid disintegration of even high positions. It can therefore be considered only a consequence and intermediate cause.

In the second place, hard-headed and practical shrewdness in the management of a given position plays a very great part. This factor manifestly explains a great deal about differences in family destiny, more specifically in three directions. Above all, the rise of many families is explained almost completely, that of others in part, by a single-minded marriage policy pursued over centuries with the object of enhancing their positions. Next, the success of such a policy, and of course success in general, requires an economic mobility that in turn presupposes shrewd and often ruthless exploitation of existing sources of revenue and rational utilization of their yield. Finally, the management of family position within the feudal system—and this means above all the energetic repression of neighboring lords, and sometimes also of vassals—presents a crucial and difficult problem which is solved with varying degrees of success. In certain outstanding cases, positions at the top are gained in this way rather than by the prior granting of privileges and rights on the part of the king— something that comes only subsequently. In other cases, the decline of a house can be explained by its failure to manage its position properly in spite of the fact that its claim to princely rank is as good as, or even better than, those that make the grade. This, in particular, explains a good deal about the varying success of princes—and, we may say in passing, about the uneven growth of territories in later ages.

In the third place, shifts in family position follow from differences in the way in which families stand up in the service of their feudal superiors. With some variations, this, of course, means almost exclusively war service. Only among the lower ranks of the knights does administrative and diplomatic skill count. High Church office is very important as a means of elevating the family—in Italy, for example, though not so much in Germany—at the time we are considering. Outstanding examples of such shifts, based on service, are obvious.

In the fourth place, success in wars undertaken on their own account elevates many families, while failure submerges others. This is quite evident at the highest levels. But even the lowliest knight, whose resources might be sufficient for only insignificant feuds and depredations, could rise in this fashion, especially if he refrained from going beyond the point at which his environment would join in league against him. Lack of restraint could ruin even families that had risen to the level, for example, of the Kuenringens in Austria below the Enns.[9]

All this is best observed in the rise and further development of the later sovereign territories. The factors which have been enumerated explain even their original size, and certainly fully account for their subsequent expansion or contraction. The fortunes of dynasties rose and fell in keeping with the success or failure of their policies. At bottom, this is really beyond argument. Who, for example, would care to dispute that even in the seventeenth century, Saxony's objective chances for hegemony were incomparably better than those of Brandenburg? Yet step by step Saxony lost its position, by persistently poor management on every hand, by ill-starred undertakings, by backing the wrong horse—in short by conduct that meant failure, or, to come right out and say so, through incompetence. Brandenburg, on the other hand, rose steadily, by conduct of the opposite kind. Yet apparent as the truth of this matter is, it can easily lead to an overestimate of the autonomy and importance of the physical individual. Nothing is more foreign in us than such an overestimate, let alone an orientation in the manner of Carlyle. We do not for a moment deny the dominance of objective social circumstances. Only the disposition of the people in general, of the stratum and of the individual family, is a part of these circumstances; and once the rest of the environment is given, this element does play the crucial role we claim for it— whether or not it be traced to other elements, which is the great question of the future, but does not here concern us.

6. In the case of the capitalist bourgeoisie of Europe—say, of the post-Napoleonic period—we also hold to the assumption that we are dealing with established data insofar as the situations of the class and of the individual families are concerned. We presume that each family already owns its enterprise, or its share in one. The only question we ask is this: how does it happen that one family rises, while the other falls—quite apart from accidents, to which we attribute a certain importance but not the crucial role? The rising and falling are facts. No matter which area we study, we always find that the relative

position of families in the class situation we have described—other
families are of no concern to us at this point—undergoes change, not
in such a way that the "big" ones grow bigger and the "small" ones
smaller, but typically the other way round. In the textile area of Brno,
the silk region of Krefeld, the iron-working district around Birming-
ham, for example, certain families have maintained their position for
more than half a century, in many cases considerably longer. Yet, by
and large, the families that led around the middle of the nineteenth
century are not on top of the heap today. Some of those that are most
successful now were than scarcely recognized as members of the class,
while some of those that were most successful then are accepted only
with reservations today. Manifestly, concentration and the formation
of corporations complicate our analysis, and it will be well if we make
a distinction between the competitive private and one-man firm, on
the one hand, and the modern large-scale enterprise and trust, on
the other.

The characteristic feature of the former is the element of family
property and the coincidence of family and business success. A first
reason for shifting family position is offered by the automatism of
accumulation, asserted by Marx. The "capitalist" who is bigger at the
outset of the period captures more profit than the smaller one. His
proportionate accumulation is therefore larger, and he improves his
productive plant more rapidly. The discrepancy grows, until the
wealthier exploiter outstrips the poorer one in the competitive field
and forces him to the wall. This view is a typical example of how bias
in favor of a theory blinds the theorist to the simplest facts, gro-
tesquely distorting their proportions. Manifestly, the captured surplus value *does not invest itself* but must *be invested*. This means on the
one hand that it must not be consumed by the capitalist, and on the
other hand that the important point is *how* it is invested. Both factors
lead away from the idea of objective automatism to the field of behavior and motive—in other words, from the *social* "force" to the *individual*—physical or family; from the *objective* to the *subjective*. It may
be objected that the logic of the social situation forces the individual
to invest his profits, that individual motivation is only a fleeting intermediate phase. This is true, as far as it goes, and must be acknowledged by any reasonable person. Naturally the individual psyche is
no more than a product, an offshoot, a reflex, and a conductor of the
inner necessities of any given situation. But the crucial factor is that
the social logic or objective situation does not unequivocally determine *how much* profit shall be invested, and *how* it shall be invested,
*unless individual disposition is taken into account.* Yet when that is done,
the logic is no longer inherent solely in the system as distinct from

the individuality of the industrialist himself. Marx, in fact, in this case as in general, implies an assumption about average behavior—an assumption that includes an economic psychology, however imperfect. The automatism as such does not exist, even though we shall presently encounter its elements—saving and the improvement of productive plant—as elements of industrial-family behavior. We can speak of an automatism, with respect to an existing class position, only in the sense that, as in the earlier example, that position does have a tendency to rise on its own, to a moderate extent, and even more a tendency to maintain itself, because the well-established firm can make better deals, attract new customers and suppliers, and so on.

There is, on the other hand, the very important fact of automatic decline. This occurs invariably when a family behaves according to Marx's description—when it persists in "plowing back into the business" a set proportion of profits, without blazing new trails, without being devoted, heart and soul, to the business alone. In that event it is bound to go under in time, though often only very slowly if the business is on a solid foundation and the mode of life frugal. A steady decline and loss of ground are first observed—what is called "being crowded out of business." This decline *is* automatic, for it is not a matter of omission or commission, but flows instead from the self-actuating logic of the competitive system, by the simple fact of profits running dry. As to the question why this is so, it is answered by the theory of entrepreneurial profit.[10] It seems to me, however, that everybody knows the type of old respectable firm, growing obsolete, despite its integrity, and slowly and inevitably sinking into limbo.

The second reason for the phenomenon with which we are concerned at the moment lies in the disposition to save, which varies from family to family. (If the term "saving" must be avoided as implying a positive value judgment, we can speak of an energetic policy of withholding.) This serves to make the class position secure, and adherence to such a policy over several generations is the factor that in many cases turns small family enterprises into large ones. It is a policy that is very conspicuous in families that practice it. Most of us have observed members of successful business families who watch with extreme care over expenditures which members of other classes, even when their incomes are incomparably smaller, do not hesitate a moment to make. In their personal lives, such families often live with curious frugality, sometimes against a background that, for reasons of prestige, may be quite luxurious and out of keeping with their parsimony. True, of itself this does not carry much weight, though contrary behavior may be one of the most important reasons for a decline.

The third reason lies in differences in efficiency—the quality of technical, commercial, and administrative leadership of the enterprise, primarily along traditional lines. Behavior giving rise to such differences may, for our purposes, be adequately described in terms of hard-headedness, concentration on profit, authority, capacity for work, and inexorable self-discipline, especially in renouncing other aspects of life. This latter feature often escapes consideration, because the outsider is likely to observe these people in the practice of compensatory and conspicuous excesses. The significance of such efficiency lies not so much in immediate results as in increased credit ratings that open up opportunities for expansion.

Actually, among the obstacles in the way of the rise of an industrial family, eventual lack of capital is the least. If it is otherwise in good condition, the family will find that in normal times capital is virtually thrust upon it. Indeed, one may say, with Marshall, that the size of an enterprise—and here that means the position of the family—tends to adapt itself to the ability of the entrepreneur. If he exceeds his personal limitations, resultant failure will trim the size of his enterprise; if he lacks the capital to exploit such personal resources as he does possess, he is likely to find the necessary credit. But in considering this process of expansion, we come upon a fourth reason for the varying success of business dynasties. Such expansion is not simply a matter of saving and efficient routine work. What it implies is precisely departure from routine. Elaboration of an established plant, the introduction of new production methods, the opening up of new markets—indeed, the successful carrying through of new business combinations in general—all these imply risk, trial and error, the overcoming of resistance, factors lacking in the treadmill of routine. Most members of the class are handicapped in this respect. They can follow suit only when someone else has already demonstrated success in practice. Such success requires a capacity for making decisions and the vision to evaluate forcefully the elements in a given situation that are relevant to the achievement of success, while ignoring all others. The rarity of such qualifications explains why competition does not function immediately even when there are no outward barriers, such as cartels; and this circumstance, in turn, explains the size of the profits that often eventuate from such success. This is the typical pattern by which industrial fortunes were made in the nineteenth century, and by which they are made even today; and these factors typically enhance family position, both absolutely and relatively. Neither saving nor efficient management as such are the crucial factors; what is crucial is the successful accomplishment of pertinent tasks. When one studies the history of great industrial families, one almost always comes upon one or more actions of this character—actions on which the family position is founded. Mere husbanding of already existing resources, no matter how painstaking, is always characteristic of a declining position.

In the second case—that of the industrial corporation with trust ramifications—individual success, on the one hand, and family and business success, on the other, do not coincide with the logical necessity that obtains in the case of family enterprises. True, qualifications that foster success vary only in part, may simply develop in other directions; but in the hierarchy of trusts and combinations, types rise that are distinct from those in family enterprises. Only in a relatively small number of cases is family ownership of a majority or even a controlling stock interest possible.[11] Yet without such control an industrialist can run a trust in the manner of an individual plant owner only if he happens to be an altogether extraordinary personality. Even then he will be acting as an individual rather than as a member of a family. In general, this development means the complete displacement of powerful family positions as a typical phenomenon, not merely the shifting of position between families. This is true despite the fact that in cartels proper, with their stabilization of income, family position often seems to be strengthened: at least, observers and often participants as well believe this to be the case—until the next quota is negotiated!

In seeking to understand the factors that account for the success of a corporation official, that lift him above his fellows, we find, first of all, that extraordinary physical and nervous energy have much more to do with outstanding success than is generally believed. It is a simple fact that such industrial leaders must shoulder an often unreasonable burden of current work, which takes up the greater part of the day. They come to their policy-making "conferences" and "negotiations" with different degrees of fatigue or freshness, which have an important bearing on individual success. Moreover, work that opens up new possibilities—the very basis of industrial leadership—falls into the evening and night hours, when few men manage to preserve their full force and originality. With most of them, critical receptivity to new facts has by then given way to a state of exhaustion, and only a few maintain the degree of resolution that leads to decisive action. This makes a great difference the next day. Apart from energy itself, that special kind of "vision" that marks the family entrepreneur also plays an important part—concentration on business to the exclusion of other interests, cool and hard-headed shrewdness, by no means irreconcilable with passion.[12]

In corporate industry it is necessary to woo support, to negotiate with and handle men with consummate skill. Elections and appointments become essential elements in the individual career. These factors are not as prominent in family enterprise, and as a result the standard type of "manager" and "president" is quite different from the proprietary factory entrepreneur of yore. The art of "advancement" counts; the skillful secretary prospers; political connections are of importance; articulateness is an asset. The man who skillfully disposes of a troublesome private matter for an important stockholder need not worry about a bungled shipment. The implications of this situation are the discrepancy between those qualities that enable a man to *reach* a leading position and those that enable him to *hold* it— a discrepancy foreign to family enterprise. There is still another discrepancy, likewise foreign to family enterprise—that between the personal success of the man at the head and the success of the enterprise itself. If this difference does not make itself more strongly felt, this is owing largely to persistence in the class of training in the methods of individually owned business, to which even men who have no such family background are assimilated and disciplined.

We should also mention that rising specialization and mechanization, reaching right up to the leading functions, has thrown open positions at the top to men with purely technical qualifications that would, of themselves, be inadequate to the needs of family enterprise. A laboratory chemist, for example, may come to head a major chemical enterprise, even though he is not at all the business leader type. A giant industry may be dominated by a lawyer who would push a simple factory to the brink of bankruptcy in no time.

Here too, however, it is always "behavior" and "aptitude" that explain shifts in the relative positions which originally existed. Only in this case, these positions are primarily individual. They affect the family position—by the opportunities opened up, the connections established, and the chances to make money which are presented—but not to the same extent as in the competitive family undertaking. Indeed, in corporate enterprise there is a tendency to evaluate negatively any orientation of leading figures toward personal aggrandizement, to put obstacles in its way, and thus to substitute for the motive of personal profit other motives of a purely personal character— prestige in expert circles, interest in "problems," the urge for action and achievement.

## III. Movement across Class Lines

7. We have assumed so far that class barriers are insurmountable. This is in accord with a very widespread popular notion that not only governs our evaluation of an emotional reaction to matters in the field of class, but has also gained entry into scientific circles—for the most part only as a half-conscious axiom, attaining the dimensions of an axiomatic rule only in the case of Marxist analysis. The modern radical critique of society often rests on this asserted law, which we must now discuss. There is, of course, also the question of whether classes as such, without respect to their component elements—their totality, apart from their component cells—endure in perpetuity and in their relative positions, or at least would so endure unless there were upheavals changing the environment. But this question we shall avoid by simply assuming that the answer is affirmative.

It is noncontroversial that the class situation in which each individual finds himself represents a limitation on his scope, tends to keep him within the class. It acts as an obstacle to any rise into a higher class, and as a pair of water wings with respect to the classes below. This is so self-evident that we shall leave it to the reader to enumerate the factors that exert this effect—class type, relations with class fellows, power over outward resources adapted to the class situation, and so on. Whatever historical period, whatever set of social circumstances we may select, we shall always be able to make two assertions that are not likely to be successfully contradicted: In the first place, only in very exceptional cases—so exceptional that they are of no particular significance to the explanation of social processes—is it possible for an individual to enter a "higher" class at a single bound. An example might be a position of sovereignty, achieved by virtue of a coup d'etat, affording the usurper immediate entry into the top levels of the aristocratic class.[13] A sudden downfall from the class to which one once belonged, constitutes, so far as I can see, no more than a mischance devoid of basic interest. In the second place, it is *as a rule* practically impossible for the physical individual to effectuate the transition to a higher class *for himself*; and in the overwhelming majority of cases it is impossible for him during his own lifetime to modify decisively the class situation of the true class individual, the family. The occasional cases, however, in which one or the other of these eventualities may occur can no longer be put aside as "basically uninteresting" exceptions.

But it is equally clear that in our case the relatively short periods under consideration eliminate the phenomenon in question. As soon as we consider longer periods—family histories, for example—the picture becomes different. There we encounter the fundamental fact that classes which in character and relative position must be considered to consist of identical *social* individuals never, in the long run, consist of the same *family* individuals—even if we subtract those that become extinct or drop down to a lower class. On the contrary, there is constant turnover. Entries and exits occur continually—the latter directed both upward and downward. Class composition is forever changing, to the point where there may be a completely new set of families. The rate at which this turnover proceeds varies greatly for different historical periods and social situations. Within each situation it varies for individual classes, and within the latter for individual families. There are cases in which membership in a given class does not even endure for the lifetime of a physical individual; and others in which it lasts for many centuries. Indeed, at first glance such cases of class longevity are unduly prominent, even though they constitute quite rare abnormalities. This difference in the rate of interchange is highly instructive and carries the greatest significance for the verification of our basic idea as well as for an understanding of important social questions. The process always goes on, though at times extremely slowly and almost imperceptibly, impeded by legal and other barriers which every class, for obvious reasons, seeks to erect. For the duration of its collective life, or the time during which its identity may be assumed, each class resembles a hotel or an omnibus, always full, but always of different people.

Precise demonstration of this fact is important not so much as an end in itself—since it can scarcely be disputed—but rather on account of the insight it affords into the rate of social upsurge and decline, and into their causes. Again, we must rest content with a few remarks on the subject. The fact that entry into and exit from a class take place on an individual basis does not violate the rule that these actions also have their corporative aspect, as it were—that they are of themselves class processes, independent of the behavior of individual families, which indeed, look upon them as "objective" processes. Nevertheless, it will be seen to be the *rule and principle* that entry and exit are *individually effected* by each family. It is not merely a matter of addition and subtraction from a basic stock of families created in some other way; the basic stock itself lives and dies solely by this process of the entry of new families and the exit of old ones. We do not deny that appearances point in the opposite direction. This is always true where a body changes by continual turnover of its parts, arising by continual building up and declining by continual tearing down. At any given moment there is a relatively stable basic stock that seems like a solid core—which it is in a certain sense, but not in the sense that concerns us here.

8. Our demonstration can best be conducted in cases where individual families can be identified and genealogically traced. This is increasingly possible, with the progress that has been made in genealogical research, though there is always likely to be an insurmountable barrier in the dim past. At the present time, really satisfactory material is available only for the aristocracy, notably the high nobility. Sources such as the Golden Book of the Roman aristocracy do offer the evidence we seek. Only a few of the original families were still listed in the seventeenth century, and we can observe precisely how the new names came to be added. In the case of the German high aristocracy, the families, as a rule, cannot be genealogically traced back beyond the year 1200. Yet the broad outlines of the picture emerge, nevertheless. We know, above all from the common law, that at their very entry into history the Germans already had a high nobility that bore the earmarks of a social class. In the case of the Bajuvari, for example, we even know the names of the families. These particular families vanished—in the case of the Bajuvari we later encounter similar names in the ministerial estate—yet a high nobility as such remained. Even earlier, however, new families entered that class, and this happened on a large scale during the Carolingian period, and again under the Ottonians and Salians. We see it more clearly after the eleventh century, when the documentary evidence for a time distinguishes between names belonging to the high and the low aristocracy. We are able to establish that in the thirteenth century the dividing line between freedom and unfreedom paled, that families that were formerly unfree household officials ascended to the high nobility. Again, by the fifteenth century virtually all the families of the thirteenth-century high aristocracy were extinct or had declined—yet the class lived on. Despite legal and economic fixations, the barriers remained in a state of flux. This is precisely what constitutes the difficult legal problem of "peerage." It is significant for our purposes that there is no clear legal method for defining either the concept or the content of the high nobility as a class—indeed, that the genealogist resists any such attempt. Whenever a family had achieved success, gained wealth and prestige, it was accepted by its superiors, whatever its origin or former status; when it went into a decline, it was suddenly no longer considered to be equal. There were frequent intermediate stages that illustrate this continual process. Occasionally connubium existed between the rising families and those already arrived, though the offspring of such unions still required the formal

act of "freeing." But after a while even this requirement lapsed, and any memory of class distinctions ceased. It remained true that the more firmly class position was established, the more difficult it was to surmount the barriers. Yet they *were* surmounted time and again, after the fifteenth century as well as before. The great Austrian families of German blood, for example, sprang almost exclusively from the ministerial estate. And more and more, proven service to the sovereign became the key that opened the door to the circles of the high nobility. Just as that class continually gained recruits from the class of knights, so this class replenished itself, down to the eleventh century, from the peasant class. Until then there was no legal barrier to prevent the peasant from becoming a "knight." All he needed to do was to secure a mount and arms, and to prove his worth in battle. Whoever reached this economic estate and demonstrated his usefulness in war service normally received a "service" fief, and though this was not the equivalent of "genuine" enfeoffment, it established his identification with the warlike master class. This particular procedure lapsed more and more, because the technical qualifications of knights steadily rose from the twelfth to the fifteenth centuries, and because the established class grew more "firm." But that does not affect our principle. And the cases of the "bourgeois knight" and the "knightly bourgeois" are analogous.

But when we make the leap to the industrial world of capitalism, the lack of genealogical material becomes even more keenly felt. True, such data are being accumulated, if only under the spur of modern genealogical interest as such; but the lack of zeal with which social scientists gather and evaluate this material is in lamentable contrast to the fact that it alone can provide a reliable knowledge of the structure and life processes of capitalist society. Only a fundamental indifference to scientific problems as such can explain the slow progress of social science, a fact which is nowhere more obvious than here, where nearly everyone is satisfied with party slogans. We do have, nevertheless, a considerable number of histories covering industrial, intellectual, and even working-class families. A beginning has also been made in preparing collections of family histories. One such collection, by Professor Haensels (Moscow), exceeds a thousand entries.[14] The picture that emerges is uniformly along the lines of the American saying: "Three generations from shirtsleeves to shirtsleeves." To an even greater degree it bears out our thesis, that the content of every "upper" class is not merely *modified* but actually *formed* by the rise and decline of individual families; and that the demonstrable transgression of class barriers is not the exception but so much the invariable rule in the life of every upper-class family that despite certain variations in detail, we are not likely to meet with great surprises.

The most interesting question, of course, is to what extent industrial families are recruited directly from the working class and, to that extent, form no more than the upper layer of that class. (In this connection it is best to avoid the term "elite" which is often and without justification used in the sense of a positive evaluation.) An ordinary census will serve to answer this question, and we have Chapman to thank for such an inquiry.[15] He studied the English cotton industry and found that between sixty-three and eighty-five percent of the entrepreneurs and other leaders had risen directly from the working class (that is, the results of the various subinquiries lay between these limits). True, the factual basis was narrow, the methods were imperfect, though painstaking and praiseworthy for a first step. The textile industry, moreover—especially the English textile industry—is not typical. But for our purposes the size of the percentage established by Chapman is not necessary—ten percent would have been entirely sufficient, provided it could be demonstrated that the *ancestors* of the remaining ninety percent had similarly risen from the working or other classes. Even then the theory of an "objective" bond between family and class would have been proved redundant. In other words, the worker, for example, would be objectively tied to his class only in the sense that he ceases to be a "worker" when he deserts his class.[16]

9. We see therefore that our earlier assumption as to the insurmountability of class barriers for individual families does not accord with the facts. The persistence of class position is an illusion, created by the slowness of change and the great stability of class character as such and of its social fluid. Class barriers *must* be surmountable, at the bottom as well as at the top. Otherwise how do we explain that at sufficiently distinct points in time we always find different people in classes that are identical as such, just as we deal forever with different individuals in families that nevertheless remain identical? Like the birth and death of individual family members, which are always events that transcend the everyday course of events and thus constitute something exceptional, entry into and exit from a class appear to us as special and in *this* sense exceptional events; but in *another* sense they are entirely normal. We see, therefore, that families *do* surmount class barriers, as *individuals* rather than as a class—though quite often in groups—and that they do this in a manner which we can, even today, study in a sufficient number of individual cases, as well as in all important groups of cases. But this process does not yet explain the formation of classes as such. It does explain, as already stated, not only the gradual *modification* of the basic family stock in a

class which might have been created in some other way, but also the *formation* of whatever stock exists at a given point in time. *Only the physical individual, not the family, is class-born.*

The question of *how* this process of surmounting class barriers takes place and why class content changes now answers itself. Primarily it happens precisely as does the shifting of position of individual families within the class. It is only necessary to examine the reasons for those shifts which we have cited in order to see at once that they are quite adequate to account for the rise and fall of individual families not only within the class but also between classes. The family in question only needs to be near the upper or lower border line of its class, and the factors that account for shifts to be strong enough to surmount the barriers peculiar to classes. These barriers are not really different in kind, only in strength, from those that limit the rise or decline of families within the class. It is seen at once that these factors actually do account for the rise or fall of a family above or below its class barriers. As a rule, such changes occur imperceptibly. Only where law or custom confers on members of certain classes certain formal qualifications—such as special political privileges or the right to perform certain religious ceremonies—is there a recognizable outward act that can be dated. And in such cases one might actually be led to believe that it is not so much a matter of voluntary ascent as a process of being pushed up the ladder from the outside. This, however, is not so. Even in such cases it is actually a matter of growth, of first creating a position which is then recognized to be a fact, in the face of which such acts as admission and appointment are merely corroborative. It is apparent that the admission of certain families to the councils of counts [*Grafenkollegien*] in the seventeenth and eighteenth centuries did not *establish* the social position of those families but were merely *expressive* of that position—although it is equally clear that such action *did* qualify the families in question for membership in those councils and for the rather insignificant privileges linked to such membership. The heart of the matter is much more clearly expressed in the essentially similar process during the Middle Ages in which a family was actually received into the circle of princely lieges, with no particular formal ceremony. The fact that certain barriers may have actually been insurmountable for centuries on end becomes a special reason why there should be no special ritual act governing the acceptance of new families. But this is the case only where ethnic differences exist—the Indian caste system is the outstanding example—and has nothing to do with the essential nature of the class phenomenon.

Yet there *is* an apparently new element, entirely absent in shifts within the class, the significance of which must be sought here. Apart from favorable or unfavorable accidents, we have considered it to be the rule, in cases of ascent or descent within the class, that the class member performs with more or less success than his fellows those activities that he must perform in any event, that are chosen by or imposed on him within his class limitations. For example, a member of a military or priestly master class may have more success than his fellows with his feuds or prophecies; a tailor may serve his customers better than other tailors; the professional may win a larger number of cases or cure a larger number of patients than other lawyers or doctors. But there is, of course, still another way that is particularly apposite to the transgression of class barriers. That is to *do something altogether different* from what is, as it were, ordained to the individual. The knight may become a statesman or administrator; the cleric may suddenly enhance the standing of his family by virtue of a career in the service of the Papal See—as a study of papal nepotism down to the end of the eighteenth century shows; artisan families like the Wurmsers and Fuggers may develop into great merchant dynasties; the modern worker may, in familiar fashion, push his son into the so-called new middle class, or, as we have seen, himself become an entrepreneur—which does not, of itself, *constitute* class position, but *leads* to class position.

Reverting to the element of chance for a moment, the likelihood of lucky accidents naturally increases when position is enhanced for other reasons, a circumstance which constitutes the other aspect of the relationship between luck and ability. The first and most important aspect we have already mentioned. Family and social history show that, in addition to the elements of chance and success along wonted and ordained lines, the method of rising into a higher class which we are now discussing is of crucial importance—the method of striking out along unconventional paths. This has always been the case, but never so much as in the world of capitalism. True, many industrial families, especially in the middle brackets, have risen from small beginnings to considerable or even great wealth by dint of hard work and unremitting attention to detail over several generations; but most of them have come up from the working and craftsman class—to a lesser degree, and then only indirectly, from the peasantry (I pass over the transition of members of the free professions to industry, because this does not necessarily imply transgression of a class barrier)—because one of their members has *done something novel*, typically the founding of a new enterprise, something that meant getting out of the conventional rut. Because of the limited opportunities open to working-class families, this is virtually the only method by which they can make the great leap out of their class.

Even though this is another and different way of rising, the conditions under which a family can follow it with success are, from our viewpoint, no different from those under which position is enhanced within the class. This statement applies only to our own viewpoint, for from other viewpoints and for other purposes it is often relevant that the method *is* a different one, that to move with assurance outside the rut, to do something special that has not been done before in essentially similar fashion, requires different qualities. This latter aspect of launching out into the unprecedented is not, by the way, necessarily implied in every case, though it does play a part in certain important cases and is basically significant to our further line of reasoning. For the present we may say that the capacity and ability to rise socially along this second line requires nothing more than a stronger endowment with the same or similar qualifications that bring success along the first line. *Those factors that account for shifts in family position within the class are the same that account for the crossing of class barriers.*

## IV. The Rise and Fall of Whole Classes

10. We observe, furthermore, that the class structure of a people also changes by virtue of the fact that the relative social position of the classes as such undergoes shifts. A question now poses itself that is analogous to the question concerning the reasons for shifts of individual families within the class. Why and how do classes change their relative position?

We see such a shift most plainly, not in cases where it is the result of a slow, organic process, but in those where it occurs by a single historical event. The most important instance of the latter process is the forcible subjugation of one social entity by another that is politically alien—usually nationally as well, though that is not essential to us now. What interests us in such an upheaval is the fact that classes that appear as "upper" or "ruling" even to superficial observation—especially *the* "ruling class"—are much more deeply affected than the "lower" classes, and in an altogether different way. True, even the lower classes may often—though not always or necessarily—be put in a worse economic plight, but their position as a class, their relative social rating, is affected only slightly or not at all, usually remaining essentially unchanged under the new overlord. The upper classes, on the other hand, are likely to lose the very core of their position—the more so, the nearer they are to the top of the social pyramid. Let us, for example, take the conquest of certain Romanized regions by the Germans during the Great Migration. The Romanized strata of the provinces of Rhaetia and Noricum, for example, usually became so-called *tributarii*—peasants compelled to offer tribute, though not necessarily unfree. As an alternative, they might keep one part of their property, if they surrendered the rest. By and large, this probably corresponded to the position the same people occupied down to the final period under Rome. Similarly, we find certain Slavs who had been tenants even under the Avari continuing in the same state under Germanic rule, while others in Carinthia and Pannonia, who had fared better before, continued as free land owners. But the situation of the upper class was severely depressed, even where the class continued to maintain itself. The position of Roman citizens of the highest class in these same regions was characterized by the fact that persons who had not been free before but were now manumitted *per cartam ingenuitatis* were declared to be their equals, while the *denariales* actually stood above them. True, these were primarily legal distinctions, but they must be considered symptoms of an altered class position. Among the above-mentioned Slavs, for example, the native aristocracy did succeed in maintaining itself, in a regime that remained largely autonomous, but it no longer carried the weight it once did. There is only one way in which the upper class can maintain its full social position under such circumstances; that is when it is received into the corresponding class of the conqueror. In our cases this came about through the cession of lands to the king, and in general it occurs quite frequently. Thus, it was a common policy of the East Roman Empire to accept the nobility of subjugated peoples (of Bulgaria, for example, in the time of the Macedonian emperors) into the imperial Byzantine nobility. But it will be seen at once that this constitutes no exception to our assertion; for it was not the old class itself that retained its social validity, but merely the sum of its members in their function as members of what now came to be the upper class.

Yet even this shift in the relative position of the classes toward each other does not quite tell us what we need to know. After all, it was the result of outside influence, which was accidental from the viewpoint of the class system in existence before. Let us, nevertheless, take note of the following two elements: to be conquered always means failure, and the failure applies particularly to the ruling classes. Apparently it is this inherent character of subjugation, so destructive to prestige, that has, in turn, much to do with the forfeiture of social position. A calamity lacking this special character—a great earthquake, for example—would not have such an effect, unless it were linked in the

public mind with a failure, on the part of the upper classes, to entertain, let us say, good relations with the gods. This offers an obvious
analogy with the effect of personal failure of a leader—a leader of
mounted nomads, for example.[17] The position of a monarchial family is typically rooted in class. Yet nothing shakes its position so much
as an unsuccessful war. It would be difficult to find any case of loss of
monarchial position that did not have, at least indirectly, some connection with this element. Again, this matter of having been subjugated or of meeting with failure is not just a question of failure in
general, failure in any field; the failure becomes relevant only when
it occurs with respect to certain definite fields—not merely those
fields which the observer, from the necessities he has grasped, deems
important, but those for which the class in question is responsible in
a way that other classes are not. Only when a class has thus been
weighed and found wanting, in the light of the circumstances of the
times, does its position toward other classes of citizens decline—all
down the line, not merely in this point alone—although, of course, a
position once gained may prove equal to quite a number of such tests.

11. Here, then, in a flash, we begin to see the underlying relationship that leads directly to an answer to our question. This is the connection between the social rank of a class and its function. Each class
is always linked to such a special function. That is the real core of all
theories of the division of labor and occupation in the field of class
phenomena—except that these theories, in our opinion, evaluate this
element incorrectly. (For this reason I ask the reader, in the interest
of avoiding troublesome misunderstandings, to impute to our line of
reasoning no part of the content of those theories, indeed, if possible,
to put them out of his mind.) Every class, in other words, has a definite function, which it must fulfill according to its whole concept and
orientation, and which it actually does discharge as a class and
through the class conduct of its members. Moreover, the position of
each class in the total national structure depends, on the one hand,
on the significance that is attributed to that function, and, on the
other hand, on the degree to which the class successfully performs
the function. Changes in relative class position are always explained
by changes along these two lines, and in no other way. For the time
being, the propositions just put forth are liable to obvious objections.
Just what their meaning is will be shown by an example which at the
same time may serve to demonstrate our line of reasoning for cases
that are not dependent on the effect of outside forces. The proof
cannot be absolute, for that would require an analysis of universal
history.

First of all, let us record the instructive fact that there are two groups of cases in which class structure is only very weakly marked. An example of the first group is furnished by the Slavs during the time they lived in the Pripet marshes. We must envision them as subdivided into very small communities, isolated by the difficult terrain, leading a highly stable existence, with untoward events quite infrequent and opportunities at home exceedingly narrow. Such dangers as did exist—invasions by Germanic or Mongol bandits and slavers—were, given the situation and the character of the people, practically beyond control. They could not be guarded against in advance. Flight was the only recourse—into some hiding place, possibly even below the water, with a hollow reed for a breathing tube. It is clear why there were no more than traces of class structure here. There was no opportunity, no occasion for class leadership. Class distinctions and social differentiations arise and have meaning only where environmental factors change with sufficient speed, where there is scope for action, decision, and service. It is different with the other group of cases, typified by the mounted nomad. Life on the steppe with its plundering forays is marked by constant change. The very physical environment alternates rapidly. The situation is always essentially new and it becomes a matter of choosing, acting, winning—or perishing. Hence individual differentiation is strongly marked. The leadership function is strongly marked, the leadership position well developed. Yet here too there are only feeble hints of class structure, even though it is much stronger than in the first group of cases. What class structure there is consists essentially of the fact that the prestige of the leaders—which is primarily graduated by their success and built up of individual successes—when once present, elevates the leader's personal circle, permitting those born into it to start with better chances than other members of the community. But all adult men are simply warriors and within the whole group—which cannot live by itself alone, in the long run always needing a host people to exploit—there are no distinguishable social functions, except for the leadership function as such. Hence we never find strongly developed stable class positions in such cases—either among the Mongol and Semitic mounted nomads, or, for example, among the Eskimos. Now let us examine our example.

12. At the time the Germans entered the limelight of history, their aristocracy was no more than the leading circle of a mounted nomad people. It was simply a circle of families of enhanced prestige—more precisely, a plurality of distinct circles, differing from one another by the degree of prestige they enjoyed. Their members had more to do with making the policies of the totality than the rest. They were more closely associated with such action as had to be taken, with such ben-

efits as accrued. It is important to emphasize that this was relative
rather than absolute, that the situation remained basically in a state
of flux. There were real or potential chieftains of larger or smaller
groups and subgroups. Yet there was one distinction as against the
case of the mounted nomads, a distinction which explains the sharply
marked character of the picture. Even when we first catch sight of
them, the Germans were in a very high stage of agriculture, normally
and preeminently living by tilling the soil. True, in *all* the German
tribes this characteristic could be temporarily subordinated during
migrations, and with *some* of them this was permanently the case, by
virtue of special circumstances, especially when a tribe, or part of a
tribe, was in a position to lead a life of banditry, or established itself
as the ruling class in some foreign land. Agriculture, to a much
higher degree than nomadic animal husbandry, destroys uniformity
of behavior among the members of a community,[18] and *adds a new
distinction to that between leaders and led.* Hence we encounter the Germanic aristocracy from the very outset in a more sharply circumscribed special function. We need scarcely fear contradiction when we
characterize this function as that of military leadership—a leadership,
however, that meant not merely the command of forces but, to an
increasing degree during the ensuing centuries, the actual execution
of combat actions. Nor need we fear contradiction when we assert
that this is the primary explanation for the generally enhanced position of the aristocracy, for its association with further functions—pre-
siding at group meetings, leadership in other group concerns. It is
plausible that the predominance of the military function, in uncom-
plicated circumstances and where the group is small in numbers, in-
hibits the emergence of positions of a different character. In the
course of the Great Migrations and the concluding Merovingian and
Carolingian successes, this social class steadily rose in power and position—it is of small moment, in this connection, that actual family
content may have turned over rather rapidly. There can be no doubt,
after all, that we are still entitled to speak of the same class. The question now at issue is no sooner put than answered. How can we explain
this rise,[19] this shift in relative class position? Evidently from the fact
that, in the circumstances of the time, the basic class function gained
in actual importance—as understood by us, the observers—and that
this importance was sensed, not necessarily consciously, by the rest of
the people. Both aspects are essential. Without the former there
would not, in the long run, be an adequate explanation, a link with
the objective facts of life of the social group; without the latter the
vital connections between those vital facts and the phenomenon they
created would be lacking.

This enhanced importance is *reflected and objectified* in the rise of a definite institution among the Germans in their new territories—the creation of great manorial estates. This is their social meaning and they become incomprehensible when this element is left out of consideration. It is for this very reason that the problem of the rise of such estates is such a complex and controversial one in the literature of legal and social history. All of a sudden, as it were, the great estates are in existence in the Carolingian period. One can only conclude from this fact that far-reaching social transformations had taken place; and, as is often the case with problems that are more apparent than real, this one has given rise to labored theories that are not always free of unconscious humor. Actually it is no more than the expression and gradual realization of an administrative system that arose independently, under the impact of our factor of a previously shifted class structure. Like the feudal system itself, the manorial estates, in one of their aspects, are only the expression of an administrative system adapted to special outward circumstances and the special class structure of the times—to the legal system in general, to passive methods of disposing of natural resources. (The methods are not necessarily passive in every case.) With the establishment of the great estates and the development of a mode of life in keeping with their conception at the time, as well as of a body of law affecting all classes—vassalage, immunity, court privilege, village law, and so on— there commenced a great social process that was subject to many fluctuations and setbacks and that ended only in the nineteenth century with the complete abolition of manorial privileges, even then leaving a heritage of established position to later times. We shall call this process *patrimonialization*.

13. There are four factors that justify the proposition that, down to the threshold of the "modern age," the relative position of our class was rising rather than sinking. I think this is apparent from the fact that, for the most part, its actual and legal privileges were on the increase, while similarly those of the remaining classes were on the decline. The only exception in this respect is the urban bourgeoisie, even though its rise did not take place in a straight line. It did, however, demonstrate the ultimate impotence of legal and political restrictions, even when the outward resources of power are at the disposal of those that impose them. It burst out of the social pyramid of feudal society, slipped from the grasp of the nobility, and enhanced its own weight and function despite all class legislation.

True, in the course of the centuries there were radical upheavals within that other class. (Technically, we should really speak in the plural, or at least distinguish between high and low aristocracy, but for the sake of simplicity in presentation we shall here speak only of a single class of feudal lords.) There were numerous shifts in the position of groups within the class—above all, a constant turnover of its constituents. There were losses as well as gains in all these respects, though in the long run the gains outweighed the losses, as far as concerns class position as such. This outcome is attributable to the following four reasons: In the first place, during this entire time war essentially retained its character as a mode of life—a character it has since increasingly lost. It was a normal thing, not a last resort, as it came to be later. War and instant readiness for war remained an indispensable element of survival in every walk of life, in all socially characteristic situations. Those who could not themselves function along these lines were dependent on the protection of some individual warlord. Because this class function was so vital, it served to enhance the significance of another factor we should like to adduce in explaining shifts in class position. The class in question exercised its function with signal success. For, in the second place, the warrior of that period grew into an expert mounted fighter.[20] Success in the profession of arms required not merely an aptitude for fighting, but constant application to technical mastery. Those who had other concerns were by that fact alone disqualified from the full exercise of this function. Today, special technical skill can be confined to the few who, in case of need, can in a short time train men drawn from their regular occupations. But that was not true then. Nor could the military rest content with working out measures for mobilization. The war lord himself constituted the machine on which everything rested. These circumstances lie at the very heart of the matter. It was no mere whim of Charles Martel that brought into being the mounted host of knights, any more than the feudal system was born of his campaigns against the Arabs. Fortunately it has at last been recognized that both phenomena merely expressed environmental and structural changes the beginnings of which can already be seen in the early Germanic period. This also disposes of the seemingly plausible notion that possession of certain "means of production"—horse and armor—was the factor that led to the formation of the class. It is only necessary to realize that one of the objectives of the system of benefices must have been to furnish not only these immediate means but also those required for the life and profession of a knight in general to those who had already been chosen for other reasons. Yet these material elements and the way in which they were provided did have the effect of elevating and securing class position. There were other mere consequences that worked in the same direction. On the one hand, the class base was broadened. Even relatively, the number of professional warriors was greater than that of the members of the nobility in the time of universal liability to military service. Then again, the qualities required and developed by the chivalric life were eminently suited to the defense of class position against other segments of the population, which in turn were in the process of losing these very qualities. A third reason for rising class position lay in the elaboration of functions that were originally subsidiary to the main function but that now, by virtue of the situation, were carefully preserved and even more closely associated with it. National horizons, interests, and tasks were expanding, and the upper class found ever new sources of activity and thus of power in the great problems of empire, which assumed reality for it alone. It should be pointed out, however, that the situation is by no means exhaustively characterized by mere reference to the interrelationship of these functions with the basic function that genetically explains class position. Two other relationships must be considered and conceptually differentiated from the one described. Quite apart from the fact that aptitude for war was necessary even for the exercise of these further functions—a qualification that gradually disappeared—it is manifestly significant that the exercise of these other functions was objectively related to the military preoccupations of a person of high rank. Here too it was a matter of deciding, commanding, leading, winning. This the knights—or at least a sufficient number of them—were able and willing to do. It was from their ranks that the emerging high nobility was recruited, and by no means exclusively nor even normally from the families of the earlier high nobility; and it was this section of the knighthood that maintained and enhanced the position of the entire knightly class. No such interrelationship was apparent in the economic sphere. The knight had neither the desire nor the ability to become a trader. Later on, as we shall presently see, this was reversed, though only in a special sense—a fact which again justifies our conception and explains the emergence of the bourgeois from the feudal class structure, as well as the already mentioned relative decline of the nobility as against this new group whose ancestors had once stood far beneath the nobility, whether they had been legally subordinate or not. The fundamental significance of this relationship to class development is evident, and it will later be formulated in general terms. Another relationship exists by virtue of the fact that, quite apart, for the moment, from the two correlations described, members of an elevated class, especially when their position has materialized even outwardly into privileges, property, and organic functions, find easier access to new functions (which they may even monopolize) than members of other classes. A fourth reason for the rise in the position of our class

lies in the opportunities it had to colonize frontier regions, either for
its own benefit or at any rate for the benefit of small subgroups, in its
capacity to exploit these opportunities, and in the fact that they *were*
exploited with success. This led to rising wealth, to a position of dominance over aliens, which in turn enhanced class position at home.[21]

14. Yet from the end of the fourteenth century down to the present
day our class has been almost without interruption on the downgrade. This is seen not so much in its legal status which even gained
rather than lost in the fifteenth, sixteenth, and seventeenth centuries
and did not begin to be systematically undermined until the eighteenth century—which agrees with the general observation that of all
the clearly marked elements of social life the "superstructure"[22] of
law, custom, and so forth is always the last to change, always lags behind changes in the actual life situation. Nor is it expressed in a decline in "social" position which, on the contrary, has been surprisingly
well maintained to the present day. Rather does this decline emerge
in the invariable subjection of the class to a new social factor—new, at
least, in this particular form—the state power. At first glance it may
seem as though this holds nothing new from the viewpoint of our
subject, as though this need not impinge on class position as such. For
primarily the "state power" meant no more than the sum total of the
powers of the sovereign; and subjection of this nature meant no more
than subjection to a superior within the class. On the one hand, such
subordination lay in the very nature of the feudal system. On the
other hand, in our view any great enhancement of the sovereign position, insofar as it elevated the sovereign as against the rest of the
nobility, would be irrelevant to the position of the class as such; while,
insofar as the sovereign was elevated with respect to other classes, it
should have enhanced the position of the nobility as a whole. But the
fact is that the sovereign did not subjugate the nobility in his capacity
as feudal overlord; he did so in his capacity as master over an entirely
different power—and it was to this power that he bent the nobility.
There arose an administrative machine, at first predominantly man-
ned by the nobility—more of this presently—but one with which it
was by no means identical. This machinery, being capable of functioning equally well and even better in other hands, could be—and
was in fact—wrested from the grasp of the nobility and even of the
sovereign. Objectively and theoretically, this was a new kind of subordination—submission to something that *ultimately turned out to be
alien and even hostile.*

What we mean by patrimonialization is the process that explains
this unfavorable change in class position—a process that must itself
be explained. The term, in other words, is used in a broader sense

than its technical application in legal and social history. We mean,
first of all, the familiar process by which, from the Carolingian period
on, vital functions became hereditary. Briefly, imperfectly, and indeed incorrectly[23] put, they tended to become objects of the law of
property. This is the *patrimonialization of office*. Second, we mean the
process by which land ownership by the nobles became—at first in
fact and then in law (in its extreme form this is the alodification of
fiefs)—a thing apart from the unified feudal system, in time simply a
source of income, a means of production, an object of traffic. This is
the *patrimonialization of landed property*. Third, we mean the process
by which the individual emerged from the obligations and attitudes
of the feudal relationship, becoming in theory a citizen left to his own
devices, shaping his private sphere more or less at will, even though
for the time being he was still invested with special privileges and tied
to fixed social forms. This is the *patrimonialization of the individual*. The
rococo period shows us an intermediate state that is highly illuminating. In many outward respects the position of the nobility was never
more splendid. Socially, legally, and materially, it rested on the very
extensive heritage of the feudal age, in part well preserved, for the
rest showing itself highly resistant even in a state of impairment. In
all three directions this position was strengthened by the fact that the
new state machine, whatever it may have taken away from the old
position of overlordship, still needed to be staffed by the nobility,
while in financial respects it proved at first to be an almost inexhaustible object of exploitation. What the historian, often quite superficially, describes as courtly extravagance at the whim of the sovereign,
was actually the very essence of a social and political system which
sought to transform the nobility from an independent gentry into a
pliant court aristocracy, not merely by force, but also by economic
temptation. Actually the time of that independence, when the nobles
stood on their own two feet, was at end. The essence and guarantee
of independence had lain in the fact that in case of need the lord
would mount his horse and defend himself, sword in hand, against
dangers from above or below—the last example, already adulterated
by other factors, is furnished by the sixteenth-century peasant wars.
The time was past when the coronation formula of Aragon was a
striking expression of an actual situation, when the concept of the
"peer" had real meaning. Now the servility of the estates just as strik-
ingly expressed a new situation of dependence on the favor and protection of the state machine. More and more the position of overlord-
ship became a derivate, even where it antedated the state and had its
foundations outside the state, even though it continued to enjoy the
glory of ancient—and otherwise to an increasing degree borrowed—

associations. In telling confirmation of our view, the complement to this situation was that the lower nobility was primarily preoccupied with its private concerns, while the higher nobility as such had nothing whatever to do. The facts are in part obscured by the circumstance that *members* of both groups were active in the service of the state, while there was an understandable tendency to continue the old functions in form rather than in substance. The rugged pugnacity of the knight remained as an ideal, to be refined into the fine arts of wielding the foil and riding according to the tenets of the classical school, utterly devoid of any further significance in the social struggle for survival. Intervention in the affairs of state became a skillful ritual, an end in itself without relevance to the task in hand. If the action had any meaning at all, this was determined, not by the great lords who actually figured in the proceedings, but by other persons and interests. It is this survival of social and material position on the one hand, and the extensive decay of underlying functions on the other, that explain the characteristic charm and high culture of that period. True, even then this group had not completely closed ranks, but it had far fewer motives for accepting newcomers than any class immediately embroiled in the struggle for survival where it must stand up and show its mettle. Yet for a while, during the time in question, the nobility could utterly ignore the nature of the relationship between ruling and serving, could temporarily surrender to the illusion that the world was its oyster, that fun was the only purpose of life, that any act that was not pure entertainment represented a graciously conferred boon. All classes, including the ruling class, exercise rights just for the sake of maintaining them. But the rococo period was characterized by the exercise of rights (which were more and more losing their function) for purely selfish reasons—and this meant that the overlord really ceased to be one, in the essential meaning of his class position. Obviously the course of events in the eighteenth century supports our contention that such a situation could continue only because it was the heritage of an altogether different situation, and also because it never existed in the pure state and was always subject to numerous corrective and weakening factors. The only alternatives would have been a timely, voluntary surrender or adaptation to a process marked by legal continuity, or loss of position by events that break such continuity—in other words, retreat or defeat; and both contingencies lead to the same final result.[24]

15. To the degree required for our purposes, we may enumerate the essential elements and causes of the process of patrimonialization under the four headings we have set forth. The scope of our study requires, however, that in each case we rest content with only the first

links in causal chains that ultimately reach very deep. Thus, we cannot immediately discuss why physical, armed combat ceased to be a mode of life inside the national community, and gradually outside it as well. But the fact that this happened did pull the foundation from under the main function of our class. One has only to ask oneself whether the competitive economy of the nineteenth century could have existed if industrial families had not had to be continually concerned over their survival and to give constant attention to current business decisions. Reflection will show why we assert that the occasional exercise of a function—no matter how frequent the occasion, how vital the preoccupation, how suitable the function to become the basis of a full-time vocation—is insufficient to intrench a special discipline and orientation in such a way that they become the very life of a class. Even when he serves in the army, the modern conscript remains at heart a civilian. The modern professional soldier is a soldier in the sense that a lawyer is a lawyer. He is *not* a warrior, even though the traditional officer corps, in order to engender or preserve such an orientation, cultivates a warrior ideology, even going so far as to keep alive the fiction of individual readiness for combat by tolerating or promoting the duel. But when combat is no longer a mode of life, when it is no longer imminent at any moment in defense of immediate, personal interests—then it is no longer *the* great task, foreordained and self-evident. Battle, even though it may still be frequent, soon becomes an emergency situation, foreign and disturbing to other spheres of life, and there is no longer occasion for every member of the class to be constantly trained in it with every fiber of his being. This carries two consequences. The basic cause for the slow demilitarization of the nobility must be sought in the whole trend of society, which more and more circumscribed the occasion and opportunity for defending individual and class position by force of arms. Ultimately this demilitarization made the armed class struggle—if one wishes to use that term—altogether impossible, and thus one of the conspicuous guarantees of class position fell by the wayside. Of far greater importance was the fact that this demilitarization, and the resulting orientation toward other interests, more and more had the effect of turning the nobility against its own basic function, causing it to undermine the very foundations of its own social importance. To an ever increasing degree military service was rejected. It was not that the obligation to render such service was denied, but it was regarded as onerous and the call to it was complied with only grudgingly, if at all. Proof is furnished by the fact that in the fifteenth and early sixteenth centuries the feudal lords used the call to military service as one of the ways of making the estates comply with their financial re-

quirements—something that can be understood only when it is realized that such duty, while acknowledged, was also resented. In this
way, a replacement was found for the nobility in that sphere where
combat still remained vital to survival—a sphere in which the nobility
might well have continued to play a role, preserving part of its social
importance. We should not overrate the significance of technical innovations in this process. On the technical side there was nothing to
keep the nobility from taking to small arms and ordnance, just as it
had once, with similar social results, mastered the technique of
mounted and armored combat. It is no valid objection to say that the
new techniques led to an increase in the number of effectives. For
apart from the fact that this was to a certain extent a consequence of
the circumstance that the people replacing the nobility were available
in greater numbers, the earlier introduction of the host of mounted
knights had itself led to a numerical increase in the nobility, a process
to which any class vigorously oriented toward its function readily sub-
mits. *It is only because this did not happen now* that we think of the nobility as clinging stubbornly to the fighting methods of the Middle
Ages and that the very idea of the nobility's adapting itself to the new
methods seems farfetched and unreal. Yet the army of knighthood
did not fail because the mercenary army came into being. Rather, the
system of mercenaries arose because the knightly host failed from
inner causes. But once the new situation existed, once the mercenary
system functioned—with the nobility in part furnishing the financial
resources (though mostly from the pockets of its own copyholders)
for the very purpose of evading military service—*then* the army of
knighthood had really grown obsolete and inferior. There was a
stronger power in existence now, and this meant a fundamental
change in the total social-class structure. As we shall presently have
occasion to discuss again, the individual knight was still the most
likely candidate for positions of leadership in the mercenary army;
and significantly enough, he endeavored for a long time, by his bearing and appearance, to convey the impression that he was prepared
at any moment to ride out full tilt with lowered lance to meet the
enemy in individual combat—though in the end he was likely to don
armor only when his portrait was to be painted. Even though this
shed glamor on the class as a whole, it was something rather different
from bearing the whole burden of combat. Yet the survival of such
conspicuous externals served to slow down the full effect of the internal change. And with this, we have disposed not only of the first two
of the four factors we enumerated as effecting changes in position,
but also of the fourth, since the possibility of private colonization is
obviously associated with the warrior function as a whole.

16. The process by which our class relinquished its basic class function implies not merely voluntary surrender and failure of will power, but also the pressure of the objective social situation which resulted in inactivity and flagging will. It implies not only *giving up*, but also, once that had begun, *taking away*. For the nobles this process was at the same time a process of individual emancipation, and it enabled the nobility as a class to loosen all the other feudal bonds—bonds which had already begun to lose meaning and to enter into a state of atrophy. This is just what we mean, in the case of the nobility, by "patrimonialization of the individual." But it is precisely because a decline in the social importance of a class function—the inadequate exercise and ultimate surrender of that function—*sets the members of the class free* that the decline in class position which might be expected occurs only if the class is unable to adapt itself to some other function that rates the same social importance as the old one. This fact, let us remark in passing, constitutes a severe limitation on the explanatory value of the relationship between class and function. There can never be any lack of new functions, unless a people chances into a stagnant social situation, free of problems. And every class that has once enjoyed an elevated position is greatly aided in seizing on new functions, because the sources and gains of its prior function survive for some time. In our own case we see at once that two such functions automatically obtruded themselves on the nobility by virtue of their relation to its former position as the warrior and master class, and to which it did, in fact, turn. These functions were the staffing of the state machine and the administration of its own landed estates. It is at once evident why these two functions were, on the one hand, able to slow down and soften the descent of the class, while, on the other hand, they were insufficient to preserve its old position. Orientation toward individually owned landed property did not occur everywhere at the same rate and in the same manner. The differences in this respect are highly instructive. Where the state machine arose on the basis of the princely domain [*Fürstenterritorium*]—which was the case precisely where the mercenary system was most strongly developed—this orientation took place much more rapidly and sharply than in cases where the state had other antecedents, the single important example of the latter being England. Longer than anywhere else, and to a certain extent down to the present day, the English nobility continued in a position of national leadership, though in the course of time it became an agent rather than a ruler. It was able to do so because it did not turn to agriculture as an occupation and thus, on the one hand, remained free of all economic activity, while, on the other, it never degenerated into a group of economic and political

partisans, as the nobility of other countries did. Nevertheless, the causes, the broad outlines, and the ultimate results of the process were everywhere the same, except that they emerge with particular clarity where the nobleman turns husbandman, where landlordism develops in its pure form. *Just as the manorial system corresponds to the type of the knightly warrior-politician and warrior-administrator, so the system of large landed estates corresponds to the type of the aristocratic businessman.* Naturally our process was determined by economic developments. Landlordism is possible only when population density has risen and when centers of consumption exist. The declining purchasing power of feudal money rents was a sharp incentive to the exploitation of inherited feudal resources for private economic gain, even though such exploitation was destructive of prestige. But the heart of the matter lies in the conquests of the period between the Merovingians and Hohenstaufens, which led to a situation in which the administration and enjoyment of what had been gained, individually and as a class, made for a full life, weakening the incentive for further headlong action—quite apart from the fact that outward opportunities for such action began to dwindle. These developments gave a calculating, private-economic direction to the nobility's attitude toward such matters as its own property, its relation to the peasantry, and the maintenance of feudal rights and duties. And all this, in turn, led to corresponding legal forms and constitutes the social content of the "patrimonialization of landed property."

17. The situation is basically similar in the case of the "patrimonialization of office." It too becomes comprehensible from the same causal nexus. Here too, in the course of time, the successful families established themselves in the positions they had temporarily acquired, as though such a situation must automatically endure—just as the bourgeoisie in the early nineteenth century established itself in the position it had created, invested those positions with appropriate legal standing, regarded individual control of the means and fruits of production as self-evident and, indeed, the whole order as permanent, because it was "natural." Yet this analogy does not extend all the way. It deserts us because of the circumstance that the old overlords, in order to administer and maintain their position, did not always have to repeat those actions that had led to the conquest of that position, while the position of the industrialists is rapidly dissipated unless it is constantly marked by the same kind of success that created it. That is the main reason why the analogy between feudal and industrial rule breaks down when applied seriously and in detail. There are, to be sure, other reasons as well, of which we shall mention the two most important. The feudal master class was once—and the

bourgeoisie was never—the supreme pinnacle of a uniformly constructed social pyramid. The feudal nobility was once lord and master in every sphere of life—which constitutes a difference in prestige that can never be made up. Moreover, the feudal nobility was once—and the bourgeoisie was never—not only the sole possessor of physical power; it *was* physical power incarnate. The aforementioned main difference, however, means, on the one hand, that in the case of the nobility, class and individual family position endured far better and longer than in the case of the bourgeoisie. It means, on the other hand, that the objective social importance of the function of the bourgeoisie as a class is not as readily destroyed by its own failure as was true in the case of the nobility. The failing bourgeois family drops out of the class so swiftly that the class itself always consists of families which are normally equal to their function. Stated in a somewhat different way, with the emphasis on another factor: The nobility *conquered* the material complement to its position, while the bourgeoisie *created* this complement for itself.

The patrimonialization of functional position can always be understood as emerging from administrative expediency rooted in contemporary circumstances. I believe that this applies even to the late Roman version though, especially in our own case, it is but a superficial explanation. Many things that would be socially expedient nevertheless do not happen. Here too the crucial point was severance from a former basic function that was losing survival value—a function that had once been the excuse for active leadership of the whole people. Viewed from this aspect, patrimonialization was the expression of incipient failure, though, from another aspect, it was the consequence and expression of an antecedent success. It reached its peak in those cases where it resulted in the constitution of princely domains—so-called patrimonial states. It is vital to recognize, however, that at bottom such cases are not essentially different from those in which this did not happen—cases of families that for some reason or other never achieved territorial ascendancy. Basically the process was the same, except that certain families simply reached greater prominence than others, and for a long time the dividing line between the two was in a state of flux. It was the same social process, too, that either deprived them altogether of their patrimonialized functional position or (in the few cases in which this did not happen until much later or did not happen at all) created something altogether new, connected with it only by outward forms, associations, and historical continuity—namely, the modern monarchy. At first glance such a conception seems puzzling and in conflict with the facts of legal history, but it immediately loses this character when we add, first, that such cases of

outstanding success, though of the same character as the less successful ones, had, in practice, different effects. They created, above all, a
special legal form for themselves, emphasizing their unique character
and elaborating precisely the consequences of this peculiarity—just
as, in an earlier age, the counts had insisted that they were counts
rather than knights. Then too, such outstanding success justified the
general taking over and vigorous exploitation of all the remaining
powers that had once belonged to superordinate authorities. With respect to the development of nonfeudal classes, such powers gained
special importance, and they helped those who had won preeminence
to consolidate their territorial position—a position that surely represented something new, distinct from the position of other families in
the same class; indeed, a position which, under pressure of the new
conditions, ceased to function along class lines and actually, as we
have seen, turned against the lesser positions of other class members.
The picture changes, secondly, when we add that the process by
which patrimonial position disintegrated in the face of outstanding
dynastic success ran quite differently when success was less sharply
marked, precisely because the peak performance ultimately led to a
position *sui generis*. The facts in point here are so familiar that we
merely have to point out the results that flow from their analysis.
Whether by slow pressure or deliberate act, prince as well as landlord
was deprived of his patrimonial position by the *same* new structural
relations that grew from the successful fulfillment of new functions.

18. Not always, but predominantly—though to a declining degree—the functions involved in the attainment of outstanding success
were exercised by members of the nobility.[25] There are many reasons
for this. The existing class relationship facilitated mutual understanding and concerted action. By tradition the nobility was fitted for
the tasks immediately in hand—quite apart from the traditions of war,
there was the lordly mode of life, the habit of command and of handling people, of much greater importance in practical action than
mere technical competence; even in our own times many outstanding
presidents of English railway companies have been members of the
court nobility. To complete the list of the most important considerations, there was finally the need to keep the nobility occupied, to tie
it to the dynasty, to maintain its prestige among the people. This led
to powerful customs and taboos which strengthened the position of
the nobility all the more, since they perpetuated certain feudal and
patrimonial elements which created the illusion of the continued existence of the old system. These customs included the long-maintained
practice of reserving high government office to the nobility, the requirement that even ordinary army officers must show descent from

a certain number of aristocratic ancestors, and so on. The practices of simony and patronage were specifically patrimonial and in most countries endured deep into the eighteenth century; in the English army, for example, they were abolished only during Gladstone's second ministry. Semi-dynastic succession in office likewise disappeared but slowly. As late as Louis XIV, Colbert and Louvois were succeeded by their sons in the same or similar offices, and the fact attracted not the slightest notice. It is nevertheless important to realize that this function of the nobility, though tending to preserve its position, merely shuffling the position of families, and serving to admit an infusion of new blood (the present-day high aristocracy was largely formed in this fashion), was something altogether different from the former warrior function of the nobility—this, of course, is self-evident—and also different from its position of leadership in public affairs during the Middle Ages. That position was then filled by warlords and by the military class generally, in their own right and with their own resources, regardless of feudal subordination. Now it was exercised at the behest, not of the feudal lord, but of the sovereign, in his borrowed right and power. The core of the system had vanished, its meaning and social content had changed. What did continue, maintaining the position of the nobility, though at a steadily declining rate, were merely accessory elements—ancient prestige, access to and fitness for certain key government jobs and political functions (now superseded by the modern trained expert), intimate contact between class members which facilitated survival, a material basis in agriculture and sometimes industry, stemming from land ownership, incidental opportunities of all kinds which were open to the individual in an "elevated" position. All this, however, tended to be swept away in time. And, confirming our basic view, the process did not take place uniformly and mechanically, but with characteristic differences, according to whether one or the other element of position could be made the basis for social function and success.

19. What we have been discussing is only an example, though one that demonstrates all the important elements essential in answering our question. It shows not only how our thesis may be proved, but also how it is meant to be understood. In particular there now emerges, much more clearly than would be possible from a general discussion, the sense in which we speak of a socially necessary function, of class activity and orientation to activity which we, the observers, understand to be necessary for the survival of the social group, under a given set of circumstances and with a given disposition on the part of the people, and which the group itself senses to be vital for survival. We have only to add the following:

*All* functions that can be distinguished in the case of a given people and in a given historical situation are "socially necessary." This criterion alone, therefore, cannot decide their relative evaluation. Evidently it is a question of how important the individual class member is in a given situation, more particularly, to what degree he can be replaced. The individual warrior in the Middle Ages was less replaceable and individually more "important" than the peasant. The individual industrialist is less replaceable and individually more "important" than the individual worker.

The social importance of class members varies with our two basic elements—the importance of the class function and the degree of success in carrying out that function. But the relation is not always a direct one. Other causes often appear to be far more conspicuous and immediate. Yet such causes, on their part, can always be reduced to those basic elements, just as, according to the economic interpretation of history, the flow of social events is always ultimately shaped by the inner logic of the economic machine, though very often this influence is anything but direct. It is especially the inertia of once solidly established positions that creates a discrepancy between theory and practice, opening up a long chapter of intermediate processes. But these positions themselves can be made comprehensible in accordance with our principle.

Only this latter element explains why the evaluation of a function and the evaluation (that is, the social value) of a class do not always run parallel; why, instead, changes in class evaluation tend to lag behind changes in the evaluation of functions. This also explains the fact that, on first impression, it is more correct to describe the evaluation of a function as dependent on the social rank of those who exercise it. We say, for example, that the social rank of a class depends on the evaluation of its function by the social group, or on its importance for survival, and that "function" often appears at first, not as the prime mover, but as an accessory factor, something quite separate.[26] And this impression is strengthened—but also fully explained—by still another factor: socially necessary functions are not simply coordinate specialties. They do not all have the same relation to the leadership of social groups. Quite apart from the question of the degree to which *individual* members of the class are replaceable, the *intensity* of this relation to leadership provides a criterion for ranking socially necessary functions above and below one another and not simply for placing them beside each other as mere social necessities. But social leadership can express itself in many different concrete activities, and those which are chosen by a once-dominant group will thereby achieve higher social evaluation.

When we survey the ideas set forth in this section, we see that the causes that account for shifts in the relative positions of classes also, *ipso facto*, account for the original order of rank—the order in which we find them at the outset of any given period. We also see why it is not always easy to establish an unequivocal class hierarchy, why there cannot always be "ruling" classes. More than that, it follows immediately that the same factors which ultimately account for shifts in class position in historical time and for the existing class structure at any given point in time, also answer the question of why there is such a phenomenon as class structure at all. For a class *gains and loses position in the same way that it emerges and passes as a class*; and only because an individual class *does* emerge and pass is there the general problem of class structure.

## V. Summary and Conclusions

20. The facts and considerations that have been presented or outlined may be summarized as follows:

Shifts of family position within a class are seen to take place everywhere, without exception. They cannot be explained by the operation of chance, nor by automatic mechanisms relating to outward position, but only as the consequences of the different degree to which families are qualified to solve the problems with which their social environment confronts them.

Class barriers are always, without exception, surmountable and are, in fact, surmounted, by virtue of the same qualifications and modes of behavior that bring about shifts of family position within the class.

The process by which the individual family crosses class barriers is the same process by which the family content of classes is formed in the first instance, and this family content is determined in no other way.

Classes themselves rise and fall according to the nature and success with which they—meaning here, their members—fulfill their characteristic function, and according to the rise and fall in the social significance of this function, or of those functions which the class members are willing and able to accept instead—the relative social significance of a function always being determined by the degree of social leadership which its fulfillment implies or creates.

These circumstances explain the evolution of individual families and the evolution of classes as such. They also explain why social classes exist at all.

We draw the following conclusions from these statements:

The ultimate foundation on which the class phenomenon rests consists of individual differences in aptitude. What is meant is not differences in an absolute sense, but differences in aptitude with respect to those functions which the environment makes "socially necessary"—in our sense—at any given time; and with respect to leadership, along lines that are in keeping with those functions. The differences, moreover, do not relate to the physical individual, but to the clan or family.

Class structure is the ranking of such individual families by their social value in accordance, ultimately, with their differing aptitudes. Actually this is more a matter of social value, once achieved, becoming firmly established. This process of entrenchment and its perpetuation constitutes a special problem that must be specifically explained—at bottom this is the immediate and specific "class problem." Yet even this entrenched position, which endures in group terms, offering the picture of a class made secure above and beyond the individual, ultimately rests on individual differences in aptitude. Entrenched positions, which constitute the class stratification of society, are attained or created by behavior,[27] which in turn is conditioned by differential aptitudes.

From other points of view—some of them still in the field of sociology, others beyond it and even beyond the field of science altogether—the essence of social classes may appear in a different light. They may seem organs of society, legal or cultural entities, conspiracies against the rest of the nation. From the explanatory viewpoint they are merely what we have described them to be. And all that is left for us to do is to particularize, illustrate, and supplement our own result in certain points.

21. First, as to aptitude, differences in aptitude, family aptitude: Insofar as "aptitude" is something that shows itself immediately in the physical individual—much like the color of hair or eyes—our line of reasoning, as already indicated, comes back to the physical individual. Insofar as, first, relevant "aptitudes" are not merely physical and, second, "aptitude" can be considered only the basis for "behavior," our argument also comes back to the individual psyche. In our presentation we have endeavored to emphasize that this implies neither the errors of individualism nor a process of "psychologization" that loses itself in surface phenomena. We cannot help those who are unable to see that the individual is a *social* fact, the psychological an *objective* fact, who cannot give up toying with the empty contrasts of the individual *vs.* the social, the subjective *vs.* the objective. But it is more important to guard against tautological confusion between "aptitude" and "success" in which only the latter is taken to be susceptible to

empirical observation, while the former becomes a mere word like the *vis soporifica* of opium. We contend that both can be empirically investigated, independently of each other. In the Goths under Teja, we recognize "aptitude" for the function of a military master class, even though history shows that they were not blessed with "success" when they encountered Narses.

To establish the presence of such an "aptitude" does not confer any laurels, nor does it testify to moral worth. From many points of view—religious, aesthetic, moral—it may have to be evaluated in a negative sense. It may, in particular, be antisocial—and this is not necessarily a value judgment, but may be a judgment based on facts. Success for the individual, the family, the class does not necessarily mean success for other segments of the population or for the nation as a whole; indeed, it may mean the very opposite. The extent to which this is true is, of course, of considerable importance, not only for our evaluation of the class phenomenon and of certain historical classes, but also for our scientific knowledge of social cause and effect. Even from the examples cited in this study it is evident that in some cases success in establishing class position does represent "social achievement"—in other words, that it enhances the position of others, as well as of those responsible for the success. In other cases this is not true, while in still others the ultimate judgment must depend on a deeper analysis, based on theoretical economics, of the consequences for which the behavior in question is responsible. Finally, a distinction must always be made *between the social significance of a given mode of behavior and the social significance of the qualities that make such behavior possible.* It is not enough merely to have a moral defect in order to become a bandit or a tyrant. As a rule, the person in question must also "have what it takes." In other words, the process of social rise or decline can be described in terms of "natural selection" only in a very restricted sense. But important as these matters are, enlightening as studies concerning them may be, this aspect of the case does not concern us here.

"Aptitude" may be "natural" or acquired. In the latter case it may be acquired individually or by family background. The relevance of these distinctions to our problem is obvious. The greater the role played by natural and family-acquired aptitude, the firmer will class position be. Its firmness will also be inversely proportional to the degree to which an acquired aptitude—of itself or by its effect on the mode and goals of life—prevents the acquisition of other aptitudes, and directly proportional to the degree of significance which outward achievements flowing from an already elevated position carry with respect to the acquisition of new aptitudes. These matters merely have to be mentioned for it to be seen that they hold a good part of class history. But for the first step which our investigation takes they are of no particular importance. Even acquired aptitude is a datum at any given time.

Aptitude determines a quality or a system of qualities only with respect to certain definite functions. The relationship is similar to that between biological adaptation and survival in a given physical environment. There are, for example, specific predispositions—those having to do with music and mathematics have been most exhaustively investigated—which have virtually no relationship to other natural endowments. Yet there are other talents that apply to a multiplicity of functions—the capacity for intellectual analysis, for example. Willpower in its various manifestations is an important element in this respect, and there is, of course, the well-known phenomenon of all-around capacity which is equally effective in the face of most of the practical demands of life. Spearman's studies of this quality have given rise to the theory of a "central factor," but actually this is no more than a word for something already empirically confirmed. From the viewpoint of class history and class theory, we are concerned, first, with the fact that class functions and their relative social necessity change only slowly. Second, we find that the socially necessary functions that succeed one another in historical time are related in important respects—administrative skill, resoluteness, and the ability to command are vital in any leading position. Third, the functions relevant to our study all have to do with the same factor, namely, social leadership. Over and above this, however, the two cited facts are of the greatest importance to an understanding of class evolution and to any "interpretive" history of class structure. The fact of the special aptitude—especially the acquired kind—emerges with particular clarity when we compare, for example, the type of the warlord of the early Middle Ages with that of the modern stock-exchange speculator. It is a fact that serves to explain why the same class does not always retain leadership—something that is by no means explained by the mere circumstance that the relative importance of functions changes. For the function alone is not the essence of the class. And the facts brought out in the central-factor theory do sometimes explain, in whole or in part, why a class often maintains its social position so well, despite a decline in the function peculiar to it, over a long period of time.

In an ethnically homogeneous environment, special and general aptitudes, physical and mental, those of will and of intellect, are probably distributed according to the normal curve. This has been carefully demonstrated with physical characteristics that are most readily susceptible to measurement, notably body height and weight. Beyond this, we have extensive experimental material only for school children. As for the capacity of adults to measure up to the tasks of daily life, we have only our general impression to go by.[28] Further investigations would be very important in advancing class research, but our present purpose is served well enough by the fact, scarcely disputed, that individual differences in aptitude do exist and that individual aptitudes do not fall into sharply marked categories, separated by empty space, but shade by imperceptible nuances from high to low. The situation is different only when there are sharp ethnical differences, such as between Mongols and Slavs, whites or Arabs and Negroes.

If it were true that individual aptitudes bear no relationship to the aptitudes of ancestors and progeny—if none were inherited and all individuals were simply sports—then the elements of position and acquired aptitude would still be capable of forming relatively stable groups, though the course of history would have been different. If aptitudes were never inherited and always distributed according to the laws of chance, the position of classes and of families within them would manifestly be far less stable than it actually is. There can scarcely be any doubt of the inheritance of physical characteristics. As for mental characteristics, we have as yet only data in the field of defects, though these are in a state of fruitful evolution. For obvious reasons, it is difficult and dangerous to go beyond them, in the field of statistics as well as of genealogy.[29] Again, therefore, we emphasize that while it may be hopeless to pass considered judgment on the cultural significance of a class—and, incidentally, on most other basic questions of the social order, past or future—until this point has been settled, the basic idea of the class theory here presented is quite independent of it.

22. As to the question of leadership, if we are to be properly understood, all the romance and gibberish surrounding this term must be discarded. We are not concerned with the individual leadership of the creative mind or of the genius. We do not care whether this phenomenon is of big or small importance in social science or whether it is irrelevant; whether it plays a causal role, direct or indirect; whether such individuals function autonomously or by their own laws. In short, the entire problem of the "great man" has no bearing on our subject. Nor do we by any means insist that group leadership, which alone concerns us here, necessarily "leads" in the direction where it desires to go of its own free will, or that it creates the realm of possibility into which it leads—a realm realized only under its leadership. We are content to say that social leadership means to decide, to com-

mand, to prevail, to advance. As such it is a special function, always clearly discernible in the actions of the individual and within the social whole. It emerges only with respect to ever new individual and social situations and would never exist if individual and national life always ran its course in the same way and by the same routine. Yet by its very nature it almost never occurs in the "pure" state. It is virtually always linked to certain other functions and offices, by virtue of which it is exercised and from which it receives its peculiar coloration and direction. But whatever the trend and the form may be, leadership always remains leadership. Ordinarily individuals differ in their capacity for it, much as they differ in their ability to sing, though it must be added that both the attainment and the practice of leadership are aided by a tradition of leadership. And, as is the case with other aptitudes, the aptitude for leadership is not necessarily strongly marked in a few individuals, and nonexistent in the rest. Most individuals possess it to a modest degree, sufficient for the simplest tasks of everyday life, while one minority has it to a stronger, another to a lesser degree. The absolute extent of aptitude for leadership in a given nation (or the qualities on which it is based) largely determines the history of that nation; and within it individual families are ranked by social value in the order in which they possess this aptitude and these qualities. It is because this aptitude is distributed continuously throughout a nation, without gaps and discontinuities, that class barriers are characteristically in a state of flux. Classes particularly deficient or altogether lacking in it secure it through talented individuals who become renegades or declassed. If such classes are already on the rise, they may be led by those of their members who would otherwise ascend to higher classes but instead now devote themselves to the task of leadership within the class. Such ranking by degree of aptitude for leadership is, immediately, one of physical individuals and can owe any supra-individual constancy only to the fact of the inheritance of characteristics. It leads to objectively defined family position and, by extension and entrenchment, to class position of those families that, by our criterion, are approximately coordinate.

23. As for the process of entrenchment, the kind of success that is the basis for the individual's rise normally tends to repeat itself, simply because as a rule the individual manages to carry out the same kind of task again and again and because success generally paves the way for further success. Even so, success, once achieved, exerts a continuing effect, without further accomplishment, for two reasons: First of all, the prestige it engenders assumes a life of its own. It does not necessarily disappear when its basis disappears—nor, for that matter, does its basis readily disappear. *This is the very heart and soul of*

*the independent organic existence of "class."* In the second place, in the vast majority of cases success brings in its wake important functional positions and other powers over material resources. The position of the physical individual becomes entrenched, and with it that of the family. This opens up further opportunities to the family, often to an even greater degree than to the successful individual himself, though these positive factors are to some extent offset by the deadening effect on the original impetus of exalted position and security, by the diversion and complication of interests, and perhaps also by the sheer exhaustion of energies which everyday experience shows to be not uncommon. *Coordinate families then merge into a social class, welded together by a bond, the substance and effect of which we now understand. This relationship assumes a life of its own and is then able to grant protection and confer prestige.* In addition to the natural endowment of the class members, there are other factors that determine the course and the firmness of class structure and class position—factors that have little or no connection with aptitude. Among those that have no such connection is the outward course of history. There are times of quietude, for example, their tranquility stemming from causes that have nothing to do with the qualities of the ruling classes, times during which class position is long maintained without effort, times during which only such events occur as the ruling classes are well able to master; and when it is otherwise, events may be entirely beyond control. Another such factor is the character of the economic base of a class. From the viewpoint of the German nobility, for example, it was pure chance that the opportunity existed for large-scale agricultural production which proved to be a very durable and relatively easily managed source of capitalist income. Third, it may likewise be mostly chance, for better or for worse, whether a suitable new function can be found at the time the old one enters into a decline. But this already passes into the other group of factors. It does have some slight connection with the capacities of the families in the class—whether, for example, the class propagates itself or withers by inbreeding. The connection with class aptitude is somewhat closer—whether or not the attainable function is a suitable basis for general leadership. The warlord was automatically the leader of his people in virtually every respect. The modern industrialist is anything but such a leader. And this explains a great deal about the stability of the former's position and the instability of the latter's. Even closer is the connection between class efficiency and adaptability to altered circumstances. There is the aristocrat, for example, who hurls himself into an election campaign as his ancestors rode into battle; and there is the aristocrat who says to himself: "I can't very well ask my valet to vote for me." Here, in fact, is the measure of two radically different types of European aristocrat. The class situation may so specialize members of the class that adaptation to new situations becomes all but impossible. From the viewpoint of this and similar factors, we can see in proper perspective why members of the ruling classes in present-day Europe so often seem to make a bad joke of our theory that class position and capacity go together. Finally, there is but a slight connection between the endowment of a class and the facility with which it grasps and handles growing power. Highly competent classes are often quite blind to the vital importance of this factor, for themselves as well as for the destiny of their people. Yet that importance is unmistakable. It is the ease with which English industrial families in the nineteenth century managed to rise into "society," by way of financial success and politics,[30] that gave England its unique leadership class. This, after all, was true even of rising intellectual talent—and the life stories of two "physical individuals," Disraeli and Lassalle, give symbolic expression to a segment of two national destinies.

## Notes

1. This essay was originally published as "Die sozialen Klassen im ethnisch homogen Milieu" in 1927 in *Archiv für Sozialwissenschaft und Sozialpolitik*. An English translation appeared in 1951 in Joseph Schumpeter, *Imperialism and Social Classes* (New York: A. M. Kelley; Oxford: Blackwell, 1951). For more information on this essay, see the section titled "The European Period: Schumpeter's Works in This Volume" in the Introduction. The translation was made by Heinz Norden.

2. We also mean to imply that a class is no mere "resultant phenomenon" [*Resultatenerscheinung*], such as a market, for example (for the same viewpoint, from another theoretical orientation, see Spann, *loc. cit.*). We are not concerned with this here, however. What does matter is the distinction between the real social phenomenon and the scientific construct.

3. In support of this criterion we may now also invoke the authority of Max Weber, who mentions it in his sociology, though only in passing.

4. We do not use the term "estate" since we have no need for it. Technically it has fixed meaning only in the sense of status and in connection with the constitution of the feudal state. For the rest, it is equated, sometimes with "profession," and sometimes with "class." Caste is merely a special elaboration of the class phenomenon, its peculiarity of no essential importance to us.

5. The theory of the "original" classless society is probably headed for a fate similar to that which has already overtaken the theory of primitive communism and primitive promiscuity. It will prove to be purely speculative, along the line of "natural law." Yet all such conceptions do receive apparent confirmation in the conditions of the "primitive horde." Where a group is

very small and its existence precarious, the situation necessarily has the aspects of classlessness, communism, and promiscuity. But this no more constitutes an organizational principle than the fact that an otherwise carnivorous species will become vegetarian when no meat is available constitutes a vegetarian principle.

6. The explanatory value of historically observable genesis must not be overrated. It does not always lead to an explanation and never offers an explanation *ipso facto*, not even when a phenomenon appears immediately in its "pure" form, which is neither inevitable nor even frequent.

7. With blood relationship the critical factor, we do not limit ourselves to the parental family here. Hence we use the terms "family," "clan," "tribe" as synonymous, though a presentation that went into greater detail would have to make distinctions.

8. More precisely: independent of positional elements that are recognizable before the event occurs. For the event may be—and generally is—tied to some one of these elements.

9. Such aggressiveness was a mode of life, important to the knightly estate as a method of natural selection. In the case cited this is seen—if evidence be needed—from the events following the capture, twice in succession, of Aggstein, robber citadel of the Kuenringens, each time by captains of the regional prince. Each time the captor, duly invested with his prize, was aping his predecessors in a matter of months.

10. I refer to my exposition of this mechanism in my *Theory of Economic Development*, which devotes a special chapter to it, though the topic is also discussed elsewhere in that treatise.

11. These cases, however, include those that are "historically" most significant and thus widely known to the public. The rule is control by a syndicate or an even weaker organizational form.

12. This is an important factor of success and social ascent in every walk of life. It is what the English gambler calls "playing to the score."

13. The monarchial position is not something *sui generis*, but simply the topmost position of the high aristocracy as a class—even though, in the individual case, the monarch may hold quite aloof from that class.

14. See Sir J. Stamp's communication in *The Economic Journal*, December 1926.

15. *Cf.* Chapman and Marquis in the *Journal of the Royal Statistical Society*, February 1912.

16. Both the fact of class struggle and the expression itself would then appear in a different light; but it is important to emphasize that they would not lose all significance.

17. Of course it is by no means a matter of indifference whether failure acts in this fashion or objectively and automatically, as in the case of a businessman, for example. But these finer distinctions, essential to an interpretation of class history, cannot be considered here.

18. Specialization along occupational lines need not, of itself, tend to form

classes. Men and women have always had distinct spheres of work, yet they never formed "classes" on the basis of mere interindividual relationships.

19. Legal and social history usually treats this rise from the opposite aspect—the decline in the position of other elements in the population.

20. True, this process was not completed until the twelfth century. Earlier techniques of war did not impose even approximately such demands, as has already been indicated. Yet while acknowledging the importance of this element, it must not be overestimated, even for later times. The equestrian art in our sense, or anything like it, did not even exist before the time of the classical school. There were then no assemblages of armored horse, no training in cavalry techniques.

21. The Saxon nobility colonized East Elbia in the same way and at about the same time as the Byzantine nobility colonized the southern and eastern border reaches of Asia Minor.

22. I employ this term, suggestive of the economic interpretation of history, in order to give expression to my belief that our line of reasoning is entirely reconcilable with that approach.

23. Incorrectly because there is implied a distinction between the spheres of private and public law, which is peculiar only to the age of capitalism. But we are here concerned only with characterizing a familiar phenomenon.

24. They do not do so at the same rate, however, as is shown by the examples of the English and French aristocracies. Sharp breaks in constitutional continuity and excesses are only symptoms of *revolution*, just as panics and depressions are symptoms of economic *crisis*; but the essential thing is a process of transformation that *may* but *need not* lead to revolution or crisis. The position of classes is not won or lost, in a causal sense, through revolutions. As Gottfried Kunwald puts it: when one already *has* the power, one can make a revolution, among other things; but power that does not exist cannot be *created* by revolution.

25. To the extent that other persons were involved, they were "elevated" and assimilated to the nobility—not always voluntarily.

26. It is more accurate, by the way, to say that class determines "occupation" than the other way round.

27. It is only this process of entrenchment that creates a special cultural background, a greater or lesser degree of promptness in concerted action, one aspect of which is expressed in the concept of the class struggle. We refrain here from passing any judgment on the actual significance of this factor.

28. The impression is not entirely a general one, for we do have concrete instances to go by, notably studies of relatively homogeneous bodies of civil servants.

29. This becomes clear in its full significance when we compare Goddard's study of the Kallikak family, for example, with Galton's *Hereditary Genius*. But both material and methods are steadily improving. Even today, we can agree that K. Pearson's pithy statement, "ability runs in stocks," is far truer than its opposite, especially since everyday experience confirms it. But should not

then class position, once established, endure *ad infinitum* in every case? Before we embarked on our study, this might have been a reasonable question. But I have no answer for those who put it at this point.

30. A noteworthy feature of this system is the elaborate "ordeal" which the rising family as a rule had to endure.

# *Five*

## Recent Developments of Political Economy

MR. PRESIDENT, colleagues and gentlemen, we shall turn today away from any particular questions, whether practical or theoretical, and try to take a survey—a bird's-eye view, of the present state of our science.[1] The questions which I shall, however imperfectly, try to deal with are, "Where do we stand? Whence do we come from and where do we go? What may our way be in the future?" A survey like this will not tell you many new facts. I have observed that Japanese scholars and students are so well informed about what happens in matters of science in other countries that I cannot hope to give you anything entirely new. What I may interest you in, is to show how the present state of the science looks to one working in the field; to show you how it looks when it is looked at through the spectacles of one particular temperament. I do not mean to say that my way of looking at it has anything to commend itself to that of another. The range of the subject is very wide. Naturally our science widens as the problems unfold, and it gets more and more difficult for one man to grasp it. But in one sense the scope is more limited than it would have been thirty years ago, because of the evolution of sociology. Sociology, much as we may have to find fault with it, has progressed in many branches in a successful way, and the consequence is that many subjects economists used to deal with are, and can be, left to the sister science. For instance, it is quite natural to think that nobody can think about economic subjects, no teacher can lecture on them, without dealing with such economic institutions as private property, inheritance, and all that sort of thing. Yet we have only to deal with these subjects as far as is necessary for practical purposes, because they form a well-defined part of sociology. There are excellent works by sociologists about private property and inheritance and what they mean to the nations and why they develop and decay, and we need not bother with these problems, as former generations had to. Generally speaking, social science is ceasing more and more to be one science. The time was when natural science was regarded as one. It is not so any more. The theoretical physicist and chemist and biologist are quite different people with different habits from practical scientists. We may regret the separation as taking away much of the splendor of

early work, as taking away much of the breadth of outlook and narrowing the work and making it less aesthetically beautiful. The compensating advantage is that it adds to efficiency. The modern man
has no choice but to specialize. We have got to do it. So the range of
questions in this sense is more limited than it was.

I must begin with the confession that I look upon economics as a
science. You may think it funny that I should think it necessary to
insist upon this, but so many people among us think that economists
derive their beliefs from their political creeds. Others think that the
philosophy of economics is a personal one. This is a point which I
shall try to unfold, that economics is a science just as any other, and
its object is, like any other science, to establish functional relations
between the phenomena that we have to observe. Empirical science,
in any case, deals with economic facts, which we simplify and more
or less put in some connection with each other—a connection which
in some mysterious way satisfies the craving of the human heart for
knowledge, and which we call scientific truth. It is not eternal truth—
a religious revelation or intuitive vision. It is only the rational connection of things. That is all. Looking at it this way, I regard economics
as having everything a physical science includes. There may be a lot
of difference in mental attitudes, but my point is that you must never
say for physiological reasons, or because economics is a social science,
and because this means something mysterious, we cannot apply natural ways, the methods usual in the natural sciences. We cannot say
whether we shall be able to apply them, we cannot judge from an *a
priori* point of view whether we shall be able to or not; it depends
upon how the experiment turns out. There are no preconceived
rules for the discovery of scientific truth but the general ones for
logic. Apart from that we are engaging in the most beautiful aspect
of science, in a kind of intellectual adventure, in which sometimes this
and sometimes the other method is useful and fruitful. No method is
good for all problems, but everyone has a place and it is for this reason that I think so little of methodological controversies. I do not
differentiate epistemologically between theorem and statistical regu-
larity, for both are empiric laws derived by definite technique from
different facts. It is absurd for the theorist to decline logical inference
and for the statistician to decline theoretical tools. Both have substantially the same empirical basis. They only look different because they
are based on a different kind of observation. As a matter of fact the
specialist may be a specialist because he has an aptitude for it and
therefore likes it, and the theorist may be a theorist because he likes
it and thinks theorizing is the nicest thing in social science, and has a
mild contempt for everything else. It is natural and good that this

should be so. I do not think science would have developed if we had not all of us overrated the importance of knowledge and knowledge of our own science and what we individually can do for it. In order to do anything in life, either to make a great scientific discovery or win a battle or be a great statesman we must overrate the importance of what we want to do, for if you look at things in too philosophical a way or from too broad a standpoint it will appear as if in the process of the centuries, very little matters really.

It is usual, if a survey is attempted of the state of our science, to distinguish between what are called schools. It is indeed convenient to do so and many have for some time followed the same practice. But before following this practice myself I ought to tell you that I disapprove of it. At the beginning of every science naturally what can be taught, what is known, what can be done is very limited. At the beginning of every science everything that can be achieved looms very big and there is the age or epoch of system building. Teachers of science build up what they are pleased to call a system, a body of general truth which they think embodies what is to be known, everything else, especially the systems of other teachers, being darkness and error. This system building ceases when the science comes of age. When it comes of age it is very soon discovered that a general standpoint matters less than one would think. For instance, modern psychology does not ask questions about the human soul; it deals with specialized phenomena. The concept of the soul is left to the philosopher. So also practical work in the service of a particular problem comes more and more to the fore and general system building sinks back into the background. It was thus that we came to distinguish schools of economic science. I hold now that we have discovered that every problem is only a technique which it imposes on us and which we cannot help making use of. It is no use before approaching a problem to form a preconceived idea of how to proceed with it. As you know, at the beginning of the eighteenth century all economists used to start in their analysis with the individual. The nineteenth-century economists also took the individualistic standpoint. It is [the creed of methodological universalism] that it is quite wrong to start from the individual. The individual is only a product of the social environment and therefore it is wrong to start from him. We know that every individual is fashioned by the social influences in which he grows up. In this sense he is the produce of the social entity or class and therefore not a free agent. That is certainly so, but it is quite uninteresting as long as it is stated in this general form, where it is nothing but a phrase. It is interesting only when we can build a concrete knowledge on the basis of that view, and my great objection to it is that we do not make anything out of preaching universalism as a creed. In some problems of sociology or political life and so on we have no choice but to start from the social whole. In other cases, such as market phenomenon and most problems of modern industry, there is no choice but to start from the individual. In the one class universalism and in the other class individualism is the indicated method. Therefore we ought to be neither individualistic nor universalistic. It is a matter of convenience; neither individualism nor universalism is an eternal truth. Both are only devices which are useful sometimes and hamper progress at other times. Therefore I do not believe in systems which are connected bodies of teaching. I do not believe in schools. I believe all competent workers in most branches of economy agree more than appears on the surface.

The trouble in economics is not that there should not be agreement among the competent workers at the science; the trouble is that while the ordinary doctor and mathematician and historian are ordinarily competent, people who talk about economics are not ordinarily competent. The amount of truth that we have about economics is not so generally recognized and accessible as in other sciences. When a new mathematical method is established it becomes the property of all other mathematicians. But when a new economic method is established it does not become common property because a great part of the economic world is so ill trained and so little gifted that it takes a great time to get the thing properly discussed and accepted or rejected. That is the whole truth. Therefore I do not think I ought to talk about schools or that they ought to exist in the sense I have discussed. What is a school? In the first and very harmless sense of the word in every university, in every institution, round every prominent teacher, naturally the pupils cluster. They are trained in the same way and naturally they acquire the habit of dealing with problems in a similar manner. They acquire a common terminology and certain mannerisms in thinking and writing. This is necessary and exists in every science. We understand by schools also something else. We distinguish—some people at least—schools according to the country, as French or German or Italian. There is no sense in that whatever, because science is of no country and does not bear any homogeneous national traits. The theorist in Germany and the theorist in England may have very much more in common than either of them have with their colleagues. To speak of a French school of economists can only be true of certain cases in past history. For instance, in the middle of the eighteenth century when the physiocrats' school arose in Paris and had a great success in France and at first nowhere else. It happened to be a specially French phenomenon. Later the whole school disappeared. We find physiocrats in other countries, but the prominent ones, who really do know things, we find only in France. Therefore we can call it a French school. The English Classical School between 1776 till 1848, the period from Adam Smith's *Wealth of Nations* to Mill's *Principles*, formed a group the members of which knew each other and had a close intercourse with one another. It is possible to speak of a school in that sense. But it is rarely the case that we can divide economists into countries or nations. This is just about the worst way to write the history of economics that can be imagined.

Another meaning [of school] is the division between economists as to political or social creeds. Some people speak of the Mercantile School, or the Liberal School, or the Socialist School, and so on. This way of looking at things is open to objection firstly because there never have been liberals or mercantilists or socialists who agreed as to their scientific standpoint, and for science it is the scientific standpoint that matters and not the conclusions they draw. The fact that Adam Smith favored a qualified method of free trade has nothing to do with its scientific importance, for if he had been in favor of protection, as he was for shipping, it would have been just the same. The fact that Ricardo held free trade views and so on neither adds nor detracts from his scientific greatness. Science means explaining and understanding and nothing else. Because an action does not depend on knowledge but on will and passion, there never is and never can be a connection—a close and stringent connection—between one's political creed and economic theory.

This is a point of importance and I want to give you an example to make my meaning clear. Many of you think it is impossible to be a socialist without being a Marxist and practically all of you think that to be a Marxist is to be a socialist. It is easy to prove that both views are wrong. Politically you may be a socialist without being a Marxist. One of the great founders of what may be styled the modern theory of economics, Vilfredo Pareto, told me that he was a socialist. He made no use of this fact in his scientific work, nor ought he to have, because if you deal with scientific questions you must deal with them in the spirit of a searcher for the truth. You can all be socialists but you need not be Marxists. But another more interesting question is whether you can be a Marxist without being a socialist. That depends upon what you mean by a socialist. If to be a socialist means that socialism has established itself as a form of organization of society, then it is true that anyone who believes can belong to the party. I know, for instance, that I shall die, but this does not mean that I shall like dying. If I say that I can prove scientifically that things have a tendency toward socialism, that does not mean that I am in sympathy with it, for I can also predict disagreeable things. Furthermore, if I am a Marxist I must hold the theory of exploitation. Does that make me a socialist? No. Let us assume that I hold the theory of exploitation, that is that I believe exploitation is necessary for human civilization. In that case I am a Marxist but I should not necessarily be a socialist because I approve of exploitation. It is not a proof of scientific conviction and therefore not an affair of Marxism or non-Marxism as far as Marxism is a scientific creed. As far as Marxism is meant to be a scientific system, as Marx meant it to be, it does not enforce socialist sympathies nor does it bind us to anti-socialist views. Yesterday, in company with some of my amiable colleagues, I was permitted to visit the city of Kyoto. There I greatly admired the works of art in the old Shogun's palace. Now from the socialist standpoint all these pictures ought never to have been painted, because naturally in order to get these pictures painted means were taken which Marx would have called exploitation. I admired the paintings with the deepest artistic approval and feel that that amount of exploitation was necessary in order that they should be painted. So you see there is no logical connection between these things.

Another meaning for the expression school is that we can divide economics according to philosophical principles. In my own country it is usual to associate Marx with the philosophy of Hegel. It is easy to show that this is not the case. Marx himself says in the preface to *Das Kapital* that there is no such connection. But although Marx uses the Hegelian terminology in the surplus value theory and the accumulation theory and so on, they are founded on economic arguments and are compatible with every philosophy. Therefore it may just as well be called Kantian as Hegelian, and take on any philosophical leanings you like or vice versa. If a man believes in a certain philosophy it does not follow that he has a certain view on economic problems. This distinction will not work.

Then there is the distinction of schools on practical lines and methods. This looks more promising, but even here I think we are approaching the time when there will be no more schools. To take an example, there was the Historical School in Germany and elsewhere. This has disappeared because we do not attach any more importance to studies in economic history. We have absorbed this school into the general body of scientific work, and few economic historians who understand their business are likely to quarrel with the theorists. It is recognized that both work toward a common end. Take the case of the experimental and theoretical physicist. The theoretical physicist knows very little about experiments and experimental work, and the experimental physicist, if he does not know how to get along with his mathematics, calls in the aid of the theoretical physicist. That is the way to cooperate. There is no sense in saying one is right and the other wrong. As I have said the Historical School has disappeared. It has disappeared in Germany and this is a nice example of how schools may and will disappear if people cease to quarrel about methods and turn to real problems. When I was at Harvard, one of the Harvard historians, Mr. Robert Blake, gave me a history of Levantine trade in which there were a lot of questions such as this: Was the Roman balance of trade from the time of Augustus, say to three thousand years after Christ, active or passive, and if passive what consequences could be expected from it? How do you explain that Byzantine coins and Persian coins penetrated certain districts and not others? All these questions require theory in the sense in which Marshall defined it, as a tool, an engine of analysis. An engine of analysis it was my privilege to supply on certain points. It is quite natural to cooperate in that way and there is no sense in distinguishing schools as practical and experimental. Therefore I will not speak about schools, which is often a catchword to cover ignorance, because membership of a school is thought sufficient by members of that school to replace talent. They are evil things in every respect and I hope that they will fall away from us as science progresses.

I will now proceed to speak about some of the groups of economists, but before doing so let me make some remarks about the state of our science in different countries. England is particularly fortunate. Her economists are so concentrated in London and Cambridge that it is easy by discussion and personal contact to establish common ground and on this common ground stood for quite a long time the greatest teacher, in the strict sense of the words, that economists ever had, Alfred Marshall, whose pupils are ninety-nine percent of the English economists. There was, of course, opposition. There was opposition from the London School of Economics, and there were single-handed opponents, among them Mr. Hobson, who is a good instance of a phenomenon that has developed in our science.[2] In other sciences if a man does not understand a thing, he does not understand and lets it alone. In our science if he does not understand he sets himself up as a differing authority. Mr. Hobson does not know what marginal analysis means, and refutes it by changing the margin not by small increments but by bigger ones. Now all marginal analysis in any science is only operating with infinite decimal quantities small in comparison with the quantity the science deals with. Now if you replace the small quantities by big ones, then of course a different logic applies and what is true for small quantities is not true for big ones. Mr. Hobson, not knowing that fact, found it easy to prove that what economists hold true for small quantities is not true for big ones. That is true. But if anyone argued like that in a classroom of a physicist he would hardly be dealt with, although a new authority on economics has been set up on the strength of this achievement. But on the whole England is on a very high level. Proceeding from the commonly accepted ground, all the pupils of Marshall, the most eminent of the economists, have developed his work. It is no use crying out for new economics; we must make it. That is what these pupils are doing, step by step. And they have developed considerable progress. How much progress has been made in the theory of economics I do not know, because there is a tradition that Marshall's teaching went further than his published work. He was very slow in publishing, and when in extreme old age he published his book he was not able to put forth quite clearly what he had before in his mind. I do not know exactly how much Pigou and others have gone beyond him in respect to money, his generous pupils always giving him the credit for the discoveries, but they have developed quite a number of pieces of apparatus, like Pigou's method of fixing in a statistical way the elasticity of demand on the data of supply and demand. Pigou has an efficient method of doing that on budget data. Further, Pigou has indicated analysis by a number of valuable theorems, so slowly rebuilding Marshall's edifice, without changing its face and foundations. Marshall himself was good in that respect, with one qualification, to which I shall refer later.

It is astonishing that our science should be in such a poor state in France, the more especially as French genius stands out so beautifully in the history of the science. The three most gifted economists that the science has had were all three Frenchmen: [Antoine Augustin Cournot, François Quesnay] and Léon Walras. Only the first had any success in his own country, as gifted people in France find it difficult to get professorships. In my own country everything is in a state of transition. The reaction against the Historical School dates quite thirty years ago, but after having left the tents of the historians people did not know how to analyze economic facts by different methods, so they started what I shall always consider one of the greatest misfortunes, they started to squabble about methods. Hundreds of books about methods appeared in Germany, and out of a hundred articles on economics in periodicals I have counted thirty-six of a methodological nature. That is dreadful. There may be some good ones, but these are cancelled by the waste of energy. If you are a good economist you ought to work on economic problems, not take up the work of the logician. If epistemology provides for our needs, why go out of the way to enter a region not our own and deal with questions we are just as well without? That is a very sorry state of things for a great nation and I am truly ashamed of it. I am only glad that other departments of science in Germany show up better.

Astonishingly much is being done in Italy. This admirable and gifted nation has overcome the limitations imposed by the economic environment. It has numberless universities, but no money to support them, and there are many professorial chairs not provided for. Yet it is astonishing how much good work is being done, how many eminent people there are always turning up. The study dates from the time of Pantaleone, on the basis of whose teaching a big host of younger men are doing excellent work.

If I had time I could also relate how much very good work is being done in the northern states of Europe, in Holland especially, Norway, Sweden, and Denmark, especially among the younger men. I know quite a number who will do great things later on.

Let me add that our science is most fortunate in the interest taken in it in America. We have the great leaders Taussig and Fischer, and many lesser men, and although there are no striking and brilliant performances, there is a tremendous amount of good laboratory work and most hopeful possibilities of putting up a collaboration between the statisticians and the theorists, which after a time of squabbling between them, is now coming to establish itself. The important thing in America is that they have both the right intentions and the means to carry the work further with the greatest possible success.

Of course things do not go on smoothly everywhere, for while in Germany that part of the work of Schmoller spoiled by errors has been put aside by most economists, there is a revival of the errors in America under the name of institutionalism. Institutionalism is nothing but the methodological errors of German historians, combined with the great and lasting contribution made to our sciences. It is only error and not achievement. This, of course, is the one dark spot in the American atmosphere.

I should not be so presumptuous as to add a picture of Japanese economics to the picture of European and American, because you know more about them than I do. I may compare the situation with the American one, however. Just as the Americans in the nineteenth century had a long spell when all their energies were taken up with practical questions, so you had to carry through a complete reorganization of the social and political structure. In such times a science like ours does not thrive. Since 1890 there has been a great evolution of which I think the whole world will hear soon.

Let me now touch upon the groups which may be called schools inasmuch as they are united to each other from a scientific standpoint. I would speak of the romantic school which centers round the name of Spann, or the school round Gottl in Berlin, or the agrarian socialism of Oppenheimer, but I have no time. The most interesting of all these schools is that called neo-Marxism. When Engels died, Marxism had just conquered German and Russian socialism. In France Marxism never conquered socialism, nor in Italy, while in England the Marxists formed a very small group. In Germany Marxism became really the official creed of the Social Democratic Party and by becoming the creed of the party naturally came into a situation which is not ordinarily the fate of a scientific theory, because a political party cannot change its creed, since a change of creed means a loss of prestige. But it is the essence of science to change. That is the difference between scientific and religious teaching. Religious teaching claims to be eternal truth, but science cannot claim that, because scientific truth is only relative to a particular kind of problem. Thus Newtonian mechanics, which was considered so long as an eternal truth, cannot any longer be held so, for the relativity theory of Einstein has shifted the ground. This being so it is useless to expect Marxism to be an everlasting canon of the science of economics. Yet the Social Democratic Party keeps to it, and ever since this pathetic state of things, the best circles in all Marxist parties in Europe have held loyalty and allegiance to the creed of Marx. But we as scientists cannot stay with Marx. We are in the disagreeable position of being condemned because we deviate from the received doctrine. This happened to Bernstein, who had a string of objections to Marx. I do not think much of Bernstein's arguments; they are superficial and inferior to Marx himself. But he had the greatest difficulty with the party and was expelled because he failed to conform with the creed, along with every one of the neo-Marxists. Marx is very much in the way of being a theologian. He talks in that prophetic voice which is usual for those who have to give eternal light. So unfortunately nothing comes of these attempts at individuality and this state of things has paralyzed a good many minds. Otto Bauer, Rosa Luxembourg, and others were of exceptional ability, but their development was stifled by fetters which no scientist can endure, because they stop the pulse of life of science. It was really a tragic thing to see all these people struggling with the best of their ability to hold what cannot be held anymore.

Now leaving the schools, I want to touch upon what is being done in that other field which in theory has competed for some time with Marxism in Germany and has expanded while Marxism has contracted. Modern socialists have more and more accepted common ground with other economists in the way of practical politics. This is as it should be. There is no truth which is only true for socialists. It is either true for both socialists and nonsocialists or wrong for both. So our general way of looking at economics is becoming more and more uniform, although we do not like to admit it. We like to stress the differences and obscure the similarities. Look, for instance, at the system of Gustav Cassel, the eminent leader of economics in Europe. What is his system? It is first of all the theory of equilibrium, which is nothing but valorization with the name of valorization left out. The work would be of great service to science were it not for the tendency to try to make out that these are new developments. If we change the name we do not change the thing. There is a little group of economists, every one of which is struggling for their new teaching and having a very hard time. In England the same thing has happened, and this means a qualification of reverence which I bear to the great name of Alfred Marshall. Marshall discovered the great theorem which Jevons published before him, independently of Jevons, as related by Keynes in his biography, a delightful book to read.[3] It is very interesting to see the great loyalty of Marshall for his classic predecessors and the care he took to assign their worth to even obscure names. I say that in order to prove a very great truth which it is important for you to know, that in economic theory there is much less of schools and differences than appear on the surface. If you know how to read Marshall you will find it is marginal utility analysis and nothing else. You may say there is the cost principle. Yes, but as there is in the marginal utility theory. If Marshall compared cost and utility to two blades of a pair of scissors, the answer is that they are both made of the same material, of utility. Marshall tried to make out in his treatment of cost that this has nothing to do with cost, but Ricardo tried to bring out this cost.

There was one who was as important for Sweden as Marshall for England—one who was free from all these blemishes—and that was Wicksell, one of the most capable and original thinkers at the end of the nineteenth century and beginning of the twentieth. His results were very much the same as the Marshallian. And in America there were the Clarkian economists. Thus, what seemed to be many schools proved to be the same teaching among all competent economists. What has become of this way of looking at things? It was developed by Walras and Jevons, and by many others in the second instance. It was thus made the object of further refinement till the marginal utility theory disappeared and the equilibrium theory emerged, which had really been stated already by Wieser, who was much superior in this regard to Jevons. What was achieved proved to be far from perfect. A more refined system was built on this by Walras, who was an engineer who late in life turned to economics and made the theory more elegant and altered it here and there in the process. Now we have in fact a very beautiful system of analysis, and it is an interesting fact that many American economists are trying to fill it up with statistical data, which was thought impossible by a former generation, who regarded it as impossible that any theory in economics should become numerical. Now we are well on the way of this being achieved. This will mean a new epoch in economic science, for it will carry quite a different authority if you can figure out the result.

Unfortunately we are very far from this goal at present and the reason is that while the facts of the physicist can be produced under certain circumstances, the facts of our science are given to us under circumstances which never recur in the same way. In other words, physical data are data subject to the fundamental laws of the probability of the norm which will not change and will only deviate from the norm according to errors of observation. Thus, in measuring the distance between two planets, slightly different results might be obtained by two or more observers resulting from errors of observation. This is corrected by taking the mathematical average between the measurements. In our own science, however, the data themselves are changed and the thing to be measured changes. It is usual to put our facts in a time series. The great question of supreme difficulty in economics as an exact science, that is as a numerical science, consists in this, to distill out of the figures a time series which will fit our theoretical law. This is a problem also known to the physical world. If you look at the waves of the ocean you will find that they are irregular. There are, for instance, the swells of the ocean, the swells due to the attraction of the moon, the ebb and flow of the tide, and finally the smaller ripples caused by the wind. If you were to measure the length of the waves you would have to eliminate such differences. But this problem would bear a smaller part in the physical science than with us. What sometimes happens in physical science always happens with us. We only see the first steps, but future generations will have to try their best, perhaps by different mathematics to those evolved in physical science, where time series plays so small a part. Our case is different; we want a different mathematical technique and it is possible for us at present to see here and there the beginning of it. There is a dropping of the barriers between history and statistics and theory. They are melting into one.

This is also the case with the facts that business administration affords—bookkeeping and cost calculations. What happens to all these calculations? Progress has been much better in some of them than would be believed. In the field of banking there has been much improvement in the use of theoretical tools, as closely and clearly stated in Mr. Keynes's volumes. Mr. Keynes is rather rigorous in his views. He once told me that there were not more than five people in the world who understood monetary theory. As he said that to me I supposed he included me among them. Who the others were I do not know. At any rate his book is a very good presentation of the Marshall type of monetary theory.[4] There you will find questions connected with statistical banking questions brought within reach by an improved collection of material. I will give you an example of how difficult it is to bring these things together. You have heard many different theories of money. One of them must be right and the others wrong. How are you to tell where the points of monetary theory are right and where they are wrong? Thus, in the quantity theory the theoretical meaning we are to give to it depends upon the statistics we have—if, for instance, I had good income statistics. As a matter of fact I have not got those figures, but I have got better figures about the quantity of legal money. I have these figures for some countries, so I can build up the theory more conveniently. This is the consideration which decides and not the right or wrong of the theory.

The theory of international trade has made great progress of late. The results are not published yet, but it is astonishing how long in this particular field we have kept to the old classical theory, working with labor values which otherwise have been discarded. This is to be changed very soon by the work of such men as [Ohlin in Sweden and Haberler] in Vienna. This tendency to introduce into the theory appropriate concepts to catch hold of statistics is most interesting—the most interesting of these tools being the barter system of trade of a pupil of Taussig, whose theory of international trade I can recommend strongly to you. The social question, as far as it relates to inequality of distribution and transfer of wealth, have received in Pigou's work a monumental basis, although the scientific method is here quite new and faults may be found with it. It may be possible some day to discuss the social question as an ideal, but the social question, as far as realities get in the way, we must hold good for socialism, and as I told you our science is not connected with political aims, but to explain things by applying to political judgments tools and arguments and facts such as we may be able already and shall supply better later, rendering to political arguments much better service than if arguing them ourselves. I do not say we ought not to be politicians, but if you are going out to battle it is well to be prepared. As long as you are doing scientific work, do it in a scientific spirit and you will be working for your ideals, for no ideal can live without a connection with scientific truth. Our whole social outlook is affected by our knowledge or otherwise of the facts of distribution. If you know nothing about distribution, as people did know nothing about it in the nineteenth century, you will look upon the upper classes as possessed of immeasurable wealth, while the masses who produce the wealth are starved on a small part of it. This is not a question of fact, but a question of scientific method. Whoever is interested ought to possess themselves of that arm. Finally we ought to be in touch with the most modern of the specialists' theories, that of business cycles, which bring with them a whole torrent of statistical facts of scientific importance, which do not consist of attempts at prevision or explanation of business cycles, but in facts accumulated by the theory of cycles. The study of cycles has an importance beyond the immediate problem of the cycle and may serve sooner or later to bring about radical changes in the way of thinking everywhere.

Then there is the study of trends. Of course here study from the statistical standpoint is most difficult. We have already made some progress. Some important contributions to this are due to a young scientist we ought not to leave out of our considerations, the Norwegian Ragnar Frisch. The more I proceed the more the path widens, but naturally the only purpose of such a lecture [as this] is to hint here and there at some point of interest and leave the rest to you.

## Notes

1. The following text is in all likelihood based on a speech that Schumpeter gave on February 9, 1931, in Osaka-kobe, Japan. It was found in the Harvard University Archives among Schumpeter's papers and is published here by permission of the Harvard University Archives. Gottfried Haberler has kindly helped to clear up some difficulties in the text. In a few places, where some explanatory words have been added, they have been marked off by brackets. For more information on this speech, see the section titled "The European Period: Schumpeter's Works in This Volume" in the Introduction.

2. For Schumpeter's opinion of John A. Hobson (1854–1940), see his *History of Economic Analysis* (London: Allen & Unwin, 1954), 823, 832–33.

3. J. M. Keynes, "Alfred Marshall," in J. M. Keynes, *Essays in Biography* 125–217 (London: Mercury Books, 1961). The essay was originally published in 1924 (ed.).

4. J. M. Keynes, *A Treatise on Money* (New York: Harcourt, Brace, 1930).

# Six

## Can Capitalism Survive?

No, LADIES AND gentlemen, it cannot. And if knowing my opinion is really all you want, I can sit down peacefully now and subside into silence.[1] Unfortunately, however, it is not so. In any such question, particularly one in which argument is so exposed to very large margins of error, the opinion of a man counts for nothing and whatever interest may attach to it is in the reasons why he holds that opinion. In fact, I do not attach any importance to whether you should, when we part, agree with my view as to the ultimate answer or not. The importance I do attach to it is in trying to stimulate your social outlook, to put problems before you, to try to make you play with them, and to contribute in this way to yourselves building up your own social world. And in this short hour I have before me [I will] do nothing but throw problems at you which cover a very wide range, unfortunately. Some are the very purest of purest economics; others are the purest of purest statistics; and others are of a historical nature; and still others are merely practical considerations drawn from observation in a life which unfortunately has now lasted for quite a time.

The first thing I want to ask you is to consider what sense [the proposition "Can capitalism survive?"] has. Do try to form such an opinion as to capitalism, or in fact anything else, that can survive in the future. Of course there is no difficulty about that in the case of a prophet. If I were a prophet in possession of light from On High, I should just give my vision, and the very fact that I stated it emphatically would have a certain psychoanalytic influence on you. But if we do not prophesy, what is the meaning of assertions about future events? The answer is as simple as it is disconcerting. Speaking quite generally, there is no meaning to such a statement. We never forecast what will happen either on social or on other [grounds]. What we do is that, if we have a set of facts before us so linked together by certain relations, then the system will go through certain processes and display in the phases of these processes certain characteristics—if the functions relating to these quantities remain invariant. This "if" spoils everything, and is another illustration of Einstein's saying that as far as our propositions are certain, they do not say anything about reality; and as far as they do say anything about reality, they are not certain.

Now, in cases where these relations are very invariant over very long periods of time, of course this kind of statement comes practically to the same as a forecast—in astronomy, for instance. But where these relations vary, there is no sense in forecasting, no sense in extrapolating in functions, and so on, if one wants to be logical and neat and correct.

The necessity of overcoming judgments about things ahead is, therefore, satisfied by a very fragile instrument. It is always the "if" that has to be taken account of. [To take an example from another field:] A doctor who examines you looks at your tongue, measures your temperature, and so on, and then says, "Well, there is not much the matter with you; your organic processes will go on about as they are for a time, which is of course not infinite but indefinite." A doctor who says that cannot in the nature of things say anything about what will actually happen to you. You might step out of his office and be run over by a motor car. Now, nothing is more likely to be run over by a motor car than economic prophecy. And therefore it would be quite unfair to blame the economist for certain difficulties about forecasting, which are incident to his subject and . . . to any subject, except a few where the system observed consists of functions which do actually remain and may safely be expected to remain invariant. . . . It is necessary to bear that in mind. And nobody, ladies and gentlemen, is so much under the necessity in his or her daily work to understand what is going on and what will happen deep down in the social processes, nobody stands so much in need of that as does the intelligent civil servant who wants to know what kind of thing he handles.

To give you an example of the uncertainty of prediction, I want to challenge any of you who is a little bit older. Has anyone, who was at a somewhat mature age in 1917, foretold that the bolshevik regime had come to stay? If he has not, that proves his incapacity and unfitness as a student of social phenomena. But no, no, the thing depended on so many variables imperfectly known then, that I am bound to say that if a man said that bolshevism had come to stay, he would be wrong for he had no business to be right on the evidence before him.

Another example: I do not think many people have foretold the great success of the present government in Germany in 1932. In 1932, everyone—myself included—saw that the National Socialist Party had passed its prime. It was slowly and at an increasing rate disintegrating. I do not admit now that I was wrong—only, of course, we must leave latitude for such events, and it is only self-evident if you bear in mind what I told you just now.

I also have to define what I mean by "capitalism." And, ladies and gentlemen, we ought really to sit down quietly and have it out, what the system we live under really means. It is astonishing how little it is done and how careless all of us become when we come to the most fundamental questions. I cannot go into this problem just now—all I can do is to define a concept, which is just useful for our purpose. But I want to say expressly that I do not mean it is bad to define the nature of capitalism. I am going to talk about the simple economic system, where economic activity goes on by private initiative for private profit. You see immediately that that sort of thing must have very many limiting causes, hardly to be distinguished from its logical contrary. But to this difficulty we shall return, when we do the last step on our way.

Well, ladies and gentlemen, now I adduce throwing problems at you strictly professionally, neither one of which I am able to solve properly. And I would be almost as bold as to ask you, or those of you who may want to use that kind of thing in future work, to jot down a few points in the questions I am going to mention.

Now, first, most people want, I think, a right social system . . . and want to find out whether it will stay or survive. Well, look to its performance. For instance, if you want to form an opinion as to how long a certain chef will stay at a certain hotel, it is rather relevant to look at the kind of menus which he turns out. This is so in our case for the following reasons, and it is very important in your social diagnosis [of] this and other countries to bear that well in mind. First, the only performance we can measure—very inexactly indeed, but with some degree of quantitative precision—is economic performance. Now, economic performance does not mean [much] to humanity. If it did, people would never have made crusades; if it did, they would not have done a lot of things. . . . Look, for instance, at Germany where they have succeeded in introducing the rationing of some important articles of food. The whole world is full of unsalable quantities of these foods and yet they stand in want of them. Besides, we have—but this I only want to touch upon—to take account of the fact that the system of course cannot be simply judged by quantitative standards of economic performance, but that it is obviously much more relevant what type of people it turns out; how happy or thwarted these people feel under it; what sort of finance it produces. And here we . . . enter fields of valuation in which no two of us agree and in which it is almost impossible to stand for rational arguments at all. But these are the things that really matter.

That is one thing. Second, as to measurable economic performance, we must not draw the conclusion that good performance will [signify] survival and bad performance will [signify] elimination for the following reasons. To begin with, what is [a] good performance? It is the term in the opinion of the masters which is suggested to them by a powerful apparatus of psychotechnics. Plenty of people know how to play them. Therefore, whatever the performance is, this does not mean it is recognized. I have often read enunciations from Russia where things, which belong to the most self-evident system of power in capitalist countries, are heralded as things which only the bolshevist state can provide. Care for the unemployed, for instance. But the people believe it, and so the performance of a system and [the] judgment of the performance are essentially [two] different things. And you must not forget that perfect performance precisely tends to make the system, that so perfectly performs, superfluous. Assume that there were an army of such tremendous efficiency as to be able to make mince pie of the rest of the world. This army would, from the standpoint of that kind of idea, certainly have an excellent performance. This, however, would not [lead] to the survival of that army. But on the contrary, after having made a mince pie of the rest of the world, this army would be superfluous however big the land may be, and what is superfluous in social life dies away as surely as superfluous organs die away. You must never forget this is very important, not only in such fundamental questions as performance but also in smaller questions which often come up in your daily work.

It is very important, I say, to take account of the fact that no social system is ever going to survive when allowed to work out according to its own logic. You need only look at the present situation. There is no firm, no industry, no country, which can live under those rules which it would assuredly live under if it were allowed. Let's take as an example a capitalist society, which has a currency based on gold. Suppose I were to say the system has broken down. Well, that would be as reasonable as to say that the motor car is no good because it does not work if you run it against the wall. The gold standard has only meaning in a peaceful and substantial free trade world. As soon as these conditions do not exist, it loses its whole meaning and cannot work. Hence, if you look at [the] performance of capitalism, we must take into account the many hardships inflicted upon the system and the many inhibitions it is exposed to. We must also take into account that in looking into economic performance, you must not only count what the system has produced in economic and cultural value but also what has been produced at the same time by noncapitalist agencies with economic means provided by capitalist evolution. Example: take a prince of the eighteenth century legislating in some cases for the peasants of the territory [and] against the aristocracy, introducing the sort of thing which we are accustomed to associate with the history of what is called in Latin absolutism, about the middle of the eighteenth century. Such a prince was nothing but a capitalist feudal lord, that is to say, he lived entirely on the surpluses of the rising bourgeois classes. If you want another example, take the social measures of Lloyd George. These must economically, though perhaps not morally, be put to the credit of the system. Now then, if we want to measure what the system has done, what are the means of doing so?

Well, if you want one other figure there is only one possible—I will be hanged if there is another. Only, I doubt very much whether this one counts for so very much, and that is to measure total output. I say "total output" and not "total consumer's output" because if you confine yourselves to that, you get too [little] as soon as you get back behind 1870. Of course you can reason and understandingly prove anything you like on postwar material, but that is of course entirely inadmissible. No illustration resting on probability assumptions can work on a span which has four or five [observations]. This is only an abuse of our refined methods, mostly resting on probability assumptions for a period like that. If, therefore, you want to know capitalism—its economics, the way it works, and especially its phenomenon of fluctuations by which it struggles on—the least you can do is to survey the material of one hundred fifty years, at least back to 1780. If in the assembling of facts you could go as far back at least as 1780, it would be one of the most useful things to do, as very often facts from the [18]40s of the nineteenth century are very much more interesting than facts from 1936 for the understanding of the most practical problems of our day. For the facts of 1840 are better embedded in a long line of comparable evidence and you can generalize only from that.

Now, this output, how can we measure it? You know that here we strike a most interesting question of modern pure theory. If the output of economic life consisted of only one commodity, then everything would be plain as day. If the output could be represented, as it were, by a matrix . . . —the elements of which would only change in proportion—all would be plain sailing. But if some elements increase more than others, then it becomes difficult to apply measurement. And if some increase and others decrease, the question whether the whole thing grows bigger or smaller from an economic standpoint becomes very doubtful. Now then what do we do? We construct indices. The Federal Reserve Board Index is one. These indices mainly rest on physical [series] evaluated on some basis or by some method in the well-known index number fashion.

I take the validity of such a proceeding for granted. If I could make you my victims for more than an hour I should show that a difficult and complicated argument really does give some support to the use of indices of total physical output but that the common sense, at first blush, of the significance of these figures is entirely misleading. And hence it is very understandable for some of the best authorities to deny any importance to this index of total output and what we accept now. I want only to tell you that we have figures, and construct such an output for England well into the eighteenth century, in a work by a Mr. Hoffman. We have such figures for this country, if you content yourself with census years, of course fairly well back, 189 years or so. . . . And of course you know Americans . . . : if they get an index or even anything that looks like an index, they are happy. . . . In Germany we have an index since about 1860; in France things are not very favorable, but we have single series which after all we might combine.

Now, I shall do something which will draw the censure and contempt of all of you down on my gilded head. I shall do what you must never do; I shall do what is the first commandment of the statistician and the economist *not* to do; I shall extrapolate in the most slipshod and uncritical fashion imaginable. I take these indices and look at them, and if you want to criticize slightly what I shall now propose, the best way is to take up that little leaflet of the Agricultural Institute by Warren A. Parsons on the physical volume of production in the United States. By a series of considerations, which I must drop, I come to the conclusion that three percent compound interest will be a fair and conservative statement of the increase of physical output in this country for the time after the Civil War. In fact, it is a conservative statement for the time. Now I take the three percent and I extrapolate for fifty years . . . and I put it on the per capita basis . . . by taking one of the more usual and one of the more reliable extrapolation estimates: the population, for instance. . . . An estimate of Mr. Dublin of the Metropolitan Insurance which leads to 130 million about 1890, is for various reasons probably a little bit too low. [But] if you take Mr. Sloan's extrapolation—published I think, if my memory serves me, in 1921—we come to a figure which we shall use. And if we take our standard from the year 1928, then in 1978—the system working as it did in the last more than fifty years—we should arrive at the conclusion that the money which in 1928 was about roughly $700, would be roughly about three times as much, or $2,100, in 1978.

Now I hold that as there is no reason to assume that if the system is left to itself distribution will change very much, and if we apply the distribution and functioning which we get now to 1978, we should stand to get an income a head which would do away with the phenomenon of poverty, in whatever sense it is at all useful to speak of poverty. This does not mean that there would not be some people suffering from poverty. This is self-evident for reasons which I can't go into and which are perhaps too obvious to state.

[In the next few pages of the speech, which are very poorly transcribed, Schumpeter goes on to discuss and refute some arguments against this way of extrapolating. He also raises the question of why only capitalism has been such an excellent economic performer. One answer is that it is built on the profit motive. Another fact to consider in this context is the way the selection of leaders is made in capitalism. In a private economy, Schumpeter says, it is clear that "a man grows with his firm." He then continues on the same theme:] The second thing which accounts for what is certainly and however we measure it a unique success, is that the private firm is the only social form of existence in which responsibility is free. Take, for instance, the very best political system, the oldest, the most famous one—England. Ministers are responsible, to be sure, but no minister that has a good majority and who knows he can make a successful speech need bother very much about it. And this indicates shortly, but clearly enough, what I would go into if I had time.

Third, however, you ladies and gentlemen of all people will be able to agree with me if I say that the possibility of following one's own judgment is of great moment in this. For this is the curse of the very best civil services I have ever known all over the world, that you can't do the things you want to do; that you must report to a committee, which will report to another committee. When the thing comes round to a string of committees the steam has gone out of you and you have no pleasure in it. I have been in the civil service myself, and I know that I immediately relapsed into the negative attitude. It was a very good civil service job I had for a time, but I immediately relapsed in the negative attitude.[2] When the various papers were piling up on my desk, well, to take the advice and agree with my undersecretary was the line of least resistance. And as to what was left of me when I could sit down to rest after working hours, were only the dregs of my energy. I would put "J.S." on such things as needed them, and put the papers away. And this is one side of it. But wherever you study a great organization of modern great industry it is just the same or develops that way. You always find that things are not as they could be in government, in business, at universities. Not so much because of bad intention, incompetence, misconduct, but mainly because quite good and competent people in this kind of work so cooperate as to interfere with each other. . . .

If all of this is so, why should not the system survive? [Well,] I came to exactly the same result as [Marx], but for a quite different reason. I do not think that the brakes would not hold because of bad performance [as in Marx]. I came to the conclusion that the system cannot hold for two reasons, and my watch tells me that I can only mention them. The first reason is that other aids to the forms of life present themselves to humanity [today], just as Christianity presented itself at a time in the Roman world when nobody could have foretold [its decline] from its economic process. So other forms present themselves at this time, and I do not care whether they are bolshevism, Hitlerism, or socialism or any shape, for in these points they are all alike.

The second group of reasons is the rationalizing effect of industrial life. The more we rationalize, the more we apply the habits of thought . . . to ourselves, to our beliefs, to the social surroundings. We apply rationalism even to our religion. We apply it to personal relations. This is soon discovered and taken advantage of by a group of people who can't stand each other. . . .

Excuse these few remarks. It is not that I could not substantiate the things. I believe [that], accustomed as you are to following a given case and to analyze an argument, you will readily see the multitude of facts which I have covered under these last two headings by a few short remarks. There is no difficulty in verifying that. The upshot of it is very simple and I may formulate the last thus: Capitalism so transforms our requirements, our cultural scheme and values, as to make those economic adjustments which economic machineries demand unbearable, as to draw away the beliefs, the social psychological basis from under the institution of property and so on for good or for ill.

And as soon as that happens, we make another discovery. Those classes directly interested in the system can't begin to appreciate the difference. In this respect you must look back to other ruling classes, say, the warlike ruling class of the Middle Ages. If, in the Middle Ages, something happened to displease the knights when their social function was threatened—and fighting produces a type which can eminently take care of its own interest—[then] they put on their armor, got on their horses, and galloped into revolting peasants as fast as it is possible to speak of galloping in the case of a horse that has three hundred pounds on his back.

But capitalists can't do that. They can just hide behind newspaper hearings, and hence capitalism . . . is an organization which can't stand on its own feet. It did work well for a time in Europe, as long as it was protected by an aristocracy and a monarchy which had free capitalistic rules, [but it] tumbled down at once when these things were removed. If it came to stay for a time here [in the United States] it was only because the fascinating sound of the opportunities for new millions drew the minds of people from other things. [But] it probably can't stand by itself yet.

And so I come to the diagnosis that the system will not survive, if by an entirely different line of reasoning [than Marx]. But the result, as far as prediction goes, is very much the [Marxian] one, although I am not a Marxist and although I have no tendency for socialist systems at all. It is of course clear that . . . such a process of dying off takes time, and that in the process of dying off . . . many intermediate points and intermediate forms of organization are likely to occur. It is futile to think that regulated capitalism can stand any more than unregulated capitalism. Political support would not be forthcoming for either.

Of course no class has a more heavy responsibility to bear than a civil service class. They have to understand which way things are [going], for this is essential in being good servants to the public. It is true that the most spectacular reforms are always those that matter [the] most. I would say [that] the success of the other schemata of life and of the workability of noncapitalistic forms of life rests largely with the success to build up an efficient civil service of well-trained, good types, removed from direct political influence, and so on. Many things might be easier if such a class can slowly rise. That the new form of socialism will be a striking measure, I have no . . . doubt.

## Discussion

*Director*: Dr. Ezekiel will lead the discussion. I think he needs no introduction to the group here.

*Dr. Ezekiel*: I am not going to attempt any prolonged discussive statement on what Dr. Schumpeter has said, but instead I am going to take the liberty of asking him a series of questions, if that's not too fatiguing, to try to draw out and develop some of the points that seem to be implicit in his statement. So I confess that it is not clear to me from his statement whether he believes that capitalism will disappear solely because of what he calls "social psychic changes" or whether he thinks it will partly disappear because of perhaps inability to function under things as they are. So I would like to ask him for the first question whether he feels [that] during the first thirty-five years of the twentieth century in this country capitalism has given evidence of ability to continue to carry forward the rate of growth in production which prevailed up to that time under the situations as they have been during that period?

*Dr. Schumpeter*: Before saying so briefly what I wish to say to the point Dr. Ezekiel raised, I want to make one general remark, ladies and gentlemen. American audiences are invariably so polite and nice to any speaker that they feel inhibitions in going for his argument and that they put their objections in the form of modest and delicate questions, which do not fully bring out the point and which therefore rob us of some of the benefits. I would urge you not to be so nice but to come out into the open and say whatever you like. I shall certainly not be offended, but on the contrary we meet in order to discuss.

Now I come back to Dr. Ezekiel's statement. I do think that if it were only a matter of the success with which the economic machine provides an ever increasing real income per head, capitalism either in this or in any other country would have nothing to fear for its life. I attach importance to the per head [income], because the distribution can be taken roughly as a constant. It may not be as constant as Vilfredo Pareto thought and it may not be well described by the Paretian alpha, but it is still a fact that distribution broadly—the distribution of income—remains constant over time and has not substantially changed, say in England where up to the war we have the data. This is the opinion of [Sir Josiah Stamp], who seems to think better of his data than I do. However there is no reason to suppose that it will be lying in the direction in which we want, and so we may take that as constant. Nor do I think that the fluctuations would constitute a deadly argument [against my way of reasoning].

You will be astonished [by this last statement], for of course America so naively enjoys her prosperity and is so down in the dumps when things go down. But it is not so in the [rest of the] world and it is not [so] everywhere, even in America. Of course, if people speculated up to 1929 and that game was up, it is quite natural that they should have thought it is . . . doomsday and deluge and the end of all things. But they are recovering now from that sort of thing. . . .

So, Doctor, the reason, the deepest reason, why I think that capitalism won't survive is the rationalizing effect the system has on our minds, the effect the system has of doing away with everything traditional. For perfectly rationalized minds there is of course no justification for plenty of points, except by difficult arguments, unacceptable to the masses. This is an important element in the situation. But there are others, and the second important element is this: I have

rightly introduced that analogy between economic life and the organization of an army. It took—if I may be permitted to use the expression—it took a hell of a brain a hundred years ago [to organize
an army]. It took in fact a Napoleon to take care of his position in a
succession of cases. Even such a thing as an army of two hundred
thousand men was, under the conditions of one hundred and fifty
years ago, by no means an easy thing to manage. You had to find new
ideas [and] you wanted a brain to do that.

That is not necessary now.

Now there is a machine for that; the thing functions alone. And
something similar happens in economic life. The entrepreneur's
hunch . . . was necessary to carry on any particular undertaking, even
fifty years ago. It is not so necessary now. The technical things are
done by technicians; you can order a textile mill as you can order a
pair of boots. There are no technical problems for the entrepreneur.
There are hardly any legal problems, because you have plenty of specialized men. There are next to no problems in forecasting the general situation, because that is so excellently done by the many services. Hence the social necessity of the type vanished, and in
vanishing, is not recognized. I think the whole thing has a tendency
to crumble. It has been a powerful element in a most important phenomenon of our time.

Are newspaper reporters here, Mr. President? There won't be any
reporting anyhow.

*Director*: Well, we can't be sure.

*Dr. Schumpeter*: There are plenty of phenomena which explain the
most strange alliances, political alliances, in some countries at the
present time, and are accounted for by the fact that plenty of leaders—very cultured men, just as good democrats as any of you—felt
convinced that the social organization of capitalism was crumbling
and needed some protection from noncapitalistic agencies.

This is one thing, but Dr. Ezekiel asked about the performance of
capitalism in this country. From the beginning of this century, from
1897 to about 1911, we have the usual phenomenon of bigger production in copper and metal going up speculatively in response to the
investment demand, according to the scheme alluded to at the present time. . . . Then comes the war period, which I always leave out,
although in this country the pulse of the phenomenon persists very
nicely even through the war period. Then comes the time where the
Kondratieff wave slides down, which is always characterized by an
increase—in some respects [a] spectacular increase—in physical production. But this physical increase doesn't show spectacularly because

it has been inhibited. It has been inhibited partly by monopolistic policies at the beginning of the century, and it has been inhibited later by conscious and unconscious regulation and so on.

This is the capitalistic machine itself. It does not show such tendencies to overproduction and to underutilization of its operations which are often attributed to it. The reason why it is attributed to it I can't go into, but I will give one reason for it. In all statistics, capacities of organization [do] not count, but only the [physical] apparatus. . . . And hence, at any given time there must be much unutilized plant.

The other most important reason, of course, is that quite a lot of operation is calculated to meet peak demands. It is calculated on the principle of a summer hotel, and therefore is of course idle for a large part of the time. I don't know whether this quite does justice to what you asked.

*Dr. Ezekiel*: The last part of your question I think began to get around to the point I had in mind. I'll just ask one more question before turning you over to the tender mercies of the audience. I want to ask the question whether one need not distinguish between capitalism and industry? This is the question that Gardner Means has raised in a lot of his work: whether the rationalism of industry—in the European use of the term: the development of very large industrial units organized in series or organized over large sectors of industry, which seems to be an inevitable outgrowth of modern machine methods— whether the organization of those large units of industrial control does not make the kind of competition under which capitalism could flourish no longer possible? Does it not presuppose a social situation in which income is not distributed to produce maximum consumption? And does it not produce a situation where the combination of what is left over of free capitalism with this newly developed or gradually developed large-scale industry, fails to function to a point where the development of some other system becomes inevitable?

*Dr. Schumpeter*: Now Dr. Ezekiel opens up a really most interesting string of questions as there are quite a number of reasons why we may suspect that the modern industrial system—call it as you please— will cease to function from internal causes. He has mentioned only one, and I will confine myself to the one which he refers to, and which of course is what may be called a prevailing opinion in all countries.

The giant concern, whether there is suppression of competitive capitalism or not, is always shown or held up as an element first of rigidity, second of restriction of output, and third as extinguisher [of competition]. This is so by the very nature of that free competition,

which is the only scheme from which all the economists were justified
... to predicate such a lot of nice things about maximum production.
I shall not do such an injustice to so eminent an economist, who is at
the same time an eminent theorist, by answering with the practical
statement that in the time since the merger movement—or what we
called the merger movement, which starts in about 1897 although
there were mergers before—the giant concern, which strives to suppress competition, shows exactly [taking the Kondratieff wave into
account] the same rate of increase of physical output as was shown
before. I will not answer that, because this does not help with what I
may term the conceptual difficulty.

To begin with, certainly if we are now revenging ourselves on the
theorists who are on the side of the pure theory of monopoly, we are
perfectly justified in predicating on those consequences. Only I want
to make the following points first as to rigidity. It is not true that a
big concern or a monopolist would have a more rigid price if he follows his pure economic interest than a competing industry. The price
of the monopoly would be higher, but it would not be less flexible.
This can be shown. If it is less flexible, you come to a very different
question of diagnosis: the question, as I explained it to myself, [is]
mainly that prices of things, etc., are agreed prices on which it was so
very difficult to agree that people would leave them when they have
all the agreement necessary. The rigidity of the other prices is often
explained by the fact that the monopolist knows he is important. He
knows that if he goes down with his price, he will never be allowed to
put it up again. So he leaves it.

And these other reasons give rise to the question whether they are
inherent to the system or to the way in which the whole cycle reacts
to the system. It is a play of words. The whole attitude we take toward
these phenomena depends on the answer we give to this question,
actually as to the phenomena arising out of the suppression of the
disappearance of free competition. This phenomenon, the reduction
of output, must first be defined as to what we are to expect. We shall
expect that a monopolist will produce and offer for sale less than industry would under perfect competition under the same circumstances. But all monopolists are mandatory and they have formed
themselves into monopolies, which are linked up with different methods of production. It is now perfectly possible that the output of the
monopolies, although smaller than the output of competition under
the same method of production, is yet larger than the output under
perfect competition that would be possible under the methods which
alone are attainable under perfect competition.

It is a little bit involved, but I think the argument is quite straight-

[forward]. And if we therefore find overcapacity phenomena or other indications of output restrictions, it is necessary to investigate every case on its merits or else we may be grievously mistaken in our conclusions. In an article, Mr. Gardner Means seems to conclude from rigid prices the presence of price regulations. That may be broadly true, but it isn't quite reliable to go by. The monopolist has quite as much interest to vary his price as competition has. But now you must not forget that a monopolist can't function as per theory, because what he faces is not the demand of economic theory but what I may call a demand of introducing an article. If you are what is called raising up a demand, you must behave very much as you would under free competition; and if the demand is elastic, you must in any case start behaving like that. And, finally, if the limited competition or the monopolistic competition is of the type of competition prevailing in the motor industry, it is probably impossible from mere factual considerations to say that you would have still cheaper and still better motors . . . if you had perfect competition.

To tell you quite frankly, my own impression is that both the value of the analytical apparatus built up—in which the names of [Edward Chamberlin] and Mrs. Joan Robinson are conspicuous— . . . has been for practical purposes much exaggerated, and that monopolies have played in this country for the last thirty years a role to send a sort of shiver down the spine of the public. . . .

*Mr. Sommers*: Now for the questions from the floor.

*Dr. Schumpeter*: Ladies and gentlemen, I have so nicely put a few little paradoxical statements before you and I have so nicely inserted for your benefit weak links in my argument, that you really ought to go for it!

*From the Floor*: When you make predictions as to the possible output of capitalism as a system—if it continues on the basis of past experience, and the basis of the increase [is] three percent compounded— don't you also assume that the economist will learn nothing that will change the course of events?

*Dr. Schumpeter*: You are quite right. That is to say, I have given you the analogy just to bring out the logical nature of this simple operation. I have told you, if you take a child, observe its rate of growth in a given, say month, and now extrapolate forth say thirty years the same rate of growth, you will get a giant—an entirely unrealistic idea. And I want to emphasize that I only haven't the same reasons to expect that this kind of growth will cease as I have to expect that the child would grow above the normal height of its race and social class and individual family. I have, although very superficially, tried to substantiate the belief in this rate of growth by showing, as I thought, the invalidity of a certain number of objections which would first suggest themselves to the economist's mind, such as the law of diminishing returns, etc. But you are perfectly right that plenty of things can happen to stop the system. So, for instance, a sufficient number of world wars would do the job excellently, and you do not even want world wars. I will go on the popular side of my statement so far as to say that the continuation of progressive taxation at the present rate in America and England is not compatible with the smooth working of capitalism. However, I quite agree with you that in no sense is what I have said more than a statement of a possible look at the cross-section. It is in no sense a prophecy.

*From the Floor*: Would I be correct in leaving this lecture with a feeling that you mean that the financial system will disappear due to old age and not being able to fight off the new diseases that will attack it?

*Dr. Schumpeter*: In a sense, I believe I might agree with this statement. But diseases [which], so to speak, do not attack the physical organs. If we are to carry out the analogy and look upon the economic system as the total of the physical organs of an organism, I do think these physical organs of the capitalist organism are remarkably free from arteriosclerosis so far. . . . I always expect the arteriosclerosis, but when I look at the figures, I'll be hanged if I can find them. And what gets old, to stick with the analogy, is the soul within, the will to fight for one's own place, the will to believe in one's self. This is only the surface, and the fact that the things people fight for—the family, the descendants, the wish to found an industrial dynasty, the love for the concrete walls of a concrete factory— . . . all that has lost its meaning. That is what I mainly mean by the rationalism of our cycles.

*From the Floor*: Do you think that when capitalism disappears in America, we will tend more toward a communistic system or a socialistic system?

*Dr. Schumpeter*: I always tell my audience that if I could I would turn out of our science the words "capitalism," "communism," "money," "commodity," "credit," and half a dozen other words. Because all these terms mean so much as to make a quite considerable percentage of our argument a quarrel about words. Hence let me put the statement in such a way as I believe will carry a clear meaning to you. I do think that the principle that economic activity and the management of industry is a private affair and left to individual initiative . . . is socially played out, and has no defenders that count at the polls;

and that therefore every conformist will be tried. Only, this being on the whole a very well-to-do and very reasonable country [where] democratic methods have become an element of the moral credo of the average American, I do not expect anything like a revolution and a dictatorship, one way or the other. But I do expect a slow progress in regulation, which will only cease when there is nothing unregulated left. You must not forget that socialism is not a uniquely determined term. . . . It is quite possible that one day, in some country, a socialism will be adopted which pays a premium on savings and introduces interest in that form, because we have quite forgotten, when we speak of socialism, that there are other socialisms than the Marxian one. But this would still be socialism. There may be greater and greater bureaus in Washington regulating all this, and there may be a wavelike movement, managing more and more economic things. Perhaps the old capitalism and private property will remain, as in England the words "His Majesty" have remained—but the essence will go out of the thing. Does that answer the question?

*From the Floor*: Would you please define the word "capitalism" as you have been using it?

*Dr. Schumpeter*: Well, I will, frankly, if it interests you, give you two definitions instead of one. I give you the one which I think defines the real, specific character of capitalism, and I repeat the one which I have been using here.

I have been calling "capitalism" here, for the purposes of my talk, a system in which the management of production is a private affair, carried on by private initiative for private profit. But I shall distinguish capitalism more restrictively as follows: Capitalism is that subspecies of all the systems characterized by private property, which carries out new combinations of factors of production and involving the creation of credit. I think that is the essential thing and I do believe, as my colleague [A. P.] Usher has shown, that capitalism is as old as the phenomenon of credit creation. That is to say, that it goes back to around the Mediterranean [in] the thirteenth century.

*From the Floor*: Is the business cycle a phenomenon peculiar to capitalism so that by shifting gradually in some other economic sense we might exaggerate it, or does the cycle become worse, or less operative?

*Dr. Schumpeter*: The answer is in the . . . affirmative, I think, in two senses. If you define capitalism as I just did, capitalism is particularly linked up with fluctuations which show, of course, particularly in monetary time series, precisely because of the alternative inflation

and deflation of credit. . . . In another sense, I also should have to
answer in the affirmative. If we had a centralized socialism—you
know I just said we must distinguish among many socialisms and you
must never speak of "socialism" but always specify which one you
mean . . . —all those industrial changes, the process of which is apparently at the bottom of the phenomenon of business cycles, could
be so planned as to come about continuously in time. You would have
one huge central bureau, and this, of course, could plan the rate of
change . . . in such a way as to make it a continuous affair, in which
case this kind of wave would cease. In Russia, it was done differently.
If you make a five-year plan during which everyone has to hunger
while the industrial apparatus is being built up, then you are doing
exactly what capitalism does—only in a much rougher way.

*From the Floor*: Doctor, I am not quite clear yet as to this distinction
between the capitalists and other orders. As [an] illustration I understand [that] the Walker Gordon Dairy, where they started handling
the entire production of milk through one management, found it
much more desirable to give the various herds and small plots of land
on which to raise the cows to individual charge, so that their managers in effect became capitalists, in order to have personal responsibility for the particular cattle. I am not sure if I am correct about this—
but it seems that there was a place where you had to go back to capitalism.

*Dr. Schumpeter*: You know, in life the evidence is never one hundred
percent. Nothing is one hundred percent in life. Russian agricultural
workers, for instance, are allowed a cow, and I believe also a little
vegetable patch around their houses. And in the feudal times, we had
after all the elements of towns, which does not properly fit in, and
was finally to bring [the feudal system] down with a crash. So, we have
always a mixed form in any particular form of organization. We have,
however, historically not much difficulty in distinguishing the thing,
but what we can define are the logical schemata which are never realized in life.[3]

## Notes

1. This lecture represents a speech that Schumpeter probably gave on January 18, 1936, in Washington, D.C., at the United States Department of Agriculture Graduate School. The manuscript on which the text is based was
found in the Harvard University Archives. There are many difficulties with
the existing transcript of the speech, which Schumpeter never corrected him-

self. Several different secretaries seem to have been involved in transcribing the speech and the discussion. Despite these difficulties, however, it has been judged worthwhile to try to give the reader a picture of Schumpeter as a lecturer. It should finally be emphasized that Professor Wolfgang Stolper went through an early version of this speech and made extremely valuable suggestions for changes.

Text within brackets has been inserted by the editor. Three ellipsis points indicate that text in the original transcript has been deleted. For more information on this speech, see the section titled "The American Period: Schumpeter's Works in This Volume" in the Introduction. The text is published by permission of the Harvard University Archives.

2. Schumpeter is here referring to his time as finance minister in the Austrian government in 1919.

3. Two more questions were asked from the floor. The transcript is however of such poor quality here that they have not been included. In the first question Schumpeter was asked by a Dr. Wenzel if his prognosis about the decay of "the soul of capitalism" was based on historical data. Schumpeter answered that his view was indeed "a very historical one," and to illustrate this he compared the decay of the feudal class to that of the bourgeois class. The second question was a follow-up question to Dr. Wenzel's. Schumpeter was now asked why the feudal class in its days of glory was so much more capable of defending itself than the bourgeoisie is today. According to Schumpeter the answer was very simple. The knights of the feudal times were trained to fight and in battle they were superior to everybody else. The only way of defending itself that the bourgeoisie, however, has "is to take up the telephone and telephone Senator X and say, 'Good God! Good God! Can't you help us?' "

# Seven

## The Meaning of Rationality
## in the Social Sciences

### I

My first thesis is that, as far as the logical quality of the analyst's fundamental attitude is concerned, rationality (rational procedure) in the social sciences does not differ from scientific rationality in general.[1] That is to say, the scientific analyst or observer of any set of phenomena will always try to behave rationally toward the subject matter of his research whatever that subject matter will be, and his fundamental procedure will always be amenable to description by rules that apply to all cases of analytic endeavor. This we shall call observer's rationality.

What that common scientific rationality consists in, I am not going to analyze beyond noting a few surface features which I will try to keep as noncommittal as possible. In the main, I shall, wherever this subject intrudes into the argument, rely on our everyday familiarity with it.

Generalizing Kirchhoff's definition of mechanics I shall define science in general as the endeavor to describe phenomena we happen to be interested in, in the way most economical with reference to an assigned degree of accuracy. The element of rationality enters by means of that minimum condition which may, I think, be so interpreted as to also include, to some extent at least, the element of predictability of future phenomena: in other respects predictability is merely a *test*, while in still others it refers to important, but logically extraneous, considerations of usefulness.

It follows that scientific procedure must necessarily reject all forms of thought that are in conflict with the rules of logic or cannot, in principle at least, be tested by these rules. But it does not necessarily follow that it also excludes reasoning on anything except verifiable "facts." Aversion to introducing any entities that cannot be observed or experimentally produced is part of the scientific attitude only so far as it is based on the principle of economy in description. If the hypothesis that planets are moved by angels opened the shortest way to describing their motions, there could be no objection to it on grounds of scientific rationality.

Both the scientific attitude and that aversion to extra-empirical cognition are, of course, sociologically related. They are both the products of "rationalist" civilizations. But logically they should be kept distinct. So should scientific rationality and rationalism in another sense that may be best visualized in the context "rationalist philosophy." Although it comprises a great number of types—among which I believe, scholastic philosophy and St. Thomas's philosophy in particular—the relevant point may be instanced by Hegelianism.[2] Illustrative examples and still another meaning will be noticed later on.

I have defined scientific endeavor with reference to "an assigned degree of accuracy." It is obvious why that was necessary. What is the most economical way of description or, in other words, the optimal way of explaining a phenomenon, cannot be determined until we have made up our mind how deeply we wish to go into it. But this is part of our choice of the goal to aim at which in itself, *and aside from questions of consistency of any particular goal with others we may at the same time wish to reach*, is not a question of rationality at all, but of "valuation."

Scientific rationality is also relative to the horizon of the analyst, that is, to the information and mental equipment at his command. What behavior is rational for a given analyst or observer can only be determined if we know what he knows. For the social sciences this entails particularly intriguing consequences, but the fundamental point holds for any science and must be noted at once. An example will illustrate it. When using infinite series, the mathematicians of the eighteenth century—until Cauchy in fact, I think—did not bother much about conditions of convergence, and only their sound horse sense (or the instinct of genius if you so please) prevented them from falling into very serious error. A modern mathematician would, if he neglected to test his series for convergence, be voted most irrational. But were the old masters any less irrational? One feels greatly tempted to say they were, and to resolve the obvious dilemma by adding that they were "objectively" irrational. Since, however, such a judgment is only arrived at by comparing their equipment with ours and since the latter has no title to "absolute" validity—whatever that may mean—we must recognize the fact that we are, in this as in other matters, acting as self-appointed judges whose verdict sometimes is and sometimes is not upheld by other equally self-appointed judges. This means more than that a strong personal equation unavoidably enters into any pronouncement about the rational quality of a given attitude or act. It means that that rational quality is by nature relative to the information and mental equipment we individually happen to possess or, if I may venture that far, which we *could* possess if we availed ourselves of all the facilities at our disposal as seen by a self-appointed judge of "higher" rank.

Value judgments enter into all this, of course. But this is not denied by anybody who, like myself, stands for excluding them from the realm of the social sciences. What is meant by "Wertfreiheit" is merely freedom from value judgments of a particular kind, viz. from judgments about how it would be *desirable* for the phenomena under study to behave. This means positing ultimate ends and, though I admit that it is more difficult in the social sciences than it is in others to prevent our ends or sympathies from influencing our results—"wishful thinking"—I cannot see that the logical position of those ultimate ends is any different in the social field. All that can be legitimately claimed for them, on the scientific plane, reduces to, first, the task of working out the consequences that action taken in order to realize any given ultimate end would have; second, the task of explaining why given people at any given time and place should feel about any given ultimate ends as they actually do. And both tasks wholly fall within the scope of scientific rationality.

Paul Sweezy raised the question whether there are "ultimate ends" at all. Their existence seems, however, to follow from a consideration of argumentative technique: Any proposition containing a value concept necessarily leads back to another proposition of the same nature—value judgments never reduce to anything else but value judgments; and since we must eventually break off this recursus—which cannot be circular—at some point, there will always be one value judgment that, for the purpose in hand, will take the position of the "ultimate" one. But as a matter of practice, it is quite true that ordinarily we do not meet with ultimate values and that the valuations we do meet with are usually intermediate ones, i.e., really refer to means to an end not itself under discussion. That is why, in apparent contradiction to the opinion submitted, we can so very often speak of the *rationality or irrationality of an end*. I will emphasize at once that this seems to me the only justifiable meaning of the phrase. But there is such a thing as *normality of an ultimate end* which it is not always easy to distinguish from rationality and which, I believe, accounts for the fact that many people are so averse to accepting the extra-rationality of ultimate ends and to seeing the difference between a madman and an ascetic.

I may as well conclude this part of my argument by pointing out what seems to me the relation between rationality of analytic procedure and rationality of the result which, as long as we speak of observer rationality only,[3] may simply be equated to "truth." Obviously, rationality of procedure is a necessary condition for rationality of the result if we except the case of chance coincidence of irrational procedure with a "true" result, such as the case of a true proposition's resulting from a formally wrong syllogism from wrong premises. No less obviously, however, rational procedure is not a sufficient condition for the emergence of a "true" result, *unless we include correctness and adequacy of both the material and the equipment at the command of the analyst which we cannot do if we admit varying horizons.* While there is thus a relation between rationality and truth, there is no congruence.

## II

So far all there is of rationality in social sciences emanates from the analyst. It is imported into the facts from the analyst's mind and the rationality of the processes of the latter is all that matters. We will emphasize at once that this observer's rationality has in itself nothing whatever to do with the presence or absence of rationality in the human types or human actions observed, or even with the applicability of the concept of rationality to the subject matter under investigation.

Now my second thesis is that there are many and important cases in which that is all, and in which the attitude of the analyzing economist or sociologist remains all along within the processes of thought that are used by the analyst of a biological species or the analyst of mechanical or electrical phenomena. Since in modern economics this type of investigation has of late acquired additional importance, I shall choose my example from that field. Everyone knows that statistical material is often presented in the form of time series, that is to say, of sequences of data, ordered in historic time. If we plot a number of such series over the same time axis, we immediately observe that there are disturbed, yet very definite relations between them. These relations can be measured and expressed analytically and this in itself suggests to us the conception of a mechanism that can be investigated as such. But we can go farther than this. We can choose these time series in a way that seems meaningful to us, replace the time series by the concepts that correspond to them, and build a rational model or theory that will display in the abstract some features of those relations and stand to reality as does, say, the scientific model of astronomy. For instance, I can take *indices* of total production, of the price level, of interest rates, and of demand deposits, and look upon the state of the economic system as characterized by them. And I can also take the *concepts* of total production, price level, interest rates, and demand deposits, and impose conditions on their behavior as against each other. These conditions I derive either directly from the statistical observation or more indirectly from relations that I, from other sources, know to subsist between these quantities or their rates of change.

Never mind whether such a theory, working with those four variables only would be satisfactory or not, that is whether it would or would not describe or account for, those phenomena for the sake of which I constructed that setup. The essential point is that here we have objectively observable quantities which do not, or at least need not, directly imply anything about human behavior and with which I can, nevertheless, derive significant economic results. It is true, of course, and has been pointed out by Professor Parsons, that further analysis of those entities and the relations that I might set up between them, would inevitably lead to acting men. But this doesn't alter the fact that meaningful arguments can be framed without such further analysis and that the mechanism of my four quantities is to a certain extent a logical world unto itself. If it is not absolutely self-contained, it shares this property with any other scientific model or theory which must always have boundaries that cut through real, as distinguished from analytic, relations. No doubt our time series have their peculiarities which are not exactly paralleled in any other material. In particular, their relations are infinitely less stable than relations are in say, physics, and the elements of disturbance and error play a role that, for the practice of research, amounts to a difference in kind. But all this does not seem to me to be relevant to the question of principle involved. In particular, if we find a certain relation between price level and total production, it is for this kind of research completely immaterial whether or not this relation can be reduced to reactions of firms that appear to us rational or not. As what I am going to say will amply prove, I do not mean that this is irrelevant from every conceivable standpoint, but it is irrelevant for the type of analysis I am now envisaging and which, of course, is not confined to economics. Wherever we have entities that can be quantitatively expressed and display regular relations to other such entities, we can get some "laws" out of them in much the same way in which the physicist does and, again, the epistemological problems that may arise do not seem to differ from those inherent in scientific procedure in general.

# III

It might seem (and some economists as well as some sociologists of the behavioristic type come near to holding this view) that we ought to confine ourselves to such objective and measurable relations as we have just been considering. My third thesis is, however, that doing so would amount to throwing away a most effective tool of analysis, the value of which is not at all impaired by the fact that it is not available in the physical sciences. Again, the tool in question can best be displayed by means of an example.

Consider a firm that produces a commodity which cannot be substituted at all and for which there exists a demand schedule which that firm cannot expect to influence. Further assume, for simplicity's sake, that there is only one way open to the firm of producing that commodity. We can construct what economists call marginal revenue and marginal cost curves, and determine from their point of intersection that quantity of output which will maximize the instantaneous profits of the firm. This is the classic case of monopoly and a number of propositions about monopoly price and monopoly output can be readily proved. Now what is the nature and the use of such a construct?

First of all, observe that we are still within the sphere of observer's rationality. The model just described is the product of the analyst's mind as much as any physical theory is, and does not in itself say anything about reality or about anybody's actual behavior or rationality. It is of particular importance to note that even if the model should fit anyone's behavior this does not mean that the individual in question consciously aims at the result and still less that he arrives at it by processes at all similar to the analytic procedure. Most businessmen, of course, do not know what a marginal cost and marginal revenue curve is; most of them would not know how to construct them, even if they knew what they meant; and it is safe to say that not a single businessman's subjective processes are correctly described by saying that he is hunting for their point of intersection. But nothing of this is necessary for the model to have sense and to be useful. For a man's behavior may conform to it and be economically described by it, even if its contents are as foreign to his mind as the law of gravitation is foreign to a stone.

Yet, second, there is a difference between the relation of the stone to its law of motion and the relation of our firm to the law of its economic behavior. In the first case we describe observed facts directly although we subject them to a purifying process of abstraction (no friction and that sort of thing). In the second case we also aim at describing observed facts but we choose a detour. We take a preliminary step which consists in setting up a norm of behavior. And this norm is not a norm in the statistical sense but a norm in the sense akin to that of a logical rule or, possibly, even to that of an ethical imperative. In order to set it up we need not only a number of factual data, *but we need also to understand a meaning.* We are setting up a model that embodies a meaning in the sense that it gives the conditions under which a certain given "goal," the maximization of profits, would be attained. Such a model may serve the purposes of description by giving us a standard with which to compare actual behavior or it might, in the most favorable case, help to describe actual behavior by giving its rationale. But in either case an element enters which is extraneous to the description or analysis of the physicist. Although the whole thing is, as has been said, still a product of the rationality of the observer, the latter makes in constructing it an assumption about a rationality present in his subject matter and the whole usefulness of the model will depend on the degree to which that hypothesis is justified by facts. To be sure it is quite sufficient that what firms want is to make money and that they would rather make more than less of it. Also we can take account of any amount of deviations as we must anyhow do also in the case of physical sciences. But that doesn't alter the fact that we have to do with the logic of an (intermediate) end and not only with the logic of a cause. The case is one of a setup that is itself supposed to be rational—of an objective rationality (rationality in the object) seen through the rationality of the observer.

The importance of models of this nature is enormous and extends far beyond the scientific sphere. We could not go through a single day if we had not constant recourse to this method of constructing, however imperfect, models that are rational in this sense. It is not too much to say that that understanding of nonphysical things which enables us to act in daily life, entirely rests upon such schemata of rationality. Objections to them can be founded only on the imperfections of a particular case or an abuse of them. But abuses can only be found out by trying. And this brings up a question of fact.

A few comments will be useful.

1. To begin with, let us restate what I meant to convey by "rationality of the object seen through the rationality of the observer." The observer visualizes an end, the instantaneous maximization of profits, which he understands and putting himself in the place of an imaginary individual that clearly perceives, and aims at, this end, he states

the means (or, in this case, conditions) that seem to him—the observer—conducive to, or logically implied by, the end (or, the conditions action would have to fulfill to produce it). If he has succeeded in "understanding" the end and if he has correctly set out its implications then he has, as we have styled it, derived a "norm" which is "valid," whether there are any facts conforming to it or not (whether it is "verified by facts" or not). This is the situation which has given rise to the distinction between what in German is referred to as *Gelten* and *Sein*. But, potentially at least, this norm is visualized as something capable of being realized by the firms which are the objects of analysis. This is an additional assumption which, e.g., the mathematician need not make. That is what I mean by rationality in the object and what distinguishes a type of rational schemata in the social sciences from, e.g., *"mécanique rationelle,"* i.e., rational schemata in the physical sciences (as well as from other types, mentioned before, of rational schemata in the social sciences).

**FIGURE 1. Schema of Rationality**

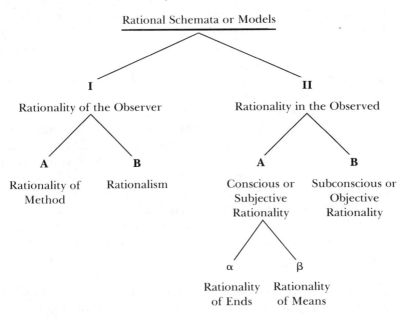

*Note*: Schumpeter used this figure in the talk he gave on "rationality in economics" on October 27 and November 13, 1939. The ideas he presented at these meetings formed the inspiration for "The Meaning of Rationality in the Social Sciences." The figure is included here because it nicely illustrates Schumpeter's argument.

2. The end need not, of course, be shared by the analyst, but we have said that it must be understood by him. For his understanding of the end is the necessary prerequisite for setting forth its implications as to means. This brings us up to the difficulty in application inherent in what I will call the infinite variety of cognate ends. Any such end like maximizing profits is not uniquely determinate. That is why I have added the word "instantaneous." The old Cournot-Marshall theory of monopoly only holds for that subcase—that is to say, practically never—and is not applicable to the cases in which monopolists wish to maximize profits over a (considerable) period of time (a case dealt with by Evans, Roos, Smithies et al.). Dissatisfaction with rational schemata in economics seems to me mainly due to the difficulty of picking appropriate rational models. Here, then, questions of fact enter after all—the rationality of a model must be supplemented by the rationality of its application which is part of the analyst's task. Many types of behavior are looked upon as irrational (not conforming to a schema of rational action), and the range of rationality in action is in consequence often underestimated because the tests of rationality have been made by means of models that failed to fit, not because they were rational but because they did not catch the right type of "Zweckrationalität."

3. Conflicting ends, modifying each other, afford another kind of instance for the same truth. An individual's or group's behavior may ideally conform to the rules of rationality and yet not seem to do so if tested by a schema embodying one end only. A social class would not consistently act according to its economic interests even if these were uniquely determined at any given point of time—which they never are—because it also has other interests to which it attaches varying weights. At a time when the agrarian interest was dominant in the class that formed English political society, the duties on foodstuffs were abolished. This was contrary to the economic interests of that class and might easily be interpreted as, from its standpoint, irrational. But a ruling class's first and foremost interest is to rule and from this angle that action was perfectly rational. The *conflict* of ends is well illustrated by the fact that the Conservative Party actually split on that issue.

The same example also illustrates another important cause of what might be called spurious failure of rational models: the faulty construction of the agent, "into the place of which" the analyst should put himself. A class never sets acts as such. It acts through politicians whom it "supports." But the personal success of politicians depends also on other things than the class interests of their supporters. Often it is best served by selling the latter down the river. And what looks very refractory to rational schematization if made to turn on class interest, may yet fit excellently into a schema of rationality if the analyst constructs his agent correctly. Such examples abound: the interest of a business corporation vs. the interests of the executives, the interest of the working class vs. the interests of trade-union officers are cases in point.

4. For many obvious reasons it is very important to distinguish again between rational behavior and rational result. Behavior can ideally conform to a rational schema and yet produce or help to produce a result which is rational only in the sense that the analyst can understand it by means of rational processes of mind but in no other. This may best be illustrated by all those cases in which the mass effect of actions, each of which may be described by a strictly rational model, spells chaos and produces results most irrational from the standpoint of the ends of the actors. Every economic crisis may be cited in verification. This illustration is particularly interesting because, far into the nineteenth century, economists used to argue that unfettered economic self-interest of individuals is bound to produce the maximum of welfare for all, *because* every individual strives to maximize his own. Such slips, by the way, may have much to do with the discredit that no doubt attaches to analysis by means of rational models in our sense.

5. Beyond very simple cases which we may hope hail from an almost universal pattern of human behavior, understanding an end and judging rationality of means often requires that the analyst "put himself" into places very far distant from his time and social location. Sometimes he has to transplant himself into another cultural world. It might well be asked what justification there can be for such "Einfühlung" in Brahmanism behavior or Hannibalian strategy, and whether sociologists or historians are writing anything else but novels. Into this I cannot go. But if we admit that when venturing into the "Sinnzusammenhang" of things so far removed from our own personal experience we are not merely stepping on clouds, we must at least recognize the risks inherent in such undertaking. Max Weber affords a good illustration of the dangers I mean to refer to, when he denies rationality to the ancient Chinese mind on the ground, among others, that examinations in classical literature were tightened as a remedy for shortcomings the bureaucracy displayed in dealing with catastrophic floods.

## IV

Workers in the field of the Social Sciences have, explicitly or implicitly, gone beyond rational schemata of the type we have been considering so far by assuming that the individuals under research—sometimes even "the people" as such—are themselves actuated by clearly perceived motives, and regulate their behavior with conscious rationality working in the full daylight of their ego's (subjective rationality). In doing so, those analysts, especially those of bygone generations, have almost invariably overrated the actual range of consciously rational action. Moreover, they so formulated their propositions as to lay them open, quite unnecessarily, to objection whenever it could be shown that their concepts were entirely foreign to the individuals whose behavior they tried to describe, whereas we have seen that, for instance, the fundamental theorem about monopolistic pricing is independent of whether or not the monopolist has any notion of marginal revenue or marginal cost curves. Finally, they almost completely overlooked the fact that the conscious motives that a man will tell himself and others are largely "rationalizations" of impulses he either is unable to diagnose or unwilling to admit. But this does not dispose of the question whether or not the distinction between objective rationality (applicability of a rational schema to the actor's behavior) and subjective rationality (conformity of the actor's mental processes to a rational schema) is completely otiose.

I answer in the negative. No doubt, the distinction *is* otiose in many cases and for many purposes. Wherever it is and where in consequence the element of subjective rationality owes its introduction into our analysis merely to the failure of analysts to perceive the fact that models of rational action do not necessarily imply conscious rationality on the part of the actors, it is sound method to discard what then turns out to be a redundant hypothesis. But all the same I believe that there are other cases and other purposes for which presence or absence of subjective rationality is not a matter of indifference. My reasons are as follows.

I have been at pains to emphasize that the propositions such as the one about the monopolist's profit maximum are independent of the subjective rationality of individual monopolists. But that is true only so long as we are interested in that proposition as such and in nothing else. If, however, we apply it as an interpretative schema, it may occur to ask *why* it does or does not fit the facts of the particular case in hand. Taking the first alternative, subjective rationality on the part of the monopolist concerned would afford a very obvious *explanatory hy-*

*pothesis:* the monopolist's conscious calculations of his own pecuniary interest would then constitute a real force ("Realgrund" as distinguished from "Erkenntnisgrund"—sorry, but for these things there are no perfectly adequate English terms). The value of that hypothesis may be inferred from the fact that if, for some reason or other, we do not feel justified in adopting it, conformity of behavior to the rational pattern becomes a puzzle, solution of which is both a laborious and a difficult task.

But the question itself why it is that reality sometimes conforms to rational schemata is by no means uninteresting. The answer makes a difference to diagnosis and especially to prediction: We control a pattern more fully, understand it *better*, handle it with more confidence, forecast its reactions to a given disturbance more surely, if we know that answer. If the monopolist acts with conscious rationality his behavior, say, in a period of rapid change will not only be easier to foretell than if he does not but it will be different from what it would be if other factors accounted for his conforming to the rational schema. In particular his—or anybody's—reactions to the element of *expectations*, especially his speed of reaction, will to a considerable extent depend on the degree to which he is "consciously rational." Of still greater importance than in the cases of often repeated everyday actions is subjective rationality in the case in which our observations are few or refer to exceptional or even unique circumstances. Suppose the task is to interpret American foreign policy. Few will deny that up to 1914, the actual behavior of the American government with respect to its relations with foreign nations almost ideally fits into a very simple rational schema. Excepting the war with Spain, we shall not be contradicted by any major factors, if we say that the "people" wanted a very understandable thing and that they rationally acted according to the implications of that goal: first they wanted independence; then they wanted to buttress it by suspiciously watching their former master and fighting him whenever there was any occasion to do so; finally they capped their policy by the Monroe doctrine and stoutly stood for it and all its implications for the rest of the period. We have here the picture of a nation that wants to be a world unto itself—to be left alone and to leave alone, and if ever rational schemata fitted any political events it does so in this case. But it makes a lot of difference for our understanding the past and for our predicting the future, whether that behavior was due to conscious rationality working for a clearly seen end or to environmental conditions, group interests, and so on that so happened to mold things as to produce, for that period, what will bear description in terms of a rational model.

The best instance for what I am trying to convey is the theory of democracy. The old theory of democracy as formulated in the seventeenth and eighteenth centuries *presupposes* degrees of awareness of one's interests, clearness of ends, rationality in the perception and use of means and, most important of all, accessibility to rational argument which are altogether unrealistic. A reformed theory of democracy could still use, to a considerable extent, rational schemata, but it would have to drop, not wholly but also to a considerable extent, the hypothesis of conscious rationality; and it would, in consequence of this, arrive at a totally different picture of democratic processes, particularly as regards the role to be assigned to rational arguments. And in such a theory the precise range of subjective rationality would constitute a vital part.

Two things must be noted here. First, it is not necessary that the subjective rationality of actors works in the same way as the rationality of the observer. The theorist of monopoly will describe the behavior of even a rational monopolist in ways that more or less differ from the actual methods by which the monopolist arrives at his decisions. We have here the germ of another distinction and another task which, however, need not detain us.

Second, it might be objective that whatever we may find out by means of subjective rationality can always be embodied in our "objectively rational" models so that there is no reason after all to stress what of subjective rationality might be in the actors we observe. I think that my examples suggest this is *not* always so. But even if it were that would only amount to saying that once we have gained full analytic control over a phenomenon we can discard conscious rationality. Heuristically, however, and so long as we are trying to gain analytic control but have not yet gained it, that hypothesis may nevertheless render valuable service. If we know how firms actually react to expectations of future prices and profits, we need perhaps no longer worry about what the subjective rationality of managers has got to do with it. But while we are trying to find out, our task will be rendered easier if we do not refuse to utilize what we may know about their subjective rationality. Similarly, modern economic theory dispenses with the concept of utility, replacing it by a single postulate about choice. But that does not alter the fact that the old marginal utility has in the past proved to be a very helpful piece of scaffolding.

The relevance of subjective rationality to analysis in the social sciences stands out perhaps still more clearly in cases in which rational schemata do not fit. Diagnosis of the reasons for the discrepancy then becomes an obviously unavoidable task of analysis. Into this diagnosis the element of subjective rationality enters, so it seems to me, in two ways. First, deficiency in subjective rationality may directly be the reason we seek, or one of these reasons. In this case it ipso facto presents its credentials as a relevant factor and, moreover, points the way to remedial interference. Second, investigation of subjective rationality may put us on to the track of other reasons and even help us to identify the right "objectively rational model." This can be best shown by an example.

Suppose we have before us a firm which neither in the method of production used (in its economy of heat and power for instance), nor in its location, nor in its cost calculation, nor in its price policy conforms to the model by which we are trying to "interpretatively describe" its behavior. In the first place, this lack of objective rationality *may* be due to lack of subjective rationality in the management, and might be remedied by an efficiency expert's pointing it out to the management.[4]

In the second place, whatever the lack of objective rationality may be due to, it is often easier to find the hitch with than it would be without the use of the concept of subjective rationality. For instance, the irrational situation may have arisen from one that perfectly conformed to the rational model applied but ceased to do so owing to a change in the commercial, technological, and so on data. Now, the firm may have failed to adapt itself, because it had as yet no time to do so or because the management is tradition-bound, lazy, lethargic, or because it thinks that the change responsible for the discrepancy is but temporary. In the latter case, if the management is right—which only means that the analyzing economist is of the same opinion—the case, though not conforming to the rational model applied, may yet be brought within the precincts of rationality by means of another model. But which we are to choose will be much easier to determine—as will in general the right one of all those varieties I have discussed before under the heading of objective rationality—if we know something, from direct observation of the types we have to deal with, of the nature, time-span, and so on of the subjective rationalities involved.

Our model may not fit a given firm also for another class of reasons. The technology of its production process may rouse the contempt of the consulting engineer, and yet the setup as a whole may be quite rational because it may not pay the leading man to bother about technology: He may have such a flair for fashions for instance and be so excellent a salesman and so entirely absorbed by filling these functions successfully that it would be sheer waste of effort for him to worry about whether or not his plant is economical of, say, power or labor. I mention this class of cases—of conflict between engineer's and economic rationality—not only because they are in themselves important and the source of much inadequate interpretation, but also because at least the engineer's rationality is so excellent an example of subjective rationality and for the importance of attending to it. Engineer's rationality turns on ends perceived with ideal clearness. It goes about devising means by ideally rational and conscious efforts. It reacts promptly to a purely rational new impulse—e.g., a new calculation published in a professional periodical. It is comparatively free from extraneous considerations. That is to say, it functions in a particular way *because* of the "conscious" quality of its intentional struggle for rationality. All the sectors in which that is the case—medicine is another example—are intimately associated with what is usually referred to as "material progress" and display mechanisms that powerfully affect the states and the behavior of social groups. They reveal the action of a distinct factor or "social force." Incidentally, they also supply an answer—which is partial only, but *almost* sufficient—to the question how we are to satisfy ourselves whether and to what extent we are in the presence of subjective rationality.

If our firm failed to adapt to the new environmental conditions from habit, laziness, lethargy, its behavior may, from the standpoint of its manager, yet conform to a rational model—he may be maximizing his welfare by not bothering. Now, just as in the case of altruistic behavior practiced from an "egotistical" wish for the satisfaction such a behavior yields or, in the case of energetic and aggressive activity pursued "hedonistically"—because it gives pleasure—so we are in cases such as the one of the lazy manager in danger of losing our criterion of rational behavior: all behavior, so it seems, would have to be looked upon as tautologically rational ex visu of suitably chosen ends and horizons. The ways to encounter this danger—which, if not successfully encountered would limit us to observer's rationality—may be many. But recourse to subjective rationality seems to me to be one of the most feasible ones.

The greatest of all the services that research into the facts of subjective rationality can render is the—possibly—melancholy one of showing up the narrow limits of its range. These limits have been sufficiently emphasized during the last half-century by writers of the most varied types, among leading economists principally by Pareto. What has not been sufficiently emphasized is that the scope of objective and of subjective rationality in action, while immeasurably smaller than our predecessors in economic and political theory thought, is at the same time wider than some of its critics would have us believe. If my points be scrutinized from this angle, it will be seen that everyone of them extends the range of application of rational models in one way or another. It is hardly necessary to add that this puts us in a better position for dealing with the subject of Error in History and with the subject of faulty practice[5] and its persistence or elimination (Taylorism).

## V

Some of the points I have touched upon may possibly be instanced and clarified by going quickly over a few of the general "systems" with which economics is usually credited. When we try to reconstruct the social world of an economist from his writings, we are likely to fall into two errors. First, we may forget that the construction of a general schema of action is not the economist's business. His schemata are devised for certain special uses and must be judged by their success in actual application, and not without reference to it. This is all the more important because the older economists have had the unfortunate habit of adding semi-philosophical obiter dicta, most of which sound horribly trite, and may easily reflect discredit on what they had really to say, especially in the eyes of a layman. Second, even where economists did construct, or adopt, what was intended to be a social philosophy, we mustn't take it for granted that they were much influenced by it in their professional work. Nobody judges Newton's performance in the world of mathematics and physics by his utterances on theology. Nobody reproaches Joule for giving as one of his reasons for belief in the conservation of energy, that it would be derogatory to God to think that anything in the creation could get lost. Similar justice must be rendered to economists and sociologists.

We will begin with the physiocrats whose positive achievement was the clear conception of economic life as a self-contained process reproducing itself in circular flows. But they looked upon their theory as an explanatory schema of the social world as a whole, with a general philosophy thrown in. The distinction between analyzing what is and postulating what ought to be, was as far from their minds (and the minds of their contemporaries) as it was from the mind of Plato. There was an ideal state of things, preordained in God's plan which at one and the same time was the natural state and yet not the existing one but one that had still to be realized. The way to realize it was to allow everyone to act according to his own self-interests while (so we ought to add) conserving the fundamentals of the existing institutional framework, in particular the land-owning class. We need not go any farther for our purposes. The case illustrates to perfection a certain number of points which keep on turning up, however the particular garb may change.

There is first that idea of an ideal state of things which, if once realized, would indefinitely continue to exist. In itself such a belief, nowadays mainly harbored by socialists, is clearly extra-scientific, which in the case of the physiocrats is made particularly obvious by the theological character impressed by them upon the *ordre naturel*.[6] But from the standpoint of the actual use made of this conception, it merely looks like a descriptive device for expressing the useful truth that the economic process is a cosmos and not a chaos. What really depends upon the concept of the ideal state and its divine sanction is only a series of value judgments which we can easily dispense with. Of course, once one believes in such an ideal state, any element of an actual state can be unequivocally labeled as right and wrong. Beyond that, however, since all the Deity was supposed to do was to lend the weight of its authority to the theorems propounded by the physiocrats, there was no theological influence whatever. Nevertheless, we have here a typically rationalist system. That is to say, a system built upon the belief that there is, underlying the empirical world, a plan or order that human reason can reveal by propositions, acceptance of which can be logically enforced. In their economic theory they clearly used a rational schema of the sort which we have tried to individualize by the phrase "rationality of the subject matter seen through the rationality of the observer." But as far as I can see no assumption about subjective rationality was necessarily involved although in common with all the thinkers of their time they certainly greatly overestimated its range of application.

Let English Utilitarianism be our next example. Here, the theological note is absent but otherwise the case is exactly similar to the preceding one. Again, there is an ideal state, which is natural though it doesn't exist, and which when reached will persist indefinitely. There is a well-nigh unlimited belief in the actual rationality of man. Most of the economic propositions of the economists of the group, Bentham himself included, could I suppose be stated in such a way as to avoid the hypothesis of conscious rationality. But the political theory of Benthamism could not. The recipe: educate people and let them vote freely and equally, presupposes, if intended to be the remedy for everything the Benthamites did not like and the key to everything they did like, that everybody knows or can be made to know what he wants and is able and willing to work for it and to discuss it with ideal rationality: thomistic rationalism has descended from the clouds, but only to reign supreme in the sphere of social action. Uncompromising intellectualism, aptly wedded to associative psychology by James Mill, is the backbone of Benthamite sociology. The observer's rationality welds with the *ratio* in the subject matter and this *ratio* is, potentially at least, subjective rationality producing, and accounting for, the objective rationality in the social patterns. Everything is conscious and what is not is being covered by a fig leaf: English tradition became so firmly set that even so modern an author—is he so very modern though?—as Professor Pigou defined welfare as a state of consciousness.

The gulf between what is and what ought to be on the one hand, and between ultimate ends and means on the other hand, is not of course narrowed thereby. But it looks smaller from the Benthamite standpoint than from almost any other. The ultimate end remains an improvable postulate but Bentham saw a particular ultimate end so ardently that he almost thought he could prove it and condemn the dissenter logically as well as ethically. What he considered a normal ultimate end became for him *the* ideal ultimate end. As everyone knows, that end was the principle, greatest happiness of the greatest number, of which Bentham speaks with the reverence of religious belief.[7]

Now the proposition that everyone seeks happiness might be considered as a factual assertion although it can be made true only at the expense of being made a tautology. But there is no real "force" that tends to realize the greatest happiness of the greatest number of people which has therefore to be realized, if at all, as a by-product of "forces" aiming at other goals. This is in fact what Bentham tried to deduce from the action of unfettered self-interests in a way so uncritical as to arouse the just criticism of the historical school. These critics were, however, primarily moved to contempt by the philosophy of life that was at the back of his value judgments and by that union of rationalism and hedonism which was of the essence of that philosophy: logically, rationalism and hedonism have nothing to do with each other; but Benthamite rationalism is essentially hedonistic, reducing as it does to a logic turning on pleasure and pain, to a logic that makes a last desperate attempt to conquer the world of ultimate ends.

Next, we will cast a glance at Marx. If we took at face value some of his Hegelian professions and then turned to the Master himself in order to allow ourselves to be impressed by the dialectic process by which Reason progresses in the Consciousness of Freedom by thesis, antithesis, and synthesis—or by the Idea which, having Being, is Nature—and that sort of thing, we might feel that we shall have done all there is to do, if we simply state that we have before us another rationalist system of the kind defined apropos of our comment on the doctrine of the physiocrats. But that would be quite wrong. For Hegelian is only Marx's garb and not the body of his thought. He tells us as much himself in the preface to the second edition of the first volume of *Das Kapital* and the ease with which that garb can be stripped off the body shows conclusively that he did not mistake the nature of his argument. In economics Quesnay and Ricardo, in sociology a number of French historians have left much clearer traces in his writings than Hegel's thought did as distinguished from Hegel's phraseology.

Marx primarily envisages a process of social evolution. The protagonist in this process is the struggle of classes, and all other factors in it are strictly impersonal too. Even economic value is carefully made so, even the labor force is. The conceptual schema is *intended* to be severely objective. Rationality enters the process to be described, in the first instance, merely as observer's rationality—it is the observer who, rationally analyzing, *understands* how blind and chaotic forces, like geological eruptions, procreate and disrupt one state of society after another until the socialist goal shall be reached. But this goal is not a teleological one nor one to be realized because it is a worthwhile ideal. That was the view of what Marx felt to be "utopian" socialism from which he was anxious to distance his own, the "scientific" socialism—the socialism which is to be understood, by means of scientific analysis, as the necessary outcome of the observed social process.[8]

Nevertheless, rational schemata enter the Marxian structure by several doors. The two most important ones may be noted. First, rational patterns are implied in many of his statements even if they are not made explicit. For instance, among the conditions under which his law of value would directly apply to actual relative prices, is the condition that all commodities are produced according to the rules of economic rationality—all firms behaving according to the ordinary classical schema as it would work out in perfect competition. This might, however, be objective rationality only. Second, when Marx attempts to explain how resources are allocated in such a way as to equalize the rate of profit on total capital he again argues from conditions of perfect competition. But in doing so he uses language which strongly suggests that he is thinking of the subjective rationality of actors who bring about the equal rate because they imagine (sich einbilden) that this must be so.

An astounding performance remains to be mentioned—it is astounding if we consider the mentality of his time and the success with which, in this point, he anticipated later thought. The word "rationalization" has by now acquired other meanings, but one type of rationalization and its baleful influence on the analysis of social phenomena he perceived with unsurpassable clearness—the type referred to as ideologies. He never ceased to preach that people invariably misconceive the events of their own time and that they do so not at random but in a systematic way: they look upon their struggles as struggles about some ideals or values and never get at the social realities below. Now, these ideologies are mostly rational schemata devised in order to marshal events into readily understandable units. To point out their treacherous character, to uncover what underlies them, to show up one kind of disservice that attempts at analysis by means of rational schemata may render—all that meant a great step forward. Such fire is dangerous to kindle however. It may well be that it burns more things than Marx had intended it to burn, and that the class struggles by which he meant to replace what he considered as pseudoexplanations, are after all nothing but another ideology.

Finally, a word or two should be said about the use of rational models by the economists who, mostly in a derogatory sense, are now looked upon as "classics." Into the modern phase I will not enter because advance, destructive and constructive, is rapid enough to have produced chaos for the time being much as—si licet parva componere magnis—it has done in physics. Suffice it then to say that in spite of the spread of the analysis that, as mentioned before, work with time-series material and with concepts designed to fit corresponding theoretical requirements, rational models in our sense have not gone out of fashion entirely. The theory of monopolistic competition, the theory of economic behavior oriented on profits over time, the theory of location and other examples could be cited in support of that statement. The only thing I should like to advert to is that modern schemata of rationality in action increasingly tend to strip the "rational" patterns of a connotation so obvious in older theory: older theory almost invariably implied that if a firm acted according to the rational pattern, such action would in fact tend to realize the goal it aimed at or, at least, would not fire back upon the actor. We are less optimistic about that and still less so about the rationality of the *social* results of rational business action.

But we will confine ourselves to the state of things in, say, 1900 or thereabouts. Very roughly, methods and results of economics may, as of that year, be identified with the teachings of Alfred Marshall and of Knut Wicksell.

Both used rational schemata very liberally and without displaying

any symptoms of doubts or of compunction. Marshall indeed professed to study humanity in its ordinary business pursuits and actually did provide tools and suggestions for the handling of deviations
from rationality. All the same a rational schema, or rather a system
of rational schemata for the behavior of individual households and
firms, is the skeleton of Marshallian economics—the skeleton worked
out much more fully by Léon Walras. Interrelations between these
schemata supply the "social" results. The same holds for Wicksell.

Both also expressed themselves in a way which suggests excessive
reliance on *subjective* rationality. Marshall's producers "each governed
under the sway of free competition by *calculations* (my italics) of his
own interest will *endeavor* (my italics) so to regulate the amount of any
commodity . . . that this amount shall be just capable on the average
of finding purchasers . . . at a remunerative price." His speculators
analyze situations rationally on the basis of strictly logical considerations. His savers save under the influence of forethought, rationality
of which is implied. And so on.

Much (though not all) of this could no doubt be formulated in
terms of objective rationality and freed from the hypothesis of subjective conscious rationality. But it is fair to suppose that this distinction did not occur to either Marshall or Wicksell and that they simply
identified the two. After all, though conscientious and neat analysts,
they were in no mind to bother about epistemological niceties. And
they paid the penalty for this, as they did for language suggestive of
hedonist premises.[9] Institutionalist critique in this country, not stay-
ing to ask how much of all that was essential and how much only a
façon de parler, bombed the whole structure on those grounds—with
more success than was fair.

It should be observed that the reform primarily associated with the
name of Pareto, though it did much to remove the hedonist stigma
and though it reduced the emphasis on conscious rationality quite a
lot, yet retained in service the objective rational schema.[10] And this
turned around the profit motive. We have, it is true, seen that it is
not essential for the applicability of the hypothesis of rationality in
action to assume any particular end. But in practice, it is almost necessary to construct a rational schema with a view to a single end—
otherwise the construct loses its main raison d'être, simplicity. Hence
the *homo oeconomicus* turned up again. Marshall obviously did not like
him. But Pareto accepted him, comforting us with the assurance that
another time we would consider the *homo religiosus*, the *homo eroticus*,
and so on in turn. This, however, only shows up a very serious limitation. Even if I could—I cannot—visualize the laborious life of a *pure*
homo eroticus, any attempt at combination of all those homines

would only serve to show, by the absence of any rational rule of combination, that life is ontologically irrational, at least as much as "nature."

## Notes

1. The following article ("still only a sketch") was found in the Harvard University Archives. It was written in 1940 for an informal discussion group on rationality, which Schumpeter had taken the initiative to start. The members of the group included Talcott Parsons, Wassily Leontief, Paul Sweezy, and a few other Harvard people. All but the first section of the article were first published in Zeitschrift für die gesamte Staatswissenschaft in 1984. For more information, see the section titled "The American Period: Schumpeter's Works in This Volume" in the Introduction. The manuscript is published by permission of the Harvard University Archives.

2. Rationalism as a philosophy (or theory of the world) is in Hegelianism wedded to the use of rational models so as to make the two practically synonymous. This is well expressed by the two famous propositions in the preface to Hegel's Philosophy of Natural Law: (1) What is rational is actual, (2) What is actual is rational.

3. This is intended to exclude not only pragmatic rationality of results ex visu of the observed individuals or groups (see infra) but also the ontological truth of, say, prophecy which might be arrived at by nonrational means.

4. I suspect that part of the opposition my theory of subjective rationality met in our group, especially from Professor Parsons, is due to my infelicitous terminology. Perhaps I should speak of personal rationality—meaning thereby rationality residing in a man rather than in a pattern—and I should not have used the word "conscious" since automatization of often repeated actions will make forms of behavior subconscious which are, nevertheless, included in my conscious rationality: If a mathematician solves a differential equation in the best known manner he is being "consciously rational" in my sense even if, in a particularly simple case, he writes down the solution quite mechanically. [In this case, Schumpeter's reference to "our group" is referring to the meetings of the group on rationality on October 27 and November 13, 1939.]

5. By faulty practice, as distinguished from error, I mean practice conforming to standards of rationality in use at the relevant time and place that themselves deviate from the correct implications of the end pursued. Example: In order to make money, a firm stands in need of correct methods of cost calculation; as a matter of fact none of the methods actually in use are correct, and business decisions that are otherwise rational and even consciously so, are often vitiated by them. Of course not everything is really irrational that appears to the economist to be so. For instance, economists often state that it is irrational for firms to insist always on charging prices that will cover overhead charges rather than take what they can get. But big business that

knows itself to be unpopular will often be driven to that course from a fear that it will not be allowed to put prices up again after having lowered them and from a desire to charge prices that can easily be "justified." This, of course, is one of those cases in which a model fails from taking inadequate account of the data before the actor and of the ends he actually pursues.

6. See in particular Francois Quesnay's *Droit Naturel*.

7. Doubtless through ignorance, I am unable to trace that "principle" (*with full realization of its implications*) farther back than to Beccaria's *Dei delitti e delle pene*.

8. Barring the one definite goal, his theory may in fact, as he himself suggested, be likened to that of Darwin. At any rate, he conceived of evolution not in a rationalist spirit but in the spirit of empirical science (*évolution créatrice*) and Marx and Darwin may both be wrong. I believe they are. But that is another matter.

9. Those, of course, are still more in evidence with Jevons who had no hesitation about talking, in the best Benthamite form, about economics as a "calculus of pleasure and pain."

10. Removal of the utility concepts did not, so I believe in spite of what one should think at first blush, alter the situation in the respect in which we are interested.

# Eight

## An Economic Interpretation of Our Time: The Lowell Lectures

### I. The Economic and Political Structure of Modern Society

In times of rapid social and economic change, the task of explaining a civilization is apt to degenerate into the explanation of a crisis.[1,2,3] But fundamentally the problem remains the same. When we behold a landslide we have still to analyze the nature of the levels from which it started. When we are shocked and bewildered by current events which we feel threaten the social world as we know it, we have still to investigate that social and economic ground that seemed solid rock forty years ago, and to the average citizen of our own country even as late as 1929. What was the structure of that rock and how did it come to crumble? To give at least partial answers to these questions is the purpose of this book.

In the first instance we may characterize the civilization whose existence is now obviously in jeopardy by a list of beliefs, attitudes, principles that, two generations ago, were not indeed universally accepted but which at least in England and America most people would have agreed in accepting as the logical consequences of those that actually prevailed.

Let us then place ourselves in the standpoint of the year 1871 when all the great national states had emerged and when the majority of storm centers in the world seemed reduced to one, or possibly two, that is to say, Turkey and the Austro-Hungarian monarchy.

To begin with international relations: the world was rapidly internationalizing itself. Though England was the only country that had adopted free trade, most economists even in the United States felt fully convinced of the virtues of the free trade system, and believed that the world was actually moving toward that goal. Free movement of commodities, restricted if at all only by custom tariffs; freedom, unquestioned in principle, of migration of people and of capital; all this facilitated by unrestricted gold currencies and protected by a growing body of international law that on principle disapproved of force or compulsion of any kind and favored peaceful settlement of international conflicts—that fairly embodies not only what was or was becoming approved practice but also what a majority of people approved. And in fact though wars continued to occur, they did not spread. The Russo-Turkish war, for instance, which in another atmosphere would have been much more likely to produce an international conflagration than was the conflict between Austria and Serbia in 1914, was localized and the result internationalized (Congress of Berlin) without much difficulty: the burning cigarette had obviously fallen into wet grass. Although imperialist policy was by no means discontinued (England acquired Egypt by force and waged war on the Boer Republic, France annexed Tunisia, and so on), the tendency yet was to consider imperialist conquest with increasing disapproval. The tendency to reduce tensions by mutual concessions asserted itself, for instance, in the policy of England toward France and Russia, associated with the names of Balfour and Lansdowne. China remained the object of imperialist attack and was by 1898 well on the way to being divided up between European powers. Yet this policy was not carried to its logical conclusion.

At home, practically all civilized nations professed allegiance to the democratic ideal. Popular education and steady extension of the franchise were generally accepted policies. The freedom of the individual to say, think, and do what he pleased was also within very wide limits, generally accepted. This freedom included the freedom of economic action: private property and inheritance, free initiative and conduct were essential elements of that civilization. What they characteristically called government interference was held to be justified only within narrow limits. The state had to provide a minimum of framework for the lives of individuals and this framework it had to provide with a minimum of expenditure. The ideal of the cheap state had its natural complement in the postulate that taxation should be kept within such limits that business and private life should develop in much the same way as they would have done if there had been no taxation at all. That roughly was the principle of Gladstonian finance.

We will add that there are many other features of that civilization which do not come within any of the headings mentioned and yet are closely linked up with them, in fact the children of the same type of mentality. That civilization was essentially rationalist and utilitarian. It was not favorable to cults of national glory, victory, and so on. That civilization required rationalist credentials for everything it was doing. It counted the cost of wars and did not back the glory as an asset. This attitude was also essentially unfavorable to religious beliefs which at that time in fact were everywhere on the retreat, being in many cases and places replaced by a crude materialism of a mechanistic type. This will also explain attitudes toward art and the success of certain types of art, particularly the naturalistic types, and the decay of others.

We need only look at the attitudes and beliefs we have just glanced at in order to realize that they are not just ideas floating in space which any man could adopt or refuse to adopt but that they are linked to a definite social and economic structure. Broadly speaking, they are the beliefs and attitudes of the business class which from small beginnings, dating from the fourteenth century, had by means of economic successes acquired the position of a ruling stratum in the nineteenth century. That does not mean that the business class actually did the governing (this happened in a comparatively few cases only) but that those who governed, even if belonging to a nonbourgeois stratum, more or less stated the interests of the business class and adapted their policies to its needs. The business class and its dependents, being in this sense the dominant social factor, impressed its own attitudes upon national domestic and foreign policy, upon art and religion, in fact upon the whole civilization of that time. The schema of ultimate values and the outlook on life, glanced at before, were not what they were believed to be at the time, namely the products of progress that should appeal to all possible types of people but they were simply the bourgeois outlook on life and the bourgeois scheme of value.

Now since the business class rose by virtue of a purely economic process which from the peasant holding and the medieval craft shop via the putting-out system had produced the privately owned and privately managed factory and bank, it seems tempting to generalize and to say that the structure and conditions of production will determine the social and political structure of society, the ideals and behavior of nations and all the manifestations of civilization. Thus, our outlook on life, our values, our beliefs, our art, seem to be a mere superstructure or emanation of economic forces—a view which has been termed the materialistic or economic interpretation of history and is primarily associated with the name of Karl Marx. Innumerable facts can be invoked in verification. For instance, it is easy to say that purely economic forces tend to eliminate the craftsman in a time of large-scale mechanized production, and with the economic position of the craftsman goes the artisan's cultural world. That is no doubt so. And the leveling, mechanizing, democratizing, rationalizing tendencies of modern civilization can certainly be accounted for on those lines.

But closer scrutiny of the end of that civilization and of the conditions that made it emerge will show that that isn't all. Before we come to that we have to take a bird's-eye view of the economic performance of that society.

The economic structure is, as has been said, characterized by private property and means of production, private enterprise, and bank credit. The core of the matter lies in the saving and investment process. The entrepreneur, the banker, the salaried employee, the workman, and the capitalist are the familiar types which account for the class stratification of capitalist society (through that also for its attitudes). And they are all of them defined in terms of economic functions.

The economic performance of the system can be best measured by what it did directly and indirectly for the masses. The sum total of real wages is not only statistically difficult to evaluate over time but it must also be borne in mind that it fails to measure adequately the performance of the economic engine because it fails to take account of such things as the shortening of hours, modern medical care, and so on. This must be pointed out because the world, having grown out of humor with the capitalist system we now frequently find that the most obvious facts about it are being made light of or even flatly denied.

Returning to our argument we must now first of all realize that that economic structure and hence the social and political structure which were based upon it, therefore also that civilization or system of values, were inherently unstable. Seventy years ago, most people were not aware of that. They looked upon their mode of life, upon the policies they espoused, and upon their whole civilization as something that, if and when fully worked out, would last forever and would be absolutely ideal. This is perfectly natural. It is a general and even an indispensable habit of mind to take much of the things around us for granted and not to ask every moment how long our world is going to last. We might even say that this is the normal attitude to take for normal man in any civilization as long as it is intact. On the other hand it is equally obvious that there cannot be such a thing as a stable social system. Any system transforms itself by its mere working and if history teaches nothing else it teaches that. But in the particular case under consideration a very simple argument carries us beyond that generality. It should not have been difficult to see that capitalist progress, embodying itself in ever larger units of control, would eventually produce a state of things in which private enterprise and the whole scheme of business action were becoming obsolete and amenable to wholesale bureaucratization. It might be added that the very increase in the standard of living and the increased leisure of all classes were producing views and attitudes essentially hostile to the capitalist engine and the people that man it. Students might differ on the details of the process that would eventually put an end to capitalist economy and capitalist society. They might differ still more about the features of the order into which capitalism tended to transform itself. But there was and is hardly much room for difference about the fact that capitalist society was going to transform itself into something else, and about the prognosis that this something would be a socialism of one kind or another. The people of that time attributed to that socialism all the pacific and democratic ideals which they held dear. In this and in other respects they were certainly guilty of wishful thinking, but if by socialism we mean nothing else but public management of economic affairs and public control of all means of production, then the prognosis was quite correct.

This teaches us one thing which is helpful in the explanation of the great landslide: the plateau that crumbled did not consist of everlasting rock. Though not necessarily in a landslide, it was bound to come down in time. But our problem is much more complicated than that.

Those liberals and radicals who, seventy years ago, believed so firmly in the social system of which they were the products and exponents that they completely overlooked how much that system and its pivotal stratum, the business class, owed to other social elements which, however much they may have allied themselves to the business class, were yet in a more fundamental sense strangers to it. The English liberal radical who looked upon the House of Lords as an anomaly and upon aristocratic cabinet ministers with distrust, was blissfully confident that the masses, when sufficiently educated and left free to vote, would recognize the excellencies of the capitalist system and keep it up of their own free will. They ignored the fact that the society in which they at that time enjoyed comparative affluence and almost unrestricted individual freedom was the product of force and of a discipline inculcated into the lower strata by the feudal predecessors of the business class, and that what remained of the aristocratic element had very much to do with the smooth functioning of that social system which they loved to represent as a pure reign of reason. The English liberal was also apt to forget that the British Empire was not the result of the enlightened self-interests of the various races in the colonies but the result of the sword wielded with a complete disregard of the moral standards of bourgeois society. Nothing illustrates better the domination of our wishfulness over our powers of rational inference than does the fact that people were able to believe that such a social organization and an empire more splendid than that of the Great Mogul, that is to say, the whole framework of English existence, could be kept together by any other means than the sword. This of course does not apply only to England. Everywhere the bourgeoisie, whether enjoying an empire or not, just looked upon the remnants of the feudal world as functionless survivals which could and should be dispensed with as soon as possible. As a matter of fact, those survivals were not functionless in the bourgeois world. Their presence made for a most useful symbiosis. They sheltered the bourgeois, regulated and occasionally exploited him, and thought that what he needed was an impressive ruler. Examples like those of Venice, the Netherlands, and most important of all, the United States may apparently be adduced in refutation of this view. But it would be easy to show that in those cases and a few others bourgeois rule prevailed for a time only owing to a combination of exceptionally favorable circumstances. There is thus a second reason for the decay of the capitalist state. We have first seen that capitalist economy tends to outgrow its own framework. But second, we have now seen that that framework had nonbourgeois girders in it which voluntarily and involuntarily the business class progressively removed.

The latter discovery, however, is of very great importance for our philosophy of history. If the social world of the businessman contained elements that were extraneous to it yet essential to it, the question naturally arises how those elements acquired that social position which enabled them to fill such a function. Well, how did the feudal world arise? Obviously it was the result of two factors. Most of the nations acquired the territories which they at present inhabit by conquest. In ancient and medieval times they moved into these territories as armed and organized bands. During the centuries which it took to conquer those territories and to settle in them as an upper stratum, the social structure of those tribes and nations was as much the reflex of the necessity to fight as the social structure of the bourgeois world is a reflex of the necessity to run factories and to trade. Successful warriors rose to positions of social leadership and they retained those positions by virtue of their social prestige when the settlement was completed. Here the second feature comes in. Circumstances being essentially agrarian in nature, the chief and all the chiefs of lower rank became large land owners in the feudal sense. This of course was a most important economic fact, determining the economic process for centuries. Yet it was in itself not the result of conditions of production or of economic achievement. This most powerful of upper classes that ever existed does not simply fit in with the economic interpretation of history and we readily see that the latter describes what is a very frequent and very important yet a special case. Men, families, and groups always do rise by achievement in lines which at the time are socially important, but business activity is only one of them and business activity induces a social rise only because and insofar as it implies leadership. Thus, we are led to generalize the economic interpretation of history and the theory of social classes associated with it and this generalized theory may prove very much more useful for explaining the events of our time than is a narrow over-emphasis of the economic element.

Finally, third, whilst substantially capitalist conservatives quarreled with substantially capitalist liberals, and substantially capitalist liberals with substantially capitalist radicals, and all of them with socialists who after all were culturally the products of the capitalist system, new tendencies appeared which were not understood by any of them. Good liberals, at the turn of the century, spoke of a recrudescence of nationalism, militarism, mercantilism. Good socialists spoke of imperialism being the last stage of capitalism and the last card of the business class. Liberals and socialists bemoaned the fact as they had every reason to. But it never occurred to them that these things might be the harbinger of a new epoch, of a new attitude of humanity toward its problems and toward life in general. Yet these things were not entirely without their complement in the realm of ideas and idealists. There had been Nietzsche, there was Bergson, and there were Sorel and Pareto. None of these was a socialist, yet none of these was a friend of either capitalism or the ethics which were congenial to capitalism. It was something that was as hostile to socialism as it was to capitalism. It was hostile to intellectualist culture.

So far as imperialism is concerned there were two theories to account for it, the socialist theory which linked it to tendencies supposedly inherent to big business capitalism and the theory which looked upon these things as atavisms. In the light of later events we may well suspect that both were wrong.

Thus it was an essentially unstable world on which the first world war impinged. From whatever standpoint we may look upon that event, first and foremost it was the result of blundering on all sides. But impinging on that particular pattern it acquired importance not naturally its own.

## II. Success and Failure in the Adjustments of 1919–1929

In the first lecture, reasons were offered for believing that the roots of the present crisis of our civilization reach far back into the past and that this crisis itself cannot be accounted for in terms of individual maladjustments, misdeeds, errors, and the like.[4] Of this, however, the world seemed completely unaware when, impoverished and disappointed, it set about to repair the damages of the 1914 hurricane.

Unlike other wars, the war of 1914–1918 had created more maladjustments than it had removed. The peace treaties were impossible instruments to handle, and by 1922 the chief problem that faced responsible men was how to get rid of them in the face of political commitments. The first attempts at workable settlements, some very meritorious ones among them, having come to nothing, we may date the period of partially successful reconstruction from 1924. Disregarding minor miscarriages and that essential insincerity of the international situation which slowed up necessary measures until they had become ineffective, it may be said that the system embodied in the League of Nations got into something like working order by means of the Locarno Pact and then, for several years, proved itself adequate to handle conflicts of great importance between small nations and conflicts of small importance between great nations. The problems of the interallied debts and of the reparations, though without the prevailing protectionism they might have been solvable, were not really solved. But provisional sham solutions paved the way toward an eventual solution by default. In spite of all barriers, the physical volume of international trade stood in 1929 at twenty-three percent above the figure of 1913. Domestic policies in Europe, fiscal policies included, adjusted themselves to a new social situation which, whatever political party happened to be in power, substantially amounted to democracy in the sense of trade-union rule, the two significant exceptions, Russia and Italy, not causing much disturbance at the time. In the United States, prosperity combined with a substantially isolationist foreign policy created a social and political situation that seemed eminently stable.

Looking back on those years we cannot fail to be struck by two ominous facts. First, the political settlements, imposed upon the world by three nations that, at the time, wielded an irresistible military power, could not be expected to last unless upheld by the continued use of military force, which, however, those three nations, or at least two of them, were unwilling to apply. The economic developments were to a great extent contingent upon the indefinite continuance of American lending, successive loans servicing preceding ones. The war having accelerated, though it had not initiated, the growth of capitalist industry outside of Europe and the United States, the long-run prospects for the recovery of international trade mentioned above, were obviously far from reassuring.

Second, the task of reconstruction had been approached in a curiously obsolete frame of mind. The admission of labor to responsible office and the reorientation of legislation in the interest of the working class was in a sense an adjustment to a new state of things. But, with the two exceptions mentioned, all nations nevertheless attempted to run their economies on capitalist lines, thus continuing to put their trust in an engine, the motive power of which was at the same time drained away by crushing taxation. But the outstanding monuments of that frame of mind were England's return to the gold standard at prewar par and the (temporarily successful) attempt to reconstruct, wherever possible, gold currencies that were bound to collapse at slight provocation, and in any case had no useful function, in a world determined not to play the international game according to the old rules. In some respects, therefore, positive adjustments were failures in proportion to their temporary success.

In the United States, both the substance and the surface phenomena of a very real internal prosperity that was largely independent of developments abroad, obliterated the true features of the social situation. But in Europe, those failures were indicative of much more than individual maladjustments that might have righted themselves in time. As weakened and distorted by the consequences of the war, the social and political machinery of the prewar system was not up to its task while there was as yet no alternative for it. Monetary specialists, experts in international relations, authorities on unemployment, collective bargaining, social security and agriculture, did their best to remedy symptoms. But their recommendations, even the sound ones among them, never came near to touching upon the fundamental difficulty which consisted in the fact that the methods indicated by economic expediency were politically unworkable while the socialist alternative was as yet economically impracticable. Of course this state of things offered unrivaled opportunities for new departures. In Russia, the contours of a despotic form of government began to emerge that had much more affinity with Ivan the Terrible than with Karl Marx. In Italy, a new form of integration of society was attempted and, for the time being at least, [was] successful. Elsewhere, similar ideologies commanded increasing allegiance. It was as much the consequence of the essentially anti-bourgeois spirit of those ideologies as of the circumstances of the "have-not" nations that those ideologies developed strongly nationalist and militarist traits.

## III. The Impact of the World Crisis

Let me recall how and why this subject brings itself to us in this course.[5] We have in the first lecture discussed from a standpoint somewhere between 1870 and 1914 the structure of capitalist society as it was at the time when it did not meet with the obstructions, that really accounted for the major spokes in the economic and political wheel. We have discussed the sort of mentality which underlied this structure, and we have finally discovered certain tendencies of change, present long before, which were sure to undermine that structure. All of this had shown in 1914 significant symptoms. In the second lecture we have discussed the question how the occurrence of the World War affected all that situation. We have seen that the War, without producing any new tendency but accelerating the existing ones and by breaking out of the structure of society certain girders that pegged it and sheltered it, in fact, created what looked like a new world. The social situation and its implications as to war in 1914 alone account certainly for what the War had done to the social fabrications all over the world. If the World War had happened to impinge on an intact society, the suffering and horror would still have been there but the lasting effects on the social structure would not.

In exact parallelism we have to consider today the effects—economic, cultural, and political—of the impact of the world depression on the social structure which had previously been shaken to its foundations by the war and which was slowly recovering, trying to do away with certain maladjustments that had been created by the war. The results of our investigations will be similar to the results we attained last time. The world depression was also really not productive of either new ideas or new factors or new situations, but impinging on a situation that was delicate independently of it, it again changed the face of the world, the only difference being that while the effects of the war had been much more serious in Europe than in this country, the effects of the world crisis were more serious in this country than in Europe. Even as the exposure to a northern gale that would do no harm and would, in fact, refresh a man in perfect health, may endanger the life of a man with tuberculosis, so a world crisis that would have freshened up the social structure in many a way endangered the life of an organism that was displaying symptoms of disease independently of the crisis. Let me elaborate. Most of us will agree that the crisis did change the face of the political world, the social scenery all over the world. Many of us, however, will add by way of explanation that that crisis was an unprecedented catastrophe spelling complete breakdown of the capitalist system which, though it might be now patched up by government action, stood discredited forever.

This theory requires qualification. In itself the world depression was not an unprecedented phenomenon. Such depressions had been experienced before, for instance, in the 1870s, and they can be fitted into the mechanism of capitalist evolution in which periods of lag alternate with periods of prosperity. Let me explain that a little more. Naturally the economic process is exposed to a lot of disturbances by external factors such as natural events, social upheavals, and that sort of thing. But there is one force inherent in the economic process which will cause it to progress or advance in wavelike fashion. This fact can be easily verified. Only imagine what economic progress consists in. Take, for instance, the railroadization of the Middle West as it was initiated by the Illinois Central. While a new thing is being built and financed, expenditure is on a supernormal level, and through a normal state of incomes we get all those symptoms which we associate with prosperity. When such a period of advance has gone on for a time, two phenomena are sure to produce themselves. On the one hand, we have the fact that the products of these new constructions, of these new methods, begin to pour out and these products compete with the products of the old methods. In fact, that's the way in which progress is accomplished in capitalism and the old eliminated. For instance, it is easy to see that the Illinois Central not only meant very good business whilst it was built and whilst new cities were built around it and land was cultivated, but it spelled the death sentence for the agriculture of the West. This is one example, but you will generalize this example readily. So we have progress bunching together in periods which we call prosperity and accounting for the speculative ardors, while when the harvest time comes, paradoxically enough, we find dislodgement of the whole structure, hence bankruptcies, recession, the business world is in the dumps.

This process so far is by no means pathological. It is a physiological process, to use the terminology of a more exact science, for reasons easy to realize always coming in ridges being followed by an absorption of these new things and exerting in the apparatus a process which goes along with falling prices, shrinking credit, unemployment, pains, and fears.

I have two more points to add and then we shall be out of the theory of business cycles which we have introduced in a sketchy form here. The one point is this: Though this process is not pathological but physical, certain pathological processes are sure to attend both the prosperity and the recession. These pathological processes consist mainly in prosperity of the fact that when everyone observes value and profits to increase, he is likely more or less to project this rate of increase into the future and to enter into commitments which will turn out to be ill-conceived and untenable as soon as that rate of increase is interrupted. So though it is not logically necessary that there should be any excesses or any swindles in prosperity, both are likely to happen in the atmosphere which is characteristic of prosperity. On the other hand, in recession it has the tendency of accelerating the recession process very much, that is to say, the bankruptcies and losses are accelerated by the fact that anything which is ill-conceived or fraudulent comes down with a crash. Instead of settling down to a new equilibrium, the system outruns it, that is, a system of ill-conceived and bad finances causes a situation in which other people's situations become endangered. You can visualize the processes by the stock market. For a time prices fall because they have fallen. The vicious spiral develops in an understandable way. This pathological process, which produces depression as distinguished from recession, is not inherent in the mechanism I have been trying to describe, but it is a thing which happens very easily and, as a matter of fact, always did happen as we can see if we look back into the history of business cycles. Observe also that the essential process is not at all catastrophic. If I could discuss past crises in this country, we would agree that the worst features of this process are not due to the normal working of the evolutionary mechanism but due to the fact that the excesses of speculation and loose banking methods make the thing much worse than it otherwise would be.

The second point is that these ups and downs are of various sorts. There are short ones; for instance, one statistical wave has an amplitude of forty months. There are medium-sized ones of from nine to ten years. There are longer ones, among them one which is very well marked and one which I call the Kondratieff cycle in honor of the Russian student who first satisfactorily distinguished that cycle. We have very few Kondratieff cycles, but it has an amplitude of roughly fifty-five years. The interesting thing about this cycle is that historians have always known it. They talk about the Industrial Revolution which was the prosperity phase of such a cycle. Around the middle of the nineteenth century another such cycles arises, the cycle of steam and steel. A third cycle arises, the cycle of electricity. In the data of the pre-existing business organism the adaptation is a long and painful process. The downswings of these cycles are always indicated and studded by a long depression. There was one in the 1820s exactly where it ought to be. There was another from 1873 to 1878, and another similar to the other two starting in 1929 and reaching the bottom in August, 1932.

This shows, though I feel very guilty for having so superficially dealt with such a problem, that the crisis was not unprecedented. Although sufferings were probably greater in 1873–1878, the agrarian sector was relatively much greater and the family tie was stronger then. The unemployed who had nothing to eat could take refuge in some family and was taken care of. It was one of the signs of decay of our society that this would not be possible any more. So the suffer-

ings were not so much bemoaned but they were not less intense.
There was nothing unprecedented in this breakdown in 1929–1932.
In fact, it was almost an exact duplication of what happened in 1873,
including the building boom and speculative mania and so on, however we may lament the occurrence of such phenomena. The crisis
was not a symptom of the breakdown of the system nor a sign of its
decreasing vitality. On the contrary, if this theory of prosperity and
depression which I have just outlined has anything to it, the intensity
of the depression will be in some way proportional to the intensity of
the preceding progress. Hence, if the violent downswing proves anything, it is that the progress was much more than the system can
stand. That isn't a sign of decay.

I have to add, however, that in the breakdown there was promise
of a harvest. For what is a breakdown? It means an elimination of
what is not able to live and hang on. It is a spring cleaning, going on
ruthlessly, ruining much, and which could live on indefinitely but for
the price and credit structure. But it is a spring cleaning, and after
such a cleaning we always observe a new avalanche of consumer's
goods. Even during the 1930s we observed some symptoms of that.
For instance, we observe a greatly increased product per man hour,
wrongly called the productivity of labor, which is a symptom of technical, organizational, commercial, and so on, progress; and the fact
that later it is quite possible to provide a larger supply of consumer's
goods to the society at large is partly a result not only of what had
been done in the past upswings in the 1920s but also of the ruthless-
ness of the spring cleaning that brushed away so much dead wood.
Capitalism is not gentle to the capitalist. Those who went down naturally don't like to tell themselves that, and hence the ideology growing around the phenomenon has taken pains to obliterate that element in the situation and put a more popular interpretation on it.

Having said all these unpopular things, I must go one step further
in unpopularity. It has become an etiquette in America to speak of
the events of the depression in superlatives. Whoever does not express horror at what happened in those years is branded as callous—
choose whatever epithet you have at your command. However, it is
important for our purpose to remind you that it is very necessary to
reduce our ideas about what happened to reasonable proportions. To
begin with, nothing very catastrophic happened in the economic organization until the spring of 1931 except the breakdown of the stock
exchange in 1929, which I personally have never been able to waste
any tears over. It was for moral reasons a most sanitary thing. Nothing happened in the economic organization, as I say, until the spring

of 1931 which can really be called catastrophic. Then the landslide
set in and hit bottom in August, 1932, after which reaction set in.
This recovery was, however, cut short and temporarily interrupted
by an event which was not of the essence of the process, the third
banking epidemic which started in October, 1932, and sent figures
down to new lows.

This is the picture. It is not the picture of an unprecedented catastrophe nor a symptom of decreased vitality of the system. I am, of
course, making now a definite point which in itself won't prevent any
indictment which you may be pleased to level at the capitalist system
as such. Call it a monster, if you please, but the monster is not dead
nor did it show by the breakdown any decrease in vitality.

In this country the breakdown was worse than in Europe. The reasons for this were, first, the speculative excesses which went before.
These greatly added to the failures which added to the downward
cumulative process. Second, the conditions in the agricultural sectors
in the United States were very unfortunate and added to the depression more so than in Europe. Third, there was the weakness of the
American banking system, by far the weakest in the world. Everywhere else the field bank has developed, which is almost insensitive
to depression; it takes a war to bring down the banks of Europe. In
America the banking system is framed by somewhat irrational ideas
about monopoly, trusts, credit, and so forth. Many small and independent banks were allowed to grow without any control. This being
so, we find the banking structure extremely sensitive to the impact of
a crisis and it is no wonder that these banks died in shoals. That was
an important element. Then there was a further reason and that was
the managing policy of the Federal Reserve system. The Federal Reserve system, following the call of business opportunity, in 1922 set
about the task of regulating the pulse of business, in particular preventing downswings. In fact it had some measure of success. Small
downswings were nipped in the bud; but adjustments were prevented, and when the great spring cleaning came, many more adjustments had to be made.

That big crisis, like any big crisis that lasts over a period of years,
has been made worse by accidents and incidents. This was no exception. In Europe, in particular, the peace treaties set up new frontiers
that had ignored old economic structures and had set up new ones
that were unstable. The growth of capitalist industries in the tropics
made European industries, particularly in England, more delicate.
When the depression came about, the effects were worse than they
otherwise would have been. The old capitalist institutions would have

had this depression sooner or later, but they wouldn't have met it so quickly and they would have adapted themselves to it. The situation was much worse, especially in England, due to the fact that the Indian cotton textile industry exerted its influence when the situation was worst and ruined the Lancashire market in England. In such a situation, long-run loans will stop and short-run balances will try to run home for cover. Even if successful, they will break down the structure which they used to support. The newly created gold clause also made things worse than they need have been. They made them worse as long as they lasted and made them worse when they broke down. Moreover, the commercial policies of the time have often been blamed for making things worse. In the middle of the depression this country introduced the Hawley-Smoot tariff. Think of the argument of America's refusal to accept her position as a creditor nation. I don't know whether too much has been made of this point. I must mention that this element has, as far as the immediate consequences for the depression are concerned, been somewhat overstressed.

But such accidents and incidents, mitigating or accelerating prosperities as well as depressions, had always attended the career of capitalism. There was nothing new in that any more than there was in the occurrence of the depression itself. What was new was the spirit in which it was met. The indictments against circumstances, groups, and individuals, remedial and punitive legislation are a general phenomenon that always presented itself, that we observe, for instance, after the South Sea Bubble in 1720. That is old stuff and perhaps does not matter very much. That is not the point, but in this case indictment was directed not against persons, groups, and circumstances but against the system itself. Private management of industry and credit was what seemed to stand condemned. It had stood condemned and prospered before, but now this spirit spread far beyond the circle of professional critics of capitalist society. Capitalism stood condemned to a point where it was hardly possible to present to any audience in 1933 a dispassionate view of events. I am a lover of observations and reactions. I very often tried the experiment and saw the reactions. The reactions were purely emotional; there was an attitude of moral indictment. There was no inclination to look at the case by an analysis of facts. In fact, anything that did not end in a condemnation of the system was out of court when the New Deal came. I am not criticizing this frame of mind of the American people and many other people; I am only drawing your attention to it. That did not happen when everything came down around people's ears in 1873. That was a sign that political beliefs and positions had been shaken. That was a sign that, just as the war had not created but accelerated many things, so the crisis had accelerated many things and eliminated resistances.

Those associated with the management of big industry understood that perfectly well. They reacted in a way that showed that they had lost their nerve. From government investigations it is clear that none of the people examined ever put his foot or his fist down. They all acted as if they had something terrible to hide. As a matter of fact, there wasn't anything very bad to be hidden. It was astonishing how few damaging facts were brought out by commissions which were firmly resolved to bring out as much as possible. And the intellectuals veered around to what they believed to be the rising sun. Definitely the intellectual interest went into the camp of social reconstruction. They had never done that before. The intellectual of the modern type emerged in the tenth century. In the sixteenth century Charles V, though he was a devoted husband, [lived the life of a gentleman]. But the world and his empress need never know provided he hand over grants of sufficient weight and number to the great critic of morals that was Pietro Aretino. But the bourgeois class was diverted by the majority of intellectuals only in our own time. In the farmer's attitudes, the intellectual's, the professional man's attitude, and even the attitude of many businessmen, though very different from each other, we have moral disruption; and economic common sense was put [out] of operation for the time. Bewildered by events they could not understand and dreaded, even sensible people believed the wildest schemes.

Inflationism is an instance. There was breakdown, there was moral disruption, and there was disorientation. That was the best atmosphere for new doctrines to arise in. You know that the dictatorial powers arose anew. But I must not be understood to mean that such a phenomenon as the rise of Hitlerism to power can ever be accounted for by preventing unemployment and people being out of temper, nor by a wider set of economic conditions. It goes much beyond that, and I have tried to show you in the first lecture that the roots of such a new religion go far back into the nineteenth century. However, it is helped both by the war and the depression, eating away the structure that they would have had to cut through otherwise, weakening the morals which would have resisted. However, it is more than ever necessary to keep in mind what is one of the fundamental principles of my exposition, to distinguish between causal factors and favoring circumstances.

## IV. Investment, Unemployment, and Planning during the Thirties

Tonight, ladies and gentlemen, we have got to look at the economic process of the 1930s.[6] The relevance of this for our subject, the analysis of the spirit of our time, will be obvious in a moment.

Everyone agrees, of course, that economic developments in the 1930s were unsatisfactory, but we have first to define in what sense they were, how far they were, and what there is really to explain. Things were not unsatisfactory, for instance, in Japan. On the contrary, Japan enjoyed through the greater part of the period a development of unheard of intensity at soaring rates of increase. Only slightly less was the increase of industrial production and employment in Germany. In fact, the unemployment problem disappeared in Germany completely by 1935. Nor did England do so badly. English economists have complained quite a lot about the social situation during the years of the world depression, but after all, the whole world subsidized England by means of furnishing her with cheap raw materials, and in 1932 a building boom started. It could not have been such a terrible depression if a building boom can start. So we can take it that at that time the worst was over and from August, 1932, on, England enjoyed increases in all the rates which economists take as symptomatic of the state of the economic system.

I have excluded Russia in these lectures for the very good reason that I don't know very much about it. When we speak, therefore, about an economically unsatisfactory performance, we are reduced to France and this country. Even in the United States the problem scales down considerably when we look closely at it. In August, 1932, the bottom of the depression was reached, but after so severe a depression of the kind that occurs in capitalist society about once in every fifty to sixty years we must expect a few years to elapse in order to get back to average rates of advance. In the particular case under discussion there was, moreover, the fact that the banking epidemic, which was the third one which started in October, 1932, did very much to retard the process of recovery. The reasons for this banking epidemic I looked at for a few minutes last time. It broke morale and made recovery much more difficult and time-consuming than it otherwise would have been.

There is another thing. If we compare the situation in this country with the comparable situation in the 1870s, we find a difference concerning the agricultural sector. The agricultural sector suffered in the current case and constituted a source of difficulties all along, whilst in the 1870s it was just the reverse. In fact, it would not be absurd to say that in the 1870s it was agriculture that pulled the economic organism out of the dumps of the depression. In 1878, for instance, a good crop in this country coinciding with a bad crop in Europe brought a lot of money to the agricultural sectors in this country, which did not happen in the 1930s.

When we consider that after a breakdown such as we had in the 1930s it takes time to get on one's feet again, we will not wonder at the first years after the depression and what we see there. The comparison with the 1870s is indeed unfavorable. In the 1870s we have the crisis in 1873, and deep depression in 1874 and 1875 for almost three years. It is quite an open question whether the depression wasn't worse than the one at the beginning of the 1930s because we were in such a good position to measure it owing to the progress in statistical information. By 1876 manufacturing output—[even if] the index is not very reliable at that time—had already reached record highs. Although at still falling prices, the economic organism was working as it never had before. Eighteen seventy-eight saw intensified prosperity which then went on in 1879, 1880, and 1881, when the thing turned down due to the crisis in the early 1880s. Eighteen seventy-six is comparable to 1933 and in 1933 the index of manufacturing output, 1923–1925 = 100, which was 127.7 in 1929, was still down that much, and during the rest of the 1930s until the beginning of the present war boom total output indices have remained under the 1929 level. Employment was just about at the level of 1929. It boils down to the fact that the upswing that set in in 1935 was out and was soon to be interrupted by the depression that set in in the last quarter of 1937, and the rest of the decrease was much faster than anything that had been witnessed in 1931. This is what we have to explain.

The explanation that has been offered by all sorts of sources and that has been accepted by economists of very high standing is that this depression and unsatisfactory recovery was not due to the unfavorable circumstances of the particular case but had a deeper meaning. It was held to be a symptom that paralysis was slowly creeping upon the economic system of capitalism and that the depressive conditions of capitalism had come to stay; and since capitalism is a state of evolution and capitalism always involves new net investment, we may just as well put the theory in the form of decreasing investment opportunity. That was held to be the matter—not, to repeat, a setback that would be a thing of the past in a few years, but an organism which could not be expected to function again. In many cases this theory, of course, was the daughter of the wish, but in other cases it was sincerely held on the basis of the facts observed by the authority.

Why should paralysis be creeping over capitalist evolution? Why should so short a period, which in itself is a few years and is not enough to establish reliable trends, have given rise to a theory of permanent relative decay? The other side of it is that government expenditure was a necessary means to keep the faltering economic apparatus going. What were the reasons which induced some of our best economists that this would be a permanent state of semi-depression? There are mainly three of them. The first was that the increase in population which offered in past periods so strong a stimulus to economic activity and investment was slackening down. We shall speak about this next week. But the increasing decrease in population as was observed in the 1930s was not a good candidate for the role it was intended for. No doubt a decreasing rate of population and its effect on economic motivations may at some future time produce a slackening of economic effort, of the rate or the pace of advance. But certainly it cannot have done so in the last decade because population, as a matter of fact, did increase considerably, though only about one-half as much as in the 1920s, and because an effect on motivation is a long-run effect. We are now only ten years from the most violent depression we have ever experienced, and economic motivation cannot be explained in such a short period; hence we cannot use this element in the explanation of the economic process of the 1930s.

Second, it was held that in the modern world there are no more new countries to capitalize, to develop. In this country, in particular, much was made of the fact that the frontier was gone that took away so much of the social tension that developed. But the frontier of the capitalist world does not exist anymore. Even if this were true, we must not forget that the economic frontier that may be conquered does not necessarily carry a geographical connotation. The conquest of the air may have greater economic consequences than the conquest of India. We must not interpret the word "frontier" literally, that is, in the geographical sense.

Third, it was said that the economic frontier was narrowing because there were no great new things in prospect such as the railroadization and electrification of the world. In a sense that is quite true, only those who stress this fact overlook that at junctures such as the 1930s it isn't great new possibilities that usually appear. Take, for instance, the comparable period of the 1870s. The railroad locomotive and the steel rail had been invested, and it may well have looked as if there was nothing more to do for capitalist enterprise. As a matter of fact, economists, who seem to have a propensity to compromise themselves, said that capitalism had done its work. No less a personage than John Stuart Mill said so in so many words. He said the task is done, possibilities have been exhausted, and it is time for radical policies, just about the same attitude which we observe in our own day. It was the same in the 1830s, another comparable period. Nothing new emerged in the 1820s and 1830s which promised business. In those periods of adaptation, absorption, development, just as in the 1870s and 1880s it was the railroads, now it is the electrification of the farm and home, and the airplane. During such times as these new things are not very much in evidence, if we may trust historical analysis. But it is said, "What is in process is not very capital consuming and therefore does not offer great opportunities for investment, and it is investment that by increasing expenditure and total incomes produces those symptoms which we associate with prosperity." That may well be, so that in the future new things will be capital saving rather than capital consuming only it's just as well to wait for it. It would not be safe to prognosticate that.

When we look at the 1930s and find in this country that new investment was not satisfactory, we must not forget that investment had been at an abnormally high level in the 1920s and that takes a lot of absorbing. This is true of investment in the financial sense as well as in the real sense. So whatever we may find unsatisfactory in the economic process of the 1930s is not satisfactorily explained by this particular theory. I want to emphasize again that the argument this theory is based upon may turn out to be true at some future time; what I'm holding now is that that cannot satisfactorily explain whatever is unsatisfactory in the 1930s.

Then what is the explanation? In order to develop what I think to be the true explanation, I have to review a part of what I told you in the first of these lectures. In the preceding lecture we saw that the Great Depression was not just a depression but a depression that happened to impinge on a social system that was tottering independently of it. In the lecture before that we saw that the World War impinged on a social system that was being undermined, and in the first lecture I tried to give the background for what I'm trying to work out in this course. In the first lecture I invited you to put yourselves anywhere from a standpoint of 1871 to 1914, and I invited you to look at the social structure—political, economic, and cultural. Look at the world of the businessman, the world of the bourgeois, with its ideas of free trade, capitalism, and all that sort of thing. I think we discovered also that that system of economic endeavor, that political structure based upon it, hence also the cultural system was inherently unstable; and I want now to report the exact reasons that prompted that diagnosis.

These depressions, though they point to an instability in another sense, need not point to an instability in the social sense. I did not mean instability in the Marxian sense; I did not mean the capitalist system was working itself to death by increasing exploitation. The facts don't justify that. I gave you a formula which was that the capitalist process by its own working produces a political atmosphere hostile to itself. The capitalist evolution first rationalizes the economic process. It supercedes less efficient technologies by increasingly more efficient technologies and more organization. The largest scale unit of control is the consequence, and the largest scale unit of control tends to develop into something akin to a department of state, that is to say, it becomes bureaucratized and mechanized and the individual in that kind of a world counts for less than before. There was a time when the personality of the leader was felt on the battlefield. In Napoleonic times every soldier felt whether Napoleon was there or not; the same applies to Wellington and also to Archduke Charles who led his troops in the Battle of Aspern. The individual who is at the head of an army today is a bureaucratic, specialized worker, so weight does not attach itself anymore to that function. The modern general would be spending his time very badly if he made himself conspicuous on a hill of the battlefield. Nothing is accomplished by that, but since nothing is accomplished by the action of a personality on other psyches, the modern general is not a danger anymore. Dictators can send out generals who are more or less successful, but they are not competitive. I will not translate my military analogy into economics, but it is the same. I made the analogy because a friend or two of mine pointed out to me that this point was not sufficiently brought out in the first lecture.

Apart from considerations of their efficiency as compared with large firms, ten thousand small steel firms made quite a political force and a political lobby. Five big firms are at the mercy of the humors of democracy. That's one thing. Another thing, five big firms could be easily socialized by [an] act of Congress. Second, capitalism not only rationalizes things in the industrial structure but also rationalizes souls. What are we acting by? What moves us? What keeps us up? Rational considerations? No, humanity is kept in its ways by traditions, beliefs, religious beliefs, by such things as honor and beauty. These things rationalize wonders. Now, for instance, and we are not at the end of this process, the average workman would not believe you if you told him that his true reward was a satisfaction of employment, loyalty to the firm, and so on. Yet these are the things that keep society together; that also has much to do with the disintegration of the family.

But there is another thing. Formerly when people were dissatisfied with a pope or a king, they would revolt against the particular pope or king but they took the institution for granted. Now we ask ourselves, "Why should there be such things as popes or kings?" The bourgeois asked this question. It did not strike him that the same question would be answered unfavorably to the capitalist; but if he had asked the popes and kings from their standpoint, they would have thought it an eminently rational arrangement that there would be popes and kings. Putting their hands behind the picture to feel whether the perspective is real or whether it is only a picture [which] goes farther and farther, the intellectuals of today are in some particularly high-minded way committing hari-kari. I have heard it from a sociologist and a Jew that freedom and class interest was an interest of intellectuals. It seems to me that this kind of analysis, this kind of opposition of principle against belief, is doing its work and a culture that does that is unstable. That's the second point.

The third point is bourgeois society is like a Gothic cathedral in one respect. I don't know how many of you have seen the cathedrals of the Ile de France with their flying buttresses—this incredible idea of a structure soaring up to the throne of God. All right, but such a structure can't stand on its own feet. That structure is kept up from the outside by flying buttresses. What are the flying buttresses of bourgeois society? The small tradesmen, small proprietors. Those small tradesmen are likely to vote for the capitalist system but they are being eliminated by the working of the machine.

Another thing is that the structure had in it a girder of noncapitalist material. The bourgeois can't rule, he can't lead. The business office does not make a success of a man in leadership. In private life the most eminent technicians and financiers, when they go home, put on their evening clothes, and go into their wives' drawing rooms, may not be able to say boo to a goose. It was the semi-aristocratic society of England that reared the society but not the bourgeois, and so on. You might say this is an exception. Exceptional about this are only the favorable circumstances incident to the explanation which did not allow these problems to adjust themselves. So this country went on without any ruling class, without such girders, so when the problem arose during the Civil War, the result was a catastrophe which was all out of proportion to the problem at stake.

Fourth, by raising standards, by living up to your own program, spreading propaganda about equality, the bourgeois raises a class of intellectuals, produces the rope which is going to hang it. This point is clear; I will leave the application to you. It is the attitude of European countries to their colonies. These colonies have been won by sword and brawn. When they were conquered, the nations educated those people, guided them in self-government, told them they were as good as anyone else, and then were astonished that people who have been told so for a hundred years believe it. It happened in the Dutch East Indies, in Egypt, in India. It is naive to wonder about this.

These four reasons account for the political, economic, and sociological instability of capitalism. What I find wrong in the theories that predict an end of the system and failure is that these theories are based on imperfect performance, while it is the success of capitalism that kills it. Here I am at the explanation of the economic process of the 1930s. What happened is this. All that I have explained to you was well under way in 1914. In Europe the war and in this country the depression accelerated it and removed the pegs and girders. This country, as other countries had before, faced a complete rift between its business and political sectors. This explains the hostility of the administration and legislative attitude toward business, and this attitude explains why business does not function as well as it could. The situation, then, in 1932–1933 was this. Of all the countries, America was the only country that was left and America had failed. We have this reduction of the prestige of the businessmen in this country just as we observe in France of the eighteenth century after the battle of Rossbach. French society of that time existed on the basis of its military glory and leadership as the glory of America's society rests upon its business leadership. That society, as this one, also was being decayed anyway. We have complete disorganization in 1933, a complete disbelief in standards, a disbelief both in the old social relationships and in the new ones; there was a moral rift.

This crystallized in legislation which may be classed under two heads. First, taxation, which in itself would be sufficient to account for decreasing investment opportunity, for whether there is no opportunity to make money or if you do make money it is taken away, comes to the same thing from the standpoint of business decision. Second, labor policies explain partly the existing unemployment and the inability of the system to absorb the unemployment of the crisis. This is an intricate subject from the standpoint of analysis. That a tendency to push up wage rates pushes up unemployment is not self-evident. It's a much more complex argument, which I couldn't think of presenting in a few minutes, which leads to the result that the wage policy has anything to do with the failure of the system to absorb the unemployment. Third, we may take all those policies under one head which in one way or another contributed to make the businessman more scared than he was before, all those measures that attacked business management. By saying this I don't mean to pronounce any opinion about the merits or the demerits of these policies. I am only trying to explain these policies and explain by them what seems unsatisfactory in the performance of the 1930s. From other standpoints these policies may be well worth the cost for what they give in economic and moral values to the masses.

Having done with this, I want to point out in verification that the only other country which was similar financially is the only other country which was similar politically. In France we find, before and after the Popular Front got into official power, the same kind of spirit and the same kind of consequences. According to all the rules of scientific inference, we should reach the diagnosis by merely looking at the facts. Popular slogans cannot be supported one hundred percent, and simplicity makes this a fact because economic life is not simple. But there is a deep truth in that slogan, although it should be observed that in the class struggles that were waged in this country there was a class interest at stake. There was the intellectual wanting to be a government servant; there was a class interest of the labor group; [and] definite economic industries being aimed at by force and economic warfare. But that is only one side of the question. Behind these economic individual aims there was a moral rift in the nation. It was two cultural worlds fighting, none of which could get the better for the time being, each of which was able to checkmate and thwart the other. General demolition of the community was the consequence.

It is natural in such a situation to try to find new ways and to try to build bridges over the rift. Planning suggests itself as a sort of compromise. What is planning? It is the replacement of the entrepreneurial decisions of how, what, and how much to produce by the decision of some other social organism. This kind of planning has assumed different forms in different countries according to the situation of those countries and the character of the different nations. It is different in England from what it is in Germany. In this country no definite line has been embarked upon, but if the N.R.A. legislation had remained, of course, it would have been a step toward the cooperative state. It would have been integrated not with Italian but with American traces—but the principle of the cooperative state would have been present here as much as in Italy. From the quick disappearance of this type of social contract, we may infer that it was not congenial to the ground, but while it lasted it was a step in the direction in which all nations, each in its own way, are moving.

Whether you say it is something else, or that it is the kind of socialism that is paradoxical, or whether you say it is the answer to Marx's prayer, it is clear that out of the moral chaos based upon the social and economic chaos of our time, constructions will arise which will answer to certain characteristics. If we assume that they will all emphasize more or less national points of view, the similarities of the contour lines looming in the future become still more impressive. Now I have touched a point where every healthy person is inclined to ask what should be done about it. That is not the purpose of pure scientific analysis. That is up to your own practical, spiritual evaluations. What I have told you today rests broadly on facts, but all the trends I have been talking about refer to comparatively short times, times shorter than the times trends take to establish themselves. So in these things perhaps analytical discretion is the better part of analytical valor.

## V. The Role of Fiscal and Monetary Policies

Ladies and gentlemen, you all have become familiar, more or less, during the last eight years with that controversy on fiscal and monetary policies that has occupied the energies of so many people.[7] This controversy, in which it isn't quite easy to find one's way, naturally deals with the immediate consequences of the particular measures that come under those headings. It is not from that standpoint that the subject turns up in our course. For us, though we must of course touch upon the immediate economic consequences, it is another angle that matters. Fiscal and monetary policies are for us mainly interesting as symptoms or as factors in that process of social transformation, in that analysis of the spirit of our time which is the subject of this course.

Let me explain; but before I explain, let me tell you that our judgment about the economic consequences of any or all of these measures is quite secondary, hence still more so is what we feel about them. The way in which a state raises and spends its revenue is one of the most important facts about that state. The budget connects everything that a nation is, does, and intends. Every national volition reflects itself in the budget, the national character, and the national past. It has been well said that the budget is the skeleton stripped of all illusory slogans and phrases of society. You could reconstruct, if you fully realized what it means, the structure and the tendencies of change of a society from the budget figures alone. For instance, the cheap state of the liberal period of the nineteenth century, because it was cheap, reflected moderate taxation and therefore a certain disposition of political power. Because it was cheap, it was also peaceful, for cheapness among other things means little expenditure on armaments. And perhaps I need not state that we could from the fiscal policies of the state not only reconstruct who rules the state, what mentality prevails in that state, but also what the state does and is going to do.

Again, the monetary circumstances and the attitude toward money and toward credit and banking are highly characteristic of bourgeois society. The sanctity of the contract in terms of money, the mechanism of the money market, and the structure of the rates of interest, the movement of the funds within and without a country—all these things are, of course, in the first instance a technical matter, and in a sense some older economists have been right in calling it the veil, the outside form, of the economic process. But they are much more than that. In the attitudes of people to money and the monetary process is reflected an attitude toward a significant social and economic organism, a certain type of morals, a certain outlook of life, a certain set of ideals—all that again you could infer from the way in which a nation handles its money, and from these aspects the subject comes into our precincts.

Well, let me begin, first as to fiscal policies and mainly as to taxation. We will then speak about the attitudes toward money, credit and banking, and finally, third, touch the problems of pump priming and of government deficit expenditure as an institution. Well, about taxation, taxation in the modern sense was born with capitalism. It is a denizen of the capitalist world, and that's quite easy to understand. Naturally, a society that leaves the economic care to the activity and responsibility of the individual presents a picture of people earning money for themselves or the purposes they set for themselves, though they may be altruistic ones. In such a society the state has really no source of livelihood of its own. It was different in the feudal state. The feudal state lived on the income, the feudal income, of its prince. The enemies of that state were—you will observe that with the English conservatism that phrase has still been retained—"the king's enemies." The expenditure of the state was the king's expenditure and if he couldn't make both ends meet, he had to ask his estates for more funds.

The capitalist state has still, and even had in its heyday, a number of functions which cost a lot of money, and to cover these there was the institution of taxation. Since the sources of means on which these taxes were laid all flowed for other purposes, since the sums that the state took for its own purposes were really earned for other purposes, it follows that in capitalist society, if it is at all to function according to design, all taxes can be only moderate with the consequence that the sum total of public revenue can only be moderate. For when you outstep moderate limits, you will interfere with those modes and arrangements by which the sums to be taxed are made. This was recognized in the nineteenth century; minimum taxation was an idea approved by everyone.

This social system, of course, takes it for granted that all these private earnings are all right. It puts social approval, within certain limits set by morals and by law, on the hunt for profits, on the earnings of the businessmen, on inheritance and saving. All these things were in themselves virtues, they were in themselves approved, and being approved, taxation was a necessary evil, an evil that had to be minimized. It was different in the nineteenth century from the state of mercantilist times, the time of Louis Quatorze, for instance, when the income of the king had to be maximized. This capitalist state with its moderate taxation commanded the moral approval of the majority of the population. It left cultural things to the individual; art was to be admired but was to be left with the private orders. The private firm and the private family home were based on these ideas, just as they produced these ideas. This attitude began to change very soon after the turn of the century. In England it is easy to see the cleavage. It came when, after the victory under Sir Henry Campbell-Bannerman, the taxes imposed during the war were not wholly repealed but were kept for social purposes, mainly for social insurance. The new policy was accelerated by Lloyd George's budget, so things were changing then. They would have gone on changing slowly, but, as we have seen, the war accelerated these changes in such a way as to cause serious economic dislocations. But in this country it was merely an intermezzo, and a return to old principles was observable in the 1920s, and from the standpoint of classical fiscal policies the secretaries of the Treasury of that time are entitled to the credit that it was a fine piece of financial steering.

But this altered abruptly in 1933, and because the transition was so abrupt and because people did not become accustomed to it, we see the effects clearly here. So it is enough to confine ourselves to the experience of this country. What are the facts? First, taxation is very high. This by itself would, however, not necessarily cause economic and social disturbances because a considerable revenue could be raised in this country by methods which do not substantially interfere with economic processes. But, secondly, this taxation was made sharply progressive not only by law but also by a change in the practice and spirit of the administration which made the laws very much more effective than they had been. Third, this taxation, this progressive taxation, showed a tendency to discriminate against savings and against inheritances, showing that it didn't see any social function in the latter or economic function in the former. On the contrary, it was a slogan of the 1930s that saving was a nonsense, creating disturbances and also injurious to the operation of the economic apparatus. Finally, we see the tendency that taxation was not so much raised for revenues. As a matter of fact, in time of deficit spending revenue was a by-product which people didn't like very much. It was mainly raised as a measure of redistribution. It was meant to change the functioning of the capitalist apparatus. In this taxation the main thing that interests us is the moral disapproval of high incomes, of capitalist profit making which it displayed whilst at the same time risky business was still based upon the profit motive.

Now let us quickly go over all the main points. The first is the least important point for the subject of the course, the immediate economic consequences. These immediate economic consequences may be described with some lack of elegance as putting a spoke into the wheels of the capitalist machine. The spoke consists, on the one hand, in an interference with capital formation, and on the other hand, in a disturbance of the allocation of resources. Let me quickly explain what I mean. The private profit mechanism will so work that more risky investments are, in case of success, attended with super-normal premia. For instance, in the year 1907 to build a huge automobile works for the production of a thing called the Model T, when nobody knew whether it would catch on or not, was a tremendous risk. The thing succeeded, and a great premium was the result. If such premia are confiscated, this means differentiating against risky investment. By and large the risky investment is investment for a new and untried purpose. It is not risky, and as a rule not profitable, to invest in something that is familiar, known by everyone, and which can be just administered. It is risky, but in case of success profitable, to start new commodities, new commercial ventures which have not yet been tried and which are an improvement on a previously existing method. Hence it follows that when you tax the cases of success to a very significant extent, this amounts to confiscation of a moderate maximum, you will find that the machine works with greater friction. Ladies and gentlemen, don't say the speaker is a reactionary or an economic royalist. I don't want to be misunderstood. I am speaking from the standpoint of a social apparatus which is eminently logical. No society can long survive that doesn't deliver the promises it holds out. This being so, this taxation is a serious spoke in the wheel.

As I said last time, the decreasing investment opportunity may have been based on this fact of taxation. This taxation may well substitute the nonexisting tendency to decrease of investment opportunity even though it may be contrary to the public will. But even if you accept the theory of decreasing investment opportunity, you must also accept my thesis that taxation was a serious obstacle to the satisfactory working of the capitalist apparatus, for the theory of decreasing investment opportunity holds that the system doesn't function if the profit margins are too small. It holds that the profit margins are too small, but it is quite immaterial in this respect whether the profit margins are too small or whether they are made so by the confiscation of the surplus gains that might be made.

But for us the point that is perhaps most interesting is the differentiation, as I have called it, the discrimination against saving. For saving, with the contingent event of leaving what you save to your children, is an element of bourgeois society. The saving-investment process is the economic basis of bourgeois evolution; it's democracy, it's what equals all we mean by the liberal bourgeois society of the nineteenth century. This taxation differentiates against savings in an economic society thinking saving injurious in various ways. The short-lived tax on undivided profits was only one example. That tax was only part of a systematic policy. For the high inheritance and progressive income taxes, in a society as energetic as ours is, means differentiation against savings because it is the incomes from which most is saved which are particularly hit by them.

Then we have the fact that there is a kind of double taxation involved whenever the saved amount is included in an income that is being saved. This has been the subject of a controversy which I can't go into here. The meaning of income is that you can satisfy your wants by spending it, that if you save it you don't satisfy wants although saving later yields returns which may then be spent to satisfy wants. By double taxation of saving I don't associate myself with other meanings that have been given to that term. For us the important thing is the symptomatic failure of this taxation. Bourgeois evaluations, tendencies, and principles being different, this kind of taxation is a proof positive, much clearer than anything else could be, of the changing spirit of the times, of a changed schema of values, of a changing moral code. Everything else can be the voice of the politician and can be so much gas, but the tax of a tax bill and the way it is administered is a hard fact. And just as you can take from the budget of a country whether it is pacific or warlike, so you can take from the budget of a country what its valuations are. You can infer them, and in this case you can infer that they are anti-capitalist. For instance, inheritance taxes which make it impossible for big fortunes to survive for a long time.

The anti-capitalist spirit is shame-faced in a sense; it is half-hearted, but at the same time it is there. Symptomatic also was the discussion that formed the opinion of this country. The discussion was carried on with a certain tactical care, but it put out all those arguments that would be adduced for a taxation which would be rational from the standpoint of a capitalist system, which of course is not a compliment to it. Such a policy has been put out of court by a discussion that it is established that big incomes ought to be taxed away, that saving is a nonsense, that there is not much to be lost by destroying those things by which capitalist advance has been financed. I am often astonished at the radical views of people who don't know how radical their views are. When a person is aware that he is being radical, you may say that he is professing radical views merely to show off, but when he doesn't know how radical he is, that shows his true soul.

You can also observe in this country that the way to a rational fiscal policy is barred. If today we had suddenly a capitalist-minded conservative government, it could here and there break off a point, release something that obviously destroys more than it helps anyone, but it couldn't give up the principle. It would be impossible, especially now when America is rapidly drawing toward the brink of the war, to introduce into the taxation system those principles that would be necessary in order to reveal rather disagreeable stains on the social fabric. For instance, first, to differentiate forced savings; to tax lightly or not at all the undivided profits of a corporation. What faces you would make if anyone proposed that, and yet I don't expect that this is the most radical audience that can be gathered together in the country. Everyone is quite convinced that to repeal a general sales tax would be a crime.

This is all said, not in a spirit of criticism; but it is said to sharpen your eyes to the symptoms of social change in that sphere, and the subject has come up again only because it is so characteristic of the changing spirit of the time. The attitude toward money and credit is of the greatest importance of bourgeois society. When I say that the principles agreeable to the law of life of that society have been given up, I mean these: first, the going off gold; second, the tendency toward the management of currency and credit by the government with a view to restoring the price level. This management found its explanation in various banking reforms, but it goes back to the Glass-Steagall Bill which permitted the Reserve Banks for a limited time to use government securities as collateral for Federal Reserve notes and under certain circumstances permitted Federal Reserve banks to make advances to member banks on its time or demand notes, which gives up a peg of that arrangement which is essential to the functioning of capitalist society. Then I mean the devaluation with the sterilization of gold, then the additions to our silver currency, the Thomas clause, the insurance of bank deposits, the reserve requirements, and finally the policy of cheap money which, together with high wages, was responsible for keeping unemployment alive.

I don't presume to judge ends. As an economist I am a technician, and I have only means. If anyone asked me how to keep alive the maximum of unemployment, I would say the best way is cheap money and a high wage policy. Perhaps I ought, at least, to sketch the argument which leads to that result, but it is fundamentally simple. The cheaper the money the cheaper the long-run machine production and the greater is the premium on avoiding the employment of labor. This sounds simple, but to defend it and to make it perfectly true is a delicate task into which we can't enter.

So we have a practically limitless expansion of the circulating medium, and it would be possible in this country to support a price level from four to five times as high as the present one. This had the consequence that the government is practically the owner of the monetary apparatus. The meaning has gone out of the old capitalist categories of borrowing and lending. The Treasury, it is true, still uses this phraseology. It borrows, for instance, but it is not a contract between two parties. It is merely a bookkeeping operation; and if there was nobody in this country except the Treasury officials, they could borrow in that sense just as well as they do now. The meaning of borrowing and the restrictions that such an arrangement is supposed to put on expenditures is entirely absent. It is a little past the hour to get excited about the proposal to nationalize the Federal Reserve banks. Whether or not they are nationalized means nothing at all just now. Similarly, it would make little difference whether we discarded the terms "borrowing" and "lending" and the shadow interest attached and simply commended the necessary means of payment.

How has this arisen? At first this monetary policy was nothing but a reaction to an emergency, intended to be temporary. This was accentuated in this country by the onslaught of inflationism. In spite of this, that might not have meant very much and those measures probably need not have been taken at all. There was also an inflationist onslaught in the 1870s, but in the 1930s the reaction was much greater than it could have been if the belief in capitalist arrangements had not been undermined before, as we have seen, and it came to be a permanent policy. And now it has developed in such a way that it would hardly be possible to reject it. I am often astonished by the fact that many otherwise excellent economists speak of a return to gold. It is meaningless in our time. It is meaningless to return to gold when nobody wants to play the gold game according to the gold rules. An economic currency with such limitless means will not necessarily lead to trouble and dire consequences. Again, economists have made too much of that from a technical standpoint. That depends on who handles that huge machine. There is no objection to forging a razor. What happens to it depends on the hands to which the razor is entrusted. The consequences of such a condition need not be injurious to the economic system.

However, it is interesting that the fact that such measures could be taken shows that all moral beliefs have gone out of capitalist life. If anyone at the time of going off gold had spoken of national honor, he would have been a laughing stock. The fact of England's going off gold and that she could do that sort of thing and nobody bemoaned it very much is of the highest symptomatic importance, whether it is good or bad. The availability of credit under these circumstances is entirely independent of either savers or banks. The government can buy of its own free will. It can regulate the monetary system, and if you regulate the monetary system of a society, you have regulated the society itself.

I will add that in most of the legislation in this country, although less than elsewhere, there was a strong nationalist element which links with the rising national religion which we observe all along. This was strong in England as it was in Germany. One of the arguments for leaving gold alone in England was that the gold standard had the disagreeable property of linking a nation's policies with those of another country. In short, gold is not popular because it ruthlessly and tactlessly always tells the truth. This being so, we have a piece of the history of our time enshrined in a little technical objection which by itself would not interest us so much. How it is that the spirit of a time, a great social process, mirrors itself in all these things is interesting to investigate because it is not always so. For instance, England after the World War tried to go back to gold. This we would consider there was not much sense in. Sometimes, however, the economic organism does show what is happening.

Finally, the pump priming expenditure. I'm afraid those economists have put their foot in it. They have entirely overlooked that an economic argument is one thing and a moral or political value is another thing. The readiness to let a budget run into a deficit in a depression by keeping up expenditures in the face of shrinking revenues is a policy which will alleviate much suffering and keep many things going which would otherwise crash. This is so and cannot be denied, and action along these lines has been taken consciously or unconsciously for more than a hundred years. In the depression of 1879 in Liverpool public works were proposed.

The interesting thing is not so much in the degree to which remedial effects can be attained in that way; the interesting fact is the spirit
in which the policy was entered in this country and the way in which
it was made permanent. I shall reserve and put aside the question,
for want of time, whether there is something in the ruthless principle
that the budget ought to be balanced under any circumstances. Action on that principle makes things worse in a depression, but who
knows whether the patient is not healthier when he gets along without it than with it. I don't want to discuss that. I want to discuss the
implications of the fact that that policy has come to stay. What's new
in the policy is the amount and the irresponsibility with which the
thing was handled. When that sort of thing is continued for four or
five years, the discontinuance of it is a process which, I am very much
afraid, bears some similarity to the treatment of a man who is given
to morphine. I have never, I am sorry to say, been a morphinist, and
I don't know what the experience is, but I am told it is unpleasant. So
when this country, having got its morphine for so long, was suddenly
left without it in 1937, we find a sharp collapse. Businessmen, standing on slippery ground, would perhaps have given all for the future
of the capitalist society. So the patient returned to his bad habits, and
we know that the bad habit will be too entrenched to be ever broken
off again. Moreover, interests have been brought up, people who are
profiting from it or living on it, which will never let it go. I should
like to see the political hero who can break that phalanx.

Now we come to the interpretation. This was not interpreted, especially after the first year, as a temporary measure. This is a theory
that has been argued by some economists and has now become the
official theory, so much so that it has even been carried into war expenditures where it defeats itself due to the reversed action of the
two hands.

Finally, fourth, the interesting thing about it is also the intention.
This kind of spending is so administered as to be incapable of effecting a capitalist recovery, for combined with a certain tax and certain
wage policies it will keep up the system, but it will never allow those
morals to grow which will make the system run again. So the same
policy which keeps up permanent spending, at the same time, sees to
it that the permanent spending will be permanently necessary unless
people are prepared to put up with a serious relapse. So what was,
no doubt, originally meant to be a temporary measure has become a
lever in the process of transforming society. The possibility of the
thing is a symptom of the process of transformation. The establishment of the thing will be a factor in the transformation, and naturally
in such a situation in which the state will always control the most im-

portant part of the total expenditure in the nation, this state will not only be master of the monetary quantities, it will be the master of the economic process in general. That is to say, the state will be the master—those who man it. It does not mean that the master is the nation.

## VI. The Falling Birth Rate

I have got the following letter:

> If possible this evening will you kindly comment on the following by Keynes: "The day is not far off when the economic problem will take the back seat, where it belongs, and the arena of the heart and head will be occupied or reoccupied by our real problems, the problems of life and human relations, of beliefs. . . ." From an economist isn't that pretty emotional?

I dare say it is, but there is something to it.[8] However, if the writer of this letter will excuse me, I would like to comment on this. Whatever we may think of the utterances of this economist, his views are worth respect and careful handling. But I am to deal for once in this course with one particular subject where this would not fit in, so I would prefer to put it off.

Now, ladies and gentlemen, we discussed last time the fiscal, financial, and monetary problems because these matters are so significant for a society and the way it runs. Much more significant and much more important from the same standpoint are population tendencies, and to these I propose to devote this lecture.

You all know that capitalist development all over the world was attended by a big upsurge in the numbers of white men. Between 1770 and 1940 the white population of the earth has increased between four and five times and is now roughly 730 million. In this country this process has been very much accentuated by immigration, of course, and a few characteristic figures are as follows. Between 1850 and 1860 the population of this country increased by a rate more than one-third, between 1900 and 1910 by a rate more than one-fifth, between 1910 and 1920 by less than one-sixth, between 1920 and 1930 by a rate more than one-seventh, and between 1930 and 1940 by a rate less than one-fourth.

Well, this development is, of course, exclusively due to the fall of the death rate, one of the great achievements of capitalist society. Naturally, the rationalist culture of capitalism, among other things, rationalized ways of living and medical methods wrought that miracle which issued in the increase in the number of white men. It is not a safe thing to say, but from historical statistics we get the impression that in ancient Rome average life expectancy was twenty-five years. Before the middle of the eighteenth century it was roughly thirty-three years, and now in this country and in Germany it is roughly sixty-two years. This would act toward the rise in population for the birth rate of earlier times before the middle of the eighteenth century was compensated by the high mortality rate, especially the child mortality rate. But the birth rate has been falling since about sixty years ago. The birth rate has been considerably falling for about thirty years. It fell first in advanced then in less advanced countries, first in dense then in open countries, first in the upper classes then in the lower classes—but everywhere and far beyond the precincts of white men the birth rate is falling.

This fall in the birth rate is imperfectly described in its consequence by what is termed the crude birth rate, that is to say, the number of births per thousand of population. For instance, in Western and Northern Europe it was between 1841 and 1890 roughly between thirty and thirty-two per thousand. It is about fifteen now. I don't want to waste any time to show that these figures mean very little. Much more significant is births per thousand women of child-bearing age, but even that doesn't take account of age distribution and can be misleading. What figures shall we then use? For that purpose we must take a cross-section and use whether the mothers at any given time produce an equal number of mothers on the average. Thus, then, the average number of mothers born to a mother of today, is referred to as the net reproduction rate. It is the birth rate per thousand women of child-bearing age corrected for the age distribution of these women. If it is one, the population replaces itself; if it is more than one, it more than replaces itself; if less than one, that population will die out although for a time, due to the change in the age distribution, the total number of population will go on increasing. There is no contradiction between the statements that a population increases and the statement that it fails to replace itself. That state of things is only temporary.

This net reproduction rate was once almost two, but in 1770 had fallen to one and is now below 0.8 in England, France, Sweden, Norway, and Switzerland. It is a little less than one in Germany and the United States, and it is 1.4 and a little more in only two of the great countries with something like statistics, Russia and Japan. That is to say, white humanity, if it keeps to its behavior, will maintain itself—only they will all be Russians some day; all others are going to die out. Only present behavior is not admissible as a basis for prediction for there is room for further decrease in the birth rate and the trend is

downward. So if we take account of the trend, which the net reproduction rate does not, the trend is downward and hence the dying
out process will go on accelerating.

This result is, of course, open to all the qualifications which must
be made in extrapolating any trend and it is also subject to cyclical
fluctuations. For instance, the low point of the net reproduction rate
was reached everywhere in 1933; births have recovered since but
characteristically only the number of first children of a marriage and
also the number of second children. The number of third children in
a marriage and over has not recovered at all. The marriage rate is
high cyclically, so this is a merely cyclical phenomenon, and if we
have an increase in births in Germany and Italy we overlook the fact
that the same phenomenon was also in this and in every other country, as far as I know.

The cause of this phenomenon of falling birth rate is simple to indicate; it is voluntary birth restriction, the spread of contraceptive
practices. But what is the cause of this cause? It is here that the subject links up with the subject of these lectures. This is a logical consequence of capitalist evaluations in two ways. First, capitalism, being
a rational form of life, rationalizes first the bookkeeping, then the
technology, then trade routes, then private life. Being a rational culture, it breaks down religious bridges and the individual draws a balance of pleasure and pain which he adds and comes to the conclusion
that the individual is better off without children. Rationalizing his
own behavior, he may style it as an increased responsibility of the
children, but the essential thing is this rationalizing of life. It would
not be relevant to object that the balance of happiness and sacrifice
which is drawn up on children is wrong because it is drawn up *ex ante*,
while the responsibility of family life and children may make a better
showing *ex post* than the individual *ex ante* expected.

This being one cause, capitalism adds another. The inventiveness
of capitalist entrepreneurs provides more effective and pleasant
means to employment than the desire to have children. Over ninety
percent may be traced to the influence of the atmosphere, aims, and
morals of the capitalist process. Capitalism kills itself by creating a
political atmosphere hostile to itself, but it kills itself also in the way
just alluded to. These tendencies are not likely to break up within the
capitalist or any other rational state culture. They are likely to be intensified.

Now I should like to discuss the consequences people are likely to
predict. The subject touches the most private spots of private life, so
people approach it with an emotional spirit, and the economist who
is afraid of the consequences will paint the economic side of it very

black. The economist who doesn't like this side of the question will palliate the consequences.

The first subjects to arise are the economic consequences, the mechanical consequences. They divide up into two parts. I will head each part by a proposition. The first proposition is that in an otherwise stationary state of the economic process, a stationary or falling population leads to a higher standard of life. Naturally if there are less workmen, work is a more valuable commodity than if there were more. Hence it is natural that in times of rapid increase, the classical instance is Malthus, the economists thought they saw the source of misery on this earth in the increase in the population. Malthus, making a fool of himself, as many economists seemed resolved to do, exaggerated his proposition. However, there is this much truth in it. If everything else remains the same only less hours of work are offered, these hours of work will be more valuable. In this sense the standard of life of the masses would be higher in a stationary state or in a state with a falling population than in a rapidly increasing one. It can be added that this higher standard of life would be realized, for these higher wages would be promptly spent.

There is another side of the picture. This side commands attention now. Other things are not equal. It has been held that the main stimulus for economic development is precisely the increasing population, that the increase in population, creating new wants, propels the economic process toward states of ever-increasing efficiency. Now again there may be something to that and also to the other, converse statement that a falling population will create difficulties, only there is much less to it than is generally held by those economists who have got into a panic about falling population. For, first, the mere increase of population, though it may increase wants, does not necessarily increase effective demand. Increasing population is valued positively by some economists because of the increase of demand which it is supposed to bring. There is a crude error in this. The mere want has nothing to do with the economic process. For instance, I would like to have a private yacht because I don't like the company I meet on a trans-Atlantic steamer. The desire for a yacht on my part has no influence on the economic process. So the fact that people want more intensively when they have many children than when they have a few does not necessarily mean there is a greater effective demand. It is absurd to say that if the population becomes stagnant now, there will be less demand for housing. This is wrong, for housing is something which people, having all the food they want, should like to have in a more plentiful and pleasant state. So the demand for housing will go on for a long time just the same whether there are many children or a few. Naturally, it is different for food. In a stagnant population there may be difficulties concerning agriculture provided this agriculture is geared to an increasing demand. The vicissitudes of American agriculture were due to the circumstance that the American farmers were accustomed for fifty or more years to an ever-expanding demand. This phenomenon we meet every day in capitalist economic life. Demand would not fall until the given population has not only begun to fall in numbers but has done so quite considerably. So these arguments are not so satisfactory as they might seem. As a matter of fact, it is not in countries with dense and quickly increasing population where we find the highest standards of life and the most effective methods of population.

Still more exaggerated is another point. We have discussed the theory of decreasing investment opportunity. It is said that if the population ceases to increase, one of the safest and most obvious kinds of investment and the one most easy to foresee will vanish, namely the provision for new families. It is easy to see the need for baby carriages in an increasing population, but this doesn't mean these investment opportunities cannot be replaced by others. The argument holds that the same nation which does not have investment opportunities continues to save, and goes into a slump. But one of the strongest incentives to save is the wife and children, and if there is no wife and children there would be a reduced tendency to save. Hence, if the population is merely drifting toward stationarity and not falling, these criticisms are not serious. Of course, if the population is falling so that at some time there will be only ten or twelve people in the United States, the picture would be serious. But for the present situation and for thirty years to come, if present trends to continue, I don't think there is much in this argument.

However, these are not the only arguments. One argument felt by everyone is that unequal rates of increase or decrease will shift the military strength and power of nations. Naturally people are concerned about this because everyone is a nationalist. What we mean by not being a nationalist is that we don't approve of the nationalism of other people, and the prospect that something as desirable as us should disappear and be replaced by something less desirable *ex definitione* is uncomfortable. Take the case of Australia and New Zealand which are just maintaining their population which is a very thin one. These populations are faced with immigration by seething masses of Asiatics. If we took our own democratic and non-national view seriously, we would say they ought to shake hands with these Asiatics and invite them to settle in their country. The idea of good Englishmen in Australia and New Zealand being swamped by Japanese is too much for us to bear. That is a matter of great political importance if we realize that politics is that form of social rationalization from which rationality is most regularly excluded.

The eugenic doubt I take more seriously. The men and women who want to do something in this life don't want children in the next room. They will be the ones to restrict families first. In fact, contraceptives first became widespread in the French society of the regency, then the bourgeoisie, then the upper working class. It was the good stock that was eliminating itself. In England we find that weak-minded mothers have about four times as many children as normal mothers. This restricts a nation not only in numbers but also in morals and intelligence. The humors of the time being what they are, it is the lower strata which will be encouraged to multiply while those who would mean more for the future of the nation are being penalized, especially in the way of inheritance taxes.

There is another point, that which I like to call the parentocracy. The parentocracy is the rule of old people. In this country in forty years we shall have only 20 million more people than we have now, but among these 150 million people, while there are now 8½ million people of and above sixty-five years of age, there will be 24 million people of sixty-five and more. That means there will be in forty years in this country for every six inhabitants, one individual above sixty-five, two children, and three in the state of being gainfully employed. What does that mean? It may not mean very much after all as far as the burden entailed in keeping these people is concerned, for on the other hand, you keep less children. The trouble is that the children don't have any votes while the old folks unfortunately have. You get in this country the lobby of the old. Townsendism is a symptom of the assertion of the interests of the indigent old. Since they are a very homogeneous group and assert themselves in Washington, they will exert a load in the way of national burdens in this country.

The expenditure on these old people, furthered by the gospel of spending as much as possible, is not much worse than what would happen on the other side of the age scale. The falling death rate is not the only result of the medical and hygienic advance during the capitalist era. People not only die later but they are stronger, more active, and more useful while they are alive, and they remain more useful to a later stage. This being so, the resources of the community are increased.

However, many people seem to be worried about the outlook in a world which will show a rule of the old. A German and a friend of mine, in sending me a reprint of his, wrote me a poem to go with it. I haven't the poem with me, but the gist of it was this: The world is getting old; even the Nazis are going to become reasonable—in a word, it is terrible. What about that? Everything we say about that is purely speculative. We don't know how a world will function which has a large number of superannuated people in it. It may have no effect, or it may have an effect in either way. I don't believe the world will be more pacific. If you have more old people, the world will be more warlike because the old people don't have to do the fighting. You hear what a beautiful façade Rome presented after Hannibal. There were eighty thousand dead, many thousands wounded, but the message from the Senate told them to fight it out to the bitter end. Once I was asked to admire that, and I probably did, but that was long ago and long life since then has told me to be careful in my allocation of admiration. I cannot help seeing now that the old gentlemen of the Senate were safely behind the walls of Rome, and to be cut to pieces by Hannibal was left to the young people who had the stern message of the senators. So a society dominated by the old may become more rather than less energetic. I am trying to show that you can't make scientific inferences as to what a society would be like which has more old people.

Much more important than anything I have mentioned so far is the fact that childlessness and the refusal to undertake the responsibilities of parenthood alter the whole psycho-sociological pattern of society. First, economic motive is changed owing to the narrowing of the time horizon. In capitalism the care of the economic future was left to the industrialist. The average family had a horizon which stretched indefinitely into the future. Many people have said that private economics takes too short a view, while a state can take a longer view. It can, but it doesn't. The economic interest of society was very much more taken care of under capitalism.

This being so, we may go further and observe the typical entrepreneur of the nineteenth century. Being a father and thinking of the conditions which he was going to leave to his children, he was fighting tooth and nail—fighting taxation, labor unions, and so on, and thereby he was safeguarding the interests of the society in the future. Now for the executive of a company, who in many cases can't leave his concern to his children but who may not have any children to leave anything to, it is better to be patted on the back and be told what a progressive individual he is and go off to Nice while there is a sit-down strike at home. The effect on the general morals of society is not for me to appraise, but I do think it is very serious and I do think we take life much less seriously than we would if we were firmly imbedded in the family that used to exist.

How far the decay has gone we can even measure. In the 1890s we have investigations showing how the unemployed found shelter in wide families, almost in clans such as you can still find in Japan. In 1930 in Japan there was little unemployment because the unemployed found shelter in the clan. That has gone. In England we can observe that in the means test in the case of the dole. The means test depended on the absence of income, but the question arose whether the criterion should be individual income or family income. One of the most popular slogans of the Labor Party and one of the most unpopular points in the Labor Party was the difference in planks on this point. The modern child doesn't care a damn what happens to his parents. They think it is just as well to leave them to public charity. This is one aspect of the thing.

The other aspect is that the reduction in the number of children sets free energies on the one hand and exasperates tempers on the other hand. In the fifteenth century twenty or more children were perfectly normal to one woman. For instance, I found a document referring to conditions in a little castle in the South of Germany which was inhabited by four knightly families—not nobility, but of knightly rank—who had all together 125 children. Naturally that absorbed quite a lot of energy, especially of the mothers. The reduction in this abundant rate of fertility set free energies for cultural and other pursuits. So far as the economic system necessitated the utilization of all the family energy set free, an explosive was put into the social system which has never been given its true value.

Another thing is this: Having children means having one of the strongest desires of the human heart. A childless family is not a healthy family; it is psychologically warped; it is subconsciously at war with God and man. Therefore, I believe the Catholic Church is entirely right in fighting contraceptive practices and wrong in relaxing the fight, as it has done in some quarters today. This explains one stream of modern radicalism. When the physiology of modern radicalism is explained, we must leave much room for many resentments, grudges, etc., which arise from that secret source, which hardly shows. It never shows because when you ask it, you get rationalizations; you would have to ask more by Freudian methods. If you ask by questionnaire, you get their rationalizations, so this element is not easy to get at. But there is no doubt that many causes of that kind of radicalism that comes from suffering nerves come from that source. The setting free of nerves and at the same time the exasperating [of] them can be traced to the rationalizing effects of capitalist evaluations.

It is not the purpose of this course to indicate measures. I merely want to present diagnoses. From the standpoint of diagnosis I think we have today discovered a major difficulty in the social situation, a difficulty which is as much a symptom as it is a cause and an effect of trends. I don't think that can be reversed in the modern society. In the society of capitalistic democracy there are no means for bringing about that conversion that would have to come about in order to eliminate this element from our moral and psychological setup. If it is not eliminated, not only is there in the future a dying out process but there is in prospect an increasing social friction, an increasing difficulty in running the social apparatus. So we come, after all, to the result to which those people come who think so much of decreasing population as a cause of economic difficulties, but we differ with them in the reasons, in the ways in which we arrive at the results.

Politically, the conservatives disapproved strongly of the phenomenon of childlessness when it was discussed. Today conservatives are more or less silent about it. Once radicals were silent about it and pressed for contraceptive practices and the repeal of prohibition. Now radicals are getting vocal about it. How shall we account for this contrary movement? The national ideals, etc., caused the conservatives to disapprove up to the World War. Fighting childlessness by putting a premium on children recommends itself to radicals for redistribution of income, while the conservatives, who stand to lose by such a redistribution, hold the opposite point of view, and it is to the discredit of both.

## VII. International Trade

Tonight, ladies and gentlemen, we have to try out our general schema, our pattern on the subject of international relations.[9] This is not particularly difficult to do in that in those times which I have dubbed the times of capitalism, roughly up to the end of the nineteenth century, the world was indeed very far from being free trade. Only one country, England, really had carried out the principle of free trade. This was due, on the one hand, to the inheritance from another social state in which this one structure had led to this view and, on the other hand, to the fact that very many people, for particular reasons which would have to be explained on the merits of each case, had never even in the most bourgeois times embraced the principles of free trade. Among the great nations the most outstanding examples are Russia and the United States.

But though free trade was not a reality, things approached a state of free trade in important respects. Free trade was the principle that summarized and explained the structural idea of bourgeois society with respect to international relations. It was the obviously right thing for very many people in very many nations, deviations from which would have to be justified in each individual case. The bourgeois world looked toward a state of free trade, and a French economist of some though not very great note, Michel Chevalier, in 1871, if my memory serves me, wrote with that lack of responsibility that often characterizes economists that the establishment of free trade will be one of the titles to glory of the nineteenth century. There were no barriers to free movement of trade, practically no custom barriers. On the other hand, there was a strong internationalist element in the gold currency that had gained ground toward the end of the century and provided a semi-automatic international standard. This economic policy, which obviously follows our pattern, was a religion of the general policy of bourgeois society, and its complement was naturally a principle of peaceful solution of such differences as might arise between the national states, a peaceful policy all around.

In such a world, ladies and gentlemen, there does not exist such a thing as a raw material problem. If you are assured of peace and substantial free trade, it does not matter a bit whether a source of raw material or foodstuff is situated within our own borders or not. You can get wool just as well from Australia and copper just as well from this country as if it were situated au beau milieu de la douce France. The question how a country is to find access to raw materials has no meaning, it does not exist.

We saw at the turn of the century a new spirit, a new attitude of life, a new religion slowly begin to exert itself. In its economic consequences it might be called neo-mercantilism. For this country, which always had the aspiration of being a world unto itself, it did not mean a great change. For other nations it meant an actual change in the direction of policy or an attempt to change the directions of policy. Some countries raised their tariff walls and entered into monetary policies that were incompatible with the autarchy of the gold policy. Other countries, like England, experienced a movement in the same direction, although in 1914 under Chamberlin it was not attended with success.

Imperialism, militarism, nationalism, etc., are the usual slogans which designate the political complement of this. This again follows a pattern. This way of thinking, feeling, making policy arose in connection with the decay of the bourgeois world and the schemas on which its survival depended. These tendencies, which we observed in other fields, were also in this field, greatly propelled by the War of 1914–1918 mainly in the following pattern. We find a thoroughly mercantilistic national policy expressed by the Allies in their Paris

Conference of 1916. They drew up a plan of how to divide the loot to which they were looking forward. Also in the Peace of Versailles and its complementary restraints there were clauses about the colonies, mandates, about the treatment of enemy assets which were in striking contrast with the old spirit of bourgeois society. Moreover, economic warfare continued for quite a time on the basis of those peace treaties. The most favored nation clause was imposed upon the vanquished powers on top of other responsibilities, and in many respects we have semi-warfare for several years following 1918. This was complemented on this side of the ocean by America's familiar refusal to accept the implications of her creditor position and to open her ports for imports. On the contrary, in the Fordney-McCumber Act this country reaffirmed its strictly protectionist attitude.

Two points merit special notice. One was the blockade, the other was the mechanism by which the policy of the League of Nations was to be made effective. Ladies and gentlemen, politics is essentially a short-run game. It was the virtue of the family that it worked for an indefinite family and hence for an indefinite national future, but the politician always thinks of the day after tomorrow. In a war the short-run view prevails, and measures are taken which may hurt national interests in the future. For a trading nation like England the blockade in 1914–1918 may have been necessary, justified, and so forth, but it had a lasting effect on her position as a trading nation. And it had another effect which accelerated the tendency toward neo-mercantilism and self-sufficiency which I have been glancing at. In Germany there was only one opinion about international trade in the future, and that was that that sort of thing shall never happen again. The consequence of that sort of education is a tendency toward autarchy, and they foster policies which have no justification in economic rationality.

On the other hand, the policy and structure of the League of Nations implied that an aggression on any member is an aggression on all, a principle first uttered in the seventeenth century, and the reaction to that aggression was a problem of considerable difficulty. The nations that concluded the covenant were not all of them ready to commit themselves to military reaction to aggression against any one of them, so by way of second best and compromise, the idea of economic sanctions was hit upon. Never was there a more unfortunate idea, if I may at least define an unfortunate idea as an idea which defeats its own purpose. Everyone who felt that such sanctions might be decreed against him was thereby turned into an autarchist; for thought from the standpoint of those nations who ran the League of Nations naturally the use of sanctions would always be a fair and just one, the thing naturally looked different to those nations who have any reason to believe that sanctions would be used against them. So a powerful impetus was given to tendencies in international trade which make for self-sufficiency and for economic preparation for war.

You need only visualize the question in a practical spirit. Every nation feels itself to be in the right in any conflict in which it may enter. Japan, for instance, feels like that; that is to say, the large majority of Japanese people, it is a safe assumption to make, feel that they are in the right in doing what they are doing. And they see that this country is trying to exert economic pressure against Japan to make her desist from aims which to this country seem unjustified and to the Japanese seem justified. This has been foreseen, so a powerful tendency toward autarchy was set up in Japan which in turn makes the waging of war easier than it otherwise would be. That is why I call that idea unfortunate. The threatening of nations with economic pressure, in case they do something which disagrees with the moral or other views of another nation, will have the consequence of pushing these people into policies of autarchy, and since in modern circumstances such a policy is always attended by success, it will make war easier. This almost childish belief that so many people hold, people who, I am glad to say, are amateur economists rather than economists, that by means of managing raw materials you can force foreign nations to their knees has been a boon to autarchists, militarists, and dictators all over the world. However, such a policy, if suddenly referred to in the short run, has the opposite result in the long run.

However, in spite of all these things world trade developed during the 1920s and in 1929 was in physical volume about twenty-five percent above, if we may trust an unreliable index, the 1913 figure. However, there is a qualification to be made. The nature of foreign trade had changed during that time; foreign trade was not quite what it had been before. The foreign trade of the 1920s partly consisted of the trade of noncapitalist countries rapidly capitalizing themselves and requiring for that purpose the equipment which capitalist countries were able to give. So that figure must not be trusted to reflect the permanent tendency of international trade at that time. Still, such as it was, it was a sign of the victory of the logic of things against the recalcitrant human will.

Next, as we have seen, the world depression further accelerated the process in question. In the depression a lot of measures were taken to shelter sickly home markets against the interlope of foreign commodities, measures which at that time were probably honestly believed to be temporary and only a reflection of the monetary emergency. However, following in with the tendency of the times these measures came to stay. There is, for instance, first the Hawley-Smoot Act. One of the first things this country did in reaction to the depressive situation was to make still higher her formidable tariff wall, thus clearly showing that she did not feel anything like economic solidarity. This was only in keeping with the existing tradition, and I for one believe there was much to be said for it.

But second, the monetary management, discussed in the last lecture but one, also came to stay and this monetary management naturally broke up one of the strongest links in the international relations of the internation automatic or semi-automatic gold currency. These monetary managements then took various forms. We have the form which was practiced in America and in England, the form of simply going off gold and regulating foreign exchanges according to what was supposed to be the national interest, and we have in other countries the direct control of foreign exchange and all that sort of thing.

Third, there was the great historical event of England's embracing protectionism and a state imperialist policy. Perhaps you have forgotten, perhaps you have not felt it so much in this country, but in Europe England's going off gold, which before had only been associated with governments of shady reputation, made an impression in Europe which I compare with what would have been if the Holy Trinity was unable to redeem its bonds. This event led far. The strong protectionist move got its nationalistic and militaristic accentuation by the imperial policy which followed the Ottawa Conference and the agreements concluded in consequence of it.

Fourth, we have Germany entering upon a similar path. The German policies, since to Germany other means were closed, consisted in forcing exports by ill-disguised subsidies, block mark arrangements, and that sort of thing, and bilateralism. Bilateralism has been severely judged by economists. So far as they are addressing an elementary class in international trade, they are right—it runs against economic rationality. But in a world where there is no economic rationality, the bilateral agreement, teaching people that you can't export without importing, has something to say for itself. Germany's bilateral agreements were concluded with countries whose economic interests gravitated toward Germany. Take Roumania. Neither England nor this country can have any use for Roumanian oil, but Germany has such a use and can pay for it by the commodities which Roumania requires. When Germany entered such agreements with Roumania, there were protests from London and Paris.

This was a movement toward regionalism, toward closed economic connections with complementary countries, or countries geographically next to each other or with common military interests. In short, the spirit of 1900 had died out of the policy of that day. The small countries did not always fare very well. For instance, in the policy followed by England with respect to the Ouchy Agreement and the Scandinavian countries in general, there is no lack of energy or consciousness of her own interests. These countries would have had, if the tendency of the Ouchy Agreement had been such, the opportunity to develop.

Finally, I want to mention the reciprocity policy of the present administration in this country, but only in order to state that it did not substantially change the picture which I was drawing, for the most important agreements concluded under the reciprocity powers were with the countries within the economic and military reach of the United States. It was only those treaties which really counted, and therefore the politico-sociological importance of the reciprocity policy is not quite what one would just assume. It was a military attempt to reduce tension all around, but the result in that direction was comparatively small.

I want to insert, however, two important points, economic facts which would militate against an expansion of international trade even in a perfectly peaceful and perfectly bourgeois and free-trade world. If it is said, as some of the writers that are grouped around the League of Nations still say, that we should expect international trade to grow in importance as the economic evolution goes its way in the capitalist world, this is not true for two reasons. First, one of the pillars of international commodity trade was the exchange of consumer's goods as well as producer's goods from capitalist countries against the raw materials of noncapitalist countries or not-yet-capitalist countries. But all those countries even in 1914 were capitalizing themselves and the war, as in India, added an impetus to that tendency. This being so, one of the main reasons for international trade was bound to get weaker and weaker for the growth of domestic industry in the tropics would decrease the balance of relative advantages and hence the amount of international trade. Second, time was—the same time when traveling was delightful on horseback—when you had to get many vital articles from the countries of their origin. The process of chemistry and of other lines have reduced this necessity to a considerable extent and are sure to reduce it at an accelerated pace later on. Indigo, rubber, and soon oil—who thinks of importing them? It will soon be possible to produce them anywhere. This being so, we cannot expect international trade to expand pro-

portionately to total output even if there were no nationalist tendencies which militate against it.

These are the facts, and now for the diagnosis and prognosis.
Frankly, at this point of my address I feel a little nervous for though
what I am going to say is perfectly simple and straightforward, it is
not easy to convey in the few minutes at my disposal. Simplifying to
the utmost, I want to put before you two propositions and make them
sound plausible at least. The one proposition is that political international relations are both the consequence and the cause of economic international relations, and second that international political relations are both the consequence and the cause of the domestic
social structure of the countries concerned. I will explain. Of course,
international relations are economically conditioned; that is a commonplace. Many well-meaning and competent Americans are trying
to explain how great an element of economic necessity enters into the
pushing forward of what are described as aggressor nations. As to
raw material markets, etc., that has become a commonplace, but this
commonplace is only true when it is complemented by its contrary.
Just as political relations are economically complementary, so economic relations are politically complementary. For instance, some
nations are described as have-not nations if they have no raw materials and such, but there would be no harm in that if the political
situation were such that we could live in a peaceful and free-trade
world. So the fact that there are have-not nations and that the possession or nonpossession of raw materials constitutes a problem, the
fact that you can speak of such a thing as access to raw materials is
politically circumstanced. In another political setup there would be
no such problem. That is what I mean that you must complement the
proposition that political international relations are economically conditioned and economic international relations are politically conditioned. That's one point.

The other point is this. International relations, economic or noneconomic, are a function of the domestic social and political structure, for what will appear to a nation as its interest in its relations to
other nations will depend entirely on its mentality and its mentality
will depend on its social structure. It makes a lot of difference
whether trade union officials dominate their nation or an army rules
that nation. Different things will be [of] national interest to them. It
is the domestic structure that determines the behavior of a country
abroad. Summing up in a sentence which sounds like a paradox
though it isn't, foreign policy is domestic policy in two senses. First,
in the sense alluded to, that the domestic structure will determine
what a nation wants to do abroad, and in another sense that the pol-

itician plays with everything and with peace and war for the purpose of the success of his party or of himself. In this sense, foreign policy must be interpreted in terms of a domestic policy. To give an example, which I am happy to say is not offensive, the Russian government in 1914 did not feel comfortable in its chair and in its skin. To take a strong stand on the Serbian trouble, which in itself was of only slight importance, was a measure to divert attention from domestic troubles to foreign happenings, to give people something else to think about. But again that would be easy to understand, and in fact Karl Marx himself would agree with most of what I have said so far. Unfortunately the agreement ends there, for the paradox that foreign policy is domestic policy must be complemented by the equally true paradox that domestic policy may be foreign policy. For instance, most of the measures of the Hitler government, most of its attempt to create a new national spirit, was prompted by the aim of national success. So those individuals whom we call politicians if they are alive and statesmen when they are dead may inspire themselves by the domestic situation in their foreign policy and they may also shape their domestic policy. Bismarck is another example, with a view to national advantage abroad. In this field there is interdependence between economic and political elements, and there is no hope of ever getting a clearcut one-way causal relationship.

Since we take the political factor as expressive of a nation's structure and spirit, an independent variable, we can see the problem in the light of the rising beliefs which spurn utilitarianism and economic rationality and take all national factors into the meaning of human life. The ethical imperialism of America and the national imperialism of Germany are only different ideological forms for the same thing. The methods may differ but the vital social phenomenon is the same.

After this digression into the sociology of politics, I return dutifully to my subject. I do expect in the near and also in the further future the economy to be the servant of the extra-economic views. Many people do not agree with me, and among them is also my collaborator in these lectures and in the book we are going to publish from them, Mrs. Schumpeter; and since she knows much more about many of these things than I do, I give my views with becoming diffidence. Free trade, or even unobstructed trade, will in the future not be likely except within areas dominated by military force, that is, within areas where no other military force can be expected to successfully put a spoke in the wheel. A return to the conditions of 1914 or, still more fantastic of 1900, would imply a return to the mentality of those times, to the structure and domestic conditions of those times, a return to capitalism. I liked those times, but since there is no use in wishful thinking, I realize that that world is dead and buried and there is no way back to it. I conclude that a return to those economic relations is practically out of the question, much as is the return to the savings and economies of intact capitalism.

What then? In order to answer this question we must make a hypothesis. There is the obvious hypothesis of a victory, in the present war, of England. That would [mean]—especially in an alliance with this country (assuming that this country would enter the empire)—world domination in a military and economic sense. It would mean that at least the extra-Russian world would be dominated and managed by Downing Street, and it is a method of establishing normal and economically rational relations in that sphere. From an economic standpoint there would be much to be said for the solution.

The other hypothesis is that from the present situation four great blocks will emerge—the Anglo-American, Russian, Japanese, and European. Taking into account all the economic policies around these blocks, all four can live. No great and terrible suffering will be entailed in any of those blocks living by themselves, and since such great blocks formed from their atmospheres naturally will have quite a lot of trouble within their borders, I may add the hope that such a four-block world may be possible. For the only way to remove war is not the garrisoning of war, it is not collective security. It is the removal of the motives of war. Let me give you an analogy. Not all of us are enthusiastic about the practices of modern labor leaders, yet we do not on that account advocate shooting them down. We may think them unreasonable and unethical, yet we accept them. Likewise, in our homes we accept the recalcitrant child. Similarly, if the great parts in which the group divides are left to themselves, that is the best chance to avoid war; or else there will be war, and to war, in a war without end, there can be only one victor, Russia and bolshevism.

This being so, let us look at the European block. It would have 400 million inhabitants. Its deficits look formidable, but they are not formidable at all. In foodstuffs there is hardly any deficit which cannot be made good with planning. The only long-run deficit is oil cakes, for since these have a lot to do with good beefsteaks, they are important; but they could be produced in the quantities desired if Asia Minor fell under this block. In other respects the people would be all right. Of course, they would have no coffee or tea, but tobacco would not be excluded. However, the raw material question is more serious. Rubber is a deficiency of one hundred percent, or it was three years ago. Now, for a long-run consideration I have to put down this deficiency with a zero, for rubber can be produced synthetically without difficulties. Copper has a deficiency of eighty-one percent, but it is not essential. There are few uses where copper has a distinct advantage over its substitutes. The manganese and tungsten problem depends on the Russian and Japanese blocks. As for wool, the death knell of wool will sound before all, but before it has sounded there is a deficit of seventy percent, a strong motive to trade. There are now a lot of less important things that sum up to considerable importance, and there is the question of oil. Soon it will be possible to produce oil as gasoline synthetically as cheaply as natural gasoline, but again with good relations with Russia and if Iraq is under the block, there would be no trouble.

Less easy is the Anglo-American block. It could live only at very great sacrifices to everyone, particularly to this country. The total exports of the hemisphere were in 1938 about 4 billion dollars, and the imports were about 3.2 [billion]. They can both be reduced, but the whole of the Americas are peculiarly uncomplementary to each other. A tremendous surplus of food and raw materials would have to be made good to its producers somehow. This country would have to pay, and the A.A.A. program would be nothing to what would be on the hands of this country. Moreover, this country would not sell its manufactures successfully to South America, or it may be able to sell them only at a price which would amount to a gift in the long run. In fact, this tendency is now spreading. Loans are being given which there is no prospect will be paid back. The sad thing is that this expenditure is one item in a total expenditure which, if expended rationally, could make this country a paradise on earth. In lacking in rationality this country has missed a great opportunity.

These blocks, while each could live within itself, could nevertheless trade with each other. The trade would be of the surplus of raw materials and foodstuffs of the Anglo-American block and of the industrial products of the European block. There would be trade and there would be perfect competition, if you please, in the Far East. So these four blocks with perfect competition would be an arrangement which would be economically possible. It is the economic aspect which interests me here. It follows that the possibilities for a very tolerable future of international relations are given. It doesn't follow from that that they will be used. The problem requires managing. All I tried to show was that the problem was not intrinsically unmanageable.

Naturally, if this country for moral or other reasons does not wish to trade with other countries, there will be no trade. There is no reason to suppose that, short of its own will, there is anything that will prevent it from trading to the extent to which it needs to trade. The United States of all nations is the one least dependent on international trade. In every respect, therefore, both as to possibilities and as to the damage which the failure of those possibilities to mature would do, there is no sense in the slogans circulated so widely which I will quote in one particular form: "If Hitler wins, our foreign trade will go. With our foreign trade our prosperity will go. With our prosperity our freedom will go." There is no justification for any one of these three statements. Whatever the result of the war, a country of the importance of this one will have pretty much the opportunities for trading and for not trading as she wants to have. Exaggerated hopes, of course, were always unjustifiable. I don't think there was any sense in trying to foster exports by the Webb Pomerene Act or the Export Act in the 1920s. But on the other hand, neither are exaggerated fears warranted.

## VIII. Possible Consequences for the United States

Ladies and gentlemen, in thanking you for your attention during this course, I must at the same time apologize in advance for what no doubt will strike you after this lecture as unsatisfactory conclusions.[10] It is natural to ask what's the upshot of all this, what does it amount to practically, and finally to ask the typically American question what should be done about it. I think that economists are much too prone to answer such questions. I want to emphasize that I don't think it my position or my right to answer them. On the other hand, data are too indefinite to warrant definite predictions, still less definite advice. What can be done is to look at possibilities under various hypotheses. On the other hand, naturally I am not so much of a pure spirit as yet that I should not hope and fear like everyone among you, but I have no right and no wish to impose any of these fears and hopes on you. These are things that are up to you. What I can do is to show up facts, tendencies, possibilities, to contribute to the result you may individually arrive at; but that is all, and it must naturally sound unsatisfactory in a subject where it is excusable if the audience expects an end with a flourish.

What we have to do tonight, ladies and gentlemen, is this. Our analytical schema, our analysis of that socio-psychological phenomenon which we have called the spirit of our time, enables us to fit in a definite pattern the present war. It especially enables us under various hypotheses to speak about certain of its possible consequences for the social structure. Now, ladies and gentlemen, such a phenomenon as this war naturally has, looked at from an analytical standpoint, two sides. They are, first, the catalyzers of the actual events, and a great element of chance factors enters into it. And then there are those attitudes based upon the social and economic structure which made the reaction to those catalyzers what it was. The catalyzers I want to deal with briefly or not at all. I want quickly to cataloguize them into three groups which I want to call the economic, political, and psychological groups.

Of the economic group of catalyzers a good instance is the raw material question. We have seen last time that the troubles about the access to raw materials are troubles only in a particular political setup. For instance, in a typically bourgeois world, free trade and all that sort of thing, these troubles would not be any trouble at all. The fact of whether you have raw materials within your borders or without them would be completely immaterial. Of the political catalyzers a good example is the problem of the town of Danzig, a town practically entirely German, wishing to join Germany, ninety percent Nazi, and not being able to do so.

Of those psycho-sociological catalyzers I shall mention only one, which to my mind is much more important than is realized. That is the resentment, however we may further analyze it sociologically and psychologically, against the Anglo-American dominion of the world. This resentment was strengthened by the first World War and by the peace and much that was done in consequence of it, but quite independently of that the mere sense of being thwarted, of not being as good as other people, acts more on domestic and foreign policies of European powers and Japan than you are prone to admit. If you look, for instance, at the Russian policy during the last thirty months, it is not to be understood unless you realize that Stalin is first of all a ruler of a great empire. He is bolshevist or anything else only in a secondary sense. The first thing is that he cannot stand a state of things in which his country has not the frontier it had in 1914. These things may be irrational—don't ask me for rationality when I am speaking of human behavior—but they are very real.

I don't know exactly how I should fit this into a general schema of historical interpretation. It would not be easy, but the attempt would start on Marxian lines. It would not end on Marxian lines. However, with this I want to dismiss this subject. It is important only to keep in mind that the attitude in which such factors are met explains both foreign and domestic policies in Europe and elsewhere. Last time I tried to familiarize you with a way of looking at foreign policy which in a nutshell can be put into two apparently contradictory sentences. Foreign policy is domestic policy. Domestic policy is foreign policy. It is a revolution, as it often has been called, what we are living through I mean, against civilization. There is some truth in that, but you must not forget that the truth looks different if you define it more closely.

It is a revolution against that civilization which capitalism, or the capitalist form of production, has created. Revolution against civilization often means setting up another civilization. Naturally to the votaries of one civilization no other civilization is civilization.

As we have seen, the first World War impinged on a social situation which contained factors of change, only these factors were working slowly and, in a sense it may be said, orderly. They were *en train* of transforming society in the direction of socialism. At the same time the first World War impinged on a society which, although harboring factors of change, was comparatively stable. The importance of the first World War consists in the fact that it accelerated and eliminated from the social structure girders that tended to keep it on its legs, so the result was what from that standpoint and in that sense, though in no other, might be called premature developments. Premature developments in Germany, for instance, were in the direction of a socialist government which found itself in an impossible situation—in a bourgeois society which it had saved. This war in Europe impinges on a social world which not only displays the factors of change more strongly than any society could have done thirty years ago but which was also weakened by the first World War and the consequences of the world depression. This weakness on the one hand means quick developments, though on the old lines, as well as free room to grow in for new religions and new tendencies.

Well, therefore, the World War, impinging on a society which can fairly be said to have been morally, intellectually, economically, politically, and sociologically in a process of rapid disintegration, cannot be expected to have only the consequence that the first World War had but can be expected to have much more radical ones. In order to fix ideas, let us look at an individual example. Nowhere is this so clear as in France. If you look at the France of the Popular Front government at the time of the premiership of Mr. Leon Blum, what do you see? You see workmen who won't work, a government which won't govern, an economic engine that won't function, women who won't bear children, intellectuals who hate every bit of the civilization that reared them and whose every word is destructive, whether they paint pictures or write in newspapers. Whatever they do has so strongly a negative connotation that the average intellectual would have felt troubled in his conscience if he had done anything that could be interpreted as a defense of that civilization. There was a disbelief by everyone of what he was and what he stood for. There was resentment by all groups for other groups. There were three minority groups—first the Catholics, the most important of the minority groups; second the communists, a smaller group; and third the fascists, a still smaller group. Breakdown was the consequence, but social breakdown and chaos would have been the consequence also were it not for the presence of a foreign army which partly did not tolerate distinction and which partly by its presence tended to close over the differences between the inhabitants. Chaos or regeneration. The likelihoods are pretty much equal as far as tangible evidence is concerned. Certain is only that from the present situation there is no way back.

At this point I will interrupt myself and answer to the note I got the other day, the note about Mr. Keynes, and I read it again. It is a quotation from an article by Keynes.

> "The day is not far off when the economic problem will take the back seat, where it belongs, and the arena of the heart and head will be occupied or reoccupied by our real problems, the problems of life and human relations, of beliefs. . . ."

From an economist isn't that pretty emotional?

Yes, for an economist it's emotional. Worse, it's not scientific and it's not the position of the economist. The economist ought to try to put the problems in order, with multiple linear correlation and all that sort of thing. But at the same time the feeling expressed in these words is highly significant as a reaction of an extremely able man. Read in its severe sense, perhaps it doesn't mean very much, but it seems to me to convey the feeling which the factors I have just adduced are no doubt apt to produce—that feeling of the meaninglessness of capitalist values for so many people, the feeling that the civilization, the achievement it was to raise the masses and the standard of life all around, has played itself out and that we ought to look for other things. I am not saying that, I am registering it; but I do think this reaction, this economic view of things, is very real all over the world, and if Keynes has formulated it he is not the only one to feel it.

In England it was different. There was no such process as there was in France owing to the fact that the girders of the social organization had not melted away. An extremely able high aristocracy, so able that it absorbed in the depths all non-aristocratic elements, has a sense of the technique of ruling, a sense of the great religion of national success and victory. Thus it keeps together, the masses following willingly. The heroic conduct of the English people obliterates the fact that the social situation was not much different in England from what it was in France. The sociologist may ask the question whether England would have gone to war, and taken such a strong stand on the Polish situation, if the ruling stratum had not felt that the ground was moving away under its feet. You must conquer Europe if you can't hold your own in your own country. As I say, the social situation was not much different.

In the vicissitudes of the war a decree has been issued from the prime minister that when the war is over, of course the interests of the working classes will be the only ones to be considered. We have a situation which is very significant, in any case, but which is precisely significant in that these things will never be undone again. Labor is conscripted, industry is perfectly controlled, national income is socialized. You may call that as you please—it is one of the principles I have acquired in an unfortunately very long life by now never to quarrel about words—you may call it as you please, only the structural pattern is the same as in Germany.

All this and the consequences of it for Europe will be largely independent of the particular issue of the war. If there is an English victory, there must be military rule over the Continent. You may ask, "Can't that be avoided by a reasonable, by a wise, by a fair peace?" Well, that is daydreaming because fairness, justice, etc., would never be accepted on the European Continent from either English or American hands. That is very silly. I don't feel like that, of course, I am only recognizing certain factors. If there is defeat, there will probably be social breakdown, but in either case there is no return to what was.

About this country, this country is of course in a very privileged position which has helped it over many of the difficulties humanity had to meet elsewhere. This country economically has substantially all it needs. Obviously this country cannot be attacked. The situation in the world adds very much to her natural weight. All these are great chances and open up many possibilities, which might be put to the good of humanity by a rational and unemotional policy. But the only hypothesis which has any realistic virtue and which I will adopt for what I am going to say is that this country will presently enter the war and keep on with the English standpoint about the European problem and add to the English standpoint only its determined hostility to Japan. This unfolds the picture of what I call ethical imperialism, an imperialism whose ethos it is to put the world into order according to American ideas. If we accept that, order will be the consequence on the pattern of American civilization.

Many people believed and still believe that this will be a comparatively simple matter. America is arming, America will then sally forth into the world as Lohengrin sallied forth for the Holy Grail, meet with success, put the world in order from the American standpoint, and then return to its ordinary pursuits, the life after being substantially the same as before. This theory might come true in either of two cases. First, if the war expenditure and war effort were managed extremely carefully and economically, the great resources of this country might be equal to a war of even ten years without substantial strain on the social fabric. But this expenditure owing to the scale of the defense program is out already. The other case is that if America enters the war and if success is very quick, say in one year or two, it is conceivable that the theory might come true and that there might be demobilization with everything going on more or less as before. This possibility I want rather to stress than to underrate. War expenditure, income creating, inflating expenditure might easily raise the national income to 90 billion dollars. It would be possible to raise 30 billion of taxation from an income of 90 billion which, if prices did not at the same time rise too much, would certainly be a possible situation. This 30 billion yearly expenditure includes all federal expenditures, civilian, state, and municipal expenditures. It is not inadequate for careful management. If it is going to be outstripped, the situation is different, but I want to make clear that I don't wish to countenance any intensely alarmist views. A country which can put up for expenditure 30 billion dollars a year is certainly in a position to get along quite all right even in a warring world.

However, if neither of these hypotheses are fulfilled, that is, if expenditure is not carefully or economically managed and if the war lasts not one or two but ten years, serious strains and disturbances on the social fabric that cannot be undone can be predicted. This danger is all the more serious because the strain of the war comes on top of ten years of unofficial and halfhearted class warfare in this country, of a process of rapid disorganization. There is now the danger of expenditure, and there will be the danger of inflation if expenditure goes on as it has done. I have already quoted one of the profoundest sayings of Lenin, "In order to destroy bourgeois society you must debauche its money." That is what inflation would do; it would bring in this country more than in other countries moral breakdown.

Some of you may ask, "That is an economist speaking to us. Doesn't he know any means to avoid it?" Good God! I know the means to avoid it, but the likelihood of their being adopted is another thing. To save my professional reputation, however, I shall say that there are six ways in which inflation can be avoided. First, wage rates must be kept down because inflation mainly comes through the wage bill. Whatever else happens in the economic organism, the great ramrod of inflation is the expenditure from the wage bill. Second, there would have to be strict economy, that is, the cutting down of public expenditures for other purposes than the war. Some of these purposes are very dear to your heart. That is sad, nevertheless it would be necessary. All the cultural expenditures, for example, would have to be reduced. Third, there would have to be restriction of civilian consumption which could be done partly by allowing prices to rise and partly by rationing.

Fourth, there would have to be drastic taxation, direct and indirect, and this taxation would have to be resorted to immediately. It has been something of a problem to me how some economists do not face the question of taxation at all at present and say, "Well, let's cross the bridge when we come to it." I can explain that only on three grounds. First, the gospel of public expenditure has gotten so much absorbed into the system of some economists that they can't reverse their position. Second, there is the point that some people are so keen on getting this country into the war that they are loath to unfold too soon all that the war may mean to this country. Third, professional economists who would agree with me but who are afraid of the kind of taxation and of its irrational nature that they would rather not have any. Incomes over $100,000 are confiscated completely already. If you count in the quota of the inheritance tax, you may say roughly that no income really stays with the receiver to an amount greater than $100,000. Incomes from $50,000 to $100,000 are also heavily taxed. Sales taxes and income taxes eat at incomes from $2,000 to $50,000. Thus a considerable revenue would accrue and that would go far toward preventing inflation.

Fifth, the anti-saving policies of taxation would have to be revised—savings being taxed, corporate savings more leniently, the sums paid out in dividends. Sixth, under six I compile any smaller measures which could be taken. To take one example, inflation could be postponed by fighting consumer credit of all kinds, by prohibiting installment contracts, by doing away with charge accounts, by insisting that everything you buy is paid for by cash or check over the counter. The reason is that in this case you will want more money for the same sum total of transactions and that would slow down the process of inflation.

I don't know how you like my six points, but I know how Congress would like them. You must make up your mind as to what the chances are of such a policy being embarked upon. That is not all. Strict control of industry will impose itself especially in a time such as this after the 1930s when the public would not stand measures taken by private business which they are going to stand when done by the government. Control of industry by the government is much further than is divined. When speaking of war industries, in particular, the investment process will have to be completely rationalized in a prolonged war. Whether you call it rationalizing or whether the investor simply gets orders of how, when, how much to invest is not important. It would be necessary to deal with strikes, slowdowns, and infractions of social discipline. It will be necessary to take control of the education of the young. Finally, it will be necessary to discipline public opinion, for the present way of discussing everything is not conducive to efficiency. We like democracy because it isn't efficient, but if America embarks on a military career this would be dead. If this is embarked upon there will be no return.

Since this will mean a different type of society, the question arises whether a document worded in 1789, when the general opinion of the country and its economic structure were based on the thesis that economic life is a private affair and personal freedom is worth having, could be kept up under these circumstances. The Constitution would not have to be rewritten, only reinterpreted as we have seen it done in the last two hundred years. I don't predict that it will be rewritten, only the whole thing will be completely different.

Now I have been speaking of possibilities. It is no more than a possibility, and I will give you my reason for believing that it is no more than a possibility presently. The upshot, however, if the reality came about along the lines indicated, should be squarely faced. It should be faced in the spirit of a reasonable problem to an old capitalist. There should be no escaping into old slogans. On the other hand, there should be no alarmist talk about bolshevism or Hitlerism, and so forth. Those who hold that there is no danger of these things in this country are right, for Hitlerism is typically German; fascism is typically, nationally Italian; bolshevism is Russian, but not American. Whatever comes will be a growth wearing the color and flavor of the soil. At the same time, it will be far removed from what used to be called the American way of life, as far as the England of the future will be from Merry Old England. The American who sees these possibilities and expects to avoid them in case the country embarks on a prolonged war is an optimist. The American who sees them but says from moral considerations that nevertheless he is going to enter upon the course he thinks is right is a saint. The American who does not see these dangers is a fool.

Now one thing, however, must be borne in mind if what I have said is to give you that impression which it is my wish to convey. All along in this course of lectures it has been my endeavor to describe a social process which offers rather hard nuts to crack to the socio-economic analyst. We have seen, on the one hand, that the course of history or the changes in the spirit of civilization or of an idea are historically and economically conditioned and that there is much that is ineluctable in these fundamental changes. For instance, when we look at the setup of 1914 it is impossible to believe, and I think no competent economist would believe, that that social structure was going to last forever. Probably that change was something which it was beyond human volition, individual volition in any case, to destroy. At the same time we have seen that the nature of the transition is much influenced by events which have not that ineluctable character and which leave much room for personal or groupwise failure or success.

For instance, in order to illustrate this, take the situation of the imperialist government of Russia in 1914. This government was in a comparatively comfortable situation. The Stolypin administration both in the energy it displayed against subversive elements and in the great revenues it had accumulated smoothed the shock of the Japanese war on the Revolution of 1905–1906. The government could have gone on for a time which there is no scientific possibility to foretell. The duma would have developed, there would have been pseudo-constitutionalism at first, real constitutionalism afterward, and so on. Why was this interrupted? Because Russia happened to be without a head at that time, and with the disorganization which that entails individuals like Sazanov had their way. They were able to drag the Empire over the Serbian affairs which had no connection with the fundamental interest of Russia, let alone of the ruling group of Russia. There was no need to go to war over Serbia. Russia did. Colleagues and friends will still explain even that event from the standpoint of a social necessity. My answer would be that that explanation is tautological. If Russia had stayed quiet, there would have been probably no events to speak of during those years and there would have been no Bolshevism. So while on the one hand we are forced to recognize the major role of ineluctable necessity, we are at the same time forced to recognize that there are chance events, success or failure of individuals or groups, ability or inefficiency in certain strata which may considerably change the course of events in the short run. But if you say that the event is changed in the short run, you must also admit that the long run consists of a succession of short runs.

So having realized that, on the one hand, we find that we cannot safely predict any concrete events. What we can predict is factors that will be operative in these events, and that's something. It is no worse than the prediction a doctor can give if you have flu that there is a possibility of pneumonia. In this respect sociological diagnosis is no worse, though it may be worse in other respects, than medical diagnosis. We have also seen that the economic society either of 1914 or later was not in itself played out. The theory is this. The capitalist process produces in various ways which we have seen a social atmo-

sphere hostile to itself, but that doesn't mean that the economic process itself is necessarily obsolete and unable to carry the strata it used
to. Hence, fighting for capitalist civilization is not a hopeless task. The
objective data for the temporary success of such a fight are still present; the strata themselves are still present. This being so, much then
depends, as it always does in such situations, on good management
by well-informed and cold rationality. As I said, the flu need not develop into pneumonia. The case is not analogous to that of the
French Revolution of 1789 when an outworn society came down with
a crash. The situation is different.

Mark the line of my argument. While I said that the fundamental
lines are probably ineluctable and while I said, second, that much in
the way in which the ever-present change comes about depends on
individuals and groups, abilities and volitions, I said, third, that no
more can be achieved by individual or group volitions than to perform transitions with a minimum of loss of human values. The latter,
the bringing about of transitions from your social structure to other
social structures with a minimum of loss of human values, that is how
I should define conservatism.

## Notes

1. The following text represents the written version of a lecture series that
Schumpeter gave in March 1941 at the Lowell Institute in Boston, Massachu-
setts. The lectures were given on Tuesdays and Fridays, starting March 4 and
ending March 28. Schumpeter intended to publish the lectures as a book but
never had the time to finish the manuscript to his satisfaction. For more information, see the section titled "The American Period: Schumpeter's Works
in This Volume" in the Introduction. Published by permission of the Harvard University Archives.

2. It seems that Schumpeter and his wife had begun to compile a bibliography for their planned volume, based on the Lowell Lectures. According to
a "List of Books Relating to *An Economic Interpretation of Our Time*," they
judged the following items to be of interest: Carl Snyder. *Capitalism the Creator: The Economic Foundations of Modern Industrial Society*. New York: Macmillan Co., 1940; Colin Clark. *The Conditions of Economic Progress*. London: Macmillan Co., 1940; Leverett Samuel Lyon, et al. *Government and Economic Life*,
2 vols. Washington, D.C.: Brookings Institution, 1939–1940; Alvin H. Hansen. *Full Recovery or Stagnation?* New York: Norton, 1938; Frank H. Simonds
and Emeny Brooks. *The Great Powers in World Politics: International Relations
and Economic Nationalism*, rev. ed. New York: American Book Co., 1937; Eu-
gene Staley. *World Economy in Transition: Technology vs. Politics, Laissez-faire vs.
Planning, Power vs. Welfare*. New York: Council on Foreign Relations, 1939;
J. B. Condliffe. *The Reconstruction of World Trade*. New York: Norton, 1940;

Cleona Lewis. *America's Stake in International Investments*. Washington, D.C.: Brookings Institution, 1938; Willy Feuerlein and Elizabeth Hannan. *Dollars in Latin America: An Old Problem in a New Setting*. New York: Council on Foreign Relations, 1941; Ernest Minor Patterson. *The Economic Bases of Peace*. New York: McGraw-Hill, 1939; T. H. Marshall, et al. *The Population Problems: The Experts and the Public*. London: G. Allen & Unwin, 1938. (This is especially good for the general reader.); Gunnar Myrdal. *Population, a Problem for Democracy*. Cambridge: Harvard University Press, 1940; Robert R. Kuczynski. *The Measurement of Population Growth: Methods and Results*. New York: Oxford University Press, 1969; A. M. Carr-Saunders. *World Population: Past Growth and Present Trends*. Oxford: Clarenden Press, 1936; the publication of the Economic Intelligence Service of the League of Nations, especially the World Economic Surveys issued annually, volumes are now available from 1931–1932 through 1938–1939.

3. This lecture was given on March 4.

4. This lecture was given on March 7. The text for this lecture seems to have been lost. Instead we here reprint an abstract of lecture 2, which Schumpeter prepared for the Lowell Institute before the course started.

5. This lecture was given on March 11.

6. This lecture was given on March 14.

7. This lecture was given on March 18.

8. This lecture was given on March 21.

9. This lecture was given on March 25.

10. This lecture was given on March 28.

# Nine

## The Future of Private Enterprise
## in the Face of Modern Socialistic Tendencies

PREDICTIONS ABOUT the future of private enterprise must be preceded by an analysis of the results produced by this system up to the present, all the more so because the unfavorable predictions formulated by socialist and quasi-socialist groups are based almost exclusively on purely economic reasoning.[1]

Here then are the essential facts.

1. The indices of total production constructed for "capitalist" countries, although imperfect, bear witness to an annual increase of approximately at least three or four percent, an increase more regular than that of the population but always higher than the latter. Under the system of private enterprise, there was then considerable progress as is indicated by the total production per inhabitant. Also, whatever may be the economic deficiencies of certain countries, it is not consumable products or the power of producing them which is lacking. Except in time of war, those who live in poverty are the people who have not known the system of private enterprise.

2. This increase in the total product, measured by the figures mentioned, has not been accompanied, in spite of Marxist predictions, by an apportionment unfavorable to the working class. Except during the depression years, wages, monetary and real, have been on the increase, so that, interestingly enough, the percentage of the total sum of wages in relation to the national income is visibly constant and this tendency (trend) varies only in the phases of the business cycle. If we take into account the effects of modern fiscal policy, this percentage has increased.

But this "economic progress," not only of societies enjoying the system of private enterprise, but also of their workers' sectors, finds itself periodically interrupted by depressions bringing with them unemployment. It is on these periodic crises and on the indifference to the lot of the victims of unemployment during the nineteenth century that the serious critics of the private enterprise system have concentrated their attacks. For the future, however, it must be noted:

(a) That enlightened cooperation between manufacturers will be able to reduce the amplitude of business fluctuations a great deal;

(b) That the increase in the national revenue, resulting from the system of private enterprise, offers us already and will offer us more completely in the future sufficient means of assuring the worker menaced by unemployment a decent standard of living;

(c) Certain economists support, however, the Secular Stagnation thesis. They have convinced themselves and have convinced part of the public that the phase of expansion of the private sector has passed, that its historic success will not repeat itself, and that, consequently, we will have to face a permanent depression which will require large-scale governmental activity to cure. It is quite natural that the bourgeois world, discouraged by the experience of 1929–1933, not knowing where to turn, profoundly anxious, has surrendered to such philosophies. It is less easy to understand the fact that these philosophies still find adherents just when we can look forward to prodigious industrial development.

If then, in these circumstances, industrial investment were lacking, it would be necessary to lay the blame on a defective business policy.

If it is true, as the statistical data would lead us to believe, that the material progress of the working class is closely allied with the success of private enterprise, it follows that "the antagonism between capital and labor" and the "class struggle" must be among the worst theories of industrial relations. Actually, considered from the scientific point of view, they are nothing but the result of defective reasoning. We shall restrict ourselves to discussion of the following phrase: THE CLASS STRUGGLE.

The conjunction of forces which make the social organism function contains elements of solidarity and antagonism. One observes this everywhere, in each family, committee, party, enterprise, etc. And it is essential to understand that the elements of antagonism are not less necessary to the functioning of a group or of the entire society than the elements of cooperation: from one point of view, there is necessarily cooperation between the primary producer and the producer of the final product; but in the act of selling the primary product, there is at the same time, within certain limits, a conflict of interests between the two, conflict evidently necessary for and inseparable from cooperation. Another instance of conflict bound necessarily to cooperation: the soldiers of a regiment and their commander cooperate in realizing a military goal; nevertheless, and necessarily incidental to this cooperation, there is conflict between the commander and a soldier who makes a mistake. The application to the case of a businessman and his workers being evident, it is only necessary to add that, in this case, the conflicts of the second kind are of particular importance. For, in real life, it is not in the role of capitalist that the businessman faces his workers. First, he is not necessarily owner of the capital which he employs; if he is not, there will be as much conflict of interest between him and his banker as there is between him and his workers, which proves that the conflicts of this type do not assume the characteristics of conflicts between *social classes*. But, even if the businessman is owner of the capital, his function and position are not those of a simple provider either of money or of the physical means of production. This is a profound error (which dates from Adam Smith but which was stressed by Karl Marx) of seeing nothing else in the activity of a captain of enterprise. Rather it is comparable to the role of a military commander; the businessman is essentially a worker who is the leader of other workers.

In the normal group or society, these conflicting elements are integrated with the cooperative elements harmoniously in the framework of a common culture and faith—which prevents the conflicts from being emphasized. As soon as the members of any group, a family for example, lose sight of the framework of individual values and beliefs and see among them only conflicts of interest we witness a social disintegration, that is, a pathological phenomenon which, in its turn, brings about other pathological phenomena. And if the phrase "class struggle" indicates a wrong theory, it indicates at the same time the presence of a real fact: namely, our society is in the process of falling apart.

But why—if on the one hand the productive forces are continuing to develop in a satisfactory manner, and if on the other hand the working class are participating in this progress as much as all the others—why is there any social conflict? To answer this question we have only to return to our example of a family, a very modern one, whose members end up hating each other. A similar situation obviously does not derive necessarily from poverty or from a conflict of economic interests. On the contrary, one often observes it among wealthy circles without the economic interests of the members revealing the slightest *objective* conflict. The diagnosis, in the individual case, can be very difficult and it may even happen that it is impossible to attribute the unsettled state of that family to well-defined faults or errors. But it is very easy to indicate the two general causes which tend to produce social decomposition: it is the lack of *faith among the governing class* and the lack of what one calls "leadership." Families, workshops, societies do not function if nobody accepts his duties, if no one knows how to make himself accepted as *leader*, and if each applies himself to constantly drawing up a balance sheet of his personal and immediate benefits and costs at any given time.

It is however precisely in this that the "utilitarian" philosophy of the last century resulted. This system of ideas, developed in the eighteenth century, recognizes no other regulatory principle than that of individual egoism. By investigating the course of history, it is doubtless possible to explain how this principle of irreligious (and also perfectly stupid) rationalism imposed itself on a long line of thinkers whose intelligence cannot be questioned. But it matters little. The essential fact is that, whether as cause or consequence, this philosophy expresses only too well the spirit of social irresponsibility which characterized the passion, and the secular, or rather secularized, state in the nineteenth century. And in the midst of moral confusion, economic success serves only to render still more serious the social and political situation which is the natural result of a century of economic liberalism.

Will the solution to this grave problem spring from authoritarian statism, which may doubtless assume more than one form but of which the perfect example is bolshevism? Not at all. Does it come from democratic socialism? Again, no. But where then is it necessary to look? It will be necessary to turn to corporate organization in the sense advocated by *Quadragesimo Anno*. It is not the economist's role to praise a moral message of the Pope. But he can draw out an economic doctrine from it. This doctrine does not call upon false theories. It does not rest on so-called tendencies that do not exist. It recognizes all the facts of the modern economy. And, while bringing a remedy to the present disorganization, it shows us the functions of private initiative in a new framework. The corporate principle organizes but it does not regiment. It is opposed to all social systems with a centralizing tendency and to all bureaucratic regimentation; it is, in fact, the only means of rendering the latter impossible.

Nevertheless, good men whose minds are completely open to the message of Pius XI see in it only the vision of an ideal. But the Pope was not speaking "from up in the clouds." He was showing us a practical method to solve practical problems of immediate urgency. They are precisely the problems which, through the impotence of economic liberalism to solve them, call for the intervention of political power. To give only one example, let us ask ourselves what happens in a depression. Business firm A cannot work because firm B is not working; B can't because C finds itself incapable of producing, and so on. No single firm can, by its own action, break the "vicious circle." Whence the closing down of an entire industry, a closing down that ends only too easily in the ruin which menaces all enterprises and of which the workers are the victims. But the corporate action of professional associations, by the fact that it guarantees to every individual enterprise that it will not be the only one to advance, that consequently it will find in the production of others the demand for its output, is the most natural remedy for the situation. It follows that the corporatism of association would eliminate the most serious of the obstacles to peaceable cooperation between worker and owner. In the economic world stabilized by corporate action, the idea of the "annual wage" would no longer meet with insurmountable obstacles and would no longer impose intolerable risks upon anyone.

One cannot deny that to succeed it will be necessary first to resolve the problem of organization. But there is in addition a much more serious difficulty. In a society that is disintegrating, centralist and authoritarian statism tends to be self-developing. It happens as a logical result of this decomposition, simply by replacing with the bureaucratic mechanism the mechanisms of laissez-faire as they cease to function. One has only to do nothing in order to assure not its success but its victory. Now, corporatism of association is not a mechanical thing. It cannot be imposed or created by legislative power. It does not tend to materialize by itself. It can be brought to birth only by the action of free men and by the faith which inspires them. To establish it and to make it succeed, willpower, energy, and a new sense of social responsibility are required. It will have to struggle against formidable obstacles, and this in a world whose largest part is dominated already by a bolshevik dictator. But its main problem, as well as its glory, is summed up in the fact that, more than an economic and social reform, it implies a moral reform.

## Notes

1. This text is based on a speech which Schumpeter gave on November 19, 1945, in Montreal at the first convention of L'Association Professionelle des Industriels. It was first published in the proceedings of the convention, *Comment sauvegarder l'entreprise privée* (Montreal 1946). A translation, by Michael G. Prime and David R. Henderson, appeared in 1975 in *History of Political Economy*. For more information about Schumpeter's Montreal speech, see the section titled "The American Period: Schumpeter's Works in This Volume" in the Introduction.

# Ten

## Comments on a Plan for the Study of Entrepreneurship

### I

In his presidential address at the 1946 meeting of the Economic History Association, Professor Arthur H. Cole leveled an indictment at economic analysis of the "theoretical" type to the effect that it has neglected throughout the phenomena of economic change.[1,2] Whatever the theorist might adduce in extenuation, substantially the indictment stands: with rare unanimity—there are very few exceptions—theorists from Cantillon onward have displayed surprisingly little interest in the causes, mechanisms, and effects of economic change as such. It should be particularly noticed that this applies also to Keynes and the Keynesians who, reasoning on a given propensity to consume, a given liquidity preference, a given marginal efficiency of a capital equipment—that is of given and unvarying amount and kind—explicitly exclude from sight what to the unbiased mind is the most striking feature of capitalist life—the incessant revolution, by a "disruptive innovating energy," of existing industrial and commercial patterns.[3]

Cole's indictment must not be confused with another which is entirely unfounded, viz., that economists believe in the permanence of the capitalist *order* and never envisage an alternative or recognize any tendency toward such an alternative, i.e., that they are blind to the actual or possible changes in economic institutions—an aspersion that can be refuted from the pages of John Stuart Mill, not to mention any modern author. Nor should Cole's indictment be interpreted to mean that theorists failed or fail to speculate about factors of purely economic change nor about the results these were supposed to produce in the long run. Adam Smith systematized older thought into a schema that, though with many modifications and changes of emphasis, persisted into Marshallian and post-Marshallian times: the factors recognized being, besides changes in public policy and institutions, increase in population, increase—through saving—in the quantity of physical means of production ("capital"), and increasing division of labor which included from the first, and was more and more replaced by, "progress of the arts" and was treated as the automatic consequence of automatically expanding markets. But it is precisely this schema which justifies Cole's indictment. For economic life most obviously is not the passive process, consisting in smooth and uniquely determined adaptation to changing data, which it should be according to that schema. If we insist that it is and that the convulsions and revolutions which we actually observe are nothing but "transitional phenomena" and have no influence upon long-run results, we are obliterating problems rather than resolving them. Moreover, we are distorting the picture of the most ordinary business practice. For, in capitalist society, economic behavior is at every point of time dominated by the effects, actual or anticipated, of technological or commercial change and cannot be understood without it. Everyone would behave differently if the main consideration were adaptation to stable conditions. Planning a production schedule, figuring out costs, depreciating one's plant and equipment, pricing one's product, struggling to protect one's market—all these things would be different matters and have different meanings but for everyone's realization that he is standing on ground which is bound to give way before long. The consequences of overlooking the fact that revolution in existing industrial and commercial patterns is the permanent state of things— instead of being something that occasionally happens to disturb the "normal" flow of economic processes—carry over, on the one hand, into our attitudes toward practical problems and, on the other hand, into the conceptual apparatus of economic theory.

As regards the first, let us consider the questions that arise in connection with price agreements. We are in the habit of treating them simply as devices to increase or maintain profits—to replace competition by monopolistic pricing. There is no objection to this view. But monopolistic pricing under supposedly stationary conditions is one thing, and monopolistic pricing under the conditions of perennial upheaval of existing industrial structures is another thing. The phenomenon, its causes and effects, cannot be fully understood if we neglect this distinction. As regards the second, let us consider the concept, Entrepreneur. Under the influence of Jean Baptiste Say, this concept—and the word for which there is no good English equivalent—has been indeed introduced into English economics by John Stuart Mill. But there is really no room for it in the economic system of the Smith-Ricardo-Mill-Marshall tradition: in a world such as these economists depicted, there is, to be sure, room for the function of administrative direction. But this is covered by the term "Management." And there is no adequate room for the entrepreneur as distinguished from the manager on the one hand, and the risk-taking capitalist on the other.[4] It is submitted that there is reason for looking askance at a theory that all but excludes from its picture of reality the most conspicuous figure in the capitalist process. Of course, this also spoils our grasp of other phenomena. For money, credit, banking, interest, employment, and other things are so closely related to enterprise that no satisfactory analysis of them is possible without reference to it. But what is the reason for these shortcomings which are not less obvious in the Keynesian teaching of today than they are in the Millian teaching of a century ago? The reason is that neither attended systematically to the details of the social processes by which industrial and commercial structures emerge and vanish. Whatever else it may be, enterprise is essentially part of the mechanism of economic change. It is only by analyzing the latter that we can see what it really is.

A satisfactory analysis of economic change—to avoid the colored word "progress"—can only be achieved by historical work. For the economic historian, even when description of a state is his immediate object, it is natural to look upon economic life as a process of change and to make his main theme out of what theorists touch but perfunctorily. Much more important is it, however, that historical work alone can furnish material from which to arrive at scientifically reliable propositions about economic change and, therefore, about entrepreneurship. A severely limited number of facts of common experience may suffice in order to build the organon of economic logic usually referred to as "theory." Even our dubious friend, the economic man, may render useful service in a field the main propositions of which can be reduced to maximum and minimum problems. But beyond this we need more than that if we are to see the true shape of our phenomena. Entrepreneurs are certainly not economic men in the theoretical sense. What they really are, how they really work, what it is that conditions their performance and their failures, how they in turn help to shape the conditions under which they work, and, above all, whether any significant generalizations may be made about all this, can be gleaned from history alone. The relation between historical and theoretical work varies widely from one type or field of economic inquiry to another. In our case the theory itself is historical in nature. Considering how much of our understanding of capitalist reality depends upon correct answers to those questions, the importance of Cole's suggestion cannot be emphasized too strongly. It may result in a new wing being added to the economist's house.

But while the suggestion itself is novel the genus to which this type of study belongs is not. Economic as well as other historians have never confined themselves to topics defined in terms of a nation or epoch. They have always also dealt with topics defined in terms of problems. The origins and functioning of the medieval manor, the rise of capitalism, the emergence of deposit banking, modern company laws are examples. The plan of a systematic study of those mechanisms of change that center in entrepreneurship, therefore, lies within the boundaries of an established and, so it seems to me, not unsuccessful practice.

## II

I have tried to trace the line of thought that leads from a perception of the inadequacy of economists' ideas about the factors, mechanisms, and effects of economic change to the proposed historical investigation into "entrepreneurship." It should be emphasized that this plan does not imply any preconception concerning the importance of the entrepreneur's role. This role is to be investigated because it constitutes an avenue to the study of economic change and, besides, presents many interesting problems, but not because there is a theory *a limine* to the effect that entrepreneurship is the motive power or creator of "economic progress." In fact, if anything is clear from the outset, it is the proposition that this cannot be so except in a very special sense—which involves the recognition of "objective" conditioning factors—that have as much claim to being dubbed "causal" as has the action they condition. Every investigator will distribute emphasis as he pleases and there are, in this as in other respects, irreducible personal equations—irreducible differences of vision: people will always differ as to whether the battle of Austerlitz was won by Napoleon, or by a social system, or by the French nation, or by a military apparatus and a technique inherited from the Revolution. This does not preclude scientific analysis of that campaign and all that need be said about this aspect of the proposed plan is that it does not imply any hero worship or in fact the acceptance of any dogma.

Investigation into the conditions that call forth, favor, impede entrepreneurial activity is therefore an essential part of the plan and may conceivably produce its most valuable results. We have all of us certain ideas about it and the introductory parts of most standard treatises—those of Mill and Marshall for instance—mention such conditioning factors as location, physical properties of the environment—climate, coal, iron, fish—social organization, "good government," freedom, and—which it is quite surprising to find in the book of a radical and utilitarian like John Stuart Mill—racial qualities. Such by-the-way generalities which are convincing only where they are trivially obvious do not amount to much. But systematic work might make something out of them. Moreover, "historical theories" of widely differing degrees of seriousness have been offered, e.g., concerning the favorable or unfavorable influence of inflation, of wars, of religion, of taxation, of protection, and the like. And scholarly economic historiography, working on the details of individual processes, has, more often by implication rather than explicitly, a lot of pertinent facts to give us. Again, what is required is, first, critical systematization of these views and these materials and, second, an organized effort to penetrate through and beyond them toward reliable generalizations. Two aspects of this type of problem deserve to be particularly noticed.

First, it is a commonplace that, in the social sciences, we are but rarely in a position to speak of clear-cut causes and effects. Instead we mostly have interaction between the elements of the social system. And this is as true within sequences as it is within a static system. But this commonplace embodies a considerable difficulty which it takes much labor to cope with and which is a source of meaningless differences of opinion. To illustrate this, let us consider such a case as Sir Robert Peel's free-trade legislation or the passing of the English company laws. In a sense these were causative factors that "conditioned"—facilitated—certain subsequent developments. But they did not fall out of the blue sky. They were themselves caused or conditioned by preexisting industrial, commercial, and financial patterns to which those subsequent developments might be *directly* linked—as their "true" causes—by any historian who chooses to emphasize this fact rather than the "relative autonomy" of the political sector of society, e.g., by a historian who adopts the theory that the economic process runs on, as it were, under its own steam, shaping legal institutions to its requirements. The same problem arises with respect to the increase of technological knowledge—which is obviously both a conditioning and a conditioned factor—and to the development of auxiliary techniques and services such as accounting or specialized trades—as, for example, the development of the wool industry conditioning the emergence of specialized wool brokers and this again conditioning further expansion of the wool industry. This applies also to the time-honored "causes," increase in capital and population. To develop a method for dealing with such hen-and-egg problems is one of the most important prerequisites for the success of the proposed study.

Second, practically all the economists of the nineteenth century believed uncritically that all that is needed in order to explain a given historical development is to indicate conditioning or causal factors such as have been mentioned above. But this is sufficient only in the rarest of cases. As a rule, no factor acts in a uniquely determined way and, whenever it does not, the necessity arises of going into the details of its modus operandi, into the *mechanisms* through which it acts. Examples will illustrate this. Sometimes an increase in population actually has no other effects than those predicated by classical theory— namely, a fall in per capita real income;[5] but, at other times, it may have an energizing effect that induces new developments with the result that per capita real income rises. Or a protective duty may have no other effect than to increase the price of the protected commodity and, in consequence, its output; but it may also induce a complete reorganization of the protected industry which eventually results in an increase in output so great as to reduce price below its initial level. Or a downward shift in the demand curve of a commodity—owing, e.g., to a change in fashion—may indeed, as traditional theory teaches, be met simply by contraction; but it may also be met by a change in the product or its method of production which *may* issue in expansion instead of in contraction; even if there be nothing but contraction, it can be effected in many different ways that produce different effects upon the industry and the employment it gives.

Before going on, let us use this opportunity to introduce an important distinction between different kinds of reaction to change in "conditions." Its common sense is immediately obvious from the examples used above. Whenever an economy or a sector of an economy adapts itself to a change in its data in the way which traditional theory describes, whenever, that is, an economy reacts to an increase in population by simply adding the new brains and hands to the working force in the existing employments, or an industry reacts to a protective duty by expansion within its existing practice or to a fall in its demand by a contraction within its existing practice, we shall speak of *adaptive response*. And whenever the economy or an industry or some firms in an industry do something else, something, namely, that is outside of the range of existing practice, we shall speak of *creative response*.

The essential points about creative response are these. First, from the standpoint of the observer who is in full possession of all relevant facts, it can always be understood *ex post*; but it can practically never be understood *ex ante*, that is to say, it cannot be predicted from the preexisting facts together with the ordinary rules of inference. This is why the "How," in what has been above called the "mechanisms," must be investigated in each case. Second, creative response shapes the whole course of subsequent events and their "long-run" outcome. It is not so that the types of responses dominate only what the economist loves to call "transitions," leaving the ultimate outcome determined by the initial data. Creative response changes social and economic situations for good, or, to put it differently, it creates situations from which there is no bridge to those situations that might have emerged in its absence. This is why creative response is an essential element in the historical process: no deterministic credo avails against this. Third, creative response—the frequency of its occurrence in a group, its intensity and success or otherwise—has obviously *something*, be that much or little, to do (a) with quality of the personnel available in a society; (b) with relative quality of personnel, that is, with quality available to a particular field of activity relatively to quality available, at the same time, to others; (c) with individual decisions, actions, patterns of behavior. And this is why it is convenient to identify creative response in business activity with entrepreneurship: the mechanisms of economic change in capitalist society[6] pivot certainly on entrepreneurial activity: however we may wish to distribute our emphasis between opportunity or conditions and individual or groupwise response, it is patently true that in capitalist society objective opportunities or conditions act *through* entrepreneurial activity, analysis of which is therefore, as previously stated, at the very least an avenue to the study of economic change in the capitalist epoch. This is compatible with widely different views as to its importance as an "ultimate cause."

## III

Viewed in this light, the entrepreneur and his function[7] are not difficult to conceptualize: the defining characteristic is simply the doing of new things or the doing of things that are already being done in a new way (innovation).[8] It is but natural, and in fact only an advantage, that such a definition does not draw any sharp line between what is and what is not "enterprise." For actual life itself knows no such sharp division, though it shows up the type well enough. It should be observed at once that the "new thing" need not be spectacular or of historic importance. It need not be Bessemer steel or the explosion motor. It can be the Deerfoot sausage. To see the phenomenon even in the humblest state of the business world is quite essential though it may be difficult to find the humble entrepreneurs historically.

Distinction from other functions with which entrepreneurship is frequently but not necessarily associated—just as "farmership" is frequently but not necessarily associated with the ownership of land and with the activity of a farm hand—does not present conceptual difficulties either. We have already adverted to the distinction between enterprise and management: evidently it is one thing to set up a concern embodying a new idea and another thing to head the administration of a going concern, however much the two may shade off into each other. Also, we have already seen that the entrepreneurial function, though facilitated by the ownership of means, is not identical with that of the capitalist.[9] New light is urgently needed on the relation between the two, especially because of the cant phrases that are current on this topic. But it is particularly important to distinguish the entrepreneur from the "inventor." Many inventors have become entrepreneurs and the relative frequency of this case is no doubt an interesting subject to investigate, but there is no necessary connection between the two functions. The inventor produces ideas, the entrepreneur "gets things done," which may but need not embody anything that is *scientifically* new. Moreover, an idea or scientific principle is not, by itself, of any importance for economic practice: the fact that Greek science had probably produced all that is necessary in order to construct a steam engine did not help the Greeks or Romans to build a steam engine; the fact that Leibnitz suggested the idea of the Suez canal exerted no influence whatever on economic history for two hundred years. And as different as the functions, are the two sociological and psychological types.[10] Finally, "getting new things done" is not only a distinct process but it is a process that produces consequences that are an essential part of capitalist reality. The whole economic history of capitalism would be different from what it is, if new ideas had been currently and smoothly adopted, as a matter of course, by all firms to whose business they were relevant. But they were not. It is in most cases only one man or a few men who see the new possibility and are able to cope with the resistances and difficulties with which action always meets outside of the ruts of established practice. This accounts, on the one hand, for the size of the gains that success often entails, and, on the other hand, for the losses and vicissitudes that it produces for other people. These things, however, are important. If, in every individual case, they may indeed be called transitional difficulties, they are transitional difficulties which are never absent in the economy as a whole and which dominate the atmosphere of capitalist life permanently. Hence it seems appropriate to keep "invention" distinct from "innovation."

The definition that equates enterprise to innovation is of course a very abstract one. Some classifications that are richer in content may be noticed because of their possible use in drawing up plans for specific pieces of research. There is, first, the obvious classification—historical and systematic—of the phenomena of enterprise according to institutional forms, such as the medieval trading company, the later "chartered companies," the partnership, the modern "corporation" and the like—on all of which there exist a vast amount of historical work.[11] The interaction of institutional forms and entrepreneurial activity—the "shaping" influence of the former and the "bursting" influence of the latter—is, as has already been stated, a major topic for further inquiry. Closely connected with this classification is, secondly, the old one according to fields of activity—commerce, industry, finance[12]—which has been refined into the following one: enterprise that introduces "new" commodities; enterprise that introduces technological novelties into the production of "old" commodities; enterprise that introduces new commercial combinations such as the opening up of new markets for products or new sources of supply of materials; enterprise that consists in reorganizing an industry, for instance, by making a monopoly out of it.[13]

But there are other classifications that may prove helpful. For instance, thirdly, we may classify entrepreneurs as to origins and sociological types: feudal lords and aristocratic landowners, civil servants—particularly important, for instance, in Germany after the Thirty Years' War, especially in mining—farmers, workmen, artisans, members of the learned professions, as has often been noticed, all embarked upon enterprise and it is from several points of view highly interesting to clear up this matter. Or, fourthly, we may try to classify entrepreneurial performances as to the precise nature of the "function" filled and the aptitudes—some may even add motivation—involved. Since all this presumably changed significantly in the course of the capitalist epoch, economic historians are particularly qualified for work on this line.[14] Though the phrase "getting a new thing done" may be adequately comprehensive, it covers a great many different activities which, as the observer stresses one more than another or as his material displays one more than another, may, locally, temporarily, or generally, lend different colors to entrepreneurship: in some cases, or to some observers, it may be the activity of "setting up" or "organizing" which stands out from the others; in other cases, or for other observers, it may be the breaking down of the resistances of the environment; in still other cases, or for still other observers, simply leadership or, again, salesmanship. Thus, it seems to me, there was a type of entrepreneur in early capitalist industry that is best described as a "fixer." Modern history furnishes many instances in which entrepreneurship was vested in a company promotor.[15] The typical industrial entrepreneur of the nineteenth century was perhaps the man who put into practice a novel method of production by embodying it in a new firm and, who, in case of success, then settled down into a position of owner-manager of a going concern or also into the position of a stockholding president of a company getting old and conservative in the process. In the large-scale corporation of today, the question that is never quite absent arises with a vengeance, namely, who should be considered as the entrepreneur. In a well-known book, Robert A. Gordon has presented much interesting material bearing upon this question.[16]

The economic nature, amount, and distribution of the returns to entrepreneurial activity constitute another set of problems on which work on the lines of Professor Cole's plan may be expected to shed much-needed light. Conceptual difficulties confront us here even before we come up against the still more formidable difficulties of fact-finding. For the "profit" of the English classics which was analyzed by John Stuart Mill into wages of management, premia for risk, and interest on owned capital, was a return to normal business activity and something quite different from, though influenced by, the gain of successful enterprise *in our sense of the term*. What the latter is, can best be explained by considering a special case. Suppose that a man, realizing the possibility of producing acceptable caviar from sawdust, sets up the Excelsior Caviar concern and makes it a success. If this concern is too small to influence the prices of either the product or the factors of production, he will sell the former and buy the latter at current prices. If, however, he turns out the unit of caviar more cheaply than his competitors, owing to his using a much cheaper raw material, he will for a time, that is, until other firms copy his method, make an (essentially temporary) surplus gain. This gain is attributable to personal exertion. Hence it might be called wages. It may with equal justice be attributed to the fact that, for a time, his method is exclusively his own. Hence it might also be called a monopoly gain. But whether we elect to call it wages or monopoly gain, we must add immediately that it is a special kind of wages or monopoly gain that differs in important respects from what we usually mean to denote by these terms. And so we had better call it simply entrepreneurial gain or profit. However, it should be observed that if this venture mean a "fortune," this fortune does not typically arise from the actual net receipts being saved up and invested in the same or some other business. Essentially, it emerges as a *capital* gain, i.e., as the discounted value of the stream of prospective returns.

In this simple case—which however does constitute a type—the investigator is not confronted with difficulties other than those involved in fact finding. Also it is clear what happens with that surplus gain: in this case the entrepreneurial gain goes to the entrepreneur,[17] and we can also see—if we have the facts—how, to use a current phrase, the "fruits of the progress involved are handed to consumers and workmen." The speed of this process of "handing on" varies widely, but it would always work, in isolated cases like the one under discussion, through a fall in the price of the product to the new level of costs which is bound to occur whenever competition steps up to the successful concern. But even here we meet the practice of innovators to keep their returns alive by means of patents and in other ways. And the gains described above shade off into gains from purposive restriction of competition and create difficulties of diagnosis that are sometimes insurmountable.[18] Cumulation of carefully analyzed historical cases is the best means to shed light on these things, to supply the theorist with strategic assumptions, and to banish slogans.

If innovations are neither relatively small nor isolated events, complications crowd upon us. Entrepreneurial activity then affects wage and interest rates from the outset and becomes a factor—the fundamental factor in my opinion—in booms and depressions. This is one reason, but not the only one, why entrepreneurial gains are not net returns (a) to the whole set of people who attempt entrepreneurial ventures; (b) to the industrial sector in which innovation occurs; (c) to the capitalist interests that finance entrepreneurial activity and to the capitalist class as a whole. Concerning the first point, I might have made my special case more realistic by assuming that several or many people try their hands at producing that caviar but that all but one fail to produce a salable product *before* the success of this one presents an example to copy. The gain of the successful entrepreneur and of the capitalists who finance him—for, whenever capital finances enterprise, the interest is paid out of the entrepreneurial gain, a fact that is very important for our grasp of the interest phenomenon—should be related not to *his* effort and *their* loan but to the effort and the loans of all the entrepreneurs and capitalists who made attempts and lost. The presence of gains to enterprise so great as to impress us as spectacular and, from the standpoint of society, irrational is then seen to be compatible with a negative return to entrepreneurs and financing capitalists as a group.[19] Concerning the second point, it is similarly clear that entrepreneurial gain is not a net accretion to the returns of the industrial sector in which it occurs. The impact of the new product or method spells losses to the "old" firms. The competition of the man with a significantly lower cost curve is, in fact, the really effective competition that in the end revolutionizes the industry. Detailed investigation of this process which may take many forms might teach us much about the actual working of capitalism that we are but dimly perceiving as yet. Concerning the third point, while we have a fair amount of information as to how the working class fares in the process of economic change—both as to real wages and as to employment—we know much less about that elusive entity, capital, that is being incessantly destroyed and re-created. That the theorist's teaching is unrealistic, according to which capital "migrates" from declining to rising industries, is obvious: the capital "invested" in railroads does not migrate into trucking and air transportation but will perish in and with the railroads. Investigation into the histories of industries, concerns, and firms—including surveys of sectors in order to point out how long a typical firm stays in business and how and why it drops out—might dispel many a preconceived notion on this subject.

In the modern corporation, entrepreneurial gains are as a rule merged with many other elements into the profit item, and the individuals who fill the entrepreneurial function are separated from them—accepting the salaries and other prerequisites of executives in lieu of them. There is, however, an interesting exception to this. If a corporation be founded in order to take over a number of existing concerns, then the difference between their combined "values" and the "value" of the new corporation should, theoretically, correspond to the entrepreneurial gain resulting from whatever it is that constitutes the entrepreneurial performance involved in the founding of the corporation. There used to be a theory to the effect that preferred stock and bonds was to represent the value of, and to pay for, the constituent concerns, whereas the common stock was to represent the incremented value.[20] But in practice this worked so little according to design that the apparent indication as to size and distribution of entrepreneurial gain is presumably next to valueless.

Finally, I beg leave to touch upon one more set of problems on which we may expect light from historical analysis, namely, the problems that come within the range of the question: Does the importance of the entrepreneurial function decline as time goes on? There are serious reasons for believing that it does. The entrepreneurial performance involves, on the one hand, the ability to perceive new opportunities that cannot be proved at the moment at which action has to be taken, and, on the other hand, willpower adequate to breaking down the resistance that the social environment offers to change. But the range of the provable expands and action upon flashes or hunches is increasingly replaced by action that is based upon "figuring out." And modern milieus *may* offer less resistance to new methods and new goods than used to be the case. So far as this is so, the element of personal intuition and force would be less essential than it was: it could be expected to yield its place to the teamwork of specialists, or, in other words, improvement could be expected to become more and more automatic. Our impression to this effect is reinforced by parallel phenomena in other fields of activity: for instance, a modern commander no doubt means less in the outcome of a war than commanders meant of old, and for the same reasons: compaigns have become more calculable than they used to be and there is less scope for personal leadership.

But this is at present only an impression. It is for the historian to establish or to refute it. If, however, it should stand up under research, this would be a result of the utmost importance. We should be led to expect that the whole mechanism of economic development will significantly change. Among other things, the economy would progressively bureaucratize itself—of which, in fact, there are many symptoms. And consequences would extend far beyond the field of economic phenomena. Just as warrior classes have declined in importance ever since warfare—and especially the management of armies in the field—began to be increasingly "mechanized," so the business class may decline in importance as its most vital figure, the entrepreneur, progressively loses his most essential function. But this would mean a different social structure.

## IV

Therefore, the sociology of enterprise reaches much further than is implied in questions concerning the conditions that produce and shape, favor or inhibit entrepreneurial activity: it extends to the structure and the very foundations of, at least, capitalist society or the capitalist sector of any given society. The quickest way of showing this starts from recognition of the facts that, just as the rise of the bourgeois class as a whole is associated with success in commercial, industrial, and financial enterprise, so the rise of an individual family to "capitalist" status within that class is typically[21] associated with entrepreneurial success; and that the elimination of a family from the "capitalist" class is typically associated with the loss of those attitudes and aptitudes of industrial leadership or alertness that enter our picture of the entrepreneurial type of businessman.

Now these facts, if they be facts, might teach us a lot about such fundamental problems as the nature of the class structure of capitalist society; the sort of class civilization which it develops and which differs so characteristically from the class civilization of feudal society; its schema of values; its politics, especially its attitudes to State and Church and War; its performance and failures; its degree of durability. But a great deal of work needs to be done in order to arrive at scientifically defensible opinions about all these and cognate things. First of all, these "facts" must be established. How far is it really true, for instance, that entrepreneurs, while not forming a social class themselves but originating in almost all existing strata, do "feed" or renew the capitalist stratum or that, to put it differently, the latter recruits itself from the entrepreneurial successes, or that, to put it still differently, the "typical" history of industrial families leads back to entrepreneurial performances that "create" a concern which will, for a time, yield capitalistic surpluses by being merely "administrated" with more or less efficiency? How much statistical truth is there in the slogan: "Three generations from overalls to overalls?" Second, what is, as measured by observable results, the economic and cultural—also political—importance of the further fact that, though the entrepreneurial *function* cannot be transmitted by inheritance—except, possibly, by biological inheritance—the financial or industrial *position* that has been created can? How much truth is there in the contention that the industrial family interest is, in capitalist society, the guardian of the nation's economic future?

These questions which could be readily multiplied have often attracted attention. Every textbook of economic history contains some material about the origins of entrepreneurs of historical standing, and there is a number of studies that have been inspired by full awareness of the importance of the answers for our understanding of capitalist society and of the ways in which it works.[22] But these studies are few and that attention has been desultory. We do not know enough in order to form valid generalizations or even enough to be sure whether there are any generalizations to form. As it is, most of us economists have some opinions on these matters. But these opinions have more to do with our preconceived ideas or ideals than with solid fact, and our habit of illustrating them by stray instances that have come under our notice is obviously but a poor substitute for serious research. Veblen's—or, for that matter, Bucharin's—*Theory of the Leisure Class* exemplifies well what I mean. It is brilliant and suggestive. But it is an impressionist essay that does not come to grips with the real problems involved. Yet there is plenty of material. A great and profitable task awaits the man or group to undertake it.

# V

Thus, historical analysis of enterprise seems to resolve itself into economic history or even social and political history in general. In a sense this is true but it is no more so than the analogous statement would be with reference to any major aspect of human behavior. An analytic history of strategy, for instance, is bound to lead its author practically everywhere if he really aims at fundamental explanations in terms of social "forces" and effects. This does not mean, however, that there is no point in writing a history of strategy per se. Similarly, the fact that all that constitutes the social process as a whole is relevant to economic enterprise, and vice versa, is no reason to despair if the goal is to work out an analytic history of enterprise that is to display all its aspects and forms and thus to give its due to a phenomenon which it is important, even for some of the most practical problems of our own day, to see in its true light whatever that may be. So many slogans, eulogistic or derogatory, hinge upon it—slogans which form an important part of the public's economics—that a scientific duty of clarifying these matters is beyond doubt. Since fulfillment of this duty requires a vast amount of historical work that will be most effective if carried out according to a definite plan, it is indeed convenient to constitute an agency—an "institute" or committee—that is to undertake the tasks of exploration and coordination, while leaving plenty of room for the initiative of individual workers.

The material that suggests itself at the outset is substantially the same as that which goes into the usual monograph on an individual industry or locality. Work on this line is perhaps more likely than any other to produce case studies of the factors, mechanisms, and effects of economic change and to show up the place of entrepreneurship within them. Beyond this a natural bifurcation comes into view. On the one hand, there is, as we have seen, the world of "conditions," physical, institutional, political, and so on, not to forget the growth of legal and business techniques such as the negotiable paper and double-entry bookkeeping; on the other hand, there is the world of types of "responses" to "objective" opportunities or barriers, the investigation of which frequently leads into the history of individual concerns and of individual men and their backgrounds and stocks. Thus, a vast amount of additional material enters the picture that includes all of what is meant by business history and much besides, even to the genealogy of industrial families. The bricks that are needed for the building are so many and so varied that contributions of the most different kinds will all fit into the comprehensive plan which therefore, however definite it may be, need not place any irksome restrictions upon the personal tastes, ideas, or methods of those who wish to cooperate. To offer suggestions to workers that want them and to keep account of results is all that is needed, at all events in the exploratory stage.

Moreover, though it is desirable that a small semi-permanent staff should be assembled to cooperate with one or more established economic historians in original research and in breaking new ground and that other established historians start work in the field under discussion on their initiative, it seems possible to solicit the cooperation, in a more detached fashion, of practically all economic historians whatever their aims or fields. This would mean no more than drawing their attention to this particular aspect of economic history and to provide them with certain questions that they may be able to answer without going out of their way. This applies also to writers of general economic histories of individual epochs or countries and to writers of textbooks. Instigation and utilization of such incidental or subsidiary research might possibly yield many valuable contributions without disturbing work on other lines and without taking anyone out of the field of his choice.

## VI

From what has been said above it follows that historical work on entrepreneurship need not start from scratch. There is a vast wealth of material scattered all over the literature of economic history and it is published source material that only awaits coordination and systematization in order to provide us with a basis from which to start further research and with the nucleus of an archive. Nor is this surprising. For it is impossible to present, e.g., a picture of the rise of capitalism or, for that matter, of the emergence of modern America without running up against *either* the entrepreneurial factor *or* those facts, practices, institutions that condition it and shape its types and modi operandi. It is not even possible to write a political history of the reign of Charles V without taking note of the doings of the Fuggers or of the reign of Napoleon III without meeting the brothers Péreire. But this amounts to saying that we are already in possession of many hundreds of case studies in entrepreneurship. And it is precisely this fact which shows both the timeliness and the hopefulness of the lead that has been given by Professor Cole. It also shows the necessity of teamwork in this field.

Therefore I beg leave to finish my comments by submitting an extremely modest suggestion. I have said above that new original work in the matter must wait upon the initiative of individual investigators and that, so far as this goes, the main things seems to be to draw the attention of economic historians to a particular point of view and to try to persuade them to contribute to the understanding of the entrepreneurial factor as opportunities for doing so occur to them in the course of their work whatever its program may be. No doubt we hope for more than this. Meanwhile, however, and as a beginning, it may be useful to start with something less than this, viz., with sifting and coordinating what we have already. This modest, yet indispensable work can be done at an expense not greater than is implied in employing three or four research assistants working under the directions of an experienced historian or of a committee of such historians.

In order to illustrate my meaning, I have, from shelves reserved for books on modern economic history, picked at random four volumes. They happen to be: (1) William T. Baxter's *The House of Hancock* (1945); (2) Fritz Redlich's *History of American Business Leaders* (1940); (3) the 3rd volume of Victor S. Clark's *History of American Manufacturers in the United States* (1929); and (4) Arthur C. Cole's and Harold F. Williamson's *The American Carpet Manufacturers* (1941).

Now, (1) is a very good example for what I mean when speaking of "case studies in entrepreneurship"—and a fully explicit one to boot. All that the hypothetical historian or committee envisaged above would have to do, or to direct his (their) research assistants to do, with this type of literature is:

(a) To compile a comprehensive catalogue (given sufficient means, the committee should of course acquire a collection of such works for the benefit of further research); (b) to analyze the contents of each item as to material, method, and quality of work; (c) to report briefly on what each item contributes to the knowledge of entrepreneurial types and of the social and economic functions of entrepreneurship (these reports being drawn up according to a preconceived plan, embodied perhaps in the form of a questionnaire);[23] and (d) to point out such lacunae, desiderata, and research opportunities as this exploratory work suggests.

[Book] (2) is, of course, as it stands a full-fledged example for one type of work to be done. Being distinguished by the clearness and "purposiveness" with which it keeps the goal in view, it might make good material for a discussion in the Committee from which suggestions for improvement and definite formulation of a "project" (not the only one, of course) could arise. However, it goes without saying that the Committee or their research assistants should work with respect to this type of analysis the same four aspects that have been mentioned sub (1).

[Book] (3) is, like all comprehensive economic histories of a country or epoch, much more difficult to deal with. It is obvious that Mr. Clark's plan of exposition did not imply any particular interest in entrepreneurship. But even a perfunctory survey of the twenty-odd sketches of industrial histories that the volume contains (Iron and Steel, chapters II–VIII, Engineering, chapter IX, Motor Cars and Electricity, chapter X, Cotton, Wool, Silk, chapters XI–XIII, Other Textiles, chapter XIV, Leather and Rubber, chapter XV, Wood, chapter XVI, Cement, Clay, Glass, chapter XVII, Food, Drink, Tobacco, chapter XVIII, Fuels, Chemistry et al., chapter XIX) brings out a great quantity of relevant material and stray facts that are extremely suggestive. Moreover, if it does not *answer* our questions—which, given the purpose of the book, should not be understood to imply adverse criticism—it *posits* them all, at least by implication. Take, e.g., the chapter on cement (XVII, first section). To an extent [that] is unusual even in this book, this chapter neglects the entrepreneurial angle. But it depicts, with Caesarian brevity, the conditions that preceded the development of a great American cement industry. It emphasizes the role of the rotary kiln. It marks the point at which one would have to dig more deeply—the point (1896) when 24 Portland cement works *were* in existence, "half of which had rotary kilns," and there sketches out the expansion that followed, with American Cement and Atlas in the van, the conquest of the home market, technological advance, and the organization of the Portland Cement Association. That is to say, it sketches out all the problems and is a boon to our hypothetical research fellows who will find in these chapters frameworks that they would otherwise have to construct themselves. Sir John Clapham's work is more helpful still—large stretches reading like preliminary histories of entrepreneurship ready-made.[24]

[Book] (4) is an excellent instance of the kind of industrial monograph that gives both material and starting points for the study of the ways of entrepreneurship. On the one hand, we get the picture of the craft-stage of the industry and of the incipient factory stage; of the early conditions and the later developments of demand; of labor conditions; and of the influence of protection: that is to say, we get a full view of the situations and factors that conditioned entrepreneurial activity in the carpet industry. On the other hand, we get with adequate emphasis upon the personal element, a full report on the development of enterprise within that framework and on the reasons why, and the manner in which, the industry eventually settled down in a "stable" or "mature" state of oligopoly, adopting the attitudes and especially the price policy (see, e.g., the highly significant incident noticed on p. 230 n.) that are characteristic of such a state. Everywhere, the interplay of invention and enterprise stands out clearly, and the authors take care to link technological and commercial changes to individual firms (e.g., the Bigelow concern) or, where this is not possible, to particular subgroups of firms (see, e.g., their quotations from Kendrick on the introduction of the "Smyrna," p. 103) and to emphasize the role of the entrepreneurial impulse, or of the absence of it, in such matters as location (e.g., pp. 151 et seq.). In short, the work comes near to being a history of enterprise in the carpet industry. In any case, it could with but little additional labor be turned into such a history. As it stands, it affords a most useful paradigma from which to develop a general schema, for the direction of our research fellows, of industry-by-industry studies of entrepreneurship. The bulk of industrial monographs does not lend itself so readily to exploitation from our standpoint. But all of them present backgrounds and suggestive facts to the student who knows what to look for. The differences in approach and the implied theories about the relative importance of conditioning circumstances and entrepreneurial responses that these monographs display are in themselves an interesting object for study.

I shall not presume to sketch the schema of questions that are to be addressed to the existing material with a view to assembling what we have and to defining what we need. It is all contained in the one question that is to be repeated with reference to every country, time, industry, and, possibly, leading concern: *who* was it that acted *how* and *why* and what were the effects that may be traced to such action? But I do venture to suggest that experiments with such schemata will soon produce a standard pattern that will greatly facilitate agreement upon definite research projects.

## Notes

1. This article was probably written in 1946 in response to a suggestion by Arthur H. Cole, who at this time was planning a research center in entrepreneurial history. Major parts of the manuscript appeared in 1947 in *The Journal of Economic History* as "The Creative Response in Economic History." The original version, which is published here, is a little more than a third longer. In particular the pages in the beginning and the end of the essay are new. More precisely, the first and fifth sections were not included in *The Journal of Economic History*, and only the latter part of section II. For more information on this article, see the section titled "The American Period: Schumpeter's Works in This Volume" in the Introduction. The manuscript is published by permission of the Harvard University Archives.
2. Cole's essay was published as "An Approach to the Study of Entrepreneurship" on pages 1–15 in a supplemental issue of *The Journal of Economic History* from 1946 on "The Tasks of Economic History."
3. The indictment is not invalidated by the fact that modern economic theory is no longer exclusively static. It is true that during the last twenty years

or so an economic dynamics has emerged. But this dynamics has nothing to do with the factors that are incessantly at work to change the structure of economic life. It merely produces models with which to analyze the functioning of any given structure. These models link indeed economic quantities such as consumers' expenditure, investment expenditure, employment, interest rates, price levels, that belong to different points of time and thus describe a process rather than a state. But though they spell a considerable improvement of the apparatus of economic theory, they still exclude what Professor Cole reproaches theory for excluding. In fact they break down when one tries to insert phenomena that pertain to the change of industrial structures.

4. The capitalist—the term was not in scientific use before the nineteenth century—is the agent that furnishes either physical or monetary capital. Therefore it is he who bears the business risks even if, as in the cases of the bondholder or simple creditor, he is, excepting bankruptcy, protected at the expense of the shareholder: that is to say, risks are always borne by those who furnish the means for a business venture although these risks may be unequally distributed among them. This obvious fact has been obscured by two circumstances. First, for a surprisingly long time, economists, consciously and unconsciously, persisted in reasoning on the paradigma of the owner-managed firm, a case in which enterprise, management, and capitalist function are easily confused and none of them stand out distinctively. Second, more modern analysts, still under the influence of a theoretical schema that really had no place for the entrepreneur, were driven back upon the functions of risk-taking because they failed to see any other and because, unrealistically accepting the legal construction, they wished to vest the entrepreneurial function in the stockholders.

5. Even within the assumptions of classical theory this is not necessarily true. We need not however go into this.

6. The function itself is not absent from other forms of society. But capitalist entrepreneurship is a sufficiently distinct phenomenon to be singled out for the purpose in hand.

7. Our definition is not the usual one. In economic literature it is usual to adopt a much wider one. But we need a distinctive word for a distinctive function. And since in traditional teaching the word "entrepreneur" is redundant we may as well make it our own.

8. An exact definition can be provided by means of the concept of production functions (on this, see Oscar Lange, "A Note on Innovations," *Review of Economic Statistics* for February, 1943).

9. It is sometimes held that entrepreneurship, although it did not require antecedent ownership of capital (or very little of it) in the early days of capitalism, tends to become dependent upon it as times goes on, especially in the epoch of giant corporations. Nothing could be farther from the truth. In the course of the nineteenth century, it became increasingly easier to secure other people's money by methods other than the partnership, and in our own time rise by promotion within the shell of existing corporations offers a much

more convenient access to the entrepreneurial functions than existed in the world of owner-managed firms. Many a would-be entrepreneur of today does not found a firm, not because he could not do so, but simply because he prefers the other method.

10. The relation between the two has attracted interest before. See, e.g., F. W. Taussig, *Inventors and Money Makers* (1st ed., 1915).

11. Gustav Schmoller introduced the subject into his general treatise (*Grundriss*) of 1904. But the novelty of this consisted only in the systematic use he made of the result of historical research. Less systematically, the subject had entered general treatises before.

12. Financial institutions and practices enter our circle of problems in three ways: they are "auxiliary and conditioning" in the first place; banking may be the object of entrepreneurial activity, in the second place, that is to say, the introduction of new banking practices may constitute enterprise; and bankers (or other "financiers") may use the means at their command in order to embark upon commercial and industrial enterprise themselves (John Law).

13. This case emphasizes the desirability—present also in others—of divesting our idea of entrepreneurial performance of any preconceived value judgment. Whether a given entrepreneurial success benefits or injures society or a particular group within society is a question that must be decided on the merits of each case. On the other hand, enterprise that results in a monopoly position, even if undertaken for the sole purpose of securing a monopoly position, is not necessarily antisocial in its total effect.

14. It seems to me that, in order to understand fully a social system or even a particular sector of it, it is necessary to go much more deeply into the details of functions, types, and performances than those analysts seem inclined to do who are content to work with types that are no more than general labels. In my youth, I did, for instance, under a man who was considered an authority, some work in the history of strategy and tactics. The one thing that still stands out in my memory is that there is no unitary type of "military man" or "great general" and that the attempt to construct such a type only falsifies our picture of military history. But let me illustrate my point by an instance that is close to our personal experience. The layman thinks he knows what a professor is. However, this term denotes a group of people who differ widely in type, function, and mentality. There is the academic administrator; the university politician; the teacher in the sense of a man who imparts current knowledge; the teacher in the sense of a man who imparts distinctive doctrines or methods; the scholar in the sense implied by "learnedness"; the organizer of research; the research worker whose strong point is ideas; the research worker whose strong point is skillful technique experimentation and its counterparts in the social sciences. And all these—and others—are very different chaps and hardly ever fully understand and appreciate one another. Yet it takes all of them to make a modern university and it takes recognition of all these types and the way they cooperate or fail to cooperate in order to understand what a university is and how it works. And he who insists

on merging them into a unitary professorial type and leaves it at that will obliterate not only secondary details but essentials.

15. In a sense, the promotor who does nothing but "setting up" new business concerns might be considered as the purest type of entrepreneur. Actually, he is mostly not more than a financial agent who has little, if any, title to entrepreneurship—no more than the lawyer who does the legal work involved. But there are important exceptions to this.

16. Robert A. Gordon, *Business Leadership in the Large Corporation* (Washington, D.C.: The Brookings Institution, 1945).

17. It should be obvious that this does not mean that the whole social gain resulting from the enterprise goes to the entrepreneur. But the question of appraisal of social gains from entrepreneurship, absolute and relative to the entrepreneurial shares in them, and of the social costs involved in a system that relies on business interests to carry out its innovations, is so complex and perhaps even hopeless that I beg to excuse myself from entering into it.

18. Still more difficult is, of course, responsible *appraisal*, that is to say appraisal that is not content with popular slogans. Measures to keep surplus gains alive no doubt slow up the process of "handing on the fruits of progress." But the knowledge that such measures are available may be necessary in order to induce anyone to embark upon certain ventures. There also may be other compensating advantages to such measures, particularly where rapid introduction into general use of new methods would involve severe dislocations of labor.

19. Whether this actually is so in any particular case is, of course, extremely difficult to establish. The successes stand out, statistically and otherwise; the failures are apt to escape notice. This is one of the reasons why economists seem so much impressed by peak successes. Another reason for faulty appraisal is neglect of the fact that spectacular prizes *may* stimulate more effectively than would the same sum if more equally distributed. This is a question that no speculation can decide. Only collection of facts can tell us how we are to frame our theory.

20. Another method of embodying the entrepreneurial capital gain was available in the French *parts de fondateurs*.

21. That is to say, successful entrepreneurship is that method of rising in the social scale that is *characteristic* of the capitalist blueprint. It is, of course, not the only method. First, there are other possibilities within the economic sphere, such as possession of an appreciating natural agent (e.g., urban land) or mere speculation or even, occasionally, success in mere administration that need not partake of the specifically entrepreneurial element. Second, there are possibilities without the business sphere, for business success is no more the only method of rising in capitalist society than knightly service was in feudal society.

22. An example is the study by F. J. Marquis and S. J. Chapman on the managerial stratum of the Lancashire cotton industry in the *Journal of the Royal Statistical Society*, February, 1912.

23. The two bracketed suggestions apply to all kinds of existing literature of published source material on entrepreneurship.

24. This is true of many general histories. A good example in P. Mantoux's *The Industrial Revolution in the Eighteenth Century* (rev. ed. 1927). [Sir John Clapham, 1873–1946, is the author, for example, of *An Economic History of Modern Britain*.]

# Eleven

## Wage and Tax Policy in Transitional States of Society

### I. The Problem

*1. Introduction*

At any given time, every nation has a certain class structure and a certain civilization.[1] The concept of a civilization comprises a system of beliefs, a schema of values, an attitude to life, a state of the arts, and so on. This class structure and this civilization will in general determine a nation's behavior in its foreign and domestic affairs, including economic affairs or, to use another word, its *policies*.

There are several theories that try to explain the causes that determine the class structure of society. The most famous one is that of Marx according to which the class structure is determined by the prevailing mode of production. But whether we accept this theory or another one, we always take it for granted that this class structure determines the salient feature of a nation's civilization and therefore also its policies. Thus, we know that a society ruled by a class of warriors will develop certain beliefs, attitudes, [and] policies and that a society ruled by a class of merchants will develop others. A society in which class structure, beliefs, values, attitudes, and policy are perfectly adjusted to each other or, to put it differently, are all consistent with each other, we shall call an *intact society*. Such a society may still have its class conflicts or its political dimensions. But the general cultural background is common to all political groups. In particular, politicians in an intact society, being all the exponents of the same class interests, will have fundamentally the same view on wages and taxes though they may differ in detail, e.g., about free trade or protection.

But this need not be so. It happens frequently that the class structure of society and its civilization or different parts of a nation's civilization cease to correspond to each other. Examples will illustrate the causes of this phenomenon which we always observe in times of rapid social change. The class structure of a warrior society may change into the class structure of a commercial society. But, protected by old habits, the beliefs and attitudes of the warriors may for a long time determine the beliefs and attitudes of their bourgeois successors. Or, the institution of private property in land may lose its original feudal meaning but its legal form may persist for a time. Or, the intelligentsia of a nation and its political sector, both of whom have group interests of their own, may develop attitudes which are at variance with the attitudes of other sectors, e.g., farmers and businessmen. Such a state of society we shall call a *transitional state*. It is evident that it creates problems which do not exist in what we have called intact society. The fact to which I want to call attention particularly is that in such a state, policies are no longer consistent with each other and with the existing economic conditions. They cannot be any longer described by such general principles as laissez-faire or socialism. And individual policies do not any longer produce the effects which they would produce in a pure or intact system.

In illustration, consider the case of the United States. The business class has lost the power it used to have, but not entirely. Organized labor has risen to power, but not completely. Labor and a government allied to the unions can indeed paralyze the business mechanism. But it cannot replace it by another mechanism. Hence we have a situation in which no class interest or viewpoint can work out the policy congenial to its social system and everybody checkmates everybody else.

## 2. Wages and Taxes

This transitional state of society manifests itself nowhere with greater clearness than in the public policy with respect to wages and taxes, the subject of this course. In order to understand what follows in the four remaining lectures, three points must be kept in mind:

(a) Economically, the effects of wage and tax policies are closely related. This is clear in the cases where taxes (such as social security taxes) increase the cost of employing labor directly. But it is true also in other cases (such as the cases of the income and inheritance taxes) where the connection is not so obvious.

(b) Politically, wage and tax policies are not less closely connected. The distribution of political power and the ideology that will prompt a government to adopt a definite policy as regards wages will also prompt the same government to adopt a related policy as regards taxes.

(c) The wage and tax policies that are popular in many countries at the present time, for instance in England and the United States, illustrate the specific problems of transitional states of society because they take no account of the organic need of a businessman's economy which is nevertheless not abolished. The contradictions involved are many, but one is of particular importance for our purpose: politically, policies that aim at high wages and high taxes go together; but economically they conflict with each other because, with certain exceptions, it is generally true that high wages are more easy to attain with low taxation and high taxes with low wages.

### 3. Wages, Taxes, and Wealth

Another point must be briefly mentioned. Wage and tax policies, like all policies, depend upon the social and political structure of the nation to which they apply. But their economic effects also depend upon the stage of economic development which a nation has reached and hence upon its accumulated wealth. Most economists are agreed that in the early stages of a nation's industrialization free enterprise and high profits will promote economic development. Marx called this a "historical necessity." Most economists are also agreed that this necessity or expediency of free enterprise and high profits decreases as industrialization is completed or, to use a word that is much in vogue in the United States, as the economy becomes *mature*. But it is not always possible to give effects to this principle. A modern nation will in general insist on a policy of high wages and of high progressive taxes even in the early stages of industrialization. Additional problems arise from this fact. It is interesting to note how they have been solved by the Russian Five-Year plans.

In the following lectures we shall first discuss how wage and tax problems presented themselves in the epoch of Laissez-faire Liberalism (second lecture). Then we shall discuss how these problems *would* present themselves in the Case of Centralist Socialism (third lecture). Finally, we shall discuss how these problems actually present themselves in modern society (fourth and fifth lectures).

## II. Wage and Tax Policies of Laissez-Faire Liberalism

### 1. Introduction

Liberalism means many different things: for instance, the liberalism of the Spanish *liberales* of 1811, of the French *liberaux* of 1820, of the English *liberals* of 1870, and of the U.S. *liberals* of 1932 are quite different things. In this course, we choose the meaning that is represented by English liberalism in the time of W. E. Gladstone. The social and political background of Gladstonian policy will be briefly sketched.[2]

*2. The Spirit of Gladstonian Finance*

(a) English free trade and currency policy. In what sense was the English gold currency "automatic"?

(b) The principle of the balanced budget.

(c) The principle of minimizing public expenditure.

(d) The principle of minimizing the effects of taxation upon the economic behavior of individuals. The English income tax in the nineteenth century. The indirect taxes and the fiscal import duties (especially on tea).

*3. The Spirit of Gladstonian Wage Policy*

(a) The principle of free contract meant flexible monetary wage rates.

(b) Limitations of this principle; protection of women and children; attitude to trade unions and strikes.

(c) The underlying theory of wages and employment.

(d) Wage policy and free trade.

*4. Effects of These Policies upon the Welfare of the Working Class*

(a) Wages per head of employee, divided by cost of living, almost exactly doubled between 1860 and 1900.[3]

(b) Difficulty of interpreting this fact; special difficulty of deciding how far it was merely historically associated with these policies and how far it was, at least in part, caused by them.

(c) It is suggested that, *under the conditions of the time and the country,* those policies brought about quicker progress of the working class than would have any others; but that this result cannot be generalized for all other times and countries.

(d) The essential point to grasp is, however, this: the class structure of England did not change greatly during that period; the political principles which follow from this class structure were accepted by the great majority of people and by nearly all politicians; in consequence, actual policies were consistent with each other; and the economic system of that particular society was allowed to work without those frictions which must always ensue if the prevailing system is challenged.

## III. Wage and Tax Policies in Centralist Socialism

*1. Introduction*

Centralist Socialism means that form of organization in which (a) all physical means of production are public property; and (b) production and distribution are controlled by a single authority which we call the Ministry of Economic Affairs. Other forms of socialism are neglected for the sake of simplicity. While in Lecture II ["Wage and Tax Policies of Laissez-faire Liberalism] we have been discussing a system that has actually existed, we are now going to discuss a system that has never existed as yet—it does not exist in Russia—and is therefore a *theoretical construction*. We shall distinguish two cases.

## 2. Case I

The Ministry decides (a) how much work, and what kind of work each comrade is to do; (b) how much of the total social product shall consist of consumers' goods and shall be handed over to the comrades for the satisfaction of their wants and how much is to be reserved, for public purposes such as hygiene or armaments, and for the improvement and extension of industrial plant and equipment. (This we shall call investment.) Whatever the comrades get in this case may be called their income. But it cannot be called "wages" because it has nothing to do with the specific "marginal productivity of labor." Therefore, there would be no wage policy in our sense, although certain questions would arise that are similar in nature to the questions that arise in capitalist society under the heading of wage policy. (c) Nor would there be any policy of taxation. Since the Ministry would withhold beforehand *and in kind* all the means of production that are necessary in order to satisfy the requirements of the public purposes and of investment, it would not have to tax the incomes which it would hand out.

## 3. Case II

The Ministry does not decide how much work and what kind of work the comrades must do nor what part of the total national production is to be reserved for public purposes and investment. The comrades are offered incomes that vary with each amount and kind of work and can take their choice. Moreover, they receive claims on the total of national production, and *they* decide afterwards how much of these claims should be given up for public purposes—this decision would have to be taken in a parliament or congress—and how much of these claims is to be reserved for investment—this decision every comrade would take individually, that is to say, he would decide how much of his income he is willing to "save," and the Ministry would simply "invest" the sum resulting from these individual decisions. It can be shown that in this case the greater part of the incomes of the comrades would be economically the same thing as capitalist *wages*. Moreover, in order to cover the requirements of public purposes, we should have to have *taxes*. It should be added that, if investments are to be covered by voluntary savings, we should also, like in Russia, have to have *interest*. If we call Case II democratic socialism, we can formulate our result by saying that democratic socialism would, in essentials, reproduce the problems of wage, interest, and tax policy of capitalist society. But whether we consider Case I or Case II, we should notice that, if either were accepted by the large majority of the people, it would work with as little friction as did the bourgeois liberalism of the nineteenth century and again we should have a logically consistent system of policies.


## IV. Wage and Tax Policies in Transitional States of Society: I

### 1. Introduction

Actually, we have neither laissez-faire liberalism nor socialism but a combination of the two that is perhaps inevitable but nevertheless illogical. The nature of the contradiction involved will be illustrated by the present condition of England.

### 2. Modern Principles of Taxation

(a) The principle of deficit financing. Its economic and sociological roots in the political structure of today. (We shall not discuss the deficits and the debts that arise from the War, but only the questions of principle involved irrespective of the situation created by the War.)

(b) The principle of maximum public service.

(c) The principle of redistribution of wealth; particularly of redistribution by means of income and inheritance taxes.

### 3. Economic Effects of These Principles

[Effects] upon industrial efficiency and the sum total of real wages in a society that is "controlled" but not "planned."

(a) The question of "inducement to invest" and of "ability to invest." Keynesian views on saving. Taxes on saving.

(b) The question of effective management, particularly with respect to risk and to organized labor.

(c) The question of the influence of modern taxation upon real wages.

(d) The question of the influence of modern taxation upon a nation's future.

# V. Wage and Tax Policies in Transitional States of Society: II

## 1. Introduction

Wage policy in transitional states of society differs from wage policy in laissez-faire liberalism in that wage rates and hours of work are no longer left to private contract. It differs from wage policy in socialism in two points. First, the socialist regime would determine wages as a part of a comprehensive plan in which the real income of the workman would be coordinated with other social needs, particularly the need for investment. Second, the socialist regime may enjoy an authority over workmen which neither employers nor governments enjoy in transitional states. Many problems arise out of this which did not exist in laissez-faire liberalism and which may disappear again in socialism. Only a few of these problems can be touched upon in this lecture. In order to simplify exposition and to make these problems stand out, we shall make the following assumptions. We assume (a) that government (by legislation or administration) determines *directly* only minimum wage rates and maximum weekly hours; and (b) that, within these limits, actual wage rates and hours are fixed by contract between employers and trade unions but that the government intervenes by putting political pressure on the employers in order to induce them to accept the terms of the trade unions so that, in effect, wage rates and hours become political questions. It is not held that this is always so in practice. But it is held that, in the United States at least, these assumptions describe the typical practice from 1932 to 1946 when fears of inflation and the result of the election caused a partial reorientation. On these assumptions we discuss the following problems.

## 2. Money Wage Rates and Total Real Wages

The wage policy of governments and trade unions is chiefly concerned with *wage rates in terms of money*. This raises two questions that have been hotly debated but can only be briefly considered here. (a) Does an increase in *money* wage per hour of work, always or normally, increase the *real* wage per hour of work? Keynes said no. Is this correct? (b) Does an increase in real wage per hour of work, always or normally, increase the total *real* income of the working class?

## 3. The Question of Full Employment

Full employment can be achieved, as it has in fact been achieved, by dictatorial governments. In a free society, i.e., in a society where workmen are at liberty to accept or refuse employment offered at given wage rates, full employment is impossible. What is really meant by a full-employment policy is a policy which regulates government expenditures in such a way as to prevent mass unemployment beyond given limits. Inflexible wage rates may be an important cause of permanently high unemployment figures. This can be remedied by inflating prices. But in this case the workman loses the advantage for the sake of which he desires those rates.

## 4. The Fundamental Question

On the surface, struggles over wages are simply struggles between opposing class interests. Fundamentally, however, they are struggles between two interests of society, the interest in present enjoyment, and the interest in the nation's economic future. In order to show this, we will now suppose that, in spite of the obstacles mentioned, wage policy succeeds in increasing the sum total of the monetary income of the working class without inflating prices. This will mean that society will produce more consumption goods and less investment goods. The question arises how society's interest in expanding its productive apparatus, that is to say, in its own future, is to be safeguarded. Laissez-faire liberalism solved this problem in one way; socialism, at least dictatorial socialism, would solve it in another way. But in a society that is in an intermediate condition, the problem is not solved automatically. Special policies must be devised for this purpose. For instance, it is possible to frame taxation in such a way that the increase in total wages will reduce the consumption of the richer classes rather than investment.

## 5. Social Security and Annual Wage

In a state of society in which individual responsibility is being increasingly replaced by public responsibility, security legislation must mean a heavy financial burden. It is therefore important to realize that in a rich society this burden does not necessarily interfere with economic progress. Whether it does or not depends largely upon how heartily it bears upon the *margin of production*. A similar statement holds true for other plans of social betterment, such as the Annual Wage, that is to say, the plan that (the) wage contract should guarantee a certain minimum annual income.[4] In itself, this plan is perfectly feasible. What makes it difficult to introduce it in the United States is that its sponsors insist on framing it so as to make it as injurious and burdensome to industry as possible.

## 6. Summary

Transitional states of society raise a particular category of problems which do not exist in societies that function according to a consistent system of principles. Thus, we still rely in the United States upon the motive and mechanisms of private-property economy. But we tax it in a way that will not allow it to function properly. We still retain the principle that wages are fixed by private contract, which means that they should vary according to the business conditions that prevail. But we do not allow them to do so. The consequences of this could be much mitigated if those contradictions were frankly realized instead of being hidden in clouds of political phrases.

## Notes

1. These five lectures were given by Schumpeter between January 16–22, 1948, at the National School of Economics of the National Autonomous University of Mexico, Mexico City. The following text is based on a typewritten version, corrected by Schumpeter himself as well as by his wife Elizabeth Boody Schumpeter. For more information, see the section titled "The American Period: Schumpeter's Works in This Volume" in the Introduction. The original manuscript was found in the Harvard University Archives, and is published by permission of the Harvard University Archives.

2. The reader who is interested in a fuller account of Schumpeter's ideas on the topic in Lecture II is referred to the section on "Gladstonian Finance" on pp. 402–5 in Schumpeter, *History of Economic Analysis* (London: George Allen & Unwin, 1954).

3. A. L. Bowley, *Wages and Income in the United Kingdom since 1860* (Cambridge: The University Press, 1937), 20, 34.

4. The last part of this sentence has been reformulated by Elizabeth Boody Schumpeter. It originally read: ". . . , the plan that no wage contract should be made for less than a whole year."

# *Twelve*

## American Institutions and Economic Progress

### I. The Factors of Economic Change

Our aim is to arrive at a diagnosis of the present social situation of the United States on the basis of an analysis of the fundamental economic and political factors and their interaction.[1] By "institutions" we mean in this course all the patterns of behavior into which individuals must fit under penalty of encountering organized resistance, and not only legal institutions (such as property or the contract) and the agencies for their production or enforcement.

Today we shall consider the motive forces of economic change (or economic growth or progress) within a given framework of institutions geared to the system of private enterprise (or capitalism). Some technical difficulties of defining and measuring economic progress will be briefly dealt with at the outset.

We shall then first survey the main features of an economic process in which there is no change in people's tastes, in their technological knowledge (technological horizon), and in their attitudes toward the future (time horizon). Under these assumptions, we shall in particular touch upon problems of the distribution of the national product, savings and investment, and the "mature economy" with a constant population.

Finally, we shall survey the phenomena that are associated with change in technological knowledge, particularly profits, the business cycle, the mechanism of bank credit, and unemployment. We shall try to formulate the conditions that make for greater or smaller economic success of such a society.

### II. The Factors of Institutional Change

When, in the first lecture, we discussed a number of problems incident to economic progress, we were of course aware all the time that economic life is never uninfluenced by institutional factors but we simplified matters by the device of "freezing" political and social conditions in a state appropriate to the kind of economy that we wished to analyze. In this lecture, we shall do exactly the same "in reverse": assuming the economic process to run along as depicted, we shall investigate the manner in which social institutions change in time, reserving the obvious interactions between the two for discussion in the next lecture. So far as the working and the changing of social institutions require the activity of distinct groups of men, we shall split each such group into politicians (who struggle for their positions by competing for the popular vote), bureaucrats (who struggle for their positions by competing for "appointment"), and a third group to be called "journalists."

Politicians, bureaucrats, and journalists are first of all concerned with routine business of which the nature may best be analyzed by analogy with an economic concept, not yet introduced, the concept of a stationary state. But even routine activity induces of itself a slow process of institutional change which it is very important to understand.

Another type of change is brought about by the responses of politicians, bureaucrats, and journalists to the impact of factors external to the given institutional pattern of a given country. The nature and mechanisms of these responses will be discussed later on. For the time being we merely note that, for instance, any major war or any major economic crisis affects a country's institutional pattern for good.

Finally, we have to recognize that sometimes it may be possible to explain observed institutional changes as adaptions to changing environmental circumstances. In such cases we speak of autonomous institutional changes and look for explanation to the habits of mind and the interests of the politicians, bureaucrats, and journalists themselves which can be shown to be entirely different from those of the people for whom these groups speak. An interesting analogy with the economic concept of profit will be noticed.

### III. The Interaction between the Factors of Economic and Institutional Change: Political Economy vs. Economics

The interaction between the two is obvious and has given rise to many "theories" which are however vitiated by the ideologies and philosophies of their proponents and also by a tendency to oversimplify things. This can be illustrated by the Marxist economic interpretation of history.

Even if we reduce this Marxist theory to its tenable elements, it is clear that economic evolution will shape human values, attitudes, legal structures, administrative practice, and so on, to some extent. Historical examples will elucidate this fact and the mechanisms through which it asserts itself.

But it must not be overlooked that institutional patterns in turn shape the economic process, a fact that can also be established historically. Therefore, neither the analysis of the economic process—economics—nor the analysis of the political process—political science—is adequate by itself to explain actual sequences of events. This is the reason why so many writers have come to plead for a political economy which is to combine both and much besides. The difficulties that beset this line of advance must be clearly understood however.

Our argument must be interpreted to mean that the economic and the "political" processes are ever patterned upon one another exactly. On the contrary, the discrepancies between the two are among the most important explanatory factors of human history. Conceptually pure systems, such as for instance the economic and political system of laissez-faire liberalism, are figments of the mind that are useful for some purposes but misleading for others: there never have been such things as a purely "feudal" or a purely "bourgeois" society. Lag phenomena are sufficient to account for this. But there are other reasons.

## IV. Groups and Classes: Policies and Politics

The environment that molds individuals is not an individual but rather a group environment; motives of the individual are not individual but group motives; actions are not simply individual actions but can, in general, be only understood as group actions. These statements, however, are liable to be misunderstood and must be interpreted with care. The groups in question are only to a minor part to be explained by purpose (such as are certain vocational groups). Mostly, sociological location and history are necessary in order to identify groups and to understand their nature and behavior. In this connection rises the modern problem of "community development." The interaction of economic and noneconomic factors is particularly clear in this connection. Illustrative examples will be taken from American political, religious, and economic groups.

A special class are social classes. Several theories of this phenomenon will be briefly mentioned and the concept of class culture will be discussed. There is no such thing as a classless society, that is to say, societies are of necessity *structured*.

Groups and classes are the real agents in the social process. By their actions or even by their mere existence, they help to determine (to restrict) the possibilities for economic and institutional change and even what is to be considered, at any time and place, as economic or institutional progress or retrogression, as good or bad, as just or unjust. There is no objective meaning to these words and it is an illusion to believe that such meaning is supplied by any rational method, such as "free discussion." This, and the true role of free discussion, will be illustrated by examples from the history of American institutions.

It follows that only in a very special case can we speak of a nation's policy or politics. In general, declared policies are nothing but verbalizations of group interests and attitudes that assert themselves in the struggles of parties and for points in the political game, though every group exalts the policies that suit it into eternal principles of a "common good" that is to be safeguarded by an imaginary kind of State. Nobody has attained political maturity who does not understand that policy is politics. Economists are particularly apt to overlook these truths.

## V. The Personal Element and the Element of Chance: A Principle of Indeterminateness

It is easy to see that the principles so far discussed are not quite adequate for explaining actual processes of change. In fact we have had already, at various turns of our argument, to appeal to sets of facts that are obviously important, but do not fit well into our schema of explanatory principles. It is the purpose of this lecture to introduce the two most important of these sets of facts.

First, we have so far neglected the element of chance. Simple examples however show that chance events may exert a powerful and lasting influence on the economic process as well as on "policy." This will be illustrated by the inflation caused in the sixteenth century by the inflow into Europe of large quantities of precious metals from the New World. Even major wars may be considered as chance events from the standpoint of countries that did not purposively plan for them. But still more important is another type of chance events. We have seen that developments in the various sectors of social life, for instance, economic and political developments, though interrelated, enjoy a limited amount of independence. Therefore, situations may arise in business and in politics the temporal coincidence of which, though to some extent fortuitous, may produce consequences that could not have been predicted from any study of either development taken separately.

Second, it stands to reason that the qualities of the human material, the intelligence, foresight, endurance, and so on, that are at any time present in it are factors of economic and institutional "progress," just as much as is the presence of certain raw materials or natural facilities for transport. This also applies to the quality of the leading stratum that the social organization and the economic process produce, from the standpoint of any particular type of activity, to the percentage of the existing "leading" personnel that social conditions attract to each pursuit. However great the weight that we may attach to the malleability of human nature and to the influence of education, it is not a matter of indifference, for instance, whether a given nation at a given time possesses "warlike qualities" and of what kind of people its military profession consists. These are important although unpopular subjects. But we have in addition to face a problem that is still more unpopular, namely, the problem of the influence that may be exerted by exceptional individuals, a problem that has hardly ever been treated without the most blatant preconceptions.

Without committing ourselves either to hero worship or to its hardly less absurd opposite, we have got to realize that, since the emergence of exceptional individuals does not lend itself to scientific generalization, there is here an element that, together with the element of random occurrences with which it may be amalgamated, seriously limits our ability to forecast the future. That is what is meant here by "a principle of indeterminateness." To put it somewhat differently: social determinism, where it is nonoperational, is a creed like any other and entirely unscientific.

## VI. Summary: How Capitalism Created and Destroyed a Civilization

The historical problem that goes under the title of the Rise of Capitalism is substantially cleared up by now and could be presented in a manner to command the unanimous assent of historians were it not for the fact that some people are enamored of certain pet theories. For us the most important thing to notice is that the rise of capitalism was not a purely economic process. This also holds true for the derivative capitalisms that developed outside of Western Europe and in particular for the colonial period of this country. Although the personal element and elements of chance must enter copiously into any analysis of details, the inherited forms of behavior of the white immigrants and the data of the environment, suffice for a substantially satisfactory explanation of American economic and institutional history through the war of independence. Any purely economic interpretation of the constitution, however, can only be partially successful.

For a time, the United States offers one of the few instances of almost perfect parallelism between economic and institutional developments, safeguarded in part by the facts that the business groups and the political groups were practically identical and that both pivoted on a relatively small circle of closely connected families that was, however, always ready to admit rising outsiders at least whenever these were of a similar type.

But in most other countries the rising business class only succeeded in transforming the preceding forms of social existence without destroying them and entered upon a symbiosis with the "feudal" classes and groups which fettered but also sheltered it. It was in this state of society that the business class achieved its unparalleled economic success and such other cultural contributions—e.g., the development of the sciences and their utilitarian applications—as may be put to its credit. At the same time, and precisely because it was for a long time not burdened with political responsibility, it developed that nineteenth-century liberalism, the fundamental principles of which offer so curious a contrast to the autocratic organization of the factory. The essential instability of this arrangement was bound to reveal itself so soon as the rising standard of life of manual labor—another result of the economic success of the business class—effected a redistribution of political weight. The provisional result is the halfway house of English laborism. The Russian case, however important with reference to international relations, is much less important so far as fundamental trends are concerned, if it does not indeed indicate one of the possible ways in which these trends may be reversed.

The application to the modern situation in the United States of the principles expounded in the five preceding lectures is easier than it would be to parallel the sketch just presented by a sketch of the American development. If time permitted, however, it could be shown that social mechanisms that became operative since the Civil War have, in spite of all the differences, produced a similar result. In particular, they have created a bureaucracy which is more powerful than any European one. That bureaucracy has been particularly successful in impressing the values and attitudes of the public servant upon the mind of the nation. The free-enterprise system is not just a technical economic arrangement that can stand, or even requires, more or less control or regulation. It is a particular scheme of values and a particular way of life. These are rapidly vanishing from the American scene. Such "chance events" as this country's participation in the first and second world wars have accelerated the process. And the process is still being accelerated by the inflationary pressure of our days, which is not a chance event. The questions of whether the process will lead to socialism and whether this socialism will be democratic or dictatorial, and whether a centralist or a guild socialism are questions for a prophet to answer, but not for an analyst, who can only list tendencies and possibilities.

## Notes

1. This text constitutes the basis for a series of lectures that Schumpeter was scheduled to give during January 9–20, 1950, at the Charles R. Walgreen Foundation in Chicago. The day before the first lecture, however, Schumpeter died. As an alternative title to this "Syllabus or Precis of a Course of Six Lectures," Schumpeter suggested "Politics and the Economic Process." The text first appeared in 1983 in *Zeitschrift für die gesamte Staatswissenschaft.* For more information on the Walgreen lectures, see the section titled "The American Period: Schumpeter's Works in this Volume" in the Introduction. Reprinted by permission of the Harvard University Archives.

# Works by Schumpeter

## Compiled by Massimo M. Augello

THE 1980s brought about a renewed and reinforced interest in the thought and work of Joseph A. Schumpeter. In particular, in-depth and systematic archival research in the United States and Germany uncovered a significant body of previously unpublished material and at the same time allowed for a reconstruction of some lesser known biographical aspects of Schumpeter's career.[1] As a result, political documents and articles written by Schumpeter while he was in Germany,[2] as well as papers and other material from the period immediately thereafter have only recently been published.[3] Richard Swedberg's anthology—which contains numerous and important unpublished works—has its place in the framework of this activity. It is of value in that it reveals various aspects of Schumpeter's personality and scientific activity, using his correspondence and other archival documents.

Thanks as well to the work of all these scholars who have dedicated themselves to meticulously researching material regarding Schumpeter, the time seems ripe to compile and publish a complete and up-to-date bibliography of all the writings of the Austrian social scientist. There has been no lack of attempts to do so. One of the first accurate reconstructions of Schumpeter's scientific production goes back as far as 1933. This was an anonymous and unpublished work[4] in which the author—probably one of Schumpeter's students at the University of Bonn—lists all of Schumpeter's writings published as of that date, as well as a considerable number of works about Schumpeter and reviews of his books.

As is well known, the bibliography of E. Boody[5] is the traditional source for scholars of Schumpeter's work. Later research has, however, made evident the gaps and imprecisions contained in this bibliography. More recent studies have only partially remedied these defects;[6] among these, M. Kanazashi's bibliography is worth noting.[7] This bibliography, updated three times after the 1976 and 1983 editions, does not, however, provide a complete picture of Schumpeter's work and indications of the various translations of his books.

Actually, there is still unpublished material in the Harvard University Archives that should be brought to light.[8] In addition, the various reprints of the Austrian economist's writings, as well as their translations into different languages (often for inclusion in anthologies), should be noted at this time. Herein lies the basis for the decision to catalogue the complete works of Schumpeter and annotate them with the most recent information possible.

The bibliography is subdivided in two sections. The first, "Books and Pamphlets," lists chronologically all the books and booklets published by Schumpeter, as well as all the collections of his essays and anthologies of his works published to date. The second section, "Articles, Reports, and Book Reviews," contains all the articles published in journals or collections, various encyclopedia and dictionary entries, and book reviews written by Schumpeter, as well as his introductions to other books, documents, and reports relative to his political activities and every other sort of writing, both published and unpublished, which I have been able to find.[9] The only materials that have been excluded are those that he used essentially for teaching purposes (notes for the most part) and articles that appeared in daily newspapers.[10]

Each entry is numbered progressively[11] and includes information on eventual reprints or new editions of the works.[12] Translations are also indicated, with the exception of partial ones of books or articles.[13] Information regarding updates and new editions to the original translations is also given.

The two tables included here provide a synthetic picture of the major characteristics of Schumpeter's bibliography. The first contains the data regarding the annual production of Schumpeter's writings, while the second gives a list of the various translations of his major works.

Thus table 1 traces the evolution of Schumpeter's activity from 1905, the year of his first writings, up to his death. This evolution can be followed better if some "phases" are defined within it. The first period ends in 1915 and includes what Schumpeter defined as "the decade of sacred fertility" in his life. In fact, this was a period of very intense scientific activity for him. He published five books, demonstrating a strong interest in methodological problems and historical research in the field of social science and political economy in particular. In addition, he actively and regularly collaborated

**TABLE 1. SCHUMPETER'S WRITINGS**

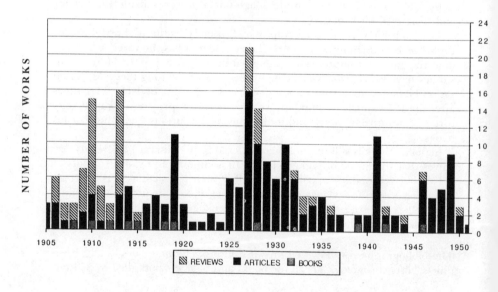

with the major German journals and provided them with reviews of the international economic literature.

A second phase extends from 1916 through 1924 and coincides with Schumpeter's political engagement and later with his professional activity as president of the Biedermann Bank. During this period Schumpeter interrupted his academic activity, his scientific production diminished considerably, and his work consisted, above all, of writings and interventions of a political nature.

After the unfortunate experience with the small Viennese banking house, which seriously damaged the state of Schumpeter's finances, the year 1925 marked the scientist's return to full-time teaching and research at the University of Bonn. This was the beginning of a period—which was to last for approximately a decade—during which Schumpeter's scientific activity was very intense. Partly to help pay his debts, he renewed and intensified his collaboration with the most important international journals and the major German periodicals. In addition, during the same years, he wrote his treatise on money—which he never published—and worked extensively on his project of publishing a textbook in economics. Since the plans for this latter venture have not previously been recounted, it is worth exploring them in greater detail.

At the beginning of 1926, Schumpeter wrote to Dr. Ferdinand Springer of the publishing house of the same name. Some months earlier Springer had proposed that Schumpeter publish a textbook in general economics.[14] Once the experience of the Biedermann Bank was over and he had again taken up university teaching, Schumpeter felt up to seriously considering this proposal. In fact, along with his letter of acceptance, he sent a long list of observations, suggestions, and requests regarding various aspects of the draft of a contract that Springer had proposed. In particular these notes concerned the length and structure of the volume, the number of copies to be printed, the eventual English edition of the textbook, and of course all the questions involving author's rights. An agreement was quickly reached, and on March 20 Schumpeter returned the signed copy, which, among other things, provided for delivering the manuscript by February of the following year.[15]

The textbook was probably never completed; what is certain is that it was never published. Further information about this affair is supplied by Schumpeter himself. In fact, in a letter to Springer dated May 17, 1929, he excuses himself for being late in delivering the manuscript of the treatise on money. Among the reasons for his tardiness he adds that he "has completed most of the textbook in general economics."[16] The fate of his manuscript is not known. Evidently Schumpeter gave up the project, but there is no trace of this decision in the later correspondence with Springer in my possession regarding the treatise on money.[17]

The last period of activity was no less intense than the preceding one. Schumpeter dedicated himself primarily to wide-ranging editorial and scientific projects such as the conclusion of his research on business cycles, the studies and thoughts on the destiny of capitalism and its relationship with socialism, and above all the writing of his monumental *History of Economic Analysis*, which he was to work on throughout the last years of his life.

Finally, table 2 provides a first synthetic picture of Schumpeter's "fortune" in an international perspective. In this table, the countries in which translations of Schumpeter's major works have been done are indicated with reference to the respective year of the first edition. The emerging data is interesting and in some ways surprising. Schumpeter's thought has been very widely diffused in various geographical and linguistic areas; probably no other twentieth-century economist has had his work translated and published in as many countries.

An analysis of the data leads to the observation that, excluding Germany and the United States—where all of Schumpeter's books were originally published—Japan and Italy are the countries in which the greatest number of his works have been translated. Brazil, Spanish-speaking countries (Spain and Mexico), and France follow. National editions of some of his major works have also been published in China, Korea, Saudi Arabia, and many other countries. Last, it should be mentioned that the book by far the most widespread in the world in terms of the number of translations is *Capitalism, Socialism and Democracy*. After this work follow *Theorie der wirtschaftlichen Entwicklung* and, with a still considerable number of translations, Schumpeter's three historical works—confirmation of their central position in his legacy. On the other hand, a scarce distribution must be observed for such works as *Business Cycles* and *Das Wesen und der Hauptinhalt der theoretischen Nationaloekonomie*.

## TABLE 2. TRANSLATIONS OF SCHUMPETER'S BOOKS

| | W.H.T. | T.W.E. | E.D.M. | V.Z.S. | K.S. | I.S.C. | B.C. | C.S.D. | M.E.S. | T.G.E. | H.E.A. |
|---|---|---|---|---|---|---|---|---|---|---|---|
| GERMANY | 1908* | 1912* | 1914* | 1915* | 1918* | 1919,1927* | 1961 | 1946 | | | 1965 |
| U.S.A. | | 1934 | 1954 | | 1954 | 1951 | 1939* | 1942* | 1946* | 1951* | 1954* |
| JAPAN | 1936 | 1937 | 1950 | 1972 | 1951 | 1956 | 1958-64 | 1951-52 | | 1952 | 1955-62 |
| ITALY | 1982 | 1932 | 1953 | | 1983 | 1972 | 1977 | 1954 | | 1953 | 1959-60 |
| BRAZIL | | 1961 | 1968 | | | 1961 | | 1961 | 1962 | 1958 | 1964 |
| SPAIN | | | 1964 | | 1970 | 1965 | | 1968 | | 1955 | 1971 |
| FRANCE | | 1935 | 1962 | | | 1972 | | 1951 | | | 1983 |
| MEXICO | | 1944 | | | | | | 1952 | 1948 | | 1971 |
| CHINA | | | | | | | | 1979 | | 1965 | 1989 |
| KOREA | | | 1965 | | | | | 1982 | | 1982 | |
| ARABIA | | | | | | | | 1963 | | 1959 | |
| YUGOSLAVIA | | | | | | | | 1981 | | | 1975 |
| SWEDEN | | | 1957 | | | | | | | 1953 | |
| ARGENTINA | | | | | | | | 1946 | | | |
| BANGLADESH | | 1974 | | | | | | | | | |
| CZECHOSLOV. | | 1987 | | | | | | | | | |
| GREECE | | | 1939 | | | | | | | | |
| HOLLAND | | | | | | | | 1963 | | | |
| HUNGARY | | 1980 | | | | | | | | | |
| INDIA | | | | | | | | 1970 | | | |
| INDONEISA | | | | | | | | | | 1963 | |
| IRAN | | | | | | | | 1976 | | | |
| POLAND | | 1960 | | | | | | | | | |
| SOVIET UNION | | 1982 | | | | | | | | | |
| TURKEY | | | | | | | | 1966 | | | |

ABBREVIATIONS: W.H.T. = *Das Wesen und der Hauptinhalt der theoretischen Nationaloekonomie*; T.W.E. = *Theorie der wirtschaftlichen Entwicklung*; E.D.M. = *Epochen der Dogmen- und Methodengeschichte*; V.Z.S. = *Vergangenheit und Zukunft der Sozialwissenschaften*; K.S. = *Die Krise des Steuerstaats*; I.S.C. = *Imperialism and Social Classes*; B.C. = *Business Cycles*; C.S.D. = *Capitalism, Socialism and Democracy*; M.E.S. = *Rudimentary Mathematics for Economists and Statisticians*; T.G.E. = *Ten Great Economists*; H.E.A. = *History of Economic Analysis*.

NOTE: *The date of publication of the first edition of each book is indicated by an asterisk.*

## Notes

1. It must be mentioned, however, that the collection of E. Boody Schumpeter's papers at the Schlesinger Library, Radcliffe College, are yet to be researched and could prove to be very useful for this purpose.

2. Cf. J. A. Schumpeter. *Aufsaetze zur Wirtschaftspolitik.* Edited by W. F. Stolper and C. Seidl. Tübingen: J.C.B. Mohr (P. Siebeck), 1985. Pp. VI–378; and J. A. Schumpeter. *Beitraege zur Sozialoekonomik.* Edited by S. Boehm. Wien: Boehlau Verlag, 1987. Pp. 375.

3. Cf. "The 'Crisis' in Economics—Fifty Years Ago." Edited by R. L. Allen. *Journal of Economic Literature,* 20, 1982, No. 3, pp. 1049–1059; "Present Developments of Political Economy." Edited by R. L. Allen (from a typescript of a lecture delivered at Kobe University, February 9, 1931). *Kobe University Economic Review,* 28, 1982, pp. 1–15; "American Institutions and Economic Progress." Edited by R. L. Allen. *Zeitschrift fuer die Gesamte Staatswissenschaft,* 139, 1983, No. 2, pp. 191–196; "The Meaning of Rationality in the Social Sciences." Edited by W. F. Stolper and R. Richter. *Zeitschrift fuer die Gesamte Staatswissenschaft,* 140, 1984, No. 4, pp. 577–593; "Some Questions of Principle." Edited by P. F. Asso and E. Barucci. *Storia del Pensiero Economico. Bollettino d'Informazione,* N.S., 1989, No. 17, pp. 46–59; and in this volume, the essays: "Can Capitalism Survive?" (1936); "An Economic Interpretation of Our Time" (1941); "Comments on a Plan for the Study of Entrepreneurship" (1947); "Wages and Tax Policy in Transitional States of Society" (1948).

4. "Verzeichnis der Schriften und Rezensionen von Joseph Schumpeter sowie ein Verzeichnis der wichtigsten Schriften und Rezensionen ueber Joseph Schumpeter." Universitaet Kiel, 1934. Pp. 26.

5. E. Boody. "Bibliography of the Writings of Joseph Alois Schumpeter." *Quarterly Journal of Economics,* 64, 1950, No. 3, pp. 373–384.

6. Nearly all these studies have been drawn directly from E. Boody's classic bibliography and are intended, for the most part, as "national" bibliographies, i.e., they furnish information relative to the various translations of Schumpeter's work in the respective languages of the different authors. See E. Schneider. *Joseph A. Schumpeter: Leben und Werk eines grossen Sozialoekonomen.* Tübingen: J.C.B. Mohr (P. Siebeck), 1970, pp. 81–93; Y. Shionoya, I. Nakayama, and S. Tobata. "Bibliography of the Writings of J. A. Schumpeter." In J. A. Schumpeter. *Keizai-hatten no Riron.* (Jap. trans. of *T.W.E.*) 2nd. ed. Tokyo: Iwanami-shoten, 1980; G. Calzoni. "Bibliografia degli scritti di J. A. Schumpeter." *Ricerche Economiche,* 37, 1983, No. 4, pp. 751–758; J. Pascual. "Bibliografia de los escritos de J. A. Schumpeter." *Cuadernos de Economía,* 12, 1984, No. 34, pp. 329–358; M. I. Stevenson. *Joseph Alois Schumpeter. A Bibliography.* Westport, CT: Greenwood Press, 1985, pp. 3–17; C. Filippini and P. Porta. "Bibliografia degli scritti di J. A. Schumpeter." In *Società Sviluppo Impresa. Saggi su Schumpeter.* Milano: Istituto IPSOA, 1985, pp. XIX–XXIX.

7. "Schumpeter chosaku mokuroku. dai 3 han." *Shogaku Shushi,* 57, 1987, No. 1, pp. 61–84.

8. See, for example, "The Future of Gold" (paper presented at the Economic Club of Detroit, April 14, 1941) and different versions of "Can Capitalism Survive?"

9. Regarding Schumpeter's unpublished or posthumously published material, it should be noted that they have been included in this bibliography according to the date at which they were written, not discovered or published, with the exception of the years 1950 and 1951. Since it was impossible to determine the order in which various works were produced in a given year, I thought it best to adopt a consistent scheme for the presentation of his various writings, which are therefore arranged in the fol-

lowing order: articles, essays, dictionary entries, introductions, documents, unpublished works, and reviews. Within each category the works are listed in as precise a chronological order as was practicable, taking into account the month of publication, especially for articles and book reviews.

10. The decision to relegate to this section works of various types (including, for example, reviews, political documents, and unpublished works along with true articles) was motivated by the desire to furnish the reader with a clear and faithful year-by-year picture of how very prolific and well rounded a writer Schumpeter was.

11. The code numbers are preceded by the letter "S" for Schumpeter (for example S.1., S.2., S.3., etc.).

12. To facilitate consultation, every catalogue entry is explained in full, that is, there is no referring the reader to other entries or earlier citations, except for anthologies or collections of Schumpeter's writings. In fact, these entries are reported in full only the first time, and thereafter only the title and year are provided. For new editions and reprints, the information provided by the entry of the first edition is not repeated unless it has changed (for example, the publisher or number of pages, etc.).

13. When listing the many foreign-language editions of Schumpeter's books (often in the same language but carried out in different countries), instead of indicating the language alone, I have indicated the country of origin. In the case of *Capitalism, Socialism and Democracy*, for example, the various Spanish-language editions published in Buenos Aires (1946), Mexico City (1952), and Madrid (1968) are indicated respectively as the "Argentine edition," "Mexican edition," and "Spanish edition." In the case of English translations, on the other hand, no distinction has been made between the British and American versions, given the substantial correspondence between them and their publication dates. These have therefore each been indicated simply as an "English translation." Information on eventual reprints by different publishing houses in the two countries has however been duly noted. Finally, the versions that represent truly new editions, such as *The Theory of Economic Development* (1934), have been indicated as "English editions."

14. Letter from Schumpeter to F. Springer (Berlin, Feb. 1, 1926).
15. Letter from Schumpeter to F. Springer (Berlin, Mar. 20, 1926).
16. Letter from Schumpeter to F. Springer (Bonn, May 17, 1929).
17. Letter from Schumpeter to F. Springer (Bonn, Feb. 21, 1930).

## I. Books and Pamphlets

### 1908

S.001. *Das Wesen und der Hauptinhalt der theoretischen Nationaloekonomie.* Muenchen und Leipzig: Duncker & Humblot, 1908. Pp. XXXII–626. (Kairo, March 2, 1908).
> Rpt. Leipzig: Duncker & Humblot, 1970.
> ———. Japanese edition (1936): *Riron Keizaigaku no Honshitsu to Shuyonaiyo.* Trans. by T. Kimura and T. Yasui. Tokyo: Nihon-hyoron-sha, 1936. Pp. 18-12-607.
> Second edition (1950).
> Revised edition (Paperback). Trans. by T. Ono, K. Kimura, and T. Yasui. 2 Vols. Tokyo: Iwanami-shoten, 1983–1984. Pp. 499, 510. Rpt. (1986).
> ———. Italian edition (1982): *L'essenza e i principi dell'economia teorica.* Ed. and introduction by G. Calzoni. Bari: Laterza, 1982. Pp. XXI–508.

### 1910

S.002. *Wie studiert man Sozialwissenschaft?* (Schriften des sozialwissen-schaftlichen akademischen Vereins in Czernowitz, Heft 2). Czernowitz: Kommisionsverlag H. Pardini, 1910. Pp. 28 + 11.
> Second edition, Muenchen und Leipzig: Duncker & Humblot, 1915. Pp. 54. Rpt. in J. A. Schumpeter. *Aufsaetze zur oekonomischen Theorie.* Ed. by E. Schneider and A. Spiethoff. Tuebingen: J.C.B. Mohr (P. Siebeck), 1952.

### 1912

S.003. *Theorie der wirtschaftlichen Entwicklung.* Leipzig: Duncker & Humblot, 1912. Pp. VIII–548. (Wien, Juli 1911).
> Second edition (revised). *Theorie der wirtschaftlichen Entwicklung: Eine Untersuchung ueber Unternehmergewinn, Kapital, Kredit, Zins und den Konjunkturzyklus.* Muenchen und Leipzig: Duncker & Humblot, 1926. Pp. XIV–369. (Bonn, October 1926).
> Third edition (reprint) (1931).
> Fourth edition (new foreword) (1935). Pp. XXI–369. (End of 1934, Cambridge, MA).
> Fifth edition, Berlin: Duncker & Humblot, 1952. Pp. XXVI–372.
> Sixth edition (1964).
> Seventh edition (1987).
> Facsimile edition (1988). Ed. by H. C. Recktenwald. Introductions by H. C. Recktenwald, F. M. Scherer, and W. F. Stolper. (Die Handelsblatt-Bibliothek "Klassiker der Nationaloekonomie.") Duesseldorf: Verlag Wirtschaft und Finanzen, 1988. Pp. VIII–548.
> ———. Italian edition (abridged) (1932): *La teoria dello sviluppo economico.* (Nuova collana di economisti stranieri e italiani. Vol. V: Dinamica economica.) Trans. by G. Demaria and K. Mayer. Introduction by G. Demaria. Torino: Utet, 1932. Pp. 17–182.
> New edition. *Teoria dello sviluppo economico. Ricerca sul profitto, il capitale,*

*il credito, l'interesse e il ciclo economico.* Trans. by L. Berti. Introduction by P. Sylos Labini. Firenze: Sansoni, 1971. Pp. XLIX–298. Rpt. (1977).

————. English edition, with a preface by the author (1934): *The Theory of Economic Development: An Inquiry into Profits, Capital, Credit, Interest, and the Business Cycle.* Trans. by R. Opie. London and New York: Oxford University Press; Cambridge, MA: Harvard University Press, 1934. Pp. XII–255.

Rpt. London and New York: Oxford University Press, 1935. (1961), (1974), (1978).

Rpt. Cambridge, MA: Harvard University Press, 1936. (1949), (1962), (1968).

Rpt. New Brunswick, NJ: Transaction Books, 1983. Introduction by J. E. Elliot. Pp. LXIV–255.

Excerpt: "The Fundamental Phenomenon of Economic Development." In P. Kilby (Ed.). *Entrepreneurship and Economic Development.* New York: Free Press. 1971. Pp. 43–70.

————. French edition (1935): *Théorie de l'évolution économique. Recherches sur le profit, le crédit, l'intéret et le cycle de la conjuncture.* Trans. by J.-J. Anstett. Introduction by F. Perroux. Paris: Librairie Dalloz, 1935. Pp. XI–589. Second edition (1983).

————. Japanese edition (1937): *Keizai-hatten no riron.* Trans. by I. Nakayama and S. Tobata. Tokyo: Iwanami-shoten, 1937. Pp. 36-6-630. Rpt. (1938), (1940), (1951), (1955).

Revised edition (Paperback). Trans. by Y. Shionoya, I. Nakayama, and S. Tobata. 2 Vols. Tokyo: Iwanami-shoten, 1977. Pp. 362, 265. Second edition (1980). Pp. 477.

————. Mexican edition (1944): *Teoria del Desenvolvimiento economico: Una investigacion sobre ganancias, capital, crédito, interés y ciclo economico.* Trans. by J. Prados Arrarte. Mexico: Fondo de Cultura Economica, 1944. Pp. 363. Second edition (1957). Pp. 255. Rpt. (1963), (1967), (1976).

————. Polish edition (1960): *Teoria rozwoju gospodarczego.* Ed. and introduction by J. Grzywicka. Warszawa: Panstow Widawn Naukowe, 1960. Pp. XLVII–405.

————. Brazilian edition (1961): *Teoria do desenvolvimento economico.* Trans. by L. Schlaepfer. Rio de Janeiro: Editora Fundo de Cultura, 1961. Pp. 330. New edition. Sao Paulo: Abril Cultural, 1982. Pp. XV–160.

————. Bangladesh edition (1974): *Arthanaitik unmayan matabad.* Trans. by T. Husain. Dacca: Bangla Academy, 1974. Pp. 314.

————. Hungarian edition (1980): *A gazdasagi fejlodes elmelete. Vizsgalodas a vallalkozoi profitrol, a tokerol, a hitelrol, a kamatrol es a konjunkturaciklusrol.* Trans. by T. Bauer. Introduction by A. Madarasz. Budapest: Kozgazdasagi es Jogi Kiado, 1980. Pp. 320.

————. Russian edition (1982): *Teorija ekonimiceskogo razvitija. Issledovanije predprinimatel skoj pribyli, kapitala, kredita, procenta i cykla konjunktury.* Trans. by V. S. Avtonomov et al. Moskva: Izd-vo Progress, 1982. Pp. 455.

————. Slovak edition (1987): *Theoria ospodarskeho vyvoja. Analiza podnikatel-*

*skeho zisku, kapitalu, uveru a kapitalistickeho cyklu.* Trans. by J. Erben. Bratislava: Pravda, 1987. Pp. 478.

### 1914

S.004. *Epochen der Dogmen- und Methodengeschichte.* In *Grundriss der Sozialoekonomik.* I. Abteilung, Wirtschaft und Wirtschaftswissenschaft. Tuebingen: J.C.B. Mohr (P. Siebeck), 1914. Pp. 19–124.

Second edition (1924). Pp. 19–125.

————. Greek edition (1939): *Istoria Oikonomikon Theorion kai Dogmaton.* Trans. by N. Giannoulatos. Athens: Argyris Papazisis, 1939. Pp. 196.

————. Japanese edition (1950): *Keizaigakushi.* Trans. by I. Nakayama and S. Tobata. Tokyo: Iwanami-shoten, 1950. Pp. 355. Rpt. (1951), (1953), (1970).

Paperback edition (1980). Pp. 379.

————. Italian edition (1953): *Epoche di storia delle dottrine e dei metodi. Dieci grandi economisti.* Ed. and introduction by G. Bruguier Pacini. Torino: Utet, 1953. Pp. XI–174. Rpt. (1971).

————. English translation (1954): *Economic Doctrine and Method: An Historical Sketch.* Trans. by R. Aris. New York: Oxford University Press; London: Allen & Unwin, 1954. Pp. 207.

Rpt. London: Allen & Unwin, 1957.

Rpt. New York: Oxford University Press, 1967.

————. Swedish edition (1957): *De ekonomiska doktrinernas historia till sekelskiftet.* Trans. by A. Byttner. Stockholm: Natur och Kultur, 1957. Pp. 240.

————. French edition (1962): *Esquisse d'une histoire de la science économique.* Ed. and introduction by G.-H. Bousquet. Paris: Dalloz, 1962. Pp. 222.

Second edition (1972). Pp. 235.

————. Spanish edition (1964): *Sintesis de la evolucion de la ciencia economica y sus metodos.* Trans. by J. Petit Fontseré. Introduction by F. Estapé. Barcelona: Ediciones de Occidente, 1964. Pp. 216.

Second edition, Barcelona: Oikos-tau, 1967. Pp. 212.

————. Korean edition (1965): *Gyeongjehagsa.* Trans. by M.-J. Kim. Seoul: Ilsinsa, 1965. Pp. 267.

————. Brazilian edition (1968): *Fundamentos do pensamento economico.* Rio de Janeiro: Zahar, 1968. Pp. 212.

### 1915

S.005. *Vergangenheit und Zukunft der Sozialwissenschaften.* (Schriften des sozialwissenschaftlichen akademischen Vereins in Czernowitz, Heft 7). Muenchen und Leipzig: Duncker & Humblot, 1915. Pp. 140. (Graz, Weihnachten, 1914).

————. Japanese translation (1972): In J. A. Schumpeter. *Shakai-kagaku no Kako to Mirai.* Ed. by Y. Tamanoi. Tokyo: Daiyamondo-sha, 1972.

Paperback edition (1980): *Shakai-kagaku no Mirai-zo.* Trans. by K. Yashima. Tokyo: Kodan-sha, 1980. Pp. 226.

*1918*

S.006. *Die Krise des Steuerstaates. (Zeitfragen aus dem Gebiete der Soziologie,* 4, 1918, Pp. 3–74.) Graz und Leipzig: Leuschner & Lubensky, 1918. Pp. 73.

Rpt. in J. A. Schumpeter. *Aufsaetze zur Soziologie.* Ed. by E. Schneider and A. Spiethoff. Tübingen: J.C.B. Mohr (P. Siebeck), 1953.

Rpt. in R. Goldscheid and J. A. Schumpeter. *Die Finanzkrise des Steuerstaats: Beitraege zur politischen Oekonomie der Staatsfinanzen.* Ed. and introduction by R. Hickel. Frankfurt: Suhrkamp, 1976. Pp. 380.

———. Japanese edition (1951): *Sozei-kokka no Kiki.* Trans. by M. Kimura. Tokyo: Keiso-shobo, 1951. Pp. 144.

Revised edition (Paperback). Trans. by M. Kimura and Y. Kotani. Tokyo: Iwanami-shoten, 1983. Pp. 141.

———. English translation (1954): *The Crisis of the Tax State.* Trans. by W. F. Stolper and A. Musgrave. In *International Economic Papers.* Vol. 4. Ed. by A. Peacock et al. London: Macmillan, 1954, 5–38.

Rpt. in J. A. Schumpeter. *The Economics and Sociology of Capitalism.* Ed. and introduction by R. Swedberg. Princeton, NJ: Princeton University Press. Forthcoming.

Rpt. in *Collected Economic Papers of Joseph A. Schumpeter.* Ed. and introduction by M. Kanazashi. Tokyo. Forthcoming.

———. Spanish translation (1970): "La crisis del Estado fiscal." *Hacienda Publica Espanola,* 1970, No. 2, 145–169.

———. Italian translation (1983): "La crisi dello Stato fiscale." Trans. by A. Marietti Solmi. In J. A. Schumpeter. *Stato e inflazione.* Ed. and introduction by N. De Vecchi. Torino: Boringhieri, 1983, 130–180.

New trans. in *Il debito pubblico.* Ed. by M. Matteuzzi and A. Simonazzi. Bologna: Il Mulino, 1988.

*1919*

S.007. *Grundlinien der Finanzpolitik fuer jetzt und die naechsten drei Jahre.* Wien: Oesterreichische Staatsdruckerei, 1919. Pp. 27. (Wien, October 17, 1919).

Rpt. in E. Maerz. *Oesterreichische Bankpolitik in der zeit der grossen Wende 1913–1923.* Wien: Verlag fuer Geschichte und Politik. 1981.

Rpt. in J. A. Schumpeter. *Aufsaetze zur Wirtschaftspolitik.* Ed. by W. F. Stolper and C. Seidl. Tuebingen: J.C.B. Mohr (P. Siebeck), 1985, 344–368.

———. Italian translation (1988): "Le linee fondamentali della politica finanziaria per ora e per i prossimi tre anni." *Rivista Milanese di Economia,* 1988, No. 25, 147–165.

S.008. *Zur Soziologie der Imperialismen.* Tuebingen: J.C.B. Mohr (P. Siebeck), 1919. Pp. 76. (First published as two articles in the *Archiv fuer Sozialwissenschaft und Sozialpolitik,* Vol. 46, 1918–1919. See: S.102).

Rpt. in *Aufsaetze zur Soziologie* (1953).

———. English translation (1951): In J. A. Schumpeter. *Imperialism and Social Classes.* Ed. and introduction by P. M. Sweezy. New York: A. M. Kelley; Oxford: Blackwell, 1951.

[See the national editions of I.S.C. (1951).]

**1928**

S.009. *Das deutsche Finanzproblem. Reich, Laender, Gemeinder.* (Der Schriften-reihe des Deutschen Volkswirt, No. 2.) Berlin: Dt. Volkswirt, 1928. Pp. 27. (First published as four articles in *Der Deutsche Volkswirt*, Vol. 1, 1927. See: S.138, S.139, S.140, S.141.)

**1939**

S.010. *Business Cycles: A Theoretical, Historical and Statistical Analysis of the Capitalist Process.* 2 Vols. New York and London: McGraw-Hill, 1939. Pp. XVI, IX–1095. Rpt. (1955), (1961).

Rpt. Philadelphia: Porcupine Press, 1982.

Abridged edition. Ed. and introduction by R. Fels. New York: McGraw-Hill, 1964. Pp. XIII–461.

———. Japanese edition (1958–1964): *Keiki-junkan-ron.* Trans. by S. Yoshida. Ed. by The Institute of Financial Economy "Kinyu Keizai Kenkyusho." 5 Vols. Tokyo: Yuhikaku, 1958–1964. Pp. 6-1653-30. Rpt. (1985).

———. German edition (1961): *Konjunkturzyklen: Eine theoretische, historische, und statistische Analyse des kapitalistischen Prozesses.* Ed. by K. Dockhorn. 2 Vols. Goettingen: Vandenhoeck & Ruprecht, 1961. Pp. XVI, XVI–1132.

———. Italian edition (abridged) (1977): *Il processo capitalistico—Cicli economici.* Trans. by G. Ricoveri. Introduction by A. Graziani. Torino: Boringhieri, 1977. Pp. 526.

**1942**

S.011. *Capitalism, Socialism and Democracy.* New York: Harper & Brothers, 1942; London: Allen & Unwin, 1943. Pp. X–381.

Further editions:

New York: Harper & Brother

Second edition (revised) (1947). ("The Consequences of the Second World War"). Pp. XIV–411.

Third edition (enlarged) (1950). ("Comments on Further Postwar Development") Pp. XIV–431. Rpt. (1962), (1970).

Fourth edition: Harper & Row, 1975.

Fifth edition (1976). Introduction by T. Bottomore. Harper & Row, 1976. ("March into Socialism" and "Prefaces and Comments on Later Development"). Rpt. (1983).

Sixth edition (1987). New introduction by T. Bottomore. Pp. XXII–437.

Reduced edition: *Can Capitalism Survive?* Ed. and introduction by R. L. Lekachman. New York: Harper & Row, 1978. Pp. XVI–103. (Part II of C.S.D.).

London: Allen & Unwin:

Second edition (revised) (1947). ("The Consequences of the Second World War"). Pp. XII–412.

Third edition (enlarged) (1950). ("Comments on Further Postwar Development"). Pp. XVIII–412.

Fourth edition (with a new chapter) (1952). ("The March into Socialism"). Pp. XVIII–431. Rpt. (1957), (1959), (1961), (1965), (1966), (1970), (1974).

Fifth edition (1976). Introduction by T. Bottomore. ("Prefaces and Comments on Later Development"). Pp. XIV–437. Rpt. (1979), (1981).

Sixth edition (1987). New introduction by T. Bottomore. Unwin Paperbacks. Pp. XXII–437.

———. Argentine edition (1946): *Capitalismo, socialismo y democracia*. Trans. by A. Sanchez. Buenos Aires: Editorial Claridad, 1946. Pp. 431.

———. German edition (1946): *Kapitalismus, Sozialismus und Democratie*. Trans. by S. Preiswerk. Introduction by E. Salin. Bern: A. Francke, 1946. Pp. 488.

Second edition (enlarged). Berlin, Muenchen: L. Lehnen; Bern: A. Francke, 1950. Pp. 498.

Third edition (1972).

Fourth edition (1977).

Fifth edition (1980).

———. French edition (1951): *Capitalisme, Socialisme et Démocratie*. Ed. and introduction by G. Fain. Paris: Payot, 1951. Pp. 462. Rpt. (1961).

Second edition (1963). Pp. 439. Rpt. (1969).

Revised edition (1979). Pp. 417.

———. Japanese edition (1951–1952): *Shihon-shugi, Shakai-shugi, Minshu-shugi*. Trans. by I. Nakayama and S. Tobata. 3 Vols. Tokyo: Toyo Keizai-shinpo-sha. Pp. 778.

Revised edition (1962). Pp. 807. Rpt. (1969).

———. Mexican edition (1952): *Capitalismo, socialismo y democracia*. Trans. by J. Diaz Garcia. Mexico: Aguilar, 1952. Pp. 512.

Second edition (1961).

Third edition (1963).

———. Italian edition (1954): *Capitalismo, Socialismo e Democrazia*. Trans. by E. Zuffi. Milano: Edizioni di Comunità, 1954. Pp. XII–392.

Second edition (1964). Pp. XII–396.

Third edition, Milano: Etas Kompass, 1967. Pp. XII–396. Rpt. (1970).

Fourth edition, Milano: Universale Etas, 1973. Rpt. (1977), (1984).

———. Brazilian edition (1961): *Capitalismo, socialismo e democracia*. Ed. and introduction by R. Jungmann. Rio de Janeiro: Editora Fundo de Cultura, 1961. Pp. XVI–512.

Second edition, Rio de Janeiro: Zahar, 1984. Pp. 534.

———. Arabian edition (1963): *Al-ra' simaliyah wa-al-ishtirakiyah wa-al-dimu-qratiyah*. Trans. by K. Hammad. Al-Qahirah: al-Dar al-Qawmiyah lil-tiba'ah wa-al-Nashr, 1963. Pp. 226.

New edition (1964). Pp. 356.

———. Dutch edition (1963): *Kapitalisme, Socialisme en Democratie*. Trans. by C. de Boer. Hilversum, De Haag, 1963. Pp. 306.

Second edition (1967–1968). Pp. 303.

Third edition, Harlem: De Haag, 1979. Pp. 412.

———. Catalan translation (1966): *Capitalisme, socialisme i democracia*. Trans.

by A. Monteserrat and J. Casajuana. Introduction by F. Estapé. Barcelona: Edicions 62, 1966. Pp. 590.

———. Turkish edition (1966): *Kapitalizm, sosyalizm ve demokrasi*. Trans. by T. Akoglu and R. Tinaz. Istanbul: Varlik Yayinevi, 1966–1967. Pp. 212.

Second edition (1968–1971). Pp. 284.

Third edition (1974). Pp. 251. Rpt. (1977).

Fourth edition, Istanbul: Eren Matbaasi, 1981. Pp. 260.

———. Spanish edition (1968): *Capitalismo, socialismo y democracia*. Trans. by J. Diaz Garcia. Madrid: Aguilar (1968). Pp. 512. Rpt. (1971).

Further editions:

Madrid: Orbis Ediciones (1983). 2 Vols.

Madrid: Folio Ediciones (1984). Pp. 512.

———. Indian edition (1970): *Punjivad, Samajavad aur Janatantra*. Trans. by Ramavinayakasimha. Lucknow: Hindi Samiti, Suchana vibhag, 1970. Pp. 680.

———. Persian edition (1976): *Capitalisme, Socialisme va Democratie*. Trans. by Hossein Mansour. Teheran: Danechgah Teheran, 1976.

———. Chinese edition (1979): *Zibenzhuyi, Shehuizhuyi, yu Minzhu*. Beijing: The Commercial Press, 1979.

———. Jugoslav edition (1981): *Kapitalizam, socijalizam i demokracija*. Trans. by A. Marusic. Zagreb: Delo OOUR Globo, 1981. Pp. 570.

———. Korean edition (1982): *Jabonjui, Sahoejui, Minjujui*. Trans. by Lee Sang-Gu. Seoul: Ilsinsa, 1982.

New edition (1985). Trans. by Lee Young-Jae. Seoul, 1985.

### *1946*

S.012. (with W. L. Crum) *Rudimentary Mathematics for Economists and Statisticians*. New York: McGraw-Hill Book Company, 1946. Pp. XI–183. (First published by W. L. Crum as Supplement to *Quarterly Journal of Economics*, 1938, March.)

———. Mexican edition (1948): *Elementos de matematicas para economistas y estadigrafos*. Trans. by C. Lara Beautell. Mexico City: Fondo de Cultura Economica, 1948. Pp. 180.

Second edition (1959).

Third edition (1968).

———. Brazilian edition (1962): *Elementos de matematica para economistas e estatisticos*. Trans. by M. do Prado Valladares. Rio de Janeiro: Fundo de Cultura, 1962. Pp. 221.

Second edition, Sao Paulo: Vertice, 1986. Pp. 219.

### *1951*

S.013. *Ten Great Economists, from Marx to Keynes*. Ed. and introduction by E. Boody Schumpeter. New York: Oxford University Press, 1951; London: Allen & Unwin, 1952. Pp. XIV–305.

Second edition (1960). Rpt. (1965), (1966), (1970), (1971), (1977).

[Contents: S.053, S.090, S.115, S.129, S.142, S.191, S.216, S.217, S.234, S.246, S.249, S.257, "The Marxian Doctrine" from C.S.D.]

S.013. Japanese edition (1952): *Judai Keizai-gakusha, Marx Kara Keynes made.* Trans. by I. Nakayama and S. Tobata. Tokyo: Nihon-hyoron-sha, 1952. Pp. 5–430. Rpt. (1953), (1966).

——. Italian edition (1953): *Epoche di storia delle dottrine e dei metodi. Dieci grandi economisti.* Ed. and introduction by G. Bruguier Pacini. Torino: Utet, 1953. Pp. 177–454.

——. Swedish edition (1953): *Stora Nationalekonomer.* Trans. by A. Byttner. Stockholm: Natur och Kultur, 1953. Pp. 353.

——. Spanish edition (1955): *Diez grandes economistas. De Marx a Keynes.* Ed. and introduction by F. Estapé. Barcelona: José M. Bosch, 1955. Pp. XX–382.

New edition. Trans. by A. de Lucas. Madrid: Alianza Editorial, 1967. Pp. 446.

Second edition (1969).

Third edition (1971).

Fourth edition (1979).

Fifth edition (1983).

——. Brazilian edition (1958): *Dez Grandes Economistas.* Trans. by J. Freire. Rio de Janeiro: Editora Civilizacao Brasileira S.A., 1958. Pp. 296.

New edition, *Teorias economicas de Marx a Keynes.* Rio de Janeiro: Zahar, 1970. Pp. 290.

——. Arabian edition (1959): *Asharah min a'immat al-Iqtisad 'min markis ila kins.* Al-qahirah: Maktabit al-Sharq bel-Fajjalah, 1959. Pp. 273.

——. Indonesian edition (1963): *Sepuluh sardjana economi terkemuka, dari Marx sempai Keynes.* Trans. by O. Bian Hong. Djakarta: Bhratara, 1963. Pp. 334.

——. Chinese edition (1965): *Cong Marx dao Keynes. Yilai de Shi Wei Zhuming Jingjixuejia.* Beijing: The Commercial Press, 1965. Pp. 312.

——. Korean edition (1982): *10 dae gyeongje hagja.* Trans. by D. Y. Chung. Seoul: Han-gilsa, 1982. Pp. 348.

S.014. *Imperialism and Social Classes.* Trans. by H. Norden. Ed. and introduction by P. M. Sweezy. New York: A. M. Kelley; Oxford: Blackwell, 1951. Pp. XXV–221. (Translation of "Zur Soziologie der Imperialismen" and "Die soziale Klassen im ethnisch homogenen Milieu," which originally were published in *Archiv fuer Sozialwissenschaft und Sozialpolitik,* 1918–1919 and 1927. See: S.102 and S.131.)

New edition, *Imperialism and Social Classes: Two Essays.* Trans. by H. Norden. Ed. and introduction by B. Hoselitz. New York: Meridian Books, 1955. Pp. X–182. Rpt. (1960).

Rpt. Cleveland: World Publishing Company, 1965. Rpt. (1968).

Rpt. New York: New American Library, 1974.

——. Japanese edition (1956): *Teikoku-shugi to Shakai-kaikyu.* Ed. by S. Tsuru. Tokyo: Iwanami-shoten, 1956. Pp. 262. Rpt. (1963), (1968), (1975), (1977), (1980).

Second edition (1983).

———. Brazilian edition (1961): *Imperalismo e classes sociais*. Rio de Janeiro: Zahar, 1961. Pp. 195.

———. Spanish edition (1965): *Imperialismo, Clases Sociales*. Trans. by V. Girbau. Ed. and introduction by F. Estapé. Madrid: Editorial Tecnos, 1965. Pp. 331.

   Second edition (1983). Pp. 336.

   Third edition (1986). Pp. 208.

———. French edition (1972): *Imperialisme et classes sociales*. Trans. by S. de Segonzac, D. Bresson, and J.-C. Passeron. Introduction by J.-C. Passeron. Paris: Minuit, 1972. Pp. 295.

   Excerpt: "Les conquetes musulmanes et l'imperialisme arabe." Ed. and introduction by G.-H. Bousquet. In *Revue Africain*, 2, 1950, 283–297.

———. Italian edition (1972): *Sociologia dell'imperialismo*. Trans. by G. Fantozzi. Preface by L. Villari. Bari: Laterza, 1972. Pp. VIII–184.

   Second edition (1974). Pp. IX–190.

S.015. *Essays of J. A. Schumpeter*. Ed. and introduction by R. V. Clemence. Cambridge, MA: Addison-Wesley, 1951. Pp. 327.

   Second edition (1969): *Essays on Economic Topics of J. A. Schumpeter*. Port Washington, NY: Kennikat Press, 1969.

   New edition (1989): *Essays on Entrepreneurs, Innovations, Business Cycles and the Evolution of Capitalism*. New introduction by R. Swedberg. New Brunswick, NJ: Transaction Publishers, 1989.

   [Contents: S.046, S.144, S.154, S.175, S.179, S.196, S.201, S.202, S.203, S.205, S.208, S.210, S.211, S.214, S.229, S.233, S.237, S.239, S.240, S.245, S.246, S.250, S.251, S.253, S.254.]

———. Spanish edition (1968): *Ensayos*. Trans. by J. Silvestre, E. Lluch Martin, and J. Planas Campos. Barcelona: Oikos-tau. Pp. 349.

*1952*

S.016. *Aufsaetze zur oekonomischen Theorie*. Ed. by E. Schneider and A. Spiethoff. Tübingen: J.C.B. Mohr (P. Siebeck), 1952. Pp. 608.

   [Contents: S.002, S.034, S.040, S.045, S.073, S.074, S.089, S.094, S.098, S.112, S.119, S.123, S.143, S.152, S.166, S.193.]

*1953*

S.017. *Aufsaetze zur Soziologie*. Ed. by E. Schneider and A. Spiethoff. Tübingen: J.C.B. Mohr (P. Siebeck), 1953. Pp. 232.

   [Contents: S.006, S.008 (S.102), S.131, S.165.]

*1954*

S.018. *Dogmenhistorische und biographische Aufsaetze*. Ed. by E. Schneider and A. Siethoff. Tübingen: J.C.B. Mohr (P. Siebeck), 1954. Pp. VIII–383.

   [Contents: S.053, S.090, S.097, S.113, S.115, S.120, S.122, S.128, S.132, S.134, S.137, S.145, S.217, S.234.]

S.019. *History of Economic Analysis*. Ed. (from manuscript) and introduction by E. Boody Schumpeter. London: Allen & Unwin; New York: Oxford Uni-

versity Press, 1954. Pp. XXV–1260. Rpt. (1959), (1961), (1963), (1966), (1968), (1972), (1976), (1981).
Paperback edition:
New York: Oxford University Press, 1986. Pp. XXV–1286.
London: Allen & Unwin, 1987. Pp. XXV–1260.
———. Japanese edition (1955–1962): *Keizai-bunseki no Rekishi*. Trans. by S. Tobata. 7 Vols. Tokyo: Iwanami-shoten, 1955–1962. Pp. 2488. Rpt. (1980).
———. Italian edition (1959 –1960): *Storia dell'analisi economica*. Ed. by P. Sylos Labini and L. Occhinero. 3 Vols. Torino: Boringhieri, 1959–1960. Pp. XXIII–1536.
New edition (abridged): Ed. by C. Napoleoni. Torino: Boringhieri, 1968. Pp. 684. Rpt. (1972), (1976).
———. Brazilian edition (1964): *Historia da analise economica*. 3 Vols. Rio de Janeiro: Fundo de Cultura, 1964.
———. German edition (1965): *Geschichte der oekonomischen Analyse*. Trans. by G. and J. Frenzel. Foreword by F. K. Mann. 2 Vols. Goettingen: Vandenhoeck und Ruprecht, 1965. Pp. VII, XIX–1520.
———. Mexican edition (1971): *Historia del analisis economico*. Trans. by L. Mantilla. Mexico City: Fondo de Cultura Economico, 1971. Pp. 810.
———. Spanish edition (1971): *Historia del analisis economico*. Trans. by M. Sacristan-Luzon, J. A. Garcia Duran, and N. Serra. Barcelona: Ediciones Ariel, 1971. Pp. 1371.
Second edition (1982). Pp. 1377.
———. Jugoslav edition (1975): *Povijest ekonomske analize*. Trans. by Z. Baletic, M. Hanzekovic, and S. Stampar. 2 Vols. Zagreb: Informator, 1975.
———. French edition (1983): *Histoire de l'analyse économique*. Preface by R. Barre. 3 Vols. Paris: Gallimard, 1983. Pp. 519, 495, 710.
———. Chinese edition (1989): *Jingji Fenxi Shi*. Beijing: The Commercial Press. Forthcoming.

*1961*

S.020. *Kahei, bunpai no Riron*. (Theory of money and distribution.) Ed. by T. Miwa. Tokyo: Toyo Keyzai Shinpo Sha, 1961. Pp. 266.
[Contents: S.094, S.098.]

*1970*

S.021. *Das Wesen des Geldes*. Ed. and introduction by F. K. Mann. Goettingen: Vandenhoeck & Ruprecht, 1970. Pp. XXVII–341.

*1972*

S.022. *Shakai-kagaku no Kako to Mirai*. (Past and future of social sciences.) Ed. by Y. Tamanoi. Tokyo: Daiyamondo-sha, 1972. Pp. 519.
[Contents: "Das Gesamtbild der Volkswirtschaft" (Chap. 7, first ed. of T.W.E.), S.005, S.128.]

*1973*

S.023. *Shihonshugi to Shakaishugi.* (Capitalism and Socialism.) Ed. by T. Ono.
Tokyo: Sobun-sha, 1973. Pp. 237.
   [Contents: S.112, S.119, S.229, S.237, S.250, S.251.]

*1977*

S.024. *Konniki ni okeru shakaishugi no Kanousei.* (Possibility of contemporary
socialism.) Ed. by T. Ono. Tokyo: Sobun-sha, 1977. Pp. 268. (Revised ed.
of *Shihonshugi to Shakaishugi,* 1973.)
   [Contents: S.112, S.119, S.229, S.236, S.237, S.250, S.251, S.258.]

*1983*

S.025. *Stato e inflazione.* (State and inflation.) Trans. by P. Castellanza, G. Cioc-
chetti, and A. Marietti Solmi. Ed. and introduction by N. De Vecchi. Torino: Boringhieri, 1983. Pp. 210.
   [Contents: S.006, S.098, S.153, S.168.]

*1984*

S.026. *Schumpeter. Antologia di scritti.* (Schumpeter. An anthology of writings.)
Ed. and introduction by M. Messori. Bologna: Il Mulino, 1984. Pp. 392.
   [Contents: S.098, S.144, S.159, S.167, S.179, S.205, S.210, S.229, S.250,
and chapters from H.E.A., T.W.E., B.C., W.G.]

*1985*

S.027. *Aufsaetze zur Wirtschaftspolitik.* Ed. and introduction by W. F. Stolper
and C. Seidl. Tübingen: J.C.B. Mohr (P. Siebeck), 1985. Pp. VI–378.
   [Contents: S.007, S.095, S.096, S.099, S.105, S.106, S.107, S.108, S.109,
S.110, S.111, S.130, S.133, S.136, S.138, S.139, S.140, S.141, S.153, S.155,
S.156, S.158, S.167, S.168, S.170, S.171, S.173, S.174, S.187, S.190, S.192.]

*1987*

S.028. *Beitraege zur Sozialoekonomik.* Ed. and introduction by S. Boehm. Fore-
word by G. Haberler. Wien: Boehlau Verlag, 1987. Pp. 375.
   [Contents: S.052, S.092, S.101, S.144, S.154, S.159, S.175, S.196, S.205,
S.210, S.237, S.238, S.239, S.240, S.248, S.250, S.253, S.254.]

*1991*

S.029. *The Economics and Sociology of Capitalism.* Ed. with an introduction by
R. Swedberg. Princeton, NJ: Princeton University Press, 1991.
   [Contents: S.006, S.102, S.113, S.131, S.186, S.209, S.215, S.218, S.219,
S.220, S.221, S.222, S.223, S.224, S.225, S.236, S.242, S.247, S.256.]

*Forthcoming*

S.030. *Collected Economic Papers of Joseph A. Schumpeter.* Ed. and introduction
by M. Kanazashi. Tokyo. Forthcoming.
   [Contents: S.006, S.036, S.098, S.125, S.151, S.176, S.177, S.178, S.181,

S.183, S.184, S.185, S.186, S.189, S.199, S.204, S.206, S.228, S.232, S.235, S.236, S.238, S.259.]

## II. Articles, Reports, and Book Reviews

### 1905

S.031. "Die Methode der Standard Population." *Statistische Monatschrift*, 31, N.S., 10, 1905, 188–191.

S.032. "Die Methode der Index-Zahlen." *Statistische Monatschrift*, 31, N.S., 10, 1905, 191–197.

S.033. "Die internationale Preisbildung." *Statistische Monatschrift*, 31, N.S., 10, 1905, 923–928.

### 1906

S.034. "Ueber die mathematische Methode der theoretischen Oekonomie." *Zeitschrift fuer Volkswirtschaft, Sozialpolitik und Verwaltung*, 15, 1906, 30–49. Rpt. in *Aufsaetze zur oekonomischen Theorie* (1952).

S.035. "Professor Clarks Verteilungstheorie." *Zeitschrift fuer Volkswirtschaft, Sozialpolitik und Verwaltung*, 15, 1906, 325–333.

S.036. "Rudolf Auspitz." *Economic Journal*, 16, 1906, Jun., 309–311. Rpt. in *Collected Economic Papers of Joseph A. Schumpeter* (Forthcoming).

S.037. "O. Karmin. *Zur Lehre von den Wirtschaftskrisen*." *Zeitschrift fuer Volkswirtschaft, Sozialpolitik und Verwaltung*, 15, 1906, 95–97.

S.038. "H. Deutsch. *Qualifizierte Arbeit und Kapitalismus*." *Zeitschrift fuer Volkswirtschaft, Sozialpolitik und Verwaltung*, 15, 1906, 98–99.

S.039. "J. Leonhard. *Neue Feststellung des Wertbegriffes und ihre Bedeutung fuer die Volkswirtschaft*." *Jahrbuch fuer Gesetzgebung, Verwaltung und Volkswirtschaft im Deutschen Reich*, 30, 1906, II, 1271.

### 1907

S.040. "Das Rentenprinzip in der Verteilungslehre." *Jahrbuch fuer Gesetzgebung, Verwaltung und Volkswirtschaft im Deutschen Reich*, 31, 1907, I, 31–65, and 591–634. Rpt. in *Aufsaetze zur oekonomischen Theorie* (1952).

S.041. "J. W. Schiele. *Ueber den natuerlichen Ursprung der Kategorien Rente, Zins und Arbeitslohn*." *Jahrbuch fuer Gesetzgebung, Verwaltung und Volkswirtschaft im Deutschen Reich*, 31, 1907, I, 395–398.

S.042. "M. E. Waxweiler. *Esquisse d'une sociologie*." *Economic Journal*, 17, 1907, Mar., 109–111.

### 1908

S.043. "Einige neuere Erscheinungen auf dem Gebiete der theoretischen Nationaloekonomie: 1. E.R.A. Seligman. *Principles of Economics*. 2. W. S. Jevons. *The Principles of Economics*. 3. L. Polier. *L'idée du juste salaire*. 4. L. Querton. *L'augmentation du rendement de la machine humaine*. 5. W. Hasbach. *Gueterverzehrung und Gueterhervorbringung*. 6. H. von Leesen. *Frédéric Bastiat*. 7. A. Rudiger-Miltenberg. *Der gerechte Lohn*. 8. T. N. Carver. *The Distribution of Wealth*. 9. F. A. Fetter. *The Principles of Economics, with Applications to Practical Problems." Zeitschrift fuer Volkswirtschaft, Sozialpolitik und Verwaltung*, 17, 1908, 402–420.

S.044. "J. B. Clark. *Essentials of Economic Theory as Applied to Modern Problems of Industry and Public Policy." Zeitschrift fuer Volkswirtschaft, Sozialpolitik und Verwaltung*, 17, 1908, 653–659.

### 1909

S.045. "Bemerkungen ueber das Zurechnungsproblem." *Zeitschrift fuer Volkswirtschaft, Sozialpolitik und Verwaltung*, 18, 1909, 79–132. Rpt. in *Aufsaetze zur oekonomischen Theorie* (1952).

S.046. "On the Concept of Social Value." *Quarterly Journal of Economics*, 23, 1909, Feb., 213–232. Rpt. in *Essays of J. A. Schumpeter*. Ed. by R. V. Clemence. Cambridge, MA: Addison-Wesley, 1951. Span. trans. in J. A. Schumpeter. *Ensayos*. Barcelona: Oikos-tau, 1968. Jap. trans. in *Takasaki Keizai Daigaku Ronshu—The Journal of Takasaki City University of Economics*, 14, 1971, No. 1-2.

S.047. "R. Kaulla. *Die geschichtliche Entwicklung der modernen Werttheorien." Jahrbuch fuer Gesetzgebung, Verwaltung und Volkswirtschaft im Deutschen Reich*, 3, 1909, II, 1261–1262.

S.048. "I. Fisher. *The Nature of Capital and Income." Zeitschrift fuer Volkswirtschaft, Sozialpolitik und Verwaltung*, 18, 1909, 679–680.

S.049. "H. Mannestaedt. *Die Kapitalistische Anwendung der Maschinerie." Zeitschrift fuer Volkswirtschaft, Sozialpolitik und Verwaltung*, 18, 1909, 680–681.

S.050. "G. de Molinari. *Questions économiques à l'ordre du jour." Zeitschrift fuer Volkswirtschaft, Sozialpolitik und Verwaltung*, 18, 1909, 681–683.

S.051. "1. I. Ryner. *On the Crises of 1837, 1847, and 1857 in England, France and the United States*. 2. M. T. England. *On Speculation in Relation to the World Prosperity, 1897–1902*. 3. W. G. Longworthy Taylor. *The Kinetic Theory of Economic Crises," Zeitschrift fuer Volkswirtschaft, Sozialpolitik und Verwaltung*, 18, 1909, 683–685.

### 1910

S.052. "Ueber das Wesen der Wirtschaftskrisen." *Zeitschrift fuer Volkswirtschaft, Sozialpolitik und Verwaltung*, 19, 1910, 271–325. Rpt. in J. A. Schumpeter. *Beitraege zur Sozialoekonomik*. Ed. and introduction by S. Boehm. Wien: Bohlau Verlag, 1987.

S.053. "Marie Esprit Léon Walras." *Zeitschrift fuer Volkswirtschaft, Sozialpolitik und Verwaltung*, 19, 1910, 397–402. Rpt. in J. A. Schumpeter. *Dogmenhistorische und biographische Aufsaetze*. Ed. by E. Schneider and A. Spiethoff. Tübingen: J.C.B. Mohr (P. Siebeck), 1954. Engl. trans. in J. A. Schumpeter. *Ten Great Economists, from Marx to Keynes*. Ed. and introduction by E. Boody Schumpeter. New York: Oxford University Press, 1951. Ital. trans. in A. Quadrio Curzio and R. Scazzieri (Eds.). *Protagonisti del pensiero economico*. Bologna: Il Mulino, 1971. [See the national editions of T.G.E.]

S.054. "Die neuere Wirtschaftstheorie in den Vereinigten Staaten." *Jahrbuch fuer Gesetzgebung, Verwaltung und Volkswirtschaft im Deutschen Reich*, 34, 1910, 913–963.

S.055. "A. Weber. *Ueber den Standort der Industrien.*" *Jahrbuch fuer Gesetzgebung, Verwaltung und Volkswirtschaft im Deutschen Reich*, 34, 1910, II, 1356–1359.

S.056. "O. Conrad. *Lohn und Rente.*" *Jahrbuecher fuer Nationaloekonomie und Statistik*, 94, 1910, 827–831.

S.057. "J. Conrad. *Leitfaden zum Studium der Nationaloekonomie. Und Grundriss zum Studium der politischen Oekonomie. 4.* Teil: *Statistik.*" *Archiv fuer Sozialwissenschaft und Sozialpolitik*, 31, 1910, 256.

S.058. "O. Neurath and A. Schapire-Neurath. *Lesebuch der Volkswirtschaftslehre.*" *Archiv fuer Sozialwissenschaft und Sozialpolitik*, 31, 1910, 256–257.

S.059. "V. Pareto. *Manuel d'économie politique.*" *Archiv fuer Sozialwissenschaft und Sozialpolitik*, 31, 1910, 257.

S.060. "G. Schmoller. *Grundriss der allgemeinen Volkswirtschaftslehre. 1.* Teil." *Archiv fuer Sozialwissenschaft und Sozialpolitik*, 31, 1910, 257–258.

S.061. "A. von Wenckstern. *Staatswissenschaftliche Probleme der Gegenwart.* Vol. 1." *Archiv fuer Sozialwissenschaft und Sozialpolitik*, 31, 1910, 258.

S.062. "E. von Boehm-Bawerk. *Kapital und Kapitalzins: Positive Theorie des Kapitals.*" *Archiv fuer Sozialwissenschaft und Sozialpolitik*, 31, 1910, 271.

S.063. "E. Fabian-Sagal. *Albert Schaeffle und seine theoretisch- national-oekonomischen Lehren.*" *Archiv fuer Sozialwissenschaft und Sozialpolitik*, 31, 1910, 271.

S.064. "H. Levy. *Monopole, Kartelle und Trusts in ihren Beziehungen zur Organisation der Kapitalischen Industrie.*" *Archiv fuer Sozialwissenschaft und Sozialpolitik*, 31, 1910, 285–286.

S.065. "A. Lansburgh. *Depositen und Spargelder.*" *Archiv fuer Sozialwissenschaft und Sozialpolitik*, 31, 1910, 297.

### 1911

S.066. "Gruendungsgewinn in Recht und Wirtschaft." *Zeitschrift fuer Notariat Oesterreich*, 4, 1911, 31.

S.067. "W. Lexis. *Allgemeine Volkswirtschaftslehre.*" *Archiv fuer Sozialwissenschaft und Sozialpolitik*, 32, 1911, 865–867.

S.068. "A. W. Small. *The Meaning of Social Science.*" *Archiv fuer Sozialwissenschaft und Sozialpolitik*, 32, 1911, 868–870.

S.069. "H. Niehuus. *Geschichte der englischen Bodenreformtheorien.*" *Archiv fuer Sozialwissenschaft und Sozialpolitik*, 32, 1911, 873–874.

S.070. "Neuere Erscheinungen auf dem Gebiete der Nationaloekonomie: F. Lifschitz. *Untersuchungen ueber die Methodologie der Wirtschaftswissenschaft.*—J. Grunzel. *Allgemeine Volkswirtschaftslehre.*—W. Hohoff. *Die Bedeutung der Marxschen Kapitalkritik.*—C. Gide. *Cours d'économie politique.*—G. Ruhland. *System der politischen Oekonomie.*—W. Jacoby. *Der Streit um den Kapitalsbegriff.*—H. Pesch. *Lehrbuch der Nationaloekonomie.*—F. Lifschitz. *Zur Kritik der Boehm-Bawerkschen Werttheorie.*—A. Weber. *Die Aufgaben der Volkswirtschaftslehre als Wissenschaft.*—S. Kiichiro. *Geld und Wert. Eine logische Studie.*—I. Fisher. *The Rate of Interest, its Nature, Determination and Relation to Economic Phenomena.*—J. H. Davenport. *Value and Distribution, a Critical and Constructive Study.*—R. Schachner. *Australien in Politik, Wirtschaft und Kul-*

*tur.*—C. A. Conant. *A History of Modern Banks of Issue.*" *Zeitschrift fuer Volkswirtschaft, Sozialpolitik und Verwaltung*, 20, 1911, 240–252.

### 1912

S.071. "Neue nationaloekonomische Lehrbuecher und Lehrbehelfe: W. Lexis. *Allgemeine Volkswirtschaftslehre.*—H. R. von Schullern zu Schrattenhofen. *Grundzuege der Volkswirtschaftslehre.*—E. Schwiedland. *Einfuehrung in die Volkswirtschaftslehre.*—F. W. Taussig. *Principles of Economics.*— L. H. Haney. *History of Economic Thought.*—O. Spann. *Haupttheorien der Volkswirtschaftslehre.*—O. und A. Neurath. *Lesebuch der Volkswirtschaftslehre.*—K. Diehl und P. Mombert. *Ausgewaehlte Lesestuecke zum Studium der politischen Oekonomie.*" *Zeitschrift fuer Volkswirtschaft, Sozialpolitik und Verwaltung*, 21, 1912, 281–292.

S.072. "R. Stolzmann. *Die soziale Kategorie in der Volkswirtschaftslehre.*— R. Stolzman. *Der Zweck in der Volkswirtschaft.*" *Jahrbuch fuer Gesetzgebung, Verwaltung und Volkswirtschaft im Deutschen Reich*, 36, 1912, I, 928-934.

### 1913

S.073. "Zinsfuss und Geldverfassung." *Jahrbuch der Gesellschaft Oesterreichischer Volkswirte*, 1913, 38–63. Rpt. in *Aufsaetze zur oekonomischen Theorie* (1952).

S.074. "Eine 'dynamische' Theorie des Kapitalzinses: Eine Entgegnung." *Zeitschrift fuer Volkswirtschaft, Sozialpolitik und Verwaltung*, 22, 1913, 599–639. Rpt. in *Aufsaetze zur oekonomischen Theorie* (1952). Span. trans. in *La nueva ciencia economica*. Madrid: Editorial Revista de Occidente, 1955. Ital. trans. in N. De Vecchi (Ed.). *La teoria austriaca del capitale e dell'interesse*. Roma: Istituto dell'Enciclopedia Italiana, 1983.

S.075. "Entgegnung auf Bundsmanns Erwiderung." *Archiv fuer Sozialwissenschaft und Sozialpolitik*, 36, 1913, 679.

S.076. "Meinungsaeusserung zur Frage des Werturteils." In *Aeusserungen zur Werturteilsdiskussion im Ausschuss des Vereins fuer Sozialpolitik*. (Paper presented at Seminar in Duesseldorf) Duesseldorf, Aus Manuskript gedruckt, 1913, 49–50.

S.077. "A. Adler. *Leitfaden der Volkswirtschaftslehre.*—Quaritsch. *Kompendium der Nationaloekonomie.*" *Archiv fuer Sozialwissenschaft und Sozialpolitik*, 36, 1913, 238–240.

S.078. "G. Mollat. *Volkswirtschaftliches Quellenbuch.*" *Archiv fuer Sozialwissenschaft und Sozialpolitik*, 36, 1913, 240.

S.079. "S.-C. Haret. *Mécanique sociale.*" *Archiv fuer Sozialwissenschaft und Sozialpolitik*, 36, 1913, 240–241.

S.080. "J. Bonar. *Disturbing Elements in the Study and Teaching of Political Economy.*" *Archiv fuer Sozialwissenschaft und Sozialpolitik*, 36, 1913, 243–244.

S.081. "E. Bundsmann. *Das Kapital, wirtschaftstheoretische Skizzen.*" *Archiv fuer Sozialwissenschaft und Sozialpolitik*, 36, 1913, 244–246.

S.082. "I. Fisher. *De la nature du capital et du revenue.*" *Archiv fuer Sozialwissenschaft und Sozialpolitik*, 36, 1913, 246–248.

S.083. "B. de Lavergne. *Théorie des Marchés Economiques.*" *Archiv fuer Sozialwissenschaft und Sozialpolitik*, 36, 1913, 249–251.

S.084. "T. Lloyd. *The Theory of Distribution and Consumption.*" *Archiv fuer Sozialwissenschaft und Sozialpolitik*, 36, 1913, 251–252.

S.085. "A. Loria. *La synthèse économique, étude sur le lois du revenu.*" *Archiv fuer Sozialwissenschaft und Sozialpolitik*, 36, 1913, 252–254.

S.086. "R. Maunier. *L'origine et la fonction économique des villes.*" *Archiv fuer Sozialwissenschaft und Sozialpolitik*, 36, 1913, 254–256.

S.087. "H. L. Moore. *Laws of Wages.*" *Archiv fuer Sozialwissenschaft und Sozialpolitik*, 36, 1913, 256–258.

S.088. "F. Oppenheimer. *Theorie der reinen und politischen Oekonomie.*" *Zeitschrift fuer Volkswirtschaft, Sozialpolitik und Verwaltung*, 22, 1913, 797.

### 1914

S.089. "Die 'positive' Methode in der Nationaloekonomie." *Deutsche Literaturzeitung*, 35, 1914, 2101–2108. Rpt. in *Aufsaetze zur oekonomischen Theorie* (1952). Span. trans. in *La nueva ciencia economica*. Madrid: Editorial Revista de Occidente, 1955.

S.090. "Das wissenschaftliche Lebenswerk Eugen von Boehm-Bawerks." *Zeitschrift fuer Volkswirtschaft, Sozialpolitik und Verwaltung*, 23, 1914, 454–528. Rpt. in *Dogmenhistorische und biographische Aufsaetze* (1954). Engl. trans. in *Ten Great Economists, from Marx to Keynes* (1951).
[See the national editions of T.G.E.]

S.091. "Railway Rate Making: Discussion." *American Economic Review*, Supplement, 4, 1914, 81–100.

S.092. "Die Wellenbewegung des Wirtschaftslebens." *Archiv fuer Sozialwissenschaft und Sozialpolitik*, 39, 1914–1915, 1–32. Rpt. in *Beitraege zur Sozialoekonomik* (1987).

### 1915

S.093. "K. Schlesinger. *Theorie der Geld- und Kreditwirtschaft.*" *Archiv fuer Sozialwissenschaft und Sozialpolitik*, 41, 1915, 239–242.

### 1916

S.094. "Das Grundprinzip der Verteilungstheorie." *Archiv fuer Sozialwissenschaft und Sozialpolitik*, 42, 1916–1917, 1–88. Rpt. in *Aufsaetze zur oekonomischen Theorie* (1952). Jap. trans. in J. A. Schumpeter. *Kahei, Bunpai no Riron*. Ed. by T. Miwa. Tokyo: Toyo Keizai-shinpo-sha, 1961.

S.095. "Memorandum I." (Graz, Feb., 1916.) In *Aufsaetze zur Wirtschaftspolitik* (1985), 251–272.

S.096. "Memorandum II." (Graz, Dec., 1916.) In *Aufsaetze zur Wirtschaftspolitik* (1985), 273–289.

### 1917

S.097. "Das Bodenmonopol. (Eine Entgegnung auf Dr. Oppenheimers Artikel.)" *Archiv fuer Sozialwissenschaft und Sozialpolitik*, 44, 1917–1918, 495–502. Rpt. in *Dogmenhistorische und biographische Aufsaetze* (1954).

S.098. "Das Sozialprodukt und die Rechenpfennige: Glossen und Beitraege zur Geldtheorie von heute." *Archiv fuer Sozialwissenschaft und Sozialpolitik*,

44, 1917–1918, 627–715. Rpt. in *Aufsaetze zur oekonomischen Theorie* (1952). Eng. trans. in *International Economic Papers*. Vol. 6. London: MacMillan, 1956. Rpt. in *Collected Economic Papers of Joseph A. Schumpeter* (Forthcoming). Jap. trans. in *Kahei, Bunpai no Riron* (1961). Ital. trans. in *Stato e Inflazione* (1983). New Ital. trans. (part.) in *Schumpeter. Antologia di scritti*. Ed. by M. Messori. Bologna: Il Mulino, 1984.

S.099. "Memorandum III: Die politische Lage und die Interessen der Monarchie." (Graz, Apr., 1917.) In *Aufsaetze zur Wirtschaftspolitik* (1985), 289–310.

S.100. "Volkswirtschaftliche Seminare." (Report presented at the University of Graz.) Graz, 1917 (Unpublished).

*1918*

S.101. "Karl Marx, der Denker." In *Arbeiterwille. Organ des arbeitenden Volkes fuer Steiermark und Kaernten*, 29, 1918, No. 120, May 5, 3. Rpt. in *Beitraege zur Sozialoekonomik* (1987).

*1919*

S.102. "Zur Soziologie der Imperialismen." *Archiv fuer Sozialwissenschaft und Sozialpolitik*, 46, 1918–1919, 1–39 and 275–310. [Also in book form, 1919. See: S.008.] Rpt. in *Aufsaetze zur Soziologie* (1953). Eng. trans. in J. A. Schumpeter. *Imperialism and Social Classes* (1951). Rpt. in *The Economics and Sociology of Capitalism* (1990).
  [See the national editions of I.S.C.]

S.103. "Finanzpolitische und wirtschaftliche Ausblicke." *Die Woche*, 21–26, 1919, 679–680.

S.104. (et al.) "Vorlaeufiger Bericht der Sozialisierungskommission ueber die Frage der Sozialisierung des Kohlenbergbaus." (Concluded on February 15, 1919.) Berlin: R. V. Decker Verlag/G. Scheuch, 1919.

S.105. "Rede in der 7. Sitzung der Konstituierenden Nationalversammlung fuer Deutschoesterreich am 2. April 1919." In *Aufsaetze zur Wirtschaftspolitik* (1985), 313–315.

S.106. "Rede in der 9. Sitzung der Konstituierenden Nationalversammlung fuer Deutschoesterreich am 4. April 1919." In *Aufsaetze zur Wirtschaftspolitik* (1985), 316–320.

S.107. "Rede in der 11. Sitzung der Konstituierenden Nationalversammlung fuer Deutschoesterreich am 25. April 1919." In *Aufsaetze zur Wirtschaftspolitik* (1985), 320–321.

S.108. "Rede in der 12. Sitzung der Konstituierenden Nationalversammlung fuer Deutschoesterreich am 6. Mai 1919." In *Aufsaetze zur Wirtschaftspolitik* (1985), 322–324.

S.109. "Rede in der 24. Sitzung der Konstituierenden Nationalversammlung fuer Deutschoesterreich am 4. Juli 1919." In *Aufsaetze zur Wirtschaftspolitik* (1985), 324–330.

S.110. "Erhoehung der Erbgebuehren, Einfuehrung eines staatlichen Noterb- und Pflichtteilsrechtes." (Jul., 1919.) In *Aufsaetze zur Wirtschaftspolitik* (1985), 330–336.

S.111. "Schreiben des Staatssekretaers Schumpeter an Staatskanzler Renner." (Undated.) In *Aufsaetze zur Wirtschaftspolitik* (1985), 337–343.

### 1920

S.112. "Sozialistische Moeglichkeiten von heute." *Archiv fuer Sozialwissenschaft und Sozialpolitik*, 48, 1920–1921, 305–360. Rpt. in *Aufsaetze zur oekonomischen Theorie* (1952). Jap. trans. in J. A. Schumpeter. *Shionshugi to Shakaishugi*. Ed. by T. Ono. Tokyo: Sobun-sha, 1973. Rpt. in J. A. Schumpeter. *Konniki ni okeru shakaishugi no Kanousei*. Ed. by T. Ono. Tokyo: Sobun-sha, 1977. Ital. trans. (part.) in *Politica ed Economia*, 18, 1988, No. 10.

S.113. "Max Webers Werk." *Der Oesterreichische Volkswirt*, 12, 1920, No. 45, Aug., 831–834. Rpt. in *Dogmenhistorische und biographische Aufsaetze* (1954). Eng. trans. in *The Economics and Sociology of Capitalism* (1990).

S.114. "Die (allgemeine) finanzpolitische Situation." *Die Boerse*, 1920, Oct.

### 1921

S.115. "Carl Menger." *Zeitschrift fuer Volkswirtschaft und Sozialpolitik*, N. F., 1, 1921, 197–206. Rpt. in *Dogmenhistorische und biographische Aufsaetze* (1954). Eng. trans. in *Ten Great Economists, from Marx to Keynes* (1951).
[See the national editions of T.G.E.]

### 1922

S.116. "Soll die Notenbank gegruendet werden." *Die Boerse*, 1922, Oct. 11.

### 1923

S.117. "Angebot." In *Handwoerterbuch der Staatswissenschaften*. 4th ed., Vol. 1. Jena: Verlag von G. Fischer, 1923, 299–303.

S.118. "Kapital." In *Handwoerterbuch der Staatswissenschaften*. 4th ed., Vol. 5, Jena: Verlag von G. Fischer, 1923, 582–584.

### 1924

S.119. "Der Sozialismus in England und bei uns." *Der Oesterreichische Volkswirt*, 16, 1924, Dec., No. 11 and 12–13, 295–297, and 327–330. Rpt. in *Aufsaetze zur oekonomischen Theorie* (1952). Jap. trans. in *Shionshugi to shakaishugi* (1973). Rpt. in *Konniki ni okeru shakaishugi no Kanousei* (1977).

### 1925

S.120. "Eugen von Boehm-Bawerk." In *Neue Oesterreichische Biographie 1815–1918*. Vol. II. Vienna, 1925, 63–80. Rpt. in *Dogmenhistorische und biographische Aufsaetze* (1954). Eng. trans. in H. W. Spiegel (Ed.). *The Development of Economic Thought*. New York: John Wiley & Sons, 1952. Jap. trans. in S. Koshimura (Ed.). *Keizai shido hatten shi*. Vol. 4. Tokyo: Toyo Keizaishinpo-sha, 1954–1955. Ital. trans. in A. Quadrio Curzio and R. Scazzieri (Eds.). *Protagonisti del pensiero economico*. Vol. I. Bologna: Il Mulino, 1977.

S.121. "Kreditpolitik und Wirtschaftslage." *Berliner Boersencourier*, 58, 1925, No. 603.

S.122. "Edgeworth und die neuere Wirtschaftstheorie." *Weltwirtschaftliches Archiv*, 22, 1925, 183–202. Rpt. in *Dogmenhistorische und biographische Aufsaetze* (1954).

S.123. "Kreditkontrolle." *Archiv fuer Sozialwissenschaft und Sozialpolitik*, 54, 1925, 289–328. Rpt. in *Aufsaetze zur oekonomischen Theorie* (1952).

S.124. "Oude en nieuwe bankpolitiek." *Economisch-Statistische Berichten*, 2, 1925, 552–554, 574–577, and 600–601.

S.125. "The Currency Situation in Austria." United States Senate. 67th Congress. Commission of Gold and Silver Inquiry. *European Currency and Finance*. S. 9, Vol. 1. Foreign Currency and Exchange Investigation. Ed. by J. P. Young. 1925, 225–231. Rpt. in *Collected Economic Papers of Joseph A. Schumpeter* (Forthcoming).

*1926*

S.126. "Subventionspolitik." *Berliner Boersencourier*, 59, 1926, No. 87.

S.127. "Konjunkturforschung." *Berliner Boersencourier*, 59, 1926, No. 157 and 159.

S.128. "Gustav v. Schmoller und die Probleme von heute." *Schmollers Jahrbuch fuer Gesetzgebung, Verwaltung und Volkswirtschaft im Deutschen Reiche*, 50, 1926, I, 337–388. Rpt. in *Dogmenhistorische und biographische Aufsaetze* (1954). Rpt. in *Gegenstand und Methoden der Nationaloekonomie*, Koeln, 1971. Jap. trans. in *Shakai-kagaku no Kako to Mirai* (1972).

S.129. "G. F. Knapp." *Economic Journal*, 36, 1926, No. 143, Sep., 512–514. Rpt. in *Ten Great Economists, from Marx to Keynes* (1951).
    [See the national editions of T.G.E.]

S.130. "Steuerkraft und nationale Zukunft." *Der Deutsche Volkswirt*, 1, 1926, Oct., 13–16. Rpt. in *Aufsaetze zur Wirtschaftspolitik* (1985).

*1927*

S.131. "Die sozialen Klassen im ethnisch homogenen Milieu." *Archiv fuer Sozialwissenschaft und Sozialpolitik*, 57, 1927, 1–67. Rpt. in *Aufsaetze zur Soziologie* (1953). Eng. trans. in *Imperialism and Social Classes* (1951). Rpt. in *The Economics and Sociology of Capitalism* (1990).
    [See the national editions of I.S.C.]

S.132. "Cassels Theoretische Sozialoekonomik." *Schmollers Jahrbuch fuer Gesetzgebung, Verwaltung und Volkswirtschaft im Deutschen Reiche*, 51, 1927, I, No. 2, 241–260. Rpt. in *Dogmenhistorische und biographische Aufsaetze* (1954).

S.133. "Die Arbeitslosigkeit." *Der Deutsche Volkswirt*, 1, 1927, No. 1, Mar., 729–732. Rpt. in *Aufsaetze zur Wirtschaftspolitik* (1985).

S.134. "Sombarts dritter Band." *Schmollers Jahrbuch fuer Gesetzgebung, Verwaltung und Volkswirtschaft im Deutschen Reiche*, 51, 1927, I, No. 3, 349–369. Rpt. in *Dogmenhistorische und biographische Aufsaetze* (1954).

S.135. "Zur Frage der Grenzproduktivitaet: Eine Entgegnung auf den vorstehenden Aufsatz von Willen Valk." *Schmollers Jahrbuch fuer Gesetzgebung, Verwaltung und Volkswirtschaft im Deutschen Reiche*, 51, I, 1927, No. 5, 671–680.

S.136. "Unternehmerfunktion und Arbeiterinteresse." *Der Arbeitgeber*, 17, 1927, No. 8, 166–170. Rpt. in *Aufsaetze zur Wirtschaftspolitik* (1985).

S.137. "Zur Einfuehrung der folgenden Arbeit Knut Wicksells: Mathematische Nationaloekonomie." *Archiv fuer Sozialwissenschaft und Sozialpolitik*, 58, 1927–1928, 238–251. Rpt. in *Dogmenhistorische und biographische Aufsaetze* (1954).

S.138. "Finanzpolitik." *Der Deutsche Volkswirt*, 1, 1927, No. 2, Apr., 827–830. Rpt. in "Das deutsche Finanzproblem." *Die Schriftenreihe des Deutschen Volkswirts*, 1928, No. 2. Rpt. in *Aufsaetze zur Wirtschaftspolitik* (1985).

S.139. "Finanzpolitik und Kabinettssystem." *Der Deutsche Volkswirt*, 1, 1927, No. 2, Apr., 865–869. Rpt. in "Das deutsche Finanzproblem." *Die Schriftenreihe des Deutschen Volkswirts*, 1928, No. 2. Rpt. in *Aufsaetze zur Wirtschaftspolitik* (1985).

S.140. "Geist und Technik der Finanzverwaltung." *Der Deutsche Volkswirt*, 1, 1927, No. 2, May, 1028–1031. Rpt. in "Das deutsche Finanzproblem." *Die Schriftenreihe des Deutschen Volkswirts*, 1928, No. 2. Rpt. in *Aufsaetze zur Wirtschaftspolitik* (1985).

S.141. "Finanzausgleich (Das deutsche Finanzproblem: Reich, Laender und Gemeinden)." *Der Deutsche Volkswirt*, 1, 1928, No. 2, Jun., 1123–1126 and 1156–1159. Rpt. in "Das deutsche Finanzproblem." *Die Schriftenreihe des Deutschen Volkswirts*, 1927, No. 2. Rpt. in *Aufsaetze zur Wirtschaftspolitik* (1985).

S.142. "Friedrich von Wieser." *Economic Journal*, 37, 1927, No. 146, Jun., 328–330. Rpt. in *Ten Great Economists, from Marx to Keynes* (1951). [See the national editions of T.G.E.]

S.143. "Die goldene Bremse an der Kreditmaschine." *Koelner Vortraege*, Vol. 1. *Die Kreditwirtschaft*, 1, 1927, 80–106. Rpt. in *Aufsaetze zur oekonomischen Theorie* (1952).

S.144. "The Explanation of the Business Cycles." *Economica*, 7, 1927, Dec., 286–311. Rpt. in *Essays of J. A. Schumpeter* (1951). Span. trans. in J. A. Schumpeter. *Ensayos*. Barcelona: Oikos-tau, 1968. Ital. trans. in *Schumpeter. Antologia di scritti* (1984). Ger. trans. in *Beitraege zur Sozialoekonomik* (1987).

S.145. "Deutschland." In H. Mayer, F. A. Fetter, and R. Reisch (Eds.). *Die Wirtschaftstheorie der Gegenwart*. Vol. 1. Wien, 1927, 1–30. Rpt. in *Dogmenhistorische und biographische Aufsaetze* (1954).

S.146. "Einfuehrung." In E. Barone. *Grundzuege der theoretischen Nationaloekonomie*. Berlin, Bonn: Duemmler, 1927, 7–10. 2nd ed. 1935.

S.147. "R. G. Hawtrey. *The Economic Problem*." *Weltwirtschaftliches Archiv*, 26, 1927, 131–133.

S.148. "H. Dietzel. *Die Bedeutung des 'Nationalen Systems' fuer die Vergangenheit und die Gegenwart*." *Archiv fuer Sozialwissenschaft und Sozialpolitik*, 58, 1927, 415–416.

S.149. "F.B.W. Hermann. *Staatswirtschaftliche Untersuchungen*." *Archiv fuer Sozialwissenschaft und Sozialpolitik*, 58, 1927, 416–417.

S.150. "E.R.A. Seligman. *Essays in Economics*." *Archiv fuer Sozialwissenschaft und Sozialpolitik*, 58, 1927, 417–418.

S.151. "C. A. Macartney. *The Social Revolution in Austria*." *Economic Journal*, 37, 1927, Jun., 290–292. Rpt. in *Collected Economic Papers of Joseph A. Schumpeter* (Forthcoming).

*1928*

S.152. "Staatsreferendar und Staatsassessor." *Schmollers Jahrbuch fuer Gesetz-gebung, Verwaltung und Volkswirtschaft im Deutschen Reiche*, 52, 1928, II, No. 2, 703–720. Rpt. in *Aufsaetze zur oekonomischen Theorie* (1952).

S.153. "Lohngestaltung und Wirtschaftsentwicklung." *Der Arbeitgeber*. 18, 1928, 479–482. Rpt. in *Aufsaetze zur Wirtschaftspolitik* (1985). Ital. trans. in *Stato e inflazione* (1983).

S.154. "The Instability of Capitalism." *Economic Journal*, 38, 1928, Sep., 361–386. Rpt. in *Essays of J. A. Schumpeter* (1951). Rpt. in R. L. Smith (Ed.). *Essays in the Economics of Socialism and Capitalism*. London, 1964. Rpt. in *The Economics of Technological Change*. Harmondsworth, 1971. Span. trans. in J. A. Schumpeter. *Ensayos*. Barcelona: Oikos-tau, 1968. Ital. trans. in L. Colletti and C. Napoleoni (Eds.). *Il futuro del capitalismo*. Bari: Laterza, 1970. Ger. trans. in *Beitraege zur Sozialoekonomik* (1987).

S.155. "Erbschaftssteuer." *Der Deutsche Volkswirt*, 3, 1928, Oct., 110–114. Rpt. in *Aufsaetze zur Wirtschaftspolitik* (1985).

S.156. "Wen trifft die Umsatzsteuer?" *Der Deutsche Volkswirt*, 3, 1928, Nov., 206–208. Span. trans. in *Hacienda Publica Espanola*, 1971, No. 12, 151–155. Rpt. in *Aufsaetze zur Wirtschaftspolitik* (1985).

S.157. "International Cartels and Their Relation to World Trade." In P. T. Moon (Ed.). *America as a Creditor Nation*. New York, 1928. Rpt. in *Academy of Political Science*, Proceedings, 12, 1928, No. 4, 908–913.

S.158. "Der Unternehmer in der Volkswirtschaft von heute." In B. Harms (Ed.). *Strukturwandlungen der Deutschen Volkswirtschaft. Vorlesungen gehalten in der Deutschen Vereinigung fuer Staatswissenschafliche Forschung*. Berlin: Verlag von Reimar Hobbing, 1928, 295–312. 2nd ed. (revised), 1929, 303–326. Rpt. in *Aufsaetze zur Wirtschaftspolitik* (1985).

S.159. "Unternehmer." In *Handwoerterbuch der Staatswissenschaften*. 4th ed., Vol. VIII. Jena: Verlag von G. Fischer, 1928, 476–487. Rpt. in *Beitraege zur Sozialoekonomik* (1987). Ital. trans. in *Schumpeter. Antologia di scritti* (1984).

S.160. "Die Tendenzen unserer sozialen Struktur." (Vortrag vor dem Verein zur Wahrung der Interessen der Chemischen Industrie Deutschlands, Dezember 8, 1928.) *Die Chemische Industrie*, 51, 1928, 1381–1387.

S.161. "C. Landauer. *Grundprobleme der funktionellen Verteilung des wirtschaftlichen Wertes.*" *Weltwirtschaftliches Archiv*, 27, 1928, 24–27.

S.162. "L. V. Birck. *The Theory of Marginal Value.*" *Weltwirtschaftliches Archiv*, 28, 1928, 24–26.

S.163. "Bonn und Palyi. *Festausgabe fuer Lujo Brentano.*" *Zeitschrift fuer Voelkerpsychologie*, 4, 1928, 101–102.

S.164. "C. Rodbertus. *Neuere Briefe ueber Grundrente.*" *Zeitschrift fuer Voelkerpsychologie*, 4, 1928, 102–103.

*1929*

S.165. "Das soziale Antlitz des Deutschen Reiches." *Bonner Mitteilungen*, 1929, No. 1, 3–14. Rpt. in *Aufsaetze zur Soziologie* (1953).

S.166. "Die Wirtschaftslehre und die reformierte Referendarpruefung." *Schmollers Jahrbuch fuer Gesetzgebung, Verwaltung und Volkswirtschaft im*

*Deutschen Reiche*, 53, 1929, II, No. 2, 637–650. Rpt. in *Aufsaetze zur oekonomischen Theorie* (1952).

S.167. "Lohnpolitik und Wissenschaft." *Der Deutsche Volkswirt*, 3, 1929, Mar., 807–810. Rpt. in *Aufsaetze zur Wirtschaftspolitik* (1985). Ital. trans. in *Schumpeter. Antologia di scritti* (1984).

S.168. "Grenzen der Lohnpolitik." *Der Deutsche Volkswirt*, 3, 1929, Mar., 847–851; *Dazu Nachbemerkung*, May, 1022–1023. Rpt. in *Aufsaetze zur Wirtschaftspolitik* (1985). Ital. trans. in *Stato e inflazione* (1983).

S.169. "Le role économique et psychologique dc l'employeur." *Informations Sociales* (Bureau International du Travail, Geneve) 31, 1929, 113–115.

S.170. "Was vermag eine Finanzreform?" *Der Deutsche Volkswirt*, 4, 1929, Oct., 75–80. Rpt. in *Aufsaetze zur Wirtschaftspolitik* (1985).

S.171. "Oekonomie und Soziologie der Einkommensteuer." *Der Deutsche Volkswirt*, 4, 1929, Dec., 380–385. Rpt. in *Aufsaetze zur Wirtschaftspolitik* (1985).

S.172. "Oekonomie und Psychologie des Unternehmers." (Vortrag in der 10. ordentlichen Mitgliederversammlung des Zentralverbandes der Deutschen Metallwalzwerks- und Huetten-Industrie E. V. in Muenchen.) Leipzig: Haberland, 1929. Pp. 15.

*1930*

S.173. "Wenn die Finanzreform misslingt . . . " *Der Deutsche Volkswirt*, 4, 1930, No.1, Feb., 695–699. Rpt. in *Aufsaetze zur Wirtschaftspolitik* (1985).

S.174. "Wandlungen der Weltwirtschaft." *Der Deutsche Volkswirt*, 4, 1930, No. 2, Sep., 1729–1733. Rpt. in *Aufsaetze zur Wirtschaftspolitik* (1985).

S.175. "Mitchell's Business Cycles." *Quarterly Journal of Economics*, 45, 1930, Nov., 150–172. Rpt. in *Essays of J. A. Schumpeter* (1951). Span. trans. in J. A. Schumpeter. *Ensayos*. Barcelona: Oikos-tau, 1968. Ger. trans. in *Beitraege zur Sozialoekonomik* (1987).

S.176. "Auspitz Rudolf (1837–1906)." In *Encyclopaedia of the Social Sciences*. Vol. 2. New York: The MacMillan Company, 1930, 317. Rpt. in *Collected Economic Papers of Joseph A. Schumpeter* (Forthcoming).

S.177. "Boehm-Bawerk Eugen von (1851–1914)." In *Encyclopaedia of the Social Sciences*. Vol. 2. New York: The MacMillan Company, 1930, 618–619. Rpt. in *Collected Economic Papers of Joseph A. Schumpeter* (Forthcoming).

S.178. "Preface." In F. Zeuthen. *Problems of Monopoly and Economic Warfare*. London: Routledge, 1930, XII–XIII. Rpt. in *Collected Economic Papers of Joseph A. Schumpeter* (Forthcoming).

*1931*

S.179. "The Present World Depression: A Tentative Diagnosis." *American Economic Review*, Supplement, 21, 1931, No. 1, Mar., 179–182. Rpt. in *Essays of J. A. Schumpeter* (1951). Span. trans. in J. A. Schumpeter. *Ensayos*. Barcelona: Oikos-tau, 1968. Ital. trans. in *Schumpeter. Antologia di scritti* (1984).

S.180. "Les possibilités actuelles du socialisme." *L'Année Politique Francaise et Etrangère*, 1931, No. 24, 385–418.

S.181. "The 'Crisis' in Economics—Fifty Years Ago." Ed. by R. L. Allen (from a typescript of a lecture delivered at Tokyo University of Commerce, January 28, 1931). *Journal of Economic Literature*, 20, 1982, No. 3, 1049–1059. Rpt. in *Collected Economic Papers of Joseph A. Schumpeter* (Forthcoming). Jap. trans. in S. Oishi (Ed.). *Schumpeter Saihakken: Seitan 100 nen kinen*. The Keizai Seminar Bessatsu. Tokyo: Nihon hyoron Sha, 1983. Span. trans. in *Hacienda Publica Espanola*, 83, 1983. Rpt. in *Informacion Comercial Espanola*, 607, 1984, No. 3.

S.182. "The World Depression with Special Reference to the United States of America." (Lecture delivered at Japan Industry Club. Tokyo, January 29, 1931.) *Nihon Kogyo Kurabu Kaiho*, 16, 1931, 14–19.

S.183. "The Theory of the Business Cycle." (Lecture delivered at the Tokyo University. Tokyo, January 30, 1931.) *Keizaigaku Ronshu—The Journal of Economics*, N. S., 4, 1931, No. 1, 1–18. Rpt. in *Collected Economic Papers of Joseph A. Schumpeter* (Forthcoming). Jap. trans., with a different title ("Kyoko no riron—Theory of economic crisis") in *Keizai Orai*, 6, 1931, No. 3.

S.184. "The Present State of International Commercial Policy." (Lecture delivered at the Kobe University. Presumably in 1931.) *The Kokumin Keizai Zasshi—Journal of Economics & Business Administration*, 50, 1931, No. 4, 481–506. Rpt. in *Collected Economic Papers of Joseph A. Schumpeter* (Forthcoming).

S.185. "The Present State of Economics. Or on Systems, Schools and Methods." (Lecture delivered at the Kobe University. February 9, 1931.) *The Kokumin Keizai Zasshi—Journal of Economics & Business Administration*, 50, 1931, No. 5, 679–705. Rpt. in *Collected Economic Papers of Joseph A. Schumpeter* (Forthcoming).

S.186. "Recent Developments of Political Economy." Ed. by R. L. Allen (from a typescript of a lecture delivered at the Kobe University, February 9, 1931). *Kobe University Economic Review*, 28, 1982, 1–15. Rpt. in *The Economics and Sociology of Capitalism* (1990). Rpt. in *Collected Economic Papers of Joseph A. Schumpeter* (Forthcoming).
[See: S.185.]

S.187. "Dauerkrise?" *Der Deutsche Volkswirt*, 6, 1931, Dec., 418–421. Rpt. in *Aufsaetze zur Wirtschaftspolitik* (1985).

S.188. "Das Kapital im wirtschaftlichen Kreislauf und in der wirtschaftlichen Entwicklung." In B. Harms (Ed.). *Kapital und Kapitalismus. Veroeffentlichungen der deutschen Vereinigung fuer Staatswissenschaftliche Fortbildung*. Vol. 1. Berlin, 1931, 187–208.

*1932*

S.189. "A German View: World Depression and Franco-German Economic Relations." *Lloyds Bank Limited Monthly Review*, Supplement, 1932, Mar., 14–35. Rpt. in *Collected Economic Papers of Joseph A. Schumpeter* (Forthcoming).

S.190. "Weltkrise und Finanzpolitik." *Der Deutsche Volkswirt*, 6, 1932, Mar., 739–742. Rpt. in *Aufsaetze zur Wirtschaftspolitik* (1985).

S.191. "Ladislaus von Bortkiewicz." *Economic Journal*, 42, 1932, Jun., 338–340. Rpt. in *Ten Great Economists, from Marx to Keynes* (1951). [See the national editions of T.G.E.]

S.192. "Kreditpolitische Krisentherapie in Amerika." *Der Deutsche Volkswirt*, 6, 1932, Jul., 1415–1418. Rpt. in *Aufsaetze zur Wirtschaftspolitik* (1985).

S.193. "Das Woher und Wohin unserer Wissenschaft." (Abschiedsrede gehalten vor der Bonner staatswissenschaftlichen Fakultaet am 20.6.1932.) Bonn, 1932. Rpt. in *Aufsaetze zur oekonomischen Theorie* (1952).

S.194. "Zur Soziologie der Aussenpolitik." Bonn, 1932. (Unpublished manuscript.)

S.195. "G.-H. Bousquet. *Institutes de science économique.*" *Economic Journal*, 42, 1932, Sep., 449–451.

*1933*

S.196. "The Common Sense of Econometrics." *Econometrica*, 1, 1933, No. 1, Jan., 5–12. Rpt. in *Essays of J. A. Schumpeter* (1951). Span. trans. in J. A. Schumpeter. *Ensayos*. Barcelona: Oikos-tau, 1968. Ger. trans. in *Beitraege zur Sozialoekonomik* (1987).

S.197. "Der Stand und die naechste Zukunft der Konjunkturforschung." In *Festschrift fuer A. Spiethoff*. Mit einem Vorwort und unter Mitwirkung von J. A. Schumpeter. Muenchen: Duncker & Humblot, 1933, 263–267.

S.198. "W. von Winkler. *Grundzuege der Statistik.*" *Schmollers Jahrbuch fuer Gesetzgebung, Verwaltung und Volkswirtschaft im Deutschen Reiche*, 57, 1933, 136–139.

S.199. "J. M. Keynes. *Essays in Biography.*" *Economic Journal*, 43, 1933, Dec., 652–657. Rpt. in *Collected Economic Papers of Joseph A. Schumpeter* (Forthcoming).

*1934*

S.200. "Imperfect Competition." (Round Table: J. A. Schumpeter Chairman.) *American Economic Review*, Supplement, 24, 1934, No. 1, Mar., 21–32.

S.201. "Depressions. Can We Learn from Past Experience?" In D. V. Brown et al. (Eds.) *The Economics of the Recovery Program*. New York and London: Whittlesey House, McGraw-Hill, 1934, 3–21. Rpt. in *Essays of J. A. Schumpeter* (1951). Ital. trans. in *Il piano Roosevelt*, Torino: Einaudi, 1935. Span. trans. in *El programa economico de Roosevelt* (N.I.R.A.). Madrid: Editorial Revista de Derecho Privado, 1935. New Span. trans. in J. A. Schumpeter. *Ensayos*. Barcelona: Oikos-tau, 1968.

S.202. "The Nature and Necessity of a Price System." In *Economic Reconstruction*. (Report of the Columbia University Commission.) New York: Columbia University Press, 1934, 170–176 (See also Schumpeter's "Addendum," 239–242). Rpt. in R. V. Clemence (Ed.). *Readings in Economic Analysis*. Cambridge, MA: Addison-Wesley, 1950. Rpt. in A. D. Gayer, C. L. Harris, and M. H. Spencer (Eds.). *Basic Economics. A Book of Readings*. Englewood Cliffs, NJ: Prentice Hall, 1951. Rpt. in *Essays of J. A. Schumpeter* (1951). Rpt. in A. A. Leeman (Ed.). *Capitalism, Market Socialism and Central Planning*. Boston:

Houghton Mifflin Co., 1963. Rpt. in *Readings in Microeconomics*. New York, London and Sydney, 1969. Jap. trans. in A. A. Leeman (Ed.). *Hikaku Keizai Taisei Ron*. Vol. 1. Tokyo: Nippon Hyhoron Sha, 1951. Span. trans. in J. A. Schumpeter. *Ensayos*. Barcelona: Oikos-tau, 1968.

S.203. "J. Robinson. *The Economics of Imperfect Competition.*" *Journal of Political Economy*, 42, 1934, Apr., 249–257. Rpt. in *Essays of J. A. Schumpeter* (1951). Span. trans. in J. A. Schumpeter. *Ensayos*. Barcelona: Oikos-tau, 1968.

### 1935

S.204. "A Theorist's Comment on the Current Business Cycle." *Journal of the American Statistical Association*, Supplement, 30, 1935, Mar., 167–168. Rpt. in *Collected Economic Papers of Joseph A. Schumpeter* (Forthcoming).

S.205. "The Analysis of Economic Change." *Review of Economic Statistics*, 17, 1935, May, 2–10. Rpt. in G. Haberler (Ed.). *Readings in Business Cycles Theory*. Philadelphia: Blakiston Company, 1944. Rpt. in *Essays of J. A. Schumpeter* (1951). Rpt. in J. J. Clark and M. Cohen (Eds.). *Business Fluctuations, Growth and Economic Stabilization*. New York, 1963. Jap. trans. in G. Haberler (Ed.). *Keiki Hendo no Riron*. Vol. 1. Tokyo: Jitsugyo no Nippon Sha, 1951. Span. trans. in G. Haberler (Ed.). *Ensayos sobre il ciclo economico*. Mexico: Fondo de Cultura economica, 1946. Rpt. in J. A. Schumpeter. *Ensayos*. Barcelona: Oikos-tau, 1968. Ital. trans. in R. Giannetti (Ed.). *Ristagno e sviluppo. Il dibattito sul ciclo economico fra le due guerre*. Firenze, La Nuova Italia, 1977. Part. rpt. in *Schumpeter. Antologia di scritti* (1984). Ger. trans. in *Beitraege zur Sozialoekonomik* (1987).

S.206. "Young, Allyn Abbott (1876–1929)." In *Encyclopaedia of the Social Sciences*. Vol. 15. New York: The MacMillan Company, 1935, 514–515. Rpt. in *Collected Economic Papers of Joseph A. Schumpeter* (Forthcoming).

S.207. "Geleitwort." In D. H. Robertson. *Das Geld*. Wien: Springer-Verlag, 1935.

### 1936

S.208. "Professor Taussig on Wages and Capital." In *Explorations in Economics: Notes and Essays Contributed in Honor of F. W. Taussig*. New York and London: McGraw-Hill, 1936, 213–222. Rpt. in *Essays of J. A. Schumpeter* (1951). Span. trans. in J. A. Schumpeter. *Ensayos*. Barcelona: Oikos-tau, 1968.

S.209. "Can Capitalism Survive?" (from a speech given in Washington, D.C., January 18, 1936). Now in *The Economics and Sociology of Capitalism* (1990). A somewhat different version has been published by the United States Department of Agriculture Graduate School. Washington, 1936. Pp. 10.

S.210. "J. M. Keynes. *General Theory of Employment, Interest and Money.*" *Journal of the American Statistical Association*, 31, 1936, Dec., 791–795. Rpt. in R. V. Clemence (Ed.). *Readings in Economic Analysis*. Cambridge, MA: Cambridge University Press, 1950. Rpt. in *Essays of J. A. Schumpeter* (1951). Rpt. in J. C. Wood (Ed.). *John Maynard Keynes. Critical Assessments*. Vol. 1. London and Canberra: Croom Helm, 1983. Span. trans. in J. A. Schumpeter. *Ensayos*. Barcelona: Oikos-tau, 1968. Ital. trans. in *Schumpeter. Antologia di scritti* (1984). Ger. trans. in *Beitraege zur Sozialoekonomik* (1987).

**1937**

S.211. "Preface." In J. A. Schumpeter. *Keizaihatten no riron.* (Jap. ed. T.W.E.) Tokyo: Iwanami-Shoten, 1937. Eng. trans. in *Essays of J. A. Schumpeter* (1951). Span. trans. in J. A. Schumpeter. *Ensayos.* Barcelona: Oikos-tau, 1968. Ital. trans. in J. A. Schumpeter. *Teoria dello sviluppo economico.* (Ital. ed. T.W.E.) Firenze: Sansoni, 1971.

S.212. "Suggestions for the Quantitative Study of the Business Cycle." (Report of the Third Annual Research Conference on Economics and Statistics.) Colorado Springs, Cowles Commission, 1937.

**1939**

S.213. "The Pure Theory of Production." (Round Table: J. A. Schumpeter Chairman.) *American Economic Review,* Supplement, 29, 1939, No. 1, Mar., 118–120.

**1940**

S.214. "The Influence of Protective Tariffs on the Industrial Development of the United States." *Academy of Political Science,* Proceedings, 19, 1940, May, 2–7. Rpt. in *Essays of J. A. Schumpeter* (1951). Span. trans. in J. A. Schumpeter. *Ensayos.* Barcelona: Oikos-tau, 1968.

S.215. "The Meaning of Rationality in the Social Sciences." Ed. and introduction by W. F. Stolper and R. Richter (from a typescript of a Faculty Seminar given at Harvard in 1940). *Zeitschrift fuer die Gesamte Staatswissenschaft,* 140, 1984, No. 4, 577–593. Rpt. in complete version in *The Economics and Sociology of Capitalism* (1990).

**1941**

S.216. (With A. H. Cole and E. S. Mason.) "Frank William Taussig." *Quarterly Journal of Economics,* 55, 1941, May, 337–363. Rpt. in *Ten Great Economists, from Marx to Keynes* (1951).
[See the national editions of T.G.E.]

S.217. "Alfred Marshall's Principles: A Semi-Centennial Appraisal." *American Economic Review,* 31, 1941, No. 2, Jun., 236–248. Rpt. in *Ten Great Economists, from Marx to Keynes* (1951). Rpt. in J. C. Wood (Ed.). *Alfred Marshall. Critical Assessments.* London and Canberra: Croom Helm, 1983. Ger. trans. in *Dogmenhistorische und biographische Aufsaetze* (1954).
[See the national editions of T.G.E.]

S.218. "An Economic Interpretation of Our Time. First Lecture." Lecture given at the Lowell Institute, Boston, MA. March 4, 1941. Pp. 12. Now in *The Economics and Sociology of Capitalism* (1990).

S.219. "An Economic Interpretation of Our Time. Second Lecture: Success and Failure in the Adjustment of 1919–1929." Lecture given at the Lowell Institute, Boston, MA. March 7, 1941. P. 4. Now in *The Economics and Sociology of Capitalism* (1990).

S.220. "The Impact of the World Crisis." Lecture given at the Lowell Institute, Boston, MA. March 11, 1941. Pp. 12. Now in *The Economics and Sociology of Capitalism* (1990).

S.221. "Investment, Unemployment, and Planning During the Thirties." Lecture given at the Lowell Institute, Boston, MA. March 14, 1941. Pp. 15. Now in *The Economics and Sociology of Capitalism* (1990).

S.222. "The Role of Fiscal and Monetary Policies." Lecture given at the Lowell Institute, Boston, MA. March 18, 1941. Pp. 16. Now in *The Economics and Sociology of Capitalism* (1990).

S.223. "The Falling Birth Rate." Lecture given at the Lowell Institute, Boston, MA. March 21, 1941. Pp. 15. Now in *The Economics and Sociology of Capitalism* (1990).

S.224. "International Trade." Lecture given at the Lowell Institute, Boston, MA. March 25, 1941. Pp. 17. Now in *The Economics and Sociology of Capitalism* (1990).

S.225. "Possible Consequences for the United States." Lecture given at the Lowell Institute, Boston, MA. March 28, 1941. Pp. 16. Now in *The Economics and Sociology of Capitalism* (1990).

S.226. "The Future of Gold." Paper presented at the Economic Club of Detroit, MI. April 14, 1941. Pp. 19. (Unpublished typescript.)

*1942*

S.227. "Cost and Demand Functions of the Individual Firm." (Round Table: J. A. Schumpeter Chairman.) *American Economic Review*, Supplement, 32, 1942, No. 1, Mar., 349–350.

S.228. "G. J. Stigler. *The Theory of Competitive Price.*" *American Economic Review*, 32, 1942, 844–847. Rpt. in *Collected Economic Papers of Joseph A. Schumpeter* (Forthcoming).

*1943*

S.229. "Capitalism in the Postwar World." In S. E. Harris (Ed.). *Postwar Economic Problems*. New York and London: McGraw-Hill, 1943, 113–126. Rpt. in *Essays of J. A. Schumpeter* (1951). Span. trans. in J. A. Schumpeter. *Ensayos*. Barcelona: Oikos-tau, 1968. Jap. trans. in *Shionshugi to shakaishugi* (1973). Rpt. in *Konniki ni okeru shakaishugi no Kanousei* (1977). Ital. trans. in *Schumpeter. Antologia di scritti* (1984).

S.230. "Preface." In B. W. Dempsey. *Interest and Usury*. Washington: American Council of Public Affairs, 1943. 2nd ed. London: Dennis Dobson, 1948.

*1944*

S.231. "Prologo." In J. A. Schumpeter. *Teoria del desenvolvimiento economico: Una investigacion sobre ganancias, capital, credito, interes y ciclo economico.* (Span. trans. T.W.E.) Mexico: Fondo de Cultura Economica, 1944.

S.232. "H. J. Laski. *Reflections on the Revolution of Our Time.*" *American Economic Review*, 34, 1944, Mar., 161–164. Rpt. in *Collected Economic Papers of Joseph A. Schumpeter* (Forthcoming).

*1946*

S.233. "The Decade of the Twenties." (In "The American Economy in the Interwar Period.") *American Economic Review*, Proceedings, 36, 1946, No. 2, May, 1–10. Rpt. in J. A. Schumpeter. *The American Economy in the Interwar Period: The Decade of the Twenties*. Indianapolis: Bobbs Merrill, 1946. Rpt. in A. H. Hansen and R. V. Clemence (Eds.). *Business Cycles and National Income*. New York: Norton, 1951. Rpt. in *Essays of J. A. Schumpeter* (1951). Span. trans. in J. A. Schumpeter. *Ensayos*. Barcelona: Oikos-tau, 1968.

S.234. "John Maynard Keynes: 1883–1946." *American Economic Review*, 36, 1946, Sep., 495–518. Rpt. in S. E. Harris (Ed.). *The New Economics: Keynes' Influence on Theory and Public Policy*. New York: A. A. Knopf, 1947. Rpt. in *Ten Great Economists, from Marx to Keynes* (1951). Rpt. in J. C. Wood (Ed.). *John Maynard Keynes. Critical Assessments*. Vol. 1. London and Canberra: Croom Helm, 1983. Jap. trans. in S. E. Harris (Ed.). *Atarasii Keizaigaku*. Ed. by Research and Statistics Department of the Bank of Japan. Vol. 1. Tokyo: Toyo Keizai Shinpo-sha, 1949–1950. Ger. trans. in *Dogmenhistorische und biographische Aufsaetze* (1954). Rpt. in C. H. Recktenwald (Ed.). *Lebensbilder grosser Nationaloekonomen*. Koeln, Berlin, 1965.
[See the national editions of T.G.E.]

S.235. "Keynes and Statistics." (In "Keynes' Contributions to Economics—Four Views.") *Review of Economic Statistics*, 28, 1946, Nov., 194–196. Rpt. in J. C. Wood (Ed.). *John Maynard Keynes. Critical Assessments*. Vol. 1. London and Canberra: Croom Helm, 1983. Rpt. in *Collected Economic Papers of Joseph A. Schumpeter* (Forthcoming).

S.236. "L'avenir de l'entreprise privée devant les tendances socialistes modernes." In *Comment sauvegarder l'entreprise privée*. (Premier Congres Patronals). Montreal: Editions Association Professionelle des Industriels, 1946. Eng. trans. in *History of Political Economy*, 7, 1975, No. 3. Rpt. in *The Economics and Sociology of Capitalism* (1990). Rpt. in *Collected Economic Papers of Joseph A. Schumpeter* (Forthcoming). Jap. trans. in *Konniki ni okeru shakaishugi no Kanousei* (1977).

S.237. "Capitalism." In *Encyclopaedia Britannica*. Vol. 4. Chicago, London, and Toronto, 1946, 801–807. Rpt. in *Essays of J. A. Schumpeter* (1951). Span. trans. in *Ensayos*. Barcelona: Oikos-tau, 1968. Jap. trans in *Shionshugi to shakaishugi* (1973). Rpt. in *Konniki ni okeru shakaishugi no Kanousei* (1977). Ger. trans. in *Beitraege zur Sozialoekonomik* (1987).

S.238. "F. A. Hayek. *The Road to Serfdom.*" *Journal of Political Economy*, 54, 1946, Jun., 269–270. Rpt. in *Collected Economic Papers of Joseph A. Schumpeter* (Forthcoming). Ger. trans. in *Beitraege zur Sozialoekonomik* (1987).

*1947*

S.239. "The Creative Response in Economic History." *Journal of Economic History*, 7, 1947, Nov., 149–159. Rpt. in *Essays of J. A. Schumpeter* (1951). Ital. trans. in A. Pagani (Ed.). *Il nuovo imprenditore*. Milano: F. Angeli, 1967. Span. trans. in J. A. Schumpeter. *Ensayos*. Barcelona: Oikos-tau, 1968. Ger. trans. in *Beitraege zur Sozialoekonomik* (1987).
[See also S.242.]

S.240. "Theoretical Problems of Economic Growth." *Journal of Economic History*, Supplement, 7, 1947, 1–9. Rpt. in *Essays of J. A. Schumpeter* (1951). Rpt. in J. T. Lambie and R. V. Clemence (Eds.). *Economic Change in America. Readings in Economic History of the United States.* Harrisburg, PA, 1954. Ger. trans. in *Beitraege zur Sozialoekonomik* (1987). Span. trans. in *El Trimestre Economico*, 25, 1958, No. 1. New Span. trans. in J. A. Schumpeter. *Ensayos.* Barcelona: Oikos-tau, 1968.

S.241. "Keynes, the Economist." In S. E. Harris (Ed.). *The New Economics: Keynes's Influence on Theory and Public Policy.* New York: A. A. Knopf, 1947, 73–101. Rpt. New York: A. M. Kelley, 1965. Rpt. in J. C. Wood (Ed.). *John Maynard Keynes. Critical Assessments.* Vol. 1. London and Canberra: Croom Helm, 1983. Jap. trans. in S. E. Harris (Ed.). *Atarasii Keizaigaku.* Ed. by Research and Statistics Department of the Bank of Japan. Tokyo: Toyo Keizai-shinpo-sha, 1949–1950. Span. trans. in *La nueva ciencia economica.* Madrid: Editorial Revista de Occidente, 1955.

S.242. "Comments on a Plan for the Study of Entrepreneurship." (Harvard University, HUH 775. January 13, 1947.) Cambridge, MA: Widener Library, 1947. (Enlarged version of "The Creative Response in Economic History," S.239). Rpt. in *The Economics and Sociology of Capitalism* (1990).

### 1948

S.243. "Broeckelnde Mauern." *Die Umschau*, 3, 1948, No. 2, 137–144.

S.244. "Der Kapitalismus und die Intellektuellen." *Deutsche Zeitschrift fuer Europaeisches Denken*, 2, 1948, 161–173.

S.245. "There Is Still Time to Stop Inflation." *Nation's Business*, 36, 1948, Jun., 33–35, 88–91. Rpt. in *Essays of J. A. Schumpeter* (1951). Span. trans. in J. A. Schumpeter. *Ensayos.* Barcelona: Oikos-tau, 1968.

S.246. "Irving Fisher's Econometrics." *Econometrica*, 16, 1948, No. 3, Jul., 219–231. Rpt. in *Ten Great Economists, from Marx to Keynes* (1951). Ital. trans. in *L'Industria*, 1948, No. 4. New Ital. trans. in A. Quadrio-Curzio and R. Scazzieri (Eds.). *Protagonisti del pensiero economico.* Vol. 2. Bologna: Il Mulino, 1977. Span. trans. in *Moneda y Credito*, 1952, No. 43.
     [See also the national editions of T.G.E.]

S.247. "Wage and Tax Policy in Transitional States of Society." (Lectures delivered at the National University of Mexico. Mexico City, January, 1948.) Now in *The Economics and Sociology of Capitalism* (1990).

### 1949

S.248. "Science and Ideology." (Presidential address delivered at the Sixty-first Annual Meeting of the American Economic Association. Cleveland, OH. December 28, 1948.) *American Economic Review*, 39, 1949, No. 2, Mar., 345–359. Rpt. in *Essays of J. A. Schumpeter* (1951). Rpt. in *The Philosophy of Economics. An Anthology.* Cambridge, New York: Cambridge University Press. 1984. Jap. trans. in *Shiso*, 303, 1949, No. 9. Ital. trans. in *L'Industria*, 1949, No. 3. New Ital. trans. in F. Caffé (Ed.). *Economisti moderni.* Milano: Garzanti, 1962. Rpt. in S. Zamagni (Ed.). *Saggi di filosofia della scienza economica.* Roma: Nuova Italia Scientifica, 1982. Span. trans. in *El Trimestre*

*Economico*, 17, 1950. No. 1. New Span. trans. in J. A. Schumpeter. *Ensayos*. Barcelona: Oikos-tau, 1968. Norw. trans. in *Stimulator*, 5, 1951, No. 1–2. Arg. trans. Buenos Aires: Eudeba, 1968. Ger. trans. in *Beitraege zur Sozialoekonomik* (1987).

S.249. "Vilfredo Pareto (1848–1920)." *Quarterly Journal of Economics*, 63, 1949, No. 2, May, 147–173. Rpt. in *Ten Great Economists, from Marx to Keynes* (1954).
[See the national editions of T.G.E.]

S.250. "The Communist Manifesto in Sociology and Economics." *Journal of Political Economy*, 57, 1949, No. 3, Jun., 199–212. Rpt. in *Essays of J. A. Schumpeter* (1951). Rpt. in E. J. Hamilton, A. Ress, and H. J. Johnson (Eds.). *Landmarks in Political Economy*. Vol. 2. Chicago and London, 1962. Span. trans. in J. A. Schumpeter. *Ensayos*. Barcelona: Oikos-tau, 1968. Jap. trans. in *Shionshugi to shakaishugi* (1973). Rpt. in *Konniki ni okeru shakaishugi no Kanousei* (1977). Ital. trans. in *Schumpeter. Antologia di scritti* (1984). Ger. trans. in *Beitraege zur Sozialoekonomik* (1987).

S.251. "English Economists and the State-Managed Economy." *Journal of Political Economy*, 57, 1949, No. 5, Oct., 371–382. Rpt. in *Essays of J. A. Schumpeter* (1951). Span. trans. in J. A. Schumpeter. *Ensayos*. Barcelona: Oikos-tau, 1968. Jap. trans. in *Shionshugi to shakaishugi* (1973). Rpt. in *Konniki ni okeru shakaishugi no Kanousei* (1977).

S.252. "Der demokratische Kurs." (Der Streit um den Sozialismus. 6 Stellungnahmen.) *Der Monat. Eine Internationale Zeitschrift*, 1, 1949, No. 5, 22–28.

S.253. "Economic Theory and Entrepreneurial History." In *Change and the Entrepreneur. Postulates and Patterns for Entrepreneurial History*. Ed. by Research Center in Entrepreneurial History. Cambridge, MA: Cambridge University Press, 1949, 63–84. Rpt. in *Essays of J. A. Schumpeter* (1951). Rpt. in H. G. Aitken (Ed.). *Explorations in Enterprise*. Cambridge, MA: Cambridge University Press, 1965. Rpt. in *Readings in United States Economic and Business History*. Boston, New York, and Atlanta, 1966. Jap. trans. in *Kinyu Keizai—The Journal of Financial Economics*, 1966, No. 100. Span. trans. in J. A. Schumpeter. *Ensayos*. Barcelona: Oikos-tau, 1968. Ital. trans. in A. Carbonaro and A. Pagani (Eds.). *Sociologia industriale e dell'organizzazione*. Milano: Feltrinelli, 1970. Rpt. in A. Cavalli (Ed.). *Economia e società*. Bologna: Il Mulino, 1972. Ger. trans. in *Beitraege zur Sozialoekonomik* (1987).

S.254. "The Historical Approach to the Analysis of Business Cycles." (Universities—National Bureau Conference on Business Cycle Research, New York. November 25–27, 1949.) In *Conference on Business Cycles*. New York: National Bureau of Economic Research, 1951, 149–162. Rpt. in *Essays of J. A. Schumpeter* (1951). Span. trans. in J. A. Schumpeter. *Ensayos*. Barcelona: Oikos-tau, 1968. Ger. trans. in *Beitraege zur Sozialoekonomik* (1987).

S.255. "Some Questions of Principle." Ed. and introduction by P. F. Asso and E. Barucci. *Storia del Pensiero Economico. Bollettino d'Informazione*, N. S., 1989, No. 17, 46–59.

S.256. "American Institutions and Economic Progress." (Outline for a series of lectures to be given in January 1950 at the Charles R. Walgreen Foundation in Chicago.) Ed. by R. L. Allen. *Zeitschrift fuer die Gesamte Staatswissenschaft*, 139, 1983, No. 2, 191–196. Rpt. in *The Economics and Sociology of Capitalism* (1990). Rpt. in *Collected Economic Papers of Joseph A. Schumpeter* (Forthcoming).

## 1950

S.257. "Wesley Clair Mitchell (1874–1948)." *Quarterly Journal of Economics*, 64, 1950, No. 1, Feb., 139–155. Rpt. in *Ten Great Economists, from Marx to Keynes* (1951). Rpt. in A. F. Burns (Ed.). *Wesley Clair Mitchell. The Economic Scientist.* New York: National Bureau Research, 1952.
   [See the national editions of T.G.E.]
S.258. "The March into Socialism." *American Economic Review*, 40, 1950, No. 2, May, 446–456. Rpt. in L. C. Harris (Ed.). *Selected Readings in Economics.* Englewood Cliffs, N.J.: Prentice Hall, 1959. Rpt. in *Capitalism, Socialism, and Democracy* (1952). Ger. trans. in *Jahrbuch fuer Sozialwissenschaft*, 1, 1950, No. 2. Jap. trans. in *Konniki ni okeru shakaishugi no Kanousei* (1977). Span. trans. in *Papeles de Economia Espanola*, 1981, No. 6.
S.259. "E. C. Bratt. *Business Cycles and Forecasting.*" *Journal of the American Statistical Association*, 45, 1950, 140–147. Rpt. in *Collected Economic Papers of Joseph A. Schumpeter* (Forthcoming).

## 1951

S.260. "Review of the Troops." *Quarterly Journal of Economics*, 65, 1951, No. 2, 149–180. Rpt. in *History of Economic Analysis* (1954).
   [See the national editions of H.E.A.]

# Index